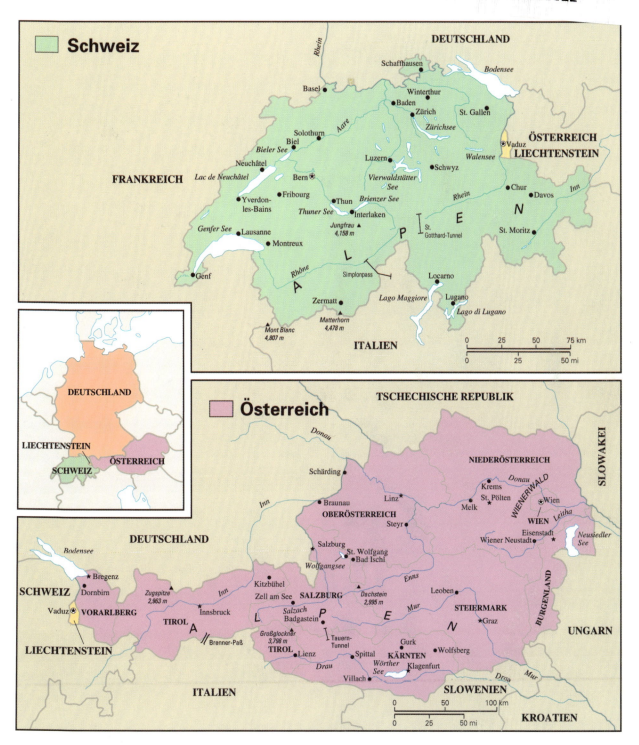

### Schweiz

DEUTSCHLAND

Schaffhausen

Bodensee

Basel

Winterthur

Baden

Zürich

St. Gallen

ÖSTERREICH

Vaduz

LIECHTENSTEIN

Zürichsee

Solothurn

Biel

Bieler See

Luzern

Walensee

Neuchâtel

Schwyz

FRANKREICH

Lac de Neuchâtel

Bern

Vierwaldstätter See

Rhein

Chur

Davos

Inn

Yverdon-les-Bains

Fribourg

Thun

Brienzer See

Thuner See

Interlaken

St. Moritz

Genfer See

Lausanne

Jungfrau 4,158 m

St. Gotthard-Tunnel

A L P E N

Montreux

Rhône

Simplonpass

Locarno

Genf

Zermatt

Lago Maggiore

Lugano

Lago di Lugano

Mont Blanc 4,807 m

Matterhorn 4,478 m

ITALIEN

0  25  50  75 km

0  25  50 mi

### Österreich

TSCHECHISCHE REPUBLIK

Donau

NIEDERÖSTERREICH

SLOWAKEI

Schärding

Donau

WIENERWALD

Krems

St. Pölten

Wien

Braunau

Linz

Melk

WIEN

OBERÖSTERREICH

Steyr

Leitha

Eisenstadt

Wiener Neustadt

Neusiedler See

Inn

Salzburg

St. Wolfgang

Bad Ischl

BURGENLAND

DEUTSCHLAND

Wolfgangsee

Enns

Bodensee

Bregenz

Leoben

SCHWEIZ

Dornbirn

Zugspitze 2,963 m

Inn

Kitzbühel

Zell am See

SALZBURG

Dachstein 2,995 m

STEIERMARK

UNGARN

Vaduz

VORARLBERG

Innsbruck

Salzach

Mur

A L P E N

LIECHTENSTEIN

TIROL

Badgastein

Großglockner 3,798 m

Tauern-Tunnel

Graz

Brenner-Paß

TIROL

Lienz

Spittal

Gurk

Wolfsberg

KÄRNTEN

Drau

Wörther See

Klagenfurt

Dras

Mur

ITALIEN

Villach

SLOWENIEN

KROATIEN

0  50  100 km

0  25  50 mi

DEUTSCHLAND

LIECHTENSTEIN

ÖSTERREICH

SCHWEIZ

# Vorsprung

## SECOND EDITION

## A Communicative Introduction to German Language and Culture

**Thomas A. Lovik**
**Michigan State University**

**J. Douglas Guy**
**Beverly High School**
**Northern Essex Community College**

**Monika Chavez**
**University of Wisconsin, Madison**

Houghton Mifflin Company   Boston   New York

**Publisher:** Rolando Hernández
**Senior Sponsoring Editor:** Glenn A. Wilson
**Associate Editor:** Caitlin McIntyre
**Project Editor:** Harriet C. Dishman/Stacy Drew
**Art and Design Manager:** Gary Crespo
**Senior Photo Editor:** Jennifer Meyer Dare
**Composition Buyer:** Chuck Dutton
**Senior Manufacturing Buyer:** Karen B. Fawcett
**Executive Marketing Director:** Eileen Bernadette Moran

**Cover image:** *Close-up of Infinity* by Friedensreich Hundertwasser, mixed media on canvas, 1994. Courtesy of Laundau Fine Art, Montreal.

Printed in the U.S.A.

Library of Congress Control Number: 2005936793

Instructor's Annotated Edition
 ISBN-10: 0-618-66908-6
 ISBN-13: 978-0-618-66908-0
For orders, use student text ISBNs
 ISBN-10: 0-618-66907-8
 ISBN-13: 978-0-618-66907-3

1 2 3 4 5 6 7 8 9-WEB-10 09 08 07 06

# Contents

## KAPITEL DREI   Was gibt es in Heidelberg und Mannheim zu tun?  74

## KAPITEL VIER   Unterwegs 115

## KAPITEL FÜNF   Freundschaften 157

## KAPITEL SECHS   Willkommen in Tübingen  196

## KAPITEL NEUN  Ein Praktikum in Wien  331

## KAPITEL ZEHN — Feste, Feiertage und Ferien 381

## KAPITEL ELF — Geschichte und Geographie Deutschlands 431

## KAPITEL ZWÖLF    Ende gut, alles gut!    474

## Reference    R-1

# Preface

*Vorsprung* is a complete first-year program designed for beginning students of German. It offers a communicative introduction to the German language and culture and provides beginning German students with the necessary skills for successful communication in today's rapidly changing world by exposing them to a wealth of spoken and written authentic textual materials. *Vorsprung* combines a focus on spoken and written texts with interactive, in-class activities that foster accuracy in the language and give students ample opportunity to practice realistic German in authentic contexts.

## Chapter Organization

The Student Text is divided into twelve chapters, each focusing on a different aspect of German culture. Each chapter is divided into three main parts, which are organized around a spoken or written text (Chapter 1 deviates slightly from this format). Extensive pre- and post-listening or reading work is provided. In addition, important structural and lexical aspects of German are systematically explored in the first two parts of each chapter (except Chapter 12, which practices material from all the other chapters).

### Chapter opener

Each chapter begins with a photo focusing on the cultural themes of the chapter. A statement of the chapter's communicative, structural, lexical, and cultural goals is included to provide students with an overview of what they can expect to learn in the chapter.

### Anlauftext *(Warm-up text)*

The first part of each chapter begins with the **Anlauftext,** an audio text in dialogue form, which can also be found recorded on the text audio program. The **Anlauftext** section presents new grammatical structures and important vocabulary in context, as well as the cultural theme of the chapter. Chapter 1 has two **Anlauftext** sections.

**Vorschau** *(Preview activities).* The **Anlauftext** section begins with the **Vorschau** activities, pre-listening activities that function as advance organizers. There is a variety of activities used for pre-listening. The **Thematische Fragen** *(Thematic questions)* help students activate prior knowledge of themes, vocabulary, and structures before listening to the **Anlauftext.** The **Wortdetektiv** or **Satzdetektiv** activities *(Word- or sentence-detective activities)* help students focus on synonyms and build their active vocabulary base. Other predictive activities help students establish context before listening to the text. The **Vorschau** section further promotes awareness of the culture of German-speaking countries and highlights cross-cultural contrasts.

**Anlauftext.**   The **Anlauftext** is recorded on the text audio program and is represented by a storyboard in the textbook. To aid comprehension, students can listen to the **Anlauftext** while following the visual cues of the storyboard in their texts. The storyboards are a unique feature of *Vorsprung*. In the **Anlauftexte,** students meet Anna Adler, an American studying for a year in Germany, along with Anna's German relatives, the Günthers, and her new friends at the university in Tübingen. All these frame the story line and unify the contents of Chapters 1–12.

**Rückblick** *(Post-viewing).*   The activities in the **Rückblick** section guide students from initial comprehension of the text to personalization of the topics in the text. The **Stimmt das?** *(True or false?)* activity, the first activity in the section, provides a quick check of the content to determine how much of the text students understood. The **Kurz gefragt** *(Short-answer questions)* activity guides students to produce more complete statements about the text. Further activities encourage students to use the **Anlauftext** as a jumping-off point for giving more personal reactions to the text. An **Ergänzen Sie** *(Fill-in)* activity in the workbook asks students to focus on new vocabulary in the context of the text.

## *Strukturen und Vokabeln* (Structures and vocabulary)

These sections (in chapters 1–11) appear after the **Rückblick** in the **Anlauftext** and **Absprungtext** sections. They are each organized around a selection of important language functions, such as describing yourself, asking for information, or expressing likes and dislikes. Each language function is identified with a roman numeral.

The grammar structures needed to perform each language function are clearly and concisely explained in English. Numerous easy-to-interpret charts and tables aid comprehension. In addition, the vocabulary needed to fulfill the language function is presented in sections called **Wissenswerte Vokabeln** *(Vocabulary worth knowing)*. Groups of thematically related words and phrases are presented in a richly illustrated format, eliminating the need for translation. This contextual approach to vocabulary presentation coincides with the functional and thematic approach of the book. A wide variety of productive and receptive activities are interspersed throughout the **Strukturen und Vokabeln** sections to aid in language development.

## *Absprungtext* (Take-off text)

The second section of each chapter revolves around the **Absprungtext,** an authentic written text produced originally for native speakers of German. (Note that there is no **Absprungtext** in Chapter 1.) The **Absprungtext** section parallels the format of the **Anlauftext** section by beginning with pre-reading activities in a **Vorschau** section. Many of the same activity types are used here to activate prior knowledge and to prepare students for reading and understanding the text. The **Absprungtext** itself is reproduced in as authentic a format as possible. Text types offered in this section include advertisements, brochures, newspaper and magazine articles, letters, short stories, time lines, Internet blog entries and articles, and fairy tales. All text types relate directly to the chapter theme and to the continuing story presented in the **Anlauftext** sections, and were selected for their high frequency of occurrence and usefulness to students.

The **Absprungtext** is followed by post-reading activities featured in a **Rückblick** section, which is very similar to the **Rückblick** section that follows the **Anlauftext.**

The **Absprungtext** section ends with another **Strukturen und Vokabeln** section, which parallels the **Strukturen und Vokabeln** section at the end of the **Anlauftext.** Additional high-frequency language functions and the grammar and vocabulary to perform them are also presented and practiced. Readings from the **Absprungtext** can also be found on the in-text audio CD.

### *Zieltext (Target text)*

The third and final part of the chapter centers on the **Zieltext,** a listening text recorded on the text audio program. As its name implies, the **Zieltext** is the culminating point of the chapter (there is no **Zieltext** for Chapter 1). **Vorschau** activities, much like those in the **Anlauftext** section, prepare students to listen to and understand the **Zieltext.** The **Zieltexte** themselves incorporate the structures and vocabulary of the chapter in a free-flowing dialogue spoken at normal speed by native speakers of German. While listening to the **Zieltexte** on the text audio program, students can look in the Student Text at art-based cues that help their listening comprehension. After listening to the **Zieltext,** students do follow-up activities in the **Rückblick** section that foster both comprehension and expansion skills. By understanding these audio texts and doing their accompanying activities, students will fulfill the communicative goals listed in the chapter opener.

### *Wortschatz (Vocabulary list)*

Each chapter ends with a **Wortschatz** section that lists all the active words and expressions taught in the chapter. The vocabulary has been categorized by semantic fields, which facilitates acquisition of new vocabulary by encouraging students to associate words and word families.

## Other Features of the Chapter

**Brennpunkt Kultur** *(Focus on culture).*  These cultural notes appear throughout the chapter, as appropriate. Each note provides background information and insightful commentaries in English on themes encountered in the chapter. They are rich in descriptive detail and include additional thematic German vocabulary. Each **Brennpunkt Kultur** note is followed by a thought-provoking cross-cultural activity called **Kulturkreuzung,** which encourages higher-level thinking about the cultural information and students' cultural assumptions. The *Vorsprung* Website provides Web addresses for additional information about the cultural notes.

**Sprache im Alltag** *(Everyday language usage).*  These short descriptions of variations in spoken German highlight useful vocabulary and expressions.

**Freie Kommunikation** *(Free communication).*  These featured activities appear at regular intervals in the chapter, especially as the culminating activities for the **Strukturen und Vokabeln** sections. Students are guided through role-play situations in which they practice the communicative functions that have been introduced.

**Schreibecke** *(Writing activities).*  These special unnumbered activities accompany the **Freie Kommunikation** activities throughout the chapter. They provide students with authentic tasks and the opportunity to practice their written skills in short, manageable writing assignments.

**Activity icons.**  With the exception of the **Freie Kommunikation** and the **Schreibecke** activities, all activities are numbered consecutively throughout the chapter. Each activity is preceded by one of three icons:

**RECEPTIVE**          **PRODUCTIVE**          **INTERACTIVE**          **AUDIO**

Receptive activities require students to recognize printed utterances. Productive activities require them to produce their own utterances. Interactive activities are productive activities that involve two or more students working together.

The Online Study Center icon *Online Study Center* at the beginning of each chapter directs students to the Web search activities to reinforce the vocabulary and grammar for each chapter in a culturally authentic context.

## Enrichment Sections

*Vorsprung, Second Edition* contains four two- or three-page special enrichment sections. **Deutsch im Beruf** *(Career German)* appears after Chapters 3 and 9. The first of these sections highlights practical vocabulary and information about using German in the tourist industry right here at home. The second offers information about finding a job in which a knowledge of German is an asset. **Literarisches Deutsch** *(Literary German)* appears after Chapter 6 and 12. These two sections offer the opportunity to read lyric poetry by well-known authors from the nineteenth and twentieth centuries and by one anonymous poet from the Middle Ages. Warm-up and comprehension activities ensure a successful first experience with the beauty of the German language as it is used in German literature.

## Supplementary Materials for Students

### Arbeitsbuch

The **Arbeitsbuch** is a two-part volume combining the Workbook and Laboratory Manual for the *Vorsprung* program. Both are coordinated with the *Vorsprung* text and appear in the Student Activities Manual (SAM).

The Workbook provides additional practice on structures, vocabulary, reading comprehension, culture, and writing skills, all designed to expand upon the work in the Student Text. The Laboratory Manual is designed to be used in conjunction with the SAM audio CDs. The activities focus on developing aural comprehension of spoken German. The audio texts reflect the themes, structures, and vocabulary encountered in the Student Text. The Video Activities (located on the Houghton Mifflin ClassPrep CD as well as the Online Teaching Center) are coordinated with the video program, *Unterwegs!* These activities guide students through their viewing of the video and assist them with comprehension of the language and structures encountered in the video.

### In-text audio

Packaged with the textbook, the in-text audio program complements the twelve chapters of *Vorsprung.* Each chapter includes the **Anlauftexte, Absprungtexte** (when appropriate), **Zieltexte,** and any applicable dialogues from the textbook chapters.

### SAM audio CDs

The SAM audio CDs contain the recorded material that coordinates with the Laboratory Manual portion of the *Vorsprung* **Arbeitsbuch** to reinforce pronunciation and listening skills, as well as provide audio for use with written exercises.

### Unterwegs! *video (on DVD and VHS)*

This exciting video program was shot on location in Tübingen, Germany. It includes twelve five- to seven-minute episodes featuring a continuing story line and cast of characters. The video is thematically linked to the *Vorsprung* Student Text and focuses on the communicative functions and vocabulary taught in the text. The video is intended to be used in conjunction with the video activity sheets located on the Online Study Center, Online Teaching Center, and instructor ClassPrep CD-ROM.

### Student Companion Website

The Online Study Center for *Vorsprung* includes a variety of activities and resources to help students practice German, review for quizzes and exams, and explore German-language websites. This site also has electronic flashcards for vocabulary practice, and video worksheets for use with the *Vorsprung* DVD/VHS.

## Authors

**Thomas A. Lovik** (University of Minnesota, M.A.; University of California, Berkeley, Ph.D.) began learning German as a second language as a junior in high school. He currently teaches German language, linguistics, and culture courses at Michigan State University. He also trains graduate teaching assistants and future teachers of German. His summers are usually spent directing a study abroad program in Mayen, Germany, a small town in the Eifel region. Professor Lovik also has close ties to the cities of Freiburg, Heidelberg, Mannheim, and Tübingen.

**J. Douglas Guy** (Indiana University, B.A.; Middlebury College, M.A.) teaches German and serves as foreign language curriculum coordinator at Beverly High School, Beverly, MA and is adjunct professor of German at Northern Essex Community College, Haverhill, MA. Mr. Guy has made significant contributions to the development of instructional text and media for German and Russian programs as an editor and ghostwriter, and has been a presenter at state and national conferences. He regularly sponsors exchange programs at the secondary level. He has also worked as a court interpreter, translator, and freelance photographer.

**Monika Lagler Chavez** was born in Austria and studied German and History at the University of Vienna. She has an M.A. in German Studies from the University of New Mexico-Albuquerque and a Ph.D. in German Applied Linguistics from the University of Texas at Austin. She is Professor of German and Second Language Acquisition at the University of Wisconsin-Madison, where she directs the first- and second-year programs in German language. Her research interests include learner and teacher variables and classroom language use.

## Acknowledgments

The original conviction that prompted the creation of the first edition of *Vorsprung*—that learning German can be enjoyable and that understanding the German language and culture can be a valuable tool in today's changing world—continues to prove itself true. The authors' efforts in writing *Vorsprung* have been bolstered by the many people who have provided support, encouragement, assistance, good humor, and vast amounts of patience. They are especially grateful to their colleagues in the profession who have the good sense to adopt *Vorsprung* for their students.

The authors are deeply indebted to the many people at Houghton Mifflin Company, who believed in their project and nurtured it along the way:

> Roland Hernández for his support and leadership of the *Second Edition;*
> Caitlin McIntyre and Glenn Wilson for their project management coordination;
> Greg Rivera for being such a strong advocate for our project.

The authors also wish to thank the many talented people, who contributed so much to the project but get so little recognition, including:

> Peggy Potter for her steady hand, good eye, and thorough developmental preparation of the *Second Edition;*
> Linda Rodolico for her all-round talent, wit, and sharp eye for photography, realia, and line art;
> Timothy C. Jones for his witty and resourceful artwork that has given *Vorsprung* its personality and edginess;
> Judith Bach for her assistance with the Web materials;
> Marcia Lord for her assistance with the artwork;
> Paul Listen for his insightful and highly informed copyediting of the manuscript for the *Second Edition;*
> Karen Hohner for her expert proofreading of galleys;

Margret Rettich for generous permission to use her illustrations for the **Aschenputtel** fairy tale;

Barbara Lasoff for her developmental work on the manuscript for the first edition of the textbook and her contributions to the Workbook/Lab Manual;

Charlotte Antibus for her careful creation of the Test Bank in the first edition;

Elizabeth Glew for her many resourceful, creative contributions to the first edition of the Workbook/Lab Manual;

Cynthia Hall Kouré for her inspired development and creativity in the original first-edition manuscript;

Harriet Dishman and Stacy Drew and the rest of the team at Elm Street Publications for their understanding, expertise, and ever-reliable, dedicated, and effective production management.

For their assistance in the acquisition of recordings and materials for the *Second Edition* as well as their native-speaker insights, the authors would like to thank the following people:

Susan Adams (Concord, MA); Gabrielle Beck (Hamburg); Karen Clausen (Hamburg); Thomas Conrad (Philadelphia, PA); Kristi Decke (Berlin); Jörg Frey (Goethe Institut, Boston, MA); who supplied us with numerous materials and magazines and supported J. Douglas Guy's study grants at the Goethe Institut Berlin and Weimar; Gerda Grimm (Hoisdorf); Karin Heidenreich and Robert Meckler (Fürth); Hans Ilmberger (Ahrensburg); Charlotte Sanford (Arlington, MA); Margita and Hans Schulz (Georgetown, MA); John Seufert (Byfield, MA); the actresses Anja Naomi Decke and Carol Jedicke (Berlin) for improvising the new **Zieltexte** for **Kapitel 9** and **11**; the German National Tourist Office (New York, NY); and numerous tourist offices through Austria, Germany, and Switzerland.

At Michigan State University: Anja Bleidorn (Jena), Minna Eschelbach, Monika Gardt (Heidelberg), Robert Gretch, Angelika Krämer, Eva Lacour, Jeannine Mickeleit, Elizabeth Mittman, Mandy Mrosek (Jena), Steve Naumann, George Peters, Carl Prestel (Tübingen), Nathan Pumplin, Marc Rathmann, Kari Richards, Theresa Schenker (Jena), Steffi Schütze, Barbara Schwenk, Matthias Steffan (Altlußheim), Julia Veltum (Jena), and Karin Wurst.

Max Coqui (Neu-Biberg), Katja Günther (Concord, MA and Frankfurt/Main), Françoise Knaack (Keltern), Christine Müller (Luzern), Silvia Solf (Stuttgart) and Florian Will (Berlin), Thomas Achternkamp, Olaf Böhlke, and Volker Langeheine for their creative improvisation work on **Zieltexte** retained from the first edition.

The authors also thank their students at Michigan State University, Northern Essex Community College (Haverhill, MA), Beverly High School (Beverly, MA), Portsmouth High School (Portsmouth, NH), and Newburyport High School (Newburyport, MA) for their involvement and feedback during the class testing of materials for the *Second Edition* of *Vorsprung.* Special thanks go to the teaching assistants and faculty at the University of Wisconsin-Madison who have taught with *Vorsprung* and whose feedback and contributions to the ancillary materials have been incorporated in the current edition.

For their valued appraisal of the manuscript in all stages of development, the authors would like to thank the following reviewers:

Manfred Bansleben, *University of Washington*
Lara Ducate, *University of South Carolina*
Hartmut Rastalsky, *University of Michigan*
Olaf Schmidt, *Tulane University*
Elizabeth Snyder, *University of North Carolina at Asheville*
Jane Sokolosky, *Brown University*

The author team would like to thank all of their family members for their support of the project and their endless patience during the months and months of work on the ***Second Edition***. These include:

My wife Mary and our kids Julianna and Will, who consider Anna Adler a member of the family.

TAL

Katherine Guy and sons Jonathan and Nicolas for their understanding while Dad was "busy" or "unavailable" taking care of ***Vorsprung***.

JDG

My parents, Franz and Helga Lagler and my brother, Franz Lagler, for helping collect materials; Gabe Chavez for accompanying me on trips for materials collection; my sisters-in-law Mari, Tita, and Mona Chavez for forwarding numerous packages during my stay in New Mexico; my parents-in-law, Gabe and Josie Chavez for housing and feeding me during various drafts; and many old friends in Austria and elsewhere for inspiration regarding characters' names and scenarios.

MLC

# To the Student

*Vorsprung*, *Second Edition*, offers students a communicative introduction to the German language and culture that fosters active use of the German language. The *Vorsprung* materials are designed to provide ample opportunity for you to practice realistic German in authentic contexts. While the program emphasizes all four language skills—listening, speaking, reading, and writing—it places a special emphasis on the development of good listening skills as a foundation for the other skills.

## *Did you know . . . ?*

- that when children learn their own language, they develop their listening skills first?
- that you spend about 40% of your time each day listening in your own language?
- that listening skills do not erode as quickly as speaking skills?
- that good listening skills can prove valuable in the development of speaking and writing skills?

## *What does this mean for learning German?*

- While doing listening activities, concentrate initially on comprehension without being too anxious about speaking. You will be asked to speak and write more German gradually, as your listening skills develop.
- Listen carefully to your instructor. He or she—along with the audio and video recordings—will be your primary models for good German.
- Listen carefully to other students in the class. You can learn a lot from them. Pay close attention to the words they use, their pronunciation, and their partner's comprehension and reaction to what they say.
- Listen carefully to what you are saying. This may seem difficult at first, but as time progresses it will become easier.

## *What else is important when learning German?*

- **Learn to focus** on what you do understand and rely on your own intuition to guess at the meanings of words. Don't become discouraged by what you don't understand.
- **Have realistic expectations.** Real fluency in another language can take years of study and may seem slow at first; during the first few weeks you may only be able to produce a word or two. However, by the end of Chapter 6, you can fully expect to be speaking in sentences about your family, your possessions, and your likes and dislikes. After two years of study you will find yourself quite comfortable conversing in German.
- **Be realistic** in your expectations of your pronunciation of German. Nobody expects you to have perfect pronunciation right away. With practice and time, your pronunciation will improve. Remember, communication is the goal of *Vorsprung.*

- **Challenge yourself.** Try to express yourself in novel ways and go beyond using language that you have rehearsed extensively.

- **Develop good study skills.** Set aside enough time each day to listen to the recordings or read the texts several times until you are comfortable with them. Let the accompanying activities guide you through different levels of comprehension. Ask your instructor for help when things are unclear.

- **Assume responsibility** for your own learning. Prepare before you come to class. For example, you are expected to read the grammar explanations on your own. Class time should be used for learning experiences you cannot get on your own, especially for communication and interaction with other students, as well as listening to authentic spoken German. Make an effort to use German whenever you can and to learn to say everyday phrases in German. Try to acquire vocabulary that is relevant to your own communicative needs.

- **Study the models** in *Vorsprung* and be sure that you understand the structures and vocabulary used in them.

- **Know your learning style.** Develop an approach to working with the information provided in *Vorsprung* that suits your particular learning style or needs. Try to assess how you learn best; for example, through visualizing concepts or associating them with each other, through listening to recordings or hearing yourself formulate statements aloud, or perhaps through writing things down and underlining them. Do whatever you find helpful for learning German.

- **Develop a vocabulary strategy.** When learning new vocabulary, practice writing new words on note cards or identifying objects in your environment with stick-on tags. You may also find it helpful to record new vocabulary and play it back to yourself. Try to organize words into small, manageable groups categorized thematically, by gender, by ranking, or by some other system. Continually test your knowledge of these new words. Avoid memorizing lists of words. Learn to associate new words with the visual or linguistic context provided in *Vorsprung.*

- **Learn to use a dictionary,** but don't let your dictionary become a substitute for effective reading strategies. This can undermine your own ability to associate meaning with new words and may inhibit your acquisition of German.

- **Keep an open mind** to new information. Much of what you learn about the German language and culture may seem different and strange at first. Maintaining an openness to new things is an important tool in learning about another language and culture.

- **Expect to make lots of errors** as you learn German. However, you will also be expected to learn from your mistakes and to make fewer and fewer errors as you progress. When you do make mistakes in class, listen carefully to what your instructor says. It should be your model for fashioning your own speech.

The authors and your instructor want to congratulate you for deciding to learn German. You have made a very exciting and valuable educational choice.

*Viel Spaß!*

# Fangen Sie bitte an.

**In this chapter you will learn to introduce yourself, ask for and spell names, identify common classroom objects, and identify and describe classmates.**

## Kommunikative Funktionen

- Understanding commands and requests
- Making polite requests with **bitte**
- Describing yourself and others
- Asking for someone's name
- Asking for information and clarification
- Identifying people, colors, and classroom objects

## Strukturen

- The imperative
- The word **bitte**
- Subject pronouns
- The verb **sein**
- The pronoun *you*
- The verb **heißen**
- Question formation (including **wie bitte?**)
- Noun gender and number
- The nominative case: definite and indefinite articles
- Negation with **nicht** and **kein**
- Subject of a sentence
- Predicate nominative
- Pronoun substitution

## Vokabeln

- The alphabet
- The numbers 0 to 1000
- Adjectives for personal description
- Classroom objects
- Colors
- Country names and nationalities

## Kulturelles

- Greetings and farewells
- Titles of address
- Where German is spoken

■ Die Studenten machen eine Pause im Uni-Café

**Online Study Center**

Go to the *Vorsprung* Website at *http://college.hmco.com/pic/vorsprung2e.*

## Annas Albtraum°

*Albtraum: nightmare*

In **Anlauftext I** you are going to meet Anna Adler, an American student from Fort Wayne, Indiana, who is planning to study in Tübingen, Germany, for a year. Although excited about her year in Tübingen, Anna is also nervous and exhausted and falls asleep. In her dream, Anna works through her fears about being in a class in Germany and not being able to say what she wants.

This previewing section helps you establish the context of the text and understand important text vocabulary. Spend a few moments considering the questions you find here before you try to read the **Anlauftext**.

The symbol for productive activities is ![] and the one for receptive activities is ![]. Interactive activities have the icon ![]. Receptive activities require that students recognize a printed utterance. Productive activities require that students produce their own sentences in German. Interactive activities usually involve two or more students talking.

*Previewing activities*

### Vorschau°

**1  Deutschtest.** (*German test.*) Find out how much German you already know. Match the following German words with their English equivalents in the right-hand column.

Most German verbs in the infinitive (the equivalent of English *to* + *verb*, e.g., *to have*) end in **-en**. All German nouns are capitalized, while German verbs and adjectives use lower case letters.

| *Deutsch* | | *Englisch* | |
|---|---|---|---|
| 1. | sprechen | a. | to come |
| 2. | der Pass | b. | German |
| 3. | kommen | c. | to speak |
| 4. | Deutsch | d. | the passport |
| | | | |
| 5. | Kanada | e. | America |
| 6. | Deutschland | f. | Germany |
| 7. | heißen | g. | Canada |
| 8. | Amerika | h. | to be called |
| | | | |
| 9. | haben | i. | from (*a country*) |
| 10. | Willkommen! | j. | car |
| 11. | aus | k. | to have |
| 12. | Auto | l. | Welcome! |
| | | | |
| 13. | fragen | m. | to say |
| 14. | Mann | n. | woman |
| 15. | Frau | o. | to ask |
| 16. | sagen | p. | man |

**2** **Thematische Fragen.** (*Topical questions.*) Discuss the following questions with your instructor or in pairs.

1. What feelings might you have if you were going to study abroad for a year in a German-speaking country? What things might excite you? What things might concern you?
2. How did you feel about coming to your first German class?

**3** **Machen Sie bitte mit.** (*Please join in.*) Listen as your instructor models the commands below and then asks you to carry them out.

Stehen Sie auf.

Setzen Sie sich.

Drehen Sie sich um.

> **Thematische Fragen.** These questions are intended as a warm-up exercise before you read the German text. They activate ideas about the topic and prepare you for the reading. Starting in **Kapitel 4** these questions will be in German.

Gehen Sie an die Tafel.

Schreiben Sie.

**4** **Wortdetektiv.** (*Word detective.*) Which words convey approximately the same meaning? Match the German word to its logical English equivalent.

| *Deutsch* | *Englisch* |
|---|---|
| 1. grau | a. Excuse me! |
| 2. Entschuldigung! | b. to ask |
| 3. fragen | c. the dream |
| 4. der Traum | d. nothing |
| 5. nichts | e. gray |
| | |
| 6. Gott sei Dank! | f. to seek, to look for |
| 7. der Hörsaal | g. quickly |
| 8. verstehen | h. the lecture hall |
| 9. schnell | i. Thank God! |
| 10. suchen | j. to understand |

> **Wortdetektiv.** Intuition can be useful when it comes to deciphering new German words. You don't need to understand every word to get the gist of a text. Look for words that may be similar to English. Also remember that German nouns begin with capital letters and that verb infinitives end with -**en** or -**n**.

*Anlauftext I*

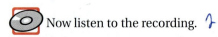 Now listen to the recording.

## Annas Albtraum

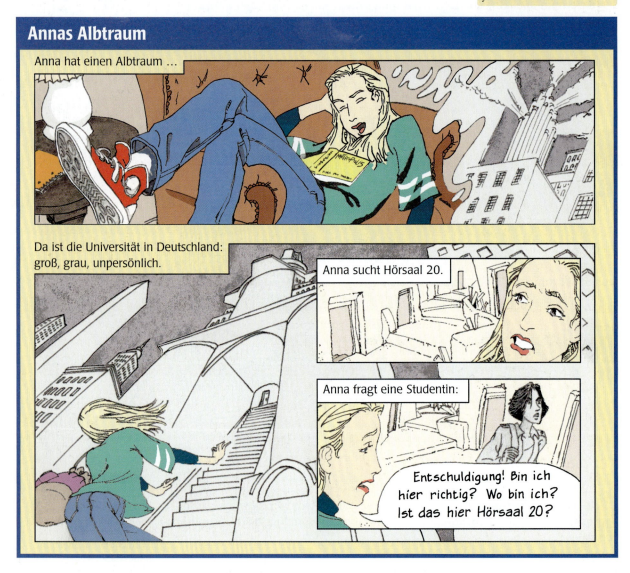

Anna hat einen Albtraum …

Da ist die Universität in Deutschland: groß, grau, unpersönlich.

Anna sucht Hörsaal 20.

Anna fragt eine Studentin:

Entschuldigung! Bin ich hier richtig? Wo bin ich? Ist das hier Hörsaal 20?

Die Studentin sagt nichts.

Anna findet Hörsaal 20 und macht die Tür auf.

Aber die Tür knallt zu. Alle drehen sich um.

Setzen Sie sich! Aber schnell!

Wie heißen Sie? Wie ist Ihr Name?

Verstehen Sie das nicht? Wie heißen Sie? Wie heißen Sie? Sprechen Sie Deutsch?

Dann gehen Sie an die Tafel! Schreiben Sie! Wie heißen Sie? Wie heißen Sie?

Anna! Anna! Anna! Wach auf!

Gott sei Dank, nur ein Traum.

*Rückblick°*

*Follow-up activities*

**5**   **Stimmt das?** (*Is that correct?*)  How much of the text can you re-member without looking back at it? Look over the following statements and mark the true statements as **Ja, das stimmt.** Mark the false statements as **Nein, das stimmt nicht.** Then, listen as your instructor reads the statements aloud and models their pronunciation. If the statement is true, say **Ja, das stimmt.** If the statement is not true, say **Nein, das stimmt nicht.**

|  | Ja, das stimmt. | Nein, das stimmt nicht. |
|---|---|---|
| 1. Anna hat einen Albtraum. | ☐ | ☐ |
| 2. Die Universität ist groß, grau und unpersönlich. | ☐ | ☐ |
| 3. Anna fragt eine Studentin: „Bin ich hier richtig?" | ☐ | ☐ |
| 4. Die Studentin sagt: „Ja." | ☐ | ☐ |
| 5. Anna findet den Hörsaal und macht die Tür auf. | ☐ | ☐ |
| 6. Die Studenten sagen: „Hallo, Anna! Willkommen in Tübingen!" | ☐ | ☐ |
| 7. Der Professor fragt: „Was suchen Sie?" | ☐ | ☐ |
| 8. Anna ist nervös und sagt nichts. | ☐ | ☐ |
| 9. Der Professor fragt Anna: „Wie heißen Sie? Wie heißen Sie?" | ☐ | ☐ |
| 10. Annas Mutter sagt: „Anna! Anna! Anna! Wach auf!" | ☐ | ☐ |

**6**   **Ergänzen Sie.** (*Complete these sentences.*)  Complete these ques-tions and statements with words from **Anlauftext I.** Look back at the text as often as you like to read the sentences and see the words in context.

1. Anna hat einen _____.
2. Da ist die _____ in Tübingen: _____, grau und _____.
3. Der Professor sagt: „ _____ Sie sich! Aber schnell!"
4. Der Professor fragt: „Wie _____ Sie?"
5. Der Professor fragt: „ _____ Sie das nicht? Wie heißen Sie?"
6. Der Professor sagt: „ _____ Sie an die Tafel!"
7. Annas Mutter sagt: „Anna! Anna! Anna! _____ _____!"

**7**   **Kurz gefragt.** (*Brief questions.*)
Now try using what you have already learned to answer some simple German questions about Anna's dream. The two question words that recur frequently are **wer** (*who*) and **was** (*what*). Be as complete in your answers as you can, but just a word or two may be enough.

„Heißen Sie zufällig° Ute?"

*by chance*

1. Was sucht Anna?
2. Wer sagt: „Bin ich hier richtig?"
3. Was sagt die Studentin?
4. Wer sagt: „Setzen Sie sich!"?
5. Was fragt der Professor?
6. Wer sagt: „Anna! Anna! Anna! Wach auf!"?

**Rückblick.** This section guides you from under-standing parts of the text to producing language based on the text.

**Stimmt das?** Do this exercise after reading the **Anlauftext** once to determine how much you understood.

## Strukturen und Vokabeln

## I Understanding commands and requests

### The imperative

#### A. Formation of the formal imperative

The infinitive (**der Infinitiv**), the basic form of all German verbs, consists of a stem plus the ending **-n** or **-en.** The infinitive is the form listed in dictionaries and in the glossary at the end of this book.

| Stem | + | Ending | | Infinitive |
|------|---|--------|---|-----------|
| geh | + | en | = | **gehen** *to go* |
| wander | + | n | = | **wandern** *to hike* |

A formal command uses the infinitive form of the verb (**das Verb**). The formal imperative (**der Imperativ**) is usually formed by placing an infinitive-like verb at the beginning of the sentence followed by the pronoun **Sie** (*you*).

> **Schreiben Sie.**　　　*Write.*
> **Gehen Sie** an die Tafel.　*Go to the blackboard.*

The formal imperative for the verb **sein** (*to be*) is **seien.**

> **Seien Sie** still.　*Be quiet.*

In German, commands are sometimes written with an exclamation point (**!**). Speakers usually lower their pitch at the end of a command. The word **nicht** (*not*) is used to make a command negative. You will learn more about the position of **nicht** in **Kapitel 2**.

> Schreiben Sie **nicht!**　*Don't write!*

#### Wissenswerte Vokabeln: Aktivitäten im Klassenzimmer°

*Understanding your instructor's requests*

*im ... : in the classroom*

Stehen Sie still.

Laufen Sie.

Lachen Sie.

**Strukturen und Vokabeln.** This section guides you through many important features of German grammar necessary for communication. Annotations tell you which structures you are expected to produce and which ones you are only expected to recognize.

See the **Arbeitsbuch** for additional practice with structures and vocabulary.

Machen Sie das Buch auf.    Machen Sie das Buch zu.    Lesen Sie das Buch.

## B. The word *bitte*

The word **bitte** (*please*) softens commands and makes them into requests. **Bitte** can appear at the beginning, in the middle, or at the end of a request.

> **Bitte** gehen Sie an die Tafel.
> Gehen Sie **bitte** an die Tafel.
> Gehen Sie an die Tafel **bitte.**

**8**    **Bitte, stehen Sie auf.**  Listen as your instructor gives the following requests. You should only carry out requests given with **bitte.**

◻ (Bitte) stehen Sie auf.

1. (Bitte) sagen Sie „Guten Tag".
2. (Bitte) setzen Sie sich (bitte).
3. (Bitte) gehen Sie (bitte) an die Tafel.
4. (Bitte) machen Sie die Tür auf.

**Anlauftext II**   ## Annas Traum°

*Traum: dream*

Now that she's awake, Anna realizes her fears were just a bad dream and that things in Tübingen will probably be a lot better. Her own experience learning German has actually been very good. In her daydream here, she knows that she will be able to say a lot in German, and she imagines how it will be to study in Germany and use the German language.

## Vorschau

**9**   **Annas Albtraum.**   Your instructor will read each question about Anna's nightmare from **Anlauftext I.** Answer with a word or two in German.

1. Wer hat einen Albtraum—Anna oder der Professor?
2. Wo ist die Universität im Albtraum?
3. Ist die Universität persönlich° oder unpersönlich? groß oder klein?
4. Was macht Anna auf?
5. Was fragt der Professor? Was sagt Anna?
6. Was sagt Annas Mutter?

*intimate*

**10**   **Thematische Fragen.**   Discuss the following questions with your instructor or in pairs.

1. What fears were causing Anna anxiety in her nightmare?
2. Now that she is awake, what kind of positive daydream images might she have concerning:
   a. studying German in the future?
   b. the professors and instructors she might have?
   c. the students in her classes?
   d. her own skill in understanding and speaking German?

**11**   **Wortdetektiv.**   Which words convey approximately the same meaning? Match the German word to its logical English equivalent.

| Deutsch | | Englisch |
|---|---|---|
| 1. freundlich | a. | to answer |
| 2. richtig | b. | right |
| 3. antworten | c. | to come in |
| 4. hereinkommen | d. | in front |
| 5. vorne | e. | friendly |
| | | |
| 6. Platz nehmen | f. | to take a seat |
| 7. hineingehen | g. | to greet |
| 8. begrüßen | h. | from where? |
| 9. schön | i. | to walk in |
| 10. woher? | j | to speak |
| 11. sprechen | k. | beautiful |

**Wortdetektiv.** Use your intuition to guide your choices. Look for similar patterns in the words, e.g., **freundlich** looks like *friendly*. Also remember what you already know about German nouns and infinitives.

## Anlauftext II

 Now listen to the recording.

**Annas Traum.** Study the pictures first, then listen to the text. You should not be reading along the first time you hear the text.

The room number is 020. A placeholder 0 is used in university buildings for ground floor room numbers.

## Annas Traum

Da ist die Universität in Tübingen: romantisch, historisch, schön.

Anna sucht den Hörsaal und fragt eine Professorin:

Ich suche Hörsaal 20. Bin ich hier richtig?

Die Professorin ist sehr freundlich und antwortet:

Ja, Sie sind hier richtig. Hörsaal 20 ist gleich da vorne.

Anna macht die Tür auf und geht hinein.

Der Professor begrüßt Anna.

Guten Morgen! Kommen Sie 'rein und nehmen Sie Platz. Setzen Sie sich, hier vorne.

**Annas Traum.** Anna has some trouble understanding the professor because he speaks with an accent typical of the dialect in the Tübingen area. This dialect is called Swabian (**Schwäbisch**).

*Rückblick*

**12  Stimmt das?** How much of the text can you remember without looking back at it? Look over the following statements and mark the true statements as **Ja, das stimmt.** Mark the false statements as **Nein, das stimmt nicht.** Then, listen as your instructor reads the statements aloud and models their pronunciation. If the statement is true, say **Ja, das stimmt.** If the statement is not true, say **Nein, das stimmt nicht.**

| | Ja, das stimmt. | Nein, das stimmt nicht. | |
|---|:---:|:---:|---|
| 1. Die Universität Tübingen ist historisch. | ☐ | ☐ | |
| 2. Anna ist nervös. Sie sagt nichts°. | ☐ | ☐ | *nothing* |
| 3. Anna fragt eine Professorin: „Bin ich hier richtig?" | ☐ | ☐ | |
| 4. Die Professorin antwortet: „Nein, Sie sind hier nicht richtig." | ☐ | ☐ | |
| 5. Der Professor heißt Professor Fachmann. | ☐ | ☐ | |
| 6. Er fragt Anna: „Wie heißen Sie?" | ☐ | ☐ | |
| 7. Anna versteht nicht und sagt: „Entschuldigung." | ☐ | ☐ | |
| 8. Der Professor fragt: „Wie heißen Sie? Wie ist Ihr Name?" | ☐ | ☐ | |
| 9. Anna antwortet: „Ich heiße Anna Adler." | ☐ | ☐ | |
| 10. Anna sagt, sie kommt aus den USA. | ☐ | ☐ | |
| 11. Der Professor sagt: „Sie sprechen gut Japanisch!" | ☐ | ☐ | |

**13  Ergänzen Sie.** Complete these questions and statements with words from **Anlauftext II.** Look back at the text as often as you like to read the sentences and see the words in context.

1. Da ist die Universität in Tübingen: historisch und _____.
2. Anna fragt eine _____: „Bin ich hier richtig?"
3. Anna macht die _____ auf.
4. Der Professor fragt: „Wie heißen _____?"
5. Anna versteht nicht und sagt: „Wie _____?"
6. Dann antwortet Anna: „Ich _____ Anna Adler."
7. Der Professor fragt: „_____ kommen Sie, Frau Adler?"
8. Anna antwortet: „Ich komme _____ Fort Wayne."
9. Der Professor sagt: „Ach, sind Sie _____?"
10. Der Professor sagt: „Sie _____ sehr gut Deutsch."
11. Anna sagt: „_____ schön!"

**14  Kurz gefragt.** Now use what you have already learned to answer some simple German questions about Anna's daydream. Be as complete as you can, but just a word or two may be enough.

1. Wie ist die Universität in Tübingen?
2. Wie ist die Professorin?
3. Wie heißt der Professor?
4. Was fragt der Professor?
5. Woher kommt Anna?
6. Wie spricht Anna Deutsch?

**15**    **Das bin ich.**  Tell a partner three things about yourself using Anna's statements about herself as your model.

Ich bin | *Amerikaner(in).*
*Student(in).*
*freundlich. / romantisch.*
*groß. / schön.*

1. Ich bin ...
2. Ich heiße ...
3. Ich komme aus ...
4. Ich spreche ...

## BRENNPUNKT KULTUR

### Greetings and farewells

Greetings such as **Guten Morgen!** and **Guten Tag!** are used to initiate conversations and to acknowledge other people, even if just in passing. In the German-speaking countries, people shake hands more often than in North America when they greet each other. Greetings differ according to geographic areas, time of day, and the social relationship of the people.

German has no single equivalent for the English greeting *hello!* Instead, German speakers use three different expressions depending on the time of day:

Until about 11 A.M.:

| | |
|---|---|
| **Guten Morgen!** | *Good morning!* |

From about 11 A.M. until sundown:

| | |
|---|---|
| **Guten Tag!** | *Good day!* |

After sundown:

| | |
|---|---|
| **Guten Abend!** | *Good evening!* |

Speakers frequently shorten these greetings to **Morgen!, Tag!, Abend!** From approximately 11 A.M. through lunch time, co-workers sometimes greet each other in passing with **Mahlzeit!** (*Have a nice meal!*).

In addition to these general greetings, many others are regionally unique. Austrians and Bavarians say **Servus!** with their friends and **Grüß Gott!** generally, instead of **Guten Tag!** The Swiss, particularly those in the region of Zurich (**Zürich**), greet everybody with **Grüezi!**

Because of the growing influence of English throughout German-speaking countries, it is now quite common to hear **Hallo!** used as a friendly, neutral greeting by younger and middle-aged speakers.

To say good-bye, speakers use several different expressions. **Auf Wiedersehen** is the generic expression for *good-bye.* **Tschüss** is more informal, although variations of it are heard by most speakers throughout Germany, Switzerland, and Austria.

| | |
|---|---|
| **Auf Wiedersehen!** | *Good-bye!* |
| **Tschüss!** | *Bye!* |
| **Gute Nacht!** | *Good night!* |

■ **Kulturkreuzung** Germans tend to greet people in situations where Americans and Canadians typically do not. Do you say "*Good morning*" when you walk into a convenience store? When do you greet the clerk in a coffee shop—when you enter the store or when you come to the counter? Do you typically shake hands when you meet a person for the first time?

**16** **Guten Morgen.** (*Good morning.*) Practice the following dialogues with a partner until you feel confident enough to perform one from memory for the class.

1. PROFESSOR KÜHLMANN:  Guten Tag, meine Damen° und Herren°.          *ladies / gentlemen*
              STUDENTEN:  Tag, Professor Kühlmann.

2. MUTTER:  Morgen, Ulla. Kaffee?
        ULLA:  Morgen, Mutter. Ja, bitte.

3. HERR LANGE (*in München*):  Grüß Gott.
        FRAU HILLGRUBER:  Grüß Gott, Herr Lange.

**17** **Grüß Gott.** Select an appropriate greeting based on the time of day, the region, and the person you are to greet. You may need to consult the maps of Germany, Switzerland, and Austria inside the front cover of your textbook. More than one answer may be possible.

Stuttgart

Berlin

Salzburg

Innsbruck

Zürich

*Strukturen und Vokabeln*

## II Describing yourself and others

### A. The verb *sein*; subject pronouns

A simple way to describe yourself or another person is to use a form of the verb **sein** (*to be*).

| | |
|---|---|
| **Ich bin** Amerikanerin. | ***I am** (an) American.* |
| **Sie sind** freundlich. | ***You are** friendly.* |

In the examples above, the words **ich** and **Sie** are called subject pronouns. They refer to individual people or things (singular pronouns) or groups of people or things (plural pronouns). Here are the present-tense forms of **sein.**

<table>
<tr><td colspan="5" align="center">sein: to be</td></tr>
<tr><td>Person</td><td colspan="2">Singular</td><td colspan="2">Plural</td></tr>
<tr><td>1st</td><td>ich bin</td><td>I am</td><td>wir sind</td><td>we are</td></tr>
<tr><td>2nd, informal</td><td>du bist</td><td>you are</td><td>ihr seid</td><td>you are</td></tr>
<tr><td>2nd, formal</td><td>Sie sind</td><td>you are</td><td>Sie sind</td><td>you are</td></tr>
<tr><td>3rd</td><td>er/sie/es ist</td><td>he/she/it is</td><td>sie sind</td><td>they are</td></tr>
</table>

See the **Arbeitsbuch** for additional practice with structures and vocabulary.

**The verb *sein*. Sein** is an infinitive.

The formal subject pronoun for *you* is **Sie**, always spelled with a capital **S**. The forms for *she* and *they* are spelled **sie** (lowercase **s**), but naturally at the beginning of a sentence, they have a capital **S**. In those cases, the verb form and context will help you avoid confusion with the formal **Sie** (*you*).

**18    Kurze Gespräche.** (*Short conversations.*)  Fill in the blanks with the correct form of the verb **sein.** With a partner, practice reading the dialogues.

1. *Im Deutschunterricht°*

   DOKTOR LANGE: Guten Abend. Ich _____ Doktor Lange. Wer _____ Sie?

   HERR ADJEMIAN: Ich _____ Herr Adjemian.

   DOKTOR LANGE: _____ Sie Frau Nakasone?

   FRAU TANAKA: Nein, ich _____ Frau Tanaka. Sie _____ Frau Nakasone.

   *In German class*

2. *An der Universität°*

   INGRID: _____ der Hörsaal da vorne?

   KARL: Ja, da _____ er.

   INGRID: Und der Professor?

   KARL: Er _____ auch schon da.

   *At the university*

3. *Vor dem Hörsaal°*

   ANNA: Pardon, _____ ihr Studenten hier?

   KARL UND ULI: Ja, wir _____ beide Studenten.

   ANNA: _____ hier Hörsaal 20?

   KARL UND ULI: Ja, gleich da vorne.

   *In front of the lecture hall*

## B. The pronoun *you*

The German language has three different words for *you*. **Du** is used when speaking to a friend, a family member, a child, a pet, or when praying to God. Students, longtime colleagues, workers, and soldiers of equal rank typically also use **du** with each other.

Bist **du** Studentin?    *Are you a student?*

The pronoun **ihr** is the plural form of **du**. Students, for example, use **ihr** when addressing more than one friend. It is used much like "*you guys*" in English.

**Ihr** seid hier richtig.    *You (guys) are in the right place.*

**Sie** is used with one or more adults when the speaker wants to show respect for them or does not know them well. When students are in about the eleventh grade, teachers begin to address them with **Sie**.

Wie heißen **Sie?**    *What is your name?* or *What are your names?*

You will use the **Sie**-form exclusively in the early chapters. Using **du** instead of **Sie** may be considered offensive by an unfamiliar person. If you are unsure which form to use, it is always safest to use **Sie** until the person to whom you are talking suggests that you use **du**.

*Sie oder du?*

It is considered inappropriate and disrespectful to address a stranger with **du**. Some people feel insulted when not addressed properly.

The pronoun **du** is also used by friends as an attention-getter; i.e., *hey*: **Du, Thomas, bist du nervös?**

**19    Du, ihr oder Sie?**  Decide whether Anna should use **du, ihr,** or **Sie** with the following people.

|  | *du* | *ihr* | *Sie* |
|---|---|---|---|
| 1. the professor she asks for directions | ☐ | ☐ | ☐ |
| 2. the student she sits next to | ☐ | ☐ | ☐ |
| 3. her dog | ☐ | ☐ | ☐ |
| 4. Professor Freund | ☐ | ☐ | ☐ |
| 5. her mother | ☐ | ☐ | ☐ |
| 6. some friends in a pub | ☐ | ☐ | ☐ |

**BRENNPUNKT KULTUR**

### Titles of address

When addressing acquaintances, most German-speaking adults use a title before the person's last name. When talking to adults, it is better to err on the side of formality at first and use the title.

| | |
|---|---|
| **Herr** (*for men*):  **Herr Müller** | *Mr. Müller* |
| **Frau** (*for women*):  **Frau Seifert** | *Mrs.* or *Ms. Seifert* |
| **Fräulein** (*for young girls*):  **Fräulein Schmidt** | *Miss Schmidt* |
| **Guten Morgen**, **Herr Müller**. | *Good morning, Mr. Müller.* |

**Fräulein,** when used with a last name, should not be used for adult women. It is outdated and carries negative connotations. In restaurants, **Frau Ober** is beginning to replace **Fräulein,** traditionally used to call the waitress.

In formal writing and speech and when talking about another person, German speakers also like to include the professional title of the person they are speaking with: **Guten Tag, Herr Professor Winkler.**

**Kulturkreuzung** Do you use names when you greet your friends? Do you use titles when greeting older people?

## III Asking for someone's name
### The verb **heißen**

Besides the verb **sein**, German speakers also use the verb **heißen** (*to be called*) to introduce themselves.

Ich **heiße** Barbara Müller.    *My name is Barbara Müller.*

These are the present-tense forms of **heißen**.

| heißen: *to be called* | | |
|---|---|---|
| **Person** | **Singular** | **Plural** |
| **1st** | ich **heiße** | wir **heißen** |
| **2nd, informal** | du **heißt** | ihr **heißt** |
| **2nd, formal** | Sie **heißen** | Sie **heißen** |
| **3rd** | er/sie/es **heißt** | sie **heißen** |

The verb *heißen*. Heißen is an infinitive.

The letter **ß** (called **Esszett**) is used to represent the **s** sound after long vowels or diphthongs. The Swiss do not use **ß**, only **ss**.

Meersburg am Bodensee

 **20**  **Wie heißen Sie?**  You are at a formal reception. Go around and ask five students what their names are using the verb **heißen.** Below are some greetings and questions to help you. Try to remember the names of the students you meet so you can introduce them to the rest of the class.

> S1: *Guten Tag. Ich heiße Thomas Conrad. Wie heißen Sie?*
> S2: *Ich heiße Clausen, Karen Clausen.*
> S1: *Guten Tag, Frau Clausen. Sehr angenehm.*
> S2: *Sehr angenehm, Herr Conrad.*
> S1 (*to S3*): *Das ist Karen Clausen.*

Guten Morgen. • Guten Tag. • Guten Abend. • Servus. • Grüezi. •
Grüß Gott. • Hallo. • Wie heißen Sie? • Wer sind Sie? • Ich bin …

> **Wie heißen Sie?** German speakers often give their family name, followed by their entire name when responding to the question **Wie heißen Sie?** or **Wer sind Sie?**

## *Wissenswerte Vokabeln: das Alphabet*

### *Spelling names*

| | | | | | | | | | | |
|---|---|---|---|---|---|---|---|---|---|---|
| **a** | ah | **h** | hah | **o** | oh | **u** | uh | **ß** | ess-tsett | **T** großes „t" |
| **b** | beh | **i** | ih | **p** | peh | **v** | fau | **ä** | ah-Umlaut | **t** kleines „t" |
| **c** | tseh | **j** | jot | **q** | kuh | **w** | weh | **ö** | oh-Umlaut | **tt** Doppel „t" |
| **d** | deh | **k** | kah | **r** | err | **x** | iks | **ü** | uh-Umlaut | |
| **e** | eh | **l** | ell | **s** | ess | **y** | üppsilon | | | |
| **f** | eff | **m** | emm | **t** | teh | **z** | tsett | | | |
| **g** | geh | **n** | enn | | | | | | | |

Wie schreiben Sie „Professor"?  *P-r-o-f-e-ss-o-r.*
Wie schreiben Sie „Professorin"?  *P-r-o-f-e-ss-o-r-i-n.*

**21**  **Das Alphabet.**  Listen as your instructor models the sounds of the alphabet. Then repeat the sounds as instructed. Practice spelling the names of students in your class as well.

**22**   **Wie bitte?** (*Excuse me?*)  You are working as a telemarketer in Vienna. Your job is to confirm the spelling of the names of people identified as winners of a trip to the United States. Choose a name from the telephone directory for Vienna and call that person to confirm the spelling of his/her name. Take turns. Follow the model below.

*Am Telefon*

S1: *Guten Morgen. Hier ist Herr (Frau) _____. Wie heißen Sie bitte?*
S2: *Beck, Hans Beck.*
S1: *Wie bitte? Wie schreiben Sie das?*
S2: *B - e - c - k.*
S1: *Danke. Auf Wiederhören°.*

*Auf …: Good-bye (on the phone)*

| | |
|---|---|
| Beck, Hans, 22, Magdeburgerstr. 63 | **233 94 37** |
| Bleisch, Ute, 16, Effingerg. 15, Stg. 2 | **456 45 32** |
| Meißner, Günter, 13, Volkg. 7, Stg. 15 | **812 69 54** |
| Schumm, Harry, 5, Marg. Gürtel 126, Stg. 2 | **45 41 47** |
| Wurmisch, Hedwig, 16, Speckbacherg. 8 | **647 04 31** |

Abbreviations are often used in telephone directories. Can you find the following address indications in the list shown here? **Effingergasse:** *Effinger Lane;* **Magdeburgerstrasse:** *Magdeburger Street;* **Margareten Gürtel:** *Margareten Loop;* **Stiege:** *stairway, floor.*

## *Wissenswerte Vokabeln: die Zahlen*

### *Asking for personal information*

| | | | |
|---|---|---|---|
| 0 = null | 10 = zehn | 20 = zwanzig | 30 = dreißig |
| 1 = eins | 11 = elf | 21 = einundzwanzig | 40 = vierzig |
| 2 = zwei | 12 = zwölf | 22 = zweiundzwanzig | 50 = fünfzig |
| 3 = drei | 13 = dreizehn | 23 = dreiundzwanzig | 60 = sechzig |
| 4 = vier | 14 = vierzehn | 24 = vierundzwanzig | 70 = siebzig |
| 5 = fünf | 15 = fünfzehn | 25 = fünfundzwanzig | 80 = achtzig |
| 6 = sechs | 16 = sechzehn | 26 = sechsundzwanzig | 90 = neunzig |
| 7 = sieben | 17 = siebzehn | 27 = siebenundzwanzig | 100 = hundert |
| 8 = acht | 18 = achtzehn | 28 = achtundzwanzig | 101 = hunderteins |
| 9 = neun | 19 = neunzehn | 29 = neunundzwanzig | 1 000 = tausend |

Wie alt sind Sie?   *Ich bin … Jahre alt.*

Was ist die Adresse?

**23**  **Autogrammspiel.** (*Autograph game.*)  Walk around and find a classmate for each age listed below. When you find someone who matches the age description, have that person sign his/her name.

☐ S1:  *Sind Sie achtzehn Jahre alt?*
   S2:  *Nein, ich bin …* (oder°)                                    *or*
        *Ja, ich bin achtzehn.* _____Christina_____

1. 18 Jahre alt _____
2. 19 Jahre alt _____
3. 20 Jahre alt _____
4. 21 Jahre alt _____
5. über 25 Jahre alt _____

Wie alt sind sie?

## *Wissenswerte Vokabeln: Aussehen*
### *Describing physical characteristics*

Ich habe … • Er hat … • Sie hat …

braune Augen

grüne Augen

blaue Augen

die Brille: *glasses*
**Er hat eine Brille.**

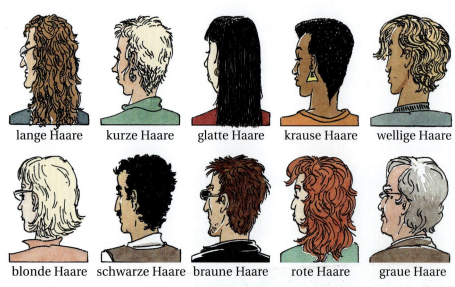

lange Haare    kurze Haare    glatte Haare    krause Haare    wellige Haare

blonde Haare    schwarze Haare    braune Haare    rote Haare    graue Haare

**die Glatze:** *bald*
**Der Professor hat eine Glatze.**

schlank/mollig

groß/klein

alt/jung

hübsch/unattraktiv

The word **hässlich** (*ugly*) is used to describe things. It is extremely rude to describe people as **hässlich**. Use the word **unattraktiv**.

**Attraktiv** is a synonym for **hübsch** and is used mostly for women. Men are referred to as **gut aussehend** (*good looking*).

🟨 Wie sehen Sie aus?°    *Ich bin (schlank). Ich habe (schwarze Haare).*    *What do you look like?*

**24**   **Wer ist das?** (*Who is that?*)  Match the descriptions below with the appropriate person in each photo.

1. Sie ist relativ jung und hübsch und hat braune, wellige Haare.
2. Er ist sehr jung und klein und hat blonde Haare.
3. Er ist 35 Jahre alt, schlank und hat kurze, braune Haare.
4. Sie ist 75 Jahre alt und mollig. Sie hat graue Haare.
5. Sie ist 32 Jahre alt, schlank und hat kurze, blonde Haare.
6. Sie ist 5 Jahre alt und hat lange, rote Haare.

Frau Winter                                              Frau Becker

Herr und Frau Zwicker und die Kinder: Baby Max und Regina

**25** **Anna ist jung.** (*Anna is young.*) Describe the characters you have encountered so far, using words from **Wissenswerte Vokabeln.** Try to use at least three descriptive words for each picture.

Anna Adler

Annas Mutter

die Professorin

Professor Freund

▪ Das ist Anna. Sie hat (*blonde Haare und blaue Augen*). Sie ist (*jung*) und sie ist (*schlank*).

**26** **Wie sehen sie aus?** (*What do they look like?*) As a class, generate a list of famous personalities that you all know. Describe one of these people to a partner and see if your partner can guess whom you are talking about.

▪ S1:  *Er ist … Er hat …*
        *Sie ist … Sie hat …*

## IV  Asking for information and clarification

### Question formation

There are two types of questions in English and German: information questions and yes/no questions.

### A. Information questions

Information questions (**Ergänzungsfragen**) require an answer that provides specific information. They begin with one of the following question words.

| | | | |
|---|---|---|---|
| **wann?** | *when?* | **Wann** ist das? | ***When** is that?* |
| **warum?** | *why?* | **Warum** sagt Anna nichts? | ***Why** doesn't Anna say anything?* |
| **was?** | *what?* | **Was** sucht Anna? | ***What** is Anna looking for?* |
| **wer?** | *who?* | **Wer** sind sie? | ***Who** are they?* |
| **wie?** | *how?* | **Wie** heißen Sie? | ***What** is your name?* |
| **wie viel?** | *how much?* | **Wie viel** ist das? | ***How much** is that?* |
| **wie viele?** | *how many?* | **Wie viele** Studenten sind hier? | ***How many** students are here?* |
| **wo?** | *where?* | **Wo** bin ich? | ***Where** am I?* |
| **woher?** | *from where?* | **Woher** kommen Sie? | ***Where** are you **from**?* |
| **wohin?** | *to where?* | **Wohin** gehen Sie? | ***Where** are you going **to**?* |

**Was für?** means *what kind of?*

Be careful not to confuse the meanings of **wer** *who* and **wo** *where*.

Information questions are formed with one of the question words, followed by the verb, then the subject. The speaker lowers his/her pitch at the end of an information question.

> Wo bin ich?    *Where am I?*

Unlike English, German does not require a helping verb (e.g., *do/ does*) to form questions.

> Was sprechen Sie?    *What **do** you speak?*
> Woher kommen Sie?    *Where **do** you come from?*

German does not always use the same question word as English does in similar expressions, and question words with prepositions are not usually separated in German as they are in English.

> **Wie** heißen Sie?    ***What** is your name?*
> **Wie** ist Ihr Name?    ***What** is your name?*
> **Woher** kommen Sie?    ***Where** are you **from**?*
> ***Where** do you come **from**?*

### The question *Wie bitte?*

**Wie bitte?** is commonly used to ask someone to repeat for clarification, much as we use *What?* or *Excuse me?* or *I beg your pardon?* in English.

> WILLI:  Guten Tag. Ich heiße Willi.
> JULIANNA:  Wie bitte?
> WILLI:  Willi. Mein Name ist Willi.

## B. Yes/no questions

Yes/no questions (**Ja/Nein-Fragen** or **Entscheidungsfragen**) give information which the person answering is expected to negate or confirm. They always begin with the verb and the pitch rises at the end of the question.

> Sind Sie Amerikanerin?    *Are you (an) American?*
> Verstehen Sie Deutsch?    *Do you understand German?*

Note again that German does not require any helping verbs (e.g., *do/does*) to form questions.

 **27** **Drei Interviews.** Ask three different students the following questions.

> S1: *Wie heißen Sie?*
> S2: *Tom.*

|  |  | *1* | *2* | *3* |  |
|---|---|---|---|---|---|
| 1.  Wie heißen Sie? |  | ____ | ____ | ____ |  |
| 2.  Woher kommen Sie? | (aus …) | ____ | ____ | ____ |  |
| 3.  Wo wohnen° Sie? | (in …) | ____ | ____ | ____ | *live* |
| 4.  Wie alt sind Sie? |  | ____ | ____ | ____ (… Jahre alt) |  |
| 5.  Wie sehen Sie aus? (Ich bin/habe …) |  | ____ | ____ | ____ |  |

# V Identifying people and classroom objects

## A. Noun gender and number

All German nouns are capitalized, and every noun is categorized into one of three genders **(das Genus):** masculine, neuter, or feminine. Nouns often are accompanied by a definite article **(der bestimmte Artikel)** meaning *the*. The form this definite article takes **(der, das,** or **die)** depends on whether the noun is masculine, neuter, or feminine.

| | |
|---|---|
| Masculine: | **der** Professor, **der** Hörsaal |
| Neuter: | **das** Buch, **das** Auto |
| Feminine: | **die** Professorin, **die** Mutter, **die** Tafel |

In German non-living things as well as living things are classified either as masculine (e.g., **der Hörsaal**), neuter (e.g., **das Zimmer**), or feminine (e.g., **die Tür, die Universität**). Some words for people are even categorized as neuter, e.g., **das Kind** (*the child*), **das Mädchen** (*the girl*). It is important to memorize the definite article (**der, das,** or **die**) that accompanies each new noun you learn. In the plural, the definite article for all nouns is **die**, regardless of their gender.

## Wissenswerte Vokabeln: das Klassenzimmer, der Hörsaal
### Naming and identifying classroom objects

🟨 Was ist das? *Das ist die Uhr.*

You will learn about the formation of plural nouns in **Kapitel 3.**

**der Tisch:** *table*

**28**   **Das Klassenzimmer.**  Listen as your instructor models the commands below and then asks you to carry them out.

> Zeigen Sie auf das Arbeitsbuch (das Buch, das Fenster).
> Zeigen Sie auf die Kreide (die Lampe, die Landkarte, die Leinwand, die Steckdose, die Tafel, die Tür, die Uhr).
> Zeigen Sie auf den Fernseher (den Overheadprojektor, den Papierkorb, den Schreibtisch, den Bleistift, den Stuhl, den DVD-Spieler).

> You may have noticed your instructor saying **auf den Stuhl** instead of **der Stuhl.** The difference will be explained in a later chapter.

**29**   **Sie sind der Professor/die Professorin.**  Ask your partner to identify as many classroom objects as possible.

> S1:  *Ist das die Kreide?*
> S2:  *Ja, das ist die Kreide.* (oder)
>       *Nein, das ist der Stuhl.* (oder)
>       *Ich weiß es nicht.°*

*Ich weiß es nicht: I don't know.*

## B. The nominative case: definite articles *der, das, die*

Nouns can have different grammatical functions in sentences, and German uses a specific *case* to highlight each function. You have already seen that the definite article identifies the gender and number of a noun. The definite article also identifies the grammatical function (or case) of a noun in a sentence. You will learn about the grammatical functions of nouns later in this chapter.

For now, you should know that the nominative case is used for nouns serving as the subject of a verb and that the definite articles **der, das,** and **die** are used for nominative-case nouns.

| **der, das, die:** *the* | | | |
|---|---|---|---|
| **Case** | **Masculine** | **Neuter** | **Feminine** | **Plural (all genders)** |
| Nominative | der | das | die | die |

**30**   **Ist das der Stuhl?** (*Is that the chair?*)  Fill in the blanks with **der, das,** or **die.**

1. Wo ist _____ Schreibtisch?
2. Ist das _____ Stuhl?
3. Wo ist _____ Uhr?
4. Wo ist _____ Papierkorb?
5. Ist das _____ Fernseher?
6. Wie heißt _____ Buch?
7. Ist _____ Steckdose kaputt?
8. Ist _____ Fenster auf°?

*open*

## Wissenswerte Vokabeln: die Farben
### Identifying objects by color

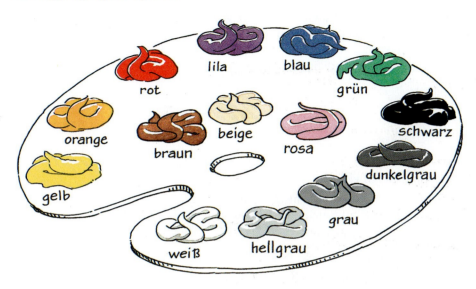

 **31** **Welche Farbe hat …?** Work with a partner to describe the color of the classroom objects you now know.

die Tafel • die Tür • der Schreibtisch • die Wand • das Buch • das Arbeitsbuch • der Papierkorb • der Stuhl • die Uhr

S1: *Welche Farbe hat der Stuhl?*
S2: *Der Stuhl ist schwarz.*
S1: *Richtig.* (oder)
  *Nein, der Stuhl ist braun.*

**32** **Annas Klassenzimmer.** Complete the following description of Anna's classroom by providing **der, das,** or **die.**

Anna lernt Deutsch an der Universität. _____ Klassenzimmer ist relativ schön. _____ Schreibtisch ist hellbraun. _____ Papierkorb ist orange. _____ Landkarte zeigt° Europa. _____ Tafel ist nicht schwarz. Sie ist grün. _____ Uhr ist kaputt. _____ Professorin heißt Ziegler. Sie sagt: „Guten Morgen. Nehmen Sie bitte Platz." _____ Stühle° stehen schon° im Halbkreis°. _____ Studenten° sprechen sehr viel Deutsch miteinander°. _____ Fernseher ist an, aber _____ DVD-Spieler ist kaputt.

*shows*

*chairs / already / **im … :** semi-circle / students / with each other*

## C. The nominative case: indefinite articles and **kein**

### 1. The indefinite article: *ein*

The indefinite article (**der unbestimmte Artikel**) identifies the typical rather than the particular.

**Ein** Klassenzimmer hat eine Tafel.    *A classroom has a blackboard.*
**Eine** Tafel ist grün oder schwarz.    *A blackboard is green or black.*

German classrooms frequently have a moveable green slate board that is cleaned with a wet sponge instead of an eraser.

The indefinite articles in German are **ein** for masculine nouns, **ein** for neuter nouns, and **eine** for feminine nouns. All three correspond to *a* and *an* in English.

As with the definite article, the indefinite article signals the gender (masculine, neuter, or feminine) and the grammatical function (or the case, e.g., nominative) of the noun in the sentence. Because **ein** literally means *one*, it cannot be used to refer to more than one item.

The following chart lists the nominative-case indefinite articles.

|  | Masculine | Neuter | Feminine | Plural |
|---|---|---|---|---|
| Nominative | ein | ein | eine | — |

### Sprache im Alltag: Abbreviated forms of ein

In everyday speech, most German speakers abbreviate the indefinite article **ein** and **eine** to **'n** and **'ne**. This is widely heard throughout the German-speaking world.

Er ist **'n** Freund von mir.
Das ist **'ne** gute Idee.

**33** **Das Klassenzimmer.** Professor Freund is talking about classroom objects with his German class. Fill in the following blanks with ein or eine.

PROFESSOR: Hier sind _____ Landkarte, _____ Leinwand und _____ Schreibtisch. Was ist das?
STUDENT: Das ist _____ Uhr.
PROFESSOR: Und was ist das?
STUDENT: Das ist _____ Stuhl.
PROFESSOR: Ist das _____ Fenster?
STUDENT: Nein, das ist _____ Fernseher, und das ist _____ DVD-Spieler.

## 2. Negating the indefinite article: *kein*

German has two ways of expressing negation. In **Anlauftexte I** and **II** you have already seen that speakers negate verbs with **nicht** (*not*).

Anna versteht **nicht.**          *Anna does **not** understand.*

To negate a non-specific noun, German speakers use a form of the word **kein** (*not a/an, no,* or *not any*).

| | |
|---|---|
| Ist das ein Stuhl? | *Is that a chair?* |
| Nein, das ist **kein** Stuhl. (Das ist ein Tisch.) | *No, that is **not a** chair. (It is a table.)* |
| Ist das eine Tür? | *Is that a door?* |
| Nein, das ist **keine** Tür. (Das ist ein Fenster.) | *No, that is **not a** door. (It is a window.)* |
| Ist das ein Deutschbuch? | *Is that a German book?* |
| Nein, das ist **kein** Deutschbuch. (Das ist ein Russischbuch.) | *No, that is **not a** German book. (It is a Russian book.)* |

The following chart lists the nominative-case forms of **kein.**

|  | Masculine | Neuter | Feminine | Plural |
|---|---|---|---|---|
| Nominative | kein | kein | keine | keine |

**34** **Ein Marsmensch° im Klassenzimmer.** Find a partner and pre-
tend one of you is a Martian who cannot get his/her "earth classroom"
vocabulary right. The "Martian" asks whether various classroom objects are
called by certain names. The "earthling" confirms what the Martian says or
contradicts with the correct information.

*Martian*

S1 (MARTIAN): *Ist das eine Tür?*
S2 (EARTHLING): *Ja, das ist eine Tür.* (oder)
*Nein, das ist keine Tür. Das ist eine Tafel.*

## Wissenswerte Vokabeln: Länder und Nationalitäten°
### Asking for personal information

*Länder ...: countries and nationalities*

|  | die Nationalität | |
|---|---|---|
| *das Land* | *Maskulin* | *Feminin* |
| die USA/Amerika | der Amerikaner | die Amerikanerin |
| England | der Engländer | die Engländerin |
| Japan | der Japaner | die Japanerin |
| Kanada | der Kanadier | die Kanadierin |
| Mexiko | der Mexikaner | die Mexikanerin |
| Österreich | der Österreicher | die Österreicherin |
| die Schweiz | der Schweizer | die Schweizerin |

*Exceptions:*

|  |  |  |
|---|---|---|
| Deutschland | der Deutsche | die Deutsche |
|  | ein Deutscher | eine Deutsche |
| Frankreich | der Franzose | die Französin |

**W. Vok.: Nationalitäten.** A
few country names like **die
Schweiz** require the article
**die.** The **die** accompanying
**die USA** is the plural article
**die,** which refers to **die
Staaten** (*the states*).

**W. Vok.: Nationalitäten.** The
feminine designation is
usually identified by the
ending **-in,** except for **die
Deutsche.** Some terms for
nationalities, among them
those describing Germans,
take different masculine
endings, depending on
whether they are used with
a definite or with an indefinite article: **der Deutsche,**
but **ein Deutscher.**

**35** **Anna ist Amerikanerin.** Make statements about the nationalities of the following people.

▫ Jennifer: aus den USA    *Jennifer ist Amerikanerin.*

1. Helena: aus der Schweiz
2. Jean-Luc: aus Frankreich
3. Margaret: aus England
4. Franz: aus Österreich
5. Robert: aus den USA
6. María: aus Mexiko
7. Jill: aus Kanada
8. Klaus: aus Deutschland

> German does not use **ein/eine** when describing people's nationalities: **Sie ist Amerikanerin.** *She is (an) American.* **Er ist Deutscher.** *He is (a) German.*

## BRENNPUNKT KULTUR

### Where German is spoken

German is the native language (**die Muttersprache**) of 100–120 million people in Germany, Austria, Switzerland, and Liechtenstein. This makes it the most widely spoken language (24%) in the European Union. German is also spoken by substantial minorities in France (Alsace-Lorraine), Italy (Southern Tyrol), Luxembourg, the Czech Republic (Bohemia), Belgium, Poland, Romania, Russia (the former East Prussia, and other areas), and by immigrant populations throughout North and South America. For many former foreign workers who have returned to their native countries, e.g., Turkey, Greece, Italy, Spain, and the former Yugoslavia, German is a second language. Because of Germany's strong economic position and leadership in the European Union, interest in learning German has increased dramatically in Eastern Europe since 1990.

■ **Kulturkreuzung** Recent census data revealed that German is the third or fourth most widely spoken language other than English in many American states, and certainly as well in many Canadian provinces. Is German spoken anywhere in your community? Are there any German-language newspapers in your community?

**Himmel Haus**
German Foods - Imported Gifts
3444 S. Main Street
Elkhart - Indiana 46517
Phone 574-293-8361

GROSSE AUSWAHL    Telefondienst zu jeder Zeit

**36** **Deutschland.** Look at the map of Germany inside the front cover of the book and match the cities on the left with their locations on the right.

1. Heidelberg ist
2. Berlin ist
3. München ist
4. Erfurt, Weimar und Jena sind
5. Hannover und Göttingen sind
6. Bonn, Köln und Düsseldorf sind
7. Rostock und Stralsund sind
8. Frankfurt, Kassel, Gießen und Mainz sind
9. Dresden und Leipzig sind
10. Bremerhaven ist

a. am Rhein in Nordrhein-Westfalen.
b. an der Nordsee.
c. an der Ostsee in Mecklenburg-Vorpommern.
d. in Baden-Württemberg.
e. in Bayern.
f. in Hessen.
g. in Niedersachsen.
h. in Sachsen.
i. in Thüringen.
j. nicht weit° von Polen.

***nicht weit:*** *not far*

**37** **Nein, sie ist keine Deutsche.** Your partner has incorrect information about the nationalities of the people listed in **Aktivität 35.** Respond to the questions with the correct information. Be sure to use **kein/keine** in your response.

◻ Robert / Deutscher   (aus den USA)
S1: *Ist Robert Deutscher?*
S2: *Nein, er ist kein Deutscher. Er ist Amerikaner.*

1. Franz / Deutscher   (aus Österreich)
2. Helena / Amerikanerin   (aus der Schweiz)
3. Klaus / Kanadier   (aus Deutschland)
4. Jill / Mexikanerin   (aus Kanada)
5. Margaret / Österreicherin   (aus England)

**38** **Auf einer Party.** (*At a party.*) Use the following cues to ask students about their nationalities.

◻ USA / Schweiz

S1: *Sind Sie Amerikaner(in)?*
S2: *Ja, ich bin Amerikaner(in). Und Sie?*
S1: *Ich bin Schweizer(in).*

1. USA / Schweiz
2. Österreich / Japan
3. Kanada / Österreich
4. Deutschland / England
5. die Schweiz / Frankreich
6. Japan / Deutschland
7. Mexiko / Schweiz
8. England / Österreich

**39** **Wer ist das?** Here are some famous personalities. Using the questions below to guide you, ask each other as many questions as you can about each person.

> Wer ist das? • Wie heißt er/sie? • Woher kommt er/sie? • Ist das … ? •
> Ist er/sie Amerikaner/Amerikanerin? • Kommt er/sie aus Österreich?

S1: *Wer ist das?*
S2: *Das ist Steffi Graf.*
S1: *Kommt sie aus Amerika?*
S2: *Nein. Sie kommt aus Deutschland.*

## D. The nominative case

### 1. Subject of a sentence

In German the subject of a sentence (**das Subjekt**) is in the nominative case. The subject is the person or thing that performs the action described by the verb. It answers the question **wer?** (*who?*) regarding people, and the question **was?** (*what?*) regarding inanimate objects.

*subject*
**Wer** macht die Tür auf?              *Who is opening the door?*

*subject*
**Der Professor** macht die Tür auf.    *The professor is opening the door.*

*subject*
**Was** ist schwarz oder grün?          *What is black or green?*

*subject*
**Eine Tafel** ist schwarz oder grün.   *A blackboard is black or green.*

In an English sentence the subject is often the first word or phrase. In a German sentence the subject is frequently not the first word or phrase. Nevertheless, the subject always determines the ending of the verb.

|                      |                           |
| -------------------- | ------------------------- |
| *subject*            | *subject*                 |
| Da vorne ist **Hörsaal 20.** | **Lecture Hall 20** *is up ahead.* |

> **Reading Strategy.** Learn to identify the subject by how it fits grammatically with the verb.

Here is a summary chart of the nominative-case definite articles, indefinite articles, and forms of **kein.**

|                    | Masculine | Neuter | Feminine | Plural |
| ------------------ | --------- | ------ | -------- | ------ |
| Definite article   | der       | das    | die      | die    |
| Indefinite article | ein       | ein    | eine     | —      |
| **kein**           | kein      | kein   | keine    | keine  |

## 2. Predicate nominative

The predicate nominative (**das Prädikatsnomen**) restates the subject of the sentence and follows the verbs **sein** (*to be*), **heißen** (*to be called*), and a few others.

| | |
| --- | --- |
| Sie ist **die Studentin aus Bonn.** | She is **the (female) student from Bonn.** |
| ***Vorsprung*** ist **ein Deutschbuch.** | ***Vorsprung*** *is **a German textbook.*** |
| Anna ist **Amerikanerin.** | *Anna is **(an) American.*** |
| Der Professor heißt **Freund.** | *The professor's name is **Freund.*** |

In the sentences above, **Sie,** *Vorsprung,* **Anna,** and **Der Professor** are all subjects, and **die Studentin, ein Deutschbuch, Amerikanerin,** and **Freund** are all predicate nouns.

In German, the indefinite article is not used when stating a person's nationality, profession, or religion.

| | |
| --- | --- |
| Er ist Amerikaner. | *He is (an) American.* |
| Sie ist Professorin. | *She is a professor.* |
| Sie sind Katholiken. | *They are Catholics.* |

 **40** **Deutsche Prominente°.** Match the prominent Germans on the left with their professions on the right.

*celebrities*

🟨 S1: *Wer ist Franka Potente?*
   S2: *Sie ist Film-Schauspielerin.*

| | |
| --- | --- |
| 1. Franka Potente | a. der Chef von DaimlerChrysler |
| 2. Roger Federer | b. Basketballspieler in der NBA |
| 3. Heidi Klum | c. ein Formel-1-Autorennfahrer |
| 4. Günter Grass | d. Model |
| 5. Dieter Zetsche | e. Autor und Nobelpreisträger° für Literatur |
| 6. Michael Schumacher | f. Tennisspieler |
| 7. Dirk Nowitzki | g. Film-Schauspielerin |

*Nobel Prize winner*

## E. Pronoun substitution

The pronouns **er, es,** and **sie** are used to replace the nouns in a sentence. By referring back to nouns, pronouns unify sentences into a tight narrative, thereby avoiding repetition and adding variety to sentences.

**Der Tisch** ist groß. **Er** ist braun.   *The table is big. It is brown.*
Wo ist **das Buch?** Hier ist **es.**   *Where is the book? Here it is.*
Das ist **die Tafel. Sie** ist schwarz.   *That is the board. It is black.*
Wo sind **die Studenten?** Hier sind **sie.**   *Where are the students? Here they are.*

**41   Wo ist der Tisch? – Hier ist er.** Ask your partner questions about the location of various people and objects using the question word **wo?** (*where?*). Use the appropriate personal pronoun (**er, es,** or **sie**) in your response.

S1: *Wo ist der Tisch?*
S2: *Hier/Da° ist er.*   *There*

das Fenster? • die Tafel? • der Professor? • die Professorin? • das Buch? • der Stuhl? • der Fernseher? • das Arbeitsbuch? • der Schreibtisch?

**Freie Kommunikation**

**Jeopardy.** Form questions in German which accompany these statements from two categories: **Prominente Deutsche oder Österreicher** and **Prominente Amerikaner/Amerikanerinnen**. The monetary value of each item is listed.

*Prominente Deutsche oder Österreicher*

$ 10   1. Er/Sie ist der/die deutsche Bundeskanzler(in).
$ 20   2. Er kommt aus Österreich. Er ist stark°. Er ist der Gouverneur von   *strong*
       Kalifornien.
$ 30   3. Sie ist sehr attraktiv. Sie hat blonde Haare und ist Model.
$ 40   4. Er ist der deutsche Vize-Kanzler und Außenminister°.   *foreign minister*

*Prominente Amerikaner/Amerikanerinnen*

$ 10   1. Er ist der Präsident der USA.
$ 20   2. Er ist Tennisspieler und der Mann von Steffi Graf.
$ 30   3. Sie ist Japano-Amerikanerin. Sie ist Eiskunstläuferin°.   *figure skater*
$ 40   4. Sie ist Afro-Amerikanerin und Rocksängerin°. Sie ist über 60 Jahre   *rock singer*
       alt und wohnt in der Schweiz.

 **S c h r e i b e c k e**

**Lesen Sie** *Stern.* Fill in the subscription information for *Stern* with your name and information under **Angaben des Werbers** and include a friend's subscription under **Angaben des neuen** *Stern***-Abonnenten.**

BEHALTEN SIE DEN ÜBERBLICK.

## Ja, wir möchten alle *stern*-Vorteile!

### Angaben des neuen *stern*-Abonnenten

Name, Vorname

Straße/Hausnummer

Postleitzahl          Wohnort

19

Telefonnummer                    Geburtsdatum

E-Mail

Schicken Sie mir 1 Jahr lang wöchentlich den *stern* samt TV-Magazin zum Einzelpreis von zzt. € 2,30 statt € 2,50 inkl. Mehrwertsteuer und Versand. Falls ich nicht 6 Wochen vor Ablauf des vereinbarten Bezugszeitraumes kündige, verlängert sich mein Abonnement um jeweils 1 weiteres Jahr. Ich war in den letzten 6 Monaten nicht Bezieher des *stern.*

Ich bin damit einverstanden, dass Sie mir auch per Telefon oder E-Mail interessante Angebote unterbreiten (ggf. streichen).

**Ich zahle bequem und bargeldlos per Bankeinzug (1/4-jährlich, zzt. € 29,90).**

Bankleitzahl                    Kontonummer

Geldinstitut

X

Datum          Unterschrift des neuen Lesers

### Angaben des Werbers

Name, Vorname

Straße/Hausnummer

Postleitzahl          Wohnort

19

Telefonnummer                    Geburtsdatum

E-Mail

Der neue *stern*-Abonnent und der Prämienempfänger dürfen nicht identisch sein. Die Zusendung meiner Prämie erfolgt nach Zahlungseingang (Zuzahlungsprämien werden per Nachnahme geliefert). Dieses Prämienangebot gilt nur innerhalb Deutschlands und solange der Vorrat reicht. Auslandspreise auf Anfrage.

Ich werbe den neuen Abonnenten. Als Prämie wähle ich:

☐ Best Choice: € 70,– Gutschein
Ohne Zuzahlung

☐ Prophete Mountainbike
Zuzahlung € 109,–

**Ausschneiden und abschicken:**
**stern Kunden-Service · 20080 Hamburg**

Bestell-Nr.: **241 947 W**

*Abonnent: subscriber; **Postleitzahl:** postal code; **Wohnort:** city or town;*
***Geburtsdatum:** date of birth*

## Wortschatz

This vocabulary list represents words from **Kapitel 1** that you may want to use. The words have been categorized according to the thematic topics in this chapter. The **Ausdrücke** and **Andere Wörter** sections will provide a list of useful expressions and words found in the chapter.

### Gruß- und Abschiedsformeln
*Greetings and Farewells*

**Guten Morgen! / Morgen!** *Good morning.*
**Hallo!** *Hello*
**Mahlzeit!** *Have a good meal.* (at lunchtime)
**Guten Tag! / Tag!** *Good afternoon; Good day.*
**Guten Abend! / Abend!** *Good evening.*
**Gute Nacht!** *Good night.*
**Auf Wiedersehen!** *Good-bye.*
**Tschüss!** *'Bye.*

### Personen *People*

**die Frau; Frau …** *woman; Mrs. …*
**das Fräulein; Fräulein …** *young girl; Miss …* (for young girls only)
**der Herr; Herr …** *gentleman; Mr. …*
**die Person** *person*
**der Professor / die Professorin**[1] *(male/female) professor*
**der Student / die Studentin** *(male/female) student*

### Länder *Countries*

**das Land** *country*
**Deutschland** *Germany*
**England** *England*
**Frankreich** *France*
**Japan** *Japan*
**Kanada** *Canada*
**Mexiko** *Mexico*
**Österreich** *Austria*
**die Schweiz** *Switzerland*
**die USA / Amerika** *United States / America*

### Nationalitäten *Nationalities*

**die Nationalität** *nationality*
**der Amerikaner / die Amerikanerin** *(male/female) American*
**der Deutsche (ein Deutscher) / die Deutsche (eine Deutsche)** *(male/female) German*
**der Engländer / die Engländerin** *(male/female) English person*
**der Franzose / die Französin** *(male/female) French person*
**der Japaner / die Japanerin** *(male/female) Japanese person*
**der Kanadier / die Kanadierin** *(male/female) Canadian*
**der Mexikaner / die Mexikanerin** *(male/female) Mexican*
**der Österreicher / die Österreicherin** *(male/female) Austrian*
**der Schweizer / die Schweizerin** *(male/female) Swiss person*

### Das Aussehen *Appearance*

**das Aussehen** *appearance*
**die Augen** *(pl.) eyes*
  **braune (grüne, blaue) Augen** *brown (green, blue) eyes*
**die Brille** *(sg.) glasses*
**die Haare** *(pl.) hair*
  **blonde (schwarze, braune, rote, graue) Haare** *blond (black, brown, red, gray) hair*
  **glatte (krause, wellige) Haare** *straight (tightly curled, wavy) hair*
  **lange (kurze) Haare** *long (short) hair*

### Farben *Colors*

**die Farbe** *color*
**beige** *beige*
**blau** *blue*
**braun** *brown*
**gelb** *yellow*
**grau** *gray*
**grün** *green*
**lila** *purple; violet*
**orange** *orange*
**rosa** *pink*
**rot** *red*
**schwarz** *black*
**weiß** *white*
**dunkel** *dark*
  **dunkelgrau** *dark gray*
**hell** *light*
  **hellgrau** *light gray*

### Im Klassenzimmer; im Hörsaal
*In the classroom; in the lecture hall*

**der Hörsaal** *lecture hall*
**das Klassenzimmer** *classroom*
**die Universität** *university*
**das Arbeitsbuch** *workbook*
**der Bleistift** *pencil*
**das Buch** *book, textbook*
**der Computer** *computer*
**der DVD-Spieler** *DVD-player*
**das Fenster** *window*
**der Fernseher** *television set*
**die Kreide** *chalk*
**der Kuli** *ballpoint pen*
**die Lampe** *lamp*
**die Landkarte** *map*
**die Leinwand** *projection screen*

---

[1] The feminine form of many professions and nationalities is formed by adding the suffix **-in** to the masculine form. Starting in **Kapitel 2**, noun plurals will also be included.

**der Overheadprojektor** *overhead projector*
**der Papierkorb** *waste basket*
**der Schreibtisch** *desk*
**die Steckdose** *electrical outlet*
**der Stuhl** *chair*
**die Tafel** *board; chalkboard*
**der Tisch** *table*
**die Tür** *door*
**die Uhr** *clock*
**die Wand** *wall*

### Fragewörter *Question words*

**wann?** *when?*
**warum?** *why?*
**was?** *what?*
**wer?** *who?*
**wie?** *how?*
**wie viel?** *how much?*
**wie viele?** *how many?*
**wo?** *where?*
**woher?** *from where?*
**wohin?** *to where?*

### Verben *Verbs*

**auf·machen** *to open*
**auf·stehen: Stehen Sie auf!** *Stand up.*
**heißen** *to be called, named*
**lachen: Lachen Sie!** *Laugh.*
**sein** *to be*
**sich setzen: Setzen Sie sich!** *Sit down.*
**stehen: Stehen Sie still!** *Stand still.*
**zeigen: Zeigen Sie …!** *Point to …*

### Adjektive *Adjectives*

**alt** *old*
**attraktiv** *attractive* (for females)
**freundlich** *friendly*
**groß** *big; tall*
**gut** *good*
    **gut aussehend** *good-looking* (for males)

**hübsch** *pretty* (for females)
**jung** *young*
**klein** *little*
**kurz** *short*
**lang** *long*
**mollig** *chubby, heavy*
**schlank** *slender, thin*
**schön** *beautiful*
**unattraktiv** *unattractive*

### Pronomen *Pronouns*

**ich** *I*
**du** *you (singular, informal)*
**Sie** *you (singular formal)*
**er** *he; it*
**es** *it (he, she)*
**sie** *she; it*
**wir** *we*
**ihr** *you (plural informal)*
**Sie** *you (plural informal)*
**sie** *they*

### Artikel *Articles*

**der, das, die (die,** *pl.***)** *the*
**ein, eine** *a, an*

### Ausdrücke *Expressions*

**bitte** *please*
**danke** *thank you*
**Das ist …** *That is …*
**Er/Sie hat …** *He/She has …*
**Er/Sie kommt aus …** *He/She comes from …*
**Ich habe …** *I have …*
**Ich komme aus …** *I come from …*
**Ich spreche …** *I speak …*
**Ich weiß nicht.** *I don't know.*
**Ist das …?** *Is that …?*
**Kommt er/sie aus …?** *Does he/she come from …?*
**Sind Sie … Jahre alt?** *Are you … years old?*
**Und Sie?** *And you?*

**Welche Farbe hat …?** *What color is …?*
**Wer ist das?** *Who is that?*
**Wer sind Sie?** *Who are you?*
**Wie bitte?** *What?; Excuse me?; Pardon?*
**Wie heißen Sie?** *What's your name?*
**Wie sehen Sie aus?** *What do you look like?*
**Woher kommt er/sie?** *Where does he/she come from?*

### Zahlen *Numbers*

**die Zahl** *number*

**null, eins, zwei, drei, vier, fünf, sechs, sieben, acht, neun**
**zehn, elf, zwölf, dreizehn, vierzehn, fünfzehn, sechzehn, siebzehn, achtzehn, neunzehn**
**zwanzig, einundzwanzig, zweiundzwanzig**
**dreißig, vierzig, fünfzig, sechzig, siebzig, achtzig, neunzig**
**hundert, hunderteins**
**tausend**

### Andere Wörter *Other Words*

**da** *there*
**ja** *yes*
**hier** *here*
**kein, keine (keine,** *pl.***)** *no, not one, not any*
**nein** *no*
**richtig** *correct*
**und** *and*

### Meine eigenen Wörter *My own words*

———————————
———————————
———————————
———————————
———————————
———————————

# Familie und Freunde

■ Am Wochenende fährt die Familie Rollerblades.

**Online Study Center**

Go to the *Vorsprung* Website at *http://college.hmco.com/pic/vorsprung2e.*

**In this chapter you will learn how to talk about your family, your possessions, activities you like or routinely do, and when certain events occur.**

## Kommunikative Funktionen

- Indicating possession or ownership
- Expressing what you like and don't like
- Describing actions
- Talking about what you like and don't like to do
- Talking about what you have and don't have

- Creating variety and shifting emphasis
- Describing daily activities
- Expressing negation
- Expressing birthdates

## Strukturen

- The verb **haben**
- Verbs (including **haben**) + the adverb **gern**
- Present tense of regular verbs
- The accusative case
- Position of subject and verb
- Separable-prefix verbs and two-verb constructions
- Position of **nicht**

## Vokabeln

- Die Familie und die Verwandten
- Studienfächer
- Die Monate
- Die Wochentage
- Zeitausdrücke
- Die Uhrzeit
- Der Alltag

## Kulturelles

- German immigration to North America
- Types of universities in Germany

## Anlauftext

## Anna Adler stellt sich vor°

*stellt ... :* *introduces herself*

Anna Adler, a German-American college student from Fort Wayne, Indiana, introduces herself and describes some of her favorite activities. She also introduces her immediate family — her father, Bob Adler, her German-born mother, Hannelore, and her teenage brother, Jeff. She talks about college, her German skills, and her anxieties and hopes as she looks ahead to a year abroad at the University of Tübingen.

## Vorschau

**1** **Thematische Fragen.** Discuss the following questions with your instructor or in pairs.

1. What do you already know about Anna Adler? Where does she come from? Where is she going to study? How does she feel about it? Who is in her family?
2. If you were going to contact family friends or relatives who lived in a foreign country and whom you had never met before, what would you tell them about yourself? What would you ask?

## Wissenswerte Vokabeln: Annas Familie
### Identifying family relationships

> **Annas Familie:** Note the absence of an apostrophe between the noun and the possessive **s.**

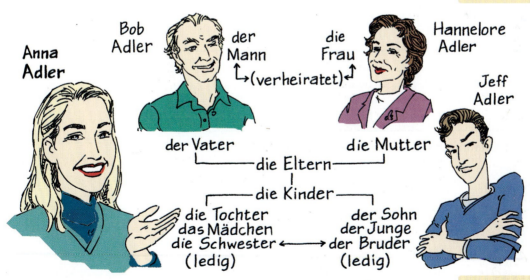

> **Wissenswerte Vokabeln:** This feature contains vocabulary that you are expected to learn and use.

Annas Eltern heißen Bob und Hannelore Adler.
Hannelore Adler ist die Mutter von Anna und Jeff.
Bob Adler ist der Vater von Anna und Jeff.

Hannelore und Bob haben zwei Kinder, Anna und Jeff.
Der Sohn heißt Jeff. Er ist der Junge in der Familie.
Die Tochter heißt Anna. Sie ist das Mädchen in der Familie.
Anna ist Jeffs Schwester. Jeff ist Annas Bruder.
Bob und Hannelore sind verheiratet. Sie sind Mann und Frau.
Anna ist nicht verheiratet. Sie ist ledig.

🔲 Sind Sie verheiratet?   *Nein, ich bin ledig.*

**2   Wer ist wer in der Familie Adler?** (*Who's who in the Adler family?*)
Complete these sentences with the correct term for each relationship.

1. Anna Adler ist die _____ von Bob und Hannelore Adler.
2. Bob und Hannelore haben zwei _____, Anna und Jeff.
3. Jeff ist der _____ von Bob und Hannelore. Er ist der _____ in der Familie.
4. Bob und Hannelore sind die _____ von Anna und Jeff.
5. Annas und Jeffs _____ heißt Bob Adler.
6. Annas und Jeffs _____ heißt Hannelore Adler.
7. Jeff ist Annas _____.
8. Anna ist Jeffs _____. Sie ist das _____ in der Familie.
9. Bob und Hannelore Adler sind verheiratet. Sie sind Mann und _____.
10. Jeff und Anna sind nicht verheiratet. Sie sind _____.

**3   Wortdetektiv.** Which words convey approximately the same
meaning? Match the German word to its logical English equivalent.

| *Deutsch* | | *Englisch* | |
|---|---|---|---|
| 1. sportlich *b* | | a. | to fly |
| 2. fliegen *a* | | b. | athletic |
| 3. meinen *d* | | c. | smart, clever |
| 4. klug *c* | | d. | to think; to mean |
| | | | |
| 5. hören *f* | | e. | history |
| 6. zu Hause *h* | | f. | to hear, listen |
| 7. die Geschichte *e* | | g. | I would like to |
| 8. ich möchte *g* | | h. | at home |
| | | | |
| 9. zwei Semester verbringen *j* | | i. | to make better, improve |
| 10. lernen *k* | | j. | to spend two semesters |
| 11. die Angst *l* | | k. | to learn; to study (*for an exam, class*) |
| 12. verbessern *i* | | l. | fear |
| | | | |
| 13. die Musik *n* | | m. | for example |
| 14. ich sehe fern *q* | | n. | music |
| 15. spielen *p* | | o. | a little bit (of) |
| 16. ein bisschen *o* | | p. | to play |
| 17. zum Beispiel *m* | | q. | I watch TV |

**Zum Beispiel** is often
abbreviated as **z.B.**

*Anlauftext*

Now listen to the recording.

## Anna Adler stellt sich vor

Ich heiße Anna Adler. Ich bin 20 Jahre alt.

Ich fliege im August nach Deutschland.

Ich komme aus den USA, aus Fort Wayne. Ich bin Amerikanerin.

Ich spiele gern Softball.

Ich gehe auch gern wandern,

Ich höre gern Musik, zum Beispiel Mozart.

aber ich sehe nicht gern fern.

Mein Vater heißt Bob Adler. Er ist 48 Jahre alt.

Ich habe auch einen Bruder. Er heißt Jeff. Er ist 16. Er meint, er ist sehr klug und sehr sportlich. Naja ...

Meine Mutter, Hannelore Adler, ist 46 Jahre alt. Sie kommt aus Deutschland, aber sie ist jetzt Amerikanerin.

Ich habe keine Schwester.

## Rückblick

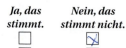 **4** **Stimmt das?** How much of the text can you remember without looking back at it? Look over the statements and mark the true statements as **Ja, das stimmt.** Mark the false statements as **Nein, das stimmt nicht.** Then, listen as your instructor reads the following statements and models their pronunciation. If the statement is true, say **Ja, das stimmt.** If the statement is not true, say **Nein, das stimmt nicht.**

|   | *Ja, das stimmt.* | *Nein, das stimmt nicht.* |
|---|---|---|
| 1. Anna Adler ist Deutsche. |  | ☒ |
| 2. Anna kommt aus Fort Wayne, Indiana. | ☒  | ☐ |

|  | *Ja, das stimmt.* | *Nein, das stimmt nicht.* |
|---|---|---|
| 3. Sie spielt gern Basketball. | ☐ | ☒ |
| 4. Sie hört gern Musik, Mozart zum Beispiel. | ☒ | ☐ |
| 5. Annas Vater Bob ist 48 Jahre alt. | ☒ | ☐ |
| 6. Annas Mutter Hannelore kommt aus Los Angeles. | ☐ | ☒ |
| 7. Annas Bruder Jeff ist 16 und meint, er ist klug. | ☒ | ☐ |
| 8. Anna möchte unbedingt ihr Deutsch verbessern. | ☒ | ☐ |
| 9. Anna verbringt ein Semester in Zürich. | ☐ | ☒ |
| 10. Anna hat etwas° Angst. | ☒ | ☐ |

*a little, somewhat*

**5** **Ergänzen Sie.** Complete these statements with words from the **Anlauftext.** Look back at the text as often as you like to read the sentences and see the words in context.

1. Ist Anna Deutsche? Nein, sie ist _____.
2. Anna kommt _____ den USA.
3. Anna sagt: „Ich spiele _____ Softball.“
4. Anna sagt: „Ich _____ gern Musik, _____ _____ Mozart.“
5. Annas Vater, Bob Adler, ist 48 _____ alt.
6. Annas Bruder _____ Jeff.
7. Anna ist Studentin. Sie studiert _____ und _____.
8. Anna sagt: „Ich spreche ein _____ Deutsch von zu Hause.“
9. Anna sagt: „Dieses Jahr _____ ich zwei Semester an der _____ in Tübingen.“
10. Anna sagt: „ _____ _____ so viel sehen und auch so viel _____.“

**6** **Kurz gefragt.** Answer the questions with just a word or two. Review the question words before you begin.

| **was?** = *what?* | **wo?** = *where?* |
|---|---|
| **wann?** = *when?* | **woher?** = *where . . . from?* |
| **wie?** = *how?* | **wohin?** = *where . . . to?* |

1. Woher kommt Anna?
2. Wann fliegt Anna?
3. Wohin fliegt Anna?
4. Was macht Anna gern? Was sind Annas Hobbys?
5. Wie alt ist Annas Vater?
6. Woher kommt Annas Mutter?
7. Was ist Annas Mutter: Deutsche oder Amerikanerin?
8. Ist Annas Bruder sportlich?
9. Was studiert Anna?
10. Wo verbringt Anna dieses Jahr zwei Semester?

**7** **Jetzt sind Sie dran.** You are introducing yourself to a German class in Germany. Complete the statements below, then read them to your partner.

1. Ich heiße _____.
2. Ich komme aus _____.
3. Ich bin _____ Jahre alt.
4. Meine Mutter heißt _____.
5. Sie ist _____ Jahre alt.
6. Sie kommt aus _____.
7. Mein Vater heißt _____.
8. Er ist _____ Jahre alt.
9. Er kommt aus _____.
10. Ich bin Student(in).

Additional vocabulary:
**ist gestorben** = *has died*

## Strukturen und Vokabeln

### *Wissenswerte Vokabeln: die Familie und die Verwandten*
*Identifying family relationships*

Friedrich Kunz
der Großvater
der Opa

Elfriede Kunz
die Großmutter
die Oma

⌐ die Großeltern ⌐

Bob Adler — der Vater

Hannelore Adler — die Mutter

Werner Kunz — der Onkel

Ursula Günther — die Tante

Johannes Günther — der Onkel

⌐ die Eltern ⌐

Anna Adler

Jeff Adler
der Bruder
der Sohn
der Enkel
der Neffe

die Schwester
die Tochter
die Enkelin
die Nichte

Katja Günther — die Kusine

Georg Günther — der Cousin

der Mann, die Männer
die Frau, die Frauen
die Eltern (*pl.*)
die Mutter, die Mütter
der Vater, die Väter
das Kind, die Kinder
die Tochter, die Töchter
das Mädchen, die Mädchen
der Sohn, die Söhne
die Schwester, die Schwestern

der Bruder, die Brüder
der Junge, die Jungen
die Großeltern (*pl.*)
die Großmutter, die Großmütter
die Oma, die Omas
der Großvater, die Großväter
der Opa, die Opas
das Enkelkind, die Enkelkinder

die Enkelin, die Enkelinnen
der Enkel, die Enkel
die Tante, die Tanten
der Onkel, die Onkel
die Nichte, die Nichten
der Neffe, die Neffen
der Cousin, die Cousins
die Kusine, die Kusinen

*der Elternteil*

*in-laws: Schwager Schwägerin*

---

See the **Arbeitsbuch** for additional practice with structures and vocabulary.

**W. Vok.** The first name of Anna's aunt is **Ursula.** However, family members and friends call her **Uschi,** which is a standard shortened version of the name.

The name **Johannes** is frequently abbreviated to **Hannes,** the name **Johann** to **Hans.**

Relationships created by remarriage of a parent (e.g., stepfather, stepsister) are indicated by the prefix **Stief-: Stiefvater, Stiefmutter, Stiefkind, Stieftochter, Stiefschwester, Stlefsohn, Stiefbruder.** Relationships where siblings share only one biological parent are indicated by the prefix **Halb-: Halbbruder, Halbschwester.** Adoptive relationships are indicated by the prefix **Adoptiv-: Adoptivsohn, Adoptivtochter.**

Note that someone who has lost a spouse is **verwitwet** (*widowed*).

A common question when people are getting to know each other is **Haben Sie Geschwister?** *Do you have siblings?*

**8** **Die Familie.** Complete the following sentences using the information provided in the family tree.

■ Anna ist die *Schwester* von Jeff.

1. Katja ist die ——— von Georg.
2. Annas ——— heißt Hannelore.
3. Katja ist Annas ———, und Georg ist Annas ———.
4. Onkel Hannes und ——— Ursula sind Katjas und Georgs ———.
5. Friedrich Kunz ist Katjas ———.
6. Bob und Hannelore Adler sind verheiratet: sie sind ——— und Frau.
7. Georg ist Katjas ———. Er ist der ——— in der Familie.
8. Bob Adler ist Katjas und Georgs ———.
9. Jeff ist Bobs und Hannelores ———.
10. Anna Adler ist Bobs und Hannelores ———. Sie ist das ——— in der Familie.
11. Anna und Jeff sind die zwei ——— von Hannelore und Bob Adler.

## German immigration to North America

*George Herman (Babe) Ruth ist ein berühmter Deutsch-Amerikaner.*

Anna, like approximately 23% of all Americans, is of German background. Germany's first immigrants to the new world, natives of the Lower Rhine city of Krefeld, settled in Philadelphia in 1683, establishing a German-speaking community called Germantown. New German, Swiss, and Austrian immigrants brought their German language and customs with them as they moved to places as diverse as southern Ontario, New York, Wisconsin, Indiana, California, Missouri, and Texas. With over 57 million Americans claiming German heritage, Germans are the largest single ethnic group in the U.S. Since 1983, German-Americans celebrate their ethnic heritage every year on October 6, German-American Day.

Many German-Americans take great pride in the continued use of the German language. In some smaller towns and rural areas, you can still hear German as their language of choice. The Amish, for example, worship in High German, but in daily conversation they use the German dialect their ancestors brought with them over 200 years ago. Cities such as New York, Chicago, and Los Angeles used to have large German-speaking communities, which have, with time, blended into the larger society. But you can still find German restaurants, bakeries, bookstores, German-speaking churches or newspapers in German, and sometimes even radio stations with a German-language program.

■ **Kulturkreuzung** Below are names from a North American telephone book. Which ones have German roots?

Adler • Chattulani • Choszczyk • Chowdhury • Choy • Ciccone • Dykstra • Fernandez • Hankinson • Kresge • Krueger • Kugler • Lehlbach • MacArthur • Manchester • Mueller • Nakamoto • O'Neill • Papadimitropoulos • Paquette • Schaefer • Schmidt • Stroh • Stuckman • Sugawara • Wagenknecht • Wang • Wilczewski • Williams • Wu

# I  Indicating possession or ownership

## The verb **haben**

The verb **haben** (*to have*) expresses possession or ownership.

| | |
|---|---|
| Ich **habe** auch einen Bruder. | *I also have a brother.* |
| Ich **habe** keine Schwester. | *I don't have a sister.* |

**Haben** has the following present tense forms.

| haben: *to have* | | |
|---|---|---|
| **Person** | **Singular** | **Plural** |
| **1st** | ich hab**e** | wir hab**en** |
| **2nd, informal** | du ha**st** | ihr hab**t** |
| **2nd, formal** | Sie hab**en** | Sie hab**en** |
| **3rd** | er/sie/es ha**t** | sie hab**en** |

**9    Wer hat was?** (*Who has what?*)  Put together meaningful sentences by matching the subjects from the left column with the correct forms of **haben** in the right column.

| | |
|---|---|
| 1. Ich ... | a.  haben eine intelligente Tochter. |
| 2. Du ... | b.  habe keine Schwester. |
| 3. Anna ... | c.  habt ein schönes Auto. |
| 4. Herr Günther, Sie ... | d.  hat etwas Angst. |
| 5. Ihr ... | e.  hast keine Verwandten in Deutschland. |

### Sprache im Alltag: Abbreviated ich-forms of verbs

In conversational German, speakers often drop the standard **-e** ending of the **ich**-form. These short forms are common in conversation, but they are considered non-standard in writing. When a colloquial conversation is written, the deleted **-e** is sometimes indicated by the use of an apostrophe.

| | |
|---|---|
| Ich **hab'** eine Frau und zwei Söhne. | Ich **hab'** keine Töchter. |
| Ich **hör'** gern Musik. | Und ich **spiel'** gern Softball. |
| Ich **hab'** Probleme mit ... | |

*with*

*money problems*

**10** **Ich habe Probleme mit ...** Complete each sentence with the correct form of **haben.**

Der Patient *hat* Probleme mit der Religion.

1. Der Psychiater fragt: „_____ Sie Probleme?"
2. Der Patient _____ viele° Probleme.  *a lot of*
3. Der Patient sagt: „Ich _____ Probleme mit meiner Identität."
4. Die Studenten sagen: „Wir _____ Probleme mit Professor Bauer."
5. _____ der Psychiater Geldprobleme?
6. Anna fragt Georg: „_____ du Geldprobleme?"
7. Georg sagt: „Nein, ich _____ keine Geldprobleme. Ich arbeite° im Sommer."  *work*
8. Anna fragt Katja und Georg: „_____ ihr Geldprobleme?"
9. Katja und Georg sagen: „Im Moment _____ wir keine Probleme."

---

**Sprache im Alltag: Expressions with the verb haben**

German uses the verb **haben** with specific nouns denoting a state of being to express a physical or emotional condition.

| | |
|---|---|
| **Angst haben** | *to be afraid* |
| Ich sehe einen Horrorfilm. Ich **habe Angst.** | |
| **Hunger haben** | *to be hungry* |
| Ich möchte essen°. Ich **habe Hunger.** | |
| **Durst haben** | *to be thirsty* |
| Ich möchte trinken°. Ich **habe Durst.** | |

To negate these expressions, use **keine(n):** Ich habe *keine* Angst. Ich habe *keinen* Hunger. Ich habe *keinen* Durst.

*eat*

*drink*

**11** **Interview.** First, fill in the information about you and your family in the column with the head **Ich.** Then, ask your partner these questions and note his/her answers in the right column.

S1: *Haben Sie Brüder?*                         S1: *Haben Sie Brüder?*
S2: *Ja, ich habe zwei Brüder (einen Bruder).*   S2: *Nein, ich habe keine Brüder.*
S1: *Wie heißen sie? (Wie heißt er?)*
S2: *Sie heißen Hans und Franz. (Er heißt Hans.)*

|  | *Ich* | *Mein Partner/Meine Partnerin* |
|---|---|---|
| 1. Haben Sie Eltern? | _____ | _____ |
| 2. Wie heißen sie? | _____ | _____ |
| 3. Wie alt sind sie? | _____ | _____ |
| 4. Haben Sie Brüder? | _____ | _____ |
| 5. Wenn° ja, wie heißen sie? | _____ | _____ |
| 6. Wie alt sind sie? | _____ | _____ |
| 7. Haben Sie Schwestern? | _____ | _____ |
| 8. Wenn ja, wie heißen sie? | _____ | _____ |
| 9. Wie alt sind sie? | _____ | _____ |
| 10. Sind Sie verheiratet? | _____ | _____ |
| 11. Wenn ja, wie heißt Ihr Mann/Ihre Frau? | _____ | _____ |

*If*

**Interview.** If you want to answer *a brother* or *a father,* say **einen Bruder** or **einen Vater.** You will learn why later in the chapter.

## *Wissenswerte Vokabeln: Studienfächer°*

### *Identifying academic interests*

*academic subjects*

Biologie • Chemie • Medizin • Mathematik (Mathe) • Philosophie • Physik • Psychologie • Soziologie

*Sprachen:* Deutsch • Englisch • Französisch • Russisch • Spanisch

| Was studieren Sie? | *Ich studiere Betriebswirtschaft.* |
|---|---|
| Welche Sprache lernen Sie? | *Ich lerne Deutsch.* |
| Was haben Sie als Hauptfach? | *Ich habe Philosophie als Hauptfach.* |
| Was haben Sie als Nebenfach? | *Ich habe Englisch als Nebenfach.* |

If your partner indicates that he or she has only one brother or sister, remember to change questions 5, 6, 8, and 9 to a singular form: **Wie heißt er/sie? Wie alt ist er/sie?**

**W. Vok.:** All sciences are feminine nouns. All languages are neuter.

If your field of study is not listed here, ask your instructor for its German name.

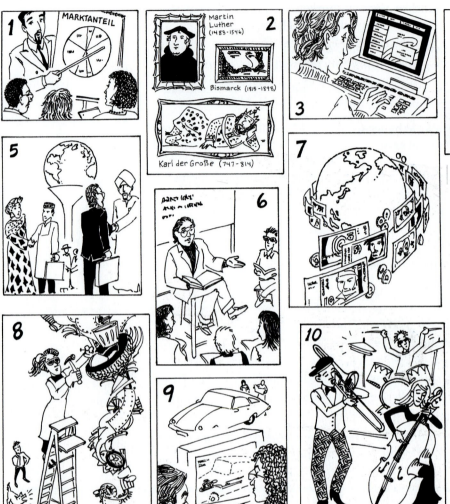

1. Betriebswirtschaft *business*
2. Geschichte
3. Informátik
4. Politikwissenschaft
5. Internationale
   Beziehungen
6. Pädagogik
7. Volkswirtschaft *econ.*
8. Kunst
9. Ingenieurwesen
10. Musik

## II  Expressing what you like and don't like

### The expression **gern haben**

When talking about what they like, German speakers use the verb **haben** with the adverb **gern. Gern** usually appears at the end of the sentence or clause.

| | |
|---|---|
| Ich **habe** meinen Deutschkurs **gern.** | *I like my German class.* |
| Meine Schwester **hat** Mozarts Musik **gern.** | *My sister likes Mozart's music.* |
| **Haben** Sie Mathe auch **gern?** | *Do you like math too?* |

When talking about what they dislike, German speakers use the verb **haben** with **nicht gern,** which appears at the end of the sentence or clause.

| | |
|---|---|
| Wir **haben** Musik **nicht gern.** | *We don't like music.* |
| Was? Ihr **habt** Musik **nicht gern?** | *What? You (guys/all) don't like music?* |

Quantifiers such as **sehr** (*a lot*), **nicht so** (*not so*), and **nicht sehr** (*not much*) can be added to specify how much one likes or dislikes something.

| | |
|---|---|
| Ich **habe** Biologie und Mathe **sehr gern.** | *I like biology and math a lot.* |
| Geschichte **haben** wir **nicht so gern.** | *We don't like history so much.* |

 **12  Interview: Studienfächer.** Ask another student the following questions.

*Fragen*

1. Was haben Sie als Hauptfach?
2. Was haben Sie als Nebenfach?
3. Welche Fächer haben Sie dieses Semester?
4. Welche Fächer haben Sie gern?
5. Welche Fächer haben Sie nicht so gern?

  **S c h r e i b e c k e**

**Was wir gern haben.** In complete sentences describe which subjects you are studying this semester, which of these you like, and which ones you dislike. Based on the interviews in **Aktivität 12,** describe which students in the class share your schedule, likes, and dislikes.

> *Ich habe Deutsch, Mathe und Chemie. Jenny hat auch Deutsch. Ben und Katie haben auch Mathe. Ich habe Deutsch gern. Jenny hat …*

**Schreibecke.** To express the notion of *also*, insert **auch** after **haben.**

## Types of universities in Germany

American and Canadian students may be surprised to see familiar academic subjects missing from the list of subjects at German universities. Until fairly recently, most German universities aspired to the ideal established by Wilhelm von Humboldt at Berlin University in 1810. Set up as an elite institution, meant for a small number of students who pursued research and study for the sake of learning alone, the university only granted advanced degrees to a limited number of students in a limited number of fields.

With increasing numbers of students since the 1960s and with changes in technology and science, this system has proved too inflexible. In response, many new types of universities were founded:

- **die technische Hochschule,** institutes of technology, for engineering and technology-driven fields with an emphasis on research;
- **die Fachhochschule,** special colleges with an emphasis on applied professions in the fields of business administration, design, engineering, health and human services, information sciences, and social work;
- creative and performing arts academies such as **die Kunsthochschule,** art academies, and **die Musikhochschule,** music conservatories, among others.

More recent reforms aim to shorten the time needed to earn a degree. By 2010 all universities will be offering shorter degree programs that lead to a Bachelor's or Master's degree. Due to political and economic pressures and competition from universities abroad, the German higher education system is creating private universities and some elite universities to attract the best and brightest German and international students.

■ **Kulturkreuzung** Which type of institution do you think German students probably attend if they want to pursue the following careers?

> accountant • computer programmer • dental technician • electrical engineer • elementary teacher • foreign language interpreter • graphic artist • lab technician • law enforcement officer • lawyer • nurse • physician • violinist

## III Describing actions

### Present tense of regular verbs

#### A. Conjugation of regular verbs in the present tense

When talking about the activities that we or other people do, a subject pronoun is used along with a conjugated verb. Often a word or phrase follows the verb. Different subject pronouns require different endings on the verbs. Here are the present tense endings of the verb **spielen** (*to play*) as an example.

**Kulturkreuzung.** Think about the different courses of study available at your college. Which ones are more theoretical in nature? Which ones are more applied or practical? Which courses of study aren't offered at your college? Why? What is different about the German system?

| | **spielen:** *to play* | |
|---|---|---|
| **Person** | **Singular** | **Plural** |
| **1st** | ich spiel**e** | wir spiel**en** |
| **2nd informal** | du spiel**st** | ihr spiel**t** |
| **2nd formal** | Sie spiel**en** | Sie spiel**en** |
| **3rd** | er/sie/es spiel**t** | sie spiel**en** |

Notice there are three forms that are always identical to the regular infinitive: **wir** (*we*), **Sie** (*you,* formal), and **sie** (*they*). As you learned in **Kapitel 1,** the infinitive is the form listed in the dictionary and is composed of two parts: the stem (**spiel-**) and the ending (**-en**). The endings are attached to the verb stem. Here are some other important verbs from the text.

| **Infinitive** | **gehen** | **heißen** | **kommen** | **meinen** | **studieren** | **verstehen** |
|---|---|---|---|---|---|---|
| | *to go* | *to be called, named* | *to come* | *to think to mean* | *to study* | *to understand* |
| **ich** | gehe | heiße | komme | meine | studiere | verstehe |
| **du** | gehst | heißt | kommst | meinst | studierst | verstehst |
| **Sie** | gehen | heißen | kommen | meinen | studieren | verstehen |
| **er/sie/es** | geht | heißt | kommt | meint | studiert | versteht |
| **wir** | gehen | heißen | kommen | meinen | studieren | verstehen |
| **ihr** | geht | heißt | kommt | meint | studiert | versteht |
| **Sie** | gehen | heißen | kommen | meinen | studieren | verstehen |
| **sie** | gehen | heißen | kommen | meinen | studieren | verstehen |

**du heißt:** Note that the typical **-st** ending for **du** is reduced to **-t** when it follows **ss, ß, s,** or **z.**

Some other verbs you have already seen and used include:

| | | | |
|---|---|---|---|
| **arbeiten** | *to work* | **lernen** | *to learn; to study (for an exam, class)* |
| **bleiben** | *to stay, remain* | | |
| **finden** | *to find; to think something is* | **machen** | *to do; to make* |
| **fliegen** | *to fly* | **schreiben** | *to write* |
| **fragen** | *to ask* | **trinken** | *to drink* |
| **hören** | *to hear; to listen to* | **verbringen** | *to spend (time)* |
| | | **wohnen** | *to reside, live* |

> Note that, in general, for verbs like **arbeiten** and **finden,** which have a **-t** or **-d** at the end of the stem, an **e** is inserted between the stem and the endings **-st** and **-t: du arbeitest, er/sie/es arbeitet, ihr arbeitet; du findest, er/sie/es findet, ihr findet.**

## B. Present tense equivalents in English and German

English has three possible meanings for one present tense German form.

Er **spielt** Mozart.
$\left\{ \begin{array}{l} \textit{He } \textbf{\textit{plays}} \textit{ Mozart.} \\ \textit{He } \textbf{\textit{is playing}} \textit{ Mozart.} \\ \textit{He } \textbf{\textit{does play}} \textit{ Mozart.} \end{array} \right.$

Wir **studieren** Kunst.
$\left\{ \begin{array}{l} \textit{We } \textbf{\textit{study}} \textit{ art.} \\ \textit{We } \textbf{\textit{are studying}} \textit{ art.} \\ \textit{We } \textbf{\textit{do study}} \textit{ art.} \end{array} \right.$

The English use of *do* or *does* emphasizes the action expressed in the infinitive: *Yes, he does play Mozart.* There is no equivalent in standard German for this use of *do* or *does.* Instead, standard present tense is used, often in conjunction with the adverb **doch: Er spielt doch Mozart.**

> You learned in **Kapitel 1** that to form a yes/no question, you reverse the position of the conjugated verb and the subject. Unlike English, German never uses helping verbs to form present-tense questions. **Spielt** er auch Bach? (*Does he play Bach, too? Is he playing Bach, too?*); **Studierst** du Chemie? (*Are you studying chemistry? Do you study chemistry?*)

**13**    **Annas Familie.**  Read Anna's statements. Then in groups or pairs, talk about Anna's family.

▪ Anna: Ich heiße Anna.
Annas Eltern (Hannelore und Bob Adler) • Annas Bruder (Jeff)

  S1:  *Annas Eltern heißen Hannelore und Bob Adler.*
  S2:  *Annas Bruder heißt Jeff.*

1. Anna: Ich heiße Anna.
   Annas Eltern (Hannelore und Bob Adler) • Annas Bruder (Jeff) • Annas Großeltern (Friedrich und Elfriede Kunz) • Annas Kusine (Katja) • Annas Cousin (Georg)
2. Anna: Ich komme aus Fort Wayne.
   Katja und Georg (Weinheim) • Annas Großeltern (Bad Krozingen)
3. Anna: Ich spiele Softball.
   Jeff (Basketball) • Katja (Feldhockey) • Georg und Katja (Tennis) • Annas Mutter (Golf)
4. Anna: Ich höre gern Rockmusik.
   Katja (Oldies) • Annas Großeltern (klassische Musik) • Annas Eltern (Country) • Tante Uschi (Schlager°) • Jeff (Rapmusik)          *easy listening hits*
5. Anna: Ich verstehe etwas Deutsch.
   Katja (Englisch) • Georg (nur° Fußball) • Annas Großeltern (kein Englisch)          *only*

## **IV** Talking about what you like and don't like to do

Verbs + the adverb **gern**

### A. Present tense of verbs with **gern**

To talk about activities they like to do, German speakers use a verb that expresses the activity and add the adverb **gern** to the sentence.

Jeff **spielt gern** Basketball.     *Jeff likes to play basketball.*
**Sind** Sie **gern** in Deutschland?    *Do you like being in Germany?*

To talk about activities they dislike, German speakers add **nicht gern.**

Ich **fliege nicht gern.**          *I **don't like to fly.***
**Hören** Sie Rapmusik **nicht gern?**    ***Don't** you **like to listen** to rap music?*

### B. Position of **gern** and **nicht gern**

Depending on the context of the sentence and the intention of the speaker, **gern** and **nicht gern** occur in different places. You will learn more about that later. For now, place **gern** and **nicht gern** as explained here. In statements, **gern** and **nicht gern** can be placed after the conjugated verb or at the end of the sentence. Placement after the conjugated verb is more common. In yes/no questions, **gern** and **nicht gern** are also placed after the conjugated verb or at the end of the sentence.

Jeff spielt gern Basketball.

Jeff spielt nicht gern Softball.

| Statement | Question |
|---|---|
| Jeff **spielt gern** Basketball. | **Spielt** Jeff **gern** Basketball? |
| Jeff **spielt** Basketball **gern.** | **Spielt** Jeff Basketball **gern?** |
| Jeff **spielt nicht gern** Softball. | **Spielt** Jeff **nicht gern** Softball? |
| Jeff **spielt** Softball **nicht gern.** | **Spielt** Jeff Softball **nicht gern?** |

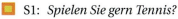 **14** **Autogrammspiel.** Walk around and find a classmate for each activity listed below. When you find someone who likes to do the activity, have that person sign his/her name.

🟨 S1: *Spielen Sie gern Tennis?*
    S2: *Nein, ich spiele nicht gern Tennis. (oder)*
       *Ja, ich spiele gern Tennis.*     _____*John*_____

1. Spielen Sie gern Tennis?     _____
2. Sprechen Sie gern Deutsch?     _____
3. Trinken Sie gern Bier?     _____
4. Gehen Sie gern einkaufen°?     _____       *shopping*
5. Hören Sie gern Rockmusik?     _____
6. Fliegen Sie gern?     _____
7. Sehen Sie gern fern?     _____

 **15** **Was meinen Sie?** Choose the following phrases that apply to you, then tell a partner in complete sentences about yourself.

🟨 *Ich höre gern klassische Musik.*

1. gern klassische Musik hören
2. aus den USA kommen
3. gern einkaufen gehen
4. Deutsch interessant finden
5. die Semesterferien° in Florida verbringen     *semester break*
6. dieses Jahr nach° Deutschland fliegen     *to*
7. eine Schwester haben
8. gern Tennis spielen

## Schreibecke

Use Katja's description of her own family as a model to write about your family.

> Meine° Familie wohnt in Weinheim.
> Mein Vater heißt Johannes Günther. Er ist 45 Jahre alt. Er ist nicht sehr alt. Er kommt aus Paderborn. Er spielt gern Tischtennis.
> Meine Mutter heißt Ursula Günther. Sie ist 48 Jahre alt. Sie ist sehr klug. Sie kommt aus Bad Krozingen. Sie spielt nicht gern Tischtennis.
> Mein Bruder heißt Georg. Er ist 16 Jahre alt. Er kommt aus Weinheim. Er meint, er ist sehr klug. Er hört gern Rockmusik. Er lernt nicht gern Englisch.
> Herzliche Grüße
> Katja

*My*

## V | Talking about what you have and don't have

### The accusative case

#### A. Definite and indefinite articles

The subject of a sentence performs the action described by the verb and is in the nominative case (**der Nominativ**). It answers the questions **wer?** (*who?*) and **was?** (*what?*). The accusative case (**der Akkusativ**) is used to designate the direct object (**das direkte Objekt**). The direct object is the target or product of the action expressed by the verb and answers the questions **wen?** (*whom?*) and **was?** (*what?*).

| | |
|---|---|
| **Was** hat Anna? | *What is Anna having?* |
|   Anna hat **einen Traum.** |   *Anna is having a dream.* |
| **Was** sucht Anna? | *What is Anna looking for?* |
|   Anna sucht **den Hörsaal.** |   *Anna is looking for the lecture hall.* |
| **Wen** fragt Anna? | *Whom does Anna ask?* |
|   Anna fragt **eine Studentin.** |   *Anna asks a (female) student.* |
| **Was** schreibt Anna? | *What is Anna writing?* |
|   Anna schreibt **eine E-Mail.** |   *Anna is writing an e-mail.* |

You can identify the accusative case by looking at the ending on the article. The ending denotes both the gender (masculine, feminine, neuter) and the number (singular or plural) of the noun, as well as its function (direct object as opposed to subject, etc.). The following chart shows all the forms of the definite and indefinite articles, plus **kein** in the nominative and accusative case.

| Case | Singular | | | Plural |
|------|----------|--|--|--------|
| | **Masculine** | **Neuter** | **Feminine** | **All Genders** |
| Nominative | **der** Mann | **das** Kind | **die** Frau | **die** Kinder |
| | **ein** Mann | **ein** Kind | **eine** Frau | — |
| | **kein** Mann | **kein** Kind | **keine** Frau | **keine** Kinder |
| Accusative | **den** Mann | **das** Kind | **die** Frau | **die** Kinder |
| | **einen** Mann | **ein** Kind | **eine** Frau | — |
| | **keinen** Mann | **kein** Kind | **keine** Frau | **keine** Kinder |

Ich habe einen Porsche, einen Audi, einen BMW, einen Mercedes und einen Trabi zu Hause.

Note that only the singular masculine forms are different in the nominative (**der, ein, kein**) and in the accusative (**den, einen, keinen**). Singular feminine and neuter forms as well as plural forms are identical in the nominative and in the accusative. Please also note that **kein** has the same endings as **ein.**

## B. Masculine N-nouns

**N-nouns** are discussed mainly for recognition.

A small group of masculine nouns adds an **-n** or **-en** ending to the noun itself to signal the change in function from subject to direct object. Pay special attention to these nouns, which include **der Herr (→ den Herrn), der Student (→ den Studenten),** and **der Junge (→ den Jungen).** In vocabulary sections, the extra accusative case ending will be noted in brackets. The second **-en** ending listed is the plural ending: **der Student, [-en], -en.**

| | |
|---|---|
| Ich kenne **den Herrn.** | *I know the (gentle)man.* |
| Sie haben **einen Jungen.** | *They have a boy.* |

**16** **Ich habe ... zu Hause.** (*I have ... at home.*) Ask what your partner has at home. Report your findings to the class. As you listen to what other students say, write down their names next to what they have.

**Ich habe ... zu Hause.** Make sure to mention things you don't have as well as things you do have.

S1: *Haben Sie einen Hund zu Hause?*
S2: *Ja, ich habe einen Hund.*

| Personen/Tiere°/Objekte | Mein Partner/ Meine Partnerin | Andere Leute° |
|---|---|---|
| 1. einen Hund | _____ | _____ |
| 2. eine Katze | _____ | _____ |
| 3. einen Bruder | _____ | _____ |
| 4. zwei (drei, vier) Brüder | _____ | _____ |
| 5. eine Schwester | _____ | _____ |
| 6. zwei (drei, vier) Schwestern | _____ | _____ |
| 7. ein Kind | _____ | _____ |
| 8. einen DVD-Spieler | _____ | _____ |
| 9. einen Fernseher | _____ | _____ |
| 10. ein Deutschbuch | _____ | _____ |

*animals / **andere ...**: other people*

**17** **Meine Familie.** Work with a partner and take turns asking each other questions. Follow the model.

Ich habe überhaupt keine Hunde zu Hause.

🔸 Schwester in Mexiko

> S1: *Haben Sie eine Schwester in Mexiko?*
> S2: *Nein, ich habe keine Schwester in Mexiko. Ich habe eine Schwester in Kanada, in Edmonton.* (oder)
> *Ich habe überhaupt keine Schwester.*

1. Onkel in Österreich
2. Großvater in Kanada
3. Großmutter in Russland
4. Tante in China

5. Kinder in England
6. Cousin in Kalifornien
7. Sohn in Japan
8. Tochter in Australien

> German speakers use the word **überhaupt** to emphasize **kein. Ich habe überhaupt keine Verwandten in Deutschland.**

---

## Absprungtext — Anna schreibt eine E-Mail

In preparation for her year in Germany, Anna Adler decides to contact her relatives in Germany. Her mother's sister, Ursula, lives with her family in Weinheim, not far from Frankfurt, where Anna's plane will land. Anna hopes to spend some time with them before her German course in Tübingen begins, but she is too unsure of her German to just call and talk on the phone. With a little help from her mother, Anna writes Tante Uschi an e-mail. Anna writes about her travel plans, her academic schedule in Germany, and her request to come for a visit. She asks Tante Uschi specifically to write back. Anna clearly wants to avoid speaking German on the phone, at least for now.

> Both **die E-Mail** and **das Mail** are used by Germans to mean *e-mail*

> Note again that the short version of **Ursula,** generally used by family and friends, is **Uschi.**

### Vorschau

**18** **Thematische Fragen.** Discuss the following questions with your instructor or in pairs.

1. If you were writing a letter or e-mail to relatives who lived in a foreign country and whom you'd never met, telling them that you wanted to come for a visit, what travel information would you include?

2. Suppose you wanted to visit these relatives before starting a study-abroad program in the country they live in. What would you tell them about yourself? What questions would you ask them?

3. Why might you prefer writing instead of calling someone abroad? Why would speaking a foreign language on the phone be more difficult than speaking it face to face with someone?

**19  Mein Tagtraum.** (*My daydream.*)  Imagine that you are going to Germany. How do you see yourself?

1. das Alter
   a. Ich bin fünfzehn Jahre alt.
   b. Ich bin zwanzig Jahre alt.
   c. Ich bin fünfzig Jahre alt.

2. der Beruf°/die Ausbildung°
   a. Ich bin Schüler(in)°.
   b. Ich bin Student(in).
   c. Ich habe einen Beruf.

3. die Personen
   a. Ich fliege allein.
   b. Ich fliege mit Freunden.
   c. Ich fliege mit meiner° Familie.

4. in Deutschland
   a. Ich gehe einkaufen.
   b. Ich studiere an der Universität.
   c. Ich besuche° meine Verwandten.

5. die Zeit
   a. Ich bleibe eine Woche.
   b. Ich bleibe einen Monat.
   c. Ich bleibe ein Jahr.

6. die Sprache°
   a. Ich spreche perfekt Deutsch.
   b. Ich spreche ein bisschen Deutsch.
   c. Ich spreche perfekt Englisch.

*am visiting*

*occupation / education*
*elementary or high-school*
  *student*

*language*

*my*

**20  Wortdetektiv.** Which words convey approximately the same meaning? Draw a line from the German word to its logical English equivalent.

| *Deutsch* | *Englisch* |
|---|---|
| 1. um 8.15 Uhr | a. to arrive |
| 2. ankommen | b. to send |
| 3. schicken | c. at 8:15 A.M. |
| 4. Verwandte | d. to get to know |
| 5. zurück | e. back |
| 6. kennen lernen | f. relatives |
| 7. ganz allein | g. immediately |
| 8. gleich | h. expensive |
| 9. teuer | i. all alone |
| 10. wunderbar | j request |
| 11. die Zeit | k. time |
| 12. die Bitte | l. wonderful |

**21  Scanning.** Scanning is a reading technique used to identify specific information, without reading every word of the text. It also helps the reader to locate the features that are typical of a certain text type.

1. When composing a letter or an e-mail the writer generally observes certain conventions. Scan Anna's e-mail for these customary elements.
   a. a subject line
   b. a date
   c. an opening greeting
   d. a closing

2. Look over Anna's e-mail for answers to these questions.
   a. When is she arriving in Germany, and where?
   b. When does her German course begin?
   c. When does the actual fall semester begin?
   d. How does she express her wish to come for a visit? How does she repeat it?

## *Absprungtext*
### *Anna schreibt eine E-Mail*

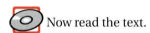 Now read the text.

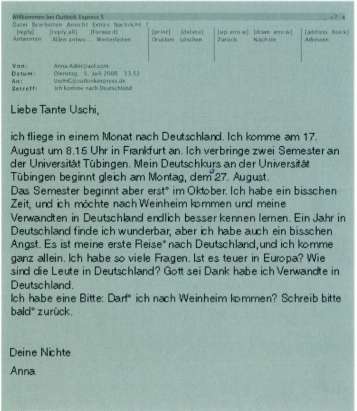

```
Willkommen bei Outlook Express 5                                    _ c? x
Datei Bearbeiten Ansicht Extras Nachricht ?
[reply]      [reply all]   [forward]    [print]   [delete]  [up arrow] [down arrow]  [address book]
Antworten    Allen antwo.... Weiterleiten  Drucken  Löschen   Zurück     Nächste      Adressen


Von:        Anna.Adler@aol.com
Datum:      Dienstag,  5. Juli 2008   13.52
An:         UschiG@outlookexpress.de
Betreff:    Ich komme nach Deutschland
```

Liebe Tante Uschi,

ich fliege in einem Monat nach Deutschland. Ich komme am 17. August um 8.15 Uhr in Frankfurt an. Ich verbringe zwei Semester an der Universität Tübingen. Mein Deutschkurs an der Universität Tübingen beginnt gleich am Montag, dem 27. August.
Das Semester beginnt aber erst° im Oktober. Ich habe ein bisschen Zeit, und ich möchte nach Weinheim kommen und meine Verwandten in Deutschland endlich besser kennen lernen. Ein Jahr in Deutschland finde ich wunderbar, aber ich habe auch ein bisschen Angst. Es ist meine erste Reise° nach Deutschland, und ich komme ganz allein. Ich habe so viele Fragen. Ist es teuer in Europa? Wie sind die Leute in Deutschland? Gott sei Dank habe ich Verwandte in Deutschland.
Ich habe eine Bitte: Darf° ich nach Weinheim kommen? Schreib bitte bald° zurück.


Deine Nichte

Anna

**Absprungtext.** In a German letter, a male is addressed with **Lieber ...** and a female with **Liebe ...** followed by that person's name (e.g., **Liebe Tante Uschi**). The plural form is **liebe** (e.g., **Liebe Großeltern!**).

"should be "dem"

*not until*

*erste ... : first trip*

*may*
*soon*

Family members close letters with **dein/deine: dein Thomas** (*your Thomas*), **deine Anna** (*your Anna*).

## *Rückblick*

**22   Stimmt das?** How much of the text do you remember without looking back at it?

| | Ja, das stimmt. | Nein, das stimmt nicht. |
|---|---|---|
| 1. Anna fliegt im Juli nach Deutschland. | ☐ | ☒ |
| 2. Anna kommt am 17. August in Frankfurt an. | ☒ | ☐ |
| 3. Annas Deutschkurs beginnt am 27. August. | ☒ | ☐ |
| 4. Anna möchte direkt nach Tübingen fahren. | ☐ | ☒ |
| 5. Anna findet ein Jahr in Deutschland wunderbar. | ☒ | ☐ |
| 6. Anna kommt ganz allein. | ☒ | ☐ |
| 7. Anna hat keine Angst; sie spricht perfekt Deutsch. | ☐ | ☒ |
| 8. Anna hat Verwandte in Deutschland. | ☒ | ☐ |
| 9. Tante Uschi soll° nicht zurückschreiben; sie soll anrufen°. | ☐ | ☒ |

*should / phone*

**23** **Ergänzen Sie.** Complete these questions and statements with words from the **Absprungtext.** Look back at the text as often as you like to read the sentences and see the words in context.

1. Ich _____ in einem Monat nach Deutschland.
2. Ich _____ am 17. August um 8 Uhr 15 in Frankfurt an.
3. Ich verbringe zwei _____ an der Universität in Tübingen.
4. Mein Deutschkurs _____ gleich am Montag, den 27. August.
5. Ich möchte nach Weinheim kommen und meine Verwandten in Deutschland endlich besser _____ _____.
6. Ein Jahr in Deutschland ist wunderbar, aber ich habe auch ein bisschen _____.
7. Ich habe so viele _____.
8. Ist es _____ in Europa?
9. Wie sind die _____ in Deutschland?
10. Ich habe eine _____: Darf ich nach Weinheim kommen?

**24** **Kurz gefragt.** Answer these questions with just a word or two.

S1: *Wann kommt Anna nach Deutschland?*
S2: *In einem Monat.* (oder)
     *Im August.*

1. Wo kommt sie an?
2. Wo studiert sie?
3. Was studiert sie?
4. Wann beginnt das Semester?
5. Hat sie Angst?
6. Wo wohnen Annas Verwandte in Deutschland?
7. Wie findet Anna ein Jahr in Deutschland?

## Wissenswerte Vokabeln: die Monate
### Talking about birthdays

**der Monat, -e**

| der Januar | ... im Januar | am ersten Januar | am elften Januar |
| der Februar | ... im Februar | am zweiten Februar | am zwölften ... |
| der März | ... im März | am dritten März | am dreizehnten ... |
| der April | ... im April | am vierten April | am vierzehnten ... |
| der Mai | ... im Mai | am fünften Mai | am fünfzehnten ... |
| der Juni | ... im Juni | am sechsten Juni | am sechzehnten ... |
| der Juli | ... im Juli | am siebten Juli | am siebzehnten ... |
| der August | ... im August | am achten August | am achtzehnten ... |
| der September | ... im September | am neunten September | am neunzehnten ... |
| der Oktober | ... im Oktober | am zehnten Oktober | am zwanzigsten ... |
| der November | ... im November | am elften November | am einundzwanzigsten ... |
| der Dezember | ... im Dezember | am zwölften Dezember | am zweiundzwanzigsten ... |

S1: *Wann haben Sie Geburtstag?*
S2: *Im Januar.*
S1: *Wann haben Sie im Januar Geburtstag?*
S2: *Ich habe am fünfundzwanzigsten Januar Geburtstag.*

**Jänner** is used in Austria for **Januar.**

**am dreiundzwanzigsten ...**
**am dreißigsten ...**
**am einunddreißigsten ...**
**am vierzigsten ...**
**am fünfzigsten ....**

When writing German, use a period following a number to indicate an ordinal number: **1.** (*1st*). Form the spoken forms of ordinal numbers for 2, 4–6, and 8–19 by adding the ending **-ten** to the number: **zweiten.** For numbers above 19, add **-sten: zwanzigsten.** Ordinal numbers that have special individual forms are: **ersten** (*first*), **dritten** (*third*), and **siebten** (*seventh*).

**Wann haben Sie Geburtstag? Ihr** and **Ihre** are the formal equivalents of *your.* You will learn more about this form in **Kapitel 3.**

**25    Wann haben Sie Geburtstag?** With a partner, state the date on which the following birthdays happen.

🟩 S1:  *Wann haben Sie Geburtstag?*
　　 S2:  *Ich habe am dritten September Geburtstag.*

To answer questions 2–6, use the subjects **Mein Vater (Bruder, Freund)** and **Meine Mutter (Schwester, Freundin)** to create full sentences. **Meine Mutter hat am zweiten April Geburtstag.**

|  | *Ich* | *Mein Partner/Meine Partnerin* |
|---|---|---|
| 1. Wann haben Sie Geburtstag? | _____ | _____ |
| 2. Wann hat Ihre Mutter Geburtstag? | _____ | _____ |
| 3. Wann hat Ihr Vater Geburtstag? | _____ | _____ |
| 4. Wann hat Ihre Schwester Geburtstag? | _____ | _____ |
| 5. Wann hat Ihr Bruder Geburtstag? | _____ | _____ |
| 6. Wann hat Ihr Freund/Ihre Freundin Geburtstag? | _____ | _____ |

## Strukturen und Vokabeln

## VI  Creating variety and shifting emphasis
### Position of subject and verb

See the **Arbeitsbuch** for additional practice with structures and vocabulary

In declarative sentences, the subject is generally the first element of the sentence, followed by the conjugated verb and the predicate (e.g., objects, prepositional phrases).

*subject*
**Ich** heiße Anna Adler.　　　　　　　*My name is Anna Adler.*

*subject*
**Ich** bin 20 Jahre alt.　　　　　　　*I am twenty years old.*

*subject*
**Ich** fliege im August nach Deutschland.　*I'm flying to Germany in August.*

However, it is also possible to begin a German sentence with something other than the subject. The first position can be occupied by a single word, a phrase, or an entire clause. The number of words in an element is not restricted. The purpose of placing an element other than the subject in first position is to emphasize that element. Regardless of the position of the subject, the position of the conjugated verb remains constant. It is always the second element of a sentence. Whenever an element other than the subject begins a sentence, the subject follows as the third element of the sentence.

|  | 1 | 2 | 3 |
|---|---|---|---|
|  |  | **Verb** | **Subject** |
| **Time phrase:** | Dieses Jahr | verbringe | **ich** zwei Semester in Deutschland. |
| **Direct object:** | Ein Jahr in Deutschland | finde | **ich** wunderbar. |

Please note that words like **ja** or **nein** and the conjunctions **und, aber, oder** (*and, but, or*) do not affect the word order.

Ja, ich heiße Anna und ich bin Amerikanerin.

**26** **Annas Pläne.** Combine the following sentence parts so they accurately reflect Anna's plans.

| | |
|---|---|
| 1. In Fort Wayne ... | a. beginnt das Semester. |
| 2. In Frankfurt ... | b. schreibe ich eine E-Mail an Tante Uschi. |
| 3. Ein Jahr ... | c. besuche ich Verwandte. |
| 4. Im Oktober ... | d. verbringe ich in Deutschland. |
| 5. In Weinheim ... | e. studiere ich in Tübingen. |
| 6. Zwei Semester ... | f. komme ich an. |

## Wissenswerte Vokabeln: die Wochentage
### Talking about weekly schedules

**der Wochentag, -e**

| | |
|---|---|
| der Sonntag | ... am Sonntag |
| der Montag | ... am Montag |
| der Dienstag | ... am Dienstag |
| der Mittwoch | ... am Mittwoch |
| der Donnerstag | ... am Donnerstag |
| der Freitag | ... am Freitag |
| der Samstag (*in Süddeutschland*) | ... am Samstag |
| der Sonnabend (*in Norddeutschland*) | ... am Sonnabend |
| das Wochenende | ... am Wochenende |

| | |
|---|---|
| Was ist heute? | *Heute ist Montag.* |
| Was haben wir heute? | *Heute haben wir Mittwoch.* |
| Wann spielt Anna Softball? | *Am Donnerstag.* |
| Wie viele Tage hat die Woche? | *Sieben.* |

The word **Wochentag** is a compound made from **die Woche** (*week*) and **der Tag** (*day*). The gender of a compound is the gender of the last word.

To find what day of the week it is, German speakers usually ask: **Was ist heute?**, or: **Was haben wir heute?** The answer states the day of the week without an article: **Heute ist Dienstag. Heute haben wir Sonnabend.**

**27** **Jetzt sind Sie dran.** (*Now it's your turn.*) Restate these sentences by positioning the underlined words in the first position and making all the necessary changes.

1. Wir verbringen ein Semester an der Universität in Göttingen.
2. Wir haben so viele Fragen!
3. Wir fliegen in drei Tagen nach Frankfurt.
4. Wir verbringen das Wochenende in Frankfurt.
5. Wir fahren dann nach Göttingen weiter°.
6. Wir kommen am Montag in Göttingen an.
7. Der Deutschkurs an der Universität beginnt gleich am Dienstag.
8. Wir spielen erst am Samstag ein bisschen Fußball.

*fahren weiter:* travel on to

**28**  **Was macht Katja heute?** (*What's Katja doing today?*) Answer these questions about Katja's activities this week. You need not answer in complete sentences.

**Was macht Katja heute?**
When one takes brief notes in German and does not make complete sentences, the infinitive appears at the end.

| Montag | Freitag |
|---|---|
| eine Postkarte schreiben | tanzen° gehen |
| Dienstag | Samstag |
| Tennis spielen | einen Spanischkurs haben |
| Mittwoch | Sonntag |
| mit Jutta Kaffee trinken | zu Hause bleiben |
| Donnerstag | Notizen |
| einen Pullover kaufen° | |

*tanzen ... : go dancing*

*buy*

🟨  Was macht Katja am Mittwoch?    *Am Mittwoch trinkt sie ...*

1. Was macht Katja am Mittwoch?
2. Wann bleibt Katja zu Hause?
3. Wann geht Katja tanzen?
4. Spielt Katja Tennis oder Fußball? Wann?
5. Was macht Katja am Montag?
6. Wann geht Katja einkaufen°? Was kauft Katja?
7. Hat Katja Samstag frei?

*shopping*

## Wissenswerte Vokabeln: Zeitausdrücke°

### Expressing repeated activities

*time expressions*

montags
dienstags
mittwochs
donnerstags
freitags
samstags, sonnabends
sonntags

**W.Vok.:** To express that an activity repeatedly or habitually takes place on a certain day, German speakers use the adverbial forms of the days of the week. They are written lower case (not capitalized) with an **-s** at the end.

🟨  Wann lernen Sie?    *Ich lerne montags und mittwochs.*

**29**   **Wann machen Sie das?** Your partner will ask you about activities you do. Answer with **am** plus the particular day of the week if you
will engage in the activity this week. Use the name of the day only plus an added
**-s** if you do the activity regularly.

🟨 S1:  *Wann haben Sie Deutsch?*
   S2:  *Ich habe montags, mittwochs und freitags Deutsch.*

| | | |
|---|---|---|
| 1. Deutsch haben | 5. Hausaufgaben° machen | *homework* |
| 2. einkaufen gehen | 6. zu Hause bleiben | |
| 3. im Restaurant essen | 7. tanzen gehen | |
| 4. Musik hören | 8. Bier trinken | |

## *Wissenswerte Vokabeln: die Uhrzeit*
### *Telling time*

Es ist sieben Uhr
morgens.

Es ist Viertel
nach eins.

Es ist Viertel
vor zwei.

12.00 = **der Mittag;** 0.00 =
**die Mitternacht.**

Fraction of hours may only
be used for the 12-hour
clock. **Viertel** (*quarter hour*)
may be used to denote a
quarter of an hour beyond
or before a full hour. **Halb**
means *half* and when used
for telling time indicates
that one half of the next full
hour has passed. Thus, **halb
zwei** means *one thirty.*
Amounts of time which
cannot be measured in
halves or quarters are
counted in minutes after
**(nach),** or short of **(vor)** the
full hour.

Es ist halb sechs.

Es ist fünf Minuten
vor sechs.

Es ist fünf Minuten
nach sechs.

In Austria, Switzerland, and
southern Germany, **viertel
zwei** means *1:15* and **drei
viertel zwei** means *1:45.*

The beginning and end of
an action is denoted by the
use of **von** (starting point)
and **bis** (end point).

Es ist zehn Uhr abends.
Es ist zweiundzwanzig
Uhr.

Es ist Mittag.

Es ist Mitternacht.

Note that points in time are
reported using the word
**Uhr: Es ist drei Uhr.** Time
periods, in contrast, are
given using the word
**Stunde,-n: Ich habe drei
Stunden Deutsch.**

🟨 Wie viel Uhr ist es?   *Es ist ...*

## Expressing time periods

| | |
|---|---|
| Wann kommt Anna in Frankfurt an? | Sie kommt um Viertel nach acht an. Sie kommt um acht Uhr fünfzehn an. |
| Wann haben Sie Deutsch? | Ich habe von acht (Uhr) bis acht Uhr fünfzig Deutsch. |
| Wann haben Sie Mathematik? | Ich habe von neun bis elf (Uhr) Mathematik. |

A point in time is denoted by the use of **um,** followed by the time.

Especially for official purposes, the 24-hour clock is used. When using the 12-hour clock, **morgens** (*in the morning*), and **abends** (*in the evening*) may be added for further clarification.

KASSE

T. 030 259004 27
täglich 12–19 Uhr
HAU ZWEI HALLESCHES UFER 32 10963 BERLIN
WWW.HEBBEL-AM-UFER.DE

Die Abendkassen an den Spielorten HAU 1, HAU 2 und HAU 3
öffnen eine Stunde vor Vorstellungsbeginn.

**30** **Georgs Stundenplan.** Georg is a student in the 11th grade at the **Johannes Kepler Gymnasium** in Weinheim. Complete the sentences below, referring to his weekly schedule for help.

| | Mo. | Di. | Mi. | Do. | Fr. |
|---|---|---|---|---|---|
| 7.45 | Mathe | — | Deutsch | — | Deutsch |
| 8.35 | Religion | Englisch | Mathe | — | Deutsch |
| 9.25 | Pause | Pause | Pause | Pause | Pause |
| 9.45 | Deutsch | Mathe | Englisch | Deutsch | Physik |
| 10.30 | Englisch | Physik | Geschichte | Sport | Sport |
| 11.15 | Geschichte | Erdkunde | — | Englisch | Erdkunde |
| 12.00 | Geschichte | Religion | Physik | Englisch | Mathe |
| 12.55 | | | Physik | Erdkunde | |

▪ Montags um _____ hat Georg Mathe.
*Montags um Viertel vor acht hat Georg Mathe.*

1. Mittwochs beginnt er um _____.
2. _____ hat er Physik um 10.30 Uhr.
3. Er geht freitags um _____ nach Hause°.
4. Religion hat er montags und _____.
5. Er hat Erdkunde freitags von _____ bis _____.
6. Montags hat er um _____ Religion.
7. Freitags hat er Mathe um _____.
8. Er hat montags bis freitags um _____ Pause.
9. Montags hat er um _____ frei.

*geht nach Hause: goes home*

**31** **Wann senden sie?** (*When do they broadcast?*) Ask your partner about the radio stations shown.

| Deutsche Radioprogramme in den U.S.A. | ILLINOIS & INDIANA | MICHIGAN | OHIO |
|---|---|---|---|

**Deutsche Radioprogramme in den U.S.A.**

**FLORIDA**
**WPIO - FM 89** Titusville
Son. von 16:30 - 18:00 Uhr
Die deutsch-polnische Stunde
Frank & Ruth Mlodzianowski

**WTIS-1110 AM** Tampa
*Deutsche Funksendung*
mit Susanne Nielsen
Son. von 13:00 - 14:00 Uhr

**ILLINOIS & INDIANA**
**WJKL- FM94.3 (Fox)**
Das Deutschlandecho
mit Armin Homann
Sam. & Son. 9:00 - 11:00 Uhr

**WKTA 1330 AM** Chicago
Der Funk am Morgen
Seit 40 Jahren
mit Alfred Richter
Samstag: 10:00 -12:30 Uhr
Österreicher Rundfunk
mit Manfred Gursch
Samstag: 12:30 -15:00 Uhr

**MICHIGAN**
**WPON 1460 AM** Detroit
"DEUTSCHE SPRACHBRÜCKE"
mit Roswitha Koch
Sa. von 9 - 10 Uhr
www.WPON.com
Email: rkochdfb@aol.com

**MISSOURI**
**WGNU 920 AM** St. Louis
Die deutsche Schlagerparade
Sprecher: Alfred Goerlich
Jeden Son. von 14:30 - 16 Uhr

**OHIO**
**WCWA 1230 AM** Toledo
DEUTSCHE RADIOSTUNDE
TOLEDO
Son. 9:00 – 10:00 Uhr
Peter Petersen, Sprecher

German-American Radio
Shows with Dr. Joe Wendel
**WCPN 90.3 FM** Cleveland
jeden Sam. 20:00 – 21:00 Uhr

**WCSB 89.3 FM** Cleveland
jeden Son. 10:00 – 12:00 Uhr
www.wcsb.org

**WQRP 89.5 FM** Dayton
jeden Sam. 10:00 – 13:00 Uhr
Melodies of Germany &
Austria with Maritta

S1: *Wie heißt der Radiosender in Tampa?*
S2: *WTIS*
S1: *Wann senden sie auf Deutsch?*
S2: *Sonntags um 13 Uhr. (Sonntags von 13 bis 14 Uhr.)*

1. Detroit
2. Chicago
3. St. Louis
4. Dayton
5. Cleveland
6. Titusville, Florida
7. Toledo
8. Illinois und Indiana

# VII Describing daily activities

## Regular present tense verbs: verbs with separable prefixes and two-verb constructions

Many German verbs that describe daily activities are composed of either a verb stem with a prefix or a two-verb construction.

- Prefixes that may be separated from the verb stem are always stressed and look like independent words, such as prepositions, e.g., **an**kommen (*to arrive*), **auf**stehen (*to get up, stand up*), **um**drehen (*to turn around*) or adverbs, e.g., **fern**sehen (*to watch TV*), **zurück**kommen (*to come back*).
- Two-verb constructions include **kennen** lernen (*to get to know*), **einkaufen** gehen (*to go shopping*), **schlafen** gehen (*to go to bed*), **spazieren** gehen (*to go for a walk*), and **wandern** gehen (*to go hiking*).

Separable prefixes and the first verb in a two-verb construction are placed at the end of the main clause in a sentence.

English has similar verbs (e.g., *stand up, get up*), but unlike German the prefix is not always part of the infinitive (e.g., *\*upstand, \*upget* do not exist but: *downplay, upgrade* are correct). Also, the placement of these prefixes within a sentence is different in English and German.

Notice that the infinitive of **wandern** is formed with the stem (**wander-**) and the ending **n.**

In the infinitive form, verbs with prefixes are written as one word; verbs in two-verb constructions are always written separately. Despite this difference, they share similarities in word placement.

| | | |
|---|---|---|
| an·kommen | Ich **komme** im August **an.** | *I arrive in August.* |
| auf·stehen | **Stehen** Sie bitte **auf.** | *Get up, please.* |
| einkaufen gehen | Wir **gehen** um 8.00 **einkaufen.** | *We're going shopping at 8:00.* |

**Gern** and **nicht gern** occur either right after the conjugated verb or right before the separable prefix or the infinitive.

Ich **stehe gern** samstags und sonntags auf. ⎫
Ich stehe samstags und sonntags **gern auf.** ⎭  *I like to get up on Saturdays and Sundays.*

Ich **stehe nicht gern** montags bis freitags auf. ⎫
Ich stehe montags bis freitags **nicht gern auf.** ⎭  *I don't like getting up Monday through Friday.*

Ich **gehe (nicht) gern** samstags einkaufen. ⎫
Ich gehe samstags **(nicht) gern einkaufen.** ⎭  *I (don't) like to go shopping on Saturday.*

> Separable-prefix verbs that occur in vocabulary lists in this book are marked with a bullet between the prefix and verb stem (e.g., **auf·stehen, zurück·kommen**). In standard German, these infinitives are written as one word (e.g., **aufstehen, zurückkommen**).

> Prefixes that do not resemble independent prepositions or adverbs are not separable. Examples are **ver-** (**verbringen:** *to spend*) or **be-** (**besuchen:** *to visit*).

## *Wissenswerte Vokabeln: Onkel Hannes' Alltag°*
### *Talking about daily activities*

*everyday life*

1.

Um halb sieben **wacht** Hannes Günther **auf.**

2.

Um Viertel nach sieben **steht** Hannes **auf.**

3.

Um zehn Minuten nach neun **kommt** er im Büro **an.**

4.

Gegen zehn Uhr **ruft** er Tante Uschi **an.**

5.

Um halb sechs **hört** die Arbeit **auf.**

6.

Er **kommt** gegen sechs Uhr **zurück.**

7.

Um Viertel nach sechs **geht** Hannes mit Uschi **spazieren.**

8.

Um Viertel vor elf **gehen** sie **schlafen.**

🟧 Wann stehen Sie auf?   *Ich stehe um ... auf.*

**32** **Das Wochenende.** Ask your classmates whether they do the following activities on the weekend. Then determine the rank of these activities based on how many people in the class engage in them. Use the numbers 1 (most popular) to 6 (least popular).

*Stehen Sie vor sieben Uhr auf?*

|  | *Person* | *Rang°* | *rank* |
|---|---|---|---|
| 1. vor sieben Uhr aufstehen | _____ | _____ | |
| 2. einkaufen gehen | _____ | _____ | |
| 3. die Eltern anrufen | _____ | _____ | |
| 4. mit Freunden spazieren gehen | _____ | _____ | |
| 5. vor zehn Uhr abends zurückkommen | _____ | _____ | |
| 6. nach elf Uhr abends schlafen gehen | _____ | _____ | |

## VIII Expressing negation

### Position of **nicht**

The following rules governing the placement of **nicht** may be helpful to you.

1. In very basic sentences, **nicht** follows the verb but precedes a separable prefix at the end of the sentence.

   Sie kommt **nicht** an.

2. In yes/no questions, **nicht** remains at the end of the sentence, even though the verb occurs at the beginning of the question.

   Kommen Sie **nicht?**

3. In statements and questions with a direct object, **nicht** usually occurs at the end of the sentence.

   Sie verstehen den Professor **nicht.**
   Verstehen Sie den Professor **nicht?**

4. **Nicht** precedes most adverbs, adjectives, and prepositional phrases.

   | | |
   |---|---|
   | Er spielt **nicht gern** Tennis. | *He doesn't like to play tennis.* |
   | Sie kommt **nicht aus Deutschland.** | *She isn't from Germany.* |
   | Wir haben **nicht so viel** Zeit. | *We don't have that much time.* |
   | Der Professor ist **nicht freundlich.** | *The professor is not friendly.* |

Remember to use a form of **kein** when you answer a question negatively about the availability or existence of someone or something.

| | |
|---|---|
| Hast du Zeit? | Nein, ich habe **keine** Zeit. |
| Haben Sie Kinder? | Nein, ich habe **keine** Kinder. |

When words like **Zeit** and **Kinder** are quantified with **viel** (*much, a lot of*) and **viele** (*many, a lot of*), however, the negation includes **nicht.**

| | |
|---|---|
| Ich habe **nicht viel** Zeit. | *I don't have much time.* |
| Ich habe **nicht viele** Kinder. | *I don't have many children.* |

**Viel** is used to quantify things that cannot be counted: **viel Angst** (*much anxiety*). **Viele** is used to quantify things that can be counted: **viele Studenten** (*many students*). The opposite expressions are **wenig** (*little*) and **wenige** (*few*): **wenig Angst** (*little anxiety*), **wenige Studenten** (*few students*).

**33** **Verstehen Sie den Professor?** Answer the following questions in the negative, using **nicht.**

S1: *Verstehen Sie den Professor?*
S2: *Nein, ich verstehe den Professor nicht.*

1. Verstehen Sie den Professor?
2. Sagen Sie gern „Guten Tag"?
3. Spielt er gern Fußball?
4. Haben Sie so viel Zeit?
5. Kommt Katja aus den USA?

6. Kommen Sie aus Deutschland?
7. Kommt Anna zurück?
8. Ist Anna sportlich?
9. Gehen Sie gern wandern?

**34** *Nicht* **oder** *kein?* Decide whether to use **nicht** or a form of **kein** in your answers to these questions.

S1: *Haben Sie einen Bruder in Sankt Petersburg?*
S2: *Nein, ich habe keinen Bruder in Sankt Petersburg.*

1. Haben Sie einen Bruder in Sankt Petersburg?
2. Sprechen Sie perfekt Deutsch?
3. Haben Sie einen Cousin in Weinheim?
4. Haben Sie Zeit?
5. Fliegen Sie heute nach Berlin?
6. Verstehen Sie Finnisch°?
7. Beginnen Sie die Hausaufgaben um sechs Uhr?
8. Stehen Sie sonntags um halb sieben auf?
9. Rufen Sie eine Tante in Istanbul an?
10. Schicken Sie Tante Ursula eine Postkarte?
11. Schreiben Sie Anna eine E-Mail?

*das Finnisch: the Finnish language*

| *Zieltext* | **Annas E-Mail** |

Anna's cousin in Weinheim, Katja Günther, finds Anna's e-mail from America, addressed to her mother. She calls her mother over to see what Anna has written.

## *Vorschau*

**35** **Das wissen wir.** (*That's what we know.*) Please review what has happened so far by checking the correct statement.

1. a. Anna schreibt eine E-Mail.
   b. Hannelore schreibt eine E-Mail.

2. a. Die E-Mail ist auf Englisch.
   b. Die E-Mail ist auf Deutsch.

The **Zieltext** in each chapter is a listening text. The text is intentionally not printed in your textbook in order to increase your understanding of spoken German. Listen carefully to the conversation. Expect to listen to the dialogue several times before you can comfortably understand it. However, remember that in order to understand a text you do not have to recognize every single word. You will be able to understand a lot of German in a fairly short time.

3. a. Anna kommt für° ein Jahr nach Deutschland.                    *for*
   b. Anna kommt für ein Semester nach Deutschland.

4. a. Annas Verwandte wohnen in Tübingen.
   b. Annas Verwandte wohnen in Weinheim.

5. a. Anna hat ein bisschen Angst.
   b. Anna hat viel Angst.

6. a. Katja und Georg haben keinen Vater.
   b. Annas Onkel, Herr Günther, heißt Hannes.

**36** **Thematische Fragen.** Discuss the following questions with your instructor or in pairs.

1. Who in the Günther family do you think receives the e-mail?
2. Who do they think wrote the e-mail?
3. How do the Günthers feel about Anna's impending visit?

**37** **Erstes Zuhören.** (*First listening.*) Read the questions below before you listen.

1. Wen hören Sie?
   a. zwei Männer
   b. zwei Frauen
   c. einen Mann und eine Frau

2. Was fragt Tante Uschi?
   a. „Von wem° ist es denn?"                    ***Von ... :*** *from whom*
   b. „Ist die E-Mail auf Englisch oder auf Deutsch?"
   c. „Ist die E-Mail lang oder kurz?"

3. Was weiß° Katja *nicht*?                    *knows*
   a. Eine E-Mail kommt an.
   b. Die E-Mail kommt aus Amerika.
   c. Anna schickt die E-Mail.

4. Was fragt Tante Uschi?
   a. „Wo möchte Anna schlafen?"
   b. „Was? Wann denn? Warum denn?"
   c. „Was möchte Anna hier machen?"

5. Katja sagt: „Das ist ja wirklich toll!" Das bedeutet ...
   a. Das ist sehr gut!
   b. Das ist nicht sehr gut.
   c. Das ist dumm!

## Zieltext
### Annas E-Mail

 Now listen to the dialogue for the first time as you listen for answers to the questions.

 Listen to the dialogue again, as often as you wish, to understand more.

## Rückblick

 **38  Stimmt das?** How much of the **Zieltext** do you understand?

|  | *Ja, das stimmt.* | *Nein, das stimmt nicht.* |
|---|:---:|:---:|
| 1. Katja und Uschi finden eine E-Mail. | ☐ | ☐ |
| 2. Tante Uschi meint, die E-Mail ist von Hannelore. | ☒ | ☐ |
| 3. Die E-Mail ist von Georg. | ☐ | ☒ |
| 4. Die E-Mail ist auf Englisch. | ☐ | ☒ |
| 5. Uschi und Katja finden es gut, dass° Anna nach Deutschland kommt. | ☒ | ☐ |

*that*

 **39  Ordnung schaffen.** (*Tidying up.*) Number these sentences from the text in the order in which you hear them.

<u>2</u>  Ich habe keine Ahnung.
<u>3</u>  Was? Wann denn? Warum denn?
<u>4</u>  Sie hat etwas Zeit.
<u>1</u>  Schau mal, Mutti!
___  Mach schon auf!
<u>5</u>  Das ist toll.

*„ Moment mal."*

**40  Austausch.** (*Exchange.*) First, check the characteristics that apply to you. Then, check the characteristics that describe an exchange student you would want to take in if you were a German speaker. Finally, ask as many students as possible about their characteristics and tell others about yours. The goal is for you to find an "exchange student" with whom you would be comfortable.

> **Austausch.** The verb **spricht** is the third person singular form of **sprechen.** You will learn more about why the stem vowel changes in **Kapitel 3.**

S1: *Sprechen Sie viel Deutsch?*
S2: *Ja, ich spreche viel Deutsch.*

**Ich ...**
1. spreche ...
   a. ein bisschen Deutsch.
   b. viel Deutsch.

**Der Austauschstudent/Die Austauschstudentin ...**
   spricht° ...
   a. ein bisschen Deutsch.
   b. viel Deutsch.

*speaks*

| *Ich ...* | *Der Austauschstudent/Die Austauschstudentin ...* |
|---|---|
| 2. spiele viel ...<br>a. Fußball.<br>b. Tennis.<br>c. Softball. | spielt viel ...<br>a. Fußball.<br>b. Tennis.<br>c. Softball. |
| 3. höre gern ...<br>a. klassische Musik.<br>b. Rockmusik.<br>c. Countrymusik. | hört gern ...<br>a. klassische Musik.<br>b. Rockmusik.<br>c. Countrymusik. |
| 4. gehe nicht gern ...<br>a. wandern.<br>b. einkaufen.<br>c. vor elf Uhr abends schlafen. | geht nicht gern ...<br>a. wandern.<br>b. einkaufen.<br>c. vor elf Uhr abends schlafen. |
| 5. trinke wenig ...<br>a. Milch.<br>b. Kaffee.<br>c. Bier. | trinkt wenig ...<br>a. Milch.<br>b. Kaffee.<br>c. Bier. |
| 6. stehe montags bis freitags ...<br>a. vor sieben Uhr auf.<br>b. vor neun Uhr auf.<br>c. nach neun Uhr auf. | steht montags bis freitags ...<br>a. vor sieben Uhr auf.<br>b. vor neun Uhr auf.<br>c. nach neun Uhr auf. |
| 7. habe ...<br>a. viele Verwandte.<br>b. wenige Verwandte. | hat ...<br>a. viele Verwandte.<br>b. wenige Verwandte. |
| 8. bin ...<br>a. ein Mann.<br>b. eine Frau. | ist ...<br>a. ein Mann.<br>b. eine Frau. |
| 9. bin ...<br>a. freundlich.<br>b. intelligent.<br>c. jung. | ist ...<br>a. freundlich.<br>b. intelligent.<br>c. jung. |
| 10. studiere ...<br>a. Deutsch.<br>b. Volkswirtschaft.<br>c. ? | studiert ...<br>a. Deutsch.<br>b. Volkswirtschaft.<br>c. ? |

 **Freie Kommunikation**

**Das bin ich.** (*That's me.*) You are giving a speech to an Austrian class that wants to know what American students are like. Describe yourself in detail.

 **Schreibecke**

**Eine E-Mail schreiben.** (*Writing an e-mail.*) You are planning to attend a summer course in Austria in July. Write an e-mail to your pen pal Annette in **Wien** (*Vienna*). Use Anna's e-mail earlier in the chapter for ideas.

> **Das bin ich.** Use items from the activity **Austausch,** but go into more detail.

> Consider recording yourself as you speak. Submit the recording to your instructor, or to peers for feedback. You may also transcribe what you have said and rerecord yourself after you have corrected your mistakes.

## *Wortschatz*

### Die Familie und die Verwandten

**der Bruder, ¨** *brother*
**der Cousin, -s** *(male) cousin*
**die Eltern** *(pl.) parents*
**der Enkel, -** *grandson*
**die Enkelin, -nen** *granddaughter*
**das Enkelkind, -er** *grandchild*
**die Frau, -en** *wife*
**die Großeltern** *(pl.) grandparents*
**die Großmutter, ¨** *grandmother*
**der Großvater, ¨** *grandfather*
**der Junge [-en], -en** *boy*
**das Kind, -er** *child*
**die Kusine, -n** *(female) cousin*
**die Leute** *(pl.), people*
**das Mädchen, -** *girl*
**der Mann, ¨er** *husband*
**die Mutter, ¨** *mother*
**der Neffe, [-n], -n** *nephew*
**die Nichte, -n** *niece*
**die Oma, -s** *grandma*
**der Onkel, -** *uncle*
**der Opa, -s** *grandpa*
**die Schwester, -n** *sister*
**der Sohn, ¨e** *son*
**die Tante, -n** *aunt*
**die Tochter, ¨** *daughter*
**der Vater, ¨** *father*

**die Familie, -n** *family*
**der Hund** *dog*
**die Katze, -n** *cat*
**die Verwandten** *(pl.) family, relatives*

### Die Universität und die Studienfächer

**das Hauptfach, ¨er** *major (area of study)*
    **Was haben Sie als Hauptfach?** *What's your major?*
**der Kurs, -e** *course*
**das Nebenfach, ¨er** *minor (area of study)*

**das Semester, -** *semester*
**das Studienfach, ¨er** *academic subject*
    **Welche Fächer haben Sie?** *What courses are you taking?*

**die Betriebswirtschaft** *business*
**die Biologie** *biology*
**die Chemie** *chemistry*
**das Deutsch** *German*
**das Englisch** *English*
**das Französisch** *French*
**die Geschichte** *history*
**die Informatik** *computer science*
**das Ingenieurwesen** *engineering*
**Internationale Beziehungen** *(pl.) international relations*
**die Kunst** *art*
**die Mathematik (Mathe)** *mathematics (math)*
**die Medizin** *medicine*
**die Musik** *music*
**die Pädagogik** *education (teaching)*
**die Philosophie** *philosophy*
**die Physik** *physics*
**die Politikwissenschaft** *political science*
**die Psychologie** *psychology*
**das Russisch** *Russian*
**die Soziologie** *sociology*
**das Spanisch** *Spanish*
**die Volkswirtschaft** *economics*

### Die Monate

**der Januar, der Februar, der März, der April, der Mai, der Juni, der Juli, der August, der September, der Oktober, der November, der Dezember**

**das Jahr, -e** *year*
**der Monat, -e** *month*

**Wann haben Sie Geburtstag?** *When is your birthday?*

**am ersten Januar** *on the first of January*
**im Januar** *in January*

### Die Wochentage

**der Montag, der Dienstag, der Mittwoch, der Donnerstag, der Freitag, der Samstag** *(Austria, Switzerland, southern Germany)***, der Sonnabend** *(northern Germany)***, der Sonntag**

**der Tag, -e** *day*
**die Woche, -n** *week*
**das Wochenende, -n** *weekend*
**der Wochentag, -e** *day of the week; weekday*

**am Sonntag** *on (this) Sunday*
**am Wochenende** *on the weekend*
**heute** *today*
    **Was haben wir heute?** *What day is it today?*
    **Was ist heute?** *What day is it today?*
**sonntags** *on Sundays (in general)*

### Die Uhrzeit

**die Uhr** *clock; (clock) time*
**die Zeit, -en** *time*
**Wie viel Uhr ist es?** *What time is it?*
**Es ist ... (Uhr).** *It's . . . (o'clock).*
**(fünf) Minuten nach (eins)** *(five) minutes after (one)*
**(fünf) Minuten vor (zwei)** *(five) minutes to (two)*
**halb (zwei)** *half past (one) (i.e., halfway to two)*
**der Mittag** *noon*
**die Mitternacht** *midnight*
**Viertel nach (eins)** *quarter past (one)*
**Viertel vor (zwei)** *quarter to (two)*
**abends** *in the evening*
**morgens** *in the morning*

**um (sechs) Uhr**  *at (six) o'clock*
**gegen (sieben) Uhr**  *around (seven) o'clock*
**von (neun Uhr) bis (zehn Uhr)**  *from (nine o'clock) until/to (ten o'clock)*

### Aktivitäten des Alltags

**an·kommen**  *to arrive*
**an·rufen**  *to call up (on the phone)*
**auf·hören**  *to stop*
**auf·stehen**  *to get up, get out of bed; to stand up*
**auf·wachen**  *to wake up*
**beginnen**  *to begin*
**bleiben**  *to stay, remain*
**ein·kaufen**  *to shop*
**fern·sehen**  *to watch TV*
**finden**  *to find; to think that something is . . .*
**fliegen**  *to fly*
**fragen**  *to ask*
**gehen**  *to go*
   **nach Hause gehen**  *to go home*
   **schlafen gehen**  *to go to bed*
   **spazieren gehen**  *to go for a walk*
**haben**  *to have*
   **Angst haben**  *to be afraid, anxious*
   **Durst haben**  *to be thirsty*
   **frei haben**  *to have time off*
   **gern haben**  *to like*
   **Hunger haben**  *to be hungry*
   **nicht gern haben**  *not to like*
**hören**  *to hear; to listen to*
**kaufen**  *to buy*
**kennen lernen**  *to get to know*
**kommen**  *to come*
**lernen**  *to learn; to study (for an exam, a class)*
**machen**  *to do; to make*
   **die Hausaufgaben machen**  *to do homework*
**meinen**  *to think; to mean*
**schlafen**  *to sleep*
**schreiben**  *to write*
**sehen**  *to see*

**spielen**  *to play*
**studieren**  *to study*
**tanzen**  *to dance*
**trinken**  *to drink*
**um·drehen**  *to turn around*
**verbessern**  *to improve*
**verbringen**  *to spend time*
**verstehen**  *to understand*
**wandern**  *to hike*
**wohnen**  *to live*
**zurück·kommen**  *to come back, return*

### Ordungszahlen

**am ersten, zweiten, dritten, vierten, fünften, sechsten, siebten, achten, neunten, zehnten, elften, zwölften, dreizehnten, …, zwanzigsten, einundzwanzigsten, …**

### Kommunikation

**die Bitte, -n**  *request*
**die E-Mail**  *e-mail (the concept)*
**die Frage, -n**  *question*
**die Leute** (pl.)  *people*
**das Mail**  *e-mail (the concept)*
**die Postkarte, -n**  *postcard*
**die Reise, -n**  *journey, trip*

### Adjektive

**besser**  *better*
**klug**  *smart*
**ledig**  *single*
**sportlich**  *athletic*
**teuer**  *expensive*
**toll**  *great*
**verheiratet**  *married*
**wunderbar**  *wonderful*

### Ausdrücke

**auf Deutsch**  *in German*
**darf ich?**  *may I?*
**ein bisschen**  *a little*
**ich bin gespannt auf**  *I'm looking forward to*

**ich möchte**  *I'd like*
**nach Hause**  *(to) home*
**nicht sehr**  *not very, not much*
**nicht so**  *not so*
**überhaupt kein**  *none at all*
**zu Hause**  *at home*
**zum Beispiel (z. B.)**  *for example*

### Andere Wörter

**aber**  *but*
**allein**  *alone*
**auch**  *also, too*
**bald**  *soon*
**dein Thomas / deine Anna**  *your Thomas/Anna (at the end of a letter)*
**doch**  *yes (for emphasis)*
**endlich**  *finally*
**etwas**  *somewhat, a little*
**für**  *for*
**ganz allein**  *all alone*
**gern**  *(after a verb) to like to do*
   **ich singe gern**  *I like to sing*
**gleich**  *right away*
**mit**  *with*
**nur**  *only*
**oder**  *or*
**sehr**  *very*
**viel**  *much, a lot*
**viele**  *many, a lot*
**von**  *of; from*
**wen?**  *whom?*
**wenig**  *little*
**wenige**  *few*

### Meine eigenen Wörter

———————————
———————————
———————————
———————————
———————————
———————————

# Was gibt es in Heidelberg und Mannheim zu tun?

- Stating personal preferences
- Expressing what you would like to do
- Expressing possibilities
- Referring to people and things
- Talking about what you know as a fact and about people, places, and things
- Talking about more than one item

## Strukturen

- Present tense of stem-changing verbs (including **wissen**)
- Nominative and accusative of possessive adjectives
- Coordinating conjunctions
- The particle **lieber**
- The modal verbs **möchte** and **können**
- Accusative pronouns
- The verb **kennen**
- Noun plurals

## Vokabeln

- Lebensmittel
- Freizeitaktivitäten

## Kulturelles

- Mealtimes in German-speaking countries
- The metric system
- Heidelberg and Mannheim

■ Ist das typisch deutsch?

### Online Study Center

Go to the *Vorsprung* Website at *http://college.hmco.com/pic/vorsprung2e.*

In this chapter you will learn how to talk about the activities of others, what you like to do, and what you can do. You will begin using the informal form of *you* (**du**) with other students. You will also read about the German cities Heidelberg and Mannheim.

## Kommunikative Funktionen

- Describing activities
- Expressing relationships or ownership
- Expressing additional and contrastive information and justifications

**Anlauftext**

## *Was halten wir von Anna? Was hält sie von uns?*

The Günthers are talking about their American relative, Anna Adler, and are making certain assumptions about her behavior and Americans in general, with whom they have had little direct contact. Anna, too, wonders about her German relatives. All of this talk reveals some glaring stereotypes about Americans and Germans.

## *Vorschau*

**1   Thematische Fragen.** Discuss the following questions with your instructor or in pairs.

1. What are some of your assumptions about Germans and German culture?
2. Think about some German characters you have seen on TV or in a movie. How were they portrayed? What stereotypes do these characterizations of the Germans perpetuate?

**2   Wortdetektiv.** Which words convey approximately the same meaning? Match the German word with its logical English equivalent.

| *Deutsch* | | *Englisch* |
|---|---|---|
| 1. das Gepäck | a. | to eat |
| 2. mit·bringen | b. | perhaps |
| 3. essen | c. | to bring along |
| 4. lächeln | d. | luggage |
| 5. vielleicht | e. | something |
| 6. etwas | f. | to smile |

| | | |
|---|---|---|
| 7. das Schweinefleisch | g. | always |
| 8. tragen | h. | train station |
| 9. der Bahnhof | i. | to wear |
| 10. immer | j. | pork |
| 11. wahrscheinlich | k. | there is |
| 12. es gibt | l. | probably |

> **Wortdetektiv.** To guess the meaning of the German words, look for similarities with English (cognates), determine which English and German words belong to the same categories (nouns, verbs, adjectives), and use a process of elimination.

**3   Kognate entdecken°.**

*discover*

1. A cognate is a word that has a similar form in two different languages, like the German **Haus** and the English *house*. Scan the statements in the **Anlauftext** (pages 76–77). Find six cognates in German.
2. Look at the statements and the drawings in the text and decide which daily habits or customs mentioned there lead to the creation of stereotypes about others.

> Try to identify any of the following words in the **Anlauftext:**
> 1. Words borrowed from English, e.g., **Popmusik.**
> 2. Cognates or words with similar forms and meanings in English and German, e.g., **trinkt, gut.**
> 3. Direct translations from English, e.g., **Kaugummi.**

## Anlauftext

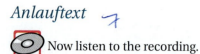

Now listen to the recording.

**Anlauftext.** Try to identify the cultural stereotypes presented in the text.

## Sprache im Alltag: Assumptions with **bestimmt, sicher, wahrscheinlich,** and **wohl**

A person who makes an assumption generally expects the listener to confirm a suspicion or thought. In German, the words **bestimmt** (*undoubtedly*), **sicher** (*certainly, surely*), **wahrscheinlich** (*most likely, probably*), and **wohl** (*in all likelihood, no doubt*) indicate that a statement is an assumption.

| | |
|---|---|
| Anna spricht **sicher** nur Englisch. | *Anna certainly speaks only English.* |
| Sie versteht **bestimmt** wenig Deutsch. | *She undoubtedly understands little German.* |
| Anna will **wahrscheinlich** mein Zimmer haben. | *Anna most likely wants to have my room.* |
| Anna sieht **wohl** immer nur fern. | *Anna no doubt watches TV all the time.* |

## *Rückblick*

**4   Stimmt das?** How much of the text can you remember without looking back at it? Look over the statements and mark the true statements as **Ja, das stimmt**. Mark the false statements as **Nein, das stimmt nicht**. Then, listen as your instructor reads the following statements and models their pronunciation. If the statement is true, say **Ja, das stimmt**. If the statement is not true, say **Nein, das stimmt nicht**.

**Stimmt das?** Do this exercise after reading the text once to determine how much you understood and how much you missed. Then reread the text until you feel confident that you understand it.

|   | Ja, das stimmt. | Nein, das stimmt nicht. |
|---|---|---|
| 1. Tante Uschi meint, Anna isst nur Bratwurst. | ☐ | ☐ |
| 2. Tante Uschi meint, Anna spricht viel Deutsch. | ☐ | ☐ |
| 3. Tante Uschi meint, Anna lächelt immer, wie alle Amerikaner. | ☐ | ☐ |
| 4. Katja meint, Anna versteht kein Deutsch. | ☐ | ☐ |
| 5. Onkel Hannes meint, Anna sieht immer fern. | ☐ | ☐ |
| 6  Georg meint, Anna trägt immer Shorts und Turnschuhe. | ☐ | ☐ |
| 7. Anna meint, die Günthers trinken nur Mineralwasser und essen vegetarisch. | ☐ | ☐ |
| 8. Anna meint, die Günthers wandern jedes Wochenende. | ☐ | ☐ |
| 9. Anna meint, es gibt gute Popmusik in Deutschland. | ☐ | ☐ |

**Nur "Bahnhof" verstehen** is a German idiom that literally means *to understand only "train station."* It means *to not have a clue.*

**5   Ergänzen Sie.** Complete these sentences with words from the **Anlauftext.**

### *Tante Uschi*
1. Anna _____ nur Hamburger mit Ketchup.
2. Anna _____ sicher nur Englisch.

### *Katja*
3. Anna ist so freundlich und optimistisch. Sie _____ immer, wie alle Amerikaner.
4. Anna _____ nicht viel Deutsch, nur „Bahnhof".

### *Onkel Hannes*
5. Anna _____ wohl immer nur _____.
6. Anna hat immer _____ im Mund.

### *Georg*
7. Vielleicht bringt Anna viel _____ mit.
8. Anna _____ bestimmt immer Shorts und Turnschuhe.

### *Anna*
9. Es _____ wahrscheinlich keine gute Popmusik in Deutschland.
10. Die Günthers _____ wahrscheinlich nur Schweinefleisch und trinken nur _____.

**6   Kurz gefragt.** Answer these questions. Try to create complete sentences.

**Kurz gefragt.** Respond with a word or phrase only.

Was, meinen die Günthers, ...

1. essen und trinken alle Amerikaner?
2. spricht Anna?
3. machen alle Amerikaner immer?

4. versteht Anna sicher nur?
5. bringt Anna mit?
6. trägt Anna bestimmt?

Was, meint Anna, ...

7. essen und trinken die Günthers?
8. machen die Günthers jedes Wochenende?
9. gibt es wahrscheinlich nicht in Deutschland?

**7**  **Bin ich typisch?**  Ask your classmates whether they are Americans. Every time a person indicates he/she is an American, confront him/her with one of the stereotypes listed below. Present these stereotypes in the form of assumptions, using **sicher, bestimmt,** and **wohl.** Your classmate says whether this stereotype applies to him/her.

▢ S1: *Sie kauen° wohl gern Kaugummi.*                                   *chew*
   S2: *Nein, ich kaue nicht gern Kaugummi.* (oder)
       *Ja, ich kaue gern Kaugummi.*

1. gern Kaugummi kauen
2. gern Rockmusik hören
3. nur Hamburger essen
4. immer Cola trinken
5. nur Englisch sprechen
6. gern Shorts und Turnschuhe tragen

---

**BRENNPUNKT KULTUR**

## Mealtimes in German-speaking countries

Since eating customs are often the most distinctive aspects of a culture, they are frequently the means by which others form stereotypes. For example, in Germany, Austria, and Switzerland, it is common to hold the knife in one hand and the fork in the other and rest the forearms on the edge of the table while eating. In the United States this may be considered rude mealtime behavior.

In German-speaking countries, three to five distinct mealtimes may be observed each day. Breakfast (**das Frühstück**) usually consists of coffee or tea, some kind of fresh-baked bread (**das Brot**) or a crusty roll (**das Brötchen** in the north and **die Semmel** in southern areas), with butter (**die Butter**), fruit jam (**die Marmelade**), honey (**der Honig**), cheese (**der Käse**), a unique German dairy spread called (**der**) **Quark,** or even cold cuts (**der Aufschnitt**). Some people round off their breakfast with a soft-boiled egg (**ein weich gekochtes Ei**), yogurt (**der/das Joghurt**), or breakfast cereal such as (**das**) **Müesli,** a Swiss whole-grain, fruit-and-nut cereal, or the American-style **Choco Krispies** or **Cornflakes.** Many Germans consider a nutritious breakfast the most important meal of the day.

Mid-morning, some people at work and school break for a snack or second breakfast (**zweites Frühstück**), which may consist of a cup of yogurt, a piece of fruit, or a **belegtes Brötchen** with cold cuts or cheese.

**Das Mittagessen** is for many the main hot meal of the day. It often has three courses: (1) an appetizer (**die Vorspeise**), most often soup (**die Suppe**); (2) the main course (**das Hauptgericht**) of meat or fish, potatoes or noodles or rice, and a vegetable; and (3) a dessert (**die Nachspeise / der Nachtisch**) of pudding, fruit, or ice cream.

On special occasions or on weekends, many people enjoy coffee and cake (**Kaffee und Kuchen**) around mid-afternoon.

The last meal of the day, around 6 P.M., is called **das Abendbrot** or **das Abendessen.** Traditionally it consists of bread, cold cuts, and cheese, along with tomatoes, salad, and cucumbers. Tea, mineral water, beer, or wine completes the meal. In a growing number of working families, the main hot meal is now prepared in the evening.

---

■ **Kulturkreuzung** Think about the differences between meals in German-speaking countries and in this country. What differences do you notice about breakfast? What kind of breakfast foods are unique to your area of the country, and to other areas of the country? Which breakfast seems healthier? What prevents people here from eating their big meal at noon? How would guests here react if you served them cold cuts and tea for supper?

Was isst man zum Frühstück?

## Strukturen und Vokabeln

### I  Describing activities

Present tense of stem-changing verbs

Was isst du gern?

Many of the most frequently occurring German verbs change their stem vowel (the main vowel of the verb) in the present tense **du-** and **er/sie/es-**forms. These verbs are called irregular verbs (**unregelmäßige Verben**) or strong verbs (**starke Verben**). Compare how the stem vowels change in the question raised by the Günthers.

*Anna*
**Essen** sie immer Schweinefleisch?
*Do they always eat pork?*

**Sehen** sie überhaupt fern?
*Do they watch TV at all?*

*Familie Günther*
**Isst** sie vielleicht nur Hamburger?
*Does she perhaps eat only hamburgers?*

**Sieht** Anna wohl immer nur fern?
*Does Anna maybe always watch TV?*

With a few exceptions that will be noted later, the stem-changing verbs use the same present tense endings as the other regular verbs (**schwache Verben**) that have been introduced so far. Here are the present tense forms of the stem-changing verb **sehen** (*to see*).

| sehen: *to see* | | |
|---|---|---|
| Person | Singular | Plural |
| **1st** | ich **sehe** (seh + **e**) | wir **sehen** (seh + **en**) |
| **2nd, informal** | du **siehst** (sieh + **st**) | ihr **seht** (seh + **t**) |
| **2nd, formal** | Sie **sehen** (seh + **en**) | Sie **sehen** (seh + **en**) |
| **3rd** | er/sie/es **sieht** (sieh + **t**) | sie **sehen** (seh + **en**) |

There are four high-frequency categories of verbs with distinct vowel changes in the stem of the verb.

| | | | |
|---|---|---|---|
| 1. | **a > ä** | **fahren** *to drive* | ich fahre, du f**ä**hrst, er/sie/es f**ä**hrt |
| | | **halten** *to stop;* **halten von** *to think about* | ich halte, du h**ä**ltst, er/sie/es h**ä**lt |
| | | **tragen** *to wear* | ich trage, du tr**ä**gst, er/sie/es tr**ä**gt |
| 2. | **au > äu** | **laufen** *to run; to walk* | ich laufe, du l**äu**fst, er/sie/es l**äu**ft |
| 3. | **e > ie** | **sehen** *to see* | ich sehe, du s**ie**hst, er/sie/es s**ie**ht |
| | | **fern·sehen** *to watch TV* | ich sehe fern, du s**ie**hst fern, er/sie/es s**ie**ht fern |
| | | **lesen** *to read* | ich lese, du l**ie**st, er/sie/es l**ie**st |
| 4. | **e > i** | **essen** *to eat* | ich esse, du **i**sst, er/sie/es **i**sst |
| | | **geben** *to give* | ich gebe, du g**i**bst, er/sie/es g**i**bt |
| | | **nehmen** *to take* | ich nehme, du n**imm**st, er/sie/es n**imm**t |
| | | **sprechen** *to speak* | ich spreche, du spr**i**chst, er/sie/es spr**i**cht |
| | | **vergessen** *to forget* | ich vergesse, du verg**i**sst, er/sie/es verg**i**sst |
| | | **werden** *to become* | ich werde, du w**i**rst, er/sie/es w**i**rd |

In the examples for categories 1–4, the **ich**-form is included to show you the vowel used in the forms other than the **du**- and **er/sie/es**-forms: **ich fahre, wir/Sie/sie fahren, ihr fahrt.**

Other verbs in category 1 are **backen** (*to bake*), **fallen** (*to fall*), **fangen** (*to catch*), **anfangen** (*to begin*), **einladen** (*to invite*), **lassen** (*to let*), **schlafen** (*to sleep*), **waschen** (*to wash*).

The **äu** is pronounced similar to the *oy* in *boy.* Another such verb is **saufen** (*to drink like an animal*).

Other verbs in category 4 are **fressen** (*to eat like an animal*) and **helfen** (*to help*).

Note that in **nehmen,** there is a consonant change from **hm** to **mm** in the present tense **du**- and **er/sie/es**-forms. Also note that the **er/sie/es**-form of **werden** uses a **-d** instead of the usual **-t** ending, and the **du**-form drops the **-d** in its stem.

**Werden:** The **-d** in the stem of **werden** disappears in the **du**-form: **du wirst.**

---

**8    Die Günthers.** Choose a partner and one of the following two **Tabellen** about the Günthers. Your partner should refer to the other **Tabelle.** Note that **Tabelle B** is printed upside down. Ask each other what the Günthers like to do.

◻ S1: *Was macht Hannes gern in der Freizeit?*
S2: *Er läuft gern Ski.*
S1: *Was macht er gern im Sommer?*
S2: *Er fährt gern Wasserski.*

**Ski** is also spelled **Schi.** Either way, the pronunciation is *Schi.*

**Tabelle A (S1):**

|  | In der Freizeit | Essen/Trinken | im Sommer |
|---|---|---|---|
| Hannes | ? | trinkt gern Weißwein | ? |
| Ursula | liest gern Zeitung° | ? | trägt gern Shorts |
| Georg | fährt gern Rad° | ? | fährt nach Italien |
| Katja | ? | isst gern vegetarisch | ? |

*the newspaper*

**fährt ... :** *likes to go bicycling*

**Tabelle B (S2):**

| In der Freizeit | Essen/Trinken | im Sommer |
|---|---|---|
| Hannes | läuft gern Ski | ? | fährt gern Wasserski |
| Ursula | ? | isst gern Hamburger | ? |
| Georg | ? | trinkt gern Cola | ? |
| Katja | spricht gern Französisch | ? | fährt nach England |

In information-gap activities, the second chart is always printed upside down. This is so you and your partner can't easily see the information in each other's charts. That way, you really have to communicate.

**9    Autogrammspiel.** Walk around and find a classmate for each activity listed below. When you find someone who likes to do the activity, have that person sign his/her name.

S1: *Trägst du gern Shorts?*
S2: *Nein, ich trage nicht gern Shorts.* (oder)
    *Ja, ich trage gern Shorts.*
S1: *Unterschreib hier bitte.*

1. Trägst du gern Turnschuhe?     _____
2. Liest du gern Zeitung?     _____
3. Siehst du gern fern?     _____
4. Sprichst du gern Deutsch?     _____
5. Isst du gern Fleisch?     _____
6. Trinkst du gern Bier?     _____
7. Vergisst du oft die Hausaufgaben?     _____

**Autogrammspiel.** From this point on you will be expected to use the informal **du** when speaking with another student.

**10    Das Interview.** You are writing an article for the student newspaper. Interview a partner who plays an Austrian exchange student. Ask the following questions about his/her habits. Circle the response that matches your partner's answer or have him/her supply one.

S1: *Was isst du gern?*
S2: *Ich esse gern Hamburger.*

| *Fragen* | *Antworten* | | | |
|---|---|---|---|---|
| 1. Was isst du gern? | Hamburger | Steak | Bratwurst | ? |
| 2. Was sprichst du gern? | Deutsch | Englisch | Spanisch | ? |
| 3. Was liest du gern? | Deutsch | Englisch | Französisch | ? |

| *Fragen* | *Antworten* | | | |
|---|---|---|---|---|
| 4. Was trägst du gern? | Shorts | Turnschuhe | Lederhosen° | ? |
| 5. Was trinkst du gern? | Kaffee | Milch | Cola | ? |
| 6. Siehst du oft fern? | Ja, oft. | Nein, nicht oft. | Nein, überhaupt nicht. | ? |
| 7. Was machst du gern? | Auto fahren | Ski laufen | einkaufen gehen | ? |

*leather pants*

## The verb **wissen**

Another verb that changes its stem vowel is **wissen** (*to know as a fact*).

| **wissen:** *to know as a fact* | | |
|---|---|---|
| **Person** | **Singular** | **Plural** |
| **1st** | ich **weiß** | wir **wissen** |
| **2nd, informal** | du **weißt** | ihr **wisst** |
| **2nd, formal** | Sie **wissen** | Sie **wissen** |
| **3rd** | er/sie/es **weiß** | sie **wissen** |

You will encounter other verbs with vowel changes that work like **wissen** both later in this chapter and in **Kapitel 4.**

Like some other stem-changing verbs, **wissen** changes its stem vowel between singular and plural forms. Because the formal **Sie** singular is really based on a plural form, it uses the same vowel as all other plural forms. For **wissen,** there also is a change in the spelling of the consonant **ss.** The singular vowel (really, a double vowel or diphthong), **ei,** requires that **ss** change to **ß.** Note, too, that **wissen,** like the other verbs that change stem vowels between singular and plural forms, has no endings in the first- and third-person singular forms.

Ich **weiß** es.                                          *I know it.*

**Wissen** generally refers to information that is expressed in a subordinate clause. The conjugated verb in the subordinate clause always occurs at the end.

Weißt du, dass Anna in
  Fort Wayne wohnt?
Ja, ich weiß, dass sie in
  Fort Wayne wohnt.

*Do you know that Anna lives
  in Fort Wayne?*
*Yes, I know that she lives
  in Fort Wayne.*

You will learn more about subordinate-clause word order in **Kapitel 5.**

**11**  **Wissen Sie das?** (*Do you know that?*)  Answer the following questions with **Ja, das weiß ich.** or **Nein, das weiß ich nicht.** If you *do* know something, provide the requested information.

◻ Wissen Sie, wie alt Anna ist?
  *Ja, das weiß ich. Sie ist zwanzig.*

1. Wissen Sie, wie alt Anna ist?
2. Wissen Sie, wann Anna nach Deutschland fährt?
3. Wissen Sie, wo Annas Großeltern wohnen?
4. Wissen Sie, wie Annas Verwandte in Deutschland heißen?
5. Wissen Sie, wo in Deutschland Annas Flugzeug landet?
6. Wissen Sie, wer Georg ist?

**12** **(Stereo)typisch.** The list below reflects stereotypical images of Americans and Germans. Determine to whom these stereotypes refer by creating ten complete sentences.

◻ *Eine typische Amerikanerin lächelt immer.*

| Ein typischer Amerikaner/Deutscher Eine typische Amerikanerin/Deutsche | spricht trinkt isst versteht hat trägt wandert sieht lächelt | eine Zigarette im Mund. jedes° Wochenende. nur Englisch. immer fern. immer Kaugummi im Mund. etwas von Softball. Cola mit viel Eis°. Schokoladeneis°. etwas von Fußball. Schweinefleisch. Deutsch und eine Fremdsprache°. nur Bier. Turnschuhe und Shorts. immer. nichts° von Politik. | *every*  *ice* *chocolate ice cream*   *foreign language*   *nothing* |

---

**Sprache im Alltag: es gibt, was gibt es … ?, was gibt's?**

**Es gibt** is a useful phrase meaning *there is, there are.*

**Es gibt** keine gute Popmusik in Deutschland.    *There's no good pop music in Germany.*
**Gibt es** frische Brötchen?    *Are there any fresh rolls?*

The phrase **was gibt es … ?** means *what is there … ?*

**Was gibt es** in Heidelberg zu tun?    *What is there to do in Heidelberg?*
**Was gibt es** Neues?    *What's new?*

The expression **was gibt's?** is used informally to ask *what's up?, what's going on?*

---

If you want to say *Nothing* in answer to the question **Was gibt's?** use the word **Nichts.**

---

## II Expressing relationships or ownership
### Nominative of possessive adjectives

German speakers use possessive adjectives (**Possessivpronomen**) to express ownership or a relationship.

Das ist **mein** Freund. Er heißt Jürgen.    *That's my friend. His name is Jürgen.*
**Meine** Freundin läuft gern Ski.    *My girlfriend likes to ski.*

The ending of a possessive adjective denotes the <u>case</u> (e.g., nominative, accusative), <u>gender</u> (masculine, neuter, feminine), and <u>number</u> (singular or plural) of the noun that follows it. Here are the nominative forms for the possessive adjectives.

|  | Masculine | Neuter | Feminine | Plural |
|---|---|---|---|---|
|  | ein/kein | ein/kein | eine/keine | —/keine |
| **Possessive Adjectives** (nominative forms) | | | | |

| Singular | | Masculine | Neuter | Feminine | Plural |
|---|---|---|---|---|---|
| Singular | *my* | **mein** Vater | **mein** Kind | **meine** Mutter | **meine** Kinder |
| | *your* (informal) | **dein** Vater | **dein** Kind | **deine** Mutter | **deine** Kinder |
| | *your* (formal) | **Ihr** Vater | **Ihr** Kind | **Ihre** Mutter | **Ihre** Kinder |
| | *his* | **sein** Vater | **sein** Kind | **seine** Mutter | **seine** Kinder |
| | *its* | **sein** Vater | **sein** Kind | **seine** Mutter | **seine** Kinder |
| | *her* | **ihr** Vater | **ihr** Kind | **ihre** Mutter | **ihre** Kinder |
| Plural | *our* | **unser** Vater | **unser** Kind | **uns(e)re** Mutter | **uns(e)re** Kinder |
| | *your* (informal) | **euer** Vater | **euer** Kind | **eure** Mutter | **eure** Kinder |
| | *your* (formal) | **Ihr** Vater | **Ihr** Kind | **Ihre** Mutter | **Ihre** Kinder |
| | *their* | **ihr** Vater | **ihr** Kind | **ihre** Mutter | **ihre** Kinder |

Note that possessive adjectives for masculine and neuter nouns are identical, as are the possessive adjectives for feminine nouns and plural nouns.

The **-er** on **unser** and **euer** is not an ending but part of the stem.

Possessive adjectives can be referred to as *ein-words* because they take the same endings for case, gender, and number as the forms of the indefinite article **ein.** This is true for all possessive adjectives (including **Ihr, ihr, unser, euer**), not just for those that are spelled with **-ein.**

**Unser** frequently and **euer** always lose the internal **-e-** when an ending is added.

|  |  |
|---|---|
| unser: | **unsere** Schwester |
| | **unsre** Schwester |
| euer: | **eure** Schwester |

**13** **Meine Freunde.** Create interesting descriptions of your friends and relatives by combining the subjects in the left column with an appropriate verb from the middle and an item from the right column. Make up a few of your own, too.

| | | |
|---|---|---|
| Mein Freund | isst | kein Schweinefleisch. |
| Meine Freundin | trägt | immer fern. |
| Mein Vater | läuft | Spanisch, Deutsch und Englisch. |
| Meine Mutter | fährt | nicht. |
| Mein Bruder | sieht | sehr schnell°. |
| Meine Schwester | liest | gern Pizza. |
| Mein Deutschlehrer | spricht | keine Lederhosen. |
| Meine Deutschlehrerin | vergisst | gern Bücher. |
| Mein Opa | | einen VW. |
| Meine Oma | | viel. |
| | | wenig. |
| | | immer das Passwort. |

*fast*

## III Expressing additional and contrastive information and justifications

### Coordinating conjunctions

German speakers use coordinating conjunctions (**nebenordnende Konjunktionen**) to provide additional information (**und**), justification (**denn**), or contrast (**sondern, aber, oder**). There are five frequently used coordinating conjunctions.

| | | | | |
|---|---|---|---|---|
| **aber** | *but* | | **sondern** | *but rather* |
| **denn** | *for, because* | | **und** | *and* |
| **oder** | *or* | | | |

Coordinating conjunctions may conjoin words, phrases, or clauses.

Meine Mutter **und** ich spielen Tennis, *My mother **and** I play tennis,*
**und** mein Vater spielt Golf. ***and** my father plays golf.*

**Aber** is commonly used in conversation to present an idea that contrasts what has been stated or implied so far.

Anna ist gespannt auf das Jahr in *Anna is excited about the year in*
Deutschland, **aber** ihre Mutter *Germany, **but** her mother is worried.*
macht sich Sorgen.

**Denn** is used to provide an indisputable reason or justification.

Mein Freund kommt nicht, **denn** *My friend isn't coming **because** he's*
er fährt nach Hause. *going home.*

**Oder** is used to provide alternative information.

Geht Hannes nach Hause, **oder** *Is Hannes going home, **or** (is he going)*
(geht er) zu Uschi? *to Uschi's?*

Do not confuse the conjunction **denn** with the particle **denn** as used in questions like: **Woher kommen Sie denn?** The particle **denn** is used to show personal interest and elicit further information. It does not join two clauses.

**Sondern** introduces a clause, phrase, or noun that contradicts a preceding negative statement which usually contains **nicht.**

| | |
|---|---|
| Anna kommt **nicht** am Montag, **sondern** am Dienstag. | *Anna isn't coming on Monday, **but** (**rather**) on Tuesday.* |

**14  Warum machen sie das?**  Match the statements in the left column with the appropriate justifications in the right column.

| | |
|---|---|
| 1. Mein Bruder isst oft Fleisch, | a. denn wir sind sehr musikalisch. |
| 2. Meine Tante isst gar kein Fleisch, | b. denn sie kommt aus Deutschland. |
| 3. Meine Familie hört gern Musik, | c. denn er kommt aus Norddeutschland. |
| 4. Meine Schwester trägt heute Shorts und Sandalen, | d. denn es ist sehr warm. |
| 5. Mein Bruder lächelt, | e. denn er ist sehr glücklich°.    *happy* |
| 6. Unsere Großeltern sehen nie fern, | f. denn sie hat Fleisch nicht gern. |
| 7. Mein Deutschlehrer trägt keine Lederhosen, | g. denn sie haben keinen Fernseher. |
| 8. Ihre Mutter spricht Deutsch, | h. denn er hat Fleisch gern. |

**15  Sie ist Amerikanerin, aber . . .**  Match the statements in the left column with the appropriate contrasting information in the right column.

| | |
|---|---|
| 1. Anna spricht Englisch, | a. aber Jeff trägt keinen Pullover. |
| 2. Anna wohnt in Fort Wayne, | b. aber sie vergisst oft ihre Brille. |
| 3. Herr Günther isst oft bei McDonalds, | c. aber sie spricht auch etwas Deutsch. |
| 4. Katja liest Shakespeare, | d. aber er trinkt nicht gern Bier. |
| 5. Georg kommt aus Deutschland, | e. aber ihr Buch ist auf Deutsch. |
| 6. Frau Adler ist gut organisiert, | f. aber sie hat Verwandte in Deutschland. |
| 7. Es ist heute kalt, | g. aber er bleibt schlank. |

# **IV**  Stating personal preferences

## The particle **lieber**

You have already learned how to use **gern** to talk about activities that you like to do.

| | |
|---|---|
| Ich spiele **gern** Tennis. | *I **like to** play tennis.* |

To express a preference for one of two options, use **lieber** with a verb.

| | |
|---|---|
| Spielst du **lieber** Tennis oder Fußball? | *Do you **prefer to** play tennis or soccer?* |
| Ich spiele **lieber** Fußball. | *I **prefer to** play soccer. (I **like to** play soccer **more.**)* |

The expression **lieber ... als** (*rather than*) is used when stating a preference for one thing over another.

| | |
|---|---|
| Ich spiele **lieber** Fußball **als** Tennis. | *I prefer to play soccer **rather than** tennis. (I **like to** play soccer **more than** tennis.)* |

**16** **Das mache ich lieber.** Ask each other about your personal preferences, using the appropriate verb. After you have finished, report back to the class.

*Was trägst du lieber, Lederhosen oder Shorts?*

🟧 Lederhosen/Shorts tragen

S1: *Trägst du lieber Lederhosen, oder trägst du lieber Shorts? (oder)*
   *Was trägst du lieber: Lederhosen oder Shorts?*
S2: *Ich trage lieber Shorts. Was trägst du lieber?*
S1: *Ich trage auch lieber Shorts.*

S1: *(Lori) sagt, sie trägt lieber Shorts.*
S2: *(Raoul) sagt, er trägt lieber Shorts.*

1. Hamburger/Bratwurst essen
2. Englisch/Deutsch sprechen
3. Cola/Bier trinken
4. klassische Musik/Rockmusik hören
5. Softball/Fußball spielen
6. Birkenstock-Sandalen/Turnschuhe tragen
7. Mathematik/Literatur lesen
8. Auto/Fahrrad° fahren

*bicycle*

## V Expressing what you would like to do

### The modal verb **möchte**

German speakers use **möchte** to express what they or somebody else would like to have or like to do. If it is used to express a preference for a certain action (what people would like to do), **möchte** acts as a modal verb. Modal verbs are helping verbs that express under which conditions an action takes place. **Möchte** implies that the action is desired by someone. The verb that expresses the desired action is used in the infinitive form. In simple declarative sentences with a modal verb, the infinitive occurs at the end of the sentence. You will be learning about other modal verbs in this chapter and **Kapitel 4.**

Ich **möchte** meine Verwandten in Deutschland **kennen lernen.**

*I would like to get to know my relatives in Germany.*

| **möchte:** *would like (to)* | | |
|---|---|---|
| **Person** | **Singular** | **Plural** |
| **1st** | ich **möchte** | wir **möchten** |
| **2nd, informal** | du **möchtest** | ihr **möchtet** |
| **2nd, formal** | Sie **möchten** | Sie **möchten** |
| **3rd** | er/sie/es **möchte** | sie **möchtet** |

When **möchte** is used, the infinitive can be omitted if it is clear from the context that an infinitive is implied. Infinitives that are commonly omitted are: **essen, trinken, fahren, gehen,** and **haben.**

Ich **möchte** bitte eine Cola (haben).
Er **möchte** nach Heidelberg (fahren).

*I would like (to have) a cola, please.*
*He would like to go to Heidelberg.*

**17** **Was möchtest du lieber?** Ask your partner questions about what he/she would prefer to do.

🟨 Cola/Kaffee trinken

S1: *Möchtest du lieber Cola oder Kaffee (trinken)?*
S2: *Ich möchte lieber Kaffee (trinken), und du?*
S1: *Ich möchte lieber Cola.*

1. Cola/Kaffee (trinken)
2. fernsehen/einen Film sehen
3. Turnschuhe/Sandalen tragen
4. Deutsch/Englisch sprechen
5. um sechs Uhr/um Mittag aufstehen
6. schwimmen/wandern (gehen)
7. Hamburger/Bratwurst (essen)
8. nach Heidelberg/nach München (fahren)
9. ins Museum/ins Restaurant (gehen)
10. ...

Was möchtest du lieber? Practice answering the questions with the book closed.

## Wissenswerte Vokabeln: Lebensmittel

*Talking about foods that we like*

🟨 Was isst du gern?  *Ich esse gern Salat.*

Wie viele Kilometer sind das?

> Notice that to specify a plural quantity, Germans use the singular form of the measurement: **500 Gramm Käse, zwei Pfund Äpfel.**

## BRENNPUNKT KULTUR

### The metric system

The metric system is used in Europe and much of the world outside the United States. Among other things, it is used when shopping, measuring body weight and height, and measuring distances between cities.

*liquids*
**der Liter (l)** = slightly more than a liquid quart
**der Zentiliter (cl)** = 0.01 liter

*mass / weight*
**das Gramm (g)** = about 35/1000 of an ounce
**das Pfund (Pf)** = 500 grams
**das Kilo(gramm) (kg)** = 1000 grams

*length / height*
**der Meter (m)** = slightly more than a yard
**der Zentimeter (cm)** = 0.01 meter

*distance*
**der Kilometer (km)** = 0.62 miles = 1000 meters

Gasoline is sold in liters, and some drinks are sold in centiliters. In a bar, wine may be ordered by a quarter/an eighth liter (**ein Viertel / ein Achtel Weißwein, bitte),** and beer may be sold by the half liter (**ein Halbes**) or in a full liter (called **eine Maß** in Bavaria).

Meats and breads are sold by the **Kilo.** Two pounds of hamburger may be ordered as **ein Kilo** or **1 000 Gramm Hackfleisch.** Germans (but not Austrians or Swiss) use pounds and might order **zwei Pfund Hackfleisch.** Amounts smaller than a pound are most frequently expressed in grams (**125 Gramm**) but can also be expressed in Germany as fractions of a pound (**ein halbes Pfund, ein Viertel Pfund**). In Austria, smaller food purchases are usually made in fractions of a **Kilo** or in **Deka** (multiples of 10), not in **Gramm** or **Pfund.** Body weight is expressed in kilos (**65,5 Kilo**) and height in meters and centimeters (**ein Meter siebzig Zentimeter**).

To say how far it is from one city to another, people use the expression **weit von** *(far from, away from):* **Konstanz ist 32 Kilometer weit von Singen und 45 Kilometer weit von hier.**

■ **Kulturkreuzung** While Canada and Great Britain converted to the metric system years ago, the United States still mostly uses the traditional English system of weights and measures. In what situations is the metric system used in the U.S.? Why has the country not converted completely to the metric system? What advantages does the metric system offer? What are the advantages of the English system? What obstacles discourage conversion to the metric system in the U.S.?

## Sprache im Alltag: Specifying amounts

In addition to metric measurement, German speakers use several other expressions with non-count nouns. As with the metric system, German does not include a word for *of* with these expressions.

| | |
|---|---|
| Die Studentin isst **ein Stück** Brot. | *The student is eating a piece of bread.* |
| Ich nehme **eine Scheibe** Schinken. | *I'll take a slice of ham.* |
| Karl trinkt **eine Tasse** Tee. | *Karl is drinking a cup of tea.* |
| Lise möchte **ein Glas** Bier. | *Lise would like a glass of beer.* |
| Frau Lehlbach kauft **eine Flasche** Olivenöl. | *Mrs. Lehlbach is buying a bottle of olive oil.* |

Masculine and neuter quantities like these (**das Glas, das Stück**) do not have separate plural forms.

| | |
|---|---|
| Der Kellner bringt **zwei Glas** Wein. | *The waiter is bringing two glasses of wine.* |
| Barbara isst **drei Stück** Käse. | *Barbara eats three pieces of cheese.* |

**18** **Was isst und trinkst du lieber?** Interview your partner about his/her preferences in food and drinks. After you have finished, report back to the class.

Schweinefleisch/Rindfleisch
S1: *Was isst du lieber: Schweinefleisch oder Rindfleisch?*
S2: *Ich esse lieber Rindfleisch als Schweinefleisch.*

S1: (Karen) *isst lieber ... als ...*
S2: (Eric) *isst lieber ... als ...*

1. Schweinefleisch/Rindfleisch
2. Fisch/Fleisch
3. Gemüse/Obst
4. Wurst/Käse
5. Hähnchen/Fisch
6. Bier/Milch
7. Kaffee/Tee
8. Honig/Marmelade

## Sprache im Alltag: Use of the metric system

German speakers usually purchase small amounts of fresh cold cuts, cheese, meat, fruit, and vegetables each day for immediate consumption. Shoppers (**Kunden**) therefore often request very small amounts and salespeople (**Verkäufer**) ask for approval if the amount on the scale is a little above or below the desired weight.

KUNDE/KUNDIN: Geben Sie mir bitte 200 Gramm Leberwurst und 150 Gramm Gouda.

VERKÄUFER(IN): Darf° es etwas mehr° sein? (*oder*)
Darf es etwas weniger° sein?

*may / more*
*less*

**19** **In der Bäckerei°.** Listen to the following dialogue, then practice it with a partner.    *bakery*

BÄCKER: Guten Tag. Bitte schön?
KUNDIN: Ich möchte ein Weißbrot und vier Brötchen.
BÄCKER: Sonst noch 'was?°                              *Sonst ... : (Would you like)*
KUNDIN: Das war's.                                       *anything else?*
BÄCKER: Das macht zwei Euro neunzig.
KUNDIN: Bitte schön.
BÄCKER: Danke. Und zehn Cent zurück.
KUNDIN: Auf Wiedersehen.
BÄCKER: Wiedersehen.

---

**Sprache im Alltag:** **Bitte schön**

The German expression **bitte schön** has several different meanings depending on the context in which it is used. German sales clerks use **Bitte schön?** *(May I help you?)* to initiate a sales dialogue. Customers use **Bitte schön** *(Here you go)* when laying their money on the counter to pay for the goods. When responding to **Danke schön,** all speakers in any situation use **Bitte schön** *( You're welcome.)*

Two common places to buy food are **das Lebensmittelgeschäft** (*grocery store*) and **der Supermarkt** (*supermarket*).

---

  **Schreibecke**

**Der Wochenkauf.** Make up a weekly food shopping list; write the amounts in **Gramm.** Use the items you have learned in the chapter and the ad from **real,–** for ideas.

**Absprungtext**   ## Heidelberg und Mannheim

In anticipation of Anna's arrival, the Günthers, who live in Weinheim just north of Heidelberg, send her tourist brochures on Heidelberg and Mannheim.

Heidelberg has many well-known attractions—a historic university, an old castle, and a scenic location on the Neckar River with vineyards nearby. Mannheim, Heidelberg's neighbor to the west on the Rhine, is known less for its tourist attractions and more for its industrial significance.

*MAGNET MANNHEIM*

## *Vorschau*

**20   Thematische Fragen.**  Discuss the following questions with your instructor or in pairs.

1. What cities do you associate with Germany? Why?
2. What do you already know about Heidelberg? Where are you likely to get information about Heidelberg?
3. Heidelberg is considered one of Germany's most romantic cities. What makes a city romantic? What sort of buildings and other tourist attractions might you find in Heidelberg that make it a "romantic city"?
4. What do you know about Mannheim?

**21   Wortdetektiv.**  Which words convey approximately the same meaning? Match the German word with its logical English equivalent.

| *Deutsch* | | *Englisch* | |
|---|---|---|---|
| 1. die Stadt (e.g., Berlin) | | a. | bicycle |
| 2. das Fahrrad | | b. | bridge |
| 3. segeln | | c. | to sail |
| 4. die Brücke | | d. | castle, palace |
| 5. das Schloss | | e. | city, town |
| | | | |
| 6. das Schwimmbad | | f. | to fish |
| 7. angeln | | g. | swimming pool |
| 8. die Bibliothek | | h. | to ride horseback |
| 9. reiten | | i. | church |
| 10. die Kirche | | j. | library |
| | | | |
| 11. die Kunsthalle | | k. | old city hall |
| 12. der Hauptbahnhof | | l. | art museum |
| 13. die Jugendherberge | | m. | youth hostel |
| 14. das Alte Rathaus | | n. | water tower |
| 15. der Wasserturm | | o. | fitness trails |
| 16. die Trimm-dich-Pfade | | p. | main train station |

## Absprungtext
### Heidelberg und Mannheim

**22    Zum Text.** Tourist brochures often list facts and figures to provide a quick overview of a city and its attractions. The following ads contain information on Heidelberg and Mannheim. Scan the texts to find . . .

1. the phone number of the tourist information offices.
2. the number of hotel beds in Heidelberg and Mannheim.
3. the year the university in Heidelberg was founded.
4. examples for how Heidelberg markets itself. (Scan the text for adjectives.)
5. the larger city: Is it Heidelberg or Mannheim?

Now read the text.

Der Zoo Heidelberg

Das Heidelberger Schloss

Das
Große Fass

Die Universität

# Heidelberg

Universitätsstadt am Neckar, 143 000 Einwohner, 3 600 Betten (davon 3 300 in Hotels, 300 in Gasthöfen und Pensionen)

**Freizeit:** Freischwimmbad°, Hallenschwimmbad°, Reiten, Tennis, Angeln, Segeln, Großgolf, Minigolf, Fahrradverleih°, Neckarschifffahrt° Zoo, Kinderparadies

**i** Verkehrsverein Heidelberg e.V.
Tourist-Information am
Hauptbahnhof
Telefon: (0 62 21) 1 94 33
Fax: (0 62 21) 1 38 81 11
E-Mail: touristinfo@cvb-heidelberg.de

**Sehenswürdigkeiten:** Heidelberger Schloss – das Große Fass – das Deutsche Apothekenmuseum, historische, romantische Altstadt am Neckar, älteste Universität Deutschlands (1386), Universitätsbibliothek, Alte Brücke, Heiliggeistkirche, Kurpfälzisches Museum, historische Studentenlokale°

**Die älteste Universität Deutschlands** means *Germany's oldest university.*

*outdoor pool*
*indoor pool*

*bicycle rental / boat ride on the Neckar River*
**Studentenlokale:** *student pubs, bars*

## Mannheim

Stadt der Quadrate° an Rhein und Neckar im Herzen der ehemaligen° Kurpfalz, 325 000 Einwohner, 2 095 Zimmer (davon 1830 in Hotels, 220 in Gasthöfen, 45 in Pensionen), 120 Betten in der Jugendherberge, Kongresszentrum „Rosengarten"

**Freizeit:** Campingplätze an Rhein und Neckar, beheizte Freischwimmbäder, Hallenbäder, Tennis, Squash, Angeln, Reiten, Segeln, Minigolf, Trimm-dich-Pfade

**Sehenswürdigkeiten:**
Friedrichsplatz (Jugendstil°) mit Wasserturm (Wahrzeichen°), Wasserspielen°, Kurfürstliches Residenzschloss (größtes Barockschloss° Deutschlands), Jesuitenkirche, Reiß-Museum, Kunsthalle, Nationaltheater, Kinder- und Jugendtheater im Kulturzentrum, Kunstverein, Altes Rathaus und Untere Pfarrkirche (Glockenspiel°) am Marktplatz, Hafen°

**i** Tourist-Information Mannheim
Willy-Brandt-Platz 3
Telefon: (06 21) 10 10 11
Telefax: (06 21) 2 41 41
E-Mail: info@tourist-mannheim.de
www.tourist-mannheim.de

*square blocks / fountains*
*former*
*Baroque palace*

*chimes*
*port*

*Art Nouveau*
*symbol*

> **Stadt der Quadrate** means *city of squares* (like in a grid).

> **Größtes Barockschloss** means *the largest baroque palace.* It is similar to **die älteste Universität.** Both are superlative forms (*the most*).

## *Rückblick*

**23   Stimmt das?** How much of the text do you remember without looking back at it?

|  | Ja, das stimmt. | Nein, das stimmt nicht. |  |
|---|:---:|:---:|---|
| 1. Heidelberg ist eine Industriestadt. | ☐ | ☐ | |
| 2. Mannheim liegt am° Rhein und am Neckar. | ☐ | ☐ | **liegt ... :** *is situated on* |
| 3. Mannheim hat 325 000 Einwohner. | ☐ | ☐ | |
| 4. In Heidelberg gibt es keinen Wassersport. | ☐ | ☐ | |
| 5. Für Kinder gibt es in Heidelberg den Zoo und das Kinderparadies. | ☐ | ☐ | |
| 6. Mannheim hat kein Schloss. | ☐ | ☐ | |
| 7. Heidelbergs Altstadt ist alt, kaputt und hässlich°. | ☐ | ☐ | *ugly* |
| 8. Mannheim hat die älteste Universität Deutschlands. | ☐ | ☐ | |
| 9. Die Alte Brücke führt über° den Neckar. | ☐ | ☐ | **führt ... :** *goes across* |
| 10. Die Tourist-Information in Heidelberg findet man in historischen Studentenlokalen. | ☐ | ☐ | |

**24  Was gibt's in Mannheim oder Heidelberg?** Compare Mannheim's attractions to those of Heidelberg. Which of the following attractions and facilities do both cities offer and which are unique to Mannheim or Heidelberg?

Theater • Squash • Schloss • Segeln • Tennis • Kirche • Minigolf
• Museum • Kunsthalle • Wasserspiele • Hallenschwimmbad • Reiten
• Universität • Motor- und Segelflugplatz • Rathaus • Trimm-dich-Pfade
• Fahrradverleih • Studentenlokal • Neckar • das Große Fass • Hafen

| Mannheim | Heidelberg | Mannheim und Heidelberg |
|----------|------------|-------------------------|
| _____ | _____ | _____ |
| _____ | _____ | _____ |
| _____ | _____ | _____ |
| _____ | _____ | _____ |
| _____ | _____ | _____ |
| _____ | _____ | _____ |

**25  Wo findet man diese Leute?** With a partner, determine where in Heidelberg or Mannheim you would most likely find these people.

1. Boris Becker          4  in der Bibliothek
2. Pastoren              7  an der Universität
3. Sportler              9  im Schloss
4. Deutsche              1  auf dem Tennisplatz
5. Professoren           2  in der Kirche
6. Studentinnen          3  im Schwimmbad
7. Touristen             7  im Museum
8. Amerikaner            6  im Lokal

> Boris Becker is a retired professional tennis player from Leimen, a suburb of Heidelberg, who won the Wimbledon Men's Tennis Singles 3 times (1985, 1986, 1989).

**26  Ergänzen Sie.** Complete these statements with words from the **Absprungtext.**

1. Heidelberg ist eine _____ mit 143 000 _____.
2. Es gibt in Heidelberg über 3 600 Betten in _____, in Gasthöfen und in _____.
3. Es gibt in Mannheim 120 Betten für junge Leute in der _____.
4. Das Heidelberger _____ ist das Symbol von Heidelberg.
5. Der _____ ist das Symbol von Mannheim.
6. Heidelberg hat eine historische, romantische _____ am Neckar.
7. Heidelbergs Altstadt ist historisch und _____.
8. Heidelbergs _____ ist die älteste in Deutschland (1386).
9. Heidelberger Studenten leihen Bücher für ihre Kurse aus der _____ aus°.
10. Sonntags gehen einige° Mannheimer Studenten in die _____.
11. In Mannheim gibt es gute Dramen von Goethe und Schiller im _____.
12. Heidelberger Studenten gehen in historische _____ und trinken dort Wein und Bier.

> *leihen ... aus = ausleihen:*
> *check out a few*

**27** **Kurz gefragt.** Answer these questions with just a word or two, or a short phrase.

1. Welche Stadt hat mehr Einwohner?
2. Welche Freizeitaktivitäten in Heidelberg und Mannheim haben mit Wasser zu tun°?
3. Welche Freizeitaktivitäten in Heidelberg haben mit Tieren° zu tun?
4. Für welche Sportarten braucht° man einen Ball?
5. Was sind zwei Sehenswürdigkeiten in der Nähe° vom Heidelberger Schloss?
6. Wo ist die Heidelberger Altstadt? Und wie ist sie?
7. Wie kommt man über den Neckar? Man geht über ...
8. Wo bekommen° Touristen Information über Heidelberg? Und wie?

*mit ... zu tun: to do with*
  *animals*
*need*
*near*

*get*

### Heidelberg and Mannheim

Heidelberg and Mannheim are a study in contrasts. Whereas Heidelberg was spared the devastation of aerial bombing in World War II, Mannheim was badly damaged. After the war Mannheim rebuilt its distinctive downtown square grid (**Quadrat)**, which resembles many American cities. Heidelberg's romantic and bustling **Hauptstraße** meanders for over a mile from the **Bismarckplatz** past the **Theaterplatz** and the **Universitätsplatz.** Many small streets and walkways make up the **Altstadt.**

Heidelberg's reputation is built on its proud academic tradition. The **Heidelberger Schloss** is one of the most popular tourist attractions in Europe. The skull of *Homo heidelbergensis,* the earliest human remains in Europe, is over 500,000 years old. Heidelberg's most famous export in recent history is Boris Becker, the world champion tennis player.

Mannheim's reputation is built on its past and current industrial innovations. In 1885, Carl Friedrich Benz invented the first automobile in Mannheim, which later evolved to become the first **Mercedes** automobile. Mannheim continues to be the home of mechanical and electrical engineering firms as well as car makers, but is also emerging as a popular music capital in Germany. Mannheim's sister city across the Rhein, Ludwigshafen, is home to BASF (Badische Anilin- und Soda-Fabrik), one of the largest chemical companies in the world.

■ **Kulturkreuzung** Can you identify two cities near one another like Heidelberg and Mannheim that represent a contrast between **Universitätsstadt** and **Industriestadt?**

**28** **Was möchtest du in Heidelberg sehen?** Use the brochure of Heidelberg on page 94 and the map below as a visual guide. Ask your partner what he/she would like to see in Heidelberg. Use the cues below.

🔲 S1: *Möchtest du das Schloss sehen?*
S2: *Ja, ich möchte das Schloss sehen, und du?*
S1: *Ja, ich auch.* (oder)
*Nein, ich nicht.*

🔲 S1: *Möchtest du die Universität sehen?*
S2: *Nein, ich möchte die Universität nicht sehen, und du?*
S1: *Nein, ich auch nicht.* (oder)
*Ja, ich möchte die Universität sehen.*

1. das Schloss
2. die Universität
3. die Alte Brücke
4. das Museum
5. den Neckar
6. die Heiliggeistkirche
7. den Zoo
8. das Große Fass
9. das Rathaus (*city hall*)

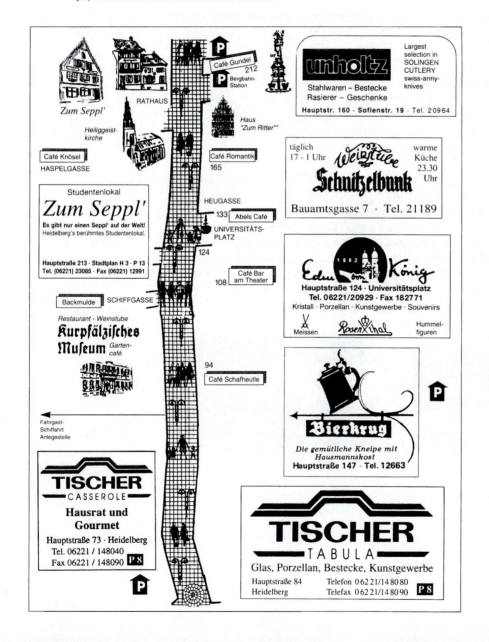

## *Strukturen und Vokabeln*

### Wissenswerte Vokabeln: Freizeitaktivitäten
*Talking about what you can do and like to do*

Karten spielen

Fußball spielen

Klavier spielen

ins Kino gehen

tanzen

Ski laufen

wandern

reiten

kochen

lesen

Rad fahren

spazieren gehen

schwimmen

singen

angeln

segeln

◻ Was spielst du gern?    *Ich spiele gern Tennis.*

**29  Das Interview.** Find out as much as you can about your partner's leisure time activities. Write **ja** if you or your partner like to do the activity, and **nein,** if you do not.

S1: *Spielst du gern Karten?*
S2: *Ja, und du?*

|  | *Ich* | *Mein Partner/Meine Partnerin* |
|---|---|---|
| Karten spielen | _____ | _____ |
| Tennis spielen | _____ | _____ |
| Klavier spielen | _____ | _____ |
| Gitarre spielen | _____ | _____ |
| ins Kino gehen | _____ | _____ |
| ins Konzert gehen | _____ | _____ |
| reiten | _____ | _____ |
| kochen | _____ | _____ |
| lesen | _____ | _____ |
| Rad fahren | _____ | _____ |
| angeln gehen | _____ | _____ |
| spazieren gehen | _____ | _____ |
| schwimmen | _____ | _____ |
| segeln | _____ | _____ |
| tanzen | _____ | _____ |
| singen | _____ | _____ |

> Similar to **Fußball spielen,** you can say **Baseball spielen, Basketball spielen, Golf spielen, Softball spielen, Tennis spielen,** and **Volleyball spielen.**

> Similar to **Klavier spielen,** you can also say **Flöte** (*flute*) **spielen** and **Gitarre** (*guitar*) **spielen.**

> Similar to **ins Kino gehen,** you can say **ins Konzert gehen** and **ins Theater gehen.**

# VI  Expressing possibilities

## The modal verb **können**

The modal verb **können** (*to be able to*) is used with an infinitive to express what a person can or cannot do or knows or doesn't know how to do.

Ich **kann** Deutsch sprechen.    *I **can (know how to)** speak German.*

Like **möchte, können** may occur without an infinitive, when the implied infinitive is clear from the context. This happens particularly often in the context of languages and musical instruments.

Angelika **kann** Deutsch (sprechen).    *Angelika **can** speak German.*
Angelika **kann** Klavier (spielen).    *Angelika **can** play the piano.*

Like other modals, **können** has stem vowels that are different in the singular and in the plural. Also, the 1st and 3rd person singular forms have no endings. You will learn more about these modal verbs in **Kapitel 4.**

| **können:** *can; to be able to* | | |
|---|---|---|
| Person | Singular | Plural |
| **1st** | ich **kann** | wir **können** |
| **2nd, informal** | du **kannst** | ihr **könnt** |
| **2nd, formal** | Sie **können** | Sie **können** |
| **3rd** | er/sie/es **kann** | sie **können** |

The pronoun **man** (*one*) is often used with **kann** to express what options are available.

In Heidelberg **kann man** segeln und Tennis spielen.    *You (one) can sail and play tennis in Heidelberg.*

 **30**    **Kannst du das machen?**  Ask a partner how well he/she can do the following activities. Then check the appropriate columns.

S1: *Kannst du Tennis spielen?*
S2: *Ja, ich kann relativ gut Tennis spielen.*

| *Aktivität* | *sehr gut* | *relativ gut* | *nicht so gut* | *gar nicht* |
|---|---|---|---|---|
| 1. Tennis spielen | ☐ | ☐ | ☐ | ☐ |
| 2. kochen | ☐ | ☐ | ☐ | ☐ |
| 3. Ski laufen | ☐ | ☐ | ☐ | ☐ |
| 4. schwimmen | ☐ | ☐ | ☐ | ☐ |
| 5. Spanisch (sprechen) | ☐ | ☐ | ☐ | ☐ |
| 6. Flöte (spielen) | ☐ | ☐ | ☐ | ☐ |
| 7. tanzen | ☐ | ☐ | ☐ | ☐ |
| 8. segeln | ☐ | ☐ | ☐ | ☐ |

> Remember, when expressing what you know how to do, especially speaking languages and playing instruments, you can drop the infinitive.

 **31**    **Was kann man in deiner Stadt machen?**  Ask a partner the following questions about his/her hometown.

ins Kino gehen

S1: *Woher kommst du?*
S2: *Aus (Detroit).*
S1: *Kann man in (Detroit) ins Kino gehen?*
S2: *Ja.*

1. ins Kino gehen
2. am Fluss° Rad fahren
3. ins Konzert gehen
4. am Abend spazieren gehen
5. ins Theater gehen
6. Studentenlokale finden
7. ins Schloss gehen
8. ins Museum gehen
9. gute Hotels finden
10. alte Kirchen besichtigen°

*am ... : at the river*

*to visit, tour*

## VII  Referring to people and things

### Accusative pronouns

In **Kapitel 1** you learned that pronouns must reflect the gender and number of the nouns they represent.

Hier ist **ein Tisch. Er** ist neu.
**Meine Mutter** heißt Helga. **Sie** spricht am Telefon.
Das ist **mein Deutschbuch. Es** hat sehr schöne Fotos.

In each of the examples above, the highlighted pronoun in the second sentence is the subject of that sentence. The subject is always in the nominative case. Now look at the pronouns highlighted in the examples on page 102. These pronouns are direct objects and are therefore in the accusative case. They are called **Akkusativpronomen.** A direct object answers the question **wen?** (*whom?*) or **was?** (*what?*).

| | |
|---|---|
| Klaus, ruf **mich** bitte zu Hause an. | *Klaus, call **me** at home, please.* |
| Hallo? Hallo? Hallo? Ich höre **dich** nicht. | *Hello? Hello? Hello? I can't hear **you**.* |
| Wo ist mein Vater? Ich sehe **ihn** nicht. | *Where is my father? I don't see **him**.* |
| Das ist meine Schwester. Möchtest du **sie** kennen lernen? | *That is my sister. Would you like to meet **her**?* |
| Hier ist mein Deutschbuch. Möchtest du **es** lesen? | *Here is my German book. Would you like to read **it**?* |

Here are the nominative and accusative forms of the personal pronouns.

| | **Singular** | | | | | | **Plural** | | |
|---|---|---|---|---|---|---|---|---|---|
| | **1st** | **2nd** | | **3rd** | | | **1st** | **2nd** | | **3rd** |
| **Nominative** | ich | du | Sie | er | es | sie | wir | ihr | Sie | sie |
| **Accusative** | **mich** | **dich** | **Sie** | **ihn** | **es** | **sie** | **uns** | **euch** | **Sie** | **sie** |
| | *me* | *you* | *you* | *him* | *it* | *her* | *us* | *you* | *you* | *them* |

**32 Kombinieren Sie.** Select a logical response from the column on the right for each statement or question in the left column.

1. Ich liebe° dich, Annette!
2. Professor Bauer spricht sehr schnell, nicht?
3. Wo ist Frau Günther?
4. Anna trägt heute Shorts.
5. Wer hat meine Zeitung?

a. Ich weiß nicht. Ich sehe sie nicht.
b. Katja trägt sie auch.
c. Ich habe dich auch sehr gern, Hannes.
d. Claudia liest sie gerade°.
e. Ja, ich verstehe ihn auch nicht so gut.

*love*

*right now*

**33 Kurze Dialoge.** Supply the appropriate accusative pronouns (**mich, dich, euch, Sie,** or **uns**) in the dialogues below.

1. PROFESSOR: Sprechen Sie Deutsch? Verstehen Sie _____?
   STUDENTEN: Ja, wir verstehen _____, Herr Professor.

2. ENKEL: Opa, hörst du _____?
   OPA: Ja, ich höre _____, Kleiner°.

   *little one*

3. SOHN: Papa, siehst du _____ nicht?
   VATER: Nein, wo bist du denn?

4. KATJA GÜNTHER: Besuchst du _____ bald, Anna?
   ANNA: Ja, ich besuche _____ im August.

5. GEORG GÜNTHER: (*am Telefon*) Du! Meine Kusine aus Amerika kommt nach Weinheim.
   FRANK: Wie bitte? Ich höre _____ nicht so gut.
   GEORG: Meine Kusine Anna aus Indiana besucht uns bald.
   FRANK: Ja? Wann besucht sie _____?

**34 Interview.** With a partner, create short dialogues about what you like to do. Use pronouns in your answers to the questions. Try to expand your answers by using **sondern** when you answer in the negative.

🟧 S1: *Liest du gern Zeitung?*
S2: *Ja, ich lese sie gern.* (oder)
*Nein, ich lese nicht Zeitung gern, sondern Bücher.*

1. Verstehst du die Professoren? *sie*
2. Sprichst du gern Deutsch? *es*
3. Liest du das Buch *Vorsprung* gern? *es*
4. Möchtest du Anna Adler kennen lernen? *sie*
5. Möchtest du die Stadt Heidelberg besichtigen? *sie*
6. Isst du gern Schweinefleisch? *es*
7. Trägst du gern Turnschuhe? *sie (Pl.)*
8. Spielst du gern Fußball? *ihn*
9. Hast du den Deutschprofessor/die Deutschprofessorin gern? *ihn/sie*

## VIII  Talking about people and things that you know

### The verb **kennen**

To express that they know people, places, films, and books, German speakers use the verb **kennen** (*to know, to be acquainted with*). Unlike **wissen** (*to know as a fact*), which refers to information described in a clause, **kennen** generally refers to information contained in a direct object. The present tense endings of **kennen** are like those of regular verbs.

| | |
|---|---|
| **Kennt** er Heidelberg? | *Does he know Heidelberg?* |
| Ja, er **kennt** es. | *Yes, he knows it.* |
| **Kennst** du unseren Nachbarn? | *Do you know our neighbor?* |
| Nein, ich **kenne** ihn nicht. | *No, I don't know him.* |

> When referring to cities by name, German speakers use the pronoun **es. Kennst du Mannheim? Ja, ich kenne *es* ziemlich gut. *Es* ist eine tolle Stadt.**

## IX  Expressing relationships or ownership

### Accusative of possessive adjectives

Earlier in this chapter, you learned about the possessive adjectives in the nominative case. Here are the accusative forms for the possessive adjectives.

| | | Masculine | Neuter | Feminine | Plural |
|---|---|---|---|---|---|
| | | einen/keinen | ein/kein | eine/keine | —/keine |
| | | **Possessive Adjectives** (accusative forms) | | | |
| **Singular** | *my* | **meinen** Vater | **mein** Kind | **meine** Mutter | **meine** Kinder |
| | *your* (informal) | **deinen** Vater | **dein** Kind | **deine** Mutter | **deine** Kinder |
| | *your* (formal) | **Ihren** Vater | **Ihr** Kind | **Ihre** Mutter | **Ihre** Kinder |
| | *his* | **seinen** Vater | **sein** Kind | **seine** Mutter | **seine** Kinder |
| | *its* | **seinen** Vater | **sein** Kind | **seine** Mutter | **seine** Kinder |
| | *her* | **ihren** Vater | **ihr** Kind | **ihre** Mutter | **ihre** Kinder |
| **Plural** | *our* | **uns(e)ren** Vater | **unser** Kind | **uns(e)re** Mutter | **uns(e)re** Kinder |
| | *your* (informal) | **euren** Vater | **euer** Kind | **eure** Mutter | **eure** Kinder |
| | *your* (formal) | **Ihren** Vater | **Ihr** Kind | **Ihre** Mutter | **Ihre** Kinder |
| | *their* | **ihren** Vater | **ihr** Kind | **ihre** Mutter | **ihre** Kinder |

> As in the nominative, the internal **e** is always dropped when adding an ending to **euer (eure, euren)** and occasionally dropped when adding one to **unser (unsre, unsren).**

**35** **Freunde und Familie.** Ask your partner these questions about friends and family members.

S1: *Hier ist mein Freund Hans. Kennst du ihn?*
S2: *Ja, ich kenne deinen Freund Hans. (oder)*
*Nein, ich kenne deinen Freund Hans nicht.*

1. mein Freund Hans
2. meine Tochter Anna
3. mein Bruder Karl
4. meine Freunde Volker und Katharina
5. meine Freundin Barbara
6. mein Partner Robert
7. meine Kinder Fabian und Helena
8. meine Eltern

## X Talking about more than one item

### Noun plurals

In **Kapitel 1** you learned that every German noun is accompanied by **der, das,** or **die,** depending on the gender of the noun. There is only one definite article for the plural in both the nominative and the accusative cases: **die.** You should memorize the gender and the plural form for each new noun as you learn it.

Here are the five basic patterns for forming noun plurals.

| Plural marker | Singular | Plural |
|---|---|---|
| no ending | der Lehrer, das Fenster, der Onkel, das Mädchen | die Lehrer, die Fenster, die Onkel, die Mädchen |
| umlaut + no ending | der Vater, die Tochter, die Mutter | die Väter, die Töchter, die Mütter |
| **-e** | der Tag, der Freund, das Lokal | die Tage, die Freunde, die Lokale |
| umlaut + **-e** ending | der Gast, der Sohn, die Wurst | die Gäste, die Söhne, die Würste |
| **-er** | das Kind | die Kinder |
| umlaut + **-er** ending | der Mann, das Schloss, das Buch | die Männer, die Schlösser, die Bücher |
| **-n** | der Neffe, die Tante, die Schwester | die Neffen, die Tanten, die Schwestern |
| **-en** | der Herr, der Professor, der Fotograf, der Automat, die Schönheit, die Möglichkeit, die Universität, die Zeitung | die Herren, die Professoren, die Fotografen, die Automaten, die Schönheiten, die Möglichkeiten, die Universitäten, die Zeitungen |
| **-nen** | die Studentin, die Professorin | die Studentinnen, die Professorinnen |
| change **-um** to **-en** | das Museum, das Studium | die Museen, die Studien |
| **-s** | der Chef, das Hotel | die Chefs, die Hotels |

Good dictionaries list the plural changes of nouns. If two endings are listed, the second one is the plural ending. (The first ending denotes the genitive, a case that you will encounter in **Kapitel 10.**) The symbol - indicates no ending, ¨ indicates an umlaut, and **-e, -er, -n, -en, -s** indicate the ending. Feminine forms ending in **-in** may not show the plural form **-nen.**

While **Vater** adds an umlaut in the plural, **Onkel** does not. The different article in the plural, however, makes singular and plural forms of **Onkel** clearly distinguishable.

The **-er** ending in **Väter** and **Lehrer** is not a plural ending; it is part of the singular form. The **-er** ending in **Kinder** however, is a plural ending.

Masculine nouns derived from Greek or Latin and ending in **-or, -f,** or **-t** often describe professions and look very similar to English.

The following simple rules may help you form certain plurals if you don't remember them. Examples of each case are included in the preceding chart.

- Neuter nouns with the suffix **-chen** add no plural ending.
- Feminine nouns ending in **-heit, -keit, -tät,** and **-ung** add **-en** in the plural.
- Nouns borrowed from English or French often (but not always) add **-s** in the plural.

> The gender of nouns is often determined by their endings. Nouns ending in the suffix **-chen** are always neuter. Nouns ending in the suffixes **-heit, -keit, -tät,** and **-ung** are always feminine.

 **36** **Wo ist der Plural?** Circle all the features that indicate that the following words are plurals. If there are no features because a plural word looks the same as its singular form, underline the word.

(Väter) • Lehrer • (Schwestern) • (Professoren) • (Studenten) • (Freunde) • (Hamburger) • (Türen) • Kinder • (Betten) • Einwohner • (Menschen) • (Straßen) • (Plätze) • (Fahrräder) • (Suppen) • (Colas)

> Most nouns that add **-s** derive from a foreign language, mostly English. However, **der Computer** does not add any ending because it ends in **-er.**

 **Schreibecke**

**Was kann man hier sehen?** You are anticipating a phone call from a young person from a Swiss village who is coming to your town for a one-year exchange. You will be speaking in German. Make some notes to yourself and write down at least five types of things in each category (**Unsere Stadt, Meine Universität**) that a person can see there. Think of all the things that might be different for your visitor.

🟨 Hier kann man viele Parks sehen.

| *Unsere Stadt* | | *Meine Universität* | |
|---|---|---|---|
| _____ | _____ | _____ | _____ |
| _____ | _____ | _____ | _____ |
| _____ | | _____ | |

**Freie Kommunikation**

**Rollenspiel: Ein Telefongespräch.** The Swiss exchange person calls you to get an understanding of life in your town. She/He is especially interested in getting a sense for the things she/he will see and need for a one-year exchange. Discuss the items you listed in the activity above. Here are some useful expressions:

Hallo
Hier ist ... ,
Ich möchte wissen ...
Was kann man dort sehen?
Gibt es viele ... ?
Vielen Dank für die Information.
Auf Wiederhören!

**Zieltext**

## Fahren wir nach Heidelberg oder nach Mannheim?

Georg is talking to his parents, Uschi and Hannes, about what to show Anna during her first weekend in Germany. They are discussing whether to take her to Heidelberg or Mannheim and what each city has to offer.

### Vorschau

**37** **Thematische Fragen.** Discuss the following questions with your instructor or in pairs.

1. When you entertain visitors from out of town, what activities are you likely to do with them?
2. What kind of place do you prefer to visit—a historic city with many sights and tourist attractions, or a modern town that offers many sports and leisure-time activities?

**38** **Wortdetektiv.** Which words convey approximately the same meaning? Match the German word with its logical English equivalent.

| *Deutsch* | *Englisch* |
|---|---|
| 1. die Fußgängerzone | a. music store |
| 2. das Rathaus | b. market square |
| 3. der Marktplatz | c. pedestrian zone |
| 4. das Musikgeschäft | d. city (town) hall |
| | |
| 5. die Idee | e. boring |
| 6. in der Nähe | f. in the vicinity |
| 7. die Aussicht | g. idea |
| 8. langweilig | h. view |
| | |
| 9. gar nicht | i. to be right |
| 10. warten | j. to wait |
| 11. Recht haben | k. first |
| 12. zuerst | l. not at all |
| | |
| 13. dann | m. main street |
| 14. die Hauptstraße | n. afterwards |
| 15. danach | o. people |
| 16. Menschen | p. then |

Die Universitätsstadt Heidelberg

Nicht weit von Heidelberg ist Mannheim. (Der Wasserturm)

**39** **Kulturkreuzung: Eine deutsche Stadt – eine amerikanische Stadt.** Which of these places and public and commercial buildings would you expect to find in an American or Canadian city and which in a German city? Decide for yourself. Then ask your partner about them.

🟨 S1: *Wo findet man ein Museum?*
S2: *Man findet ein Museum in einer deutschen Stadt und auch in einer amerikanischen/kanadischen Stadt.*

ein Museum • ein Schloss • ein China-Restaurant • eine Fußgängerzone • Cafés • einen Marktplatz • ein Theater • eine Universität • eine Disko • ein Rathaus • ein Musikgeschäft • eine Bibliothek • eine Altstadt • eine Kirche • einen Fahrradverleih • einen McDonald's • ein historisches Studentenlokal • ein Hallenschwimmbad

## *Zieltext*

### *Fahren wir nach Mannheim oder nach Heidelberg?*

**40** **Erstes Zuhören.** Read the questions below before you listen.

1. Who are the speakers?
2. Who suggests going to see Mannheim and why?
3. Who prefers Heidelberg and why?
4. Where do they intend to eat and when?

Now listen to the conversation for the first time as you listen for answers to the questions.

 Listen to the conversation again, as often as you wish, to understand more.

## Rückblick

**41** **Ist das in Heidelberg oder in Mannheim?** Check **Heidelberg** or **Mannheim** to indicate where you can find these items that were mentioned in the dialogue.

| | Heidelberg | Mannheim |
|---|:---:|:---:|
| 1. das Schloss | ☒ | ☐ |
| 2. das Museum | ☒ | ☐ |
| 3. das Rathaus | ☐ | ☒ |
| 4. der Marktplatz | ☐ | ☒ |
| 5. die Fußgängerzone | ☐ | ☒ |
| 6. Musikgeschäfte | ☐ | ☒ |
| 7. die Universität (Uni) | ☒ | ☐ |
| 8. viele Menschen | ☒ | ☐ |
| 9. die Hauptstraße | ☒ | ☐ |
| 10. eine Disko | ☒ | ☐ |

**42** **Stimmt das?** How much of the text can you remember?

| | Ja, das stimmt. | Nein, das stimmt nicht. |
|---|:---:|:---:|
| Georg meint, ... | | |
| 1. Anna kommt am Samstag aus Amerika. | ☒ | ☐ |
| 2. in Mannheim gibt es tolle Schuhgeschäfte. | ☐ | ☒ |
| 3. sie sollen zuerst ins Schloss gehen und danach ins Restaurant gehen. | ☐ | ☒ |
| Hannes meint, ... | | |
| 4. sie sollen lieber nach Mannheim fahren. | ☒ | ☐ |
| 5. Heidelberg ist wahrscheinlich besser als Mannheim. | ☒ | ☐ |

|  | Ja, das stimmt. | Nein, das stimmt nicht. | |
|---|---|---|---|
| 6. er isst lieber im Café am Theater als im Restaurant. | ☒ | ☐ | |
| 7. er fährt lieber am Sonntag nach Heidelberg, denn samstags sind zu viele° Menschen da. | ☒ | ☐ | **zu ...** : *too many* |

Uschi meint, ...

|  | | | |
|---|---|---|---|
| 8. in Heidelberg gibt es viel zu sehen: das Schloss, die Universität, das Museum und das Große Fass. | ☒ | ☐ | |
| 9. sie isst lieber im Restaurant in der Nähe vom Schloss, denn da hat man eine schöne Aussicht auf den Neckar. | ☒ | ☐ | |
| 10. sie gehen zuerst in den Supermarkt, dann ins Schloss und zuletzt° essen. | ☐ | ☒ | *lastly* |

**43** **Ergänzen Sie: Diktat.** Complete these sentences with words from the **Zieltext.**

1. HANNES: Warum fahren wir nicht nach Mannheim? Das ist sehr schön und _____ _____ dort viel zu sehen.
2. USCHI: Ich habe gedacht, wir _____ nach Heidelberg.
3. HANNES: Aber es gibt nicht viel zu _____ in Heidelberg. Das Schloss vielleicht und die Uni.
4. USCHI: _____! Es gibt viel zu sehen in Heidelberg: das Schloss, das Museum, und dann ...
5. GEORG: Das Museum ist _____.
6. HANNES: Du _____ das Museum in Heidelberg doch _____ nicht.
7. HANNES: Heidelberg ist _____, wahrscheinlich besser als Mannheim. Wir _____ doch einfach ein bisschen spazieren gehen in der _____.
8. USCHI: Und ich _____ ein sehr gutes kleines Restaurant in der Nähe vom Heidelberger _____. Man hat eine schöne Aussicht auf den Neckar. Das ist eine gute _____.
9. HANNES: Gehen wir doch _____ ins Café am Theater.
10. USCHI: Das stimmt, und es ist auch in der Nähe von der _____.

**44** **Kurz gefragt.** Answer these questions with just a few words, a phrase, or a complete sentence.

1. Wer sagt zuerst, die Günthers sollen° Pläne für Anna machen?    *should*
2. Warum fährt Hannes lieber nach Mannheim als nach Heidelberg?
3. Was gibt es in Heidelberg zu sehen?
4. Was kennt Georg in Heidelberg gar nicht?
5. Was wollen sie zuerst in Heidelberg machen?
6. Was sind die zwei Möglichkeiten° zum Essen?    *possibilities*
7. Warum geht Hannes lieber ins Café in der Hauptstraße?
8. Warum geht Uschi lieber ins Restaurant in der Nähe vom Heidelberger Schloss?
9. Fährt Hannes lieber am Samstag oder am Sonntag nach Heidelberg? Warum?
10. Wann möchte Georg mit Anna in die Disko gehen?

**45** **Was machen wir zuerst?** You will be accompanying the Günthers on their excursion with Anna. With another student, decide in which order you will do the following activities.

a. das Schloss ansehen       b. das Museum besuchen     c. im Restaurant essen

d. in der Fußgängerzone spazieren gehen     e. in der Disko tanzen

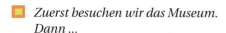 *Zuerst besuchen wir das Museum.*
*Dann ...*

1. Zuerst ...          3. Danach ...          5. Zuletzt ...
2. Dann ...            4. Später° ...                                      *later*

 **║║║ F r e i e   K o m m u n i k a t i o n**

**Der neue Mitbewohner / Die neue Mitbewohnerin.** Your German roommate has just told you that one of his/her friends is coming to live with you. Since you feel your apartment is quite small and you know nothing about this person, ask your roommate questions about the new roommate's eating and drinking preferences, TV viewing habits, free-time activities, and any other personal traits. Discuss these issues in German.

**║║║ S c h r e i b e c k e**

**Meine Stadt: Information für Touristen.** Write a description of your home town or college/university town that you would like to send to some German friends. Include all the information that is relevant to tourists, e.g., about sports facilities, cultural events, historic sights, restaurants, number of inhabitants.

## Wortschatz

### Das Essen

**das Frühstück** *breakfast*

**das Mittagessen** *lunch*

**das Abendbrot** *light evening meal, supper*

**das Abendessen** *evening meal, supper*

**die Vorspeise, -n** *appetizer*

**das Hauptgericht, -e** *main course, entree*

**die Nachspeise, -n** *dessert*

**der Nachtisch, -e** *dessert*

**der Apfel, ⸚** *apple*

**die Apfelsine, -n** *orange*

**der Aufschnitt** *cold cuts*

**die Banane, -n** *banana*

**das Bier, -e** *beer*

**die Bratwurst, ⸚e** *bratwurst*

**das Brot, -e** *bread*

**das Brötchen, -** *hard roll*

   **ein belegtes Brötchen** *roll spread with butter, jam, meat, etc.*

**die Butter** *butter*

**die Cola, -s** *cola*

**das Ei, -er** *egg*

   **ein weich (hart) gekochtes Ei** *soft-boiled (hard-boiled) egg*

**das Eis** *ice; ice cream*

**die Erbse, -n** *pea*

**der Fisch** *fish*

**das Fleisch** *meat*

**das Geflügel** *poultry, fowl*

**das Gemüse** *vegetable(s)*

**das Getränk, -e** *beverage, drink*

**das Hackfleisch** *ground beef*

**das Hähnchen, -** *chicken*

**der Hamburger, -** *hamburger*

**der Honig** *honey*

**der/das Joghurt** *yogurt*

**der Kaffee** *coffee*

**die Karotte, -n** *carrot*

**die Kartoffel, -n** *potato*

**der Käse** *cheese*

**der Kaugummi, -s** *chewing gum*

**die Kirsche, -n** *cherry*

**der Kuchen** *cake*

**die Marmelade, -n** *fruit jam, preserves*

**die Milch** *milk*

**das Müesli** *muesli (grain cereal)*

**das Obst** *fruit*

**die Orange, -n** *orange*

**die Pute, -n** *turkey*

**der Quark** *(a special German dairy spread)*

**das Rindfleisch** *beef*

**der Saft, ⸚e** *juice*

**der Salat, -e** *lettuce; salad*

**das Schweinefleisch** *pork*

**die Semmel, -n** *hard roll (in southern Germany and Austria)*

**die Suppe, -n** *soup*

**der Tee** *tea*

**die Tomate, -n** *tomato*

**die Traube, -n** *grape*

**das Wasser, ⸚** *water*

   **das Mineralwasser** *mineral water*

**der Wein, -e** *wine*

**die Wurst, ⸚e** *sausage*

### Verben und Freizeitaktivitäten

**die Freizeitaktivität, -en** *leisure activity*

**angeln** *to fish*

**besuchen** *to visit*

**essen (er isst)** *to eat*

**fahren (er fährt)** *to travel*

   **Rad fahren (er fährt Rad)** *to ride a bicycle (he's riding a bicycle)*

**fern·sehen (er sieht fern)** *to watch television*

**geben (er gibt)** *to give*

   **Es gibt ...** *There is/are ...*

   **Was gibt es ... ?** *What is (there) ... ?*

   **Was gibt's?** *What's up?*

**ins Kino (Konzert, Theater) gehen** *to go to the movies (concert, theater)*

**halten (er hält)** *to hold*

   **halten von** *to think of, have an opinion of*

**Kaugummi kauen** *to chew gum*

**kennen** *to know, be acquainted with (a person, a city)*

**kochen** *to cook*

**können** *to be able to, can*

**lächeln** *to smile*

**laufen (er läuft)** *to run*

   **Ski laufen** *to ski*

**lesen (er liest)** *to read*

**mit·bringen** *to bring along*

**möchte** *would like to*

**nehmen (er nimmt)** *to take*

**reiten** *to ride (horseback)*

**schwimmen** *to swim*

**segeln** *to sail*

**sehen (er sieht)** *to see*

**singen** *to sing*

**spielen** *to play*

   **Fußball (Baseball, Basketball, Golf, Tennis, Volleyball) spielen** *to play soccer (baseball, basketball, golf, tennis, volleyball)*

   **Karten spielen** *to play cards*

   **Klavier (Flöte, Gitarre) spielen** *to play piano (flute, guitar)*

**sprechen (er spricht)** *to speak*

**tragen (er trägt)** *to wear*

   **Turnschuhe (Shorts) tragen** *to wear athletic shoes (shorts)*

**tun** *to do*

   **haben mit ... zu tun** *to have ... to do with*

**vergessen (er vergisst)** *to forget*

**warten** *to wait*

**werden (er wird)** *to become*

**wissen (er weiß)** *to know as a fact*

## Die Stadt

**der Bahnhof, ¨e** *train station*
**die Bibliothek, -en** *library*
**die Brücke, -n** *bridge*
**das Café, -s** *café*
**die Disko, -s** *disco*
**der Einwohner, -** *inhabitant (male)*
**die Einwohnerin, -nen** *inhabitant (female)*
**die Fußgängerzone, -n** *pedestrian zone*
**das Geschäft, -e** *store*
  **das Lebensmittelgeschäft (Musikgeschäft, Schuhgeschäft)** *grocery store (music store, shoe store)*
**die Hauptstraße, -n** *main street*
**die Kirche, -n** *church*
**die Kunsthalle, -n** *art museum*
**das Lokal, -e** *pub*
**der Marktplatz, ¨e** *market place*
**das Museum, *pl.* Museen** *museum*
**der Platz, ¨e** *plaza, square*
**das Rathaus, ¨er** *city hall*
**das Restaurant, -s** *restaurant*
  **im Restaurant** *in (at) a restaurant*
**das Schwimmbad, ¨er** *swimming pool*
**die Stadt, ¨e** *city*
  **die Altstadt** *historic district*
**der Supermarkt, ¨e** *supermarket*
**das Theater, -** *theater*
**der Turm, ¨er** *tower*
  **der Wasserturm** *water tower*

## Für den Touristen / Für die Touristin

**die Aussicht, -en** *view*
**das Bett, -en** *bed*
**der Gasthof, ¨e** *inn*
**das Gepäck** *luggage, baggage*
**das Hotel, -s** *hotel*
**die Jugendherberge, -n** *youth hostel*
**die Pension, -en** *guesthouse*
**das Schloss, ¨er** *castle, palace*
**die Sehenswürdigkeit, -en** *sightseeing attraction*
**der Zoo, -s** *zoo*

## Im Geschäft und im Restaurant

**die Flasche** *bottle*
**das Glas** *glass*
**das Gramm** *gram*
**das Kilo(gramm)** *kilo(gram)*
**der Kilometer** *kilometer*
**der Liter** *liter*
**der Meter** *meter*
**das Pfund** *pound*
**die Scheibe** *slice*
**das Stück** *piece*
**die Tasse** *cup*

## Personalpronomen im Akkusativ

**dich** *you (sg. informal)*
**es** *it*
**euch** *you (pl. informal)*
**ihn** *him*
**mich** *me*
**sie** *her; them*
**Sie** *you (sg. & pl. formal)*
**uns** *us*

## Possessivpronomen

**dein** *your (sg. informal)*
**euer** *your (pl. informal)*
**ihr** *her; their*
**Ihr** *your (sg. & pl. formal)*
**mein** *my*
**sein** *his; its*
**unser** *our*

## Andere Ausdrücke

**gar nicht** *not at all*
**in der Nähe (von)** *in the vicinity (of)*

## Andere Wörter

**die Idee, -n** *idea*
**der Mensch, [-en], -en** *person*
**besser** *better*
**bestimmt** *undoubtedly*
**danach** *afterward*
**denn** *because; then* (particle)
**etwas** *some(thing)*
**immer** *always*
**langweilig** *boring*
**lieber** *rather*
  **lieber ... als ...** *rather ... than ...*
**man** *one; you*
**nichts** *nothing*
**sicher** *certainly, surely*
**sondern** *but, rather*
**vielleicht** *perhaps, maybe*
**wahrscheinlich** *most likely, probably*
**wohl** *in all likelihood, no doubt*
**zuerst** *first of all, firstly*
**zuletzt** *lastly*
**zu viele** *too many*

## Meine eigenen Wörter

_____

_____

_____

_____

_____

_____

Many tourists who come to the United States and Canada are German speakers who love to visit, especially when a weak dollar makes food, lodging, and transportation a bargain. Major cities such as New York, Toronto, San Francisco, Atlanta, Montreal, New Orleans, Philadelphia, Washington, D.C., and Los Angeles are popular travel destinations. However, tourists from Germany, Austria, and Switzerland also flock to the sunny beaches of Florida and California, and to the wide-open spaces of the American Southwest.

Knowledge of German is often useful in the tourist industry for writing advertising copy, such as the ads you see here for San Francisco. It is also useful for interpreting for and assisting travelers whose command of English may be limited.

The **Deutsch im Beruf** section will provide you with specific information about jobs in which you can use your language skills and will help develop language skills that are important on the job. In **Deutsch im Beruf 1,** you will read about employment opportunities in the tourist industry in the United States and as office support in German-speaking countries.

 **1** **Wo sind die Touristen?** Have you heard anyone speak German where you live? The following is a list of places where you might encounter German-speaking tourists in the U.S. and Canada. Check the places where you have heard German spoken.

___ auf einem Oktoberfest
___ am Bahnhof
___ auf der Straße
___ auf einem Campingplatz
___ am Strand *(beach)*

___ am Flughafen (z.B., O'Hare in Chicago)
___ im Hotel
___ im Restaurant
___ in einer Bank
___ im Bus

**2** **Sehenswürdigkeit Nr. 1: Pier 39.** Tourist advertisements emphasize the positive and use colorful descriptive adjectives. Find the adjectives used to describe San Francisco's Pier 39. Which German words in the descriptions match which pictures?

1. Die _____ Attraktion San Franciscos
2. _____ Aussichten° auf die Bucht°
3. _____ Restaurants
4. von _____ Fischgerichten°
5. bis zu _____ Speisen
6. _____ Shopping
7. _____ Unterhaltung°

*Aussichten: views*
*Bucht: bay*
*Fischgerichten: fish dishes*
*Unterhaltung: enjoyment*

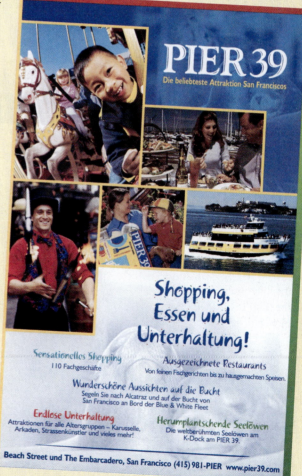

PIER 39
Die beliebteste Attraktion San Franciscos

**Shopping, Essen und Unterhaltung!**

Sensationelles Shopping
110 Fachgeschäfte

Ausgezeichnete Restaurants
Von feinen Fischgerichten bis zu hausgemachten Speisen.

Wunderschöne Aussichten auf die Bucht
Segeln Sie nach Alcatraz und auf der Bucht von San Francisco an Bord der Blue & White Fleet

Endlose Unterhaltung
Attraktionen für alle Altersgruppen – Karusselle, Arkaden, Strassenkünstler und vieles mehr!

Herumplantschende Seelöwen
Die weltberühmten Seelöwen am K-Dock am PIER 39.

Beach Street und The Embarcadero, San Francisco (415) 981-PIER www.pier39.com

**3  Sprechen Sie das deutlich aus.** One important skill you should develop in order to use your German successfully on the job is clear pronunciation of the language. Practice the following expressions from the Pier 39 and Cliff House ads.

1. Shopping, Essen und Unterhaltung!
2. Wunderschöne Aussichten auf die Bucht
3. Attraktionen für alle Altersgruppen
4. Segeln Sie nach Alcatraz.
5. eine romantische Atmosphäre
6. in unserer Bar

**4  Kommen Sie bitte mit nach San Francisco!** Tourist ads often use verbs that describe activities tourists can do while visiting their destination. Find the verbs used in these ads to engage the reader and invite him or her to experience San Francisco actively.

1. _____ Sie nach Alcatraz und auf der Bucht von San Francisco.
2. _____ Sie° einen Aperitif und den Sonnenuntergang° in unserer Bar.
3. _____ Sie auf dem Fahrradweg über die Golden Gate Bridge nach Sausalito und Tiburon.

*enjoy / sunset*

4. _____ Sie Yosemite an einem Tag: _____ Sie mit dem Zug bis nach Merced …

114

# Unterwegs

**In this chapter you will learn how to make informal requests and express what you can, must, want to, should, and may do.**

## Kommunikative Funktionen

- Telling friends or relatives to do something
- Making inclusive suggestions
- Expressing ability, fondness, expected obligation, permission, prohibition, necessity, and strong desire
- Expressing spatial movement, the recipient of something, opposition, and omission

## Strukturen

- The informal (**du-, ihr-**) imperative
- Particles with the imperative
- Inclusive suggestions (**wir-**imperative)
- Modal verbs (**können, mögen/möchte, sollen, dürfen, müssen, wollen**)
- Accusative prepositions

## Vokabeln

- Das Gepäck
- Eigenschaften

## Kulturelles

- Studienmöglichkeiten in Deutschland
- Fahrschule und Fahrrad fahren
- Mit der Bahn fahren
- Frankfurt am Main

■ Mit der Bahn kommt man schnell in die Stadt.

**Online Study Center**

Go to the *Vorsprung* Website at *http:// college.hmco.com/pic/ vorsprung2e.*

# Mutters Ratschläge°

*Ratschläge: advice*

Anna packt die Koffer für ihre Reise nach Deutschland. Sie ist gespannt auf das Jahr in Deutschland, aber ihre Mutter macht sich Sorgen wegen° Anna und der Reise. Sie gibt Anna Ratschläge, aber Anna reagiert wie viele Jugendliche: sie möchte das alles nicht hören. Tante Uschi hat auch ein paar Ratschläge für Katja und Georg.

*macht ... : is worried about*

Beginning in **Kapitel 4,** all activity directions are given in German. Try to learn the meanings of the words used. They are used frequently.

## Vorschau

**1** **Thematische Fragen.** Beantworten° Sie die folgenden° Fragen auf Deutsch.

*answer / following*

A. Anna ist noch° zu Hause in Indiana. Sie packt für zwei Semester in Tübingen. Was kommt mit nach Deutschland? Was bleibt zu Hause? Kreuzen Sie die passende Kategorie an° und bilden Sie dann Sätze.

*still*

*kreuzen Sie ... an: check the appropriate category*

■ *Der warme Pullover kommt mit nach Deutschland.*
*Der Familienhund bleibt zu Hause.*

| | Nach Deutschland | Bleibt zu Hause |
|---|---|---|
| 1. der warme Pullover | ☐ | ☐ |
| 2. die digitale Kamera | ☐ | ☐ |
| 3. die Kreditkarte | ☐ | ☐ |
| 4. der Reisepass° | ☐ | ☐ |
| 5. das Auto | ☐ | ☐ |
| 6. der Fernseher | ☐ | ☐ |
| 7. der Familienhund | ☐ | ☐ |
| 8. die Familienfotos | ☐ | ☐ |
| 9. das Adressbuch | ☐ | ☐ |
| 10. der Laptop | ☐ | ☐ |

*passport*

B. Eine Mutter wie Hannelore Adler macht sich oft Sorgen, wenn die Kinder verreisen° – besonders° für ein Jahr. Sind die Sorgen realistisch oder unrealistisch? Kreuzen Sie an, was stimmt.

*take a trip / especially*

| | Realistisch | Unrealistisch |
|---|---|---|
| 1. Probleme mit der Sprache | ☐ | ☐ |
| 2. Probleme mit Alkohol oder Drogen | ☐ | ☐ |
| 3. Kriminalität | ☐ | ☐ |
| 4. Fremdenhass° | ☐ | ☐ |
| 5. Freunde im Ausland° | ☐ | ☐ |
| 6. Liebe° im Ausland | ☐ | ☐ |
| 7. nicht genug Geld | ☐ | ☐ |
| 8. politische Revolutionen | ☐ | ☐ |
| 9. Terrorismus | ☐ | ☐ |
| 10. Anti-Amerikanismus | ☐ | ☐ |

*xenophobia*

*abroad*

*love*

**2** **Für die Reise.** Was ist wichtig° für Sie, wenn Sie eine Reise machen? Kreuzen Sie an, was für Sie stimmt.

*important*

| | Wichtig | Nicht wichtig | |
|---|---|---|---|
| 1. Verwandte besuchen | ☐ | ☐ | |
| 2. Geld ausgeben | ☐ | ☐ | |
| 3. Andenken° kaufen | ☐ | ☐ | *souvenirs* |
| 4. Sehenswürdigkeiten (z. B. Schlösser) sehen | ☐ | ☐ | |
| 5. Ansichtskarten° schreiben | ☐ | ☐ | *post cards* |
| 6. Alkohol trinken | ☐ | ☐ | |
| 7. zu Hause anrufen | ☐ | ☐ | |
| 8. Fotos machen | ☐ | ☐ | |
| 9. schönes Wetter° haben | ☐ | ☐ | *good weather* |
| 10. Freunde besuchen | ☐ | ☐ | |
| 11. neue Leute kennen lernen | ☐ | ☐ | |
| 12. tanzen gehen | ☐ | ☐ | |

**3** **Wortdetektiv.** Welche Wörter und Ausdrücke° bedeuten° ungefähr° das Gleiche?

*expressions / mean*
*approximately*

| Deutsch | Englisch |
|---|---|
| 1. mit·nehmen | a. carefully |
| 2. die Kleidung | b. clothing |
| 3. ich muss | c. to take along |
| 4. vorsichtig | d. I have to |

| | |
|---|---|
| 5. sich Sorgen machen | e. to hitchhike |
| 6. per Anhalter fahren | f. to worry |
| 7. Andenken kaufen | g. glove |
| 8. der Handschuh | h. to buy souvenirs |

| | |
|---|---|
| 9. Geld aus·geben | i. to help |
| 10. ich soll | j. surrounding area |
| 11. helfen | k. I should |
| 12. die Umgebung | l. to spend money |

*Anlauftext*

 Hören Sie gut zu.°                                    *Listen carefully.*

**Mutters Ratschläge**

Hannelore Adler hat viele Ratschläge für Anna, aber Anna interpretiert sie anders.

*Frau Adler sagt:*            *Anna denkt:*

Trink nicht so viel Cola!

Dann muss ich wohl Bier trinken, aber das mag ich nicht.

Nimm genug warme Kleidung mit!

Ich darf meine Handschuhe nicht vergessen.

Gib nicht zu viel Geld für Andenken aus!

Ich will aber Andenken kaufen.

Fahr nie per Anhalter!

Dann muss ich wohl ein Fahrrad haben.

> **Sprache im Alltag: Assumptions with wohl and wahrscheinlich**
>
> A person who makes an assumption generally expects the listener to confirm a suspicion or thought. The words **wohl** (*in all likelihood, probably*) and **wahrscheinlich** (*most likely*) mark statements as assumptions in German.
>
> Dann müssen wir **wohl** 100 Schlösser besuchen.
> *Then we'll probably have to visit 100 castles.*
>
> Anna will **wahrscheinlich** mein Zimmer haben.
> *Anna most likely wants to have my room.*

## *Rückblick*

**4** **Stimmt das?** Stimmen diese Aussagen° zum Text oder nicht? Wenn nicht, was stimmt?

*statements*

|  | Ja, das stimmt. | Nein, das stimmt nicht. |
|---|:---:|:---:|
| 1. Annas Mutter sagt, Anna soll Bier trinken. | ☐ | ☒ |
| 2. Anna denkt, sie darf ihre Schuhe nicht vergessen°. | ☐ | ☒ |
| 3. Anna denkt, sie will Andenken kaufen. | ☒ | ☐ |
| 4. Anna denkt, sie muss ein Auto kaufen. | ☐ | ☒ |
| 5. Anna denkt, sie soll hin und wieder eine Postkarte schreiben. | ☐ | ☒ |
| 6. Annas Mutter sagt, Anna soll in Deutschland vorsichtig sein. | ☒ | ☐ |
| 7. Katja denkt, Anna kann kein Deutsch. | ☐ | ☒ |
| 8. Onkel Hannes möchte gern viele Schlösser besuchen. | ☒ | ☒ |
| 9. Georg möchte Anna sein Zimmer geben. | ☐ | ☒ |

*darf ... : must not forget her shoes*

Complete the **Ergänzen Sie** activity in your workbook for this text before doing the next activity.

**5** **Kurz gefragt.** Beantworten Sie diese Fragen auf Deutsch.

1. Was soll Anna mitnehmen?
2. Warum soll Anna nicht so viele Andenken kaufen?
3. Muss Anna ein Fahrrad haben? Warum? Warum nicht?
4. Wen soll Anna nicht vergessen?
5. Wie soll Anna mit den Eltern in Kontakt bleiben?
6. Was müssen die Günthers wohl mit Anna besuchen?

**Kurz gefragt.** Try to answer these questions in complete sentences.

U.S. cell phones do not work in Europe without installation of the appropriate chip.

**6** **Interview.** Stellen Sie einem Partner/einer Partnerin die folgenden Fragen.

1. Du machst eine Reise. Welches Transportmittel benutzt° du?
   a. ein Auto
   b. einen Autobus
   c. ein Flugzeug°
   d. einen Zug°

*use*
*airplane*
*train*

2. Wie bleibst du mit deinen Eltern in Kontakt?
   a. Ich wohne zu Hause.
   b. Ich rufe sie oft an.
   c. Ich besuche sie oft.
   d. Ich schreibe viele Briefe° und E-Mails.

*letters*

3. Was möchtest du in Deutschland sehen?
   a. eine Stadt
   b. ein Schloss
   c. die Natur
   d. typische Deutsche

4. Was machst du, wenn Besucher° kommen?

    a. Wir gehen ins Kino.    c. Wir besuchen Freunde oder Familie.

    b. Wir besuchen die Stadt.    d. Wir treiben Sport°.

5. Du fährst nächste° Woche nach Europa: Was vergisst du sicher nicht?

    a. mein Wörterbuch°    c. warme Kleidung

    b. mein Adressbuch    d. ein Familienfoto

*visitors*

***wir ... :*** *we do sports*

*next*
*dictionary*

**BRENNPUNKT KULTUR**

## Studienmöglichkeiten° in Deutschland

*study options*

Named for Germany's most famous classical author and playwright, Johann Wolfgang von Goethe (1749–1832), the **Goethe-Institut** promotes the study of German language and culture around the world while supporting international cultural cooperation. Students of the German language can enroll in classes at seven sites in the U.S., three in Canada, and sixteen in Germany, representative of the 142 **Goethe-Institute** in seventy-seven countries around the world. In addition to classes, the institutes maintain lending libraries and organize cultural events such as film series, concerts, lectures, and traditional celebrations to enhance understanding of German culture in the local community. Working on behalf of Austria, the **Austrian Cultural Institute** of New York City also organizes exhibits, film festivals, and lectures and facilitates student exchanges and dissemination of information about Austria. The **Swiss Institute** in New York, Switzerland's foremost cultural institute in the United States, promotes artistic dialogue between Switzerland and the U.S. through various cultural programs.

In an era of global education, the demand for well-educated, multilingual professionals has never been greater. On the list of "Top Ten" qualifications for new employees of German firms are communicative fluency in several foreign languages and experience studying abroad. Many **Hochschulen** and **Universitäten** in Germany, Austria, and Switzerland offer "year abroad" programs for their students and also welcome students from the U.S., Canada, and other countries. In fact, the enrollment of foreign students at some German universities exceeds 30%. Many U.S. and Canadian colleges also offer study and internship programs abroad. A year abroad enriches student appreciation for the German language and culture while raising that student's language skills to their highest level. The **Deutscher Akademischer Austauschdienst** *(German Academic Exchange Service),* with offices in Bonn and New York, arranges study and research grants for scholars and graduate students.

■ Vor dem Berliner Goethe-Institut.

IHR PARTNER FÜR DEUTSCH
GOETHE-INSTITUT

**DAAD**
Deutscher Akademischer Austausch Dienst
German Academic Exchange Service
Kennedyallee 50 · 53175 Bonn
Postfach 20 04 04 · 53134 Bonn
Deutschland / Germany

*www.daad.de*

■ **Kulturkreuzung** Wo in Deutschland, Österreich oder der Schweiz hat Ihre Universität Studienprogramme? Kennen Sie Studenten oder Studentinnen an Ihrer Universität aus Europa? Warum, meinen Sie, kommen diese Studenten an Ihre Universität?

## Strukturen und Vokabeln

**Im** is a contraction that means *in the*. It will be explained in **Kapitel 6.**

Additional articles of clothing for men are: **der Anzug, -, -̈e** *suit,* **die Badehose,** *swim trunks,* **die Krawatte, -n** *necktie,* **der/das Sakko, -s** *sportcoat.*

### Wissenswerte Vokabeln: das Gepäck
*Identifying personal items*

Im Koffer hat Anna …

Im Kulturbeutel hat Anna …

Im Rucksack hat Anna …

In der Handtasche hat Anna ...

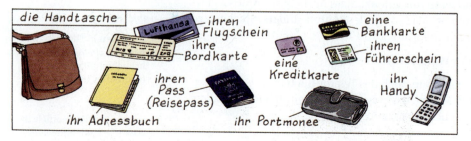

◻ Was hat Anna im Rucksack? *Sie hat ihre digitale Kamera, ...*

**7 Was trägt man wahrscheinlich?** Wählen° Sie das beste Wort.

*choose*

1. Karl geht ins Theater. Er trägt:
   a. ein Kleid          b. einen Sakko          c. einen Rock

2. Barbara geht Ski laufen. Sie trägt:
   a. Sandalen          b. Turnschuhe          c. Skistiefel

3. Monika geht zur Universität. Sie trägt:
   a. Jeans          b. ein Abendkleid          c. einen Mini-Rock

4. Das ist mein Freund Stefan. Er trägt:
   a. ein Hemd          b. eine Bluse          c. eine Strumpfhose

5. Herr Professor Schmidt ist konservativ. Er trägt:
   a. ein T-Shirt und Shorts          b. einen Pullover und Jeans          c. einen Sakko, eine Krawatte und eine Hose

**8 Wer trägt das heute?** Wer in der Klasse trägt heute die folgenden Kleidungsstücke°?

Wer trägt heute:

1. einen blauen Pullover
2. eine Krawatte
3. Jeans
4. Sandalen
5. eine weiße Bluse
6. einen Rock
7. ein gelbes Hemd
8. keine Turnschuhe
9. schwarze Stiefel
10. ein Kleid

*clothes (lit., pieces of clothing)*

**Wer trägt das heute?** Use **niemand** (*nobody*) if necessary.

**9 Interview:** Was trägst du gern? Stellen Sie einem Partner/einer Partnerin die folgenden Fragen.

◻ S1: *Was trägst du, wenn es kalt° ist?*
   S2: *Ich trage einen Mantel.*

*cold*

1. Was trägst du, wenn es kalt ist?
2. Was trägst du gern?
3. Was trägst du nicht so gern?
4. Was trägst du heute?
5. Was trägst du sehr oft?
6. Was trägst du nie°?

*never*

**10   Aber Mama!** Frau Adler denkt, dass Anna bestimmte Gegen- | objects / needs
stände° in Deutschland braucht°. Wie so oft, denkt Anna anders. Spielen Sie mit
einer Partnerin / mit einem Partner Mutter und Tochter.

◾ – das Telefonbuch   + das Wörterbuch

> S1 (FRAU ADLER):  Anna, nimm doch das Telefonbuch mit!
> S2 (ANNA):  Aber Mama. Ich brauche doch kein Telefonbuch. Ich
> brauche ein Wörterbuch.

| – *Frau Adler:* | + *Anna:* |
|---|---|
| 1. das Telefonbuch | das Wörterbuch |
| 2. der Kuli | der Laptop |
| 3. das Parfüm | das Deospray |
| 4. das Kleid | die Jeans |
| 5. das Scheckbuch | die Kreditkarte |
| 6. die Haarbürste | die Zahnbürste |
| 7. der Kassettenrecorder | der CD-Player |
| 8. der Führerschein | der Pass |
| 9. die Handschuhe | der Lippenstift |
| 10. der Rock | das T-Shirt |

**Aber Mama!** The verbs **mitnehmen** (*to take along*) and **brauchen** (*to need*) are followed by the accusative case.

Use the indefinite article to refer to an indefinite item and the definite article to refer to a specific item: **Nimm doch das Telefonbuch mit.**

**7.** Europe has 220 volt circuits instead of 120 volts as in the U.S. The plugs are also shaped differently. American appliances require a voltage converter and a plug adapter.

## I   Telling friends or relatives to do something

### The informal imperative

#### A. The *du*-imperative

In **Kapitel 1,** you learned how the formal imperative is formed for commands **(Befehlsformen)** and polite requests by placing the verb first and using the pronoun **Sie.**

> Stehen Sie auf.
> Setzen Sie sich bitte.

In this chapter Anna and her family use the informal **du**-imperative (**der informelle Imperativ).**

| *Mrs. Adler advises Anna:* | Trink nicht so viel Cola. | *Don't drink so much cola.* |
|---|---|---|
| *Anna tells her mother:* | Mach dir keine Sorgen. | *Don't worry.* |

German speakers use the **du**-imperative whenever the situation requires the use of **du.**

1. when speaking to a family member, a friend, any child up to adolescence or when talking to their peers (e.g., students, athletes, workers, soldiers):

> Vergiss deine Eltern nicht. *Don't forget your parents.*
> Gib mir den Ball. *Give me the ball.*

2. when praying to God:

> Komm, Herr Jesu, sei unser Gast! *Come, Lord Jesus, be our guest!*

3. when intentionally showing disrespect or insulting someone:

> Geh weg!    *Scram!*

4. when speaking to animals, e.g., to a dog:

> Rollo, komm her!    *Rollo, come here!*

For most verbs (all but the stem-changing verbs with an **a** or **au** in the infinitive), the **du**-imperative is formed by dropping the **st**-ending (or just the **-t** if the stem ends in **-s, -ss, -ß, -x, -z**) and the personal pronoun **du** from the **du**-form of the present tense of the verb.

| Infinitive | Present tense | *du*-imperative | |
|---|---|---|---|
| machen | du machst | **Mach** dir keine Sorgen. | *Don't worry.* |
| lesen | du liest | **Lies** das Deutschbuch. | *Read the German book.* |
| vergessen | du vergisst | **Vergiss** deine Eltern nicht. | *Don't forget your parents.* |
| antworten | du antwortest | **Antworte** auf Deutsch. | *Answer in German.* |
| öffnen | du öffnest | **Öffne** die Tür. | *Open the door.* |

Verbs with stem-vowel changes from **a** or **au** to **ä/äu** in the present-tense **du**-form revert to the **a/au** spelling in the **du**-imperative.

| Infinitive | Present tense | *du*-imperative | |
|---|---|---|---|
| fahren | du fährst | **Fahr** nie per Anhalter. | *Don't ever hitchhike.* |
| tragen | du trägst | **Trag** warme Kleidung. | *Wear warm clothes.* |
| laufen | du läufst | **Lauf** schnell. | *Run fast.* |

| Infinitive | *du*-imperative | |
|---|---|---|
| sein | **Sei** immer vorsichtig! | *Always be careful!* |
| haben | **Hab** keine Angst! | *Don't be afraid!* |

Verbs with separable prefixes (e.g., **an·kommen, an·rufen, auf·hören, auf·stehen, auf·wachen, mit·bringen, mit·nehmen**) place the prefix at the end of the phrase.

| | |
|---|---|
| **Ruf** doch mal **an!** | *Give a call!* |
| Anna, **wach auf!** | *Anna, wake up!* |
| **Gib** nicht zu viel Geld **aus!** | *Don't spend too much money!* |
| **Nimm** genug warme Kleidung **mit!** | *Take enough warm clothes along!* |

German speakers use **nicht** or **kein** when telling somebody what <u>not</u> to do.

| | |
|---|---|
| Vergiss bitte deine Eltern **nicht!** | *Please don't forget your parents!* |
| Mach dir **keine** Sorgen! | *Don't worry!* |

---

Notice that even many verbs with stem changes follow this basic rule. Shown in the examples to the left are **lesen, vergessen, antworten, öffnen.** Others are:
sehen, du si̲e̲hst, **si̲e̲h**
essen, du i̲sst, **i̲ss**
geben, du gi̲bst, **gib**
helfen, du hi̲lfst, **hi̲lf**
nehmen, du ni̲mmst, **ni̲mm**
sprechen, du spri̲chst,
    **spri̲ch**
finden, du finde̲st, **finde̲**

Note verbs like **lächeln** (*to laugh*) and **ändern** (*to change*), whose stems end in **-el** or **-er.** The present tense **du**-form includes the internal **e,** but the **du**-imperative does not and instead adds an **e** at the end: **du läche̲lst** but lächle, du ände̲rst but **änd(e)re.**

Also: halten, du hältst, **halt;** schlafen, du schläfst, **schlaf;** waschen, du wäschst, **wasch.**
These are the **du**-imperative forms of the verbs **sein** (*to be*) and **haben** (*to have*).

Remember the **Sie**-imperative forms of **sein** and **haben: Seien Sie pünktlich!** (*Please be punctual!*) or **Haben Sie keine Angst!** (*Don't be afraid!*)

**11** **Was sagt man zu Karl?** Ein Student/Eine Studentin spielt die Rolle von Karl. Karl hat Probleme im Deutschkurs. Ein anderer Student/Eine andere Studentin gibt Ratschläge. Wählen Sie die passende Antwort.

S1 (KARL):  *Ich komme immer zu spät.*
S2 (SIE):  *Steh früh auf!*

| *Karl* | *Sie* |
|---|---|
| 1. Ich komme immer zu spät. | a. Steh früh auf. |
| | b. Bleib bis mittags im Bett. |
| 2. Ich bin so nervös. | a. Trink drei Tassen Kaffee. |
| | b. Mach dir keine Sorgen. |
| 3. Ich habe morgen um acht Uhr Deutsch. | a. Bring dein Buch nicht mit. |
| | b. Vergiss dein Buch nicht. |
| 4. Ich schreibe morgen einen Test. | a. Lies heute Abend dein Buch. |
| | b. Fahr heute Abend nach Deutschland. |
| 5. Ich bin heute krank°. | a. Geh in eine Bar. |
| | b. Ruf den Professor an. |

*sick*

**12** **Hast du einen Ratschlag für mich?** Was sagen Sie in diesen Situationen? Formen Sie passende **du**-Imperative.

> **Hast du einen Ratschlag für mich?** Note that some of these verbs contain separable prefixes.

S1:  *Es ist kalt heute.*
S2:  *Trag warme Kleidung.*

1. Es ist kalt heute. F. Trag
2. Ich fahre dein Auto. G. Fahr
3. Es ist spät°. Der Deutschkurs beginnt bald°. A. Fahr
4. Meine Eltern sind traurig. D. Ruf
5. Ich gehe heute Abend auf eine elegante Party. E. Trag
6. Morgen habe ich eine Deutschprüfung°. C. Lies
7. Ich habe Hunger. B. Iss
8. Ich kaufe ein schönes Geschenk. H. Gib

a. schnell° zur Uni fahren
b. eine Pizza essen
c. heute Abend dein Deutschbuch lesen
d. deine Eltern (sie) doch mal anrufen
e. ein Kleid/ein Sakko und eine Krawatte tragen
f. warme Kleidung tragen
g. vorsichtig fahren
h. nicht zu viel Geld ausgeben

*fast*

*late*

*soon*

*German test*

## B. The **ihr**-imperative

When speaking informally with more than one person, German speakers use the **ihr**-imperative. The **ihr**-imperative forms are identical to the present tense **ihr**-forms of all verbs including **sein** and **haben.** As in the **du**-imperative, the personal pronoun (**ihr**) is dropped.

| Infinitive | Present tense | *ihr*-imperative | |
|---|---|---|---|
| machen | ihr macht | **Macht** euch keine Sorgen. | *Don't (you, pl. inf.) worry.* |
| essen | ihr esst | **Esst** kein Fleisch. | *Don't eat any meat.* |
| antworten | ihr antwortet | **Antwortet** auf Deutsch. | *Answer in German.* |
| öffnen | ihr öffnet | **Öffnet** die Tür! | *Open the door!* |
| sein | ihr seid | **Seid** immer vorsichtig! | *Always be careful!* |
| haben | ihr habt | **Habt** keine Angst. | *Don't (you all) be afraid.* |

Verbs with a separable prefix place the prefix at the end of the phrase.

**Ruft** doch mal **an.**                          *Give a call.*
Anna und Katja, **wacht auf.**            *Anna and Katja, wake up.*
**Gebt** nicht zu viel Geld **aus.**        *Don't spend too much money.*
**Nehmt** genug warme Kleidung **mit.**   *Take enough warm clothes along.*

German speakers use **nicht** or **kein** when telling somebody what <u>not</u> to do.

Vergesst eure Eltern **nicht.**       *Don't forget your parents.*
Macht euch **keine** Sorgen.        *Don't (you all) worry.*

**13   Reisetipps.** Diese Personen machen eine Reise. Was sollen sie machen/nicht machen? Geben Sie diesen Personen Ratschläge und benutzen Sie **du-, ihr-** oder **Sie**-Imperative.

- das Wasser nicht trinken (Dieter und Ingrid)
  *Trinkt das Wasser nicht.*

- dort keine Andenken kaufen (Herr und Frau Mertens)
  *Kaufen Sie dort keine Andenken.*

1. das Wasser nicht trinken (Dieter und Ingrid)
2. den Fisch nicht essen (Heiner)
3. den Pass nicht vergessen (Professor Steinhuber)
4. kein Deutsch sprechen (Sigrid und Mario)
5. die Andenken nicht vergessen (Claus)
6. nicht in einem billigen° Hotel schlafen (Herr und Frau Günther)
7. den Kölner Dom° besuchen (Monika und Gabriel)
8. die Kreditkarte nicht mitnehmen (Martina)
9. Helga und Wilhelm in Bonn anrufen (Greta und Thomas)
10. nicht so viel Geld für Hummel-Figuren ausgeben (Tante Frieda)
11. nicht so viel Gepäck mitnehmen (Katja und Georg)
12. Dieter eine Ansichtskarte schreiben (Onkel Fritz)

## C. Particles with the imperative

German speakers frequently use the words **bitte, doch,** or **mal** to modify a request. Only **bitte** has a direct English translation: *please.* It ensures that a request is expressed in a polite manner.

Mach dir **bitte** keine Sorgen.    *Please don't worry.*

The word **doch** makes a request more persuasive. It indicates that the speaker may be anticipating opposition from the listener.

Zeigen wir Anna **doch** die Umgebung.    *Let's show Anna the area.*

The word **mal** makes a request more emphatic. **Mal** is related to **ein Mal** (*one time*) and leaves the time of when to carry out the request vague.

Schau **mal!**    *Look!*

In combination with **doch, mal** adds insistence to a request.

Ruf **doch mal** an!    *Call sometime!*

Reisetipps. Remember to use the **du-** or **ihr-** imperative forms when first names are provided and the **Sie**-imperative forms when last names are provided.

*inexpensive*
**Kölner Dom:** *cathedral in Cologne*

Hummel figurines are stereotypical porcelain figures of sentimentalized young boys and girls. Originally designed by Berta Hummel in the early 20th century, they are produced at the *Goebel Porzellanfabrik* and sold worldwide as collectibles.

**14** **Lest bitte das Buch.** Kennen Sie das Spiel „Simon sagt …"? Hier spielen wir eine deutsche Version. Ein Student /Eine Studentin gibt die Befehle. Die anderen machen mit, solange er/sie **bitte** sagt. Wer etwas tut, ohne **bitte** zu hören°, muss sich setzen. Der Gewinner/Die Gewinnerin gibt dann die Befehle in der nächsten Runde.

*Ohne ... hören: without hearing **bitte***

🟧 aufstehen    S1:   *Steht auf!*       (oder)    *Steht **bitte** auf!*
                       *Stehen Sie auf!*   (oder)    *Stehen Sie **bitte** auf!*

1. die Tür aufmachen
2. den Kuli nehmen
3. zur Tür gehen
4. die Hand zeigen
5. das Buch lesen
6. die Nummer aufschreiben
7. den Lehrer/die Lehrerin anrufen
8. schnell laufen

## D. Inclusive suggestions: the **wir**-imperative

German speakers form inclusive suggestions, also called **wir**-imperatives, by placing the **wir**-form of a verb followed by the pronoun **wir** at the beginning of the sentence. The word order is identical to that of a yes/no question, but the speaker's voice drops instead of rises at the end. The **wir**-imperative corresponds to the *let's* construction in English.

**Zeigen wir** Anna doch die Umgebung.    *Let's show Anna the area.*

**15** **Gute Idee! Machen wir das.** Machen Sie mit einem Partner/ einer Partnerin Pläne für heute Abend. Benutzen Sie den **wir**-Imperativ.

🟧 heute Abend ins Kino/Theater gehen

   S1:  *Gehen wir heute Abend ins Kino oder ins Theater?*
   S2:  *Gehen wir doch ins Kino.*

1. heute Abend in die Disko/Oper gehen
2. Klaus/Franz anrufen
3. die Cornelia/den Jürgen mitnehmen
4. mit dem Bus/Auto fahren
5. vorher° Karl/Professor Steinhuber besuchen
6. nachher° eine Pizza/einen Hamburger essen
7. nachher im Studentenlokal einen Wein/eine Cola trinken
8. nachher die Hausaufgaben machen/fernsehen

> **Gute Idee! Machen wir das.** Try to use the particle **doch** in your responses. Place it right after **wir**.

*beforehand*
*afterwards*

## **II** **Expressing ability, fondness, and expected obligation**

### Modal verbs (I)

You already learned in **Kapitel 3** about the modal verbs **können** and **möchte (mögen).** Modal verbs in German, as in English, modify the meaning of another verb by indicating ability (**können**), fondness (**mögen**), obligation (**sollen**), permission (**dürfen**), necessity (**müssen**), or desire (**wollen**) to carry out the action. In German the other verb appears in its infinitive form at the end of the sentence.

> Ich **kann** Deutsch **sprechen.**    *I can (am able to) speak German.*
> Ich **möchte** so viel **lernen.**    *I would like to learn so much.*

Here are the modal verbs that you encountered in the **Anlauftext:**

**dürfen:**    Ich **darf** meine Handschuhe nicht vergessen.
  *I must not forget my gloves.*
**können:**    Anna **kann** ja ein bisschen Deutsch.
  *Anna can speak a little German.*
**mögen:**    Das **mag** ich nicht.
  *I don't like that.*
**müssen:**    Dann **müssen** wir wohl 100 Schlösser besuchen.
  *Then we probably have to visit a hundred castles.*
**sollen:**    Ich **soll** mein Handy **mitnehmen** und sie hin und wieder **anrufen.**
  *I should take along my cell phone and call them now and then.*
**wollen:**    Ich **will** aber Andenken **kaufen.**
  *But I want to buy souvenirs.*

> **Muß** is the old spelling for **muss.**

> The use of **mögen** without an infinitive will be explained later in this chapter.

Modal verbs may occur without the infinitive of the main verb when the meaning of the missing infinitive is clear from the context.

> Anna **kann** schon etwas        *Anna can already speak some*
>   Deutsch (sprechen).            *German.*
> Anna **muss** jetzt nach Hause (gehen).    *Anna has to go home now.*

Modals have no endings in the **ich**- and **er/sie/es**-forms. The **ich**- and **er/sie/ es**-forms are identical: **ich (er/sie/es) darf, kann, mag, muss, soll, will.**

### A. Expressing ability: *können*

We will start with the review of the modal verb **können** (*can, to be able to*), which you already encountered in **Kapitel 3.**

| **können:** *can, to be able to* | |
|---|---|
| **Singular** | **Plural** |
| ich **kann** | wir **können** |
| du **kannst** | ihr **könnt** |
| Sie **können** | Sie **können** |
| er/sie/es **kann** | sie **können** |

**16    Anna kann nicht Ski laufen.** Was können diese Personen machen/nicht machen? Was können *Sie* machen/nicht machen? Diskutieren Sie das mit einem Partner/einer Partnerin. Benutzen Sie die folgenden Ausdrücke.

| + | +/− | − |
|---|---|---|
| sehr gut | ziemlich gut, nicht so gut | nicht gut, überhaupt nicht |

| | Anna | Katja | Georg | **ich** | Partner/ Partnerin |
|---|---|---|---|---|---|
| | − | + | + | | |
| | + | − | − | | |
| | + | + | + | | |
| | − | − | + | | |
| | + | − | − | | |
| | + | + | + | | |
| | + | − | + | | |
| | + | + | + | | |
| | + | − | + | | |

S1: *Wer kann Ski laufen? Wer kann nicht Ski laufen?*
S2: *Katja und Georg können Ski laufen, aber Anna kann nicht Ski laufen.*
S1: *Ich kann gut Ski laufen, aber meine Partnerin, Sara, kann überhaupt nicht Ski laufen.*

**17** **Was kann man nicht machen?** Welche Aktivitäten können diese Personen nicht machen?

▪ Ingrid hat ihre Kontaktlinsen nicht.  *Ingrid kann nicht sehen.*

1. Ingrid hat ihre Kontaktlinsen nicht.           Lars anrufen
2. Dieter hat keine Gitarre.                       einkaufen
3. Roland hat die Telefonnummer nicht.            nach Berlin fahren
4. Jörg und Thomas haben kein Auto.               zur Party kommen
5. Oskar hat kein Geld.                            schwimmen
6. Marion und Angelika haben keine Zeit.          Musik machen
7. Sophie hat Angst vor dem Wasser.               in den Deutschkurs kommen
8. Die Studentin ist heute krank.                 sehen

## B. Expressing fondness and desire: *mögen* and *möchte*

The modal verb **mögen** expresses general liking. Its special form **möchte** expresses an immediate desire and specific preference.

In standard German, **mögen** generally occurs with a noun and **möchte** can be used with or without an infinitive (see **Kapitel 3**).

| | |
|---|---|
| Ich **mag** Bier. | *I (generally) like beer.* |
| Ich **möchte** ein Bier (haben). | *I would like to have a beer (right now).* |
| Ich **möchte** Deutsch sprechen. | *I would like to speak German.* |

> **Möchte** is used to express politeness when offering something to someone: **Möchten Sie ein Stück Kuchen?**

Remember to use the particle **gern** when talking about an activity you like in general (for which you would use a verb). When talking about an object you like (for which you would use a noun), use a form of **mögen.**

| | |
|---|---|
| Ich **spreche gern** Deutsch. | *I (generally) enjoy speaking German.* |
| Sie **mag** klassische Musik. | *She likes classical music.* |

| mögen: *to like* | |
|---|---|
| **Singular** | **Plural** |
| ich **mag** | wir **mögen** |
| du **magst** | ihr **mögt** |
| Sie **mögen** | Sie **mögen** |
| er/sie/es **mag** | sie **mögen** |

**18** **Was mögen Sie?** Markieren Sie Ihre Interessen mit +, +/ − oder −. Finden Sie dann einen Studenten/eine Studentin mit mindestens drei gleichen° Interessen.

*similar*

S1: *Ich mag Deutsch sehr. Magst du Deutsch auch?*
S2: *Nein, ich mag Deutsch nicht so sehr.*

| + | +/− | − |
|---|---|---|
| sehr | nicht so sehr | überhaupt nicht |

*auch nur: "ich mag X"*

|  | *Ich* | *Mein(e) Partner(in)* |
|---|---|---|
| Deutsch | ☐ | ☐ |
| Tennis | ☐ | ☐ |
| Fußball | ☐ | ☐ |
| Extremsportarten | ☐ | ☐ |
| Shakespeare | ☐ | ☐ |
| Stephen King | ☐ | ☐ |
| Hermann Hesse | ☐ | ☐ |
| Horrorfilme | ☐ | ☐ |
| Theater | ☐ | ☐ |
| Jazzmusik | ☐ | ☐ |
| Brokkoli | ☐ | ☐ |
| Pizza | ☐ | ☐ |
| Bier | ☐ | ☐ |
| Kaffee | ☐ | ☐ |

> **Hermann Hesse** was born on July 2, 1877, in Calw near Stuttgart. In 1946 he won the Nobel Prize for Literature. His works include *Der Steppenwolf, Siddhartha,* and *Narziss und Goldmund.*

You already encountered **möchte** in **Kapitel 3.** Here are the present tense forms again, presented for review.

| möchte: *would like (to)* | |
|---|---|
| **Singular** | **Plural** |
| ich **möchte** | wir **möchten** |
| du **möchtest** | ihr **möchtet** |
| Sie **möchten** | Sie **möchten** |
| er/sie/es **möchte** | sie **möchten** |

German speakers use **möchte** to extend invitations and, often together with **lieber,** to inquire about or to express preferences.

**Möchtest** du nach Paris fahren?          *Would you like to go to Paris?*
Nein, ich **möchte lieber** nach Wien fahren.    *No, I would rather go to Vienna.*

**19**   **Was möchten Sie machen?**  Sie reisen nach Deutschland. Geld ist kein Problem für Sie. Kreuzen Sie Ihre Wünsche° an. Planen Sie dann eine Reise zusammen mit einem Partner/einer Partnerin.

*wishes*

S1: *Möchtest du nach Tübingen oder nach Berlin fahren?*
S2: *Ich möchte nach Tübingen fahren.*
S1: *Ich möchte auch nach Tübingen fahren.* (oder)
    *Ich möchte lieber nach Berlin fahren.*

| | Ich | Mein(e) Partner(in) |
|---|---|---|
| 1. nach Tübingen/Berlin fahren | ☐ | ☐ |
| 2. Verwandte/Freunde besuchen | ☐ | ☐ |
| 3. wenig Geld ausgeben/viele Andenken kaufen | ☐ | ☐ |
| 4. viel essen/viel trinken | ☐ | ☐ |
| 5. einen Mercedes/einen VW kaufen | ☐ | ☐ |
| 6. viele Schlösser sehen/viele Menschen kennen lernen | ☐ | ☐ |
| 7. in den Alpen wandern/in Mannheim einkaufen | ☐ | ☐ |
| 8. München ansehen/in München wohnen | ☐ | ☐ |

## C. Expressing expected obligation: *sollen*

The modal verb **sollen** expresses an obligation that one has. Here are the present tense forms of the modal verb **sollen.**

| sollen: *should; to be supposed to* | |
|---|---|
| **Singular** | **Plural** |
| ich **soll** | wir **sollen** |
| du **sollst** | ihr **sollt** |
| Sie **sollen** | Sie **sollen** |
| er/sie/es **soll** | sie **sollen** |

Ich **soll** mein Handy mitnehmen.   *I should take my cell phone along.*

**20**   **Hausarbeit.**  Frau Günther hat eine Liste für Georg und Katja. Was sollen sie machen? Und was sollen *Sie* machen? Kreuzen Sie Ihre Aufgaben an. Fragen Sie dann einen Partner/eine Partnerin.

S1: *Wer soll das Zimmer aufräumen°?*
S2: *Georg soll das Zimmer aufräumen.*
S1: *Und du? Sollst du das Zimmer aufräumen?*
S2: *Ja, das soll ich machen.* (oder) *Nein, ich soll das nicht machen.*

*tidy up*

| | Georg | Katja | Ich | Partner/ Partnerin |
|---|---|---|---|---|
| das Zimmer aufräumen | ✔ | ☐ | ☐ | ☐ |
| das Bett machen | ✔ | ✔ | ☐ | ☐ |
| das Essen kochen | ✔ | ✔ | ☐ | ☐ |
| Hausaufgaben machen | ✔ | ✔ | ☐ | ☐ |
| die Katze füttern° | ✔ | ☐ | ☐ | ☐ |
| die Wäsche° waschen | ☐ | ✔ | ☐ | ☐ |
| Staub saugen° | ✔ | ☐ | ☐ | ☐ |

*feed*
*laundry*
*vacuum*

**F r e i e   K o m m u n i k a t i o n**

**Rollenspiel: Die Einladung°.** Sie sind neu in Hannover. Frau Meyer ruft Sie an und lädt Sie zu Kaffee und Kuchen ein. Sie möchten kommen, aber Sie haben viel zu tun – die Kinder abholen, Essen kaufen und zur Bank gehen. Fragen Sie Frau Meyer, wann Sie kommen sollen und was Sie bringen können. Sagen Sie Frau Meyer, was Sie machen sollen und wann Sie kommen können.

*invitation*

  **S c h r e i b e c k e**

**In diesem Alter.** Was können Sie in diesem Alter° machen? Was sollen Sie machen? Was möchten Sie machen?

*in ... : at this age*

1. Sie sind fünf Jahre alt.
2. Sie sind zehn Jahre alt.
3. Sie sind fünfzehn Jahre alt.

> **Absprungtext. Nr.** is an abbreviation for **Nummer.**

**Absprungtext**

## FAHRRAD fahren: Sicherheitsinfo° Nr. 8

*Sicherheitsinfo: safety information*

In den USA fährt Anna sehr gern Rad. In Deutschland ist Radfahren sehr populär, sogar° populärer als in den USA. Junge Leute fahren mit dem Rad zur Schule, alte Menschen fahren oft mit dem Rad zum Einkauf oder zur Arbeit. Aber Radfahren in der Stadt kann gefährlich° sein. Tante Uschi schickt Anna diese Broschüre.

*even*

*dangerous*

### Vorschau

  **21** **Thematische Fragen.** Beantworten Sie die folgenden Fragen auf Deutsch.

1. Haben Sie ein Fahrrad? Fahren Sie mit dem Rad zum Campus oder fahren Sie lieber Auto?
2. Fahren viele Leute an Ihrer Uni mit dem Rad zum Campus? Warum? Warum nicht?
3. Welche Probleme gibt es für Radfahrer auf der Straße? Auf dem Campus? In der Stadt? Auf dem Land?

**22 Satzdetektiv.** Welche Sätze bedeuten ungefähr das Gleiche°? Wählen Sie für jeden Satz **a** oder **b**.

*ungefähr … : about the same*

1. Radfahren ist gesund, es macht Spaß und ist umweltfreundlich.
   a. Radfahren ist nicht gut für die Gesundheit°, ist nicht lustig° und ist nicht gut für den Planeten.
   b. Radfahren ist gut für die Gesundheit, ist lustig und ist gut für den Planeten.

   *health / fun*

2. Das Fahrrad kann man selbst warten und pflegen.
   a. Profi-Mechaniker müssen Fahrrad-Reparaturen machen.
   b. Radfahrer können Fahrrad-Reparaturen selber machen.

3. Das heißt ganz einfach: So fahren, dass man immer bremsen° kann und sein Rad vollständig° beherrscht.
   a. Radfahrer sollen ihr Rad immer unter Kontrolle haben.
   b. Radfahrer sollen so schnell fahren, wie sie wollen.

   *halten*
   *completely*

4. Natürlich müssen Radfahrer Verkehrszeichen° beachten.
   a. Nur Autofahrer müssen Verkehrszeichen verstehen und machen, was auf dem Zeichen steht.
   b. Autofahrer und auch Radfahrer müssen Verkehrszeichen verstehen und machen, was auf dem Zeichen steht.

   *traffic signs*

5. Auf einem gemeinsamen Fuß- und Radweg müssen Radfahrer auf Fußgänger Rücksicht nehmen.
   a. Radfahrer dürfen die Fußgänger auf einem kombinierten Weg nicht ignorieren.
   b. Radfahrer dürfen die Fußgänger ignorieren.

6. Für Radwege°, die mit diesen Zeichen gekennzeichnet sind, besteht Benutzungspflicht.
   a. Radfahrer dürfen hier machen, was sie wollen.
   b. Radfahrer müssen hier machen, was auf dem Verkehrszeichen steht.

   *Fahrradstraßen*

7. Radfahrer müssen immer den rechten Radweg benutzen.
   a. Man soll immer rechts° fahren.
   b. Man kann rechts oder links° fahren.

   *on the right*
   *on the left*

8. Radfahrer dürfen auf „ihren" Straßen auch nebeneinander° fahren.
   a. Auf Fahrradstraßen darf man nebeneinander oder hintereinander Rad fahren.
   b. Auf Fahrradstraßen muss man nebeneinander Rad fahren.

   *next to each other*

## Absprungtext
### FAHRRAD fahren: Sicherheitsinfo Nr. 8

Lesen Sie jetzt den Text.

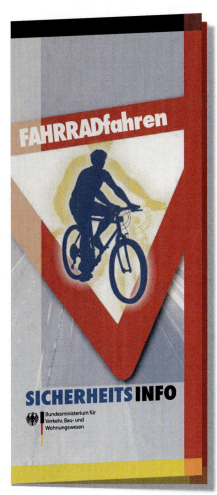

### Radfahren: beliebt, aber auch gefährlich

Radfahren ist gesund, es macht Spaß und ist umweltfreundlich. Wer mit dem Fahrrad fährt, verbraucht kein Öl und Benzin. Das Fahrrad kann man selbst warten und pflegen. Ein Fahrrad braucht wenig Platz. Vieles spricht also für das Radfahren, das immer beliebter° wird. Inzwischen dürfte es in Deutschland rund 75 Millionen Fahrräder geben.

Immer mehr Menschen steigen in ihrer Freizeit aufs Rad oder benutzen es zum Einkauf, auf dem Weg zur Schule oder Arbeit. Radfahren ist allerdings leider° auch nicht ungefährlich.

Das heißt ganz einfach: So fahren, dass man immer bremsen kann und sein Rad vollständig beherrscht. An Bushaltestellen müssen Radfahrer anhalten oder vorsichtig vorbeifahren.

### Verkehrszeichen

Natürlich müssen auch Radfahrer Verkehrszeichen beachten.

Autobahn    Kraftfahrstraße    Verbot für Radfahrer

Fußgängerbereich    Verbot für Fahrzeuge aller Art

### Sonderwege für Radfahrer

Neben reinen Radwegen gibt es auch kombinierte Wege für Fußgänger und Radfahrer. Auf einem gemeinsamen Fuß- und Radweg müssen Radfahrer auf Fußgänger Rücksicht nehmen.

Für Radwege, die mit diesen Zeichen gekennzeichnet sind, besteht Benutzungspflicht:

Sonderweg Radfahrer    Getrennter Rad- und Fußweg    Gemeinsamer Fuß- und Radweg

### Straßen für Radfahrer

Radler° haben jetzt sogar ihre „eigenen" Straßen. Dafür wurde das neue Verkehrszeichen „Fahrradstraße" eingeführt°. Radfahrer dürfen auf „ihren" Straßen auch nebeneinander fahren.

Fahrradstraße    Fahrradstraße

***immer ... :*** *more and more popular*
***leider:*** *unfortunately*

***Radler = Radfahrer***
***eingeführt:*** *introduced*

From **Kapitel 3** on, all of the reading texts in *Vorsprung* were written by native speakers of German for a native speaker audience. This reading activity requires you to skim the text to locate enough information to answer the questions. You are not expected to understand every word or even every sentence. Try to understand the main gist of the reading.

*Rückblick*

**23** **Stimmt das?** Stimmen diese Aussagen zum Text oder nicht? Wenn nicht, was stimmt?

|  | Ja, das stimmt. | Nein, das stimmt nicht. |
|---|---|---|
| 1. Radfahren ist dumm, es macht keinen Spaß und ist ungesund. | ☐ | ☒ |
| 2. Radfahren ist gut für den Planeten. | ☒ | ☐ |
| 3. Radfahrer können das Rad selbst pflegen und reparieren. | ☒ | ☐ |
| 4. Man braucht eine große Garage für ein Fahrrad. | ☐ | ☒ |
| 5. Immer weniger Menschen fahren Rad in Deutschland. | ☐ | ☒ |
| 6. Das Radfahren ist 100 Prozent sicher und ungefährlich. | ☐ | ☒ |
| 7. Ein Radfahrer soll immer bremsen können und das Rad unter Kontrolle haben. | ☒ | ☐ |
| 8. Radfahrer dürfen alle Verkehrszeichen ignorieren – sie sind nur für Autofahrer da. | ☐ | ☒ |
| 9. Auf kombinierten Wegen gibt es Radfahrer und Fußgänger. | ☒ | ☐ |
| 10. Radfahrer sollen rechts fahren, wenn zwei Wege existieren. *not in text* | ☒ | ☐ |
| 11. In Deutschland gibt es keine exklusiven Straßen und Wege für Radfahren. | ☐ | ☒ |

**24** **Kurz gefragt.** Beantworten Sie die folgenden Fragen auf Deutsch.

1. Wer im Deutschkurs hat ein Fahrrad? Welche Farbe hat es?

2. Wo benutzen Studenten ihre Fahrräder: in der Stadt, auf dem Campus, auf dem Land oder zum Extrem-Sport?

3. Halten Sie Radfahren für gesund oder ungesund? Gefährlich oder ungefährlich? Interessant oder uninteressant?

4. Was sollen, Ihrer Meinung nach°, Radfahrer / Radfahrerinnen tragen?
   a. Einen Schal oder einen Sicherheitshelm°?
   b. Shorts oder Jeans?
   c. Handschuhe oder keine Handschuhe?
   d. Turnschuhe oder Sandalen?
   e. Knie- und Ellenbogenschutz° oder nichts?

*Ihrer ... : in your opinion*
*bike helmet*

*Knie ... : knee and elbow pads*

**25** **Interview** Stellen Sie einem Partner / einer Partnerin die folgenden Fragen.

1. Hast du ein Auto? Welche Farbe hat es? Wie alt ist es?
2. Wie viel kostet die Versicherung? das Benzin? das Parken?
3. Hast du ein Fahrrad? Welche Farbe hat es? Wie alt ist es?
4. Kann man hier per Anhalter fahren, oder ist das gefährlich?
5. Fährst du lieber Rad oder Auto? Warum? Und deine Freunde und Familie? Was fahren sie lieber?

A common word for **das Benzin** is **der Sprit.** Gas mileage in Germany is measured in liters / 100 km.

## Fahrschule und Fahrrad fahren

Bicycling is an inexpensive and convenient alternative to owning a car in Germany. The high price of driving in Germany begins with driver's education. To get a driver's license **(der Führerschein)**, applicants must be at least 18 years old to sign up for the required 8 hours of classroom instruction and 35 hours of practice driving with an instructor at a private driving school **(die Fahrschule).** Tuition is steep and includes night driving and driving on **die Autobahn.** After completing driver's education, a first aid course, and an eye test, applicants take a written test and a road test **(die Fahrprüfung).** Only one in three applicants passes the test on the first try. All others have to take more classes before taking the test again. The **Klasse III** license permits drivers to operate a passenger vehicle **(der Personenkraftwagen, der PKW)** for life. Other driving related expenses—including insurance **(die Versicherung),** an automobile tax **(die Autosteuer),** gasoline **(das Benzin),** oil **(das Öl),** parking fees, and the occasional fine **(die Strafe)**—make car ownership very expensive.

Because of urban congestion and the high cost of owning a car, many city dwellers do not own a car. They choose instead to take public transportation or to ride a bicycle or moped, for which they can obtain a license at age 16. Bicycling in the city is not just for speedster couriers; little old ladies with baskets of groceries can be seen almost as often as children and university students on their way to school. Many businesses keep bicycle parking racks out front, and most German cities have their own bicycle paths, separate from the sidewalk, with their own sets of traffic lights!

*Junge Leute dürfen erst mit 18 den Führerschein machen.*

**■ Kulturkreuzung** Fährt man in Ihrem Land lieber Rad oder Auto? Warum ist Autofahren so beliebt und relativ billig? Warum ist es relativ schwierig Fahrrad zu fahren? Ist man umweltbewusst° und warum (nicht)?

*environmentally aware*

## III Expressing permission, prohibition, necessity, and strong desire

Modal verbs (II)

### A. Expressing permission: *dürfen*

The modal verb **dürfen** expresses that an action is permitted. These are the present tense forms of **dürfen.**

| dürfen: *may; to be permitted to* | |
|---|---|
| **Singular** | **Plural** |
| ich **darf** | wir **dürfen** |
| du **darfst** | ihr **dürft** |
| Sie **dürfen** | Sie **dürfen** |
| er/sie/es **darf** | sie **dürfen** |

German speakers use **man darf nicht** and **man darf kein** to indicate that an action is not permitted.

> **Man darf keinen** Alkohol trinken.  *One is not permitted to drink any alcohol.*
>
> Hier **darf man nicht** parken.  *No parking allowed here. (You're not allowed to park here.)*

**26**  **Was bedeutet das Verkehrsschild?**  Verbinden° Sie jeden Satz      *connect*
(unten) mit einem Schild.

a. Autobahn    b. Kraftfahrstraße    c. Fußgängerzone    d. Parkplatz    e. Halteverbot

1. Hier beginnt die Autobahn. Hier darf man schnell fahren. _____
2. Hier dürfen keine Radfahrer und keine Autofahrer fahren. _____
3. Hier darf man parken. _____
4. Hier dürfen nur Autos fahren. _____
5. Hier darf man nicht halten. _____

**27** **Ist das erlaubt°?** Die Klasse hat viele Ideen, wie man Deutsch-lernen leichter machen kann. Aber der Lehrer/die Lehrerin findet diese Ideen nicht immer gut. Spielen Sie Student/Studentin und Lehrer/Lehrerin.

*permitted*

🔸 ich / die Hausaufgaben hin und wieder vergessen?

S1 (STUDENT/STUDENTIN): *Darf ich die Hausaufgaben° hin und wieder vergessen?*
S2 (LEHRER/LEHRERIN): *Nein, Sie dürfen die Hausaufgaben nie vergessen.*

*homework*

1. die anderen Studenten / die Hausaufgaben später machen?
2. alle Studenten / im Deutschkurs Englisch sprechen?
3. die neue Studentin / die Prüfung zu Hause machen?
4. ich / ein Wörterbuch zur Prüfung mitbringen?
5. alle Studenten / heute früher nach Hause gehen?

**28** **Die Regeln° im Deutschunterricht.** Schreiben Sie mit einem Partner/einer Partnerin eine Liste von zehn Regeln für den Deutschunterricht.

*rules*

🔸 *Wir dürfen nicht zu spät kommen.*

zu spät° kommen
Englisch sprechen
Cola trinken
zu dem Professor / die Professorin
　**du** sagen

eine Baseball-Mütze° tragen
die Hausaufgaben vergessen
im Klassenzimmer essen
Kaugummi kauen
?

***zu ...:*** *too late / cap*

## B. Expressing necessity: *müssen*

The modal verb **müssen** expresses necessity. Here are the present tense forms.

| **müssen:** *must, to have to, need to* | |
|---|---|
| **Singular** | **Plural** |
| ich **muss** | wir **müssen** |
| du **musst** | ihr **müsst** |
| Sie **müssen** | Sie **müssen** |
| er/sie/es **muss** | sie **müssen** |

Note that when *must, have to,* and *need to* are negated in English, different German verbs are used for each specific meaning.

You **must not** do that.　　*Das **darfst** du **nicht**.*
You **don't have to** do that.　*Das **brauchst** du **nicht** zu tun.*
You **don't need** to do that.　*Das **musst** du **nicht** tun.*

Unlike **muss nicht,** which states that something need not be done, **darf nicht** expresses a strong prohibition. Thus, *must not* and **muss nicht** have entirely different meanings and should not be confused.

**29** **Was bedeutet das Verkehrsschild?** Verbinden Sie jeden Satz (unten) mit einem Schild (rechts).

a. Kinder    b. Sonderweg Radfahrer

1. Hier muss man halten. _____
2. Hier dürfen nur Radfahrer fahren. _____
3. Hier müssen Fahrräder links fahren und Fußgänger rechts gehen. _____
4. Hier muss man langsam fahren. _____

 **30** **Verkehrsregeln.** Was muss man beim Autofahren tun oder sein?

c. Getrennter Rad- und Fußweg    d. Stop

🟨 bei Rot/Grün halten    *Man muss bei Rot halten.*

1. bei Rot/Grün fahren
2. bei Gelb/Blau aufpassen°
3. im Schulbereich° langsam/schnell fahren
4. im Parkhaus schnell/langsam fahren
5. in der Stadt links/rechts überholen°
6. im Nebel° schnell/vorsichtig° fahren
7. 16/18/21 Jahre alt sein

*pay attention*
*in a school zone*

*pass*
*fog / carefully*

 **31** **Darf ich nicht oder muss ich nicht?** Wählen Sie die beste Antwort.

1. Es ist warm heute.
   a. Du darfst keine Jacke tragen.    b. Du musst keine Jacke tragen.
2. Darf ich hier rauchen°?
   a. Nein, das dürfen Sie nicht.    b. Nein, das müssen Sie nicht.
3. Warum geht Jürgen zur Party?
   a. Er darf heute nicht lernen.    b. Er muss heute nicht lernen.
4. Warum steht sie so spät auf?
   a. Sie muss heute nicht arbeiten.    b. Sie darf heute nicht arbeiten.
5. Was bedeutet das Schild?
   a. Du musst nicht rauchen.    b. Du darfst nicht rauchen.

*smoke*

## C. Expressing strong desire: *wollen*

The modal verb **wollen** expresses a strong desire to do something. Here are the present tense forms.

| **wollen:** *to want to, wish to* | |
|---|---|
| **Singular** | **Plural** |
| ich **will** | wir **wollen** |
| du **willst** | ihr **wollt** |
| Sie **wollen** | Sie **wollen** |
| er/sie/es **will** | sie **wollen** |

**32** **Was wollen Barbara, Karl und Thomas?** Bilden Sie Sätze mit **will** oder **wollen.**

S1: *Barbara hat Hunger. Sie will essen. Und du?*
S2: *Ich will auch essen.* (oder)
   *Ich will nicht essen.*

| | |
|---|---|
| 1. Barbara hat Hunger. | lesen |
| 2. Karl hat Durst. | viel ausgeben |
| 3. Thomas hat seinen Tennisschläger°. | etwas essen |
| 4. Barbara und Karl haben ihre Fahrräder. | Tennis spielen |
| 5. Thomas hat eine englische Zeitung. | etwas trinken |
| 6. Thomas denkt an° seine Familie in den USA. | anrufen |
| 7. Karl nimmt viel Geld mit. | Rad fahren |

*tennis racket*

***denkt ... :*** *thinks about*

## D. Modal verb summary

| Modal verbs summary chart | | |
|---|---|---|
| Permission | **dürfen** | *may; to be permitted to, allowed to* |
| Prohibition | **darf nicht** | *may not; must not* |
| Ability | **können** | *can; to be able to* |
| General fondness *(with nouns only)* | **mögen** | *to like* |
| Immediate desire *(with nouns and verbs)* | **möchte** | *would like* |
| Necessity | **müssen** | *must; to have to* |
| Expected obligation | **sollen** | *should; to be supposed to* |
| Strong desire | **wollen** | *to want to, wish to* |

**33** **Babysitten.** Es ist 6 Uhr abends. Sie sind der Babysitter/die Babysitterin von drei Kindern. Die Kinder sind 3, 10 und 13 Jahre alt. Fragen Sie einen Partner/eine Partnerin, was die Kinder machen dürfen, können, möchten, müssen, sollen oder wollen. Dann informieren Sie sich über Ihren Partner/Ihre Partnerin.

S1: *Was darf die 3-jährige Tochter machen?*    S2: *Sie darf fernsehen.*
S1: *Was darfst du machen?*    S2: *Ich darf ...*

**Tabelle A (S1):**

| | Die 3-jährige Tochter ... | Der 10-jährige Sohn ... | Der 13-jährige Sohn ... | Ich ... |
|---|---|---|---|---|
| **darf** | ? | online gehen | Computer-Spiele spielen | _____ |
| **muss** | um 7 ins Bett gehen | ? | Abendessen kochen | _____ |
| **soll** | ? | Hausaufgaben machen | ? | _____ |
| **kann** | gut sprechen | ? | ? | _____ |
| **möchte** | ? | Freunde anrufen | ein Buch lesen | _____ |
| **will** | im Haus Rad fahren | ? | ? | _____ |

**Tabelle B (S2):**

_(Note: In this information-gap activity the second chart is printed upside down.)_

| | Die 3-jährige Tochter ... | Der 10-jährige Sohn ... | Der 13-jährige Sohn ... | Ich ... |
|---|---|---|---|---|
| **will** | ? | ins Kino gehen | fernsehen | ——— |
| **möchte** | um 9 ins Bett gehen | ? | ? | ——— |
| **kann** | ? | gut schwimmen | gut kochen | ——— |
| **soll** | etwas essen | ? | sein Zimmer aufräumen | ——— |
| **muss** | ? | um 9 zu Hause sein | ? | ——— |
| **darf** | fernsehen | ? | ? | ——— |

> In information-gap activities, the second chart is always printed upside down to encourage you and your partner to communicate orally without reading each other's charts.

## BRENNPUNKT KULTUR

### Mit der Bahn fahren

Germany is much smaller in land area than the U.S. or Canada—it is roughly the size of Montana. For that reason many travelers prefer the convenience of taking a train (**mit der Bahn fahren**) rather than traveling by plane. The German Federal Railway (**DB = Deutsche Bahn AG**), a private enterprise, maintains an extensive rail system, including excellent connections from the Frankfurt airport. Because of the frequent and prompt arrival and departure times, many people prefer to commute to work by train, making the main train station (**der Hauptbahnhof**) a bustling hub of activity in German cities. Young people, students, and retired persons are eligible for substantial discounts for train travel. Non-Europeans can purchase a Eurail Pass, which allows for unlimited first- or second-class rail travel throughout Europe, or a Flexi-Pass, which is valid for a specified number of days over a longer time period.

_Der Hauptbahnhof in Frankfurt: Mit dem Inter-City-Express kann man schnell von Stadt zu Stadt fahren._

**■ Kulturkreuzung** Wie kommen die meisten° Leute von New York nach Chicago, von Vancouver nach Toronto oder von Atlanta nach San Francisco – mit dem Auto, mit der Bahn oder mit dem Flugzeug? Warum? Hat Ihre Stadt einen Hauptbahnhof? Hat Ihre Stadt eine zentrale Stelle, wo sich viele/alle Verkehrsmittel treffen°? Warum? Warum nicht?

*die meisten: most*

*wo ... : where many/all of the means of transportation converge*

**34   Regeln für den Deutschunterricht.**  Lesen Sie die Regeln, und diskutieren Sie sie mit der Klasse. Entscheiden Sie, ob° die Regeln gut oder nicht so gut sind.

*entscheiden ... : decide if*

◻ Man soll im Unterricht nur Deutsch sprechen.

S1: *Ja, das stimmt. Man soll im Unterricht nur Deutsch sprechen.* (oder)
*Nein, das stimmt nicht. Man kann im Unterricht ein bisschen Englisch sprechen.*

1. Man soll im Unterricht nur Deutsch sprechen.
2. Man darf nicht zum Unterricht kommen.
3. Man soll mit anderen Studenten kein Deutsch sprechen.
4. Man soll nicht viele deutsche Bücher lesen.
5. Man darf jeden Tag Deutsch lernen.
6. Man muss die Grammatik nicht lernen.
7. Man soll alle neuen Wörter auswendig lernen°.
8. Man muss viele Fragen stellen.

*auswendig ... : memorize*

**35   Schönes-Wochenende-Ticket.**
Lesen Sie die Broschüre und füllen Sie die Tabelle mit den richtigen Informationen aus.

| Schönes-Wochenende-Ticket | |
|---|---|
| Preis? | 30 Euro |
| Familie? (ja? nein?) | |
| Tag(e)? | |
| Kosten pro Fahrt? | |
| Rabatt° für Automatenkauf oder Internetkauf? | 2 Euro pro Ticket |
| Bahnmöglichkeiten°? | |
| Klasse? | |
| Web-Adresse? | |

*Rabatt: discount*
*Bahnmöglichkeiten: train options*

Preiswert reisen am Wochenende: Natur oder Kultur? Allein, mit der Familie oder mit Freunden? Egal welche Freizeitaktivitäten Sie am Wochenende planen, das Schönes-Wochenende-Ticket für 30 Euro eignet sich ideal für Ihre Wochenendausflüge. Doppelt vorteilhaft: mit Preisnachlass und ganz flexibel erhältlich für 28 Euro an allen DB Fahrkartenautomaten und im Internet unter www.bahn.de/fahrkarten.

Es gilt bundesweit in allen Nahverkehrszügen der Deutschen Bahn (InterRegioExpress [IRE], Regional-Express [RE], RegionalBahn [RB] und S-Bahn [S]) in der 2. Klasse ohne Kilometerbegrenzung. In vielen Verkehrsverbünden können Sie auch S-/U-Bahnen, Straßenbahnen und Busse nutzen.

**Infotipp:** Aktuelle Informationen rund um das Schönes-Wochenende-Ticket finden Sie im Internet unter www.bahn.de/swt.

**36** **Zugverbindungen°.** Sie möchten vom Frankfurter Hauptbahn-    *train connections*
hof zum Münchener Hauptbahnhof fahren.

| Frankfurt(Main)Hbf → München Hbf | | | | | | | Die Bahn DB | |
|---|---|---|---|---|---|---|---|---|
| **Ab** | **Zug** | **Umsteigen** | **An** | **Ab** | **Zug** | | **An** | **Verkehrstage** |
| 4.45 | RB 15241 | Aschaffenburg | 5.40 | 5.45 | IC 2521 🍴 | | 9.21 | Mo - Fr 01 |
| 5.01 | IC 2521 🍴 | | | | | | 9.21 | Mo 02 |
| 5.13 | RE 36001 | Mannheim Hbf | 6.23 | 7.11 | IC 2293 🍴 | | 10.18 | Mo - Sa 03 |
| 5.33 | ICE 991 🍴 | | | | | | 9.21 | täglich |
| 6.19 | IC 2021 | Nürnberg Hbf | 8.24 | 8.28 | ICE 781 🍴 | | 10.14 | Mo - Sa 04 |
| 6.19 | IC 2021 | Regensburg Hbf | 9.24 | 9.44 | RE 26019 | | 11.18 | täglich |
| 6.23 | ICE 1099 R🍴 | | | | | | 9.46 | Mo - Fr 05 |
| 6.44 | EC 52 | Mannheim Hbf | 7.37 | 7.54 | IC 2053 🍴 | | | Mo - Sa 04 |
| | | Stuttgart Hbf | 8.46 | 8.53 | EC 61 🍴 | | 11.13 | |
| 6.50 | ICE 271 🍴 | Mannheim Hbf | 7.28 | 7.31 | ICE 511 🍴 | | 10.25 | täglich |
| 7.13 | ICE 827 🍴 | Würzburg Hbf | 8.26 | 8.31 | ICE 581 🍴 | | 11.00 | So 06 |
| 7.13 | ICE 825 🍴 | Würzburg Hbf | 8.26 | 8.31 | ICE 581 🍴 | | 11.00 | Mo - Sa 04 |
| 7.30 | RE 20095 | Würzburg Hbf | 9.25 | 9.41 | RB 20011 | | | Sa, So 07 |
| | | Treuchtlingen | 11.29 | 11.34 | RE 31237 | | 13.28 | |
| 7.30 | RB 15205 | Frankf(M) Süd | 7.35 | 7.41 | RE 20065 | | | Mo - Fr 01 |
| | | Würzburg Hbf | 9.25 | 9.41 | RB 20011 | | | |
| | | Treuchtlingen | 11.29 | 11.34 | RE 31237 | | 13.28 | |
| 7.50 | ICE 591 🍴 | | | | | | 11.24 | Mo - Sa 08 |
| 8.19 | IC 2295 🍴 | | | | | | 12.18 | täglich |
| 8.50 | ICE 871 🍴 | Mannheim Hbf | 9.28 | 9.31 | ICE 513 🍴 | | 12.25 | täglich |
| 8.57 | Ⓢ 6 | Frankf(M) Süd | 9.07 | 9.20 | ICE 721 🍴 | | | täglich 09 |
| | | Würzburg Hbf | 10.26 | 10.31 | ICE 583 🍴 | | 13.01 | |
| 9.02 | RB 15265 | Frankf(M) Süd | 9.07 | 9.20 | ICE 721 🍴 | | | Mo - Sa 03 |
| | | Würzburg Hbf | 10.26 | 10.31 | ICE 583 🍴 | | 13.01 | |
| 9.05 | ICE 571 🍴 | Stuttgart Hbf | 10.33 | 10.52 | EC 115 🍴 | | 13.14 | Mo - Sa 04 |
| 9.50 | ICE 593 🍴 | | | | | | 13.24 | Sa, So 10 |
| 9.50 | ICE 1091 🍴 | | | | | | 13.24 | Mo - Fr 11 |
| 10.19 | IC 329 🍴 | | | | | | 14.13 | täglich |
| 10.19 | IC 2297 🍴 | | | | | | 14.18 | täglich |

1. Sie fahren um 7.13 Uhr von Frankfurt ab. Um wie viel Uhr kommen Sie in
   München an?
2. Sie haben um 12 Uhr Mittag ein Treffen° bei BMW in München. Wann kön-    *meeting*
   nen Sie spätestens° abfahren, damit Sie rechtzeitig° zum Treffen in München    *at the latest /*
   ankommen?    *on time*
3. Sie möchten am Sonntag gegen 10 Uhr nach München fahren. Um wie viel
   Uhr fährt der Zug am Sonntag?
4. Sie wollen nach München fahren. Sie fahren um 6.44 Uhr von Frankfurt ab.
   Wo müssen Sie umsteigen°?    *change trains*
5. Können Sie im Zug etwas zu essen kaufen?
6. Können Sie am Samstag mit dem Zug fahren?

**37** **Eine Reise planen.** Spielen Sie diese Situation mit einem Partner/einer Partnerin.

Drehscheibe Frankfurt.
Hier ballt sich der Verkehr.

**S1:** *Tourist (Touristin)*

Sie planen eine Reise im Sommer nach Spanien (Mexiko, Österreich usw.). Sie haben wenig Geld und viel Zeit, und Sie möchten viel sehen.

1. Ich möchte nach ... fahren.
2. Wann soll ich nach ... fahren?
3. Was kann ich in ... machen?
4. Was soll ich in ... sehen?
5. Was kann ich in ... essen?
6. Was soll ich in ... trinken?
7. Was muss ich in ... nicht machen?
8. Was darf ich in ... nicht machen?

**S2:** *Experte (Expertin)*

Sie kennen Spanien (Mexiko, Österreich usw.) gut. Geben Sie viele Reisetipps.

1. a.  Das ist eine gute Idee!
   b.  Das ist eine schlechte Idee! Fahr doch lieber nach ... !
2. Fahr doch im Januar.
3. am Strand° liegen (Sehenswürdigkeiten besuchen, Ski laufen, schwimmen, Rad fahren, Leute kennen lernen, tanzen usw.)
4. das Museum (das Schloss, die Altstadt usw.)
5. das Brot (das Obst, den Kuchen usw.)
6. den Kaffee (den Wein, das Bier usw.)
7. dein Zimmer aufräumen (Hausaufgaben machen, zur Uni gehen, arbeiten usw.)
8. gefährliche° Wanderungen° machen (das Wasser trinken, zu lange in der Sonne° liegen, viel Geld ausgeben usw.)

*on the beach*

*dangerous / hikes*
*sun*

## Wissenswerte Vokabeln: Eigenschaften
### Identifying personal characteristics

freundlich/unfreundlich

sportlich/unsportlich

locker/steif

offen (gesellig)/schüchtern

selbstsicher/unsicher (nervös)

ruhig/laut

kreativ/einfallslos          musikalisch/unmusikalisch          klug (intelligent)/dumm

heiter (lustig)/ernst          fleißig/faul          sympathisch/unsympathisch

interessant/langweilig          glücklich/unglücklich

🟧 Ist Anna glücklich?      *Ja, sie ist glücklich.*
   Ist Anna unglücklich?   *Nein, sie ist nicht unglücklich.*

*Künstlerisch*

**38**   **Katja ist freundlich.** Welche Adjektive beschreiben° Katja,      *describe*
welche beschreiben Georg?

🟧 *Katja mag andere Leute und hat viele Freunde. Sie ist freundlich.*

Katja ...

1. mag andere Leute und hat viele Freunde. Sie ...
2. kann Klavier spielen. Sie ...
3. kann gut Tennis und Fußball spielen. Sie ...
4. geht gern auf Partys. Sie ...

Georg ...

5. kann Physik verstehen. Er ...
6. macht immer Hausaufgaben. Er ...
7. kann gut zeichnen°. Er ...      *sketch*
8. ist informell in formellen Situationen. Er ...

**39**  **Georg ist nicht dumm!**  Beschreiben Sie, wie diese Personen wirklich sind. Benutzen Sie Argumente aus der Liste.

> S1: *Katja denkt, Georg ist dumm.*
> S2: *Georg ist nicht dumm, sondern klug. Er kann Mathematik verstehen und Spanisch sprechen.*

kann gut Witze° erzählen° • kann 60 Meter in sieben Sekunden laufen • kann Spanisch sprechen • möchte oft allein sein • will immer singen • will nie laut sprechen • muss oft lachen • möchte immer Hausaufgaben machen • kann fantastisch Klavier spielen • möchte jeden Tag schwimmen • kann Mathematik verstehen • will immer nur arbeiten

*jokes / tell*

1. KATJA: Georg ist dumm.
2. GEORG: Anna ist faul.
3. ANNA: Onkel Hannes ist ernst.
4. ANNA: Jeff ist unsportlich.
5. HANNES: Uschi ist laut.
6. HANNELORE: Bob ist unmusikalisch.

**40**  **Zwanzig Fragen: Wie heißt er/sie?**  Bilden Sie Gruppen von vier bis fünf Personen. Ein Student/Eine Studentin denkt an eine prominente Person. Die anderen Studenten/Studentinnen stellen maximal zwanzig Fragen. Hier sind einige Fragen:

Ist es eine Frau?  Ist sie tot°?  *dead*
Ist sie kreativ?  Kann sie Klavier spielen?

> S1: *Ich denke an eine Person. Der Name beginnt mit B.*
> S2: *Ist es ein Mann?*

## IV Expressing spatial movement, the recipient of something, opposition, and omission

### Prepositions with the accusative

German has a group of five prepositions that are always followed by the accusative case.

| | | | |
|---|---|---|---|
| **durch** | *through* | **ohne** | *without* |
| **für** | *for* | **um** | *around* |
| **gegen** | *against* | | |

1. **für:** German speakers use the preposition **für** to denote a recipient.

   Anna bringt ein Geschenk **für** die Günthers.   *Anna is bringing a present for the Günthers.*

2. **ohne:** Omission is expressed with the preposition **ohne.**

   Anna kommt **ohne** ihr Fahrrad.   *Anna is coming without her bicycle.*

3. **durch, um:** Spatial movement is expressed in German with the prepositions **durch** and **um.**

   Anna geht **durch** das Zimmer.   *Anna is walking through the room.*
   Anna geht **um** den Tisch.   *Anna is walking around the table.*

   As you learned in **Kapitel 2, um** is also used in time expressions, e.g., **um drei Uhr.**

> The word **doof** is often used for **dumm** to characterize a person as *goofy.*

**4. gegen:** Opposition to an action or an object is expressed with the preposition **gegen.**

Papa hat nichts **gegen** meine Reise.    *Papa has nothing against my trip.*

**Gegen** can also be used to express a position against something concrete or abstract.

| | |
|---|---|
| Das Auto fährt **gegen** das Fahrrad. | *The car is driving into the bicycle.* |
| Mein warmer Pullover hält mich warm **gegen** den kalten Wind. | *My warm sweater keeps me warm in a cold wind.* |
| Nächste Woche spielen sie Fußball **gegen** uns. | *Next week, they're playing soccer against us.* |

**Gegen** is also used in time expressions to express approximate time.

**gegen** drei Uhr    *around three o'clock*

**41   Geschenke.** Für wen bringt Anna die Geschenke? Für ihre Kusine, ihren Cousin, ihren Onkel oder ihre Tante? Was sagt Anna?

◻ *Katja liest gern. Das Buch ist für meine Kusine.*

1. Katja liest gern. E.
2. Georg kann gut zeichnen. C.
3. Tante Uschi mag Musik. D.
4. Onkel Hannes will Spanisch lernen. B.
5. Katja kann gut Tennis. A.

a. die Tennisbälle
b. das spanisch-deutsche Wörterbuch
c. der Zeichenblock°          *drawing pad*
d. die CDs
e. das Buch

**42   Mutters Hilfe.** Annas Mutter hilft Anna beim Packen. Im Flugzeug hat Anna aber nicht viel Platz. Ohne welche Sachen kann Anna fahren oder nicht fahren? Bilden Sie Sätze mit **ohne.**

◻ S1:  *Hier sind deine Rollerblades, Anna.*
  S2:  *Ach, Mutti, ich kann ohne meine Rollerblades fahren.*
  S1:  *Hier ist dein Laptop, Anna.*
  S2:  *Danke, Mutti, ich kann ohne meinen Laptop nicht fahren.*

1. deine Rollerblades
2. dein Laptop
3. dein Pass
4. deine Bordkarte
5. dein Handy

6. deine Kamera
7. deine Deutschbücher
8. dein Fahrrad
9. deine Zahnbürste
10. deine Wasserflasche°          *water bottle*

**43   Was passiert in Annas Leben?** Schreiben Sie eine passende Präposition (**durch, für, gegen, ohne, um**) in die Lücke.

1. Anna fliegt _ohne_ ihre Eltern nach Deutschland.
2. Hannelore hat viele Ratschläge _für_ Anna.
3. Hannelore ist _gegen_ Cola und Geldausgeben.
4. In Deutschland muss Anna _durch_ den Zoll°.          *customs*
5. Anna gibt gern Geld _für_ Andenken aus.
6. Anna kommt _durch_ die Tür.

**Freie Kommunikation**

**Rollenspiel: Eine Abschiedsparty°.** Annas Deutschklasse in Indiana plant eine Abschiedsparty für Anna. Diskutieren Sie die Details für die Party (Essen, Trinken, Aktivitäten usw.) in kleinen Gruppen. Benutzen Sie diese Ausdrücke:

*bon voyage party*

> Wer kann ...? • Wer soll ...? • Wer möchte ...? • Wer will ...? • Kannst du ...? • Möchtest du ...?

  **Schreibecke**

**Das Fotoalbum.** Die Günthers sehen sich Annas Familienfotos im Fotoalbum an. Hier spricht Frau Günther über ihre Schwester Hannelore in Indiana. Lesen Sie, was Tante Uschi sagt, und schreiben Sie dann etwas über Ihre Schwester (Ihren Bruder, einen Cousin/eine Kusine, einen Freund/eine Freundin). Benutzen Sie Tante Uschis Aussagen als Beispiele.

*in ... : in some ways*

In mancher Hinsicht° sind meine Schwester und ich gleich:

> Ich bin groß und schlank und sie auch.
> Ich habe braune Augen und braunes Haar und sie auch.
> Ich habe einen Mann und eine Familie und sie auch.
> Ich habe einen Sohn und eine Tochter und sie auch.
> Ich bin relativ ruhig und sie auch.

Und in mancher Hinsicht sind meine Schwester und ich verschieden°:

*different*

> Ich mag klassische Musik, aber sie nicht.
> Ich bin unsportlich, aber sie ist sehr sportlich.
> Ich bin relativ unsicher, aber sie ist sehr selbstsicher.
> Sie ist sehr locker und lustig, aber ich bin relativ steif und ernst.
> Sie ist sehr offen und gesellig, aber ich bin schüchtern.

  **Schreibecke**

**Eine Zeitungsannonce.** Suchen Sie einen Freund/eine Freundin durch die Zeitung. Schreiben Sie eine Anzeige° und sagen Sie, wie diese ideale Person sein soll.

*want ad*

🟨 *Ich suche einen Freund/eine Freundin. Er/Sie muss intelligent sein. Er/Sie soll viel Kaffee trinken. Er/Sie soll kein Bier trinken. Er/Sie soll nur vegetarisch essen usw.*

**Zieltext**    # Endlich unterwegs!°

Anna ist endlich unterwegs nach Deutschland. Hier kommt sie am Flughafen in Frankfurt an. Die Günthers holen Anna ab°. In dem Dialog sprechen die Günthers zuerst über Anna. Anna trifft° die Günthers. Sie sprechen kurz miteinander° und dann fahren sie alle nach Hause.

*Endlich unterwegs: Finally, on the way!*
**holen ... :** *pick Anna up*
*meets*
*with each other*

## Vorschau

 **44** **Thematische Fragen.** Beantworten Sie die folgenden Fragen.

1. Wo kommen Passagiere im Flughafen an?
   a. in Halle A
   b. beim Abflug°                                        *departure*
   c. an der Ankunft

2. Durch welche Kontrolle müssen ankommende Auslands-Passagiere *nicht* gehen?
   a. durch die Passkontrolle
   b. durch die Bordkartenkontrolle
   c. durch die Zollkontrolle

3. Passagiere müssen ihre Koffer selbst _____.
   a. holen°                                              *retrieve, pick up*
   b. kaufen
   c. vergessen

4. Was kann man als Geschenk für einen Gast zum Flughafen bringen?
   a. einen Computer
   b. eine Hose
   c. Rosen

5. Was kann man für einen Gast im Flughafen machen, wenn man helfen will?
   a. Koffer tragen
   b. ein Taxi rufen
   c. das Flugticket kaufen

6. Wo parkt man Autos am Flughafen?
   a. im Park
   b. im Parkhaus
   c. auf der Straße

**45** **Zur Orientierung.** Schauen Sie sich die Zeichnung° zum Zieltext     *sketch*
an und beantworten Sie diese Fragen.

1. Wie viele Personen sind da? Wer sind diese Personen?
2. Wo sind die Personen: auf der Uni? auf einem Bahnhof? auf einem Flughafen?
3. Was machen sie: essen, warten, schlafen, sprechen?

**46** **Satzdetektiv.** Welche Sätze bedeuten ungefähr das Gleiche?

1. Wie können wir sie denn **erkennen?** *E*
2. Das kann nicht mehr so lange **dauern.** *b*
3. Anna muss durch den **Zoll.** *A*
4. Gib ihr doch die **Blumen!** *C*
5. Wie war dein **Flug?** *D*

    a. Anna muss durch die Kontrolle gehen.
    b. Das kann nicht so lange sein.
    c. Gib ihr die Rosen!
    d. Wie war deine Reise?
    e. Wie wissen wir, wer Anna ist?

6. Ich bin jetzt **todmüde.** *G*
7. Du **siehst wirklich aus wie** Hannelore. *I*
8. Tu die Koffer da in den **Kofferraum.** *F*
9. Wir müssen erst die **Parkgebühr bezahlen.** *H*

    f. Stell die Taschen und Koffer hinten° ins Auto.    *in the rear*
    g. Ich bin extrem müde°.    *tired*
    h. Man muss für das Parken Geld ausgeben.
    i. Du und Hannelore sehen sehr ähnlich° aus.    *similar*

## BRENNPUNKT KULTUR

### Frankfurt am Main

Frankfurt am Main, located in the heart of Germany, on the banks of the Main River (**der Main**) in the state of Hesse (**Hessen**), is both the geographic crossroads of the country and one of its key economic centers. As the major gateway to Germany and the nation's most important transportation center, Frankfurt is home to Europe's busiest international airport, **der Frankfurter Flughafen,** and to the German international airline **Deutsche Lufthansa,** as well as to the German Federal Railway, **die Deutsche Bahn.** Frankfurt is also the hub of the German business community: the German federal bank (**die Bundesbank**), the national stock market (**die Börse**), and many large corporations and publishing houses. In recognition of the city's important role in international finance, the Monetary Institute of the European Community (**Europäisches Währungsinstitut**) and the central bank of the European Community (**EZB = die Europäische Zentralbank**) are situated in Frankfurt.

   Frankfurt is also a center of German culture and history. Germany's most famous author, Johann Wolfgang von Goethe, was born in Frankfurt am Main. In 1848 Frankfurt was the site of the first attempt to establish a united German nation through a representative assembly. Frankfurt's university is renowned for its reputation in the social sciences, reflecting a long, liberal tradition in **Hessen.**

   The people of Frankfurt enjoy a lively theater, opera, and music season, along with some of the best jazz in Germany. They relax by visiting the numerous museums along the Main River (**das Museumsufer**), taking their children to the world-class **Frankfurter Zoo,** spending a day in the glass-enclosed **Palmengarten** terrarium, and sipping the popular local apple wine (**Äppelwoi**) in the cozy pubs of Sachsenhausen, the part of Frankfurt that is most famous for its ambience.

*Der Römer in Frankfurt am Main: Diese junge Familie geht mit ihrem Kind spazieren.*

■ **Kulturkreuzung** Welche Städte in den USA oder in Kanada kann man mit Frankfurt vergleichen°? Wo ist die Börse in Kanada? In den USA? Wo ist der größte° Flughafen in den USA? In Kanada? Wie heißt der/die bekannteste Schriftsteller(in)° von Kanada? Von den USA?

*compare*
*largest*
**bekannteste ... :** *most famous writer*

## Zieltext
### Endlich unterwegs!

 **47  Erstes Zuhören.**  Lesen Sie die folgenden Fragen, bevor Sie den Dialog anhören.

1. Wie sollen die Günthers Anna erkennen? Was hat sie?
2. Was sagen die Günthers, wenn Anna endlich ankommt?
3. Wie geht es Anna? Was will sie jetzt machen?

Hören Sie sich den Dialog jetzt an und beantworten Sie die Fragen.

Hören Sie sich den Dialog noch einmal° an, um mehr zu verstehen.

*noch ... : again*

## Rückblick

**48  Was hören Sie wann?**  Bringen Sie diese Sätze aus dem Text in die richtige Reihenfolge°.

*order*

<u>4</u>  Georg, gib ihr doch die Blumen!
<u>2</u>  Hat sie nicht so einen lila Rucksack?
<u>1</u>  Da vorne steht's: Ankunft.
<u>5</u>  Hier, links, gehen wir zum Parkhaus.
<u>3</u>  Da kommen die ersten Leute 'raus.

> Complete the **Ergänzen Sie** activity in your workbook for this text before doing the next activity.

**49  Stimmt das?**  Stimmen diese Aussagen zum Text oder nicht? Wenn nicht, was stimmt?

|  | Ja, das stimmt. | Nein, das stimmt nicht. |
|---|---|---|
| 1. Katja sieht das Schild „Ankunft". | ☒ | ☐ |
| 2. Anna soll einen lila Rucksack tragen. | ☒ | ☐ |
| 3. Anna soll lange braune Haare haben. | ☐ | ☒ |
| 4. Anna muss durch den Zoo. | ☐ | ☒ |
| 5. Georg hat Blumen für Anna. | ☒ | ☐ |
| 6. Anna ist todmüde nach dem Flug. | ☒ | ☐ |
| 7. Anna trägt die Koffer zum Parkhaus. | ☐ | ☒ |
| 8. Anna soll vorne im Auto sitzen; da hat sie mehr Platz. | ☒ | ☐ |

**50** **Wer muss/will/soll was?** Hören Sie sich den Dialog noch einmal an und bilden Sie dann Sätze über die Situation am Flughafen.

 *Die Günthers können Anna erkennen.*

| Die Günthers | sollen (müssen, können) | Anna erkennen. |
|---|---|---|
| Anna | soll (muss, kann) | das Gepäck holen. |
| Onkel Hannes | | durch den Zoll gehen. |
| Tante Uschi | | Annas Koffer tragen. |
| Katja | | die Parkgebühr bezahlen. |
| Georg | | Anna Blumen geben. |

die Koffer in den Kofferraum
    stellen°.              *put*
warten°.              *wait*
das Schild sehen.

 **51** **Kurz gefragt.** Beantworten Sie diese Fragen auf Deutsch.

1. Warum müssen die Günthers lange auf Anna warten?
2. Wie fühlt sich° Anna nach° dem Flug?          *fühlt ... : feels / after*
3. Wie fahren die Günthers nach Weinheim zurück?
4. Wo sitzt Anna im Wagen? Warum?
5. Wer hat ein Geschenk für wen?

 **F r e i e  K o m m u n i k a t i o n**

**Mutter/Vater und Tochter/Sohn.** Machen Sie dieses Rollenspiel mit einem Partner/einer Partnerin: Ihr Sohn/Ihre Tochter fährt bald nach Frankfurt. Welche Ratschläge haben Sie für ihn/sie? Wie reagiert Ihr Sohn/Ihre Tochter auf die Ratschläge?

S1 (MUTTER/VATER): *Sprich nicht mit Fremden!*
S2 (SOHN/TOCHTER): *Was? Ich soll nicht mit Fremden sprechen?*
                 *Wie kann ich neue Leute kennen lernen?*
S1 (MUTTER/VATER): *Geh auf die Uni und sprich nur mit den*
                 *Professoren und mit Studenten.*

 **S c h r e i b e c k e**

**Anna im Flugzeug.** Sie sind Anna im Flugzeug nach Frankfurt. Das Flugzeug landet in einer Stunde. Sie wissen, Sie sehen bald Ihre Verwandten und müssen dann Deutsch sprechen. Sie sind ein bisschen nervös. Was können Sie wohl sagen? Machen Sie sich zu den folgenden Fragen Notizen°.       *notes*

1. Was sollen Sie in Deutschland machen? Was denken Sie? Was denken Ihre Eltern?
2. Was dürfen Sie in Deutschland nicht machen? Was denken Sie? Und Ihre Eltern?
3. Wie fühlen Sie sich jetzt?
4. Was wollen Sie machen, sobald° Sie in Weinheim sind?       *as soon as*

# Wortschatz

### Die Reise

**das Adressbuch, ¨er** *address book*
**das Andenken, -** *souvenir*
**die Bahn** *railroad*
**die Bordkarte, -n** *boarding pass*
**der Brief, -e** *letter*
**der Flug, ¨e** *flight*
**der Flughafen, ¨** *airport*
**der Flugschein, -e** *airline ticket*
**das Flugzeug, -e** *airplane*
**das Geschenk, -e** *gift*
**der Hauptbahnhof, ¨e** *main train station*
**der Pass (Reisepass), ¨e** *passport*
**der Platz, ¨e** *seat, place; space, room*
**die Reise, -n** *trip*
**der Zug, ¨e** *train*

**mit der Bahn fahren** *to travel by train*
**per Anhalter fahren (er fährt per Anhalter)** *to hitchhike*
**unterwegs** *underway*

### Das Gepäck

**die Handtasche, -n** *handbag, purse*
**der Koffer, -** *suitcase, trunk*
**der Kulturbeutel, -** *cosmetics / toiletries case*
**der Rucksack, ¨e** *backpack*
**die Tasche, -n** *bag*

### Die Kleidung

**der Anzug, ¨e** *suit*
**der Badeanzug, ¨e** *(woman's) bathing suit*
**die Badehose, -n** *(man's) bathing suit*
**die Bluse, -n** *blouse*
**der Handschuh, -e** *glove*
**das Hemd, -en** *shirt*
**die Hose, -n** *trousers, pants*
**die Jacke, -n** *jacket*

**die Jeans** *(pl.) jeans*
**das Kleid, -er** *dress*
**die Kleidung, -en** *clothing, clothes*
**die Krawatte, -n** *tie*
**der Mantel, ¨** *overcoat*
**der Pullover, -s** *pullover sweater*
**der Rock, ¨e** *skirt*
**der/das Sakko, -s** *sports jacket*
**die Sandale, -n** *sandal*
**der Schal, -s** *scarf*
**der Schuh, -e** *shoe*
**die Socke, -n** *sock*
**der Stiefel, -** *boot*
**die Strumpfhose, -n** *panty hose, stockings*
**das T-Shirt, -s** *tee-shirt*
**die Unterwäsche** *(pl.) underwear*

### Die Toilettenartikel

**das Deo, -s** *deodorant*
**die Haarbürste, -n** *hair brush*
**der Kamm, ¨e** *comb*
**der Lippenstift, -e** *lipstick*
**der Nagellack** *nail polish*
**der Spiegel, -** *mirror*
**die Zahnbürste, -n** *toothbrush*
**die Zahnpasta, -pasten** *toothpaste*

### Persönliche Gegenstände

**die Bankkarte, -n** *bank card, ATM card*
**die CD, -s** *CD*
**der CD-Player, -** *CD player*
**der Gegenstand, ¨e** *object*
**das Geld, -er** *money*
**das Handy, -s** *cell phone*
**die (digitale) Kamera, -s** *(digital) camera*
**die Kreditkarte, -n** *credit card*
**der Laptop, -s** *laptop computer*
**das Portmonee, -s** *wallet*
**das Wörterbuch, ¨er** *dictionary*

### Die Eigenschaften

**die Eigenschaft, -en** *personal trait, quality, characteristic*

**doof** *goofy*
**dumm** *dumb*
**einfallslos** *uncreative*
**ernst** *serious*
**faul** *lazy*
**fleißig** *hardworking, industrious; busy*
**gesellig** *gregarious, sociable*
**glücklich** *happy*
**heiter** *funny, cheerful*
**intelligent** *intelligent*
**interessant** *interesting*
**kreativ** *creative*
**laut** *loud, noisy*
**locker** *relaxed, cool*
**lustig** *funny, jovial*
**müde** *tired*
**musikalisch** *musical*
**nervös** *nervous*
**offen** *open*
**ruhig** *quiet, peaceful, calm*
**schüchtern** *shy*
**selbstsicher** *self-assured*
**sportlich** *athletic*
**steif** *stiff, ill-at-ease*
**sympathisch** *likeable, pleasant, nice*
**tot** *dead*
**unfreundlich** *unfriendly*
**unglücklich** *unhappy*
**unmusikalisch** *unmusical*
**unsicher** *unsure, insecure*
**unsportlich** *unathletic*
**unsympathisch** *unlikeable, disagreeable*

### Radfahren, Autos und Verkehr

**das Auto, -s** *automobile, car*
**die Autobahn, -en** *autobahn, freeway*

**der (Auto)bus** *bus*
**das Benzin** *gasoline*
**das Fahrrad, ̈-er** *bicycle*
**der Führerschein, -e** *driver's license*
**der Fußgänger, -** *pedestrian*
**der Radfahrer, - / die Radfahrerin,
  -nen** *cyclist, bicycle rider*
**die Regel, -n** *rule, regulation*
**der Sicherheitshelm** *safety helmet*
**das Verbot, -e** *ban, prohibition*
**der Verkehr** *traffic*
**das Verkehrszeichen, -** *traffic sign*
**der Wagen, -** *car*
**der Weg, -e** *path*
  **der Fußweg** *footpath*
  **der Radweg** *bicycle path*

**gefährlich** *dangerous*
**langsam** *slow*
**links** *left*
**rechts** *right*
**schnell** *fast*

### Akkusativpräpositionen

**durch** *through*
**für** *for*
**gegen** *against; around (a time)*
**ohne** *without*
**um** *around; at (a time)*

### Modalverben

**dürfen (er darf)** *may; to be allowed
  to, permitted to*
  **ich darf nicht** *I must not*
**können (er kann)** *can; to be able to*

**möchte (ich möchte, du möchtest,
  er/sie möchte,** *etc.) would like to
  (immediate relevance)*
**mögen (ich mag, du magst, er/sie
  mag,** *etc.) to like (a thing, a person)
  (generally)*
**müssen (er muss)** *must; to have to,
  be required to*
  **ich muss nicht** *I don't need to*
**sollen** *should, ought to; to be supposed to*
**wollen (er will)** *to want to*

### Andere Verben

**auf·passen** *to pay attention*
**aus·geben (er gibt aus)** *to spend
  (money)*
**bedeuten** *to mean, have the meaning of*
**benutzen** *to use*
**beschreiben** *to describe*
**bezahlen** *to pay*
**brauchen** *to need*
  **ich brauche nicht** *I don't have to*
**denken** *to think*
  **denken an ...** *to think about ...*
**helfen (er hilft)** *to help*
**mit·nehmen (er nimmt mit)** *to take
  (something) along*
**packen** *to pack*
**schicken** *to send*

### Andere Wörter

**besonders** *especially*
**genug** *enough*

**gleich** *similar, same*
**leider** *unfortunately*
**mal** *once*
**neu** *new*
**nie** *never*
**niemand** *nobody, no one*
**noch** *still; again*
**oft** *often*
**spät (später)** *late (later)*
  **spätestens** *at the latest*
**ungefähr** *approximately*
**vorsichtig** *careful*
**wichtig** *important*
**ziemlich** *somewhat*

### Andere Ausdrücke

**das heißt (d.h.)** *that is (to say)*
**hin und wieder** *now and then*
**Mach dir keine Sorgen!** *Don't worry.*
**noch einmal** *once again*

### Meine eigenen Wörter

_____
_____
_____
_____
_____
_____

# Freundschaften

**In this chapter you will learn how to talk about events in the past, about personal relationships, the weather, and the seasons.**

## Kommunikative Funktionen

- Talking about past events
- Describing weather conditions and seasons
- Describing personal relationships
- Expressing what you know and don't know
- Expanding on an opinion or idea
- Giving reasons
- Positioning information in a German sentence
- Talking about activities that continue from the past into the present

## Strukturen

- The conversational past
- The verbs **kennen** and **wissen**
- Subordinate clauses with **ob, dass, weil,** and **zu** + infinitive
- Word order: subject-verb inversion, two-part verbs, and verb forms in subordinate clauses
- Present tense verbs with **seit, schon,** and **erst**

## Vokabeln

- Das Wetter
- Die Jahreszeiten
- Freundschaft und Liebe

## Kulturelles

- Hansestadt Hamburg
- **Bekannte** oder **Freunde?**

■ Zwei gute Freundinnen lachen beim Eis essen.

**Online Study Center**

Go to the *Vorsprung* Website at *http://college.hmco.com/pic/vorsprung2e.*

## Anlauftext    Die Geschichte von Tante Uschi und Onkel Hannes

Onkel Hannes und Tante Uschi sitzen an einem Abend mit Anna zu Hause in Weinheim und sprechen über ihre Studienzeit in Hamburg. Hier erzählen° sie Anna, wie sie sich kennen gelernt haben.

*tell*

### Vorschau

**1   Thematische Fragen: Meine Jobs.**  Viele Studenten müssen arbeiten° und ihr Studium selbst° finanzieren. Kreuzen Sie die Jobs an, die Sie auch schon° gehabt haben. Bei welchen Jobs trifft° man interessante Leute°?

*work / themselves*
*already / meets / people*

|  | Meine Jobs | Jobs mit interessanten Leuten |  |
|---|---|---|---|
| 1. in einer Kneipe° als Kellner(in)° arbeiten | ☐ | ☐ | *pub / waiter (waitress)* |
| 2. in der Bibliothek° arbeiten | ☐ | ☐ | *library* |
| 3. in einem Geschäft° arbeiten | ☐ | ☐ | *store* |
| 4. in einem Krankenhaus° arbeiten | ☐ | ☐ | *hospital* |
| 5. Pizza ausfahren° | ☐ | ☐ | *deliver* |
| 6. Nachhilfestunden geben° | ☐ | ☐ | **Nachhilfestunden … :** *to tutor* |
| 7. im Restaurant kochen | ☐ | ☐ | |
| 8. babysitten | ☐ | ☐ | |
| 9. Karten spielen und Geld gewinnen | ☐ | ☐ | |
| 10. Taxi fahren | ☐ | ☐ | |

**2   Kennen lernen.**  Sie finden jemanden attraktiv. Was machen Sie?

|  | Das mache ich. | Das mache ich nicht. |  |
|---|---|---|---|
| 1. etwas fallen lassen° | ☐ | ☐ | **fallen lassen:** *to drop* |
| 2. viel Bier trinken | ☐ | ☐ | |
| 3. tolle° Kleider tragen | ☐ | ☐ | *cool* |
| 4. freundlich sein | ☐ | ☐ | |
| 5. die Person direkt ansprechen | ☐ | ☐ | |
| 6. wild tanzen | ☐ | ☐ | |
| 7. viel Geld ausgeben | ☐ | ☐ | |
| 8. etwas Intelligentes sagen° | ☐ | ☐ | *say* |
| 9. Komplimente machen | ☐ | ☐ | |
| 10. anstarren° und warten | ☐ | ☐ | *stare* |

**3   Zeitdetektiv.**  Hier sind Sätze im Präsens. Welche Sätze im Perfekt° bedeuten ungefähr das gleiche?

*conversational past*

| Präsens | Perfekt | |
|---|---|---|
| 1. Du hast eine Erkältung°. *B* | a. Er hat nie Trinkgeld gegeben. | *cold* |
| 2. Du tust mir Leid°. *D* | b. Du hast eine Erkältung gehabt. | *I feel sorry for you.* |
| 3. Er gibt nie Trinkgeld°. *A* | c. Ich war in Tante Uschi verliebt. | *tips* |
| 4. Danach heiraten° wir. *E* | d. Du hast mir Leid getan. | *marry* |
| 5. Ich bin in Tante Uschi verliebt°. *C* | e. Danach haben wir geheiratet. | *in love* |

*Präsens*

6. Er küsst° mich. ⏴*I*

7. Er sieht gut aus. ⏴*H*

8. Ich gehe oft in die Kneipe. ⏴*G*

9. Wir verbringen viel Zeit miteinander. ⏴*J*

10. Ich lade sie ins Theater ein. ⏴*F*

*Perfekt*

f. Ich habe sie ins Theater eingeladen.

g. Ich bin oft in die Kneipe gegangen.

h. Er hat gut ausgesehen.

i. Er hat mich geküsst.

j. Wir haben viel Zeit miteinander verbracht.

*kisses*

> **Zeitdetektiv.** You will learn how to form the conversational past later in this chapter. For now, recognizing it is sufficient.

 **4**  **Gegensätze.**  Finden Sie das Wort mit der umgekehrten° Bedeutung.

*opposite*

🟨  Geld verdienen  *Geld ausgeben*

1. ganz schlimm ⏴*E*
2. dort ⏴*D*
3. zusammen ⏴*A*
4. bald ⏴*B*
5. arbeiten ⏴*C*

a. allein

b. später

c. spielen

d. hier

e. sehr gut

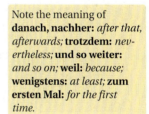

> Note the meaning of **danach, nachher:** *after that, afterwards;* **trotzdem:** *nevertheless;* **und so weiter:** *and so on;* **weil:** *because;* **wenigstens:** *at least;* **zum ersten Mal:** *for the first time.*

## *Anlauftext*

  Hören Sie gut zu. ⏴*15*

> **War** (*was*) is frequently used in speech.

Und dann habe ich sie eines Tages ins Theater eingeladen, und nachher haben wir zusammen ein Bier getrunken. Wir haben leidenschaftlich diskutiert ...

Ja, aber nach dem zweiten Bier war ich etwas mutiger.

Leidenschaftlich diskutiert? Du warst so nervös, du hast keine drei Worte gesagt.

Und später haben wir einen romantischen Spaziergang an der Alster gemacht. Dort haben wir einander zum ersten Mal geküsst.

Romantisch, sagst du? Es hat die ganze Zeit geregnet, und du hast eine ganz schlimme Erkältung gehabt.

Aber du hast mich trotzdem geküsst!

Ich habe dich nur geküsst, weil du mir so Leid getan hast.

Na, trotzdem ... Von da an haben wir viel Zeit miteinander verbracht. Wir haben oft zusammen gekocht und gegessen und sind auch abends ausgegangen.

Und sonntags sind wir immer zum Fischmarkt gegangen ...

Ja, wir haben tolle Nächte in St. Pauli durchgemacht. Getanzt, getrunken und so weiter ...

... und an der Elbe spazieren gegangen.

*Rückblick*

**Sprache im Alltag: Article with first names**

German speakers frequently use a definite article with first names to signal familiarity.

**Die Uschi** hat als Kellnerin gearbeitet.
**Der Hannes** war nervös.

**5**   **Stimmt das?** Stimmen diese Aussagen zum Text oder nicht? Wenn nicht, was stimmt?

Complete the **Ergänzen Sie** activity in your workbook for this text before doing the next activity.

|  | Ja, das stimmt. | Nein, das stimmt nicht. |  |
|---|:---:|:---:|---|
| 1. Uschi hat in Heidelberg studiert. | ☐ | ☒ | |
| 2. Hannes hat Uschi sehr viel Trinkgeld gegeben. | ☐ | ☒ | |
| 3. Hannes und Uschi sind zusammen ins Kino gegangen. | ☐ | ☒ | |
| 4. Nachher haben Hannes und Uschi einen Spaziergang gemacht. | ☐ | ☒ | |
| 5. Hannes hat Uschi zum ersten Mal im Regen geküsst. | ☒ | ☐ | |
| 6. Uschi war krank° und sie hat Hannes Leid getan. | ☒ | ☐ | *sick* |
| 7. Uschi und Hannes haben viel Zeit zusammen verbracht. | ☒ | ☐ | |
| 8. Uschi hat ein Gedicht für Hannes geschrieben. | ☐ | ☒ | |
| 9. Hannes war in Uschi verliebt. | ☒ | ☐ | |
| 10. Uschi und Hannes haben geheiratet. | ☒ | ☐ | |

**6** **Gut organisiert.** Was ist die korrekte Reihenfolge°? — *sequence*

_____ haben in St. Pauli Musik gehört, getanzt, getrunken
_____ sind in die Kneipe gegangen
_1_ hat in der Kneipe gearbeitet
_____ haben einen romantischen Spaziergang an der Alster gemacht
_____ haben einander zum ersten Mal geküsst
_____ haben geheiratet
_____ hat Uschi ins Theater eingeladen
_____ haben viel Zeit zusammen verbracht

**7** **Kurz gefragt.** Beantworten Sie diese Fragen auf Deutsch.

1. Was hat Tante Uschi in Hamburg gemacht?
2. Wie hat Onkel Hannes Tante Uschi kennen gelernt?
3. Was war ihre erste Verabredung°? Wer hat wen eingeladen? — *date*
4. Was haben sie nachher zusammen gemacht?
5. Wo haben sie einander zum ersten Mal geküsst? Wer hat wen geküsst?
6. Was haben sie von da an gemacht?
7. Was hat Onkel Hannes für Tante Uschi geschrieben?

**8** **Romantisch?** Welche Aktivitäten, die Uschi und Hannes zusammen gemacht haben, finden Sie romantisch? Welche langweilig? Kreuzen Sie **Romantisch** oder **Langweilig** an. Dann fragen Sie einen Partner/eine Partnerin.

🟨 S1: *Findest du es romantisch oder langweilig ins Theater zu gehen?*
S2: *Das finde ich romantisch (langweilig).*

> **Finden Sie/Findest du … ?** is used to ask for a person's opinion. Insert **zu** before the last verb in your questions.

| | Romantisch | | Langweilig | |
|---|---|---|---|---|
| | Ich | Partner(in) | Ich | Partner(in) |
| 1. ins Theater gehen | ☐ | ☐ | ☐ | ☐ |
| 2. zusammen ein Bier trinken | ☐ | ☐ | ☐ | ☐ |
| 3. einen Spaziergang im Regen machen | ☐ | ☐ | ☐ | ☐ |
| 4. eine Person küssen | ☐ | ☐ | ☐ | ☐ |
| 5. ein Liebesgedicht schreiben | ☐ | ☐ | ☐ | ☐ |
| 6. tanzen gehen | ☐ | ☐ | ☐ | ☐ |
| 7. auf einen Fischmarkt gehen | ☐ | ☐ | ☐ | ☐ |
| 8. zusammen kochen und essen | ☐ | ☐ | ☐ | ☐ |

**9** ***Ach, es tut mir Leid°* oder *Ja, das macht Spaß.*** Finden Sie einen Partner oder eine Partnerin. Ihr Partner/Ihre Partnerin lädt Sie zu einer Aktivität ein. Sie können die Einladung° akzeptieren oder auch nicht. Geben Sie eine Entschuldigung oder sagen Sie, warum Sie die Einladung akzeptieren wollen. Beispiele gibt es unten. Wechseln° Sie die Rollen. — *I'm sorry.* — *invitation* — *switch*

*Man kann sich so entschuldigen:*
Ich habe leider keine Zeit. • Ich muss mir die Haare waschen°. • Ich muss viel lernen. • Das kann ich nicht machen. • Ich bin leider krank. • Ich habe leider schon andere Pläne. — *I have to wash my hair.*

*Man kann so eine Einladung annehmen:*
Das ist eine tolle Idee! • Das macht sicher Spaß! • Das hat mich schon immer interessiert. • Das möchte ich unbedingt° machen. • Das klingt romantisch. — *for sure*

S1:  *Möchtest du ins Theater gehen?*
S2:  *Ach, es tut mir Leid. Ich bin leider° krank.*                    *unfortunately*

1. ins Theater gehen
2. zusammen Deutsch lernen
3. einen Spaziergang machen
4. eine Studentenkneipe besuchen

5. tanzen gehen
6. zum Fischmarkt gehen
7. etwas Zeit zusammen verbringen
8. zusammen einen Kaffee trinken

## BRENNPUNKT KULTUR

### Hansestadt Hamburg

Hamburg (**die Freie und Hansestadt Hamburg**), Germany's largest seaport and second largest city (1.7 million inhabitants) constitutes one of the 16 states (**Länder**) of the Federal Republic of Germany. Hamburg, as well as Berlin and Bremen, is a city-state with an independent status, which it owes to its history as a Hanseatic city.

The Hanseatic League (**die Hanse**) originated in the 13th century, when Hamburg and Lübeck agreed to reduce the trade barriers between them in order to foster trade in the North Sea and throughout the Baltic region. **Die Hanse** actively promoted trade, international contacts, and the accumulation of wealth, along with the relative independence that such economic wealth provided in a feudal society. Eventually over 200 cities, including Bergen (Norway), Novgorod (Russia), London (England), Bruges (Belgium), and Gdansk (Poland) joined the league and profited from the trade network. Strategically located on the Elbe River (**die Elbe**) between the North Sea (**die Nordsee**) and the Baltic Sea (**die Ostsee**), Hamburg became a hub of Hanseatic trade and has proudly maintained its role as a center of international trade into the 21st century.

*Das Hamburger Rathaus dominiert das Stadtbild von der Alster her.*

From its center along the banks of the Alster (**die Alster**), which is now dammed and forms a large lake in the center of the city, Hamburg revels in its maritime history and its position as Germany's window on the world. Being a port city has fostered a cosmopolitan image and a tolerant tradition for which Hamburg is famous. The copper-roofed, neo-renaissance city hall (**das Rathaus**) serves as the seat of city-state government and dominates the skyline from the Alster. The **Jungfernstieg** is home to Hamburg's most exclusive shops and hotels. It passes over the canals (**Fleete**) that crisscross Hamburg and leads to the main shopping street, **Mönckebergstraße.**

The harbor section, **St. Pauli,** is home to the city's shipping and shipbuilding industries, its immense historic warehouse district (**die Speicherstadt**), and the symbol (**das Wahrzeichen**) of Hamburg, **die Sankt Michaeliskirche (der Michel)**, the largest Baroque church in the city. It is also the location of northern Europe's largest entertainment and red light district, **die Reeperbahn.** The nearby St. Pauli Fish Market (**der Fischmarkt**) is held every Sunday morning from six to ten o'clock.

Hamburg is the birthplace of composers Johannes Brahms and Felix Mendelssohn, author Gotthold Ephraim Lessing, and Chancellor Angela Merkel. In addition to being an important media, TV, and filmmaking center, Hamburg has over twenty theaters, the oldest opera house in Germany, three symphony orchestras, a ballet company, and numerous art museums and galleries. Hamburg is also home to one of Germany's largest urban universities (**die Universität Hamburg**). And not to be forgotten, Hamburg is the birthplace of the **Hamburger Steak,** chopped beef topped with a fried egg, which traveled to America, where it abandoned the egg but added a bun, mustard, and ketchup to become an American staple: the hamburger.

■ **Kulturkreuzung** In der Geschichte Hamburgs spielt das Wasser eine große Rolle: die Elbe, die Alster, die Fleete, die Nähe° zur Nordsee und zur Ostsee. Ist Ihre Stadt an einem See° oder an einem Fluss, oder gibt es nur einen kleinen Bach° in der Nähe? Wie heißen diese Gewässer? Wie wichtig sind sie im wirtschaftlichen° Leben von der Stadt? Was kann man dort in der Freizeit machen? Was haben Sie dort schon gemacht°?

**die See** = *sea;* **der See** = *lake*

*proximity*
*lake*
*brook*
*economic*
*have done*

## Strukturen und Vokabeln

# I  Talking about past events
## The conversational past

When speaking or writing informally about past events, German speakers often use the conversational past, which is also sometimes called the present perfect tense (**das Perfekt**). The conversational past is formed with a present tense form of the auxiliary verb **haben** or **sein** and the past participle of the verb (**das Partizip**). The past participle is frequently, although not always, identifiable by a **ge-** prefix and either a **-t** or **-en** ending.

| | |
|---|---|
| Onkel Hannes **ist** in die Kneipe **gegangen.** | *Uncle Hannes went to the pub.* |
| Onkel Hannes **hat** Tante Uschi **geküsst.** | *Uncle Hannes kissed Aunt Uschi.* |

The German conversational past (e.g., **sie hat geschrieben**) looks like the English present perfect *(she has written)*, but it does not have the same meaning. It is most commonly used for actions completed in the past. In contrast, the English present perfect often expresses uncompleted actions that continue into the present.

*German conversational past*
Ich **habe** einen Brief **geschrieben.**    *I **wrote** a letter.*

*English present perfect*
*I **have known** him for three years.*    Ich **kenne** ihn seit drei Jahren.

A few common verbs, such as **sein** and **haben,** seldom occur in their conversational past forms, even in informal language. Instead, they frequently appear in the simple past forms: e.g., **ich war** (*I was*) and **er hatte** (*he had*).

## A. The auxiliaries *haben* and *sein*

As mentioned above, German speakers use the two auxiliaries **haben** and **sein** to form the conversational past. **Haben** is used most frequently and is always used with a *transitive* verb (any verb that takes a direct object).

| | |
|---|---|
| Uschi **hat** Pharmazie studiert. | *Uschi studied pharmaceutics.* |
| Uschi und Hannes **haben** Bier getrunken. | *Uschi and Hannes drank beer.* |

**Sein** is used with verbs that express a change of location. Such verbs do not have a direct object and are called *intransitive* verbs.

| Infinitive | Conversational past | |
|---|---|---|
| **fahren** | Ich bin gefahren. | *I drove; I went.* |
| **fliegen** | Ich bin geflogen. | *I flew.* |
| **gehen** | Ich bin gegangen. | *I walked; I went.* |
| **kommen** | Ich bin gekommen. | *I came.* |
| **laufen** | Ich bin gelaufen. | *I ran.* |

In general, the simple past is used more frequently (even in speaking) in northern regions, while the conversational past is used more frequently (even in writing) in southern regions.

You will learn more about the simple past in **Kapitel 10**.

The form of the past participle in no way affects whether one uses **haben** or **sein** as the auxiliary of the conversational past.

When the verbs **fahren, fliegen, reiten, schwimmen,** and **segeln** are used with a direct object, they require **haben: Ich bin nach Hause gefahren** vs. **Ich habe dein Auto gefahren.**

| Infinitive | Conversational past | |
|---|---|---|
| **reiten** | Ich bin geritten. | *I rode horseback.* |
| **schwimmen** | Ich bin geschwommen. | *I swam.* |
| **segeln** | Ich bin gesegelt. | *I sailed.* |

Verbs that express a change of condition also require **sein.** The verb **bleiben** also uses **sein** even though it does not show a change of location, but instead the absence of a change of location.

| Infinitive | Conversational past | |
|---|---|---|
| **auf·stehen** | Ich bin früh aufgestanden. | *I got up early.* |
| **auf·wachen** | Ich bin aufgewacht. | *I woke up.* |
| **bleiben** | Wir sind zu Hause geblieben. | *We stayed home.* |
| **sterben°** | Sie ist gestorben. | *She died.* |
| **werden** | Sie ist böse geworden. | *She became angry.* |

In standard German all verbs expressing non-motion, e.g., **stehen** *(to stand),* **sitzen** *(to sit),* **liegen** *(to lie, recline),* and **hängen** *(to hang),* use the auxiliary **haben.** However, in the southern regions these verbs use the auxiliary **sein.**

*to die*

*Note:* Verbs requiring **sein** appear in the vocabulary lists with the auxiliary verb **ist,** including the exception **bleiben (ist geblieben)** *to stay, remain.*

In the conversational past, the auxiliary is conjugated to agree with the subject. The past participle never changes.

> Wir **sind** auf den Fischmarkt **gegangen.** *We went to the fish market.*
> Anna **ist** mit Katja ins Kino **gegangen.** *Anna went to the movies with Katja.*

The position of the subject has no influence on the position of the auxiliary or the past participle. Like all conjugated verbs, the auxiliary occurs in the second position in statements and in the first position in questions. The past participle always appears at the end of the clause or sentence.

| *Statement* | *Question* |
|---|---|
| subject | subject |
| <u>Hannes</u> **hat** Uschi **geküsst.** | **Hat** <u>Hannes</u> Uschi **geküsst**? |
|        subject |      subject |
| Bald danach **haben** <u>sie</u> **geheiratet.** | **Haben** <u>sie</u> bald danach **geheiratet**? |

**10** **Was ist passiert°?** Verbinden Sie einen Satz in der linken Spalte° mit einem Satz in der rechten Spalte.

*happened / column*

1. Die Kellnerin ist heute morgen sehr müde.
2. Tante Uschi ist heute Apothekerin° in Weinheim.
3. Hannelore Adler hat eine E-Mail von Anna.
4. Anna kann nicht schlafen.
5. Barbara und Anna finden den Film sehr gut.
6. Tante Uschi liebt° Onkel Hannes.

a. Anna hat letzte Woche eine E-Mail geschrieben.
b. Onkel Hannes hat Tante Uschi geküsst.
c. Sie hat gestern Abend bis spät in der Kneipe gearbeitet.
d. Sie hat in Hamburg Pharmazie studiert.
e. Sie hat zu viel Kaffee getrunken.
f. Sie sind gestern° ins Kino gegangen.

*pharmacist*

*loves / yesterday*

**11**    **Wo hast du studiert?** Ergänzen Sie diese Sätze mit den passenden Formen von **haben** und **sein.**

1. KARL:   Wo _haben_ deine Eltern studiert?
2. BEATE:  Mein Vater _ist_ in Heilbronn zur Schule gegangen, aber er _hat_ in München Chemie studiert.
3. KARL:   Aber du _bist_ doch hier zur Schule gegangen, nicht?
4. BEATE:  Eigentlich° _bin_ ich in Amerika in den Kindergarten gegangen. Mein Vater _hat_ dort zwei Semester verbracht.  *Actually*
5. KARL:   Wirklich?° Was _hat_ er dort gemacht?  *Really?*
6. BEATE:  Er _hat_ seine Dissertation geschrieben. Wir _haben_ ein Jahr in Cambridge in Massachusetts gelebt. Dort _habe_ ich Englisch gelernt.

## B. Past participles

All verbs can be classified as regular (weak—**schwach**), irregular (strong—**stark**), or mixed (combining characteristics of weak and strong verbs—**gemischt**). Whether a verb is regular, irregular, or mixed affects the form of the past participle, particularly its stem and its ending.

### 1. Regular (weak) verbs

Regular verbs (**regelmäßige Verben**), which include many verbs that have been recently incorporated into the German language, are sometimes referred to as weak verbs (**schwache Verben**).

- Most regular verbs form the past participle by keeping the present tense stem and adding the **ge-** prefix and the ending **-t.**

| Infinitive | Conversational past | |
|---|---|---|
| **mailen**° | hat **ge** + mail + **t** | Sie hat uns gemailt. |
| **spielen** | hat **ge** + spiel + **t** | Die Kinder haben gespielt. |
| **surfen** | hat **ge** + surf + **t** | Ich habe gestern im Internet gesurft. |
| **wandern** | ist **ge** + wander + **t** | Anna ist viel gewandert. |

*to e-mail*

| | | | |
|---|---|---|---|
| angeln | **hat geangelt** | machen | **hat gemacht** |
| brauchen | **hat gebraucht** | meinen | **hat gemeint** |
| fragen | **hat gefragt** | packen | **hat gepackt** |
| hören | **hat gehört** | schicken | **hat geschickt** |
| kaufen | **hat gekauft** | setzen | **hat gesetzt** |
| kochen | **hat gekocht** | tanzen | **hat getanzt** |
| lachen | **hat gelacht** | wohnen | **hat gewohnt** |
| lächeln | **hat gelächelt** | zeigen | **hat gezeigt** |
| lernen | **hat gelernt** | | |

- Regular verbs whose stem ends in **-t, -d, -gn, -chn,** or **-fn** require the ending **-et** to form the past participle.

| Infinitive | Conversational past | | |
|---|---|---|---|
| **arbeiten** | hat **ge** + arbeit + **et** | Ich habe gearbeitet. | |
| **downloaden** | hat **ge** + download + **et** | Mutti hat die Software gedownloadet. | |
| **flirten** | hat **ge** + flirt + **et** | Uschi und Hannes haben geflirtet. | |
| **öffnen°** | hat **ge** + öffn + **et** | Georg hat die Tür geöffnet. | *to open* |
| **regnen** | hat **ge** + regn + **et** | Es hat so viel geregnet | |
| **warten** | hat **ge** + wart + **et** | Anna hat lange gewartet. | |

- Most verbs ending in **-ieren** are regular, but they do not add the prefix **ge-.**

| Infinitive | Conversational past | |
|---|---|---|
| **studieren** | hat studier + **t** | Sie haben studiert. |

**12  Katjas Freund Roland.**  Hier erzählt Katja, wie sie ihren Freund Roland kennen gelernt hat. Schreiben Sie das richtige Partizip.

arbeiten • kaufen • lernen • machen • öffnen • regnen • spielen

Ich habe Roland im Jugendklub kennen gelernt. Er hat dort als Kellner _gearbeitet_. Es war im September. Das Wetter war miserabel. Es hat _geregnet_, und ich war total nass. Er hat mir die Tür _geöffnet_, denn ich habe gerade (*just*) im Kaufhaus neue Kleidung _gekauft_ und ich hatte keine freie Hand. Er war ein richtiger Gentleman!
   Danach haben wir viel zusammen _gemacht_. Für die Schule haben wir beide (*both*) zusammen Mathe _gelernt_. Am Wochenende haben wir oft Tennis _gespielt_.

**13  Gestern Abend.**  Was haben Barbara, Karl, Christina und Thomas gestern Abend gemacht? Fragen Sie einen Partner/eine Partnerin nach° einer Aktivität mit einem Fragezeichen. Beantworten Sie dann eine Frage von Ihrem Partner/Ihrer Partnerin.    *about*

S1:  *Was hat Barbara gestern Abend gemacht?*
S2:  *Sie hat Spaghetti gekocht.*
     *Und was hat Thomas gemacht?*
S1:  *Er hat telefoniert.*

**Tabelle A (S1):**

| | Gespielt | Gemacht | Gelernt |
|---|---|---|---|
| Barbara | Billard gespielt | ? | Mathe gelernt |
| Thomas | ? | telefoniert | ? |
| Karl | Karten gespielt | ? | Physik gelernt |
| Christina | ? | zu Hause gearbeitet | ? |

**Tabelle B (S2):**

| | Gespielt | Gemacht | Gelernt |
|---|---|---|---|
| Barbara | ? | Spaghetti gekocht | ? |
| Thomas | Tischtennis gespielt | ? | nichts gelernt |
| Karl | ? | ein Buch gekauft | ? |
| Christina | Gitarre gespielt | ? | Deutsch gelernt |

## 2. Irregular (strong) and mixed verbs

- Irregular verbs (**unregelmäßige Verben**), namely those verbs with a stem-vowel change in the present tense or one of the past tenses, are also called strong verbs (**starke Verben**). They generally include **ge-** and have the ending **-en** on the past participle.

| Infinitive | Conversational past | |
|---|---|---|
| **geben** | hat **ge** + geb + **en** | Was hast du ihm gegeben? |
| **lesen** | hat **ge** + les + **en** | Ich habe das ganze Buch gelesen. |

> halten, gehalten; heißen, geheißen; schlafen, geschlafen; tragen, getragen

For many verbs, the vowel in the present tense stem changes in the past participle. For some verbs, one or more consonants change as well. There is no way to recognize which verbs change the stem vowel or consonant in the past participle. They must be memorized.

| Infinitive | Conversational past | |
|---|---|---|
| **gehen** | ist ge + **gang** + en | Er ist mit mir ins Kino gegangen. |
| **trinken** | hat ge + tr**u**nk + en | Wir haben doch kein Bier getrunken. |

> helfen, geholfen; singen, gesungen; tun, getan.

> There are approximately 35 high-frequency irregular and mixed verbs. You will need to memorize their stem changes. Some English verbs can help you remember the German verb forms (e.g., *speak, spoken:* **sprechen, gesprochen**).

- Mixed verbs combine features of both regular and irregular verbs to form their past participles. Like regular verbs, they add a **-t** in the past participle and, like some irregular verbs, they change the stem in the past participle.

| Infinitive | Conversational past | |
|---|---|---|
| **bringen** | hat ge + br**ach** + t | Was hast du mir gebracht? |
| **denken** | hat ge + d**ach** + t | Ich habe oft an dich gedacht. |
| **kennen** | hat ge + k**a**nn + t | Hast du sie gut gekannt? |
| **wissen** | hat ge + w**u**ss + t | Ich habe das nicht gewusst. |

The following list shows irregular and mixed verbs with their stem changes. You will find the complete list of irregular and mixed verbs in the Appendix.

| | Infinitive | Conversational past | |
|---|---|---|---|
| **No stem-vowel change** | **e**ssen | hat geg**e**ssen | Hast du gegessen? |
| | f**a**hren | ist gef**a**hren | Sie ist gefahren. |
| | l**e**sen | hat gel**e**sen | Haben Sie das Buch gelesen? |

HABEN SIE DAS SCHILD NICHT GESEHEN ?!

HAB ICH EIN ROTES AUTO ?

Notice that the past participle of **essen** has an extra **g** to facilitate pronunciation: ge**g**essen.

| | Infinitive | Conversational past | |
|---|---|---|---|
| **ei > ie** | schr**ei**ben | hat geschr**ie**ben | Anna hat einen Brief geschrieben. |
| **e > a** | g**e**hen | ist geg**a**ngen | Er ist nach Hause gegangen. |
| | st**e**hen | hat gest**a**nden | Wir haben hier gestanden. |
| **e > o** | n**e**hmen | hat gen**o**mmen | Petra hat es genommen. |
| | spr**e**chen | hat gespr**o**chen | Die Studenten haben Deutsch gesprochen. |
| **i > u** | f**i**nden | hat gef**u**nden | Herr Meyer hat sein Auto gefunden. |
| | tr**i**nken | hat getr**u**nken | Habt ihr alles getrunken? |

**nehmen:** Note the change in consonant spelling in the past participle: **mm.**

**e > o:** Note also: **werden, geworden.**

---

**14**    **Autogrammspiel: Was hast du heute gemacht?**  Finden Sie
für jede° Frage eine Person, die mit **Ja** antwortet. Bitten Sie diese Person    *each*
um ihre Unterschrift.

S1:  *Hast du heute Kaffee getrunken?*
S2:  *Ja, ich habe heute Kaffee getrunken.*
S1:  *Unterschreib hier bitte.*

1. Kaffee getrunken          _____
2. Hausaufgaben gemacht      _____
3. Pizza gegessen            _____
4. mit dem Bus zur Uni gefahren  _____
5. das Bett° gemacht         _____          *bed*
6. Musik gehört              _____
7. eine Zeitung° gekauft     _____          *newspaper*
8. Vokabeln gelernt          _____
9. gut geschlafen            _____
10. Deutsch gesprochen       _____

---

**15**    **Übertreibungen°.**  Ein alter Freund beschreibt seine Kindheit°,    *exaggerations /*
aber er übertreibt auch gern. Sie müssen ihn oft an die Realität erinnern.          *childhood*

perfekt Deutsch sprechen / gar kein Deutsch sprechen

S1 (DER FREUND):  *Ich habe als Kind perfekt Deutsch gesprochen.*
       S2 (SIE):  *Nein, du hast als Kind gar kein Deutsch gesprochen.*

1. ein Auto kaufen / ein Fahrrad kaufen
2. viele Bücher lesen / Comichefte° lesen          *comic books*
3. jeden Morgen ein Bier trinken / jeden Morgen Orangensaft trinken
4. gesund° essen / ungesund essen          *healthy*
5. immer zur Schule laufen / immer zur Schule fahren
6. nie am Wochenende zu Hause bleiben / oft am Wochenende zu Hause bleiben
7. das Abendessen immer kochen / das Abendessen nie kochen
8. viele Briefe schreiben / viele E-Mails schreiben

## C. Prefixes of past participles

### 1. Separable-prefix verbs

As you know, most verbs add **ge-** to form the past participle. A verb with a separable prefix (**trennbares Präfix**) inserts this **-ge-** between the prefix and the stem.

> Hannes hat Uschi ins Theater ein**ge**laden.    *Hannes invited Uschi to the theater.*

Here is a list of past participles of common verbs with separable prefixes. When spoken, the stress in the infinitive and in the past participle is always on the prefix: **an**kommen, **an**gekommen.

| Infinitive | Conversational past | | |
|---|---|---|---|
| **an·fangen°** | hat an + **ge** + fangen | Der Film hat schon angefangen. | *to begin* |
| **an·kommen** | ist an + **ge** + kommen | Magda ist schon angekommen. | |
| **an·rufen** | hat an + **ge** + rufen | Anna hat uns angerufen. | |
| **auf·hören** | hat auf + **ge** + hört | Der Professor hat gerade aufgehört. | |
| **auf·stehen** | ist auf + **ge** + standen | Wann bist du aufgestanden? | |
| **aus·geben** | hat aus + **ge** + geben | Hast du viel Geld ausgegeben? | |
| **aus·gehen°** | ist aus + **ge** + gangen | Claudia ist mit Karl ausgegangen. | *to go out* |
| **aus·sehen°** | hat aus + **ge** + sehen | Ihr habt gut ausgesehen. | *to appear, look* |
| **durch·machen°** | hat durch + **ge** + macht | Sie haben die Nacht durchgemacht. | *to get through* |
| **ein·kaufen** | hat ein + **ge** + kauft | Katja hat viel eingekauft. | |
| **ein·laden°** | hat ein + **ge** + laden | Wen hast du zur Party eingeladen? | *to invite* |
| **fern·sehen** | hat fern + **ge** + sehen | Wir haben ferngesehen. | |
| **los·fahren°** | ist los + **ge** + fahren | Wann ist er losgefahren? | *to leave, set out* |
| **heim·kommen°** | ist heim + **ge** + kommen | Ich bin um zwei Uhr heimgekommen. | *to come home* |
| **mit·bringen** | hat mit + **ge** + bracht | Sie haben nichts mitgebracht. | |
| **mit·nehmen** | hat mit + **ge** + nommen | Was hast du mitgenommen? | |
| **zurück·kommen** | ist zurück + **ge** + kommen | Franz ist schon zurückgekommen. | |

> The most common separable prefixes are: **ab-, an-, auf-, aus-, ein-, mit-, um-, zu-, zurück-.**

> Irregular and mixed verbs with separable prefixes undergo the same stem changes as the forms that have no separable prefix: **nehmen** (*to take*) → **hat genommen; annehmen** (*to assume*) → **hat angenommen.**

> Other separable-prefix verbs you may already know are **aufpassen** (**hat aufgepasst**) and **umdrehen** (**hat umgedreht**).

**16   Ein Einkaufsbummel° in Hamburg.**  Es ist Abend. Onkel Hannes und Tante Uschi besuchen Hamburg. Katja ist zu Hause in Weinheim. Katja spricht am Telefon mit ihrer Mutter. Was sagt Katja? Was sagt Tante Uschi?

*shopping spree*

S1 (KATJA):　　　　*Was hast du heute gemacht, Mama?*
S2 (TANTE USCHI):　*Ich bin früh aufgestanden. Und was hast du gemacht, Katja?*
S1 (KATJA):　　　　*Ich habe lange geschlafen. Und was hast du noch°*
　　　　　　　　　　*gemacht, Mama?*

*was noch: what else*

**Tabelle A (S1, Katja):**

| Katja | Tante Uschi |
|---|---|
| lange geschlafen | ? |
| zur Schule losgefahren | ? |
| heimgekommen | ? |
| mit Claudia ferngesehen | ? |

**Tabelle B (S2, Tante Uschi):**

| Katja | Tante Uschi |
|---|---|
| ? | viel Geld ausgegeben |
| ? | viele Sachen eingekauft |
| ? | an der Elbe spazieren gegangen |
| ? | früh aufgestanden |

**17** **Interview.** Stellen Sie einem Partner/einer Partnerin die folgenden Fragen.

S1: *Hast du heute gut oder schlecht° geschlafen?*                    *badly, poorly*
S2: *Ich habe heute gut geschlafen.*

1. Hast du heute gut oder schlecht geschlafen?
2. Wann bist du aufgestanden?
3. Wann bist du zur Uni losgefahren?
4. Wann bist du gestern zurückgekommen?
5. Hast du heute oder gestern eingekauft?
6. Wie viel Geld hast du gestern ausgegeben?
7. Hast du gestern Abend ferngesehen oder bist du ausgegangen?
8. Wann hast du zuletzt deine Eltern angerufen?

## 2. Inseparable-prefix and *-ieren* verbs

A verb with an inseparable prefix (**untrennbares Präfix**) does not add **ge-** in the past participle. When spoken, the stress in the past participle is always on the stem, not on the inseparable prefix: **be***sucht*, **ver***stand***en.**

| Infinitive | Conversational past | |
|---|---|---|
| **besuchen** | hat besuch + t | Er hat uns besucht. |
| **erzählen** | hat erzähl + t | Mutti hat uns die Geschichte erzählt. |
| **verbringen** | hat verbrach + t | Sie hat ein Jahr in Afrika verbracht. |
| **verdienen°** | hat verdien + t | Uschi hat viel Geld verdient. |
| **vergessen** | hat vergess + en | Monika hat Annas Geburtstag vergessen. |
| **verlieren°** | hat verlor + en | Sie hat ihr Handy verloren. |
| **verstehen** | hat verstand + en | Hast du den Professor verstanden? |

The most common inseparable prefixes are: **be-, ent-, er-, ge-, ver-, zer-.**

*to earn*

*to lose*

For verbs ending in **-ieren,** stress is placed on **-iert: stud***iert.*

| Infinitive | Conversational past | |
|---|---|---|
| **buchstabieren°** | hat buchstabier + t | Fabian hat das Wort richtig buchstabiert. |
| **diskutieren** | hat diskutier + t | Sie haben Politik diskutiert. |
| **studieren** | hat studier + t | Wo hat Franz in den USA studiert? |

Other verbs in this group that you may already know are **bedeuten (hat bedeutet), beginnen (hat begonnen), benutzen (hat benutzt),** and **bezahlen (hat bezahlt).**

*to spell*

**18** **Das Happyend: Ein Rätsel°.** Onkel Hannes und Tante Uschi haben einander in Hamburg kennen gelernt. Sie sind jetzt 25 Jahre verheiratet. Zum 25. Hochzeitstag° besuchen sie die Stadt wieder. Rekonstruieren Sie mit einem Partner/einer Partnerin die korrekte Reihenfolge der Geschichte von Uschi Kunz und Hannes Günther in Hamburg.

*riddle*

*wedding anniversary*

*Vor 25 Jahren*
___ Hannes Günther und Uschi Kunz haben sich verliebt.
___ Sie haben sich verlobt.
_1_ Uschi hat in Hamburg Pharmazie studiert.
___ Uschi hat als Kellnerin wenig Geld verdient.
___ Sie sind im Regen spazieren gegangen.
___ Hannes hat Uschi ins Theater eingeladen.

*Gestern*

___ Am Abend haben sie das Hamburger Ballett besucht.

___ Hannes hat die Karten im Hotel vergessen und Uschi war böse°.        *angry, upset*

___ Sie haben das Ballett nicht verstanden.

___ Hannes hat die Karten wieder gefunden und Uschi war wieder glücklich.

_1_ Sie haben den Tag an der Alster verbracht.

___ Sie haben in einer Kneipe etwas getrunken und über das Ballett diskutiert.

## D. Past participles of **sein** and **haben**

The past participle of **sein** is **gewesen.** The past participle of **haben** is **gehabt.**

| | |
|---|---|
| Tante Uschi **ist** in Hamburg Studentin **gewesen.** | *Aunt Uschi was a student in Hamburg.* |
| Du **hast** eine ganz schlimme Erkältung **gehabt.** | *You had a really bad cold.* |

In spoken German, the simple past tense forms of **sein (war, warst, waren)** and **haben (hatte, hattest, hatten),** discussed in **Kapitel 10,** are frequently used instead of the conversational past to express the past tense.

Er **hat** Geburtstag **gehabt.**
Er **hatte** Geburtstag.  } *He had a birthday.*

Sie **ist** krank **gewesen.**
Sie **war** krank.  } *She was sick.*

**19   Meine Kindheit.** Sprechen Sie zusammen über Ihre Kindheit. Benutzen Sie **sein** und **haben.**

S1:  *Als Kind bin ich selten krank gewesen. Und du?*
S2:  *Als Kind war ich auch selten krank.* (oder)
    *Als Kind war ich oft krank.*

| | |
|---|---|
| 1. oft/selten krank | 5. viele/wenige Erkältungen |
| 2. sehr aktiv/sehr ruhig | 6. viele/wenige Regeln |
| 3. oft im Kino/selten im Kino | 7. viele/wenige Spielsachen° |
| 4. sehr sportlich/nicht sehr sportlich | 8. viele/ein paar° Spielkameraden° |

*toys*
***ein paar:** a few / playmates*

**20   Herrn Günthers Geschäftsreise°.** Ergänzen Sie diese Sätze mit der korrekten Partizipform.        *business trip*

Herr Günther war letzte Woche auf Geschäftsreise in München. Dort hat er die letzten fünf Tage _____ (verbringen). Er ist gestern Abend aus München _____ (zurückkommen). Er ist um 21.15 Uhr am Bahnhof in Weinheim _____ (ankommen). In München hat er mit Kollegen an einem Projekt _____ (arbeiten). Das Projekt haben sie vor einem Jahr _____ (anfangen). Die beiden Kollegen haben viel _____ (diskutieren). Aber zum Schluss° haben beide sehr gut an dem Projekt _____ (verdienen).        ***zum ...:** in the end*

    In München hat Herr Günther auch etwas Zeit für die Sehenswürdigkeiten _____ (haben). Am Samstag hat er das BMW-Museum _____ (besuchen). Dort hat er viele alte Autos und Flugzeuge _____ (sehen). Er ist sehr lange im Museum _____ (bleiben). Für seine Kinder hat er auch Andenken _____ (kaufen). Für Georg hat er ein Buch über den BMW Autokonzern _____ (finden). Für Katja hat er eine CD mit südamerikanischer Flötenmusik _____ (mitbringen). Seine Frau hat er auch nicht _____ (vergessen). Für sie hat er einen Schal _____ (kaufen). Er hat relativ viel Geld _____ (ausgeben).

## Wissenswerte Vokabeln: das Wetter
### Describing weather conditions

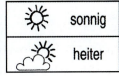

| | |
|---|---|
| ☀ | sonnig |
| ⛅ | heiter |

Wie ist das Wetter heute?

Heute ist es | sonnig.
              | heiter.

Die Sonne scheint.

Es wird heiß und schwül°. Die Temperatur liegt° um vierunddreißig Grad Celsius.

Heute ist es | wolkig.
              | bedeckt.
              | windig.

Es gibt | viele Wolken.
        | Nebel.

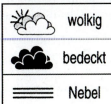

| | |
|---|---|
| ⛅ | wolkig |
| ☁ | bedeckt |
| ≡ | Nebel |

Es wird kühl. Die Temperatur | fällt.
                                     | sinkt.

**Die Sonne hat gestern geschienen.**

*humid / is* (lit. *lies*)

**Es hat gestern viele Wolken gegeben.**

**Die Temperatur fällt (ist gefallen). Die Temperatur sinkt (ist gesunken).**

| | |
|---|---|
|  | Regen |
| | Schauer |
| | Gewitter |

Heute regnet es.
Wir haben Regen.
Es gibt | Schauer.
        | Gewitter.
Das Wetter ist schlecht°.
Es blitzt und donnert.

Es ist | ganz nass°.
       | nicht trocken°.
       | wirklich mies°.

Es wird aber warm. Die Temperatur steigt°.

*bad*

*wet*
*dry*
*rotten, lousy*

*is rising*

Heute schneit es.
Wir haben Schnee.

Es wird kalt. Die Temperatur liegt um null Grad Celsius (um den Gefrierpunkt).

Morgen soll es sonnig aber kalt sein.

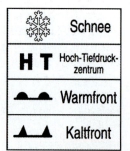

| | |
|---|---|
| | Schnee |
| H T | Hoch-Tiefdruck-zentrum |
| | Warmfront |
| | Kaltfront |

### Sprache im Alltag: *ganz*

The word **ganz** is used (quite) frequently in German. It can be used as an adjective (to mean *whole* or *all*) and as an adverb (to mean *really, quite,* or *very*).

| | |
|---|---|
| Es hat den **ganzen** Tag geregnet. | *It rained **all** day.* |
| Das ist meine **ganze** Familie. | *This is my **whole** family.* |
| Ja, das finde ich **ganz** gut. | *Yes, I think that's **quite** good.* |
| Du hast eine **ganz** schlimme Erkältung gehabt. | *You had a **really** (**very**) bad cold.* |

**21** **Wie ist das Wetter in Oslo?** Das Wetter in Tübingen ist momentan nicht so gut. Anna sucht schönes Wetter! Sie liest die *Frankfurter Allgemeine Zeitung* und findet den Wetterbericht für Europa. Beantworten Sie die Fragen.

1. Wien
2. Dublin
3. Bordeaux
4. Moskau
5. Rom
6. Istanbul
7. Athen
8. Madrid
9. München
10. Berlin
11. Nizza
12. Paris

S1: *Wie ist das Wetter in Oslo?*
S2: *In Oslo ist es bedeckt. Die Temperatur liegt um drei Grad.*

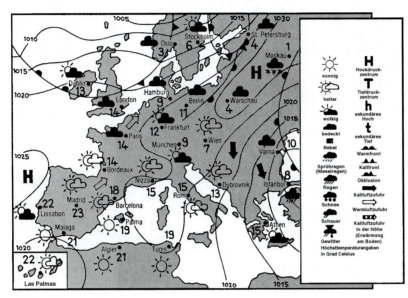

**22** **Das Wetter hier.** Beantworten Sie die Fragen.

1. Wie ist das Wetter heute?
2. Ist es heute bedeckt oder heiter?
3. Was ist die Temperatur heute in Fahrenheit? In Celsius?
4. Haben wir heute Morgen Nebel gehabt?
5. Wie ist das Wetter gestern gewesen?
6. Wann hat es zuletzt geregnet?
7. Wann hat es zuletzt geschneit?
8. Wie soll das Wetter morgen° (und übermorgen) sein?          *tomorrow*

## Wissenswerte Vokabeln: die Jahreszeiten
### Talking about the seasons

der Frühling

der Sommer

der Herbst

der Winter

Wie ist das Wetter im Winter?

**23** **Fragen zum Wetter.** Stellen Sie einem Partner/einer Partnerin diese Fragen über das Wetter.

1. Wie ist es im Sommer in Atlanta?
2. Wie ist das Wetter im Winter in Buffalo, New York?
3. Wie ist es im Frühling in Washington, D.C.?
4. Wie ist das Wetter im Herbst im Mittelwesten?
5. In welcher Jahreszeit regnet es hier am meisten?
6. In welcher Jahreszeit ist das Wetter hier sehr schlecht?
7. Wann haben wir das beste Wetter? Warum meinst du das?

> Vocabulary that might be important for your region: **der Sturm** (*storm*), **der Orkan** (*hurricane*), **der Tornado** (*tornado*), **der Wirbelsturm** (*whirlwind*).

  ### Freie Kommunikation

**Rollenspiel: Gestern Abend.** Sie treffen° einen Freund/eine Freundin an der Uni. Der Freund/Die Freundin sieht sehr müde aus. Beginnen Sie die Konversation mit „Guten Tag". Stellen Sie dann die Frage: „Wie geht's?" Der Freund/Die Freundin erzählt, was er/sie gestern Abend gemacht hat. Hier sind einige Ideen.

*meet*

> **Freie Kommunikation.** Remember to use the informal **du-** and **ihr-**forms of the verbs when talking to one another.

| | |
|---|---|
| nicht so gut geschlafen | bis spät gearbeitet |
| für eine Prüfung gelernt | Basketball gespielt |
| in die Kneipe gegangen | Hausaufgaben gemacht |
| eine Party besucht | die ganze Nacht mit Freunden telefoniert |

**Rollenspiel: Letzten Sommer.** Sie treffen einen Freund/eine Freundin und sprechen über letzten Sommer. Beginnen Sie die Konversation mit: „Hallo." Hier sind einige Ideen.

| | | |
|---|---|---|
| im Sommer gemacht | zum Strand° gefahren | *beach* |
| fast° immer geregnet | die Sonne hat geschienen | *almost* |
| Wasserski gefahren | Baseball gespielt | |
| eine Reise gemacht | mit Freunden ausgegangen | |
| nichts Interessantes gemacht | viel gearbeitet und wenig verdient | |

**Ein Pechtag°.** Beschreiben Sie einen Tag, an dem nichts gut gegangen ist. Eine Person beginnt mit „Hallo, _____. Du siehst nicht so gut aus. Was ist los?°" Hier sind einige Ideen.

*unlucky, bad day*
***Was ... :*** *What's the matter?*

| | |
|---|---|
| zu spät aufgestanden | kein Buch gehabt |
| Wasser nur kalt gewesen | Geld vergessen |
| das Handy verloren | krank geworden |
| keinen freien Parkplatz gefunden | usw.° |

***und so weiter***

  ### Schreibecke

**Einen Brief schreiben.** Sie sind heute nicht in den Deutschkurs gekommen. Schreiben Sie Ihrem Lehrer/Ihrer Lehrerin eine kurze E-Mail. Erklären° Sie, warum Sie nicht da waren. Was haben Sie gemacht?

*explain*

> zu lange schlafen • Auto kaputt • das Buch vergessen • Hausaufgaben nicht machen • krank sein

📧 *Lieber Herr ... (Liebe Frau ...),*

**Absprungtext** | **Freundschaft! Was bedeutet sie?**

Anna besucht ein Online-Forum, wo sie sieht, was junge Deutsche von Freundschaft halten. Ist die Terminologie für Freundschaft in Deutschland anders als hier? Sie möchte sich informieren.

## Vorschau

**24** **Thematische Fragen: Eigenschaften° eines Freundes/einer Freundin.** Welche Dinge° finden Sie gut, welche schlecht für Freundschaften, und welche sind nicht wichtig?

*characteristics*

*things*

|  | Gut | Schlecht | Nicht wichtig |  |
|---|---|---|---|---|
| 1. Vertrauen° haben | ☐ | ☐ | ☐ | *trust* |
| 2. ineinander verliebt sein | ☐ | ☐ | ☐ |  |
| 3. offen miteinander sprechen | ☐ | ☐ | ☐ |  |
| 4. einander nie enttäuschen° | ☐ | ☐ | ☐ | *disappoint* |
| 5. einander sehr lange kennen | ☐ | ☐ | ☐ |  |
| 6. einander gern haben | ☐ | ☐ | ☐ |  |
| 7. jeden Tag miteinander sprechen | ☐ | ☐ | ☐ |  |
| 8. Gefühle° offen zeigen | ☐ | ☐ | ☐ | *feelings* |
| 9. die gleichen Interessen haben | ☐ | ☐ | ☐ |  |
| 10. in der gleichen Stadt wohnen | ☐ | ☐ | ☐ |  |
| 11. einander treu° sein | ☐ | ☐ | ☐ | *faithful, loyal* |
| 12. Energie in die Freundschaft investieren | ☐ | ☐ | ☐ |  |

**25** **Satzdetektiv.** Welche Sätze bedeuten ungefähr das Gleiche?

1. Was **versteht ihr unter** Freundschaft?  C
2. Man kann mit Freunden über fast alles **reden.** D
3. **Echte** Freundschaft **erfordert** viel Energie.  A
4. Ich **frage mich, ob** es **wahre** Freundschaft überhaupt noch gibt. B
5. Früher haben wir uns **täglich** gesehen.  E

a. Man muss in eine richtige Freundschaft viel Energie investieren.
b. Ich möchte wissen: Existiert richtige Freundschaft wirklich?
c. Was bedeutet Freundschaft für euch?
d. Gute Freunde können über praktisch alles sprechen.
e. Wir haben uns jeden Tag gesehen.

---

6. **Doch** dann bin ich **weggezogen.** G
7. **Unterhalten sich** hier nur Mädchen? H
8. Dicke Freundschaften zwischen Jungs sind sehr **selten.** I
9. Es **ist schade.** J
10. Ich freu' mich auf **Stellungnahmen.** F

f. Ich möchte wissen, was ihr denkt.
g. Aber dann bin ich in eine andere Stadt gegangen.
h. Sprechen hier nur Mädchen miteinander?
i. Wahre Freundschaften zwischen Jungen gibt es nicht oft.
j. Das tut mir Leid.

## Absprungtext
### Freundschaft! Was bedeutet sie??

Lesen Sie jetzt den Text.

These blogs are from *freundschafts.net* and *crazy-board.de.*

**Plauderei**

**MYSTICIA**
Freundschaft! Was bedeutet sie??
Alle reden darüber[1], doch was Freundschaft ist, weiß eigentlich keiner[2] so genau[3]. Ist Freundschaft Treue[4]? Ist Freundschaft einfach nur Sympathie[5]? Ist Freundschaft Respekt? Ist Freundschaft offene Kommunikation – über alles? Was versteht ihr unter einer Freundschaft? Ich meine jetzt nicht die Liebe zu einer anderen Person! Was macht bei euch eine Freundschaft aus[6]?

**SCOOBY**
Freunde sind für mich Leute, mit denen man über fast[7] alles reden kann, man muss sie schon länger kennen und richtiges Vertrauen zu ihnen haben! Bekannte[8] sind alle anderen.

**SCHNEEWITTCHEN**
Freundschaft ist mir wichtiger als Liebe, weil es so verdammt einfach ist, verliebt zu sein. Aber eine echte Freundschaft erfordert[9] viel mehr Energie. Ein Philosoph[10] hat einmal gesagt, dass es die wahre Liebe selten[11] gibt, aber dass die wahre Freundschaft noch viel seltener ist. Ich jedoch[12] frage mich, ob es in der heutigen Zeit die wahre Freundschaft überhaupt noch[13] gibt, denn ich wurde schon oft enttäuscht.[14]

**DORNRÖSCHEN**
Ich denke auch, dass es die wahre Freundschaft noch gibt. Meine beste Freundin kenne ich schon seit[15] dem Kindergarten und seit dem[16] sind wir auch schon die besten Freunde. Also schon so 11 Jahre. Früher[17] haben wir uns täglich gesehen, doch dann bin ich weggezogen, 500 km entfernt. Und wir sind trotzdem noch die besten Freunde, auch wenn wir uns nur in den Ferien[18] oder so sehen. Wir haben trotzdem fast täglich Kontakt. Und ich kann mit ihr über fast alles reden.

**ANDRÉ 2001**
Hallo, darf ich mal fragen ob sich hier nur Mädchen unterhalten? Es hört sich jedenfalls[19] so an. Und ich als Großstädter[20] aus Hamburg kann nur sagen, dass es zwischen Jungs[21] sehr selten hier dicke Freundschaften gibt. Hab sowas noch nie gesehen, außer bei[22] Mädchen. Was jetzt nicht heißt, dass ich das gut finde. Es ist eher Schade. Ich freu' mich auf Stellungnahmen.[23]

**STERNCHEN**
Hallo André
ich weiß nicht, aber ich glaube,[24] es gibt auch unter Jungs dicke Freundschaften, nur ist es UNCOOL, es zu sagen oder Gefühle zu zeigen.

Send

---

[1]*about it*  [2]*no one*  [3]*exactly*  [4]*loyalty*  [5]*likeability*  [6]***macht … aus:*** *make a difference*
[7]*almost*  [8]*acquaintances*  [9]*requires*  [10]*philosopher*  [11]*rarely*  [12]*however*  [13]*still*
[14]***wurde… enttäuscht:*** *was disappointed*  [15]*since*  [16]*ever since*  [17]*back then*  [18]***in den Ferien:***
*during vacation*  [19]*in any case*  [20]*city dweller*  [21]*guys, boys*  [22]***außer bei:*** *except for*
[23]*opinions*  [24]*believe*

The language used in e-mails and electronic messaging reflects the spoken language, e.g., **hab'** = **habe;** **so 11 Jahre** = *about 11 years;* **oder so** = *or such;* **Jungs** = **Jungen** = *guys.*

*Rückblick*

**26** **Wer hat die Aussage gemacht?** Geben Sie die richtige Person/richtigen Personen an. *Achtung:* Zwei Aussagen werden von zwei Personen gemacht.

| | Mysticia | Scooby | Schneewittchen | Dornröschen | André 2001 | Sternchen | |
|---|---|---|---|---|---|---|---|
| 1. Mit Freunden kann man über fast alles reden. | | ☒ | | ☒ | | | |
| 2. Ich wohne in Hamburg. | | | | | ☒ | | |
| 3. Jungen können auch gute Freundschaften haben. | | | | | | ☒ | |
| 4. Mir ist Freundschaft wichtiger als Liebe. | | | ☒ | | | | |
| 5. Meine beste Freundin wohnt weit weg.° | | | | ☒ | | | ***weit ... :*** *far away* |
| 6. Was bedeutet eigentlich Freundschaft? | ☒ | | | | | | |
| 7. Jungen haben nur sehr selten gute Freundschaften. | | | | | ☒ | | |
| 8. Ich kenne meine beste Freundin schon seit dem Kindergarten. | | | | ☒ | | | |
| 9. Wahre Freundschaft gibt es nicht oft. | | | ☒ | | ☒ | | |
| 10. Freunde sind Menschen, die ich schon lange kenne. | | ☒ | | | | | |
| 11. Jungen finden es nicht cool, Gefühle zu zeigen. | | | | | | ☒ | |
| 12. Ich bin oft enttäuscht geworden. | | | | ☒ | | | |
| 13. Freunde sind Menschen, denen° ich vertraue. | | ☒ | | | | | *whom* |
| 14. Wir sehen uns in den Ferien. | | | | | ☒ | | |

**27** **Interview: Der beste Freund/Die beste Freundin.** Stellen Sie einem Partner/einer Partnerin die folgenden Fragen.

1. Wie heißt dein bester Freund oder deine beste Freundin?
2. Wie, wann und wo habt ihr euch kennen gelernt? Wie lange seid ihr schon die besten Freunde oder Freundinnen? Wohnt ihr jetzt in der gleichen Stadt?
3. Warum seid ihr Freunde? Habt ihr die gleichen Interessen? Was macht ihr gern zusammen?
4. Welche Eigenschaften findest du an deinem besten Freund/an deiner besten Freundin am besten?
5. Wie ist dein bester Freund oder deine beste Freundin anders als° deine anderen Freunde oder Freundinnen?
6. Ist dein bester Freund/deine beste Freundin ein Mann oder eine Frau? Glaubst° du, dass es Freundschaft (nicht Liebe) zwischen einem Mann und einer Frau gibt? Glaubst du, dass Freundschaften unter Männern oder unter Frauen dicker sind?
7. Ist dir die Freundschaft zu deinem besten Freund/deiner besten Freundin wichtiger als Liebe?

> Complete the **Ergänzen Sie** activity in your workbook for this text before doing the next activity.

***anders ... :*** *different from*

*believe*

## Bekannte oder Freunde?

In North America it is common to call most of the people you know reasonably well your "friends." German speakers distinguish between two types of "friends." **Bekannte** (*acquaintances*) may be people you know quite well or those you have seen only once in your life: classmates, co-workers, members of a club, or people you know only superficially. Even when the first name is used, a **Bekanntschaft** (*acquaintance relationship*) of this type maintains a certain emotional distance as indicated by the continued use of **Sie** in conversation. While German speakers may have many **Bekannte,** they have only a few **Freunde.** A **Freund** or **Freundin** is an intimate friend or a person with whom one shares a very special, permanent bond that is rare and treasured. Young people may also call such a friend their **Kumpel.**

In the relatively stable, less mobile cultures of central Europe, students often go through school with the same classmates, growing up together and evolving into a close circle of friends (**der Freundeskreis, eine Clique**). Whether they are of the same sex or opposite sex, such **Freunde** acquired in school often become close friends for life. When a **Bekanntschaft** among adults evolves into a **Freundschaft,** the new friends may acknowledge their special relationship with a ceremonial drink (**Brüderschaft trinken**). From this point on, they will use **du** with each other. Close friends of this type are usually referred to as **ein Freund von mir/eine Freundin von mir.** When German speakers refer to **mein Freund** or **meine Freundin,** they are talking about a person with whom they have a close relationship or even an intimate or romantic relationship.

Meine Freundin heißt Annette.

■ **Kulturkreuzung** Ist es im College leicht°, Freundschaften zu schließen°? Warum? Warum nicht? Machen Sie viel mit einer kleinen Clique oder sind Sie lieber mit ein oder zwei Personen zusammen? Haben Sie noch Kontakt zu Freunden aus der Schulzeit? Haben Sie lieber viele Bekannte oder nur ein paar gute Freunde? Mit wem sprechen Sie lieber über persönliche Dinge – mit Personen am College, mit Freunden von der Schule, mit Ihrer Familie?

*easy / **Freundschaften … :** to make friends*

**28**   **Diskussion: Zusammen ausgehen.**  In Europa geht man oft mit einer Gruppe aus. Bilden Sie eine Gruppe von drei Personen. Diskutieren Sie, welche Dinge man besser zu zweit° macht, und welche man in der Gruppe machen kann. Welche Dinge machen Sie alle lieber zu zweit, welche lieber in der Gruppe?

*zu zweit: two people together*

S1: *Gehst du lieber zu zweit oder in einer Gruppe ins Kino?*
S2: *Ich gehe lieber zu zweit ins Kino. Und du?*
S3: *Ich gehe auch lieber zu zweit ins Kino.* (oder)
    *Ich gehe lieber in einer Gruppe ins Kino.*

| *Aktivität* | *Zu zweit* | *In der Gruppe* |
|---|---|---|
| 1. ins Kino gehen | ☐ | ☐ |
| 2. tanzen | ☐ | ☐ |
| 3. in ein Restaurant gehen | ☐ | ☐ |
| 4. spazieren gehen | ☐ | ☐ |
| 5. fernsehen | ☐ | ☐ |
| 6. für eine Prüfung lernen | ☐ | ☐ |
| 7. ... | ☐ | ☐ |

## Wissenswerte Vokabeln: Freundschaft und Liebe
### Describing personal relationships

Sie sieht gut aus.
Er findet sie attraktiv.

Sie spricht ihn an.
Sie flirtet mit ihm.

Sie umarmt ihn.
Er küsst sie. Sie küsst ihn.
Sie schmusen.

Sie mögen einander.
Sie haben einander
lieb. Er hat sie lieb.
Sie hat ihn lieb.

Sie verlieben sich
ineinander. Es wird
ernst. Er zieht ein.
Sie leben zusammen.

Sie haben
Krach/Streit
miteinander.

Er hat Liebes-
kummer.

Sie ver-
söhnen sich.

*Das ist meine Verlobte!*

Sie verloben sich.

Sie lernen die Verwandten kennen.

Sie heiraten: Sie werden Mann und Frau.

---

**Sprache im Alltag: Expressing fondness or love**

German speakers use three expressions to describe fondness or love for a person. Expressions with **mögen** indicate fondness, while expressions with **lieb haben** indicate fondness verging on love. **Lieben** is used explicitly to indicate romantic love.

| | |
|---|---|
| Ich mag dich. | *I like you.* |
| Ich hab' dich lieb. | *I am really fond of you.* |
| Ich liebe dich. | *I love you.* |

**W. Vok.** Although the German reference to one's husband or wife as **mein Mann** or **meine Frau** may strike you as odd, it is in fact correct German for *my husband* or *my wife.*

**Additional vocabulary: schwul** *(gay)*, **lesbisch** *(lesbian)* **die Braut** *(bride)*, **der Bräutigam** *(groom).*

---

🟧 Du hast einen neuen Freund? Wie findest du ihn?

**29    Ein Liebesgedicht.** Schreiben Sie ein Liebesgedicht mit sechs Zeilen und lesen Sie dann das Gedicht der Klasse vor. Bilden Sie Sätze mit den folgenden Verben.

| | | |
|---|---|---|
| geheiratet | schön ausgesehen | angesprochen |
| ernst geworden | geküsst | attraktiv gefunden |
| gut ausgesehen | geschmust | sich verliebt |
| Liebeskummer gehabt | sich verlobt | angesehen |

🟧 *Er hat gut ausgesehen.*

**30    Aktivitäten mit Freunden.** Kreuzen Sie an, wie oft Sie die folgenden Aktivitäten mit einem (Ihrem) Freund/mit einer (Ihrer) Freundin im letzten Jahr gemacht haben. Dann fragen Sie einen Partner/eine Partnerin.

🟧 S1: *Wie oft bist du mit deinem Freund (deiner Freundin) Rad gefahren?*
  S2: *Wir sind selten miteinander Rad gefahren. Und du?*
  S1: *Wir sind oft miteinander Rad gefahren.*

**Aktivitäten mit Freunden.** Remember that **ein Freund/ eine Freundin** generally refer to good friends while **mein Freund/meine Freundin** mostly refer to a romantic relationship.

| | Nie 0% | Selten 20% | Oft 60% | Sehr oft 80% | Immer 100% | |
|---|:---:|:---:|:---:|:---:|:---:|---|
| 1. Rad gefahren | ☐ | ☐ | ☐ | ☐ | ☐ | |
| 2. ins Kino gegangen | ☐ | ☐ | ☐ | ☐ | ☐ | |
| 3. ins Restaurant gegangen | ☐ | ☐ | ☐ | ☐ | ☐ | |
| 4. zusammen ein Bier getrunken | ☐ | ☐ | ☐ | ☐ | ☐ | |
| 5. Hausaufgaben gemacht | ☐ | ☐ | ☐ | ☐ | ☐ | |
| 6. ein Buch gelesen | ☐ | ☐ | ☐ | ☐ | ☐ | |
| 7. ein Theaterstück° gesehen | ☐ | ☐ | ☐ | ☐ | ☐ | *play* |

| | Nie 0% | Selten 20% | Oft 60% | Sehr oft 80% | Immer 100% | |
|---|---|---|---|---|---|---|
| 8. Verwandte besucht | ☐ | ☐ | ☐ | ☐ | ☐ | |
| 9. über andere Leute gesprochen | ☐ | ☐ | ☐ | ☐ | ☐ | |
| 10. Pläne für die Zukunft° diskutiert | ☐ | ☐ | ☐ | ☐ | ☐ | *future* |

## Freie Kommunikation

**Die Einladung.** Sie finden eine Person attraktiv und möchten sie in die Kneipe einladen. Die andere Person hat wenig Interesse. Sie sind aber sehr motiviert und geben nicht auf°.

*geben … : don't give up*

## Schreibecke

**Eine Seifenoper° schreiben.** Schreiben Sie eine kurze Seifenoper (fünf bis acht Sätze). Benutzen Sie die Fragen unten und Wörter und Ausdrücke aus **Wissenswerte Vokabeln: Freundschaft und Liebe.** Viel Spaß!

*soap opera*

1. Was ist der Titel der Seifenoper?
2. Wie heißen die Personen? Was sind die Eigenschaften jeder° Person?
3. Was ist vorher passiert°?
4. Was sind die momentanen Beziehungen°?

*of each*
*ist … : already happened*
*relationships*

🟨 **Lieben und Leben:** *Die Personen heißen Beate, Torsten, Hanno und Sabine. Hanno findet viele Frauen attraktiv und sieht sehr gut aus. Beate ist hübsch und ziemlich lustig. Torsten […] Vorher war Beate in Hanno verliebt, aber Hanno hat Sabine geküsst. […] Beate ist jetzt böse° auf Hanno. Sie geht mit Torsten aus und er ist in sie verliebt.*

*angry*

## Strukturen und Vokabeln

## II Expressing what you know and don't know
### The verbs **kennen** and **wissen**

German uses two separate verbs meaning to *know*. **Kennen** is used when referring to "knowing" people or places and occurs with a direct object.

> **Kennst** du meinen Freund Lars?   *Do you **know** my friend Lars?*
> Ja, ich **kenne** ihn.   *Yes, I **know** him.*

In contrast, German speakers use the verb **wissen** to express factual knowledge.

> Es ist kalt heute. **Weißt** du das nicht?   *It's cold today. Don't you **know** that?*

> Both **wissen** and **kennen** are mixed verbs. Their past participles are **gewusst** and **gekannt**.

> **Wissen Sie** or **Weißt du** may be used in a narrative to hold the listener's attention, the same way that English speakers use *you know* … : **Und dann, weißt du, haben wir uns geküsst.**

## Subordinate clauses with **ob** and **dass**

### A. The subordinating conjunction **dass**

Frequently the factual knowledge expressed by speakers with the verbs **wissen, glauben,** or **denken** is in the form of an entire sentence or clause.

> Ich **weiß, dass** es heute kalt ist.     *I know that it's cold today.*

A clause usually has a subject and a verb. When a clause stands by itself it is known as a sentence or main clause (**Hauptsatz**). A dependent or subordinate clause (**Nebensatz**) cannot stand alone; it depends upon a main clause and is introduced by a subordinating conjunction, e.g., **dass** (*that*) followed by the subject of the subordinate clause. A comma always separates a dependent clause from the main clause.

The conjugated verb of a subordinate clause comes at the end. Separable prefixes are reunited with the conjugated verb at the end of the clause. Auxiliary verbs follow past participles because they are conjugated.

> Ich weiß, **dass** er gut **aussieht.**     *I know that he is good-looking.*
> Weißt du, **dass** ich ein neues     *Do you know that I bought a*
>     Auto **gekauft habe?**     *new car?*

Speakers also often use a **dass**-clause to express that something is good (**gut**), interesting (**interessant**), important (**wichtig**), etc., or that a person is disappointed (**enttäuscht**), happy (**froh**), sad (**traurig**), etc.

> Es ist wichtig, **dass** wir Deutsch     *It is important **that** we speak*
>     sprechen.     *German.*

**Dass** may be omitted. In that case, the verb reverts to main clause position.

> Ich glaube, **dass es** dicke Freundschaften zwischen Jungs **gibt.**
> Ich glaube, **es gibt** dicke Freundschaften zwischen Jungs.

### B. The subordinating conjunction **ob**

To express that they do not know something, German speakers use a negated form of the verb **wissen** with the subordinating conjunction **ob** (*if, whether*), followed by a reference to the missing information. This is, in essence, an indirect yes/no question.

> Ich **weiß nicht, ob** sie heute     *I don't know whether she is coming*
>     kommt.     *today.*

German speakers also use **ob** with the affirmative expressions **fragen, will wissen,** and **möchte wissen** to obtain more information.

> Ich **frage** euch, **ob** es die wahre     *I'm asking you if true friendship*
>     Freundschaft noch gibt.     *still exists.*
> Sie **will wissen, ob** er sie wirklich     *She wants to know whether he really*
>     geliebt hat.     *loved her.*

**31** **Traumpartner(in).** Welche Eigenschaften hat Ihr Traumpartner/ Ihre Traumpartnerin? Wie wichtig sind diese Eigenschaften für Sie? Kreuzen Sie **Gar nicht wichtig/Wichtig/Sehr wichtig** an. Fragen Sie dann einen Partner/eine Partnerin.

S1:  *Ist es wichtig, dass dein Traumpartner sportlich ist?*
S2:  *Nein, es ist gar nicht wichtig. Ist es wichtig, dass deine Traumpartnerin viel Geld hat?*
S1:  *Nein, es ist nicht wichtig, dass sie viel Geld hat. Ist es wichtig, dass …?*

| | *Gar nicht wichtig* | *Wichtig* | *Sehr wichtig* | |
|---|---|---|---|---|
| 1.  Er/Sie ist unternehmungslustig°. | ☐ | ☐ | ☐ | *likes to do things* |
| 2.  Er/Sie ist ehrlich°. | ☐ | ☐ | ☐ | *honest* |
| 3.  Er/Sie ist sportlich. | ☐ | ☐ | ☐ | |
| 4.  Er/Sie hat viel Geld. | ☐ | ☐ | ☐ | |
| 5.  Er/Sie sieht gut aus. | ☐ | ☐ | ☐ | |
| 6.  Meine Eltern mögen ihn/sie. | ☐ | ☐ | ☐ | |
| 7.  Er/Sie mag die Natur. | ☐ | ☐ | ☐ | |
| 8.  Er/Sie liest viel. | ☐ | ☐ | ☐ | |
| 9.  Er/Sie trinkt keinen Alkohol. | ☐ | ☐ | ☐ | |
| 10.  Er/Sie spricht Deutsch und Englisch. | ☐ | ☐ | ☐ | |
| 11.  Er/Sie ist romantisch. | ☐ | ☐ | ☐ | |
| 12.  Er/Sie hat viel Humor. | ☐ | ☐ | ☐ | |
| 13.  Meine Katze (Mein Hund) mag ihn/sie. | ☐ | ☐ | ☐ | |

**Schreibecke**

**Freund(in) oder Traumpartner(in)?** Gute Freunde sind nicht unbedingt Traumpartner. Beschreiben Sie in zehn Sätzen einen guten Freund/eine gute Freundin mit dem Vokabular aus der Aktivität „Traumpartner(in)".

## III Expanding on an opinion or idea
### Infinitive clauses with **zu**

A variant of the subordinate clause is the **zu** clause. **Zu** is frequently used after an adjective or a noun with an infinitive to expand on an idea. While the verb still occurs at the end of the clause, it is not conjugated and occurs in the infinitive form after **zu.**

| | |
|---|---|
| Es ist *einfach*, verliebt **zu sein.** | *It is easy to be in love.* |
| Es ist *uncool*, es **zu sagen.** | *It is uncool to say it.* |
| Anna *hat Zeit*, eine E-Mail **zu schreiben.** | *Anna has time to write an e-mail.* |

Verbs with a separable prefix insert **zu** between the prefix and the stem in infinitive clauses.

Es ist einfach, ihn an**zu**rufen.    *It is easy to call him up.*

„Meint ihr, dass er der Richtige für mich ist?"

**32  Ist es cool?** Kombinieren Sie zwei Satzteile and fragen Sie einen Partner/eine Partnerin.

🟨 Ist es cool? Du lernst Deutsch.

S1:  *Ist es cool, Deutsch zu lernen?*

S2:  *O, ja! Es ist sehr cool, Deutsch zu lernen. Hast du Interesse, Japanisch zu lernen?*

1. Ist es cool?        Du kommst am Samstag mit.
2. Hast du Interesse?   Du liest das Buch.
3. Hast du Zeit?        Du lernst Japanisch.
4. Seid ihr froh°?      Ihr fahrt im Sommer nach Italien.          *glücklich*
5. Ist es schwierig°?   Du besuchst Südamerika.                    *difficult*
6. Ist es leicht?       Du lernst Deutsch/Arabisch.
7. Ist es gut?          Du hast wenige Freunde.
8. Bist du neugierig°?  Du machst viel mit deinen Freunden.        *curious*

## IV  Giving reasons

### Subordinate clauses with **weil**

To state a reason or a justification, German speakers use the subordinating conjunction **weil** *(because)*. The verb in the subordinate clause occurs at the end of the clause.

| | |
|---|---|
| Ich habe dich geküsst, **weil** du mir Leid getan hast. | *I kissed you because I felt sorry for you.* |
| Onkel Hannes hat ein Bier getrunken, **weil** er Durst hatte. | *Uncle Hannes drank a beer because he was thirsty.* |

> You learned about the coordinating conjunction **denn** *(because, for)* in **Kapitel 3.** Because it is a coordinating conjunction, it uses main clause word order rather than requiring the conjugated verb to come at the end of the clause. More and more, many German speakers are now using main clause word order after **weil** as well.

**33  Warum machen sie das?** Geben Sie einen Grund° für die folgenden Handlungen°.          *reason*
*actions*

🟨 *Uschi und Hannes sind nach Hamburg gefahren, weil sie ihren Hochzeitstag haben.*

1. Uschi und Hannes sind nach Hamburg gefahren,
2. Hannes ist zum Hotel zurückgegangen,
3. Uschi hat an der Alster einen Spaziergang gemacht,
4. Uschi hat eine Cola bestellt°,
5. Uschi ruft das Deutsche Schauspielhaus an,
6. Uschi und Hannes müssen um 17.00 Uhr zurück im Hotel sein,

a. er hat sein Geld im Hotelzimmer vergessen.
b. das Wetter heute ist so schön.
c. Katja ruft heute Nachmittag an.
d. sie haben ihren Hochzeitstag.
e. sie hat Durst.
f. sie möchte für heute Abend Karten bestellen.

> Other subordinating conjunctions are **bevor** *(before)*, **nachdem** *(after)*, and **obwohl** *(although)*. They require placement of the verb at the end of the subordinate clause.

*ordered*

**34  Warum lernst du Deutsch?** Stellen Sie einem Partner/einer Partnerin die folgenden Fragen. Er/Sie gibt als Antwort einen Grund an.

🟨 S1:  *Warum lernst du Deutsch?*

S2:  *Ich lerne Deutsch, weil …*

1. Warum lernst du Deutsch?
    a. Ich möchte Deutschland besuchen.
    b. Ich habe deutsche Verwandte.
    c. Ich möchte gut Deutsch sprechen.
    d. Ich möchte Deutschlehrer(in) werden.
    e. Ich muss es für Chemie (Musik, Geschichte usw.) lernen.
    f. …

2. Warum ist Deutsch wichtig?
    a. Meine Eltern (Großeltern) sprechen Deutsch.
    b. Über 90 Millionen Europäer sprechen Deutsch.
    c. Mein Freund/Meine Freundin spricht Deutsch.
    d. Die deutsche Industrie ist sehr stark°.                              *strong*
    e. …

3. Warum besuchen viele Deutsche die USA?
    a. Sie haben Verwandte in den USA.
    b. Sie möchten die Nationalparks besuchen.
    c. Die USA haben viele Attraktionen.
    d. Sie wollen Englisch sprechen.
    e. …

## V   Positioning information in a German sentence

### Features of German word order

You have learned three important features of German word order (**Wortstellung**).

### A. Subject-verb inversion

In **Kapitel 2** you learned that in a main clause the conjugated verb always comes in the second position.

> Hannes **liebt** Uschi.    *Hannes loves Uschi.*

The subject may appear *after* the verb when the sentence begins with other elements.

> *direct object*          *verb*    *subject*
> Meine beste Freundin **kenne** ich schon seit dem Kindergarten.
> *I've known my best friend since kindergarten.*

> *adverb   verb    subject*
> Früher **haben** wir einander täglich gesehen.
> *We used to see each other daily.*

### B. Two-part placement of German verbs

Some verb forms occur at the end of the main clause. In **Kapitel 4** you learned that in modal + infinitive constructions, the infinitive is placed at the end of a main clause.

> Man **muss** sie schon länger **kennen**          *You have to know them*
> und richtiges Vertrauen zu ihnen                      *for a while and have real*
> **haben.**                                                      *trust in them.*

Remember that verbs with separable prefixes place the prefix at the end of the clause in the present tense.

Herr Günther **ruft** Uschi um 10 Uhr **an**.    *Herr Günther calls up Uschi at 10:00.*

Earlier in this chapter you learned that the past participle is placed at the end of a main clause in the conversational past.

Uschi **hat** in Hamburg Pharmazie **studiert** und als Kellnerin in einer Studentenkneipe **gearbeitet**.    *Uschi studied pharmaceutics in Hamburg and worked as a waitress in a student bar.*

## C. Verb forms at the end of a subordinate clause

You learned earlier in this chapter that in German the conjugated verb is placed at the end of a subordinate clause.

Ein Philosoph hat einmal gesagt, dass es die wahre Liebe selten **gibt.**
*A philosopher once said that true love is rare.*

A subordinate clause may begin with a subordinating conjunction (e.g., **dass, ob, weil**) or with a question word (e.g., **wann, warum, was, wie,** or **wo).**

ANNA:    Weißt du, **wo** sie wohnt?    *Do you know where she lives?*

KATJA:    Nein. Ich weiß auch nicht, **wie** sie heißt.    *No. I don't know her name either.*

The separable prefix appears joined with the verb at the end of a subordinate clause.

USCHI:    Weißt du, wann Anna **ankommt?**    *Do you know when Anna is arriving?*

KATJA:    Nein, nur, dass sie vorher **anruft.**    *No, only that she will call first.*

**35    Ob sie mich liebt?** Karl und Inge sind Studenten an der Universität in Tübingen. Karl hat Inge kennen gelernt und jetzt hat er Liebeskummer. Stellen Sie einem Partner/einer Partnerin Fragen.

S1:    *Was weiß Karl über Inge?*
S2:    *Er weiß, dass sie aus Ulm kommt. Und was weiß er nicht?*
S1:    *Er weiß nicht, wie alt sie ist. Und was möchte er wissen?*
S2:    *Er möchte wissen, ob sie gern italienisch isst.*

| *Karl weiß* | *Karl weiß nicht* | *Karl möchte wissen* |
| --- | --- | --- |
| 1. Sie kommt aus Ulm. | Wie alt ist sie? | Isst sie gern italienisch? |
| 2. Sie sieht gut aus. | Ist sie romantisch? | Geht sie gern spazieren? |
| 3. Sie hat viel Humor. | Ist sie sportlich? | Tanzt sie gern? |
| 4. Sie studiert Betriebswirtschaft. | Wohnt sie schon lange hier? | Mag sie die Natur? |

## VI Talking about activities that continue from the past into the present

### Present tense verbs with **seit, schon,** and **erst**

English and German speakers have different ways of expressing past activities that still have relevance in the present. Where English speakers use the present perfect (e.g., *have known*), German speakers use the present tense (e.g., **kennen**) together with the preposition **seit** (*since, for*).

> Meine beste Freundin kenne ich schon     *I have (already) known my best*
>    seit dem Kindergarten.     *friend since kindergarten.*

An accusative time expression (e.g, **drei Jahre**) may be used in place of **seit.**

> Ich kenne Uli **drei Jahre.**     *I've known Uli for three years.*

German speakers use **schon** (*already*) to add emphasis, indicating that the speaker perceives the stated duration to be long. If the speaker perceives the duration to be short, he/she uses the word **erst** (*only*). **Schon** and **erst** can be used with or without **seit.**

> Ich kenne Uli **schon drei Jahre.**     *I've already known Uli for three years.*
>           **schon seit drei Jahren.**
> Ich kenne Uli **erst drei Jahre.**     *I've only known Uli for three years.*
>           **erst seit drei Jahren.**

> The preposition **seit** requires the dative case. The dative case and dative endings of words will be explained in **Kapitel 6.**

> Because of the dative with **seit, Jahren** ends in an **-n.** The accusative expression does not: **Jahre.**

English verbs such as *to learn, to live, to eat, to smoke, to write,* etc., express activities that may have started in the past and continue into the present. The idea of duration in English is expressed with the present perfect continuous form (*have been learning,* etc.). German does not have an equivalent verbal form for the English continuous *-ing* form and uses the present tense with phrases using **schon/erst** + accusative or **seit** + dative instead.

> Ich lerne **seit sechs Monaten** Deutsch.     *I have been learning German*
>       **schon sechs Monate**     *for six months.*
>       **erst sechs Monate**

**36 Wie lange machst du das schon?** Sie möchten Ihren Partner/Ihre Partnerin besser kennen lernen. Stellen Sie einander die folgenden Fragen.

> **Wie lange machst du das schon?** The question requires **schon,** however, you can answer with **schon** or **erst,** depending on whether you feel the duration is long or short.

> ▪ S1:  *Wie lange lernst du schon Deutsch?*
>    S2:  *Ich lerne (erst) seit vier Monaten Deutsch.*

| **Was?** | **Wie lange?** |
|---|---|
| 1. Deutsch lernen | schon/erst seit _____ Jahren/Monaten/Tagen |
| 2. (nicht/nicht mehr) rauchen° | schon/erst _____ Jahre/Monate/Tage |
| 3. Auto fahren | schon/erst seit _____ Minuten/Stunden |
| 4. an dieser Uni studieren | schon/erst _____ Minuten/Stunden |
| 5. mit dem Computer schreiben | |
| 6. keinen Alkohol trinken | |
| 7. im Studentenwohnheim wohnen | |

*smoke*

**F r e i e   K o m m u n i k a t i o n**

**Stolze° Eltern.** Sie sind eine stolze Mutter (ein stolzer Vater). Ihr Partner/Ihre Partnerin ist auch eine stolze Mutter (ein stolzer Vater). Vergleichen Sie Ihre tollen Kinder. Was hat Ihr Sohn (Ihre Tochter) schon gemacht?

*proud*

- S1:  *Ich bin stolz darauf, dass mein Sohn schon drei Jahre Deutsch lernt.*
  S2:  *Und meine Tochter hat schon vier Bücher auf Deutsch, Englisch, Franzö-sisch und Chinesisch geschrieben.*

  **S c h r e i b e c k e**

**Reisetagebuch.** Sie sind in Deutschland. Schreiben Sie in ein Reisetagebuch, was Sie schon gemacht, gesehen und gelernt haben. Schreiben Sie auch auf, was Sie noch wissen oder sehen wollen. Verwenden Sie Konjunktionen wie **dass, ob** und **weil** und die Fragewörter als Konjunktionen. Verwenden Sie auch die folgenden Konstruktionen: **Ich möchte/will wissen, ob … ; Ich frage mich** (*wonder*), **ob … ; In Deutschland ist es leicht, … zu ….**

- Ich habe schon gesehen, wie freundlich die Leute sind. Ich habe schon viele nette° Leute kennen gelernt. Ich möchte aber auch wissen, ob …

*nice*

## *Zieltext*    Ein Gespräch° mit Opa und Oma Kunz

*Gespräch = die Konversation*

Anna ist nach Bad Krozingen zu ihren Großeltern gefahren. Alle drei sind froh, dass sie einander endlich sehen. Anna hört, wie ihre Eltern einander in Heidel-berg kennen gelernt haben. Sie will auch wissen, warum Oma und Opa Kunz noch nie nach Amerika gekommen sind.

### *Vorschau*

**37    Thematische Fragen: Deine Großeltern.**  Beantworten Sie die folgenden Fragen mit einem Partner/mit einer Partnerin auf Deutsch.

> **Thematische Fragen.** If your grandparents have passed away, answer these questions in the conversa-tional past (e.g., **Meine Großeltern haben in Iowa gewohnt**).

- S1:  *Leben deine Großeltern noch?*
  S2:  *Ja, sie leben noch.* (oder)
        *Nein, sie sind gestorben.*

1. Leben deine Großeltern noch?
2. Wohnen deine Großeltern weit weg?
3. Wie oft sprichst du mit deinen Großeltern? Bekommst° du oft Post von den Großeltern?
4. Besuchst du deine Großeltern oft? Wie oft? Sind sie froh, dich zu sehen?
5. Hast du mal° mit deinen Großeltern über deine Eltern gesprochen?

*receive*

*ever*

6. Hast du Fotos von deinen Eltern als Kinder gesehen? Wie haben sie ausgesehen?

7. Hast du eine gute Beziehung zu anderen älteren Menschen? Welche Rolle spielen sie in deinem Leben?

**38** **Annas Familienstammbaum°.** Können Sie sich noch an Annas Familie erinnern°? Füllen Sie den Stammbaum aus.

*family tree*
*remember*

1.
_____

2.
_____

3.
_____

4.
_____

5.
_____

6.
_____

7.
_____

8.
_____

9.
_____

10.
_____

**39** **Ein Gespräch mit Oma und Opa Kunz.** Wie wahrscheinlich ist es, dass Oma und Opa mit Anna über folgende Themen sprechen?

|  | *Sehr unwahrscheinlich* | *Vielleicht* | *Sehr wahrscheinlich* | |
|---|---|---|---|---|
| 1. Annas Mutter und Vater | ☐ | ☐ | ☐ | |
| 2. Annas Freund in den USA | ☐ | ☐ | ☐ | |
| 3. Rockmusik | ☐ | ☐ | ☐ | |
| 4. Gewalt° in den USA | ☐ | ☐ | ☐ | *violence* |
| 5. die deutsche Sprache | ☐ | ☐ | ☐ | |
| 6. das Wetter | ☐ | ☐ | ☐ | |
| 7. junge Leute | ☐ | ☐ | ☐ | |
| 8. Opas Gesundheit | ☐ | ☐ | ☐ | |
| 9. Omas Freundin | ☐ | ☐ | ☐ | |
| 10. Annas Studium | ☐ | ☐ | ☐ | |
| 11. Geld | ☐ | ☐ | ☐ | |
| 12. Annas Probleme | ☐ | ☐ | ☐ | |

**40** **Satzdetektiv.** Welche Sätze bedeuten ungefähr das Gleiche?

1. Mit dem Flugzeug **dauert** es nur sieben Stunden. *b*
2. Das war keine leichte **Entscheidung.** *A*
3. Wir waren eigentlich **dagegen.** *D*
4. Nachher **schwätzen** deine Kinder dann nur Englisch. *c*

a. Das war nicht einfach zu tun.
b. Mit Lufthansa fliegt man sieben Stunden von den USA nach Deutschland.
c. Später sprechen deine Kinder kein Deutsch.
d. Oma und Opa haben es nicht gut gefunden, dass Hannelore einen Amerikaner geheiratet hat.

5. Der Opa war überhaupt nicht **begeistert** von der Idee. *f*
6. Ich habe ihm dann **zugeredet.** *e*
7. Wir müssen schließlich damit **fertig werden.** *H*
8. Warum kommt ihr uns nicht **besuchen** in Amerika? *G*

e. Oma hat Opa gezeigt, dass das auch gut sein kann.
f. Opa hat nicht gedacht, dass das eine gute Idee war.
g. Warum kommt ihr nicht nach Amerika, um uns zu sehen?
h. Opa und Oma müssen das eben akzeptieren.

## Zieltext

### Ein Gespräch mit Opa und Oma Kunz

Anna besucht ihre Großeltern in Bad Krozingen. Sie sprechen über Annas Mutter Hannelore.

 Hören Sie gut zu.

> The **Zieltext** contains two simple past tense verb forms that will be explained in more detail in **Kapitel 10: war** *(was)*, **wollten** *(wanted)*.

## Rückblick

 **41** **Gemischte Sätze.** Bringen Sie diese Sätze aus dem Dialog in die richtige Reihenfolge.

_4_ Wir wollten° unsere Kinder eben hier behalten°.          *wanted / to keep*
_2_ Mit dem Flugzeug dauert es nur sieben Stunden.
_1_ Ach, Anna, es ist schön, dass du da bist.
_5_ Wie hat Mama Papa überhaupt kennen gelernt?
_6_ Ja, wir bekommen so viel aus Amerika.
_3_ Was habt ihr gedacht?

**42    Stimmt das?** Stimmen diese Aussagen zum Text oder nicht? Wenn nicht, was stimmt?

|  | Ja, das stimmt. | Nein, das stimmt nicht. |
|---|---|---|
| 1. Oma findet, Amerika ist nicht sehr weit weg. | ☐ | ☒ |
| 2. Oma und Opa Kunz mögen Bob nicht. | ☐ | ☒ |
| 3. Hannelore und Bob haben einander in Berlin kennen gelernt. | ☐ | ☒ |
| 4. Oma und Opa Kunz wollen bald nach Denver oder Dallas fahren. | ☐ | ☒ |
| 5. Oma und Opa Kunz sind noch nie° in Amerika gewesen. | ☒ | ☐ |
| 6. Oma und Opa Kunz haben Amerika schon oft im Fernsehen gesehen. | ☒ | ☐ |
| 7. Sie mögen Amerika nicht – da gibt es zu viel Gewalt und Hektik. | ☒ | ☐ |

*noch ... : never yet*

**43    Kurz gefragt.** Beantworten Sie diese Fragen auf Deutsch.

1. Warum sind Anna und ihre Großeltern glücklich?
2. Warum finden die Großeltern es nicht so gut, dass ihre Tochter Hannelore jetzt in den USA wohnt? Welche Probleme nennen sie?
3. Welches Kommunikationsproblem erwähnen° die Großeltern?
4. Warum kommen sie nicht nach Amerika?
5. Warum haben Oma und Opa die amerikanischen Städte Denver, Dallas, San Francisco und Miami im Fernsehen gesehen?
6. Welche Vorstellungen° haben die Großeltern von Amerika?

*mention*

*impressions*

## Freie Kommunikation

**Rollenspiel: Heimweh°.** Sie sind Austauschstudent(in) und studieren zur Zeit in Luzern in der Schweiz. Sie vermissen Ihre Heimat° und haben Heimweh. Erzählen Sie einem Studenten/einer Studentin über Ihre Heimat und Ihre Familie zu Hause. Was haben Sie zu Hause alles gemacht? Wie ist das Wetter? Was haben Sie im Frühling, Sommer, Herbst und Winter gemacht? Der Partner/Die Partnerin stellt viele Fragen.

*homesickness*
*hometown*

## Schreibecke

**Wir sind verliebt!** Sie studieren in Berlin und haben dort eine sehr nette Person kennen gelernt. Sie verbringen schon viel Zeit miteinander, und Sie möchten bei dieser Person einziehen und mit ihr zusammenleben. Schreiben Sie einen Brief an Ihre Eltern. Informieren Sie Ihre Eltern über die Fragen:

• Wie und wo haben Sie sich kennen gelernt?
• Was haben Sie zusammen gemacht?

Fragen Sie Ihre Eltern, ob sie dafür oder dagegen sind.

> Complete the **Ergänzen Sie** activity in your workbook for this text before doing the next activity.

## Wortschatz

### In der Kneipe

**der Kellner, - / die Kellnerin, -nen** *waiter / waitress*

**die Kneipe, -n** *pub, bar*

**das Trinkgeld, -er** *tip, gratuity*

**arbeiten (hat gearbeitet)** *to work*

**bestellen (hat bestellt)** *to order*

**verdienen (hat verdient)** *to earn*

**verkaufen (hat verkauft)** *to sell*

### Freundschaft, Liebe und Leute

**der / die Bekannte, -n** *acquaintance, casual friend*

**die Einladung, -en** *invitation*

**die Frau, -en** *wife; woman*

**der Freund, -e / die Freundin, -nen** *friend*

**die Freundschaft, -en** *friendship*
  **dicke Freundschaften** *close, intimate friendships*
  **eine Freundschaft schließen** *to form a friendship*

**der Junge, [-n], -n** *boy, guy;* **die Jungs** *boys, guys (slang)*

**der Kontakt** *contact*

**der Krach, ⁚e** *argument, quarrel; noise*
  **Krach haben** *to have a fight, quarrel*

**der Kumpel, -s** *buddy, pal*

**die Leute** *(pl.) people*

**die Liebe, -n** *love*

**der Liebeskummer** *lovesickness; heartbreak*

**das Mädchen, -** *girl*

**der Mann, ⁚er** *husband; man*

**der Respekt** *respect*

**der Streit** *argument*

**die Sympathie** *likeability*

**die Treue** *loyalty*

**die Verabredung, -en** *date; appointment*

**der / die Verlobte** *fiancé(e)*

**das Vertrauen** *trust*

**an·sprechen (spricht an, hat angesprochen)** *to initiate a conversation (with someone)*

**aus·gehen (ist ausgegangen)** *to go out*

**aus·sehen (sieht aus, hat ausgesehen)** *to look, appear*

**diskutieren (hat diskutiert) (über + acc.)** *to discuss (a topic)*

**ein·laden (lädt ein, hat eingeladen)** *to invite; ask out*

**ein·ziehen (ist eingezogen)** *to move in*

**fertig werden (wird, ist geworden)** *to accept, come to grips with*

**flirten (hat geflirtet)** *to flirt*

**heiraten (hat geheiratet)** *to marry, get married*

**küssen (hat geküsst)** *to kiss*

**leben (hat gelebt)** *to live*
  **zusammen·leben (hat zusammengelebt)** *to live together*

**lieben (hat geliebt)** *to love*

**reden (hat geredet) (über + acc.)** *to talk (about a topic)*

**schmusen (hat geschmust)** *to cuddle, make out*

**treffen (trifft, hat getroffen)** *to meet*

**umarmen (hat umarmt)** *to embrace, hug*

**(sich) unterhalten (unterhält, hat unterhalten)** *to discuss, talk*

**verliebt (in + acc.) sein** *to be in love (with somebody)*

**weg·ziehen (ist weggezogen)** *to move away*

**attraktiv** *attractive*

**beide** *both*

**einander** *each other*

**ernst** *serious*

**selten** *rare, seldom*

**täglich** *daily, every day*

**treu** *loyal, true*

**wahr** *authentic, real*

**zusammen** *together*

**Ich habe dich lieb.** *I am really fond of you.*

**Ich liebe dich.** *I love you.*

**Ich mag dich.** *I like you.*

**Sie verlieben sich ineinander.** *They fall in love with each other.*

**Sie verloben sich.** *They get engaged.*

**Sie versöhnen sich.** *They reconcile, make up.*

**Vertrauen haben (zu + dat.)** *to trust*

**weit weg** *far away*

**zu zweit** *as a couple; in twos*

**zum ersten Mal** *for the first time*

### Das Gefühl

**böse** *angry*

**enttäuscht** *disappointed*

**froh** *happy*

**stolz** *proud*

**traurig** *sad*

### Das Wetter

**Wie ist das Wetter heute?** *What's the weather like today?*

**der Gefrierpunkt** *freezing point*

**das Gewitter** *electrical storm, thunderstorm*

**der Grad** *degree*

**der Nebel** *fog*

**der Regen** *rain*

**der Schauer, -** *rain shower*

**der Schnee** *snow*

**die Sonne, -n** *sun*

**der Sturm, ⁚e** *storm*

**die Temperatur, -en** *temperature*

**das Wetter** *weather*

**die Wolke, -n** *cloud*

**blitzen: es blitzt (es hat geblitzt)** *there is lightning*

**donnern (es hat gedonnert)** *to thunder*

**fallen (fällt, ist gefallen)** *to drop; to fall*

**regnen (es hat geregnet)** *to rain*

**scheinen (hat geschienen)** *to shine*

**schneien (es hat geschneit)** *to snow*
**sinken (ist gesunken)** *to sink; to drop*
**steigen (ist gestiegen)** *to rise; climb*

**bedeckt** *overcast*
**heiß** *hot*
**heiter** *clear*
**kalt** *cold*
**kühl** *cool*
**mies** *rotten, lousy*
**nass** *wet, damp*
**schwül** *humid*
**sonnig** *sunny*
**trocken** *dry*
**warm** *warm*
**windig** *windy*
**wolkig** *cloudy*

**Die Temperatur liegt um [zehn] Grad Celcius.** *The temperature is [ten] degrees Celcius.*

### Die Jahreszeiten

**die Jahreszeit, -en** *season*

**der Frühling** *spring*
**der Herbst** *autumn, fall*
**der Sommer** *summer*
**der Winter** *winter*

### Zeitausdrücke

**bald** *soon*
**bevor** *before*
**früher** *earlier, in the past*
**gestern** *yesterday*
**jetzt** *now*
**morgen** *tomorrow*

**erst** *only just;* **erst (seit)** *just since*
**schon** *already;* **schon (seit) Jahren** *for years*
**seit (erst seit, schon seit)** *since (+ time phrase); for (+ time phrase)*

### Andere Verben

**an·fangen (fängt an, hat ange-fangen)** *to start, begin*
**beginnen (hat begonnen)** *to begin*
**bekommen (hat bekommen)** *to get*
**bringen (hat gebracht)** *to bring*
**erfordern (hat erfordert)** *to require, demand*
**erzählen (hat erzählt)** *to tell, relate*
**glauben (hat geglaubt)** *to believe*
**heim·kommen (ist heimgekommen)** *to come home*
**liegen (hat gelegen)** *to lie*
**los·fahren (fährt los, ist losgefahren)** *to set off (on a trip)*
**mailen (hat gemailt)** *to e-mail*
**öffnen (hat geöffnet)** *to open*
**passieren (ist passiert)** *to happen*
**sagen (hat gesagt)** *to say*
**sitzen (hat gesessen)** *to sit*
**sterben (stirbt, ist gestorben)** *to die*
**surfen (hat gesurft)** *to surf*
**verlieren (hat verloren)** *to lose*

### Andere Wörter

**die Ferien** *(pl.) school vacation*
**die Zeitung, -en** *newspaper*

**außer** *except for*
**zwischen** *between, among*

**dass** *that*
**ob** *whether, if*
**trotzdem** *nevertheless, in spite of that*
**weil** *because*
**zu** *(+ inf.) to*

**einfach** *simple*
**erst (seit)** *only for*
**fertig** *finished*
**frei** *free*
**jede(r)** *each*

**leicht** *easy; light*
**richtig** *right, proper; real*
**schade** *too bad, unfortunate*
**schlecht** *bad*
**schlimm** *bad, nasty*
**schwierig** *difficult, hard*
**toll** *fantastic, great*

**eigentlich** *actually*
**fast** *almost, practically*
**ganz** *really, very; whole*
  **ganz nass** *completely wet*
  **ganz schlimm** *really bad*
  **die ganze Zeit** *the whole time*
**wenigstens** *at least*
**wirklich** *really*

### Andere Ausdrücke

**ein paar** *a few*
**ich frage mich, ob …** *I wonder if …*
**und so weiter (usw.)** *and so on, etcetera (etc.)*
**Was ist los?** *What's the matter?*
**Was noch?** *What else?*

### Meine eigenen Wörter

_____
_____
_____
_____
_____
_____

# Willkommen in Tübingen

■ Tübingen bietet viele Sehenswürdigkeiten.

**Online Study Center**

Go to the *Vorsprung* Website at *http:// college.hmco.com/pic/ vorsprung2e.*

**In this chapter you will learn to express giving or lending to others, talk about the location of things, express when something happens, make compliments, and talk about ailments.**

## Kommunikative Funktionen

• Expressing the beneficiary or recipient of an action
• Indicating location
• Expressing when we do things
• Expressing temporal and spatial relationships with dative prepositions
• Expressing gratitude, pleasure, ownership, and need for assistance
• Specifying what you are talking about

## Strukturen

• The dative case
• The subordinating conjunction **wenn**
• Dative prepositions
• Dative verbs and expressions
• **Der**-words

## Vokabeln

• Das Studentenzimmer
• Ein Einfamilienhaus
• Körperteile

## Kulturelles

• Wo Studenten wohnen
• Tübingen
• Ausländer in Deutschland

# Anna zieht ins Wohnheim ein

Anna zieht in ein Tübinger Studentenwohnheim ein. Es heißt Waldhäuser-Ost. Barbara, eine Studentin im ersten Semester aus Dresden, hat das Zimmer neben Anna. Sie hilft Anna beim Einzug°.

*Vorschau*

*Wissenswerte Vokabeln: das Studentenzimmer und die Möbel*
*Identifying objects*

> *hilft … : helps Anna move in*

> **W. Vok.** In northern Germany, **der Stuhl** (regular chair) and **der Sessel** (arm-chair) refer to different types of chairs. In Austria **der** *Stuhl is rarely used at all.*

🟧 Was für° Möbel hast du im Zimmer?   *Ich habe …*

> *What kind of*

**1   Hast du das im Zimmer?**  Fragen Sie einen Partner/eine Partnerin, was er/sie im Zimmer hat. Benutzen Sie die Akkusativformen: einen/keinen, ein/kein, eine/keine.

🟧 S1:  *Hast du eine Stereoanlage im Zimmer?*
   S2:  *Ja, ich habe eine Stereoanlage. Und du?* (oder)
      *Nein, ich habe keine Stereoanlage. Und du?*

**2   Thematische Fragen.**  Beantworten Sie diese Fragen auf Deutsch.

1. Was brauchen Studenten für die Universität? Machen Sie eine Liste.
2. Wohnen Sie mit anderen Studenten in einem Studentenwohnheim? Wie finden Sie das? Was können Sie da alles machen? Was ist verboten°?
3. Wohnen Sie zu Hause? Was können Sie da machen? Was ist verboten?

> Ask your partner whether he/she has these additional items: **das Wasserbett, der Farbfernseher, das Telefon, der Mikrowellenherd, das Handy, die Kaffee-maschine, der Mini-Kühlschrank** (*mini-refrigerator*).

> *forbidden*

**3**    **Satzdetektiv.** Welche Sätze bedeuten ungefähr das Gleiche?

1. Anna **zieht** ins Wohnheim **ein.** *A*
2. Ich bin selber **erst vor** einer **Woche** hier **eingezogen.** *C*
3. Ich **krieg'** die Tür nicht **auf.** *B*
4. Gib mir deinen Schlüssel. Ich **schließ'** dir die Tür **auf.** *F*
5. Hier, **guck mal**, Anna! *D*
6. **Gefällt dir** dein Zimmer denn nicht? *E*

a. Von jetzt an wohnt Anna im Studentenwohnheim.
b. Ich kann die Tür nicht öffnen.
c. Ich wohne erst seit einer Woche im Wohnheim.
d. Schau mal, Anna!
e. Findest du dein Zimmer nicht schön?
f. Gib mir den Schlüssel. Ich mache die Tür auf.

---

7. Du hast einen Schrank für deine **Klamotten.** *H*
8. Also, jetzt zeig' ich dir das Badezimmer, **wenn es dir recht ist.** *J*
9. Du hast wirklich **Schwein gehabt.** *I*
10. Du hast ein **Privatbad** bekommen: **Klo, Dusche** und Waschbecken. *G*
11. Du, ich **danke dir** echt für die Hilfe! *L*
12. Kannst du mir einen Stift **leihen?** *K*

g. Das Badezimmer hast du für dich allein: Toilette, Dusche und Waschbecken.
h. Du hast einen Schrank für deine Kleidung.
i. Du hast wirklich Glück gehabt.
j. Ich zeige dir das Badezimmer, wenn das O.K. ist.
k. Kannst du mir einen Stift geben?
l. Vielen Dank für deine Hilfe.

*Anlauftext*

    Hören Sie gut zu.

In German-speaking countries, floors are counted as follows: **das Erdgeschoss** *(first floor),* **erster Stock** *(second floor),* **zweiter Stock** *(third floor),* etc.

German door locks often include a deadbolt, which must be turned twice to lock the door.

**Zum** + verb in the infinitive (**ein Bett zum Schlafen**) is the equivalent of *for* + *-ing* verb (*a bed for sleeping*).

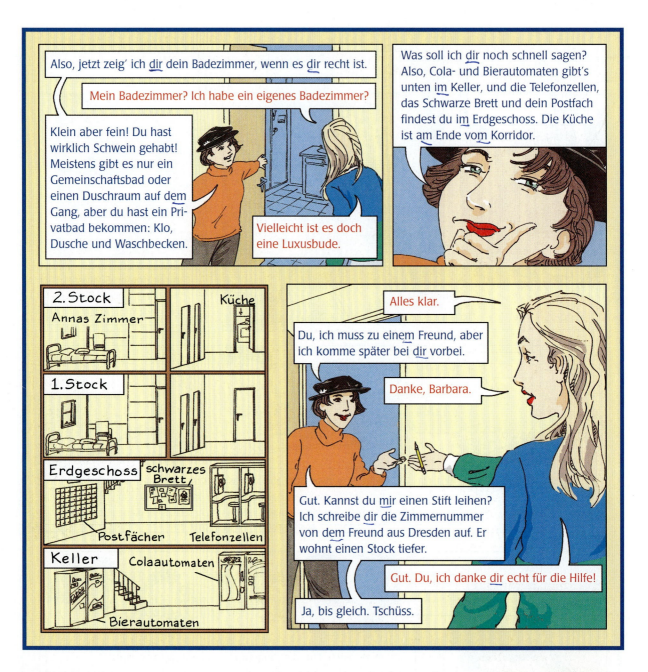

## Rückblick

**4** **Stimmt das?** Stimmen diese Aussagen zum Text oder nicht? Wenn nicht, was stimmt?

Because the legal drinking age in Germany for beer and wine is 16, it is quite common to find machines that dispense beer in residence halls.

|  | Ja, das stimmt. | Nein, das stimmt nicht. |
|---|---|---|
| 1. Anna muss den Weg zu ihrem Zimmer alleine finden. | ☐ | ☒ |
| 2. Barbara studiert schon lange in Tübingen. | ☐ | ☒ |

|  | Ja, das stimmt. | Nein, das stimmt nicht. |
|---|---|---|
| 3. Annas Zimmer ist gleich neben Barbaras Zimmer im zweiten Stock. | ☒ | ☐ |
| 4. Anna kann die Tür nicht aufschließen. Barbara nimmt den Schlüssel und hilft. | ☒ | ☐ |
| 5. Anna und Barbara finden, sie haben Luxusbuden im Studentenwohnheim. | ☒ | ☐ |
| 6. Barbara meint es ironisch, wenn sie sagt, deutsche Studenten stehen erst gegen Mittag auf und schlafen in den Vorlesungen. | ☒ | ☐ |
| 7. In diesem Wohnheim haben alle Zimmer ein Privatbad. | ☐ | ☒ |
| 8. Es gibt Milch- und Zigarettenautomaten im Erdgeschoss. | ☐ | ☒ |
| 9. Die Studenten können am Ende vom Korridor selber kochen. | ☒ | ☐ |
| 10. Anna leiht Barbara eine Zigarette. | ☐ | ☒ |

> Complete the **Ergänzen Sie** activity in your workbook for this text before doing the next activity.

---

### Sprache im Alltag: Expressions with animals

German speakers like to use colorful expressions involving animals.

| | |
|---|---|
| **Schwein haben** | *to be lucky* |
| Du **hast Schwein gehabt.** | |
| **einen Bärenhunger haben** | *to be hungry as a bear* |
| Er **hat einen Bärenhunger.** | |
| **einen Vogel haben** | *to be crazy* |
| Er **hat einen Vogel.** | |
| **(einen) Kater haben** | *to have a hangover* |
| Wir **haben** heute **einen Kater.** | |
| **hundemüde sein** | *to be dog-tired* |
| Ich **bin hundemüde.** | |

---

**5**  **Sie/Er weiß (nicht), dass …**  Welche Dinge weiß ein deutscher Student/eine deutsche Studentin wahrscheinlich nicht, wenn er/sie zuerst in ein amerikanisches Studentenwohnheim kommt? Welche Dinge weiß er/sie?

S1: *Weiß ein deutscher Student (eine deutsche Studentin), dass es keine Bierautomaten gibt?*

S2: *Nein, er (sie) weiß nicht, dass es keine Bierautomaten gibt.* (oder)
*Ja, er (sie) weiß, dass es keine Bierautomaten gibt.*

1. Es gibt keine Bierautomaten.
2. Man schläft in einem Bett.
3. *First floor* ist das Erdgeschoss.
4. Man kann Türen ohne Schlüssel abschließen.
5. Das Zimmer hat meistens° ein Telefon.
6. Das Badezimmer hat ein Klo.
7. Die Studenten essen zusammen in der *cafeteria.*
8. Man darf oft nicht rauchen.

*mostly, usually*

**6    Der Studentenalltag.** Was machen Sie als Student/ Studentin jeden Tag? Kreuzen Sie zuerst an, was Sie jeden Tag machen. Notieren Sie dann die Reihenfolge (zuerst … , dann … , später …). Fragen Sie dann einen Partner/eine Partnerin.

S1: *Was machst du zuerst?*
S2: *Zuerst stehe ich auf.*
S1: *Und dann?*

| | **Was?** | **Jeden Tag?** | **In welcher Reihenfolge?** | |
|---|---|---|---|---|
| 1. | frühstücken | ☐ | _____ | |
| 2. | Kaffee trinken | ☐ | _____ | |
| 3. | duschen° | ☐ | _____ | *to shower* |
| 4. | weggehen | ☐ | _____ | |
| 5. | Radio hören | ☐ | _____ | |
| 6. | aufstehen | ☐ | _____ | |
| 7. | den Wecker abstellen° | ☐ | _____ | *turn off* |
| 8. | Deutsch lernen | ☐ | _____ | |

**BRENNPUNKT KULTUR**

## Wo Studenten wohnen

Most universities in German-speaking countries are located in the center of town, surrounded by unrelated buildings, and are rarely arranged in an insular, campus-like setting. Because the universities do not assume responsibility for housing all students, students must compete for a limited number of subsidized dorm rooms or find their own housing on the more expensive open market (**der Wohnungsmarkt**). The shortage of space in town near the classroom buildings has resulted in the construction of many residence halls (**Studentenwohnheime**), as well as many research buildings, on the outskirts of town. Most residence halls consist primarily of single rooms (**Einzelzimmer**), which contain a bed, a desk, a bookcase, and a small table and chair. Separate from the sleeping quarters is a small entryway, which contains closet space or a freestanding wardrobe and a small sink. In older residence halls everyone living on the floor typically has to share the toilets (**die Toiletten/die WCs**) and the shower room (**der Duschraum**). Each floor is also equipped with a communal kitchen (**die Gemeinschaftsküche**) where students can store food and cooking utensils and cook their own meals. In general, student dormitories do not provide warm meals; instead, **die Mensa**, located at or near the university, serves both students and faculty.

According to the student census taken by Deutsches Studentenwerk in 2003, Tübingen dormitories can house only 19% of the student body. The majority of the student body must look for other accommodations. Many universities offer a placement service for rooms and apartments in town (**Zimmer- und Wohnungsvermittlung**) free of charge and often have a special placement office for foreign students. Nonetheless, many students still have to find creative solutions to their housing problems. Roughly 16% of all students live at home with their parents or relatives. 5% rent rooms in private homes or apartments (**zur Untermiete wohnen**), which often excludes cooking privileges and allows for little privacy. Another 23% of the student body shares apartments or private houses in residential cooperatives (**Wohngemeinschaften** or **WGs**), in which the housemates share costs and often the cooking, shopping, and cleaning responsibilities. The largest group of Tübingen students, 36%, simply get their own apartment and assume the responsibilities of paying rent and keeping up the household. Students have often staged demonstrations to focus government attention on the housing shortage, which has worsened since unification in 1990.

**Brennpunkt Kultur.** Students' expenses vary from city to city. In Tübingen, for example, single rooms in residence halls start at 180 Euros/month. A room in a private home usually costs much less. Real estate agencies (**Immobilienmakler**) require a 1- to 2-month rent fee. The daily meal offering in the **Mensa** in Tübingen costs 2.40 Euros.

■ **Kulturkreuzung** Wo wohnen Sie – privat oder im Studentenwohnheim? Wie viele Jahre muss man an Ihrer Universität im Studentenwohnheim wohnen? Welche Vorteile° bietet° das Studentenwohnheim: Telefonzellen? Einzelzimmer? Doppelzimmer? Gruppenzimmer? Was kostet ein Zimmer im Studentenwohnheim? Was kostet ein privates Zimmer? Gibt es viele Studenten, die lieber zu Hause wohnen und jeden Tag mit dem Auto zum Campus fahren?

*advantages / offers*

*„... und wenn, liebe Eltern, mein Vermieter° mit dem Auto unterwegs ist, dann ist es sogar richtig gemütlich° hier..."*            Zeichnung: Buchegger

*landlord*
*cozy*

 **7** **Unser Traumzimmer.** Sprechen Sie in einer Gruppe von drei Personen über Ihr Traumzimmer. Was haben Sie alles im Zimmer? Schreiben Sie eine Liste. Machen Sie dann eine Skizze° des Zimmers.

*sketch*

🔶 *In unserem Traumzimmer gibt es ein Wasserbett, eine ...*
*Das Zimmer ist ...*
*Das Zimmer hat ...*

### Freie Kommunikation

**Interview.** Stellen Sie einem Partner/einer Partnerin die folgenden Fragen.

1. Hast du eine Luxusbude? Wenn ja (nein), warum kann man das sagen?
2. Hat man hier im Wohnheim eine Küche auf dem Gang?
3. Gibt es Bierautomaten an unserer Uni? Kann man an der Uni überhaupt Bier kaufen oder trinken?
4. Kann man an der Uni Zigaretten kaufen?
5. Was hast du in deinem Zimmer?

**Rollenspiel: Neu im Wohnheim.** S1 ist neu im Wohnheim und sucht sein/ihr Zimmer. S2 wohnt schon im Wohnheim und hilft S1, das Zimmer zu finden. Was sagen Sie? Hier sind einige Ausdrücke.

> Kannst du mir bitte helfen? • Das ist nett von dir. • Ich zeige dir ... • Gib mir ...
> • Hast du auch so ein ... im Zimmer?

**Schreibecke**

**Eine E-Mail an Katja.** Anna schreibt Katja Günther eine E-Mail. Sie will über ihren ersten Tag im Studentenwohnheim, über Barbara, ihr Zimmer und die Dinge im Keller und im Erdgeschoss schreiben. Aber Anna wird müde. Schreiben Sie Annas E-Mail fertig.

Liebe Katja,

heute bin ich im Studentenwohnheim Waldhäuser-Ost angekommen. Ich habe eine nette Studentin kennen gelernt. Sie heißt Barbara Müller und kommt aus Dresden. Sie hat mir geholfen. Sie hat …

## Strukturen und Vokabeln

## I Expressing the beneficiary or recipient of an action

### The dative case

You have already learned that the nominative case is used for the subject of a sentence and the accusative case is used for the direct object. A third case, called the dative (**der Dativ**), is used for an indirect object, the beneficiary or recipient of an action, which is usually a person or an animal.

| | |
|---|---|
| Komm, ich zeig' **dir** dein Zimmer. | *Come on, I'll show your room to you.* (*Come on, I'll show you your room.*) |
| Gib' **mir** deinen Schlüssel. | *Give your key to me.* (*Give me your key.*) |
| Ich schließ' **dir** die Tür auf. | *I'll open the door for you.* |

> The direct objects in these sentences are inanimate objects (**dein Zimmer, deinen Schlüssel, die Tür, einen Stift**) and appear in the accusative case.

The dative answers the question **wem?** (*to whom? for whom?*).

| | |
|---|---|
| **Wem** leiht Anna einen Stift? | *To whom is Anna lending a pen?* |
| Sie leiht **Barbara** einen Stift. | *She's lending a pen to Barbara.* |
| Sie leiht **ihr** einen Stift. | *She's lending her a pen.* |

### A. The dative case: personal pronouns

The indirect object in the dative case is often expressed as a personal pronoun. Here are the nominative, accusative, and dative forms of the personal pronouns.

> In English, indirect objects that follow direct objects usually include either *to* or *for* before the noun or pronoun (*to you, for him*). Notice that the German dative case, when used with people, doesn't need an accompanying preposition (**dir, ihm**).

> Note that the dative forms **ihm** and **ihr** resemble their English counterparts *him* and *her*. Remember that the English forms *him* and *her* also correspond to the German accusative forms **ihn** and **sie**.

| | Singular | | | | | | Plural | | | |
|---|---|---|---|---|---|---|---|---|---|---|
| | 1st | 2nd | | 3rd | | | 1st | 2nd | | 3rd |
| **Nom.** | ich | du | Sie | er | es | sie | wir | ihr | Sie | sie |
| **Acc.** | mich | dich | Sie | ihn | es | sie | uns | euch | Sie | sie |
| **Dat.** | mir | dir | Ihnen | ihm | ihm | ihr | uns | euch | Ihnen | ihnen |
| | *(to/for) me* | *(to/for) you* | *(to/for) you* | *(to/for) him* | *(to/for) it* | *(to/for) her* | *(to/for) us* | *(to/for) you* | *(to/for) you* | *(to/for) them* |

When the direct object is a pronoun, it precedes the indirect object.

Kannst du **mir** *deinen Stift* leihen?    *Can you lend me your pen?*
Kannst du *ihn* **mir** leihen?    *Can you lend it to me?*

**8   Was leihen sie einander?** Was leihen die folgenden
Studenten/Studentinnen einander? Unterhalten Sie sich mit einem Partner/einer
Partnerin und benutzen Sie Personalpronomen in den Antworten.

S1: *Was leiht Rolf Barbara?*
S2: *Er leiht ihr seinen Computer.*

**Tabelle A (S1):**

|  | Rolf | Barbara | Carlos und Karla | Torsten | Anna |
|---|---|---|---|---|---|
| Rolf |  | ? | seine Sporttasche | ? | 5 Euro |
| Barbara | nichts |  | ? | ihre Zeitung | ? |
| Carlos und Karla | ? | ihre Gitarre |  | ihr Radio | ? |
| Torsten | sein Handy | ? | ? |  | sein Wörterbuch |
| Anna | ? | ihre Haar-bürste | ihr Shampoo | ? |  |

**Tabelle B (S2):**

|  | Rolf | Barbara | Carlos und Karla | Torsten | Anna |
|---|---|---|---|---|---|
| Rolf |  | seinen Computer | ? | sein Auto | ? |
| Barbara | ? |  | ihre Karten | ? | ihren Schlüssel |
| Carlos und Karla | 20 Euro | ? |  | ? | ihr Fahrrad |
| Torsten | ? | seinen Fernseher | seine CDs |  | ? |
| Anna | ihr Auto | ? | ? | Geld |  |

**9   Leihst du mir das?** Leihen Sie Freunden oft etwas? Ein Part-
ner/Eine Partnerin fragt, ob er/sie sich die folgenden Gegenstände von
Ihnen leihen kann. Was antworten Sie?

S1: *Leihst du mir bitte dein Deutschbuch?*
S2: *Na klar! Ich leihe dir mein Deutschbuch.* (oder)
    *Nein. Mein Deutschbuch leihe ich dir nicht.*

1. dein neues Auto
2. dein Fahrrad
3. deine Zahnbürste
4. deine Haarbürste
5. dein Shampoo
6. zehn Dollar
7. 100 Euro
8. 1 000 Dollar
9. deinen Pullover
10. deine Schuhe

**10** **Geburtstagsgeschenke.** Wem schenken° Sie die folgenden Gegenstände zum Geburtstag? Besprechen° Sie mit einem Partner / einer Partnerin, welche Leute welche Geschenke bekommen sollen. Besprechen Sie auch, warum.

*give (a gift)*
*discuss*

- S1: *Wem schenkst du ein Auto zum Geburtstag?*
- S2: *Ich schenke Mary ein Auto.*
- S1: *Warum schenkst du ihr ein Auto?*
- S2: *Weil ihr Auto kaputt ist.*

> Remember that **ihr** is a possessive adjective (**ihr Auto:** *her car*) as well as a dative personal pronoun, (**Ich gebe ihr das Auto:** *I give her the car*).

1. ein Auto
2. ein Flugticket nach Frankreich
3. Bart-Simpson Aufkleber°
4. ein Fahrrad
5. einen Computer
6. Blumen°
7. einen Fernseher
8. ein Buch über Deutschland
9. einen Reisekoffer

a. Frankie ist ein großer Simpsons-Fan.
b. Luise ist sehr sportlich.
c. Sabine ist Hobbygärtnerin.
d. Bastian ist ein Internet-Fan.
e. Holger sieht gern Seifenopern.
f. Elke fliegt nach Spanien.
g. Stefan studiert Deutsch.
h. James studiert Französisch.
i. Marys Auto ist kaputt.

*stickers*

*flowers*

> **Geburtstagsgeschenke.** Remember that **weil** is a subordinating conjunction and requires the conjugated verb to be placed at the end of the clause.

## B. The dative case: definite and indefinite articles, and possessive adjectives

You can identify the dative case of a noun by looking at the ending on the article or possessive adjective. The following chart summarizes the dative forms of the definite and indefinite articles, **kein,** and the possessive adjectives.

|  | Masculine | Neuter | Feminine | Plural |
|---|---|---|---|---|
| **Nominative** | der Vater | das Kind | die Mutter | die Freunde |
| **Accusative** | den Vater | das Kind | die Mutter | die Freunde |
| **Dative** | dem Vater | dem Kind | der Mutter | den Freunden |
|  | einem Vater | einem Kind | einer Mutter | keinen Freunden |
|  | meinem Vater | meinem Kind | meiner Mutter | meinen Freunden |
|  | deinem Vater | deinem Kind | deiner Mutter | deinen Freunden |
|  | Ihrem Vater | Ihrem Kind | Ihrer Mutter | Ihren Freunden |
|  | seinem Vater | seinem Kind | seiner Mutter | seinen Freunden |
|  | ihrem Vater | ihrem Kind | ihrer Mutter | ihren Freunden |
|  | unserem Vater | unserem Kind | unserer Mutter | unseren Freunden |
|  | eurem Vater | eurem Kind | eurer Mutter | euren Freunden |

Nouns in the dative plural add the ending **-n (den Freunden, den Kindern)**, unless

1. the regular plural is formed by adding **-s: die Autos → den Autos**
2. the plural already ends in **-n: die Tanten → den Tanten**

Just as they do in the nominative plural and in the accusative singular and plural, masculine N-nouns

1. add **-n** or **-en** in the dative singular: **dem Herrn, dem Neffen, dem Studenten**
2. add **-n** or **-en** in the dative plural: **den Herren, den Neffen, den Studenten**

**11** **Wem gibt Stefan den Schlüssel?** Was ist die logische Antwort? Fragen Sie einen Partner/eine Partnerin.

S1:  *Wem gibt Stefan die Seminararbeit?*
S2:  *Er gibt der Professorin die Seminararbeit.*

1. Stefan / die Seminararbeit geben
   a. seinen Eltern        b. der Professorin        c. einer Studentin

2. Barbara / ihre Haarbürste leihen
   a. der neuen Studentin  b. ihrer Katze            c. dem Professor

3. Anna / ein Kleid schenken
   a. ihrem Freund Karl    b. ihrer Freundin         c. ihrer Professorin

4. Karl / einen CD-Player kaufen
   a. seiner Tochter       b. seinem Bruder          c. seinem Hund

5. Barbara / einen Computer schenken
   a. ihrer Nachbarin      b. ihrer Katze            c. ihrem Vater

6. Anna / ein Poster von einer Rockgruppe schenken
   a. einer Freundin       b. ihrer Mutter           c. ihrem Physikprofessor

7. der Professor / die Prüfungen zurückgeben
   a. den Eltern           b. den Studenten          c. seiner Frau

8. Barbara / die Postkarte aus Italien schreiben
   a. der Bank in Tübingen  b. der Bundeskanzlerin°  c. den Eltern in Dresden        *chancellor*

9. Karl / das Bier bringen
   a. den Studenten        b. den Kindern            c. dem Hund

## **II** Indicating location

### Dative of location: **in der, im/in dem, in den**

The preposition **in** belongs to a group of prepositions called *two-case prepositions* (**die Wechselpräpositionen**) that can occur with either the accusative case or the dative case. To indicate the location of a person, animal, object, or action, German speakers use **in** with a definite article in the dative case.

> Two-case prepositions will be explained more thoroughly in **Kapitel 7.**

Die Studenten essen **in der** Küche.    *The students eat in the kitchen.*
Abends sind sie **in den** Kneipen.    *In the evening, they're in the bars.*

For the dative case of masculine and neuter nouns, a contracted form of **in dem** is frequently used: **im.**

Bierautomaten gibt's **im** Keller.    *There are beer machines in the basement.*
Was hast du **im** Zimmer?    *What do you have in the room?*

When referring to countries (**Deutschland**) or cities (**Tübingen**) as locations, German speakers use the preposition **in** without the definite article.

**Tübingen:** Anna ist **in** Tübingen.
**Deutschland:** Tübingen ist **in** Deutschland.

However, certain countries always occur with a definite article, e.g., **die Elfenbeinküste** (*fem.*), **die Schweiz** (*fem.*), **die Türkei** (*fem.*), or **die Vereinigten**

Staaten (**die USA**) (*pl.*). When they are used in expressions indicating locations, the article must be changed to the dative case.

> **die Elfenbeinküste:** Abidjan ist eine Stadt **in der** Elfenbeinküste.
> **die Schweiz:** Bern ist eine Stadt **in der** Schweiz.
> **die Türkei:** Birsens Großeltern leben **in der** Türkei.
> **die Vereinigten Staaten (die USA):** Annas Familie lebt **in den** Vereinigten Staaten (**in den USA**).

## Wissenswerte Vokabeln: ein Einfamilienhaus, die Stockwerke
*Describing the features of a house*

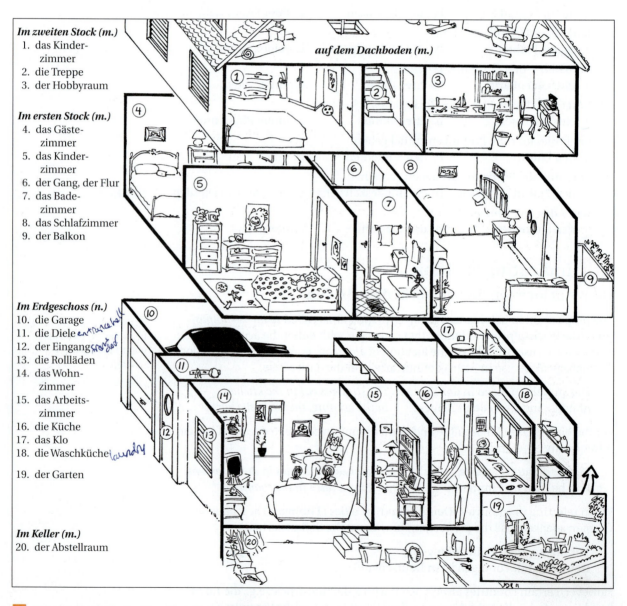

*Im zweiten Stock (m.)*
1. das Kinderzimmer
2. die Treppe
3. der Hobbyraum

*Im ersten Stock (m.)*
4. das Gästezimmer
5. das Kinderzimmer
6. der Gang, der Flur
7. das Badezimmer
8. das Schlafzimmer
9. der Balkon

*Im Erdgeschoss (n.)*
10. die Garage
11. die Diele
12. der Eingang
13. die Rollläden
14. das Wohnzimmer
15. das Arbeitszimmer
16. die Küche
17. das Klo
18. die Waschküche
19. der Garten

*Im Keller (m.)*
20. der Abstellraum

*auf dem Dachboden (m.)*

■ Was ist im Keller?   *Der Abstellraum ist im Keller.*
  Wo schläfst du?   *Ich schlafe im Gästezimmer.*

**12** **Wo machst du das?** Kreuzen Sie das Zimmer an, in dem Sie diese Aktivitäten machen.

S1: *Wo schläfst du?*
S2: *Ich schlafe im Schlafzimmer.*

|  | *Im Schlafzimmer* | *Im Badezimmer* | *In der Küche* | *Im Wohnzimmer* |
|---|---|---|---|---|
| 1. schlafen | ☐ | ☐ | ☐ | ☐ |
| 2. Kaffee trinken | ☐ | ☐ | ☐ | ☐ |
| 3. baden | ☐ | ☐ | ☐ | ☐ |
| 4. fernsehen | ☐ | ☐ | ☐ | ☐ |
| 5. die Zeitung lesen | ☐ | ☐ | ☐ | ☐ |
| 6. frühstücken | ☐ | ☐ | ☐ | ☐ |
| 7. aufstehen | ☐ | ☐ | ☐ | ☐ |
| 8. duschen | ☐ | ☐ | ☐ | ☐ |
| 9. die Hausaufgaben machen | ☐ | ☐ | ☐ | ☐ |
| 10. die Kleidung aufhängen° | ☐ | ☐ | ☐ | ☐ |

*hang up*

**13** **Wo ist das Auto?** Wo findet man normalerweise die folgenden Gegenstände?

S1: *Wo ist das Auto?*
S2: *In der Garage.*

das Auto • der Farbfernseher • die Waschmaschine
• die Kaffeemaschine • der Rasierapparat • das Doppelbett
• die Stereoanlage • der Mikrowellenherd • die Rolle Toilettenpapier
• die Couch • das Waschbecken • das Bücherregal
• die Rosen, Tulpen und Tomaten • die Zahnbürsten
• die alten Klamotten • das Kinderbett • das Handy

**14** **Interview.** Stellen Sie einem Partner/einer Partnerin die folgenden Fragen.

1. Wohnst du in einem Haus, in einer Wohnung° oder in einem Studentenwohnheim?

   *apartment*

2. Wie viele Schlafzimmer hat dein Haus, deine Wohnung, dein Studentenwohnheim?
3. Wie viele Badezimmer hat dein Haus, deine Wohnung, dein Studentenwohnheim?
4. Hast du eine Küche?
5. Wo isst du normalerweise?
6. Was für Möbel hast du in deinem Zimmer?

BRENNPUNKT KULTUR

## Tübingen

Located approximately 40 kilometers south of Stuttgart, Baden-Württemberg's urban capital and economic powerhouse, the old university city of Tübingen is distinguished by its historical town center (**die Altstadt**). Straddling the Neckar and Ammer rivers, Tübingen contains a historic town hall (**das Rathaus**), a castle (**Schloss Hohentübingen**), and a myriad of half-timbered houses (**Fachwerkhäuser**) on narrow, winding streets. While the city boasts a population of 80,000, it owes its fame to the 25,000 students at the **Eberhard-Karls-Universität,** who are continually drawn to this dynamic educational institution. Founded in 1477 with only 300 students, the university established a reputation for outstanding scholarship and teaching. It has attracted significant German intellectuals: the astronomer and mathematician Johannes Kepler; the philosopher G.W.F. Hegel; the Romantic author Ludwig Uhland; the 20th century novelist Hermann Hesse; and the contemporary theologian Hans Küng. In the 18th century, the impassioned German poet Friedrich Hölderlin attended the university, but later descended into mental illness, spending the last 36 years of his life in a tower on the banks of the Neckar, now known as the **Hölderlinturm.** After the collapse of the Nazi government in 1945, the university at Tübingen was the first in Germany to reopen its doors. Since then the university has pursued international cooperation and collaborative projects, establishing academic partnerships with numerous American universities. The city of Tübingen has a partnership with the city of Ann Arbor, Michigan, in the U.S.

Stocherkahnfahren ist eine von den beliebtesten Traditionen von Tübinger Studenten.

Seit Jahrhunderten genießen Studenten die malerische Atmosphäre von Tübingen.

■ **Kulturkreuzung** Tübingen ist als Universitätsstadt sehr bekannt. Ist die Stadt, wo Sie jetzt studieren, auch als Universitätsstadt bekannt? Wie kann man die Stadt sonst noch beschreiben? Die Eberhard-Karls-Universität ist über 500 Jahre alt. Wie alt ist Ihre Uni? Was studieren besonders viele Leute an Ihrer Uni? Welche bekannten Leute haben an Ihrer Uni studiert?

**15** **Entschuldigung, können Sie mir sagen, wo der Hölderlinturm ist?** Sie und ein Partner/eine Partnerin sind Touristen und fragen einige Tübinger nach Sehenswürdigkeiten in Tübingen. Benutzen Sie den Stadtplan von Tübingen.

German addresses give the number following the street name.

## Theater

**1  Landestheater Württemberg-Hohenzollern**, Eberhardtstr. 8
Theaterkasse Tel.: 9313149

**2  Zimmertheater**
Bursagasse 16
Tel.: 92730

## Kinos

**3  Kino Arsenal**
Eine Institution. Programmkino. Anspruchsvolles° Programm, Kinokneipe
Am Stadtgraben 33, Tel.: 51073

**4  Kino Atelier**
Das Programmkino und Café Haag, der American Diner
Am Haagtor, Tel.: 21225

**5  Museum 1 + 2**
**Studio Museum** Die Kino's mit Niveau° Am Stadtgraben 2, Tel.: 23661

**6  Blaue Brücke 1 - 3**
Friedrichstr., Tel.: 23661

**7  Kino Löwen**
Kornhausstr., Tel.: 22410

## Discotheken

**8  Musicclub Patty**
Di, Do + Sa. stimmungsvolle brasilianische Nächte. Fr. Hits Hits Hits
Schlachthausstr. 9, Tel.: 51612

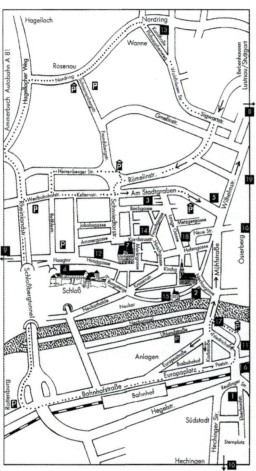

## Veranstaltung/Konzert

**9  Zentrum Zoo** Diskothek, Kneipe, Konzerte. Schleifmühleweg 86. Tel.: 40539

**10 Sudhaus** Veranstaltungen, Konzerte, Kabarett. Hechinger Str. 203 Tel.: 74696

**11 Tübinger Matinee** Konzerte und Vorträge. Casino, Wöhrdtstr. 25

**12 Club Voltaire** Kleinkunst, Konzerte. Haagasse 26b, Tel.:51524

## Ausstellungen

**13 Kunsthalle Tübingen**, Philosophenweg 76

**14 Stadtmuseum Kornhaus**, Kornhausstr. 10

**15 Hölderlinturm**, Bursagasse 6

**16 Institut Culturel Franco-Allemand**, Doblerstr. 25

**17 Deutsch-Amerikanisches Institut**, Karlstr. 3

**18 Galerie im Alten Schlachthaus**, Metzgergasse 3

**19 Auto- und Spielzeugmuseum Boxenstop** Autos, Motorräder, Puppen°, (Blech) Eisenbahnen, Spielsachen° präsentiert in toller Atmosphäre Brunnenstr. 18, Tel.: 21996

*Anspruchsvolles:* sophisticated

*mit ... :* with high standards

*Puppen:* dolls
*Spielsachen:* toys

---

S1:  *Entschuldigung, können Sie mir sagen, wo der Hölderlinturm ist?*
S2:  *Der Hölderlinturm? Ja. In der Bursagasse 6.*
S1:  *Danke schön.*

**Entschuldigung, ...** Note: **die Gasse** *(lane),* **die Straße** *(street),* **der Weg** *(way, path).*

1.  das Zimmertheater
2.  die Blaue Brücke
3.  der Club Voltaire
4.  die Kunsthalle Tübingen
5.  das Deutsch-Amerikanische Institut
6.  das Stadtmuseum Kornhaus

**16** **Fragen über Tübingen.** Benutzen Sie den Stadtplan und beantworten Sie die Fragen über Tübingen.

■ S1: *Wo kann man ein anspruchsvolles Kinoprogramm finden?*
  S2: *Im Kino Arsenal.*

1. Wo kann man Motorräder, Puppen und Spielsachen finden?
2. Wo kann man zwei Kinos mit Niveau finden?
3. Wo kann man Konzerte hören?
4. Wo kann man Kleinkunst° finden?                          *craftwork*
5. Wo kann man amerikanisches Essen finden?
6. Was möchten Sie in Tübingen sehen?

  **Freie Kommunikation**

**Neu im Studentenwohnheim.** Florian ist neu im Studentenwohnheim. Er zieht gerade ein. Heribert wohnt schon seit zwei Jahren im Studentenwohnheim. Heribert gibt Florian viele Tipps. Spielen Sie die drei Dialoge zu Ende.

FLORIAN: Was kann man hier im Studentenwohnheim machen?
HERIBERT: …
FLORIAN: Mein Gepäck ist noch am Bahnhof. Ich brauche es dringend° …    *urgently*
         Was soll ich machen?
HERIBERT: …
FLORIAN: Mein Zimmer ist total leer°!                                    *empty*
HERIBERT: Kein Problem, …

**Ein Telefongespräch.** Sie haben eine neue Wohnung in Frankfurt. Sie rufen zu Hause an und sprechen mit Ihrer Mutter. Erzählen Sie ihr von der neuen Wohnung. Ihre Mutter ist sehr neugierig° und stellt viele Fragen.    *curious*

**In unserer Stadt.** Ein Student/Eine Studentin ist neu in Ihrer Stadt. Welche interessanten Dinge soll er/sie machen? Und wo?

**Schreibecke**

**Mein Zimmer.** Beschreiben Sie Ihr Zimmer. Was haben Sie alles?

■ *In meinem Zimmer habe ich …*

EBERHARD KARLS
UNIVERSITÄT
TÜBINGEN

ZIMMER FREI?

Semesterbeginn in Tübingen. Viele Studierende haben noch keine Bleibe.

Vermieten Sie freien Wohnraum! Unsere Vermittlung ist kostenlos.

Sprechzeiten: montags bis freitags 9.00 – 14.45 Uhr
Telefon (0 70 71) 29-7 38 71
Telefax (0 70 71) 29-38 15

Studentenwerk Tübingen
Anstalt des öffentlichen Rechts
Wilhelmstraße 13 (Mensa)
72074 Tübingen

**Absprungtext**

## Integration und multikulturelles Leben

Deutsche Universitäten sind unter ausländischen Studenten sehr beliebt. Im Jahre 2002 waren 11% von allen Studenten an deutschen Universitäten (1 868 666) Ausländer. Das Online-Magazin *campusmagazin.de* hat ein Interview zum Thema Integration und multikulturelles Leben an der FH-Darmstadt mit zwei ausländischen Studenten geführt.

> German has only one term for Native Americans: **Indianer (indianischer Abstammung)**. **Inder** refers to Asian Indians (**indischer Abstammung**).

## Vorschau

**17**   **Thematische Fragen.**   Beantworten Sie die folgenden Fragen auf Deutsch.

1. Zu welcher Gruppe gehören Sie? Ich bin ... Abstammung°.   *descent*
   a. afrikanischer
   b. asiatischer
   c. europäischer
   d. hispanischer
   e. indianischer
   f. gemischter°   *mixed*

2. Gibt es viele Austauschstudenten° an Ihrer Uni? Gibt es jetzt mehr oder weniger ausländische° Studenten als vor dem 11. September 2001? Warum?   *exchange students*
   *foreign*

3. Welche Probleme haben ausländische Studenten vielleicht an Ihrer Uni? Die soziale Integration? Probleme mit dem Visum? Finanzielle Probleme? Heimweh°? Ausländerfeindlichkeit°? Andere Probleme?   *homesickness / xenophobia*

4. Warum finden vielleicht viele ausländische Studenten die soziale Integration schwierig? Weil sie die Kultur nicht so gut kennen? Weil sie die Sprache nicht so gut sprechen? Weil manche Leute nicht offen sind? Weil ... ?

5. Was finden ausländische Studenten an Ihrer Universität wahrscheinlich sehr positiv? Die Studienfächer? Die Professoren? Die anderen Studenten? Die Unterhaltungsmöglichkeiten° (die Kinos, die Kneipen, die Sportanlagen, die Einkaufsmöglichkeiten) in der Stadt? Das Klima? Etwas anderes?   *die Möglichkeit = opportunity*

6. Glauben Sie, dass ausländische Studenten an amerikanischen oder kanadischen Universitäten andere Probleme haben, als ausländische Studenten an einer deutschen Universität? Warum?

7. Glauben Sie, dass ausländische Studenten an kanadischen oder amerikanischen Universitäten andere Dinge° positiv finden als ausländische Studenten an einer deutschen Universität? Was?   *things*

8. Was finden Sie persönlich besonders positiv an einem Studium oder einem Studienjahr im Ausland?

**Sprache im Alltag: Ausländer**

**Ausländer** generally means *foreigner(s)*. However, an accurate definition of the word is complex because there is no clear distinction between ethnicity and nationality. German citizenship is automatically bestowed by way of German parentage. Thus, children born to parents of German descent in Romania or Russia are recognized as German citizens. With the introduction of liberalized citizenship laws on Jan. 1, 2000, children born in Germany to foreign-born parents may become German citizens as long as one parent has lived in Germany for eight years.

The term **Bildungsinländer** (foreigners with German secondary education) refers to the children of immigrant workers and refugees who are raised, educated, and often born in Germany. They may speak perfect German but often remain cultural outsiders, even if they have been granted citizenship. Unlike **Ausländer,** who can return home after college, **Bildungsinländer** may have no other home than Germany.

 **18** **Satzdetektiv.** Welche Sätze und Satzteile bedeuten ungefähr das Gleiche?

1. Wie war **die Einreise** nach Deutschland?
2. Hat es **eventuell** Probleme gegeben?
3. **Die Voraussetzungen,** ein Visum zu bekommen, sind sehr **schwer.**
4. Ich musste° **eine Kaution hinterlegen.**
5. Ich kann **meinen Unterhalt** selber bezahlen.
6. Hast du **negative Erfahrungen** gemacht?

a. Ich musste Geld in Reserve halten.
b. Es gibt viele Konditionen, wenn man ein Visum braucht.
c. Hat es vielleicht Probleme gegeben?
d. Wie war die Immigration nach Deutschland?
e. Ich kann mein Leben allein finanzieren.
f. Ist dir etwas Schlechtes passiert?

*had to*

---

7. Es ist **eine Bereicherung.**
8. Ganz egal, woher man **abstammt** oder welche Hautfarbe man hat.
9. Musstest du auch bestimmte **Zulassungskriterien erfüllen?**
10. Die Leute **schauen** mich auf der Straße **schief an.**
11. Es **hält sich in Grenzen.**
12. Bist du **auf** Ausländerfeindlichkeit **gestoßen?**

g. Hast du ausländerfeindliche Leute getroffen?
h. Ich habe viel gelernt. Es hat mein Leben reicher gemacht.
i. Es ist nicht so schlimm.
j. Es macht nichts aus, woher man kommt oder ob man weiße, braune, schwarze, gelbe oder rote Haut° hat.
k. Die Leute sehen mich komisch an, wenn ich auf der Straße gehe.
l. Musstest du viele Papiere ausfüllen, um nach Deutschland einzureisen?

*skin*

## *Absprungtext*
### *Integration und multikulturelles Leben*

Lesen Sie jetzt den Text.

### An der Fachhochschule°-Darmstadt: Eine Bestandsaufnahme°

An der FH-Darmstadt studieren Gaststudenten aus über 70 verschiedenen
Nationen. In den letzten drei Monaten haben wir sie als interessante
Gesprächspartner kennen gelernt, die° uns über ihre Erfahrungen, Probleme und
Sorgen als StudentInnen der FH berichteten°: Was sind die Probleme, mit denen
ausländische StudentInnen zu kämpfen° haben, bevor sie in Deutschland
studieren können? Was sind die Gründe° für die Wahl° des Studienortes°? Aus
welchen Ländern kommen ausländische Studenten?

*specialized university /
  assessment, snapshot*

*who*
*reported*
*fight*
*reasons / choice /
  place of study*

**Constant Charles Dathe** ist 30 Jahre alt
und kommt von der Elfenbeinküste in Afrika.
Er studiert Informations- und Wissensmanage-
ment im fünften Semester.

> **StudentInnen** is an attempt
> to use inclusive language to
> refer to both male (**Studen-
> ten**) and female students
> (**Studentinnen**).

CAMPUSMAGAZIN.DE (CM):   Constant, wie lange lebst du schon in Deutschland?

CONSTANT:   Seit ca.° drei Jahren.

*ca. = **zirka**: approximately*

CM:   Wie war das mit der Einreise nach Deutschland, mit dem Visum?
Hat es eventuell Probleme gegeben?

5   CONSTANT:   Nein, mit dem Visum hatte ich keine Probleme, aber die Voraussetzungen, um überhaupt ein Visum zu bekommen, waren sehr
schwer. Ich musste eine Art Kaution hinterlegen von 6 000 Euro,
damals° 12 000 DM. Als Beweis°, dass ich hier keinem auf der
Tasche liegen werde°, sondern meinen Unterhalt selber bezahlen
10   kann.

*at that time / proof*
**keinem ... :** *won't live off of
  somebody else*

CM:   Hast du irgendwelche negativen Erfahrungen an der FH-
Darmstadt gemacht?

CONSTANT:   Hier an der FH? Nein, an der FH nicht. Aber außerhalb° der FH.

*outside, beyond*

CM:   Was waren das für Erfahrungen?

15   CONSTANT:   Man hat mich auf der Straße angepöbelt°, angeglotzt°, ich musste
mir dumme Sprüche anhören, wie zum Beispiel „Hat es hier ge-
brannt°?." Aber so Sprüche amüsieren mich nur, meistens muss
ich darüber lachen. Die Menschen sind teilweise intolerant und
unsicher. Sie wissen nicht, wie sie auf mich zukommen sollen.

*pestered / stared at*

**brennen** = *to burn*

20   CM:   Haben dir die Studenten bei der Integration geholfen?

CONSTANT:   Die Studenten waren nett° und hilfsbereit°. Diejenigen Studenten, die freundlich sind, zu denen bin ich auch freundlich. Man
nimmt was kommt.

*nice / helpful*

CM:   Wie würdest° du deinen Freundeskreis° beschreiben?

*would / circle of friends*

25   CONSTANT:   Ich würde sagen, mein Freundeskreis ist multikulturell. Wobei°
ich sagen muss, dass ich viele deutsche Freunde habe, vor allem
in der FH. An der FH habe ich nicht so viel Kontakt zu meinen
Landsleuten, da° es dort° auch nicht so viele gibt. Aber privat
kenne ich schon ein paar.

*in addition*

*since / there*

30     CM:  Was bedeutet für dich multikulturelles Leben?

CONSTANT:  Völkerverständigung. Dass Menschen zusammenkommen und dabei alles vergessen, Hautfarbe, Herkunft, Religion. Ich denke, wir Menschen sind im Grund alle gleich, da wir alle rotes Blut haben. Ich kenne keinen Menschen, der grünes oder schwarzes

35     Blut hat. Es gibt nur rotes Blut, ganz egal woher man abstammt und welche Hautfarbe man hat. Es wäre° doch sehr langweilig,   *would be* wenn alle Menschen gleich wären! Es ist doch eine Bereicherung, wenn man die Möglichkeit hat, andere Kulturen und andere Menschen kennen zu lernen.

**Khalid El Abdi** ist 23 Jahre alt, stammt ursprünglich° aus Marokko. Er studiert hier   *originally* an der FH-Darmstadt Telekommunikation im ersten Semester.

40     CM:  Bist du als Austauschstudent nach Darmstadt gekommen?

KHALID:  Nein, ich bin durch kein Austauschprogramm nach Darmstadt gekommen. Ich habe ursprünglich in Hannover studiert und bin dann nach Darmstadt gezogen, weil ich hier Freunde habe, die mir nur Gutes über die FH erzählt haben.

45     CM:  Wie lange lebst du schon in Deutschland?

KHALID:  Seit etwa zwei Jahren und drei Monaten.

CM:  Da du kein Austauschstudent bist, hattest du damals Probleme mit der Einreise nach Deutschland? Und musstest du auch bestimmte Zulassungskriterien erfüllen?

50     KHALID:  Nein, ich hatte zu der Zeit° keine Probleme mit dem Visum, es ist   ***zu ... :** at that time* relativ schnell gegangen. Wenn alles in Ordnung ist°, hat man   ***Wenn ... :** If everything's* eigentlich auch keine Probleme. Probleme kann es geben, wenn   *okay (in order)* man das Visum verlängern möchte.

CM:  Bist du an der FH-Darmstadt auf Ausländerfeindlichkeit gestoßen?

55     KHALID:  Nein, hier an der FH habe ich solche Erfahrungen nicht gemacht. Aber in Dresden, dort habe ich einen Sprachkurs gemacht und ein Semester Maschinenbau studiert. An der FH-Darmstadt habe ich nur positive Erfahrungen gemacht, vor allem mit den Studenten. Ich denke, unter den Studenten gibt es auch keine Probleme, da

60     viele Kulturen in der FH aufeinander stoßen. Aber außerhalb der FH sieht das Ganze etwas anders aus, gerade nach dem 11. September schauen mich manchmal° auf der Straße die Leute schief an. Aber   *sometimes* es hält sich in Grenzen.

On July 1, 1993, restrictions on asylum-seekers were tightened when **Artikel 16a** of the German **Grundgesetz** was amended. It now requires that asylum-seekers must enter Germany directly from their country of origin. The liberalized citizenship laws introduced on Jan. 1, 2000, allow children born in Germany to foreign-born parents to be German citizens. They also obtain the citizenship of their parents. By age 23 they must choose one citizenship.

**BRENNPUNKT KULTUR**

## Ausländer in Deutschland

Over the last 50 years, Germany has become a multicultural society that includes a variety of ethnic groups, races, and religions. About two million people of Turkish descent (**die Türken**) live and work in Germany. In addition, thousands of people from Italy, the former Yugoslavia, Greece, Poland, Spain, Romania, Portugal, Russia, and many other countries call Germany their home.

In the 1950s and 1960s, the German economy experienced unparalleled economic growth (**das Wirtschaftswunder**). Recruited by German businesses, many so-called "guest workers" (**Gastarbeiter**) from poorer southern European countries came to Germany as a temporary work force to replace those German workers killed in the war. By the 1970s the children of the workers, particularly those from Turkey (**die Türkei**), found it difficult to return to a country they hardly knew. At the same time, the Turks, more than any other ethnic group, maintained their ethnic identity through language, the Islamic religion (**der Islam**), their customs and their social isolation. For many younger Turkish people, the conflict between their ethnic background and where they lived was heightened by laws that prevented them until Jan. 1, 2000 from obtaining full German citizenship. The struggles of ethnic minorities are reflected in the literature of immigrant authors writing in German, such as the Turkish author Ermine Özdamar or the **Afro-Deutsche** author May Opitz.

Bolstered by the former West Germany's liberal asylum policy, the number of foreigners living in Germany swelled in the 1970s with political asylum-seekers from Iran and the Soviet Union. By 1992, nearly 80% of all immigrants seeking asylum in European countries were coming to Germany. Before long, the drain on government resources was straining German good will. Following German unification in 1990, the ethnic diversity of Germany had expanded to include communities of Russians, Poles, Chinese, Vietnamese, Africans, and Arabs from the former German Democratic Republic (**die Deutsche Demokratische Republik**). Shelters where these people were housed soon became targets of right-wing extremist attacks. In 1991 a young African was murdered in Hoyerswerda. In 1992 a shelter for asylum seekers in Rostock was firebombed, and members of a family of Turks living in an apartment building in Mölin were killed by arsonists. Following the beating death of an African immigrant in Dessau by three Neo-Nazis in June 2000, a German court sentenced the ringleader to the maximum sentence of life in prison and the underage accomplices to nine years each. The current German government is attempting to crack down on right-wing extremism in Germany. Outraged Germans around the country held candlelight vigils and demonstrations to protest rising anti-foreigner sentiment (**Ausländerfeindlichkeit**), forcing many people to acknowledge openly the persistent, subtle racism around them. While skinhead attacks on foreigners make the headlines, multiculturalism has been embraced and accepted as a positive development by many people in Germany and the rest of German-speaking **Mitteleuropa**.

*Etwa zwei Millionen Türken bilden die größte Minderheit in Deutschland.*

**Kulturkreuzung** Die USA, Kanada und Australien haben alle zuerst europäische Einwanderer akzeptiert und später Einwanderer aus vielen anderen Ländern. Aus welchen Ländern kommen Einwanderer in Ihrer Stadt oder in Ihrem Staat? Welche Einwanderer sind gut integriert, welche nicht so gut integriert? Was bedeutet „integriert" für Sie – Englisch sprechen? Etwas Spezielles (nicht) essen? Etwas Spezielles (nicht) feiern? Bestimmte Kleidung (nicht) tragen? Warum sind Ihrer Meinung nach verschiedene Einwanderer gut oder nicht gut integriert?

## Rückblick

**19** **Constant und Khalid.** Welche Aussagen° stimmen für Constant, welche für Khalid? Welche für beide und welche für keinen? Kreuzen Sie sie an.

*statements*

|  | Constant | Khalid |
|---|---|---|
| 1. ... kommt aus Afrika. | ☐ | ☐ |
| 2. ... lebt schon länger in Deutschland. | ☐ | ☐ |
| 3. ... hat schon an zwei deutschen Unis studiert. | ☐ | ☐ |
| 4. ... ist weiter in seinem Studium. | ☐ | ☐ |
| 5. ... hat Probleme mit dem Visum gehabt. | ☐ | ☐ |
| 6. ... glaubt, dass nach dem 11. September alles anders ist. | ☐ | ☐ |
| 7. ... findet Multikulturalismus wichtig. | ☐ | ☐ |
| 8. ... ist sozial isoliert und hat keine Freunde. | ☐ | ☐ |
| 9. ... findet die Uni und die anderen Studenten weniger ausländerfeindlich als die Leute in der Universitätsstadt. | ☐ | ☐ |

**20** **Kurz gefragt.** Beantworten Sie die folgenden Fragen auf Deutsch.

> Complete the **Ergänzen Sie** activity in your workbook for this text before doing the next activity.

1. Warum, glauben Sie, studieren Constant und Khalid in Deutschland?
2. Glauben Sie, dass ausländische Studentinnen andere Erfahrungen machen als Constant und Khalid. Welche?
3. Glauben Sie, dass Studenten aus den USA und Kanada andere Erfahrungen als Constant und Khalid machen, wenn sie an deutschsprachigen Universitäten studieren? Alle amerikanischen und kanadischen Studenten? Wie hängen Erfahrungen von der Nationalität oder von der Hautfarbe ab°?

   *ab ... hängen: depend on*

4. Glauben Sie, dass Studenten in den USA und Kanada weniger ausländerfeindlich sind als Europäer? Warum oder warum nicht?
5. Finden Sie es gut, wenn eine Universität viele ausländische Studenten hat? Warum (nicht)?
6. Finden Sie es gut, wenn eine Universität viele ausländische Professoren hat? Warum (nicht)?
7. Welchen Rat° können Sie einem ausländischen Studenten oder einer ausländischen Studentin an Ihrer Universität geben? Was soll er oder sie machen oder wissen? Und was soll er oder sie nicht machen?

   *advice*

## Strukturen und Vokabeln

# III Expressing when we do things

## The subordinating conjunction **wenn**

German speakers use the subordinating conjunction **wenn** *(when, whenever, as soon as, if)* to express when they do things and to express certain conditions. As in all subordinate clauses, the conjugated verb comes at the end of a **wenn**-clause.

| | |
|---|---|
| Wir fahren nach Hause, **wenn** er zurückkommt. | *We'll go home as soon as (when) he returns.* |
| Jetzt zeig' ich dir das Badezimmer, **wenn** es dir recht ist. | *Now I'll show you your bathroom, if that's all right with you.* |

The **wenn**-clause may also come at the beginning of the sentence, in which case the verb of the main clause precedes the subject.

| | |
|---|---|
| **Wenn** alles in Ordnung ist, hat man eigentlich keine Probleme. | *If (When) everything's in order, you don't have any problems.* |

**21  Was passiert, wenn man in Deutschland studiert?** Kombinieren Sie die beiden Satzteile, um Sätze über das Studium in Deutschland zu bilden.

1. Ausländer aus Afrika brauchen ein Visum,
2. In Darmstadt kann man viele ausländische Studenten sehen,
3. Einige Ausländer können in Deutschland Ausländerfeindlichkeit erfahren,
4. Constant lacht nur,
5. Khalid sagt, es kann Probleme geben,

a. wenn man an der FH-Darmstadt ist.
b. wenn man das Visum verlängern möchte.
c. wenn Menschen ihn auf der Straße komisch ansehen.
d. wenn sie außerhalb der Uni sind.
e. wenn sie nach Deutschland einreisen möchten.

**22  Wann?** Sie spielen ein zwölfjähriges Kind. Ein Partner/Eine Partnerin spielt Ihren Vater/Ihre Mutter. Stellen Sie einander Fragen und geben Sie passende Antworten.

S1 (VATER/MUTTER): *Wann machst du dein Zimmer sauber?*
    S2 (KIND): *Wenn ich meinen Computer nicht mehr finden kann.*

**Vater/Mutter:**
1. Wann machst du dein Zimmer sauber?
2. Wann machst du deine Hausaufgaben?
3. Wann bekommst du eine gute Note?
4. Wann gehen deine Freunde nach Hause?
5. Wann wäschst du dir endlich die Hände?

**Kind:**
Mein Lehrer versteht mich besser.
Ich kann meinen Computer nicht mehr finden.
Wir haben den Videofilm zu Ende gesehen.
Das Essen ist fertig.
Die Hausaufgaben machen mehr Spaß.

**Kind:**
1. Wann darf ich bis drei Uhr morgens aufbleiben°?
2. Wann darf ich Auto fahren?
3. Wann bekomme ich mehr Taschengeld°?
4. Wann darf ich ins Kino gehen?
5. Wann muss ich nicht in die Schule gehen?

**Vater/Mutter:**
Du bist achtzehn.
Du hast deine Hausaufgaben gemacht.
Du bist dreißig.
Du bist sehr krank.
Du bekommst nur gute Noten.

*stay up*

*allowance*

# IV Expressing temporal and spatial relationships

## Dative prepositions

There are eight prepositions that are always followed by the dative case (**die Dativpräpositionen**). You already encountered some in earlier chapters.

aus        nach
außer      seit
bei        von
mit        zu

1. Expressing origin: **aus** *(from, out of)*

   Khalid stammt ursprünglich **aus** Marokko.    *Khalid originally comes **from** Morocco.*

2. Expressing exclusion: **außer** *(except for)*

   **Außer** ihm sprechen alle Studenten Deutsch.    ***Except for** him all the students speak German.*

3. Expressing location: **bei** *(at, near, with)*

   Das Studentenwohnheim ist **bei** der Autobahn.    *The dorm is **near** the freeway.*

   Barbara hat **bei** einer Frau in Moskau gewohnt.    *Barbara lived **with** a woman in Moscow.*

   Some common verbs used with **bei** are **arbeiten, essen, vorbeikommen** *(to stop by)*, and **wohnen.**

   Wir essen **bei** Stefanie.    *We're eating **at** Stefanie's.*
   Werner arbeitet **bei** der Bank.    *Werner works **at** the bank.*
   Karl kommt morgen **bei** uns vorbei.    *Karl is stopping by (**at** our place) tomorrow.*

4. Expressing accompaniment: **mit** *(with)*

   **Mit** meinen Freunden kann ich über alles reden.    *I can talk about everything **with** my friends.*

   Expressing means: **mit** *(by)*

   Wir fahren **mit** der Bahn nach Rostock.    *We're going **by** train to Rostock.*

5. Expressing time: **nach** *(after, past)*

   Es ist fünf **nach** drei.    *It's five after (past) three.*
   **Nach** der Vorlesung gehen wir nach Hause.    *After the lecture we'll go home.*

6. Expressing destination: **zu, nach** *(to)*

   *People and institutions*
   Wir gehen **zu** Karl.    *We're going **to** Karl's (house).*
   Anna geht **zur** (= **zu der**) Universität.    *Anna is going **to** the university.*

   *Cities, countries, and home*
   Ich bin dann **nach** Darmstadt gezogen.    *Then I moved **to** Darmstadt.*
   Ich gehe **nach** Hause.    *I'm going home.*

   Remember: The expression **zu Hause** means *at home*.

The translations of these prepositions are only approximate. The scope of their meanings generally varies depending on the context.

As with the preposition **in**, be sure to alter the endings of articles that accompany country names (e.g., **aus den USA/Vereinigten Staaten, aus der Türkei, aus der Schweiz, aus der Elfenbeinküste).**

When **außer** occurs in the same sentence with **auch** *(also)*, it means *in addition to*: **Außer ihm sind auch Anna und Barbara hier.** *(In addition to him, Anna and Barbara are also here.)*

There are two translations of *to live with*: **leben/wohnen bei** and **zusammenleben/wohnen mit.** The first (**bei**) indicates a relationship of dependency, as in **Jeff lebt/wohnt bei seinen Eltern.** The second (**mit**) implies a relationship of shared responsibilities: **Franz lebt/wohnt mit seiner Freundin (zusammen).**

**Wir essen bei Stefanie.** *(We're eating at Stefanie's.)*: Note that German does not add a possessive *s* to the nouns or names describing a location. The same applies to destinations: **Wir gehen zu Karl.** *(We're going to Karl's house.)*

The dative case—not **zu**—is used for the recipient of an action. **Gib' mir deinen Schlüssel.**

7. Expressing duration: **seit** *(since, for)*

| | |
|---|---|
| Wir kennen uns schon **seit** dem Kindergarten. | *We have known each other **since** kindergarten.* |
| Ich lebe **seit** etwa zwei Jahren in Deutschland. | *I've been living in Germany **for** about two years.* |

8. Expressing possession, association, or connection: **von** *(of, by, from)*

| | |
|---|---|
| Der Bruder **von** Barbara wohnt noch zu Hause. | *Barbara's brother still lives at home.* |
| Das ist nett **von** dir. | *That's nice **of** you.* |
| Das Lied ist **von** Beethoven. | *The song is **by** Beethoven.* |
| Das Geschenk ist **von** Karl. | *The present is **from** Karl.* |

> Remember that **ein** (*a*) takes endings when used as a number (*one*), e.g., **seit einem Jahr.** No other number takes endings, but the plural noun in the dative has an ending, e.g., **seit zwei Jahren.**

The prepositions **von, zu,** and **bei** frequently form contractions with the definite article.

| | | | |
|---|---|---|---|
| **von + dem** | **= vom** | am Ende **vom** Korridor | *at the end of the hall* |
| **zu + dem** | **= zum** | ein Bett **zum** Schlafen | *a bed for sleeping* |
| **zu + der** | **= zur** | Sie geht **zur** Universität. | *She's going to the university.* |
| **bei + dem** | **= beim** | Karl war **beim** Arzt. | *Karl was at the doctor's.* |

> In colloquial German, speakers often use **von** to indicate possession. Standard German uses the possessive *s:* **Barbaras Bruder wohnt noch zu Hause.**

When used with an infinitive, **beim** means *while,* and **zum** means *for.*

| | |
|---|---|
| beim Essen | *while eating* |
| beim Lesen | *while reading* |

| | |
|---|---|
| zum Schlafen | *for sleeping* |
| zum Lernen | *for learning* |

**23** **Anna spricht mit Oma und Opa.** Wählen Sie die richtige Dativpräposition.

1. Anna spricht (aus/seit/mit) ihren Großeltern.
2. OMA: Wir sind so froh, dass du (nach/zu/aus) uns gekommen bist, Anna.
3. OPA: Wir haben auch so gern die Briefe (aus/mit/von) dir und deiner Mutter gelesen. Wir sind wirklich froh, dass du da bist. Es ist nur schade, dass deine Mutter nicht auch gekommen ist.
4. OMA: Ja, die Hannelore haben wir (seit/von/außer) fünf Jahren nicht mehr gesehen.
5. ANNA: Meiner Meinung nach wollte Mama im Dezember (zu/mit/bei) Papa (zu/aus/nach) Deutschland kommen, aber er muss Mitte Dezember für zwei Wochen nach Florida fahren und sie weiß nicht, wann sie endlich° kommen können.
6. OMA: Also, von mir aus kommen sie hoffentlich bald. Wie lange dauert° der Flug (außer/von/zu) Amerika?
7. ANNA: (Bei/Nach/Mit) dem Flugzeug dauert es sieben Stunden. Also nicht so lange.
8. OPA: Sieben Stunden! Meine Güte!°

*finally*
*lasts*

*My Goodness!*

**Sprache im Alltag: Emphasizing one's opinion**

German speakers frequently use expressions with dative prepositions to express or emphasize an opinion.

| | |
|---|---|
| meiner Meinung nach | *in my opinion* |
| mit anderen Worten | *in other words* |
| von mir aus | *as far as I am concerned* |
| (von) daher | *therefore* |
| aus diesem Grund | *therefore, that's the reason why* |

Note that in the expression **meiner Meinung nach** the preposition **nach** occurs at the end of the prepositional phrase.

 **24** **Wie ich wohne und lebe.** Bilden Sie Sätze mit den folgenden Elementen.

1. Ich wohne
   a. bei meinen Eltern zu Hause.
   b. mit Freunden zusammen.
   c. alleine
2. Ich wohne … hier.
   a. seit wenigen Wochen
   b. seit vielen Monaten
   c. seit einigen Jahren
3. Ich arbeite
   a. bei (McDonald's).
   b. in der Mensa.
   c. zu Hause.
4. Ich esse oft
   a. mit meinem Mitbewohner.
   b. mit meiner Mitbewohnerin.
   c. allein.
5. Ich fahre … zur Uni.
   a. mit dem Rad
   b. mit dem Bus
   c. mit dem Auto

 **25** **Neue Leute kennen lernen.** Kreuzen Sie die beste Antwort an.

S1: *Wann lernst du neue Leute kennen?*
S2: *Beim Essen.*

| | Beim Lernen | Beim Schlafen | In der Freizeit | Beim Essen | |
|---|---|---|---|---|---|
| 1. neue Leute kennen lernen | ☐ | ☐ | ☐ | ☐ | |
| 2. vom Sommer träumen | ☐ | ☐ | ☐ | ☐ | |
| 3. Kollegen aus Kursen erkennen° | ☐ | ☐ | ☐ | ☐ | *see, recognize* |
| 4. Kleingeld brauchen | ☐ | ☐ | ☐ | ☐ | |
| 5. ungeduldig° werden | ☐ | ☐ | ☐ | ☐ | *impatient* |
| 6. über Physik und Deutsch lesen | ☐ | ☐ | ☐ | ☐ | |
| 7. mit Ausländern sprechen | ☐ | ☐ | ☐ | ☐ | |
| 8. einem Partner den Ball geben | ☐ | ☐ | ☐ | ☐ | |

**26**   **Das ist nett von ihm.** Geben Sie eine passende Antwort zu den folgenden Bemerkungen°.   *observations*

■   Karl hilft Anna mit den Hausaufgaben.
*Das ist nett von ihm.*

| Das ist | nett | von … |
|---|---|---|
| | freundlich | |
| | nicht nett | |
| | unfair | |

1. Karl hilft Anna mit den Hausaufgaben.
2. Barbara hilft Anna beim Einzug.
3. Inge leiht sich° immer das Fahrrad von Barbara.   ***sich leihen (von):** to borrow (from)*
4. Wir leihen unseren Freunden gern Geld.
5. Karl gibt Carlos seine 20 Euro nicht zurück.
6. Die Studenten haben den Test vor der Prüfung° gesehen.   *exam*
7. Ich habe meiner Freundin Blumen geschenkt.
8. Der Professor gibt gar keine Prüfungen!

**27**   **Mein Tagesablauf.** Denken Sie an einen ganz normalen Tag. Schreiben Sie sechs Aktivitäten oder Termine° auf sechs Karten auf, z.B.   *appointments* (das) Aufstehen, die Vorlesung. Geben Sie dann einem Partner/einer Partnerin die gemischten Karten. Der Partner/Die Partnerin versucht, mit Fragen die richtige Reihenfolge der Aktivitäten und Termine festzustellen°. Benutzen Sie im-   *determine* mer die Präposition **nach**.

■   S1: *Was machst du nach der Vorlesung?*
S2: *Nach der Vorlesung esse ich.*
S1: *Was machst du nach …?*

**28**   **Interview.** Stellen Sie einem Partner/einer Partnerin die folgenden Fragen.

1. Bei wem wohnst du oder mit wem wohnst du zusammen?
2. Wie lange wohnst du schon in dieser Stadt? *~seit*
3. Hast du einen Job? Wo arbeitest du? *~bei*
4. Mit wem lernst du oft?
5. Wohin gehst du nach dem Unterricht°? *~zu/nach*   *lecture, class*
6. Zu wem fährst du gern?
7. Wohin möchtest du fahren, wenn du Geld hast? *zu/nach*
8. Aus welchem Land kommst du? Deine Eltern? Deine Großeltern?
9. Von wem bekommst du jedes Jahr ein Geschenk zum Geburtstag?
10. Zu wem gehst du, wenn du persönliche Probleme hast?

> **Interview.** German speakers use the question word **wohin** to ask for destinations (e.g., **Wohin fährst du?**). They use **wo** to ask for locations (e.g., **Wo wohnst du?**).

## V Expressing attitudes and conditions such as gratitude, pleasure, ownership, and need for assistance

Dative verbs and expressions

### A. Dative verbs

There are five common verbs in German that always occur with the dative (**Dativverben**).

1. Expressing gratitude: **danken (hat gedankt)** *(to thank)*

   Ich **danke dir** für die Hilfe!     *Thanks for your help!*

2. Expressing pleasure: **gefallen (gefällt; hat gefallen)** *(to be appealing, pleasing)*

   **Gefällt dir** dein Zimmer denn nicht?     *Don't you like your room?*

3. Expressing like and dislike for food: **schmecken (hat geschmeckt)** *(to taste good)*

   Schokolade **schmeckt mir** immer.     *Chocolate always tastes good to me.*
   Milch **schmeckt mir** nicht.     *Milk doesn't taste good to me.*

4. Expressing ownership: **gehören (hat gehört)** *(to belong to)*

   Der Bleistift **gehört ihr.**     *The pencil belongs to her.*

5. Expressing the need for assistance: **helfen (hilft; hat geholfen)** *(to help)*

   Kannst du **mir** bitte **helfen?**     *Can you help me, please?*
   Das ist wirklich nett von dir, dass du     *It's really nice that you're helping*
      **mir hilfst.**     *me.*

German speakers often use expressions with **gefallen** or **schmecken** to compliment another person. The other person then responds with a comment or detail, or sometimes downplays the compliment.

| | |
|---|---|
| KARL: Dein Pullover gefällt mir echt°. | *really* |
| BARBARA: Danke. Er ist aus Norwegen. *(oder)* | |
| Danke. Aber er ist schon alt. | |

| | |
|---|---|
| BARBARA: Deine Spaghettisauce schmeckt mir wirklich gut. | |
| KARL: Danke. Ich habe sie dir extra° gekocht. *(oder)* | *just for you* |
| Danke. Aber ich hab' sie nur im Supermarkt gekauft. | |

 **29** **Komplimente machen.** Machen Sie Komplimente. Verwenden Sie **gefallen** oder **schmecken.**

S1: *Dein Pullover gefällt mir echt gut.*
S2: *Danke. Ich habe ihn erst vor ein paar Tagen gekauft.* (oder)
   *Ich danke dir, aber er ist schon alt.* (oder)
   *Danke, mir auch.*

1. dein Pullover gefällt
2. deine Schuhe gefallen
3. dein Kuchen schmeckt
4. deine Freunde gefallen
5. dein Poster gefällt
6. dein Haus gefällt
7. dieser Wein schmeckt
8. diese Tomaten schmecken

**30**    **Ein Ratespiel.**  Bilden Sie Gruppen von vier bis sechs Leuten. Eine Person ist der Gruppenleiter/die Gruppenleiterin. Jede Person in der Gruppe gibt dem Leiter/der Leiterin einen oder zwei Gegenstände. Dann zeigt der Leiter/die Leiterin der Gruppe jeden Gegenstand und fragt: „Wem gehört das?" Die anderen Leute in der Gruppe beschreiben den Besitzer°/die Besitzerin. Nennen Sie keine Namen!

**Ein Ratespiel.** The noun **der Student** adds **-en** in all cases but the nominative singular.

*owner*

S1: *Wem gehört das Buch?*
S2: *Das gehört einem Studenten mit schwarzen Haaren.*
S3: *Gehört das Buch einem Studenten mit einer Brille?*
S1: *Ja.*
S4: *Ist es Jeremy?*
S1: *Ja.*

| ein Student | mit | schwarzen (blonden, roten, braunen) Haaren |
| eine Studentin | | blauen (braunen, grünen, grauen) Augen |
| | | einer Brille |

## B. Adjectives with the dative case

Some adjectives appear in conjunction with the dative in order to indicate a temporary condition rather than a permanent quality. When used with the dative case, these adjectives always refer to people. They are **warm, heiß, kalt, schlecht,** and **langweilig.**

*Temporary condition*
| Mir ist langweilig. | *I am bored.* |
| Ihr ist schlecht. | *She feels ill (nauseous).* |
| Mir ist kalt. | *I'm (feeling) cold.* |

It is important to use the dative with these adjectives. Incorrect use with **heiß, kalt,** and **warm** may lead to unintended meanings.

*Permanent quality*
| Ich bin langweilig. | *I am a boring person.* |
| Sie ist schlecht. | *She is a bad person.* |
| Eis ist kalt. | *Ice is cold.* |

**31**    **So fühle ich mich° jetzt.**  Beschreiben Sie, wie Sie sich in dieser Situation fühlen.

*sich fühlen = to feel*

Kannst du bitte das Fenster aufmachen?
*Mir ist heiß.*

1. Kannst du bitte das Fenster zumachen?
2. Kannst du bitte die Heizung° anmachen?
3. Ich möchte etwas Interessantes machen.
4. Ich kann jetzt nichts essen.

*heat*

## C. Idiomatic expressions with the dative case

Here are some common idiomatic expressions that require the dative case.

| Wie geht es Ihnen/dir? | *How are you?* |
| Es/Das tut mir Leid. | *I'm sorry.* |
| Der Arm tut mir weh. | *My arm hurts.* |
| Die frische Luft tut ihm gut. | *Fresh air is good for him.* |
| Das ist mir peinlich. | *That's embarrassing for me.* |

## *Wissenswerte Vokabeln: Körperteile*
*Describing your body; talking about physical discomfort*

das Haar, -e
der Kopf, ¨ e
das Ohr, -en
die Schulter, -n
der Hals, ¨ e
die Brust, ¨ e
der Arm, -e
die Hand, ¨ e
der Finger, -
der Rücken, -
die Stirn
der Hintern
das Auge, -n
der Bauch, ¨ e
das Gesicht, -er
das Bein, -e
die Nase, -n
das Knie, -
der Mund, ¨ er
der Fuß, Füße
der Zeh, -en
der Zahn, ¨ e
die Lippe, -n
das Kinn

**die Haut** = *skin*;
**das Herz** = *heart*

◻ Was tut dir weh?
*Mir tun die Füße (die Augen) weh.* (oder)
*Ich habe mir das Bein gebrochen.*

**32    Ursache° und Wirkung°: Mir tut der Arm weh.** Verbinden Sie    *cause / effect*
eine Ursache mit einer Wirkung.

◻ Karl hat sich das Bein gebrochen.
*Ihm tut das Bein weh.*

1. Karl hat sich das Bein gebrochen. *B*     a. Mir tut der Kopf noch weh.
2. Die Studenten haben heute sehr            b. Ihm tut das Bein weh.
   viel gelesen. *C*                          c. Ihnen tun die Augen weh.
3. Frau Müller geht heute zum Zahnarzt°. *D*  d. Ihr tun die Zähne weh.    *dentist*
4. Ich habe ein Aspirin eingenommen. *A*

5. Monika ist vom Fahrrad gefallen. *E*       e. Ihr tun die Knie noch weh.
6. Stefan hat seine Wohnung                    f. Den Zuhörern tun die Ohren weh.
   eingerichtet und viele Möbel                g. Ihm tun die Schultern und
   getragen. *G*                                  die Arme weh.
7. Wir haben viel zu viel gegessen. *I*        h. Ihnen tun die Füße weh.
8. Anna und Barbara sind heute                 i. Uns tut der Bauch weh.
   sehr weit gelaufen. *H*
9. Die Musik im Konzert war zu laut. *F*

**33    Hast du Lust mitzumachen?** Ihr Mitbewohner/Ihre Mitbewohnerin hat Pläne für den Abend. Sie haben aber gar keine Lust mitzumachen. Beantworten Sie die Fragen mit einer Ausrede° und sagen Sie, was Ihnen       *excuse*
wehtut.

> S1:  *Ich gehe heute Abend essen. Hast du auch Lust zu essen?*
> S2:  *Nein, danke. Mein Bauch tut mir weh.*

**Hast du Lust mitzu-
machen?** Select these situations at random and take
turns.

1. heute Abend essen gehen
2. mit Freunden Basketball spielen
3. einer Freundin beim Einziehen ins Studentenwohnheim helfen
4. um acht Uhr ins Hard-Rock-Konzert gehen
5. in einer Stunde eine Fahrradtour machen
6. am Samstag wandern gehen
7. Karten spielen
8. Bier trinken gehen

## VI    Specifying what you are talking about

### Der-words

**Der**-words have case endings similar to those of **der/das/die.** You have already
encountered three common **der**-words in exercise direction lines in this text.

| | | | |
|---|---|---|---|
| **dieser/dieses/diese** | *this, that* | **diese** | *these, those* |
| **jeder/jedes/jede** | *each, every* | **alle** | *all (pl.)* |
| **welcher/welches/welche** | *which* | **welche** | *which (pl.)* |

The literal translation of
*that* is **jener/jenes/jene**
(e.g., **jener Mann, jenes
Kind, jene Frau**). It is used
almost exclusively in written German. Generally,
**dieser/dieses/diese** stands
for both *this* and *that*.

| | |
|---|---|
| Wie fühlen Sie sich in **dieser** Situation? | *How do you feel in this situation?* |
| **Welche** Sätze bedeuten das Gleiche? | *Which sentences mean the same thing?* |
| **Welcher** Student kommt aus der Elfenbeinküste? | *Which student is from Ivory Coast?* |
| **Alle** Studenten müssen eine Arbeit schreiben. | *All students have to write a paper.* |
| Ich kenne **diesen** Professor. | *I know that professor.* |
| Er steht **jeden** Tag um 6 Uhr auf. | *He gets up every day at 6:00.* |
| Kannst du **diesem** Studenten helfen? | *Can you help this student?* |

Time phrases with **dieser**
and **jeder** employ the accusative case: **Anna ruft
Stefan diesen Freitag /
jeden Morgen an.**

Here are the nominative, accusative, and dative endings for **der**-words:

| | Masculine | Neuter | Feminine | Plural |
|---|---|---|---|---|
| **Nominative** | dies**er** Mann | dies**es** Kind | dies**e** Frau | dies**e** Kinder |
| | jed**er** Mann | jed**es** Kind | jed**e** Frau | all**e** Kinder |
| | welch**er** Mann | welch**es** Kind | welch**e** Frau | welch**e** Kinder |
| **Accusative** | dies**en** Mann | dies**es** Kind | dies**e** Frau | dies**e** Kinder |
| | jed**en** Mann | jed**es** Kind | jed**e** Frau | all**e** Kinder |
| | welch**en** Mann | welch**es** Kind | welch**e** Frau | welch**e** Kinder |
| **Dative** | dies**em** Mann | dies**em** Kind | dies**er** Frau | dies**en** Kinder**n** |
| | jed**em** Mann | jed**em** Kind | jed**er** Frau | all**en** Kinder**n** |
| | welch**em** Mann | welch**em** Kind | welch**er** Frau | welch**en** Kinder**n** |

Remember that plural
nouns add an **-n** in the
dative unless they already
end in **-n: dieses Kind,
diese Kinder, mit diesen
Kindern.**

**34  Nimm diesen hier!**  Fragen Sie einen Freund/eine Freundin, ob er/sie Ihnen diese Gegenstände leihen kann.

■  einen Stift

> S1:  *Kannst du mir einen Stift leihen?*
> S2:  *Ja, nimm diesen Stift hier.*

1. einen Stift
2. ein Buch über Deutschland
3. ein Radio
4. ein Fahrrad
5. einen Laptop
6. eine Cola
7. einen 20-Euro-Schein
8. eine Lampe

**35  Entscheidungen° am Bahnhof.**  Barbara ist am Bahnhof. Sie hat aber noch keine konkreten Reisepläne. Karl hilft ihr. Finden Sie einen Partner/eine Partnerin, und spielen Sie Barbara und Karl. Setzen Sie auch eine richtige Form von **welcher/welches/welche** in Barbaras Fragen ein.

*decisions*

■  S1 (BARBARA):  *Um welche Zeit soll ich nur abfahren: um vier Uhr oder um vier Uhr dreißig?*
   S2 (KARL):  *Fahr um vier Uhr ab.*

1. Um _____ Zeit soll ich nur abfahren: um vier Uhr oder um vier Uhr dreißig?
2. Mit _____ Zug soll ich nur fahren: mit einem Eilzug oder mit einem Lokalzug?
3. _____ Stadt soll ich nur besuchen: Bonn oder Hamburg?
4. _____ Buch soll ich im Zug lesen: mein Deutschbuch oder einen Roman?
5. _____ CDs soll ich für die Reise mitbringen: Jazz oder Rock?
6. _____ Freund oder _____ Freundin soll ich ein Souvenir kaufen: dir oder Anna?
7. Mit _____ Leuten soll ich im Abteil° sitzen: mit jungen oder mit alten?

*compartment*

> **Entscheidungen am Bahnhof. Der Lokalzug** stops in every train station. **Der Eilzug** is a faster train with stops in larger towns and cities only. In addition, there are **Intercityzüge,** which stop only in very large cities. They require an extra fee (**der Zuschlag**) of about 5 Euros.

**36  Übertreibungen°.**  Barbara beschreibt das deutsche Studenten-leben. Sie übertreibt ein bisschen. Setzen Sie eine richtige Form von **jeder/jedes/jede** und **alle** ein. Benutzen Sie **alle** für Nominativ und Akkusativ Plural und **allen** für Dativ Plural.

*exaggerations*

1. _____ Tag müssen die Studenten um fünf Uhr morgens aufstehen.
2. Dann lernen _____ Studenten zwei bis drei Stunden.
3. Danach isst _____ Student und _____ Studentin nur ein Stück Brot mit Käse.
4. Dann gehen die Studenten zur Uni: sie gehen zu _____ Vorlesung.
5. Die Studenten stellen° viele Fragen und _____ Frage ist intelligent und wichtig.
6. _____ Professoren freuen sich° über die Fragen. Sie helfen _____ Studenten gern.
7. _____ Abend arbeiten die Studenten schwer.
8. Und _____ Wochenende lernen oder arbeiten sie auch. Sie haben keine Freizeit.

*pose, ask*

**sich freuen** = to be happy

**Freie Kommunikation**

**Rollenspiel: Ausländer.**  Sie treffen in der Küche im Studentenwohnheim einen Ausländer/eine Ausländerin. Er/Sie ist neu. Er/Sie möchte wissen, wo man einkaufen kann, wo man telefonieren kann, wie man in die Stadt kommt usw. Helfen Sie ihm/ihr. Sagen Sie, dass Sie auch ein Ausländer/eine Ausländerin sind.

**Rollenspiel: Beim Arzt°.**  Patient(in): Sie sind ein Hypochonder. Sie gehen zum Arzt, denn Sie fühlen sich schon wieder° nicht sehr wohl. Beschreiben Sie dem Arzt Ihre Symptome. Arzt (Ärztin): Sie kennen diesen Patienten/diese Patientin sehr gut. Er/Sie ist ein Hypochonder. Sie wissen, dass die beste Lösung° ist, wenn Sie gut zuhören und viele Fragen über die Probleme stellen.

*Doktor*
*again*

*solution*

> ARZT (ÄRZTIN):  *Wie fühlen Sie sich heute?*
> PATIENT(IN):  *Mir tut der Bauch weh.*
>  (oder)
> PATIENT(IN):  *Können Sie mir helfen?*
> ARZT (ÄRZTIN):  *Wo tut es Ihnen weh?*

> **Rundherum in dieser Stadt.** Helpful words not shown in art: **die Schule** (*school*), **der Wald** (*forest*), **das Theater, der Zoo, der Club, das Stadtmuseum** (*city museum*).

## Schreibecke

**Rundherum in dieser Stadt: eine Werbebroschüre**.  Sie haben einen neuen Job bei einer Werbeagentur° und müssen Ihrer Chefin° den Text für eine Broschüre für eine kleine Fantasiestadt in Deutschland schreiben. Die Stadt heißt Neuheim am Main. In der Broschüre sollen Sie viele Informationen über Neuheim am Main geben. Geben Sie an, wo man gut essen und trinken kann (und was die Spezialitäten der Stadt sind), was für Musik man hören kann (und wo), wo man einen Spaziergang machen kann (und in welchen Jahreszeiten), was man mit Kindern tun kann (und wo), usw. Benutzen Sie den Imperativ, wenn Sie wollen. Beginnen Sie die Broschüre mit dem folgenden Satz.

*ad agency /*
*(female) boss*

> *Neuheim am Main bietet° dem Besucher viele Attraktionen und Sehenswürdigkeiten.*

*offers*

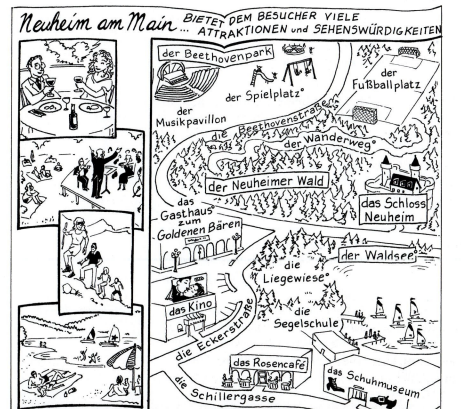

*playground*

*hiking path*

*inn*

**der See** = *lake*
*meadow*

**Zieltext**

## Gespräch in der Gemeinschaftsküche

Anna hat inzwischen° ihr Zimmer eingerichtet° und hat jetzt Hunger. Sie geht mit          *in the meantime / furnished*
Barbara in die Gemeinschaftsküche. In der Küche lernen sie Karl und Inge
kennen. Barbara möchte etwas zu essen machen, aber sie weiß nicht so genau,
wo alles ist. Karl und Inge geben Anna und Barbara viele Tipps über die Küche
und das Wohnheim. Aber zuerst trinken sie zusammen einen Tee.

## Vorschau

**37    Thematische Fragen: Ein Gespräch mit Karl und Inge.**
Kreuzen Sie an, wie wahrscheinlich es ist, dass Karl und Inge mit Anna und
Barbara über die folgenden Themen sprechen.

|  | *Sehr wahrscheinlich* | *Vielleicht* | *Sehr unwahrscheinlich* |
|---|---|---|---|
| 1. Tübingen | ☐ | ☐ | ☐ |
| 2. die Sachen in der Küche | ☐ | ☐ | ☐ |
| 3. Ausländer im Studentenwohnheim | ☐ | ☐ | ☐ |
| 4. den Islam | ☐ | ☐ | ☐ |
| 5. Hunger haben | ☐ | ☐ | ☐ |
| 6. die Organisation in der Küche | ☐ | ☐ | ☐ |
| 7. Annas Kochen | ☐ | ☐ | ☐ |
| 8. das Essen in der Mensa | ☐ | ☐ | ☐ |

**38    Satzdetektiv.** Welche Sätze bedeuten ungefähr das gleiche?

1. Hier wohnen eigentlich viele **Ausländer** im Haus.

2. Ich weiß nicht, wo die **Töpfe** sind.

3. Es gibt zwei **Kühlschränke** hier.

4. Ich hoffe, dass dir der Hauswart° einen Schlüssel **mitgegeben** hat.

a. Du kannst das Essen in diesen beiden Schränken kühl halten.

b. Hoffentlich° hast du vom Hausmeister einen Schlüssel bekommen.          *I/we hope*

c. Studenten aus vielen Ländern wohnen im Studentenheim.          *caretaker*

d. Wo sind die Pfannen und anderen Sachen° in der Küche?          *things*

5. Also du kannst nur **das Notwendigste reinstellen**.

6. Das ist dein **Fach** für Brot und Reis und so.

7. Die Küche ist immer offen, deswegen musst du eben dein Fach immer **unter Verschluss halten.**

8. Sonst kommen die Leute rein und **nehmen** dir einfach **das Zeug weg.**

e. Das ist dein Platz im Schrank für Brot und Reis und andere Sachen.

f. Du hast nur Platz für die wichtigsten Sachen.

g. Schließ dein Fach immer ab°, weil jeder in die Küche gehen kann.          ***abschließen*** *= to lock*

h. Wenn du das nicht machst, kommen andere Studenten und essen deine Sachen.

## Zieltext

### Gespräch in der Gemeinschaftsküche

 Hören Sie gut zu.

## Rückblick

**39 Gemischte Sätze.** Bringen Sie diese Sätze aus dem Dialog in die richtige Reihenfolge.

_____ Also, ich muss mal etwas Essen kaufen.

_____ Anna hat ein bisschen Hunger, wir wollen uns eigentlich 'was zu essen machen.

_____ Guten Appetit!

_____ Ich hab' mir gerade einen Tee gekocht.

__1__ Ich glaube, ich habe euch auch schon mal gesehen.

_____ Und ich hoffe, dass dir der Hauswart einen Schlüssel mitgegeben hat.

_____ Wir sind am Ende vom Gang.

> German speakers generally say **Guten Appetit!** before eating.

**40 Stimmt das?** Stimmen diese Aussagen zum Text oder nicht? Wenn nicht, was stimmt?

| | Ja, das stimmt. | Nein, das stimmt nicht. | |
|---|:---:|:---:|---|
| 1. Anna weiß, wo die Küche im Studentenheim ist. | ☐ | ☐ | |
| 2. Barbara hat Karl und Inge noch nie vorher im Leben gesehen. | ☐ | ☐ | |
| 3. Karl und Inge wohnen beide am Ende vom Flur. | ☐ | ☐ | |
| 4. Im Studentenwohnheim gibt es viele Ausländer. | ☐ | ☐ | |
| 5. Karl lädt Anna und Barbara zu einem Kaffee ein. | ☐ | ☐ | |
| 6. In der Gemeinschaftsküche gibt es zwei Kühlschränke mit einem Fach für jeden Studenten. | ☐ | ☐ | |
| 7. Alle Studenten im Heim müssen sich diese Küche teilen°. | ☐ | ☐ | *share* |
| 8. Die Küche ist nur für wenige Stunden am Tag offen. | ☐ | ☐ | |
| 9. Man muss sein Essen unter Verschluss halten, sonst nehmen es die anderen weg. | ☐ | ☐ | |

**41**    **Der aktive Zuhörer.** Hören Sie sich den Text noch einmal an, und ergänzen Sie die Sätze mit Wörtern aus dem **Zieltext**.

1.    ANNA:    Barbara, ich habe Hunger. Weißt du, _____ ich essen kann?
2.    BARBARA:    Wir können _____ hier etwas zu essen machen.
3.    INGE:    Du bist da _____, ja?
4.    KARL:    Hier wohnen eigentlich viele _____ im Haus.
5.    KARL:    Dann können wir _____ das erklären.
6.    KARL:    Und _____ du die Tür aufmachst, hat _____ sein Fach.
7.    KARL:    Ich hoffe, dass _____ der Hauswart einen Schlüssel mitgegeben hat.
8.    BARBARA:    Sonst kommen die Leute rein und nehmen _____ einfach das Zeug weg.

 **|||** **F r e i e   K o m m u n i k a t i o n**

**Rollenspiel: In der Küche.** Sie sind mit einem Freund/einer Freundin in der Küche und möchten eine Pizza für eine Party machen. Ihr Freund/Ihre Freundin hilft Ihnen und gibt Ihnen, was Sie brauchen. Hier sind einige Ausdrücke.

der Teig

das Mehl

die Tomaten

der Käse

die Wurst

die Pilze *(pl.)*

die Oliven *(pl.)*

Salz und Pfeffer

das Öl

das Wasser

der Topf

der Löffel

das Messer

die Gabel

der Teller

der Herd

| | |
|---|---|
| Kannst du mir helfen ? | Ich helfe dir gern. |
| Wo ist/sind … ? | Leider haben wir das nicht. |
| Wem gehört/gehören … ? | Im Kühlschrank. |
| Gefällt/Gefallen dir … ? | Ich weiß nicht. |
| Kannst du mir … geben ? | Ich kann (den Käse) nicht finden. |
| Kannst du … | finden? | Ja, klar. |
| | waschen? | Leider, nein. |
| | schneiden°? | |

*cut*

In der Gemeinschaftsküche darf man jederzeit kochen.

  S c h r e i b e c k e

**Wie heißt mein Studentenwohnheim?**  Beschreiben Sie Ihr Studentenwohnheim in zehn Sätzen, aber schreiben Sie nicht den Namen von dem Wohnheim! In welchem Stock wohnen Sie? Seit wann wohnen Sie dort? Was haben Sie alles? Welche Zimmernummer haben Sie? Was gefällt Ihnen gut/nicht gut? Dann geben Sie die Beschreibung einem Partner/einer Partnerin, und er/sie soll erraten°, in welchem Wohnheim Sie wohnen.

*guess*

**Die Küche.**  In der Küche fehlen° viele Sachen. Der Hausmeister will wissen, was die Studenten in der Küche haben und was sie brauchen. Anna, Barbara, Karl und Inge schreiben eine Liste für den Hausmeister. Schreiben Sie an den Hausmeister für sie.

*are missing*

ein Herd • ein Fernseher • Töpfe • ein Faxgerät • ein Bett • ein Mikrowellenherd • Kochbücher • Fächer für Brot und Reis • ein Kühlschrank • eine Geschirrspülmaschine° • eine Kaffeemaschine • Tee und Kaffee • ein Spiegel° • ein Spülbecken° • ein Teppich • eine Brot- und Wurstschneidemaschine°

*dishwasher / mirror*
*sink / bread and meat slicer*

## Wortschatz

### Das Studentenleben, -

**der Austauschstudent, [-en], -en**
*foreign exchange student*
**die Fachhochschule, -n (die FH)**
*specialized university*
**die Party, -s** *party*
**die Prüfung, -en** *test, examination*
**der Unterricht, -e** *lesson, instruction, class*
**die Vorlesung, -en** *lecture, class*

### Das Studentenzimmer, -

**das Bett, -en** *bed*
**das Bild, -er** *picture*
**die Blume, -n** *flower*
**der Computer, -** *computer*
**die Couch** or (Sw.) **der Couch, -s** or **-en** *couch*
**der Drucker, -** *printer*
**die Gardine, -n** *curtain*
**der Internet-Anschluss, ¨e** *Internet connection*
**die Klamotten** (pl.) *things to wear, duds*
**die Kommode, -n** *chest of drawers*
**die Möbel** (pl.) *furniture*
**die Pflanze, -n** *green plant*
**das Radio, -s** *radio*
**das Regal, -e** *set of shelves*
  **das Bücherregal** *bookcase*
**der Schrank, ¨e** *closet*
  **der Kleiderschrank** *wardrobe*
  **der Kühlschrank** *refrigerator*
**der Schreibtisch, -e** *desk*
**der Sessel, -** *armchair (North), chair (South)*
**die Stereoanlage, -n** *stereo set*
**das Telefon, -e** *telephone*
**der Teppich, -e** *rug, carpet*
**das Waschbecken, -** *(bathroom) sink*
**der Wecker, -** *alarm clock*
**die Wohnung, -en** *apartment*

### Das Studentenwohnheim, -e

**der Automat, [-en], -en** *vending machine*
**das Brett, ¨er** *board*
  **das Schwarze Brett** *bulletin board*
**die (Luxus)bude, -n** *(luxury) student room (slang)*
**der Duschraum, ¨e** *shower room*
**das Einzelzimmer, -** *single room*
**das Fach, ¨er** *compartment, cupboard, container, shelf*
**das Gemeinschaftsbad, ¨er** *shared/communal bathroom*
**die Gemeinschaftsküche, -n** *shared/communal kitchen*
**die Mensa,** pl. **die Mensen** *university cafeteria*
**das Postfach, ¨er** *mailbox*
**der Schlüssel, -** *key*
**das Studentenwohnheim, -e** *residence hall*
**das Studentenzimmer** *student's room*
**die Telefonzelle, -n** *telephone booth*
**auf·kriegen (hat aufgekriegt)** *to open (slang)*
**auf·schließen (hat aufgeschlossen)** *to unlock*
**auf·schreiben (hat aufgeschrieben)** *to write down*
**ein·ziehen (ist eingezogen)** *to move in*
**leihen (hat geliehen)** *to lend, loan*

### Das Einfamilienhaus, ¨er

**das Bad, ¨er** *bath*
**der Balkon, -s** *balcony*
**der Boden, ¨** *floor; ground*
**der Dachboden, ¨** *attic*
  **auf dem Dachboden** *in the attic*
**die Diele, -n** *entrance hall*
**die Dusche, -n** *shower*
**der Eingang, ¨e** *entrance, front door*

**das Erdgeschoss, -e** *ground floor*
  **im Erdgeschoss** *on the first (ground) floor*
**der Flur, -e** *hallway, corridor*
**der Gang, ¨** *hallway, corridor*
**der Garten, ¨** *garden; yard*
**das Haus, ¨er** *house*
  **das Einfamilienhaus** *single-family home*
**der Keller, -** *basement, cellar*
**das Klo, -s (das Klosett)** *toilet (colloq.)*
**die Küche, -n** *kitchen*
**der Raum, ¨e** *room*
  **der Abstellraum** *storage room*
**der Rollladen, ¨** *roll-top shutter*
**der Stock,** pl. **die Stockwerke** *floor, story*
  **im ersten (zweiten) Stock** *on the second (third) floor*
**die Toilette, -n** *toilet*
**die Treppe, -n** *step; stairway*
**die Waschküche, -n** *laundry room*
**das WC, -s** *toilet*
**das Zimmer, -** *room*
  **das Badezimmer** *bathroom*
  **das Schlafzimmer** *bedroom*
  **das Wohnzimmer** *living room*

### In der Küche

**die Gabel, -n** *fork*
**der Herd, -e** *stove*
**der Löffel, -** *spoon*
**das Messer, -** *knife*
**der Pfeffer** *pepper*
**das Salz** *salt*
**der Teller, -** *plate*
**der Topf, ¨e** *pot*

**Guten Appetit!** *Enjoy your meal., Bon appétit.*

### Der Körperteil, -e

**der Arm, -e** *arm*
**das Auge, -n** *eye*

**der Bauch, ¨-e** *stomach*
**das Bein, -e** *leg*
**die Brust, ¨-e** *chest*
**der Finger, -** *finger*
**der Fuß, ¨-e** *foot*
**das Gesicht, -er** *face*
**das Haar, -e** *hair*
**der Hals, ¨-e** *throat*
**die Hand, ¨-e** *hand*
**die Haut** *skin*
**das Herz, -en** *heart*
**das Kinn,** *chin*
**das Knie, -** *knee*
**der Kopf, ¨-e** *head*
**der Mund, ¨-er** *mouth*
**die Nase, -n** *nose*
**das Ohr, -en** *ear*
**der Rücken, -** *back*
**die Schulter, -n** *shoulder*
**die Stirn,** *forehead*
**der Zahn, ¨-e** *tooth*
**der Zeh, -en** *toe*

## *Der*-Wörter

**alle,** *pl. all*
**dieser/dieses/diese** *this, that (pl. these, those)*
**jeder/jedes/jede** *each, every*
**welcher?/welches?/welche?** *which?*

## Dativpronomen

**dir** *(to/for) you (informal)*
**euch** *(to/for) you (guys)*
**ihm** *(to/for) him/it*
**ihnen** *(to/for) them*
**Ihnen** *(to/for) you (formal)*
**ihr** *(to/for) her*
**mir** *(to/for) me*
**uns** *(to/for) us*
**wem?** *(to/for) whom?*

## Dativpräpositionen

**aus** *from; out of*
**außer** *except for*
**bei** *at; by; near; with*
**mit** *with*
**nach** *after; past; to*
**seit** *since, for*
**von** *from, of, by*
**zu** *to*

## Dativverben

**danken (hat gedankt)** + *dat. to thank*
**gefallen (gefällt, hat gefallen)** + *dat. to please, to appeal to*
**gehören (hat gehört)** + *dat. to belong to*
**helfen (hilft, hat geholfen)** + *dat. to help*
**schmecken (hat geschmeckt)** + *dat. to taste good*
**weh·tun (hat wehgetan)** *to hurt*

## Andere Verben

**dauern (hat gedauert)** *to last (a length of time)*
**rauchen (hat geraucht)** *to smoke*
**schenken (hat geschenkt)** *to give (a gift)*
**eine Frage stellen (hat gestellt)** *to ask a question*

## Ausländer

**der Ausländer, -/die Ausländerin, -nen** *foreigner*
**die Ausländerfeindlichkeit** *xenophobia*
**ausländisch** *foreign*
**das Austauschprogramm, -e** *study abroad exchange program*
**die Bereicherung** *enrichment*
**die Erfahrung, -en** *experience*
**der Freundeskreis, -e** *circle of friends, clique*
**die Hautfarbe, -n** *skin color*
**die Herkunft** *origin*
**die Kaution** *deposit*
**der Mensch, [-en], -en** *human being, person*
**die Völkerverständigung** *international understanding*
**die Voraussetzung, -en** *prerequisite*
**die Zulassungskriterien** *admissions requirements*
**ab·stammen (ist abgestammt)** *to originate from*
**an·schauen (hat angeschaut)** *to look at*
**schief an·schauen** *to look at (someone) funny*
**erfüllen (hat erfüllt)** *to fulfill*
**multikulturell** *multicultural*

## Andere Ausdrücke

**alles in Ordnung** *everything's in order, okay*
**Alles klar!** *Okay!, Great!*
**Bis gleich!** *See you soon!*
**(Der Arm) tut mir weh.** *My (arm) hurts.*
**Es/Das tut mir Leid.** *I'm sorry.*
**Entschuldigung.** *Excuse me.*
**gleich neben** *right next to*
**Guck mal!** *Look!*
**(einen) Kater haben** *to have a hangover*
**meiner Meinung nach** *in my opinion*
**na ja** *oh well*
**Schwein haben** *to be really lucky*
**Vielen Dank.** *Thanks a lot.*
**einen Vogel haben** *to be crazy, nuts*
**Wie geht es Ihnen/dir?** *How are you?, How's it going?*

## Andere Wörter

**das Ding, -e** *thing*
**die Möglichkeit, -en** *possibility*
**die Reihenfolge, -n** *sequence, order*
**die Sache, -n** *thing*
**allein** *alone*
**alles** *everything, all*
**egal** *no difference*
**endlich** *finally*
**eventuell** *possibly, by chance*
**gerade** *just now, directly*
**hoffentlich** *I/we hope*
**klar** *sure, all clear*
**manchmal** *sometimes*
**nett** *nice*
**schwer** *hard, difficult; heavy*
**ursprünglich** *originally*
**vor** + *dat. before; in front of; (of time) ago*
**wenn** *when, whenever, as soon as; if*
**wieder** *again*

## Meine eigenen Wörter

________________
________________
________________
________________
________________

## Gedicht 1

### Ein Liebesgedicht
*Autor unbekannt, ca. 1200*

1 dû bist mîn, ich bin dîn,
2 des solt dû gewis sîn.
3 dû bist beslozzen
4 in mînem herzen;
5 verlorn ist daz slüzzelîn
6 dû muost immer drinne sîn.

  **1** **Modern gesagt.** Die Sprache in diesem Gedicht° ist aus dem Mittelalter°. Welche Zeile° im Gedicht sagt das Gleiche wie diese Sätze?

*poem*
*Middle Ages / line*

| Satz | Zeile im Gedicht | |
|---|---|---|
| 1. In meinem Herzen° | — | *heart* |
| 2. Dessen sollst du gewiss° sein | — | *certain* |
| 3. Verloren ist das Schlüsselein° | — | *little key* |
| 4. Du bist mein, ich bin dein | 1 | |
| 5. Du bist eingeschlossen° | — | *locked in* |
| 6. Du musst immer drinnen° sein | — | *inside* |

 **2** **Die Bedeutung.** Wovon erzählt das Gedicht?

1. Jemand hat seinen Hausschlüssel verloren.
2. Jemand hatte einen Herzanfall°.
3. Jemand hat sich schwer verliebt.
4. Jemand kann nicht aus dem Haus.

*heart attack*

**3** **Die Sprache.** Die deutsche Sprache im Mittelalter war anders. Man hat zum Beispiel keinen Unterschied° zwischen Großbuchstaben° und Kleinbuchstaben gemacht. Die Laute° waren auch anders als heute (z.B. **sl → schl, î → ei, zz → ss, uo → u** usw.). Wie heißen die folgenden Wörter vom Gedicht im modernen Deutschen?
mîn • dîn • sîn • beslozzen • mînem • slüzzelîn • muost

*distinction / capital letters*
*sounds*

## Gedicht 2

### Ein Jüngling liebt ein Mädchen
*Heinrich Heine, 1797–1856*

Harry Heine was born into a Jewish family on December 13, 1797, in Düsseldorf, but was later baptized as a Protestant to promote his career, a decision about which he remained ambivalent throughout his life. Following the baptism he was known as Heinrich Heine. Although he earned his doctorate in law, he chose a career as a writer and spent most of his life in financial straits. In 1831, Heine moved to Paris and died there in 1856. First associated with German Romanticism, his later writings became increasingly political and many were banned in Prussia, Austria, and other states in the German Confederation.

*Heinrich Heine*

**4** **Eine unglückliche Liebesgeschichte.** Das Gedicht „Ein Jüngling liebt ein Mädchen" endet mit dieser Zeile: „dem bricht das Herz° entzwei°."

*heart / in two*

1. Klingt das optimistisch oder pessimistisch?
2. Erwartet° man das in einem Liebesgedicht?
3. Was erwartet man normalerweise von Liebe?
4. Ein Mädchen heiratet „den nächsten besten Mann". Ist das eine gute Motivation? Kennen Sie ein Beispiel aus den Hollywood-Zeitungen dafür?

*expects*

### Ein Jüngling° liebt ein Mädchen

*young man*

1  Ein Jüngling liebt ein Mädchen,
2  Die hat einen anderen erwählt°;
3  Der andre liebt eine andere.
4  Und hat sich mit dieser vermählt°.

*hat erwählt: chose*

*hat sich vermählt: wed*

5  Das Mädchen heiratet aus Ärger°
6  Den nächsten besten Mann,
7  Der ihr in den Weg gelaufen°;
8  Der Jüngling ist übel dran°.

*aus ...: out of annoyance*

*der ...: who crosses her path*
*ist ...: is upset about it*

9  Es ist eine alte Geschichte,
10 Doch bleibt sie immer neu;
11 Und wem sie just passiert°,
12 Dem bricht das Herz entzwei.

*just ...: happens this way*

**5** **Was ist passiert?** Was passiert im Gedicht zuerst und dann später? Nummerieren Sie die Sätze von **1** bis **5**.

> The original poem had these spellings: *andern* (2), *eine andre* (3), *passieret* (11).

___ ein junger Mann liebt und heiratet ein Mädchen
___ ein Mädchen heiratet einen jungen Mann, aber sie liebt ihn nicht
_1_ ein junger Mann liebt ein Mädchen, aber sie liebt ihn nicht
___ ein Mädchen liebt einen jungen Mann, aber er liebt sie nicht
___ ein junger Mann ist unglücklich

**6** **Was glauben Sie?** Diskutieren Sie die folgenden Fragen mit der Klasse oder mit einem Partner/einer Partnerin mit Hilfe der Grafik.

1. Wer kennt wen und wer kennt wen nicht? Wer heiratet wen zum Schluss?
2. Welche Ehe ist (un)glücklich? Warum?
3. Kennen Sie diese Geschichte aus einem Film, aus einem Buch oder aus dem wirklichen Leben?
4. Das mittelalterliche Gedicht ist optimistisch. Heines Gedicht ist pessimistisch. Welches ist Ihrer Meinung nach realistisch? Wie ist Liebe wirklich?

# Man kann alles in der Stadt finden

Diese Frau kauft beim Metzger ein.

**In this chapter you will learn where to do errands and where to spend free time in a city, how to ask for and give directions, and how to talk about travel and transportation.**

## Kommunikative Funktionen

- Expressing location and destination
- Talking about when events happen
- Talking about means of transportation
- Expressing time, manner, and place
- Giving directions
- Expressing the purpose for an action

## Strukturen

- Two-case prepositions
- **Wo?** and **wohin?**
- The prefixes **hin** and **her**
- Verbs used with two-case prepositions
- The verbs **hängen/hängen, legen/liegen, setzen/sitzen,** and **stellen/stehen**
- Time expressions in the dative and accusative
- The preposition **mit** with the dative case
- Word order: time, manner, place
- Prepositional phrases of location
- The subordinating conjunction **damit**

## Vokabeln

- Wo gehst du gern hin?
- Wo macht man das in der Stadt?
- Wie kommt man dahin?
- Literatur und Film

## Kulturelles

- Studentenermäßigungen
- Einkaufen
- Stuttgart
- Fußball und Profi-Sport in Mitteleuropa
- München

**Anlauftext**   **Barbara muss ein Konto eröffnen**

Barbara, die neue Studentin aus Dresden, sucht° eine Bank, denn sie will in Tübingen ein Konto eröffnen. Auf dem Weg zur Bushaltestelle° trifft sie Stefan und Karl. Zusammen fahren sie mit dem Bus in die Stadt. Karl und Stefan geben Barbara ein paar gute Tipps, zum Beispiel, wo sie eine gute Buchhandlung° finden kann und wo sie ein Semesterticket für den Bus kaufen kann.

*is looking for*
*bus stop*

*bookstore*

## Vorschau

  **1**   **Thematische Fragen.**  Beantworten Sie die folgenden Fragen auf Deutsch.

1. Wie kommen Sie zur Universität: mit dem Auto, mit dem Rad, mit dem Bus oder zu Fuß?
2. Was für Verkehrsmittel° gibt es in Ihrer Stadt – Busse, eine U-Bahn, Privatautos?
3. Wie kaufen Sie Ihre Bücher für die Uni: mit Bargeld°, mit einem Scheck, mit einer Kreditkarte?
4. Wie bekommen Sie Bargeld, wenn Sie es brauchen: von den Eltern, von Freunden, vom Bankautomaten, direkt von der Bank?
5. Wie viel Geld brauchen Sie pro Woche? Wie viel pro Monat?

*means of transportation*
*cash*

 **2**   **Satzdetektiv.**  Welche Sätze bedeuten ungefähr das Gleiche?

1. Karl will auf der Bank Geld **abheben.**
2. Barbara muss auf der Bank ein **Konto eröffnen.**
3. Könnt ihr mir eine Bank **empfehlen?**
4. Die Sparkasse hat eine **Filiale** ganz in der Nähe von der Uni.

a. Bei der Uni gibt es auch eine Sparkasse.
b. Karl möchte von der Bank Geld holen°.
c. Barbara braucht ein neues Bankkonto.
d. Kennt ihr eine gute Bank?

*pick up*

---

5. Ich hab' ein **Semesterticket.**
6. Wo kann ich mir ein Semesterticket **besorgen?**
7. Am **Kiosk** gibt es Semestertickets.
8. Dann kann ich praktisch alles in der Stadt **erledigen.**

e. Fast alles, was ich brauche, kann ich in der Stadt machen.
f. Ich habe einen Buspass für Studenten.
g. Wo kann ich mir ein Semesterticket für den Bus kaufen?
h. Semestertickets kann man an einem Stand für Zigaretten, Zeitschriften usw. kaufen.

**Satzdetektiv.** A **Kiosk** offers a variety of items, such as stamps, magazines, newspapers, stationery, cigarettes, and lottery and bus tickets.

## *Anlauftext*

 Hören Sie gut zu.

### Barbara muss ein Konto eröffnen

## Rückblick

**3** **Stimmt das?** Stimmen diese Aussagen zum Text oder nicht? Wenn nicht, was stimmt?

| | Ja, das stimmt. | Nein, das stimmt nicht. |
|---|---|---|
| 1. Stefan muss auf die Post. | ☐ | ☐ |
| 2. Karl braucht Geld von seinem Bankkonto. | ☐ | ☐ |
| 3. Barbara sucht ein Buch, und dann will sie auch ein Bankkonto eröffnen. | ☐ | ☐ |
| 4. Stefan und Karl empfehlen Barbara die Kreissparkasse. | ☐ | ☐ |
| 5. Die Kreissparkasse hat eine Filiale ganz in der Nähe von der Universität. | ☐ | ☐ |
| 6. Karl und Stefan fahren immer mit dem Bus in die Stadt. | ☐ | ☐ |
| 7. In der Kreissparkasse kann Barbara ein Semesterticket für den Bus kaufen. | ☑ | ☐ |
| 8. Gleich gegenüber von der Sparkasse ist der Hauptbahnhof. | ☐ | ☐ |

Complete the **Ergänzen Sie** activity in your workbook for this text before doing the next activity.

Germans, Swiss, and Austrians typically pay for purchases with cash (**Bargeld**), while credit cards (**Kreditkarten**) are used less frequently. Money can be withdrawn from a debit account (**das Girokonto**) using an ATM card (**die Bankkarte**) at an automated teller machine (**der Bankautomat**), or it can be deposited in a savings account (**das Sparkonto**).

**4** **Kurz gefragt.** Beantworten Sie diese Fragen auf Deutsch.

1. Warum fahren Karl und Stefan in die Stadt?
2. Was will Barbara alles in der Stadt erledigen?
3. Warum empfiehlt Karl die Kreissparkasse?
4. Wie fährt Karl meistens in die Stadt?
5. Warum fährt Stefan meistens mit dem Bus?
6. Wo kann Barbara ein Semesterticket kaufen?
7. Wo gibt es eine gute Buchhandlung?

**5** **Das Semesterticket.** Lesen Sie die Informationen über das Semesterticket für Tübingen und schreiben Sie die Sätze unten fertig.

**Sehr geehrte Kundin, sehr geehrter Kunde,**

bitte füllen Sie Ihr Semesterticket beim Kauf unauslöschlich und vollständig aus. Das Semesterticket ist nur vollständig ausgefüllt, mit Unterschrift und in Verbindung mit Ihrem Studentenausweis mit Lichtbild gültig. Die Gültigkeitsdauer muss mit der Semesterdauer übereinstimmen.

Das Semesterticket gilt für das Sommersemester 2004 in allen Bussen, Stadtverkehren und Bahnen des naldo-Verbundgebietes*¹. Bei Anmeldeverkehren (z.B. Nacht-SAM, Anrufsammeltaxi) können Aufpreise erhoben werden bzw. wird das Semesterticket nicht anerkannt.

**Bei Verlust ist kein kostenloser Ersatz der Fahrkarte möglich.**

Bei Missbrauch wird die Fahrkarte eingezogen. Strafrechtliche Schritte bleiben vorbehalten.

Bei Fragen, Anregungen und Wünschen wenden Sie sich einfach an uns:

Tübinger Straße 14
72379 Hechingen
Tel.: 07471/93 01 96 96
Fax: 07471/93 01 96 20
E-Mail: verkehrsverbund@naldo.de

**naldo**
Verkehrsverbund
Neckar-Alb-Donau GmbH

*¹ Das naldo-Gebiet umfasst:
Die Landkreise Tübingen, Reutlingen, Sigmaringen und den Zollernalbkreis. Im Landkreis Böblingen die Ammertalbahn von/nach Herrenberg, die Buslinien 777 (bis Gäufelden), 791, 794 und 7631 sowie die Gemeinde Bondorf über die Buslinie 7627. Im Landkreis Esslingen die Buslinien X 3 und 7556 von/zum Flughafen Stuttgart-Echterdingen.
Im Landkreis Rottweil die Buslinien 7430 und 7440. Außerdem wird das Semesterticket im Landkreis Rottweil auf weiteren Linien anerkannt, bitte beachten Sie dazu den jeweils aktuellen Liniennetzplan.

1. Das Semesterticket ist gültig° von April bis _____.  *valid*
2. Mit welchen Infos müssen Studenten das Ticket ausfüllen?
3. Der Preis ist _____.
4. Die Klasse ist _____.
5. Naldo steht für drei Namen. Welche drei? Sind das Städte, Flüsse° oder  *rivers*
   Menschen?
6. Was bedeutet wohl „Nicht übertragbar"?
   a. *not transferable*     b. *not useable*     c. *not returnable*

### Studentenermäßigungen°

*student discounts*

*Studenten und Schüler reisen billig mit der Bahn und mit dem Bus.*

In the German-speaking countries, all students receive a student identification card (**der Studentenausweis** for university students and **der Schülerausweis** for high school students and apprentices). With this ID, students are entitled to receive discounts for museums, theaters, movie theaters, ballet and music performances, but not popular music concerts. Students may also purchase a **Semesterkarte** (called a **Semesterticket** in Tübingen), which is a discounted ticket for use on public transportation such as subways (**die Untergrundbahn** or **U-Bahn**), trains, or busses during the semester. Students also pay low rates for rooms in university residence halls, and the mandatory usage fees for television and radio may be waived for financially-strapped students. The federal government subsidizes many of these benefits.

> **Brennpunkt Kultur.** Remember that German speakers distinguish between university students (**Studenten, Studierende**) and all elementary and secondary school pupils (**Schüler**). Similarly, when a person says **ich gehe zur Schule,** he/she refers to a primary or secondary school. Attending university is called **auf die Universität gehen** or simply **studieren.**

■ **Kulturkreuzung** Bekommen Sie als Student/Studentin Ermäßigungen? Wann? Wo? In Europa haben Studenten einen relativ hohen Status und die Finanzierung des Studiums ist eine soziale Verantwortung°. Ist das auch der Fall° in Ihrem Land? Warum? Warum nicht?

*responsibility / case*

## Strukturen und Vokabeln

### I Expressing location and destination

Two-case prepositions: **wo?** versus **wohin?**

> Two-case prepositions are also known as two-way prepositions.

#### A. Two-case prepositions

In **Kapitel 6,** you learned that the two-case preposition (**Wechselpräposition**) **in,** when used with the dative case, expresses location. The preposition **an** is also used frequently in the dative case to show location.

    **an der** FH-Darmstadt    *at the Fachhochschule Darmstadt*

When used with the accusative case and a verb of forward motion, however, these prepositions express destination. Location or destination is not expressed by the preposition itself but rather by the case ending of the article that follows.

    Sie steht **an der** Tafel.    *She is standing at the chalkboard.*
    Sie geht **an die** Tafel.    *She is going to the chalkboard.*

To ask about location, German speakers use **wo**? (*where?*). To ask about destination, they use **wohin?** (*where . . . to?*). In both situations, a two-case preposition with the appropriate case is commonly part of the answer.

In English, ***Where*** *are you going?* is used to mean ***Where*** *are you going* ***to?*** In German, however, the distinction between **wo** and **wohin** must be strictly observed. An old English equivalent of German **wohin** is *whither*.

| | |
|---|---|
| **Wo** stehen Karl und Stefan? | *Where are Karl and Stefan standing?* |
| **An der** Haltestelle. | *At the bus stop.* |
| **Wohin** fahren sie? | *Where are they driving to?* |
| **In die** Stadt. | *(In) to town.* |

German has nine two-case prepositions.

| | | | | |
|---|---|---|---|---|
| an | *at, on; to* | über | *above, over* |
| auf | *at, on; onto; to* | unter | *under, underneath* |
| hinter | *behind, to/in the back of* | vor | *in front of* |
| in | *at, in; into; to* | zwischen | *between* |
| neben | *beside, next to* | | |

**Wohin?**                           **Wo?**

**an**      Barbara geht **an die** Ampel.        Das Auto steht **an der** Ampel.
         *Barbara walks up to the traffic light.*   *The car is stopped at the traffic light.*

It is also common to split the interrogative **wohin: Wo fahren sie *hin?***

**auf**     Die Kinder laufen **auf den**          Das Kind spielt **auf dem**
         Spielplatz.                          Spielplatz.

         *The children are running*            *The child is playing on the*
         *(on)to the playground.*              *playground.*

English has only two preposition pairs that are comparable to the German two-case prepositions: *in/into* and *on/onto.*

**hinter**   Der Tankwart fährt den Wagen         Der Tankwart wäscht den
          **hinter die** Tankstelle.            Wagen **hinter der** Tankstelle.

          *The station attendant is driving*    *The station attendant is washing*
          *the car to the back of the gas station.*   *the car behind the gas station.*

| **Wohin?** | **Wo?** |
|---|---|

**in**

Die Familie steigt **ins (in das)** Auto.

*The family is getting into the car.*

Die Familie sitzt **im (in dem)** Auto.

*The family is in the car.*

Except for **ans** and **aufs**, the following contractions are mandatory.

am = an dem
ans = an das
aufs = auf das
im = in dem
ins = in das

You have already used **ins Kino / Konzert / Theater / Museum / Schloss gehen** in **Kapitel 3**.

**neben**

Er hängt den Fahrplan **neben das** Poster.

*He is hanging the train schedule next to the poster.*

Der Fahrplan hängt **neben dem** Poster.

*The train schedule is hanging next to the poster.*

**über**

Der Bus fährt **über die** Brücke.

*The bus is driving over the bridge.*

**Über der** Bäckerei ist ein China-Restaurant.

*There's a Chinese restaurant above the bakery.*

**unter**

Der Ball rollt **unter das** Auto.

*The ball is rolling under the car.*

Der Ball ist **unter dem** Auto.

*The ball is underneath the car.*

|  | **Wohin?** | **Wo?** |
|---|---|---|
|  |  |  |
| **vor** | Der BMW fährt **vor den** Hoteleingang vor.<br><br>*The BMW is driving up to the hotel entrance.* | Der Mercedes steht **vor dem** Hoteleingang.<br><br>*The Mercedes is standing in front of the hotel entrance.* |
|  |  |  |
| **zwischen** | Der Ball rollt **zwischen die** Autos.<br><br>*The ball is rolling between the cars.* | Der Kiosk steht **zwischen dem** Theater und **der** Bank.<br><br>*The kiosk is between the theater and the bank.* |

 **6** **Wo sind die Bücher?** Anna sucht ihre Bücher in ihrem Zimmer. Wo sind sie alle?

🟨 *Ein Buch ist unter dem Bett.*

> **Wo sind die Bücher?** Useful words: **das Bett, der Schreibtisch, die Lampe, der Spiegel, der Schrank, der Computer, der Stuhl, die Tür, der Tennisschläger** (*tennis racket*), **die Bettdecke** (*bedspread*).

## B. More about *an, auf,* and *in*

**An, auf,** and **in** are the three most common two-case prepositions. **An** is often used to talk about objects on vertical surfaces, such as a wall or a door, or the edge of something, such as a body of water. **Auf** is used to refer to objects on horizontal surfaces such as a table, the floor, or a desk. **Auf** is also used with certain locations (**die Post, der Fußballplatz, der Markt, die Uni**) and events (**das Fest, die Fete, die Party**). **In** is used to refer to an enclosed space, such as a room or car, or a very defined space, such as a store or a city.

|  | *Dative of location* |  | *Accusative of destination* |
|---|---|---|---|
| *at* | Uwe sitzt **an der** Tür (**am** Fenster). | *to* | Uwe geht **an die** Tür (**ans** Fenster). |
|  | *Uwe is sitting at the door (at the window).* |  | *Uwe is going to the door (to the window).* |
|  | Bert arbeitet **auf der** Post. |  | Bert geht **auf die** Post. |
|  | *Bert works at the post office.* |  | *Bert is going to the post office.* |
| *on* | Die Nummer ist **an der** Tür. | *on(to)* | Er schreibt die Nummer **an die** Tür. |
|  | *The number is on the door.* |  | *He's writing the number on(to) the door.* |
|  | Das Buch liegt **auf dem** Tisch. |  | Sie legt das Buch **auf den** Tisch. |
|  | *The book is on (top of) the table.* |  | *She puts the book on(to) the table.* |
| *in* | Er sitzt **in der** Küche. | *in(to)* | Er geht **in die** Küche. |
|  | *He's sitting in the kitchen.* |  | *He's going in(to) the kitchen.* |
|  | Er sitzt **im** Kino. |  | Er geht **ins** Kino. |
|  | *He's sitting in the movie theater.* |  | *He's going to the movies.* |

> The preposition **an** is used for bodies of water, e.g., **an die Nordsee fahren** *to drive to the North Sea.*

> The preposition **in** is used for country names that have an article, **Wir fahren in die Schweiz** *We're driving to Switzerland.*

## *Wissenswerte Vokabeln: Wo gehst du gern hin?*
### *Talking about where you like to go in your free time*

in die Kirche (Synagoge, Moschee) gehen

ins Konzert gehen

ins Museum gehen

in den Jazzkeller gehen

in die Oper gehen

ins Theater gehen

ins Kino gehen

ins Schwimmbad gehen

ins Stadion gehen

ins Fitnessstudio gehen

in die Disko(thek) gehen

in die Kneipe gehen

ins Restaurant gehen

auf eine Party (Fete) gehen

🔲 *Wohin gehst du (nicht) gern?*

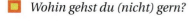 **7** **Wohin gehen Karl und Stefan?** Finden Sie für jede Situation einen passenden Ort°.

*place*

🔲 *Wenn Karl und Stefan Durst haben, gehen sie in die Kneipe.*

| | |
|---|---|
| 1. Wenn sie Durst haben, gehen sie | auf den Fußballplatz. |
| 2. Wenn sie billig° essen wollen, gehen sie | in den Hörsaal. |
| 3. Wenn sie gut essen wollen, gehen sie | in die Mensa. |
| 4. Wenn sie einen Film sehen wollen, gehen sie | in die Oper. |
| 5. Wenn sie ein Buch suchen müssen, gehen sie | in die Kneipe. |
| 6. Wenn sie Fußball spielen wollen, gehen sie | ins Kino. |
| 7. Wenn Karl kochen will, geht er | ins Restaurant. |
| 8. Wenn Stefan Musik hören will, geht er | in die Bibliothek. |
| 9. Wenn sie eine Vorlesung haben, gehen sie | in die Küche. |
| 10. Wenn sie auf eine Hochzeit° gehen, gehen sie | in die Kirche. |

*inexpensively*

*wedding*

**8** **Interview.** Stellen Sie einem Partner/einer Partnerin die folgenden Fragen.

1.  Wohin gehst du, wenn du lernen willst?
2.  Wohin gehst du, wenn du mit jemandem° ausgehst?                 *someone*
3.  Wohin gehst du am Freitag, am Samstag, am Sonntag?
4.  Wohin gehst du, wenn es im Sommer sehr heiß ist?
5.  Wohin gehst du, wenn du Sport treiben° willst?                 *Sport treiben: to do sports*
6.  Wohin gehst du, wenn du einen Kurs oder ein Seminar hast?

> ### Sprache im Alltag: Names of cities with an/am
>
> A few prominent German cities indicate their location on a major river (**der Fluss**) by using the preposition **an/am** and the name of the river in their name. The two Frankfurts rely on this designation to distinguish between them.
>
> | | |
> |---|---|
> | Frankfurt am Main | Fluss: der Main |
> | Frankfurt an der Oder | Fluss: die Oder |
> | Marburg an der Lahn | Fluss: die Lahn |

## Wissenswerte Vokabeln: Wo macht man das in der Stadt?
### Talking about where to run errands

**Am Bahnhof kauft** man Fahrscheine.

**An der Haltestelle** wartet man auf den Bus.

**Auf der Post** kauft man Briefmarken und gibt Pakete auf.

**Auf der Bank (Auf der Sparkasse)** zahlt man Geld ein°, oder man hebt es ab.

*zahlt … ein: deposit*

**Am Kiosk (Am Zeitungsstand)** kauft man Zeitungen, Zeitschriften und Studentenpässe.

**In der Buchhandlung** kauft man Bücher.

**Im Reformhaus (Im Bioladen)** bekommt man gesunde, natürliche Kost°.

**In der Bäckerei** kauft man Brot, Brötchen und Brezeln.

*Essen*

**In der Konditorei** kauft man Kuchen und Torten.

**Im Supermarkt** hat man eine große Auswahl°.

*selection*

**In der Fleischerei (In der Metzgerei)** bekommt man Fleisch, Wurst und Geflügel.

**Auf dem Markt** kauft man alles frisch vom Lande: Obst, Gemüse, Käse, Eier.

🔲 *Wo kauft man Bücher?*

**BRENNPUNKT KULTUR**

### Einkaufen

*"Am besten ist die eigene Tasche!"*

While **der Supermarkt** has found its niche for one-stop grocery shopping throughout German-speaking Europe, many customers prefer the higher quality and personal service available in smaller specialty shops. Shoppers often make daily trips to their local stores to purchase fresh goods. Since shops and residential housing are well integrated, many people walk to stores and carry their groceries home. Many customers use their own bag (**die Einkaufstasche**), a mesh shopping bag (**das Einkaufsnetz**), or a basket (**der Einkaufskorb**) for shopping, since stores charge for each plastic bag (**die Tragetasche**). Customers also bag their own groceries and a deposit is charged for a shopping cart (**der Einkaufswagen**). While these frequent shopping trips reduce the need to purchase large quantities of groceries at one time, the higher cost and effort required have also given rise to the growth of discount marketers like Aldi and Wal-Mart.

die Tasche = die Tüte

■ **Kulturkreuzung** Wie oft gehen Sie einkaufen? Gehen Sie oder fahren Sie zum Supermarkt? Warum? Was meinen Sie: Ist es eine gute Idee, dass man die eigene Tragetasche zum Einkaufen mitbringt? Machen Sie das? Warum (nicht)?

**9**   **Wo treffen sie einander?**  Lesen Sie die Liste von Stefan und die von Barbara und fragen Sie dann einen Partner/eine Partnerin, wo die beiden einander treffen. Wählen Sie Orte aus der **wo?**-Liste.

**Wo?**

| | | |
|---|---|---|
| auf ____ Markt | auf ____ Post | in ____ Konditorei   in ____ Bäckerei |
| in ____ Metzgerei | auf ____ Bank | an ____ Kiosk |

□ S1:  *Stefan holt Briefmarken und Barbara muss ein Paket schicken. Wo treffen sie einander?*

   S2:  *Sie treffen einander auf der Post.*

*Stefans Liste*

1. Briefmarken holen
2. Geld abheben
3. frische Landeier kaufen
4. eine Zeitung kaufen
5. Fleisch kaufen
6. Boot kaufen
7. einen Apfelkuchen kaufen

*Barbaras Liste*

1. ein Paket schicken
2. ein Konto eröffnen
3. Gemüse kaufen
4. einen Studentenpass kaufen
5. Wurst kaufen
6. Brötchen holen
7. eine Schokoladentorte kaufen

*pick, get*

**10    Wohin müssen sie gehen?** Klaus, Barbara und Anna müssen vieles erledigen. Stellen Sie einem Partner/einer Partnerin Fragen über Klaus, Barbara und Anna.

Wohin müssen sie gehen?

| | | |
|---|---|---|
| in _die_ Bäckerei | in _die_ Bibliothek | auf _die_ Post |
| in _den_ Supermarkt | in _die_ Konditorei | auf _den_ Markt |
| auf _die_ Bank | in _die_ Metzgerei | in _die_ Apotheke° |

*pharmacy*

**Wohin müssen sie gehen?**
Note that you are talking about destinations. Therefore, the two-case prepositions require the accusative case.

S1:  *Klaus muss Briefmarken kaufen. Wohin muss er gehen?*
S2:  *Er muss auf die Post (gehen).*

| Klaus muss | Briefmarken kaufen. | Anna muss | Kuchen holen. |
|---|---|---|---|
| | eine EC-Karte holen. | | Brot kaufen. |
| | Medikamente kaufen. | | frische Eier kaufen. |

| Barbara muss | Kaffee und Käse kaufen. |
|---|---|
| | Bücher zurückgeben. |
| | Wurst und Fleisch kaufen. |

An **EC-Karte** is a debit card that can be used to access cash and make purchases in Europe.

**11    Rätsel: Wo ist die Buchhandlung?** Lesen Sie die Sätze und bestimmen° Sie, wo die Buchhandlung ist.

*determine*

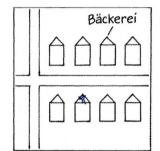

Rechts neben der Bäckerei ist die Metzgerei.
Direkt gegenüber von der Metzgerei ist die
    Konditorei.
Die Buchhandlung ist zwischen dem Zeitungs-
    kiosk und der Apotheke.
Die Bank ist an der Ecke°.
Rechts von der Buchhandlung ist die Apotheke.
Die Buchhandlung ist nicht an der Ecke.
Die Post ist zwischen der Bank und der
    Bäckerei.
Quer gegenüber von° der Post ist der
    Zeitungskiosk.

*corner*

***Quer… :*** *diagonally across
    from*

**12    Stuttgart.** Anna, Barbara, Karl und Stefan besuchen Stuttgart. Helfen Sie Anna und Barbara, die folgenden Sehenswürdigkeiten in Stuttgart zu finden. (Siehe Seite 253.)

*Der zentrale Omnibusbahnhof ist neben dem Hauptbahnhof.*

1. Der zentrale Omnibusbahnhof
2. Der Schlossplatz
3. Die Universitätsbibliothek
4. Das Alte Schloss
5. Das Rathaus
6. Die Markthalle
7. Die Staatsgalerie

a.  am Karlsplatz.
b.  am Marktplatz.
c.  hinter dem Staatstheater.
d.  im Stadtgarten.
e.  neben dem Hauptbahnhof.
f.  vor dem Postamt.
g.  zwischen dem Alten Schloss und
      dem Rathaus.

# STUTTGART

**Schloß:** This map uses the old spelling.

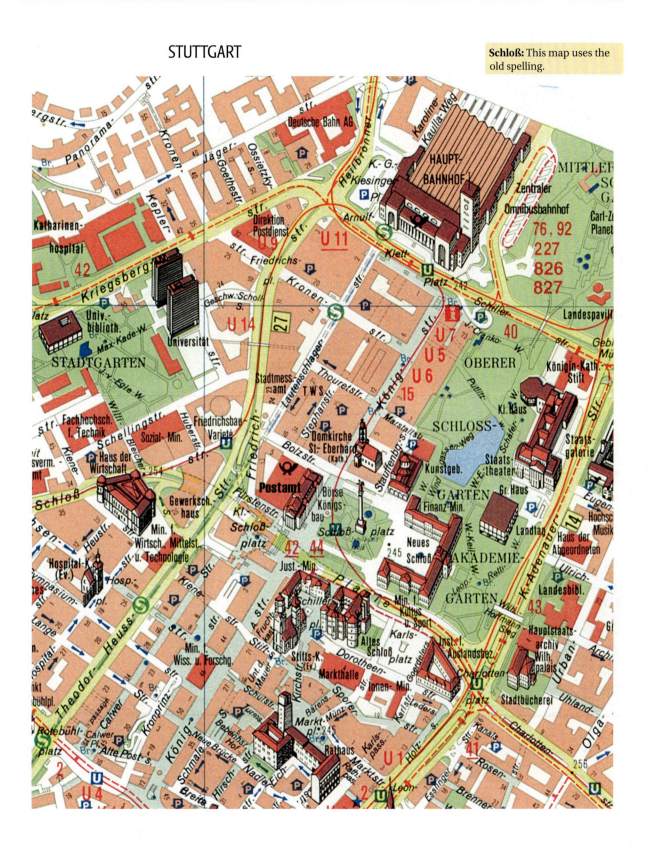

BRENNPUNKT KULTUR

## Stuttgart

Baden-Württemberg, bordering on France to its west and Switzerland to its south, is Germany's southwesternmost state. The city of Stuttgart, located an hour north of Tübingen, is the capital (**die Landeshauptstadt**) of Baden-Württemberg and cultural center of the dialect region called Swabia (**Schwaben**), noteworthy for its industrious, ingenious, and thrifty people. With a population of 589,395, Stuttgart ranks as Germany's eighth largest city. It is home to two of the world's most famous carmakers, DaimlerChrysler and Porsche, and to automobile parts manufacturer Robert Bosch. The city's fame in the automotive industry is further enhanced by the Porsche and Mercedes-Benz Museums.

Largely destroyed in World War II, Stuttgart has since emerged as an attractive regional metropolis with distinctly southern charms and a leisurely pace of life. Nestled in the Neckar River valley, the city exudes a sense of calm that is created by the surrounding forests and hills, many of which were home to working vineyards through the 19th century. Climbing the stairways (**die Weinbergstäffele**) through these old vineyards is one of the best ways to discover Stuttgart's romantic charm. Downtown Stuttgart maintains the calm of nature with its massive **Schlossgärten** and **Schlossplatz**, dominated by the majestic baroque **Neues Schloss**, located adjacent to Stuttgart's main shopping area, **die Königstraße**. Culturally, Stuttgart has gained international fame for its ballet troupe, **Stuttgarter Ballett**, for its outstanding theater, **Staatstheater Stuttgart**, and for the architecture and art collections of **die Staatsgalerie**. The outstanding opera company, **Staatsoper Stuttgart**, was named "opera house of the year" four times from 1998 to 2002, and **die Internationale Bachakademie Stuttgart** under the direction of Helmut Ruling has achieved worldwide recognition for authentic performances of Bach's music. Stuttgarters also love sports, and none more passionately than their soccer team, **VfB Stuttgart**.

**Kulturkreuzung** Stuttgart ist eine bekannte deutsche Auto-Stadt. Welche deutschen Autos kommen aus Stuttgart? Wie ist die Qualität von diesen Autos? Welche US-Stadt assoziiert man mit Autos? Welche Sportmannschaften° sind in dieser Stadt wichtig?

*sports teams*

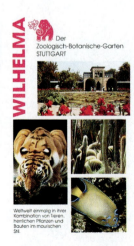

... ein Park zum Verlieben

**13** **Wohin gehen sie in Stuttgart?** Barbara und die anderen machen Pläne. Hier sind ihre Interessen. Wohin gehen sie wahrscheinlich in Stuttgart?

S1: *Anna möchte frisches Obst finden. Wohin möchte sie gehen?*
S2: *Sie möchte in die Markthalle gehen.*

| Anna | Barbara | Karl | Stefan | du |
|------|---------|------|--------|-----|
| frisches Obst finden | Uni-Bücher finden | ein Theaterstück sehen | mit dem Bus fahren | ? |
| einen Picasso sehen | ein altes Schloss sehen | Briefmarken kaufen | den Bürgermeister besuchen | ? |

# II  Giving directions

## Prepositional phrases; **hin** and **her**

### A. Prepositional phrases indicating location

When you visit an unfamiliar city in Germany you will need to ask for and understand directions. German speakers frequently use two-case prepositions with the accusative when giving directions.

> Gehen Sie **über die Brücke in die Stadt.**    *Go over the bridge into town.*

Other prepositions, such as **um** and **zu,** are common, too. Here are some useful prepositional phrases for asking for and giving directions.

| | |
|---|---|
| Wie komme ich zur/zum …? | *How do I get to . . . ?* |
| bis zur Kreuzung/Ampel | *as far as (up to) the intersection/traffic light* |
| links/rechts ab·biegen | *turn left/right* |
| →die Straße entlang | *down the street* |
| über die Straße | *across the street* |
| geradeaus | *straight ahead* |
| →(gleich) um die Ecke | *(right) around the corner* |
| an der Ecke | *at the corner* |

> Note that the preposition **zu** (e.g., **bis zur Kreuzung**) always occurs with the dative, while the preposition **um** (e.g., **um die Ecke**) always occurs with the accusative.

**14** **Wie kommt Anna zur Staatsgalerie?** Anna ist in Stuttgart und möchte vieles sehen. Welche Wegbeschreibung° ist richtig?

*direction*

Use the map on page 253.

*Anna ist …*

1. am Hauptbahnhof und möchte zur Staatsgalerie.
2. am Marktplatz und möchte zum Karlsplatz.
3. am Postamt und möchte zum Hauptbahnhof.
4. in der Markthalle und möchte zum Karlsplatz.
5. im Neuen Schloss und möchte zum Königsbau.
6. am Marktplatz und möchte zum Rathaus.

*Ein Stuttgarter/Eine Stuttgarterin sagt:*

a. „Sie stehen doch direkt vor dem Rathaus!"
b. „Gehen Sie über den Schlossplatz."
c. „Gehen Sie die Münzstraße entlang."
d. „Nehmen Sie die Boltzstraße bis zur Königstraße, biegen Sie links ab und gehen Sie dann geradeaus."
e. „Gehen Sie die Schillerstraße entlang bis zur Konrad-Adenauer-Straße und biegen Sie dann rechts ab."
f. „Gehen Sie über die Dorotheen-straße."

**15** **Wie komme ich zum Bahnhof?** Sie sind in Stuttgart am Schloss-platz vor dem Neuen Schloss. Ein Tourist/Eine Touristin fragt nach dem Weg. Beschreiben Sie, wie man dahin kommt. Bcnutzen Sie den Stadtplan von Stuttgart.

🟧 S1 (TOURIST/TOURISTIN): *Entschuldigung, wie komme ich zum Bahnhof?*
　　　　　　　S2 (SIE): *Fahren Sie geradeaus in die Königstraße.* (oder)
　　　　　　　　　　　　*Gehen Sie die Königstraße entlang.*

*S1 (Tourist/Touristin):*
　zum Bahnhof • zum Schillerplatz • zum Staatstheater • zur Markthalle

Use the map on page 253.

## B. The prefixes **hin** and **her**

You have already encountered **hin** and **her** in the question words **wohin** *(where to)* and **woher** *(where from)*.

Wo**her** kommst du?　Ich komme aus Berlin.
Wo**hin** fährst du?　Ich fahre in die Stadt.

Both **hin** and **her** also occur as separable prefixes on verbs of motion expressing the notion of origin, (e.g., **her·kommen**) and destination (e.g., **hin·fahren**).

Komm mal **her!**　　　　　　　*Come over here!*
Möchtest du dort **hin**fahren?　*Would you like to go (drive) there?*
Wo soll ich das Buch **hin**legen?　*Where should I put the book?*

**16** **Der neugierige° Zimmernachbar.** Karls Nachbar im Studenten-wohnheim ist sehr neugierig. Er möchte alles ganz genau wissen. Welche Fragen hat er gestellt und was hat Karl geantwortet? Verbinden Sie seine Fragen mit den passenden Antworten von Karl und lesen Sie sie dann laut mit einem Partner/einer Partnerin.

*nosy, curious*

🟧 S1 (NACHBAR): *Woher hast du deine Schecks?*
　　　S2 (KARL): *Von der Sparkasse bei der Uni.*

1. Woher hast du deine Schecks?
2. Woher hast du das gute Brot?
3. Wohin gehst du, wenn du eine Semesterkarte brauchst?
4. Woher hast du diese interessante Zeitschrift?
5. Wohin bringst du das Geld?
6. Wohin gehst du, wenn du schnell einige Brötchen brauchst?

a. Vom Kiosk bei der Kreuzung.
b. Zum Kiosk bei der Kreuzung.
c. Auf die Sparkasse bei der Uni.
d. Von der Sparkasse bei der Uni.
e. Aus der Bäckerei gleich um die Ecke.
f. In die Bäckerei gleich um die Ecke.

Any of these verbs may oc-cur with prepositions other than two-case prepositions. The prepositions may be followed by a dative or an accusative, as appropriate, e.g., **Ich fliege über das Meer** (two-case preposition with the accusative), **ich fliege mit dem Flugzeug** (**mit** = dative preposition), **ich fliege ohne meinen Bruder** (**ohne** = accusative preposition).

## C. Verbs commonly used with two-case prepositions

### 1. Verbs with prepositions followed by the accusative

Verbs that express movement toward a destination occur with two-case preposi-tions followed by the accusative case. Such sentences always answer the question **wohin?** Some of the verbs that frequently trigger accusatives after two-case prepositions are: **gehen, fahren, fallen, fliegen, laufen,** and **springen** *(to jump).*

While these verbs mostly occur with a two-case preposition followed by the accusative, a dative is ap-propriate if the movement is not directed towards a destination: **Stefan läuft im Park.** (*Stefan is running in-side the park.*)

| Question | Sentence |
|---|---|
| **Wohin** gehen Stefan und Karl? | Sie gehen **auf die Bank.** |
| | *They are going to the bank.* |
| **Wohin** fahren sie? | Sie fahren **in die Stadt.** |
| | *They are driving into town.* |
| **Wohin** ist Anna gefahren? | Anna ist **an die Nordsee** gefahren. |
| | *Anna drove to the North Sea.* |
| **Wohin** springt das Kind? | Das Kind springt **in das Wasser.** |
| | *The child is jumping into the water.* |

## 2. Expressions with prepositions followed by the accusative

There are also idiomatic expressions that involve two-case prepositions. These expressions combine verbs and specific prepositions and are frequently followed by the accusative case.

| | |
|---|---|
| Er **achtet** nie **auf** das Wetter. | *He never pays attention to the weather.* |
| Sie **bittet** mich **um** meine Telefonnumer. | *She's asking me for my phone number.* |
| Ich **denke** oft **an** dich. | *I think of you a lot.* |
| Er **erinnert** mich **an** meinen Vater. | *He reminds me of my father.* |
| Sie **schreibt an** ihren Freund. | *She's writing to her boyfriend.* |
| Ich bin **böse auf** meine Schwester. | *I'm mad at my sister.* |
| Wir **hoffen auf** eine Tochter. | *We're hoping for a daughter.* |
| Ich muss immer **auf** sie **warten.** | *I always have to wait for them.* |
| Sie **lachen über** den Film. | *They are laughing about the movie.* |
| Er **spricht über** das Problem. | *He's talking about the problem.* |

> Idiomatic expressions shown here use two-case prepositions. Other expressions use dative or accusative prepositions: For example: **Sie bittet uns um 10 Euro.** *She is asking us for 10 euros.*

**17   Als Tourist in Stuttgart.**  Verbinden Sie mit einem Partner/einer Partnerin die richtigen Satzteile.

1. Stuttgart erinnert mich ein bisschen …
2. Es regnet seit Tagen. Wir hoffen …
3. Vergiss nicht! Du sollst eine E-Mail …
4. Pass auf! Du musst besser …
5. Ich bin wirklich böse …
6. Wir warten noch fünf Minuten …
7. Unser Busfahrer bittet uns …
8. Gehen wir ins Hallenbad. Dann springe ich gleich …
9. Wenn ich dieses Foto wieder zu Hause sehe, werde ich immer …

a. auf die Verkehrszeichen achten.
b. ins warme Wasser.
c. an meine Heimatstadt – Pittsburgh.
d. um etwas Geduld.
e. auf ihn, dann laufen wir!
f. auf gutes Wetter.
g. an deinen Freund zu Hause schreiben.
h. an die schöne Zeit in Stuttgart denken.
i. auf unseren Reiseleiter°. Er kommt zu spät.

*tour guide*

## 3. Verbs with prepositions followed by the dative

Verbs that express location are used with two-case prepositions followed by the dative case. **Sein** and **wohnen** are among the verbs that frequently trigger datives after two-case prepositions.

| | |
|---|---|
| Wo **wohnt** Cornelia? | Sie wohnt **in der** Stadt. |
| *Where does Cornelia live?* | *She lives in town.* |

## 4. The verbs *hängen/hängen; legen/liegen; setzen/sitzen; stellen/stehen*

There are four verb pairs that demonstrate the difference between location and movement toward a destination. To show location, an irregular (strong) verb (e.g., **hängen [hat gehangen]; liegen [hat gelegen]; sitzen [hat gesessen]; stehen [hat gestanden]**) is used with the dative case. To show movement toward a destination, a regular (weak) verb (e.g., **hängen [hat gehängt]; legen [hat gelegt]; setzen [hat gesetzt]; stellen [hat gestellt]**) is used with the accusative case. All of these verbs when used with the accusative essentially mean *to put*. In standard German, **haben** is used to form the conversational past of all these verbs, e.g., **ich habe gestanden.** In Southern German, however, verbs that express an action take **haben,** but verbs that express location take **sein,** e.g., **ich bin dort gestanden.**

| | |
|---|---|
| **legen** | to lay or put something (e.g., a newspaper) in(to) a horizontal position |
| **setzen** | to seat, set, or put someone (e.g., a person, a child, a doll) down |
| **stellen** | to put something (e.g., a bottle or suitcase) in(to) an upright position |

One use of **stellen** is idiomatic: **Er stellt** (not **legt**) **den Teller auf den Tisch.**

> Please note that even in colloquial German, speakers always distinguish between verbs that express actions and verbs that express results. Confusions such as the one between *to lie* (**liegen**) and *to lay* (**legen**) in colloquial English are not typical in German.

*Accusative of destination*

Er **hängt** den Fahrplan an die Wand.

*Dative of location*

Der Fahrplan **hängt** an der Wand.

Er **legt** die Zeitung auf den Sitz.

Die Zeitung **liegt** auf dem Sitz.

Er **setzt** das Kind auf die Bank.

Das Kind **sitzt** auf der Bank.

> The verbs **stehen** and **liegen** both mean *is* when describing locations. **Stehen** is used with buildings; **liegen** is used to state the location of streets, cities, states, and countries. **Die Post steht an der Ecke.** *The post office is on the corner.* **Heidelberg liegt am Neckar.** *Heidelberg is on the Neckar.* **Deutschland liegt im Herzen Europas.** *Germany is in the heart of Europe.*

*Accusative of destination*

Sie **stellt** den Koffer
in den Bahnhof.

*Dative of location*

Der Koffer **steht** im
Bahnhof.

 **18** **Mein Zimmer.** Machen Sie eine Zeichnung von Ihrem Zimmer und beschreiben Sie es dann für einen Partner/eine Partnerin. Der Partner/Die Partnerin soll Ihr Zimmer zeichnen. Stimmt die Zeichnung? Wechseln Sie die Rollen.

 S1:  *Das Bett steht an der Wand.*

| Das | Bett | steht | in der | Ecke. |
|-----|------|-------|--------|-------|
|  | Poster | liegt | auf dem | Tisch. |
| Der | Schreibtisch | hängt | am | Boden. |
|  | Stuhl | ist | an der | Stuhl. |
|  | Computer | sind |  | Fenster. |
| Die | Lampe | stehen |  | Wand. |
|  | Stereoanlage |  |  | Tür. |
|  | Bücher |  |  |  |

 **19** **Annas Zimmer.** Annas Zimmer ist durcheinander°. Was soll Anna machen? Helfen Sie Anna das Zimmer aufzuräumen°.      *messy*
*clean up*

Die Papiere liegen auf dem Boden. Sie liegen nicht auf dem Tisch.
*Sie soll die Papiere auf den Tisch legen.*

1. Die Papiere liegen auf dem Boden. Sie liegen nicht auf dem Tisch.
2. Das Poster liegt auf dem Bett. Es hängt nicht an der Wand.
3. Die Zeitung liegt unter dem Stuhl. Sie ist nicht auf dem Stuhl.
4. Der Stuhl steht an der Tür. Er steht nicht am Tisch.
5. Das Radio steht neben dem Bett. Es steht nicht auf dem Nachttisch.
6. Die Uhr liegt auf dem Teppich. Sie hängt nicht über dem Bett.
7. Die Pflanze steht in der Ecke. Sie steht nicht am Fenster.
8. Die Flaschen liegen neben dem Stuhl. Sie stehen nicht im Schrank.
9. Mein Hund liegt unter dem Bett. Er sitzt nicht auf dem Bett.

## Freie Kommunikation

**Rollenspiel: Bett frei.** Sie haben ein Zimmer in einem Haus frei und suchen einen Mitbewohner/eine Mitbewohnerin. Eine Person ruft an und möchte mehr über das Zimmer wissen. Beschreiben Sie der Person das Zimmer.

## Schreibecke

**An meinen Lehrer/meine Lehrerin.** Schreiben Sie eine Postkarte an Ihren Deutschlehrer/Ihre Deutschlehrerin. Beschreiben Sie, was Sie schon alles in Tübingen gemacht haben: Wo und was haben Sie eingekauft? Wie haben Sie Ihr Zimmer eingerichtet? Was haben Sie schon alles gesehen? Wen haben Sie schon kennen gelernt? Schreiben Sie in einem sehr positiven Ton.

---

**Absprungtext**

# Die Entdeckung° des Benjamin Lauth

Das Wochenende rückt immer näher°, und schon überlegen Anna und Barbara, was sie am Wochenende machen. Stefan schlägt vor°, sie fahren alle nach München zu einem Heimspiel von „1860 München". Stefan und Karl sind leidenschaftliche Fußball-Fans, und Stefan bleibt seiner 1860 München-Mannschaft treu. Und auch wenn Barbara nicht viel von Fußball hält, ist sie von Benjamin Lauth begeistert, seitdem° sie diesen Artikel über ihn im *Focus* gelesen hat. Und Anna freut sich, die bayrische Hauptstadt München zu besuchen. Da haben sie alle Grund° genug, in den Wagen zu steigen und nach München zu fahren.

*Entdeckung: discovery*
*is getting closer*
***schlägt ... = vorschlagen:***
  *suggests*

*ever since*

*reason*

## Vorschau

**20** **Sportarten: Was halten Sie davon?** Identifizieren Sie 5 bis 10 Sportarten, die Sie interessieren. Fragen sie dann einen Partner/eine Partnerin, ob er/sie diese Sportart auch interessant findet.

*Sportarten:*
  amerikanischer Football • Angeln • Baseball • Basketball • Boxen • Eishockey • Feldhockey • Fußball • Golf • Lacrosse • Mountain-Bike-Fahren • Schwimmen • Segeln • Skifahren • Surfen • Tennis • Volleyball • Wandern • Wasserskifahren

*Aussagen:*
  *Positiv:* ... finde ich toll.
  *Neutral:* ... finde ich so lala.
  *Negativ:* ... gefällt mir gar nicht.

S1: *Ich finde Eishockey wirklich toll. Und du? Wie findest du Eishockey?*
S2: *Eishockey gefällt mir gar nicht. Ich spiele lieber Lacrosse. Und du?*
S1: *Lacrosse finde ich so lala.*

**Turnvereine** (p. 261) started by German immigrants in the United States during the 19th century introduced the sport of gymnastics to North America.

**BRENNPUNKT KULTUR**

## Fußball und Profi-Sport in Mitteleuropa

*Spieler aus verschiedenen Ländern finden in Deutschland loyale Fußball-Fans.*

Even though Anna's friends may not understand her love of baseball and what is so interesting about it, they all share their love of the national pastime of Germany, Austria, Switzerland and almost every other country around the world. That pastime is soccer (**der Fußball**), called football everywhere outside of North America. Soccer has mass appeal because it doesn't involve complicated or expensive equipment. It can be played on any flat, open surface, and in most weather other than snow. As long as the players are able to run and kick a ball, there can be a soccer match. As a result, many preschoolers learn the rudiments at a very early age. In school, children who are interested in developing their skills and playing real games join the town soccer club (**der Fußballverein**). There is no interscholastic play of any sort. As children increase in age and ability, they work their way up the league structure and can continue to play on adult teams all the way to semi-professional regional leagues. In larger cities, the clubs sponsor professional teams for national-level competition. In Germany these are called the **Bundesliga** 1 and **2**.

European fans are rabidly loyal to their teams. On nights when important matches are broadcast, streets and restaurants are virtually empty as friends and families crowd around the television to cheer on their team. The pinnacle of international play in soccer is the World Cup (**die Weltmeisterschaft**, **die WM**), which takes place every four years. Germany was world champion (**Weltmeister**) in the 1974 World Cup under the leadership of Franz Beckenbauer, who later became the coach (**Trainer**) of the national team and a national celebrity and hero. Germany won the World Cup again in 1990. The nation was chosen as host of the 2006 World Cup, with games played in Berlin, Dortmund, Frankfurt, Gelsenkirchen, Hamburg, Hannover, Kaiserslautern, Köln, Leipzig, München, Nürnberg, and Stuttgart.

Other sports, both team and individual, are very popular in Central Europe, but all of them require membership in the local athletic club (**Sportverein**) to play. Gymnastics clubs (**Turnvereine**), highly popular in the 19th century, continue to exist in many towns, as do clubs for sports as diverse as judo (**Judo**), fencing (**Fechten**), and volleyball (**Volleyball**). Many of these clubs post schedules and game results on the Internet. Professional **Basketball** has a huge following and a national league, as does **Eishockey** and **amerikanischer Football**, all especially popular in areas that once housed U.S. military personnel. The interest in **Tennis** skyrocketed with the international success of German players Boris Becker and Steffi Graf, a tradition carried on today by Swiss tennis pro Roger Federer. Austria provided a world-class bodybuilder in Mr. Universe, Arnold Schwarzenegger, who later became an actor and governor of California. In addition, Germany is home to the world's most successful Formula I race car driver, Michael Schumacher.

■ **Kulturkreuzung** Was hält man hier für den Nationalsport? Was ist wichtiger: Vereinssport oder Schulsport? Warum ist das so? Inwiefern° ist Studentensport wichtig im Studentenleben auf Ihrem Campus? Was sind die Möglichkeiten für Studenten/Studentinnen, die sich nicht für den „Leistungssport°" interessieren aber trotzdem gern aktiv bleiben wollen? Welche Unis sind die traditionellen Rivalen Ihrer Uni? Europäische Unis haben normalerweise keine eigenen Sportmannschaften. Was halten Sie davon?

*to what extent*

*competitive sport*

**21** **Thematische Fragen.** Beantworten Sie die folgenden Fragen auf Deutsch.

1. Was ist Ihr Lieblingssport°? Spielen Sie gern aktiv mit, oder sind Sie lieber Zuschauer°?

2. Haben Sie als Kind viel Sport gemacht? Zu welchen Jahreszeiten haben Sie gespielt? Wenn nicht, warum nicht? Haben Sie andere Interessen gehabt?

3. Was für Sport werden Sie wohl treiben können, wenn Sie älter sind?

4. Welche Sportarten kann man als Nationalsport betrachten°? Welche Sportarten sind regional besonders populär? Spielen Sie diese Sportarten gern?

5. Wie heißen die professionellen Sportmannschaften in Ihrer Gegend? Sind Sie ein Anhänger°/eine Anhängerin von diesen Teams? Oder nicht?

6. Was sind die populärsten Sportarten auf Ihrem Campus? Was kosten die Eintrittskarten für die Spiele? Wie oft gehen Sie selber hin?

*favorite sport*
*spectator*

*view*

*fan*

> **Thematische Fragen.** By asking you to answer short questions in German, this activity will help you establish the context for understanding the reading.

## Lesestrategien: „Die Entdeckung des Benjamin Lauth"

Good readers do not necessarily know more words. They are, however, more adept at guessing the meaning of new words and understanding the gist of what they are reading, even if they do not actually understand all of it. They use several skills to help them read.

Use the following reading strategies to improve your comprehension level of the text **Die Entdeckung des Benjamin Lauth.**

**22** **Den Kontext verstehen.** Understanding the context is an important first step in approaching a new reading. Begin by scanning **Die Entdeckung des Benjamin Lauth** for answers to the following questions.

| Wer? | Wo? | Sonstiges°? |
|------|-----|-------------|
| Was? | Wann? | Kognate? |

*other information*

**23** **Neue Wörter lernen: erster Versuch.** Once you understand the context of a reading, it is easier to decode some of the new words. You know this reading focuses on the talents of a young up-and-coming soccer star. What do you think the following words and phrases from the article mean?

1. die Bundesliga
2. der Cheftrainer
3. die Nationalmannschaft
4. der Stadionsprecher
5. der Stürmer
6. das „Tor des Jahres"
7. eines der größten Talente in der Bundesliga
8. im Stadion … sitzen 36 000 Zuschauer
9. er schießt zwei Tore
10. mit rechts schießt und trifft
11. fünf Spiele und vier Treffer später

**24**   **Neue Wörter lernen: Vier Strategien.**   Listed here are four strategies that will sometimes enable you to determine the exact meaning and at other times the general meaning of a word.

### Background knowledge

This is the strategy you just used above. Guess at the meaning of unfamiliar words by using what you already know about the topic at hand, in this case professional sports and/or soccer in particular.

1. „Manche hatten ihn bemerkenswert° genannt, als er, **eingewechselt** in der 80. Minute gegen Hannover 96, am 17. August 2002 sein erstes Bundesliga-**Tor macht**.“   *noteworthy*

   In team sports, players frequently come on and off the playing field. Knowing that, what might **eingewechselt** mean? _____ How does a team score in soccer? **Tor macht** probably means _____.

2. „Er träumt°, wie er sein erstes Bundesliga-**Tor schießt** und wie zehntausende Zuschauer **jubeln** ...“   *dreams*

   Different sports have different ways of scoring. If **Tor schießt** is more specific than **Tor macht,** it probably means _____. How do fans react when their team scores? **Jubeln** probably means _____.

### Similar words

Guess at the meaning of unfamilar words by using what you know about other German words that look similar or by considering possible English cognates.

1. „... in einem **Benefizspiel** der **Nationalmannschaft** ...“

   If you know that **Spiel** means *game,* what is **Benefizspiel** likely to mean? _____ **Nationalmannschaft** = **national** + **Mann** + **-schaft**. It probably means _____.

2. „... als ich den Benny zum **Training** der **Profis** geholt hab’ ...“

   **Training** is a word borrowed from English. The word **der Trainer,** however, is used for another English word. What do you think it means? _____ German speakers often use abbreviations, such as **Profi**. **Profis** are _____ players.

3. „Hans Lauth wirkt froh darüber, dass sein Sohn Benjamin **die Karriere** gemacht hat ...“

   **Die Karriere** likely means _____.

4. „Vor einem Jahr spielte er noch in der Bayern-**Liga**.“

   **Liga** is a cognate of an English word that sounds similar. What is it? _____

### Context

Guess at the meaning of unfamiliar words in a sentence by using your knowledge of other, surrounding German words as clues.

   „Jetzt **gilt** der 21-jährige **Stürmer** von 1860 München **als** eines der größten Talente in der Bundesliga und Hoffnung für die WM 2006.“

The most famous athletes are usually the ones who score for their team. Knowing that, one could guess that the position of **Stürmer** on a soccer team is _____. Good players quickly build reputations based on their performance. Fans talk about their opinions of that performance and that reputation and whether it's earned or not. In that context, *gilt* **der ... Stürmer ...** *als* **eines der größten Talente ...** probably means _____.

*Grammatical cues*

Guess at the meaning of unfamiliar words by using your knowledge of grammar. For example, try to identify the part of speech of the unfamiliar word. Recurring words often provide clues for comprehending unfamiliar structures.

> „Seit dem Debüt des Torjägers° Benjamin Lauth sind gerade einmal hundert Tage **vergangen**.“     *goal scorer*

In **Kapitel 5,** you learned that the conversational past form for the verb **gehen** is **ist gegangen**. What is the most likely infinitive of the past participle **vergangen**? _____ Based on its context in the sentence, what is its probable meaning? _____

**25** **Wichtige Wörter finden: Verben.** As you read, focus your attention on words that seem to convey important information. Verbs are important, for example, because they explain the action involved. How many of these verbs from the article do you know already? Can you guess the meaning of the others, based on other words in the sentence? Look for clues and use associations to make some logical guesses.

1. „Peter Pacult, der ihn **entdeckt hat,** sitzt in seinem Cheftrainer-Büro° …“     ***Büro:*** *office*
   „„Warum sollte ich stolz sein, den Benny **entdeckt zu haben**?'“
2. „Viele **nannten** ihn bemerkenswert, als er gegen Schalke° zwei Tore **schießt**.“     *(name of another team)*
3. „**Schaun** S', als ich den Benny zum Training der Profis **geholt hab, ist** der mehr im Dreck° **gelegen** als vorwärts **gekommen**.“     *dirt*
4. „Jeden Schritt°, den der Sohn in Richtung Zukunft° **tat, hat** der Vater **vorausgedacht**.“     *step /* ***Richtung … :*** *direction of the future*
5. „Als Benjamin Lauth fünf Jahre alt ist, **verkündet** er seinen Eltern, dass er höchstens° vier Jahre zur Schule **gehen wird**.“     *at the most*

**26** **Satzdetektiv.** Welche Sätze bedeuten ungefähr das Gleiche?

1. **Entdeckt** hat er ihn.
2. Manche hatten ihn **bemerkenswert genannt**.
3. Alle sind sich **darüber einig, dass** …
4. … als … [er] aufsteigt und sich in die Luft legt und dreht und mit rechts **schießt und trifft.**
5. Der ist mehr **im Dreck gelegen** als vorwärts gekommen.
6. Wenn den einer **angespielt** hat, ist der gleich **ausgerutscht.**

a. Er springt hoch, dreht sich flach°, kickt mit dem rechten Fuß und macht ein Tor.     *low*
b. Alle Zuschauer denken gleich, dass …
c. Wenn ein anderer Spieler ihm den Ball zugespielt hat, ist er hingefallen.
d. Er hat ihn zuerst gefunden.
e. Er hat nicht gut gespielt und hat sich nicht verbessert.
f. Manche Leute haben gesagt, er ist etwas Besonderes.

TSV München von 1860

7. Hans Lauth wirkt froh darüber, dass sein Sohn die Karriere gemacht hat, **für die er selber nicht den Mut gehabt hätte.**

8. Jeden Schritt, den der Sohn in Richtung Zukunft tat, hat der Vater **vorausgedacht.**

9. Im Juli 1992 erfährt Hans Lauth durch ein Zeitungsinserat von einem **Probetraining** beim TSV 1860 München.

10. Die Trainer wollen nach einer **Sichtung** die Entdeckung des Hans Lauth gleich **da behalten.**

11. Er träumt, wie zehntausende **Zuschauer jubeln.**

g. Der Vater hat über wirklich alles zum Thema Fußball gedacht, bevor sein Sohn es gemacht hat.

h. Wenn sie Benjamin Lauth sehen, wollen die Trainer, dass er in München bei ihnen bleibt.

i. Im Schlaf träumt Benjamin, wie die vielen Fans schreien°. *are cheering*

j. Hans Lauth liest in der Zeitung dass junge Leute bei TSV 1860 in München spielen können.

k. Der Vater freut sich°, dass sein Sohn die Karriere hat, die für ihn zu stressig war. *sich freuen: to be happy*

 **27** **Im Wiener Dialekt.** Welche Sätze bedeuten ungefähr das Gleiche wie die Sätze im Wiener Dialekt?

1. Schaun S'.
2. Ich habe mir dacht, naaa, des geht ned guad.
3. … Briaf austrogn hat …
4. Jetzt muaß ea aufpassen, dass ea eam de Fiaß ned wegga ziagt.

a. … Briefe ausgetragen° hat … *delivered*
b. Jetzt muss er aufpassen, dass er ihm die Füße nicht wegzieht.
c. Sehen Sie.
d. Ich habe mir gedacht, na, das geht nicht gut.

## *Absprungtext*

Lesen Sie jetzt den Artikel aus dem Magazin *Focus*.

### *Die Entdeckung des Benjamin Lauth*

Vor einem Jahr spielte er noch in der Bayern-Liga. Jetzt gilt der 21-jährige Stürmer von 1860 München als eines der größten Talente in der Bundesliga und Hoffnung für die WM 2006. Einige haben das schon immer gewusst.

**Der 1860-Trainer**
Entdeckt hat *er* ihn.

Manche hatten ihn bemerkenswert genannt, als er, eingewechselt in der 80. Minute gegen Hannover 96, am 17. August 2002 sein erstes Bundesliga-Tor macht. Viele nannten ihn bemerkenswert, als er gegen Schalke zwei Tore schießt. Fünf Spiele und vier Treffer später sind sich alle darüber einig, dass er bemerkenswert ist. Seit dem Debüt des Torjägers Benjamin Lauth sind gerade einmal hundert Tage vergangen.

Und dann, es ist der 16. Dezember und in einem Benefizspiel der Nationalmannschaft, im Stadion AufSchalke sitzen 36 000 Zuschauer und 5,6 Millionen vor dem Fernseher, als der 21-jährige Nationalstürmer-Neuling von 1860 München in Minute 23 nach

*Der junge Star vom deutschen Fußball: Benjamin Lauth.*

seiner Einwechslung aufsteigt und sich in die Luft legt und dreht und mit rechts schießt und trifft. Und das „Tor des Jahres" erzielt ...

Alle, die ihn bis dahin bemerkenswert nannten, beginnen ihn jetzt, hundertundzweiundzwanzig Tage nach seinem Debüt, mit den Heiligenfiguren° des Fußballs zu erdrücken°.

*sacred figures*
*overwhelm*

Cheftrainer Peter Pacult, der ihn entdeckt hat, sitzt in seinem Cheftrainer-Büro im dritten Stock der gläsernen TSV-1860-Geschäftsstelle und ... lächelt. Er lächelt wie einer, der Zahnschmerzen hat und dennoch tapfer sein will. „Warum sollte ich stolz sein, den Benny entdeckt zu haben?"

„Schaun S', als ich den Benny zum Training der Profis geholt hab', ist der mehr im Dreck gelegen als vorwärts gekommen", sagt er. „Wenn den einer angespielt hat, ist der gleich ausgerutscht." Den Rest der Aufklärung komponiert der 43-Jährige in schönster Wiener Melodie: „Ich habe mir dacht, naaa, des geht ned guad." Sagt er. Und hat damit gesagt, dass es mit dem Entdecken allein nicht getan war°. Dann zieht er sein Leidenslächeln auf.

*nicht ... : wasn't enough*

Der Trainer Pacult mag Spieler, die fleißig sind. Geradlinig. Spieler, die dem Verein dienen° und ansonsten den Ball flach halten. Spieler, wie der Spieler Lauth einer ist. Spieler, wie der Spieler Pacult einer war. Der als Postbote° morgens um sechs „Briaf austrogn" hat und abends für den Wiener Sportklub siegte° und dafür mit 3 750 Schilling, umgerechnet 260 Euro, zufrieden° war.

*serve*
*mail carrier*
*won*
*content*

„Das Schwierigste kommt doch erst beim Benny", sagt er. „Jetzt muaß er aufpassen, dass er eam de Fiaß ned wegga ziagt." Dann lächelt er. Sein Leidenslächeln.

## Der Vater

Entdeckt hat *er* ihn.

Hans Lauth wirkt froh darüber, dass sein Sohn Benjamin die Karriere gemacht hat, für die er selber nicht den Mut gehabt hätte. Der heute 54-Jährige wollte lieber bei seiner Familie und den Freunden in Fischbachau sein, nahe dem Schliersee und den Bergen.

Hans Lauth lebt noch immer in dem Haus, das sein Vater 1962 für die ganze Familie gebaut hat. ...

Jeden Schritt, den der Sohn in Richtung Zukunft tat, hat der Vater vorausgedacht. Er hat gesehen, wann es an der Zeit war, den schmächtigen° Jungen, der jeden Tag stundenlang gegen Garage und Gartentor boltzte°, ins Kindertraining zu schicken. Er hat gesehen, wann es an der Zeit war, den kleinen Fußballer, der als Elfjähriger keine gleichwertigen Partner mehr hatte, in professionellere Hände zu geben. Im Juli 1992 erfährt Hans Lauth durch ein Zeitungsinserat von einem Probetraining beim TSV 1860 München. Der Vater ist schon immer ein Anhänger der „Löwen°". Benny liebt den FC Bayern.

*lanky*
*kicked (the ball)*

*name of soccer team*
**1860 München**

Die Trainer in München wollen nach einer Sichtung die Entdeckung des Hans Lauth gleich da behalten. Der Vater fühlt sich ein wenig überrumpelt°. ... Acht Jahre chauffiert er seinen Sohn dreimal die Woche zum Training nach München-Giesing. Es sind insgesamt rund 200 000 Kilometer, ein ganzes Autoleben.

*taken by surprise*

Als Franz Beckenbauer, die wohl unentbehrlichste° Heiligenfigur des Fußballs, im Dezember 2002 aus dem sehr großen Fernseher des Hans Lauth die sehr großen Worte spricht, Benjamin Lauth „ist für mich der Spieler der Hinrunde°", weiß der Vater, dass er alles richtig gemacht hat.

*most indispensable*

*first round*

**Der Star**

Entdeckt hat *er* sich.

Als kleiner Junge schläft er in FC-Bayern-Bettwäsche und träumt sich seine Zukunft schön. Er träumt, wie er sein erstes Bundesliga-Tor schießt und wie zehntausende Zuschauer jubeln und der Stadionsprecher seinen Namen ruft.

Als Benjamin Lauth fünf Jahre alt ist, verkündet er seinen Eltern, dass er höchstens vier Jahre zur Schule gehen wird. Dass es ihm genügt, Lesen und Schreiben und Rechnen zu lernen. Weil er ein Fußballspieler werden will.

Als Benjamin Lauth am 17. August 2002 sein erstes Bundesliga-Tor schießt, ist es im Stadion fast still. Sein erstes Bundesliga-Tor ist ein Auswärtstor°.

> An **Auswärtstor** is a goal scored in an away game against the home team. It is considered a particularly hard score to make, even for seasoned professionals, and in championship play it can count double. This made Lauth's first professional goal in the **Bundesliga** an especially impressive feat.
>
> *goal at an away-game*

von Carin Pawlak und Stefan Pielow, *Focus,* Nr. 9: 24. Februar 2003

## *Rückblick*

**28**   **Stimmt das?**  Stimmen die folgenden Aussagen zum Text oder nicht? Wenn nicht, was stimmt dann?

|  | Ja, das stimmt. | Nein, das stimmt nicht. |  |
|---|---|---|---|
| 1. Benjamin Lauth spielt seit 20 Jahren Profi-Fußball. | ☐ | ☐ | |
| 2. Viele Leute haben ihn sofort° bemerkenswert gefunden. | ☐ | ☐ | *immediately* |
| 3. Nach 120 Tagen als Profi haben viele Leute gemeint, Lauth ist einer der besten Spieler in der Geschichte vom deutschen Fußball. | ☐ | ☐ | |
| 4. Der Trainer Peter Pacult meint, Lauth hatte in der Bundesliga nicht viel zu lernen. | ☐ | ☐ | |
| 5. Pacult meint, Lauth hat gute Arbeitsmoral und Disziplin und macht das, was gut für das Team ist. | ☐ | ☐ | |
| 6. Das größte Problem für Lauth, sagt Pacult, ist, dass er weiter hinfällt und ausrutscht. | ☐ | ☐ | |
| 7. Der Vater hat Benjamins Karriere vorsichtig geplant. | ☐ | ☐ | |
| 8. Hans Lauth war der Einzige, der den Benjamin Lauth trainieren durfte. | ☐ | ☐ | |
| 9. Hans Lauth war immer ein Fan von TSV-1860, aber als Kind war Benjamin ein Fan von FC Bayern. | ☐ | ☐ | |
| 10. Der Vater hat acht Jahre lang dreimal in der Woche den Benjamin nach München zum Training gefahren. | ☐ | ☐ | |
| 11. Franz Beckenbauers Aussagen über Benjamin Lauth waren für den Vater unbedeutend° und uninteressant. | ☐ | ☐ | *unimportant* |
| 12. Schon als kleines Kind hat Benjamin Lauth Fußball-Kommentator werden wollen. | ☐ | ☐ | |

**29** **Kurz gefragt.** Beantworten Sie die folgenden Fragen auf Deutsch.

1. Wie lange spielt Benjamin Lauth schon in der Bundesliga, und was halten die Fans von ihm?
2. Welche Probleme hat der Trainer Peter Pacult bei dem jungen Spieler entdeckt, als er zu den Profis gekommen ist?
3. Was hat dem Trainer Pacult an Benjamin Lauth gefallen?
4. Was für ein Spieler ist Pacult selbst als junger Mann gewesen? Woher kommt er?
5. Warum hat Hans Lauth selber nie Profi-Fußball gespielt?
6. Wie hat der Vater das Training und die Karriere von seinem Sohn organisiert?
7. Was hat der Vater machen müssen, um Benjamin das bestmögliche Training zu ermöglichen?
8. Seit wann hat der Vater gewusst, dass er alles richtig gemacht hat?
9. Was für Träume hat Benjamin Lauth als kleiner Junge gehabt?
10. Warum war es ganz still, als Lauth sein erstes Bundesliga-Tor geschossen hat?

> Complete the **Ergänzen Sie** activity in your workbook for this text before doing the next activity.

## BRENNPUNKT KULTUR

### München

*Am Marienplatz im Herzen Münchens steht das Neue Rathaus mit dem Glockenspiel quer gegenüber vom Alten Rathaus.*

Munich (**München**), a city with a population of over 1,260,000, is officially the capital of the Free State of Bavaria (**der Freistaat Bayern**), the largest of Germany's 16 **Bundesländer** in land mass and second largest in population. But to many non-Bavarians, it's considered "**die heimliche Hauptstadt**" of the nation. Graced with a gentle climate and a location near the Alps, Munich is a historic city of great charm and ambience while also being a first-class center of business development and the service industry. With 26 universities and other **Hochschulen** and many research institutions, such as eleven Max Planck Institutes and seven Fraunhofer Gesellschaft institutions, Munich is very science- and technology-friendly, attracting talented young people from all over Germany and the world, who are drawn to its outstanding quality of life. Munich maintains a uniquely Bavarian atmosphere: cozy, comfortable, inviting, exciting.

The city's three 14th-century gates still stand, creating the connection to Munich's past. On the central **Marienplatz** square, the **Altes Rathaus** is within sight of the **Neues Rathaus,** whose 260-foot tower and **Glockenspiel** attract hoardes of visitors. Along with the new City Hall, Munich's most recognizable building is the **Frauenkirche,** whose twin onion-domed towers are the symbol (**das Wahrzeichen**) of the city. Nearby, **das Hofbräuhaus** draws locals and tourists with its traditional Bavarian cuisine, oom-pah bands, and its famous beer, and the 900-acre **Englischer Garten** provides respite for busy city-dwellers with its walking paths, ponds, and four beer gardens. Sports-minded Münchners may be split in their loyalty to soccer teams FC Bayern-München and TSV 1860, but they all enjoy easy access to abundant winter sports in the nearby Alps. Museum lovers will find a treasure trove in Munich, with everything from the science and technology collections of the **Deutsches Museum** and the automotive history at the **BMW-Museum** to the extraordinary art collections of the **Alte und Neue Pinakothek.** But for many visitors, Munich's greatest attraction will always be **das Oktoberfest,** a mixture of county fair and traditional costume festival celebrated beginning each September on the **Theresienwiesen,** fondly known to locals as **die Wies'n.** Each brewery headquartered in Munich sets up an immense beer tent (**das Bierzelt**) that can hold thousands of patrons who come to savor a one-liter **Maß** of beer and sway in harmony to traditional Bavarian bands.

■ **Kulturkreuzung** München liegt in Bayern und für viele Amerikaner und Kanadier ist München oder Bayern „typisch deutsch". Was assoziieren Sie mit München? Vieles aus Bayern ist nur ein Klischee, d.h°. es ist nicht repräsentativ für ganz Deutschland. Welche Aspekte vom Leben in den USA oder in Kanada dienen als° Klischees für Europäer? Wie finden Sie das? Haben Sie etwas Neues über München aus **Brennpunkt Kultur** gelernt?

*das heißt*

*dienen … : serve as*

## *Strukturen und Vokabeln*

## III **Talking about when events happen**
### Time expressions in the dative and accusative case

### A. Time expressions in the dative case

German speakers use the two-case prepositions **in/im, am,** and **vor** with the dative case to express a time when an event occurs. These expressions answer the question **wann?** *(when?)*.

> **Wann** hast du Geburtstag? — **Im** Mai.
> *When is your birthday? — In May.*
> **Wann** kommen die Schmidts? — **In einer** Stunde.
> *When are the Schmidts coming? — In an hour.*
> **Wann** hast du Geburtstag? — **Am** 11. Mai. (**Am** elften Mai.)
> *When is your birthday? — On the 11th of May. (On the eleventh of May.)*
> **Wann** hast du in Zürich studiert? — **Vor einem** Jahr.
> *When did you study in Zurich? — A year ago.*

The preposition **in/im** can be used two ways.

1. It can define the point in time of an event happening.

   Ich bin **im Jahre** 1986 geboren.    *I was born in the year 1986.*

2. It can also define the length of time before which an event occurs.

   Er kommt **in einem Monat**.    *He's coming in one month.*

German speakers use **am** to describe an event that happens on a specific day or date or on the weekend.

| | |
|---|---|
| Manche hatten ihn bemerkenswert genannt, als er, eingewechselt in der 80. Minute gegen Hannover 96, **am 17. (siebzehnten) August 2002** sein erstes Bundesliga-Tor macht. | *Many people called him noteworthy when, substituted in in the 80th minute of the match with Hannover 96 on August 17, 2002, he shot his first goal.* |
| Weihnachten ist immer **am 25. (fünfundzwanzigsten) Dezember.** | *Christmas is always on the 25th of December.* |
| **Am Wochenende** spielen wir Fußball. | *We're going to play soccer on the weekend.* |

Use **in/im** when referring to years, seasons, months, and weeks. Use **am** when referring to days, dates, and weekends. Remember to use the accusative preposition **um** when referring to hours and minutes: **um zwei Uhr; um drei Minuten nach zwei.**

Note that **in/im** (when used to define a length of time) and **vor** (when used to mean *ago*) have opposite meanings. **Vor** refers to a point in time at which events took place in the past while **in/im** refers to a point in time at which events *will take* place in the future: **Jetzt bin ich 30 Jahre alt. Vor einem Jahr war ich 29 Jahre alt. In einem Jahr bin ich 31 Jahre alt.**

The preposition **vor** expresses time in the past in the way that *ago* does in English.

| | |
|---|---|
| Ich habe die Karten schon **vor einer Woche** abgeholt. | *I picked up the tickets a week ago.* |
| **Vor einem Jahr** spielte er noch in der Bayern-Liga. | *A year ago he was still playing in the Bavarian Regional League.* |

---

**Sprache im Alltag: Expressing regularity**

German speakers use the expressions **einmal** (*once*), **zweimal** (*twice*), **dreimal** (*three times*), etc. before non-specific time expressions (e.g., **im Sommer, im Jahr, am Tag, am Wochenende, in der Woche**) to tell how often they do an activity.

| | |
|---|---|
| Acht Jahre chauffiert er seinen Sohn **dreimal die Woche** zum Training nach München-Giesing. | *Eight years he chauffeurs his son to practice in Munich-Giesing three times a week.* |
| Karl wäscht sein Auto **einmal im Monat.** | *Karl washes his car once a month.* |

For special emphasis or to express their exasperation, speakers use the expressions **hundertmal** *(a hundred times),* **zigmal,** or **x-mal** *(umpteen times).*

| | |
|---|---|
| Ich habe dir schon **x-mal** gesagt: Du musst um zehn Uhr zu Hause sein. | *I've told you umpteen times: You have to be home by ten.* |

---

## B. Time expressions in the accusative case

The accusative case without a preposition may also be used in a time expression to express definite time in German. These time expressions often correspond to an expression with the preposition *for* in English.

| | |
|---|---|
| **Diesen Samstag** fahren wir nach Stuttgart. | *We are driving to Stuttgart this Saturday.* |
| Ich habe **ein Jahr** in Heidelberg gewohnt. | *I lived in Heidelberg for one year.* |
| Er bleibt **eine Woche** bei uns. | *He's staying with us for one week.* |

For emphasis, speakers also say **ein Jahr lang.**

**30** **Wann ist Barbara zu Hause gewesen?** Fragen Sie einen Partner/eine Partnerin nach einer Aktivität mit einem Fragezeichen. Beantworten Sie dann eine Frage von Ihrem Partner/Ihrer Partnerin.

S1: *Wann ist Stefan zu Hause gewesen?*
S2: *Stefan ist vor einer Woche zu Hause gewesen.*
S1: *Wann bist du zu Hause gewesen?*
S2: *Ich bin am Wochenende zu Hause gewesen.*

**Tabelle A (S1):**

|  | Barbara | Stefan | Partner(in) 2 |
|---|---|---|---|
| zu Hause gewesen | am Freitag | ? | ? |
| Freunde in Berlin besucht | ? | vor einem Jahr | ? |
| in die Stadt gefahren | ? | vor einer Stunde | ? |
| ein gutes Buch gelesen | vor einem Monat | ? | ? |
| ein Konto eröffnet | ? | vor zwei Wochen | ? |
| auf die Post gegangen | gestern | ? | ? |
| an der Uni gewesen | heute Morgen | ? | ? |
| einen Film gesehen | ? | am Samstag | ? |
| mit dem Rad gefahren | dieses Wochenende | ? | ? |

**Tabelle B (S2):**

|  | Barbara | Stefan | Partner(in) 1 |
|---|---|---|---|
| zu Hause gewesen | ? | vor einer Woche | (am Wochenende) |
| Freunde in Berlin besucht | im Sommer | ? | ? |
| in die Stadt gefahren | vor 25 Minuten | ? | ? |
| ein gutes Buch gelesen | ? | am Wochenende | ? |
| ein Konto eröffnet | gestern | ? | ? |
| auf die Post gegangen | ? | vor zehn Minuten | ? |
| an der Uni gewesen | ? | um zehn Uhr | ? |
| einen Film gesehen | gestern Abend | ? | ? |
| mit dem Rad gefahren | ? | am Sonntag | ? |

**31** **Oft oder nie?** Notieren Sie, wie oft Sie die folgenden Aktivitäten machen: **einmal (zweimal** usw.**) am Tag (in der Woche, im Monat, im Jahr)** oder **nie?** Fragen Sie dann einen Partner/eine Partnerin, wie oft er/sie das macht.

> **Oft oder nie?** In sentences referring to both a time and a place, Germans mention the time *before* the place. **Ich fahre um sieben Uhr nach Hause.**

S1: *Wie oft gehst du in eine Buchhandlung?*
S2: *Ich gehe (einmal in der Woche) in eine Buchhandlung.*

|  | Ich | Partner(in) |
|---|---|---|
| 1. in eine Buchhandlung gehen | _____ | _____ |
| 2. ins Restaurant gehen | _____ | _____ |
| 3. ins Kino gehen | _____ | _____ |
| 4. zu Fuß zur Uni gehen | _____ | _____ |
| 5. auf eine Party gehen | _____ | _____ |
| 6. in die Kneipe gehen | _____ | _____ |
| 7. ins Fitnessstudio gehen | _____ | _____ |
| 8. auf die Bank gehen | _____ | _____ |
| 9. in die Kirche (Synagoge, Moschee) gehen | _____ | _____ |
| 10. ins Stadion zum Profispiel gehen | _____ | _____ |

**32** **Interview.** Stellen Sie einem Partner/einer Partnerin die folgenden Fragen.

**Interview.** Remember that **wenn** (*if*) is a subordinating conjunction in German. The verb always occurs at the end of the subordinate clause.

🟨 S1: *Wohin gehst du am Montag, wenn du Bücher ausleihen willst?*
S2: *Ich gehe am Montag in die Bibliothek, wenn ich Bücher ausleihen will.*

1. Wohin gehst du am Montag, wenn du Bücher ausleihen willst?
2. Wohin gehst du am Freitagabend, wenn du einen neuen Film sehen willst?
3. Wohin gehst du am Wochenende, wenn du ein Theaterstück sehen willst?
4. Wohin gehst du am Samstag, wenn du tanzen willst?
5. Wohin gehst du im Sommer, wenn du ein Bier trinken willst?
6. Wohin gehst du am Freitagabend, wenn du gute Musik hören willst?
7. Wohin gehst du am Sonntagabend, wenn du ein Theaterstück sehen willst?
8. Wohin gehst du im August, wenn du schwimmen willst?
9. Wohin gehst du im Winter, wenn du Bodybuilding machen willst?

# IV Talking about means of transportation
## The preposition **mit** with the dative case

German speakers use the dative preposition **mit** *(with, by)* to talk about means of transportation.

| | |
|---|---|
| Barbara fährt **mit dem Bus** in die Stadt. | *Barbara is taking the bus downtown.* |
| Stefan kommt **mit dem Auto** nach Hause. | *Stefan is driving his car home.* |

To ask about means of transportation German speakers use the question words **wie?** *(how?)* or **womit?** *(with what?)*.

| | |
|---|---|
| **Wie** kommst du nach Hause? | Mit dem Taxi. |
| **Womit** fährt Stefan in die Stadt? | Mit dem Fahrrad. |

In answers to a question that contains a **mit** expression, speakers often use **da + mit: damit.**

Kannst du **mit deinem alten Fahrrad** noch fahren?
Klar. Ich fahre jeden Tag **damit.**

To talk about travel on foot, speakers most commonly use the expression **zu Fuß** with the verbs **gehen** or **laufen.**

Wir gehen **zu Fuß.**     *We walk (are walking).*

## *Wissenswerte Vokabeln: Wie kommt man dahin?*
### *Talking about means of transportation*

mit dem Fahrrad (Rad)

mit dem Auto (Wagen, PKW)

mit dem Bus

mit der Bahn (dem Zug)

mit der Straßenbahn

mit der U-Bahn (Untergrundbahn)

mit dem Schiff

mit dem Flugzeug

mit dem Taxi

mit dem Motorrad

mit Rollerblades

zu Fuß

 Womit fährst du? *Ich fahre mit dem Bus.*
Wie kommst du? *Ich komme mit dem Taxi.*

**33** **Interview.** Stellen Sie einem Partner/einer Partnerin die folgenden Fragen.

S1: *Womit fährst du am Vormittag zur Uni?*
S2: *Ich fahre mit dem Rad. Und du?*
S1: *Ich fahre mit dem Bus.*

| | Ich | Partner(in) | |
|---|---|---|---|
| 1. Womit fährst du am Vormittag zur Uni? | ____ | ____ | |
| 2. Womit kommst du im Winter zur Uni? | ____ | ____ | |
| 3. Womit fährst du nach Hause? | ____ | ____ | |
| 4. Womit fährst du lieber: mit der Straßenbahn oder mit der U-Bahn? | ____ | ____ | |
| 5. Womit kommt man am besten° nach Europa? | ____ | ____ | **am ...:** *the best way* |

**34**  **Fahren Sie am besten mit dem Taxi.**  Sie arbeiten in einem Luxushotel in Köln und geben den Hotelgästen Rat, womit sie fahren sollen.

S1:  *Wir müssen in fünf Minuten im Stadttheater sein. Aber das ist am anderen Stadtende. Wie kommen wir am schnellsten dahin?*
S2:  *Dann fahren Sie am besten mit dem Taxi.*

1. Wir wollen den Kölner Dom besuchen. Aber mit kleinen Kindern können wir nicht den ganzen Weg laufen. Wie kommen wir dahin?
2. Heute Nachmittag muss ich in Düsseldorf sein, aber ich habe kein Auto. Das ist aber nicht so weit – weniger als eine Stunde von hier. Wie fährt man dahin?
3. Ich möchte so gern die Schlösser und die Weinberge am Rhein sehen!
4. Wir suchen ein kleines Café oder eine Konditorei hier gleich in der Nähe.
5. Wie kommt man von Köln nach Bonn?
6. In drei Stunden muss ich in London sein! Was soll ich machen?

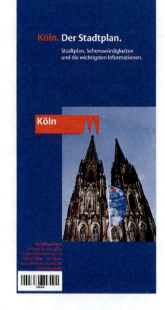

# V  Expressing time, manner, and place

## Word order for time, manner, and place

References to time in German often occur at the beginning of a main clause, followed by the conjugated verb and the subject.

> *time    verb    subject*
> **Heute** fahren wir in die Stadt.    *We are going (driving) into town today.*

Such time references may also appear after the verb in the interior of the sentence.

> Wir fahren **heute** in die Stadt.

Information about how an action occurs (the manner) follows the time reference.

> *1        2*
> *time    manner*
> Wir fahren **heute mit dem Auto** in die Stadt. (*or* **Heute** fahren wir **mit dem Auto** in die Stadt.)

Information about where an action occurs follows the references to time and manner. In summary, information in a German sentence follows the sequence: (1) time, (2) manner, (3) place.

> *1        2            3*
> *time    manner      place*
> Wir fahren **heute mit dem Auto in die Stadt.**

> The sequence of information in an English sentence is organized in the opposite order: (1) place, (2) manner, (3) time.
> We are driving **to town by car today.**

**35** **Wann, wie und wo lesen Sie das?** Wählen Sie aus jeder Spalte°   *column*
ein Element und formulieren Sie eine passende Antwort.

S1: *Liest du dein Deutschbuch?*
S2: *Ja, ich lese mein Deutschbuch so oft wie möglich laut in meinem Zimmer.*

eine deutsche Zeitung • ***Vorsprung*** • eine Wirtschaftszeitung (z.B. *Money Magazine*) • ein Mathematikbuch • eine Lokalzeitung • eine Frauenzeitschrift (z.B. *Cosmopolitan*) • ein Automagazin • ein Physikbuch • einen
Roman von Stephen King • einen Krimi von Agatha Christie • Gedichte von
Goethe • einen Roman von Danielle Steele • eine Tratschzeitschrift°   *gossip magazine*
(z.B. *People Magazine*) • ein Nachrichtenmagazin (z.B. *Time Magazine*)

| *Wann?* | *Wie?* | *Wo?* | |
|---|---|---|---|
| jeden Abend | leise° | im Wohnzimmer | *quietly* |
| jeden Tag | laut | auf der Post | |
| am Morgen | im Kopf | im Bett | |
| einmal im Monat | mit den Kindern | vor dem Fernseher | |
| nie | allein | in meinem Zimmer | |
| immer | mit großem Interesse | an der Uni | |
| jede Woche | ohne großes Interesse | im Schwimmbad | |
| einmal am Abend | mit dem Lehrer | im Café | |

## Schreibecke

**Eine Postkarte schreiben.** Sie sind in München und vermissen Ihren
Deutschlehrer/Ihre Deutschlehrerin sehr. Schreiben Sie ihm/ihr wieder eine
Postkarte. Verwenden Sie die folgenden Vokabeln und Ausdrücke.

| | | | | | |
|---|---|---|---|---|---|
| | | | | Auto | |
| | | ich | | Bus | ins Museum |
| Letzte Woche | bin | mein Freund | mit dem | Fuß | ins Theater | gegangen. |
| Gestern | ist | meine Freundin | mit der | Schiff | in die Kneipe | gefahren. |
| Heute Morgen | sind | meine Freunde | zu | Straßenbahn | in die Oper |
| Heute | | meine Freundinnen | | Taxi | auf die Uni |
| | | | | U-Bahn | |

## Freie Kommunikation

**In die Sprechstunde gehen.** Ihr Partner/Ihre Partnerin möchte nach der Stunde
mit dem Deutschlehrer/der Deutschlehrerin sprechen. Erklären Sie ihm/ihr, wie
man vom Klassenzimmer dorthin kommt.

## *Wissenswerte Vokabeln: Literatur und Film*
### *Talking about literature and film*

der Roman, -e

der Kriminalroman
(der Krimi, -s)

der Liebesroman

die Biographie, -n/
Autobiographie

die Erzählung, -en

die
Kurzgeschichte, -n

das Märchen, -

das Gedicht, -e

das Theaterstück, -e

das Drama,
(*pl.*) Dramen

die Komödie, -n

der Film, -e

der Abenteuerfilm

der
Dokumentarfilm

der Horrorfilm
der Gruselfilm

der
Zeichentrickfilm

spannend

lustig

unterhaltend

> Other types of movies are: **der Actionfilm, der Kriegsfilm, der Liebesfilm, der Western, der Sciencefictionfilm.**

◼ Was liest du gern?          *Ich lese gern Abenteuerromane.*
   Siehst du gern Horrorfilme?   *Nein, ich sehe lieber Dokumentarfilme.*

**36  Fantasietitel.** Der Titel von einem Buch oder Film sagt oft etwas über das Genre aus. Aus welchem Genre kommen die Filme und Bücher mit dem folgenden Titel?

*Filmtitel*

1. Die Invasion der Killer-Elefanten
2. 101 Elefanten
3. Illinois Jones und der Elefant des Maharadschas
4. Die Elefanten Afrikas
5. Ein Elefant sieht rot

*Genre*

a. der Zeichentrickfilm
b. der Abenteuerfilm
c. der Dokumentarfilm
d. der Actionfilm
e. der Horrorfilm

*Buchtitel*

1. Der Elefantenprinz
2. Der Elefantenmord
3. Ode an den Elefanten
4. Warten auf Elefanten
5. Mein Leben als Elefant

a. ein Gedicht
b. ein Theaterstück
c. ein Kriminalroman
d. eine Autobiographie
e. ein Märchen

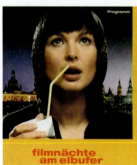 

**filmnächte am elbufer**

**Sonntag, 7. August**    MÄRCHENKULTFILMNACHT
**FEUER, WASSER UND POSAUNEN**
R: Alexander Rou, Märchen, UdSSR 1976, 76 min, FSK 6
D: Georgi Millar (Gerippe Unsterblich), Natalja Sedych (Aljonuschka), Alexej Katyschew (Wassja)
Aljona, ein schönes Hirtenmädchen, trifft auf der Suche nach ihrem entlaufenen Zicklein den jungen Wassja. Sie verlieben sich ineinander, doch „Gerippe", der böse Zauberer Kastschej, will Aljona schon heiraten. So belegt er Wassja mit einem Fluch, dass er durch Feuer, Wasser und Posaunen sterben solle.

**Montag, 8. August**    DREWAG ❈ KINOTAG
**KEBAB CONNECTION**
R: Anno Saul, Komödie, D 2004 , 95 min, FSK 12
D: Denis Moschitto, Nora Tschirner, Güven Kiraç
Culture-Clash-Komödie vom Hamburger Kiez: Ein verhinderter türkisch-deutscher Kung-Fu-Regisseur träumt vom Actionfilm – und muss die Vaterrolle spielen.
Einlass: 20.00 Uhr, Beginn: 21.00 Uhr, Abendkasse: 5,– Euro, VVK: 5,– Euro
>> www.kebabconnection.de

# VI  Expressing the purpose for an action

## The subordinating conjunction **damit**

A clause introduced by the subordinating conjunction **damit** *(so that)* stresses one's intent or purpose in carrying out an action. This differs somewhat from **weil** *(because)*, which stresses the reason for the action.

> Barbara geht in die Buchhandlung, **damit** sie *Fitness für faule Säcke°* kaufen kann.
> *Barbara is going to the bookstore so that she can buy* Fitness für faule Säcke.

*faule Säcke:* "lazy bones," "couch potatoes"

> Barbara geht in die Buchhandlung, **weil** sie *Fitness für faule Säcke* sucht.
> *Barbara is going to the bookstore because she is looking for* Fitness für faule Säcke.

The subordinating conjunction **damit** must not be confused with the compound **damit,** which substitutes for **mit +** a noun and cannot join clauses.

> Hier sind die Papiere. Was soll ich **damit** machen?
> *Here are the papers. What should I do with them?*

**37** **Lesen nur zum Spaß?** Warum lesen Sie das? Benutzen Sie **weil** oder **damit** in Ihrer Antwort.

 *Ich lese eine deutsche Zeitung, weil ich sie gern lese.*

Ich lese ...

| | |
|---|---|
| 1. eine deutsche Zeitung, | damit ich gute Noten bekomme. |
| 2. mein Deutschbuch, | weil es mich interessiert. |
| 3. das Mathematikbuch, | weil ich (sie/es) gern lese. |
| 4. die Lokalzeitung, | weil ich neue Ideen suche. |
| 5. Frauenzeitschriften | damit ich neue Informationen finden kann. |
| (z. B. *Cosmopolitan*), | damit ich etwas Neues lernen kann. |
| 6. ein Automagazin, | weil ich Stephen Kings (Danielle Steeles |
| 7. Wirtschaftszeitschriften | usw.) Romane liebe. |
| (z. B. *Money Magazine*), | weil es lustig ist. |
| 8. Romane von Stephen King | weil es mir gefällt. |
| (Danielle Steele usw.), | weil ... |
| 9. das Horoskop, | damit ... |
| 10. Gedichte von Goethe, | |
| 11. eine Geschichte von Agatha Christie, | |
| 12. Nachrichtenmagazine (z. B. *Time Magazine*), | |

 **F r e i e   K o m m u n i k a t i o n**

**Rollenspiel: In die Stadt fahren.** Es ist Samstag. Sie müssen vieles erledigen (z. B. Bücher und Lebensmittel einkaufen, Geld abheben). Sie möchten aber nicht allein in die Stadt fahren. Ihr Partner/Ihre Partnerin möchte nicht mitkommen, denn es sind immer so viele Leute in der Stadt und es ist zu hektisch **(Ich will nicht kommen, weil ...).** Versuchen Sie, Ihren Partner/Ihre Partnerin zu über-reden°, dass er/sie mitkommt. Erklären Sie, womit Sie fahren, wohin Sie in der Stadt gehen und wann Sie zurückkommen.

*persuade*

 **S c h r e i b e c k e**

**Meine Biographie/Autobiographie.** Beschreiben Sie Ihre Biographie/Auto-biographie für einen Buchkatalog.

1. Was ist der Titel?
2. Was ist die Länge?
3. Wie heißt der Autor/die Autorin? (Schreiben Sie selbst? Wenn nicht, wer schreibt? Warum?)
4. Was ist der Preis?
5. Was steht in der Biographie/Autobiographie?
6. Was ist passiert? Wann? Wie oft?
7. Wohin sind Sie (oft, selten) gefahren? Womit?

**Schreibecke.** Provide basic information such as where and when you were born, how and where you spent your early years, etc. Use the conversational past.

**Zieltext**    **In der Buchhandlung**

Barbara hat von einem Buch über Fitness für faule Menschen gelesen. Sie geht in eine Buchhandlung, denn sie möchte das Buch kaufen. Sie braucht auch ein Vorlesungsverzeichnis für die Uni. Ihr Freund Karl kommt mit und wartet draußen auf Barbara.

## Vorschau

 **38** **Thematische Fragen.** Beantworten Sie die folgenden Fragen auf Deutsch.

1. Was lesen Sie gern?
2. Welche Autoren sind im Moment populär?
3. Wo finden Sie neue Bücher über aktuelle Themen, z. B. Bestseller?
4. Nennen Sie einige berühmte deutsche Autoren/Autorinnen.

 **39** **Satzdetektiv.** Welche Sätze bedeuten ungefähr das Gleiche?

1. Also, wir haben **momentan** *Fitness für faule Säcke* von Dr. Michael Despeghel-Schöne.
2. Das Buch *Fitness für faule Säcke* ist **hochaktuell**.
3. Es **beschreibt ein paar leichte Tipps**, wie man gesund leben kann.
4. Viele Leute **schwören darauf**.

a. Das Buch *Fitness für faule Säcke* ist sehr relevant und neu.
b. Viele Leute finden das Buch sehr, sehr gut.
c. *Fitness für faule Säcke* von Dr. Michael Despeghel-Schöne ist im Moment neu im Buchhandel.
d. Es erklärt, wie man gesund leben kann.

---

5. Kommen Sie bitte mit zur **Kasse.**
6. **Manche haben's im Kopf, andere in den Beinen.**
7. Ich brauch' noch ein **Vorlesungsverzeichnis.**
8. Möchten Sie eine **Tüte** oder geht's auch ohne?
9. **Die Quittung** liegt auf der ersten Seite.

e. Der Zettel° mit dem Preis darauf ist im Buch.                    *slip of paper*
f. Ich möchte ein Buch über Universitätskurse kaufen.
g. Kommen Sie bitte mit. Sie können das Buch dort bezahlen.
h. Manche Leute vergessen nichts und andere Leute vergessen alles.
i. Möchten Sie auch eine Plastiktasche haben?

**Wo man in Tübingen Bücher kauft.**

OSIANDER
Bücher seit 1596

## Zieltext
### In der Buchhandlung

 Hören Sie gut zu.

## Rückblick

**40** **Stimmt das?** Stimmen diese Aussagen zum Text oder nicht? Wenn nicht, was stimmt?

|  | Ja, das stimmt. | Nein, das stimmt nicht. |
|---|:---:|:---:|
| 1. Barbara sucht ein Buch in der Buchhandlung. | ☐ | ☐ |
| 2. Barbara hat *Fitness für faule Säcke* schon gelesen. | ☐ | ☐ |
| 3. *Fitness für faule Säcke* ist sehr alt. | ☐ | ☐ |
| 4. Die Buchhandlung hat *Fitness für faule Säcke* nicht. | ☐ | ☐ |
| 5. Barbara kauft das Buch nicht. | ☐ | ☐ |
| 6. Das Buch kostet 14,90 Euro. | ☐ | ☐ |
| 7. Karl geht mit in die Buchhandlung. | ☐ | ☐ |
| 8. Barbara hat schon ein Vorlesungsverzeichnis. | ☐ | ☐ |
| 9. Karl kauft das Vorlesungsverzeichnis für Barbara. | ☐ | ☐ |
| 10. Barbara hat keinen Rucksack. | ☐ | ☐ |

**41** **Wann sagt man das?** Wann hört man diese Sätze aus dem Zieltext? Kreuzen Sie für jeden Satz eine passende Situation an.

*Eine Person sagt:*                                      *Man hört es,*

1. „Kommen Sie bitte mit zur Kasse.“
   _____ a. wenn man ein Buch bezahlen will.
   _____ b. wenn man ein Buch sucht.

2. „Sie bekommen 20 Cent zurück.“
   _____ a. wenn ein Buch 19 Euro 80 kostet und man mit einem 20-Euro-Schein bezahlt.
   _____ b. wenn ein Buch 19 Euro 80 kostet und man mit einem 10-Euro-Schein bezahlt.

*Eine Person sagt:*                          *Man hört es,*

3. „Entschuldigen Sie       ____  a. wenn der Deutschlehrer/die Deutsch-
bitte, ich muss Sie                     lehrerin in das Klassenzimmer kommt.
noch einmal stören.“     ____  b. wenn man aus einem Geschäft schon
                                        hinausgegangen ist, aber dann gleich
                                        wieder zurückkommt.

4. „Möchten Sie eine        ____  a. wenn man Schokolade kauft.
Tüte?“                   ____  b. wenn man einen Hund kauft.

5. „Die Quittung liegt auf  ____  a. wenn ein Freund/eine Freundin Ihnen
der ersten Seite.“                      ein Buch leiht.
                          ____  b. wenn man ein Buch in einer
                                        Buchhandlung kauft.

## Freie Kommunikation

**Rollenspiel: In der Buchhandlung.** Spielen Sie eine von diesen Situationen in einer Buchhandlung mit einem Partner/mit einer Partnerin. S1 ist der Kunde/die Kundin°, S2 arbeitet in der Buchhandlung.

*customer*

S1: Wählen Sie eine von diesen Personen und spielen Sie sie in der Buchhandlung.

1. Sie suchen ein Buch als ein Geschenk für einen Freund/eine Freundin. Der Freund/die Freundin ist sehr sportlich und reist° gern. Sie wollen ein gutes Buch finden; der Preis ist nicht so wichtig.

*travels*

2. Sie haben eine Einladung zu einer Party. Sie brauchen ein Geschenk für den Gastgeber/die Gastgeberin°. Sie kennen ihn/sie nicht gut und suchen ein Buch, das teuer° aussieht aber wirklich wenig kostet.

*host*
*expensive*

3. Sie machen bald eine lange Reise. Sie verbringen viel Zeit im Flugzeug (im Zug) und brauchen etwas zum Lesen, damit Ihnen nicht so langweilig wird.

S2: Sie arbeiten in einer Buchhandlung. Wählen Sie eine von diesen Personen und spielen Sie sie.

1. Sie helfen dem Kunden/der Kundin gern, sind sehr freundlich und kennen sich gut mit Büchern aus.

2. Es ist spät am Nachmittag und Sie wollen lieber nach Hause gehen. Sie haben wenig Interesse an Ihrem Kunden/Ihrer Kundin und sind ziemlich unhöflich (*impolite*).

3. Sie arbeiten erst seit ein paar Stunden in der Buchhandlung. Sie wissen fast nichts von Büchern. Sie wollen helfen, können es aber nicht.

**Erlesenes**
aus Tübingen

- Große Auswahl vom Roman bis zum Fachbuch
- Qualifizierte und freundliche Beratung
- direkter Draht zum Buchmarkt in England und Amerika
- Versandservice in alle Welt

**400 Jahre**
**Freude am Lesen**
**Osiandersche**
BUCHHANDLUNG
Tübingen
Wilhelmstr. 12 und Uni Morgenstelle
Tel. 07071/9201-0, Fax 9201-92
http://www.osiander.de

## Schreibecke

**Eine Campusbroschüre.** Mithilfe des Computers° schreiben Sie eine Broschüre für neue Studentinnen und Studenten an Ihrer Universität. Erklären Sie, wo die Deutschkurse sind und wie man von den Studentenwohnheimen dahin kommt. Beschreiben Sie auch, wo man Deutsch lernen kann und wie man dahin kommt.

*Mit... : Using a computer*

## Wortschatz

### Das Studentenleben

**der Mitbewohner, - / die Mitbewohnerin, -nen** *roommate, apartment mate, cohabitant*

**der Schüler, - / die Schülerin, -nen** *school pupil*

**das Semesterticket, -s** *semester pass (for city transportation)*

**der Studentenausweis (Schülerausweis), -e** *student ID*

### Wechselpräpositionen

**an** *at, on; to*
**auf** *at, on; onto, to*
**hinter** *behind, to/in the back of*
**in** *at, in; into; to*
**neben** *beside, next to*
**über** *above, over*
**unter** *under, underneath*
**vor** *in front of; ago*
**zwischen** *between*

### Wo gehst du gern hin?

**die Fete, -n** *party*
**das Fitnessstudio, -s** *health club*
**der Fluss, ¨e** *river*
**der Jazzkeller, -** *jazz club*
**die Moschee, -n** *mosque*
**die Oper, -n** *opera*
**das Stadion,** *pl.* **Stadien** *stadium*
**die Synagoge, -n** *synagogue*
***Noch einmal:*** **die Disko(thek), das Kino, die Kirche, die Kneipe, das Konzert, das Museum, die Party, das Restaurant, das Schwimmbad, das Theater**

**auf /in … gehen** *to go to …*

### Wo macht man das in der Stadt?

**die Apotheke, -n** *pharmacy*
**die Bäckerei, -en** *bakery*
**die Bank, -en** *bank*
**der Bioladen, ¨** *health food store*
**die Buchhandlung, -en** *bookstore*

**das Büro, -s** *office*
**die Fleischerei, -en** *butcher shop*
**die Haltestelle, -n** *bus stop*
**der Kiosk, -s** *kiosk, stand*
**die Konditorei, -en** *pastry shop*
**der Markt, ¨e** *market*
**die Metzgerei, -en** *butcher shop*
**die Post** *post office*
**das Reformhaus, ¨er** *health food store*
**die Sparkasse, -n** *savings bank*
**der Zeitungsstand, ¨e** *newspaper stand*
***Noch einmal:*** **der Bahnhof, der Supermarkt**

### Verkehrsmittel

**das Motorrad, ¨er** *motorcycle*
**der PKW (Personenkraftwagen), -s** *car*
**die Rollerblades** *pl. in-line skates*
**das Schiff, -e** *boat*
**die Straßenbahn, -en** *streetcar*
**das Taxi, -s** *taxi*
**die U-Bahn (Untergrundbahn), -en** *subway*
***Noch einmal:*** **das Auto, die Bahn, der Bus, das Fahrrad (Rad), das Flugzeug, der Wagen, der Zug**

**zu Fuß** *on foot*

### Literatur und Film

**die Biographie, -n (Autobiographie)** *biography (autobiography)*
**das Drama,** *pl.* **Dramen** *drama, play*
**die Erzählung, -en** *story*
**der Film, -e** *film, movie*
   **der Abenteuerfilm, -e** *adventure film*
   **der Dokumentarfilm, -e** *documentary film*
   **der Gruselfilm, -e** *horror movie*
   **der Horrorfilm, -e** *horror movie*
   **der Zeichentrickfilm, -e** *animated cartoon*

**das Gedicht, -e** *poem*
**die Komödie, -n** *comedy*
**die Kurzgeschichte, -n** *short story*
**die Literatur** *literature*
**das Märchen, -** *fairy tale*
**der Roman, -e** *novel*
   **der Kriminalroman, -e (der Krimi, -s)** *crime novel, detective story*
   **der Liebesroman, -e** *romance novel, love story*
**das Theaterstück, -e** *(theatrical) play*
**die Zeitschrift, -en** *magazine*

**lustig** *funny, comical*
**spannend** *exciting*
**unterhaltend** *entertaining*

### Der Sport

**der amerikanische Football** *American football*
**das Eishockey** *ice hockey*
**das Feldhockey** *field hockey*
**das Lacrosse** *lacrosse*
***Noch einmal:*** **der Baseball, der Basketball, der Fußball, das Golf, das Tennis, der Volleyball**

**behalten (behält, hat behalten)** *to keep*
**jubeln (hat gejubelt)** *to cheer*
**schießen (hat geschossen)** *to shoot*
**siegen (hat gesiegt)** *to win*
**Ski fahren (fährt, ist gefahren)** *to ski*
**Sport treiben (hat getrieben)** *to do sports*
**treffen (trifft, hat getroffen)** *to score (in a game); to meet*
***Noch einmal:*** **angeln, schwimmen, segeln, surfen, wandern**

**der Anhänger, - / die Anhängerin, -nen** *follower, supporter*
**der Ball, ¨e** *ball*
**der Dreck** *dirt, mud*
**der Fußballplatz, ¨e** *soccer field*
**die Liga,** *pl.* **Ligen** *league*
**die Mannschaft, -en** *team*
**der Mut** *courage*

**der Profi, -s** *professional*

**das Spiel, -e** *game, match*

**der Spielplatz, ˝e** *playground*

**das Stadion,** *pl.* **Stadien** *stadium*

**das Tor, -e** *goal*

**der Trainer, -** *coach*

**der Verein, -e (Sportverein, Turn-verein, Fußballverein, usw.)** *club (sports club, gymnastics club, soccer club, etc.)*

**der Zuschauer, - / die Zuschauerin, -nen** *spectator*

### In welcher Richtung?

**die Richtung** *direction*

**Wie komme ich zur/zum … ?** *How do I get to … ?*

**an der Ecke** *at/on the corner*

**bis zur Ampel** *as far as (up to) the traffic light*

**bis zur Kreuzung** *as far as (up to) the intersection*

**die Straße entlang** *down the street*

**gegenüber (von +** *dat.***)** *across from*

**geradeaus** *straight ahead*

**(gleich) um die Ecke** *right around the corner*

**links/rechts ab·biegen (ist abgebo-gen)** *to turn to the left/right*

**näher** *nearer, closer*

**quer gegenüber von** *diagonally across from*

### Auf der Post

**die Briefmarke, -n** *postage stamp*

**das Paket, -e** *package*

### Beim Einkaufen

**das Einkaufsnetz, -e** *mesh shopping bag*

**die Kasse, -n** *check-out counter; cash register*

**der Kunde, [-n], -n / die Kundin, -nen** *customer*

**die Quittung, -en** *receipt*

**die Tragetasche, -n** *plastic store bag*

**die Tüte, -n** *sack, bag*

**billig** *inexpensive, cheap*

**teuer** *expensive*

### Auf der Bank

**das Bargeld** *cash*

**das Konto,** *pl.* **Konten** *bank account*

**das Girokonto, -konten** *checking/debit account*

**das Sparkonto, -konten** *savings account*

**der Scheck, -s** *check*

*Noch einmal:* **die Bankkarte, die Kreditkarte**

**ab·heben (hat abgehoben)** *to with-draw (money)*

**(ein Konto) eröffnen (hat eröffnet)** *to open (an account)*

**ein·zahlen (hat eingezahlt)** *to de-posit (money)*

### Die Meinung geben

**(Das) finde ich so lala.** *I find (that) so-so.*

**(Das) finde ich toll.** *I think (that) is great/fantastic.*

**(Das) gefällt mir gar nicht.** *I don't like (that) at all.*

### Zeitausdrücke

**einmal, zweimal, dreimal** usw. *once, twice, three times, etc.*

**zigmal (x-mal)** *umpteen times*

### Eigenschaften

**bemerkenswert** *noteworthy*

**gesund** *healthy*

**hochaktuell** *very current, very timely*

**neugierig** *nosy, curious*

**praktisch** *practical; practically*

**unhöflich** *impolite*

**zufrieden** *happy, satisfied*

### Andere Verben

**empfehlen (empfiehlt, hat emp-fohlen)** *to recommend*

**entdecken (hat entdeckt)** *to discover*

**erklären (hat erklärt)** *to explain*

**erledigen (hat erledigt)** *to take care of*

**gelten (gilt, hat gegolten) als** *to be considered as*

**hängen (hat gehangen)** *to be hanging*

**hängen (hat gehängt)** *to hang (something) up*

**hoffen (hat gehofft) auf +** *acc.* *to hope for*

**holen (hat geholt)** *to fetch, get, pick up*

**lachen (hat gelacht) über +** *acc.* *to laugh about, at*

**legen (hat gelegt)** *to lay (something) down, put down*

**liegen (hat gelegen)** *to be lying down, lie*

**nennen (hat genannt)** *to name, to call someone something*

**reisen (ist gereist)** *to travel*

**schauen (hat geschaut)** *to look at, watch*

**setzen (hat gesetzt)** *to set (some-thing) down*

**sitzen (hat gesessen)** *to be sitting*

**springen (ist gesprungen)** *to jump*

**stehen (hat gestanden)** *to stand, be standing*

**steigen (ist gestiegen)** *to climb*

**stellen (hat gestellt)** *to stand (some-thing), put*

**suchen (hat gesucht)** *to look for*

**vor·schlagen (schlägt vor, hat vorgeschlagen)** *to suggest*

*Noch einmal:* **beschreiben, denken an, gehen in/auf/an, fahren in/nach, fallen auf, fliegen, laufen in/nach, schreiben an, sein in/an/auf, sprechen über, warten auf, wohnen in**

### Andere Wörter

**damit** *with it/that; so that*

**her** *here*

**hin** *there*

### Meine eigenen Wörter

_____

_____

_____

_____

_____

_____

# An der Uni studieren

In this chapter you will learn to talk about your daily routine, about issues of personal health, and what you will do in the future. You will also learn to talk about university-related activities.

## Kommunikative Funktionen

- Talking about activities we do for ourselves
- Talking about daily hygiene routines
- Talking about future events
- Expressing probability
- Specifying additional information about actions

## Strukturen

- Reflexive verbs
- Reflexive pronouns
- Future time and time expressions
- The verb **werden + wohl**
- Verbs with prepositional objects
- **Da-** and **wo-**compounds

## Vokabeln

- Die tägliche Routine
- Im Badezimmer
- Krank sein

## Kulturelles

- Universitätskurse
- Das deutsche Universitätssystem
- Wie Studierende ihr Studium finanzieren
- Das deutsche Schulsystem

■ Du, ich muss mich beeilen. Die Vorlesung fängt gleich an.

**Online Study Center**

Go to the *Vorsprung* Website at *http:// college.hmco.com/pic/ vorsprung2e.*

**Anlauftext**   ## Ein Gruppenreferat°

*Gruppenreferat: group presentation*

Karl und Stefan sind Partner in einem Betriebswirtschaftsproseminar. Ihre Arbeitsgruppe soll nächste Woche ein Referat halten; sie müssen im Proseminar über ihr gemeinsames° Projekt sprechen, aber sie haben noch gar nichts geschrieben. Karl geht zu seiner Dozentin, Frau Dr. Osswald, in die Sprechstunde° und erfindet Ausreden°, warum er und Stefan noch nicht viel gemacht haben.

*joint*
*office hours*
*erfindet ... : makes excuses*

## Vorschau

 **1**   **Thematische Fragen.** Beantworten Sie die folgenden Fragen auf Deutsch.

1. Mit wem sprechen Sie zuerst, wenn Sie Probleme in einem Kurs haben?
   a. mit Freunden
   b. mit Kommilitonen°
   c. mit dem Professor/der Professorin
   d. mit den Eltern
   e. mit dem Dekan°
   f. mit dem Institutsleiter/der Institutsleiterin°
2. Besuchen Sie Professoren/Professorinnen in der Sprechstunde? Warum? Warum nicht? Wie oft haben Ihre Professoren/Professorinnen Sprechstunden?
3. Haben Sie schon mal ein Gruppenprojekt gemacht? Was ist passiert? Was war gut? Was war schlecht?
   a. Wir haben nicht genug Zeit für das Projekt gehabt.
   b. Manche Leute haben mehr gearbeitet als andere.
   c. Wir haben viele gute Ideen gehabt.
   d. Wir haben viele Talente in der Gruppe gehabt.
   e. Wir haben verschiedene° Interessen gehabt.
   f. Wir haben Konflikte gehabt.

*college classmates*

*dean*
*chairperson*

*different*

**2**   **Die Seminararbeit°.** Was muss man machen, wenn man eine gute Seminararbeit schreiben will? Ordnen Sie die Faktoren nach ihrer Wichtigkeit von 1 (sehr wichtig) bis 10 (unwichtig).

*term paper*

|                                            | *Wichtigkeit* |               |
| ------------------------------------------ | ------------- | ------------- |
| ein Thema wählen°                          | _____       | *select*      |
| einen Partner/eine Partnerin finden        | _____       |               |
| Notizen machen                             | _____       |               |
| in die Bibliothek gehen                    | _____       |               |
| im Internet recherchieren°                 | _____       | *to do research* |
| Bücher und Artikel lesen                   | _____       |               |
| ein paar Versionen schreiben               | _____       |               |
| mit dem Professor/der Professorin sprechen | _____       |               |
| Folien° und Handouts vorbereiten           | _____       | *transparencies* |
| eine PowerPoint-Präsentation vorbereiten   | _____       |               |
| eine Tabelle° oder eine Grafik zeichnen    | _____       | *table, chart* |

**3**    **Satzdetektiv.** Welche Sätze bedeuten ungefähr das Gleiche?

1. Schön, dass Sie **sich** endlich **melden.** A
2. Wie sieht es mit Ihrem **Referat** aus? D
3. Ich habe **mich** schwer **erkältet.** B
4. Sie haben wirklich **Pech gehabt!** C

a. Es ist gut, dass Sie jetzt zu mir gekommen sind.
b. Ich war krank – ich habe eine schlimme Erkältung gehabt.
c. Das war wirklich eine schlechte Situation für Sie!
d. Wie weit sind Sie mit Ihrem Projekt?

5. Haben Sie **sich** überhaupt **für** ein Thema **entschieden?** H
6. Wie lange wird das Referat **dauern?** G
7. Ich **freue mich** schon **auf** Ihr Referat. I
8. Wir müssen unser **Referat** schon nächste Woche **halten.** F
9. Das werden wir bis nächste Woche nie **schaffen.** E

e. Das können wir bis nächste Woche nicht zu Ende machen!
f. Nächste Woche müssen wir unsere Arbeit mündlich° präsentieren.    *orally*
g. Wie viel Zeit werden Sie für das Referat brauchen?
h. Wissen Sie schon, über welches Thema Sie sprechen werden?
i. Ich bin auf Ihren Vortrag° gespannt.    *presentation*

## *Anlauftext*

    Hören Sie gut zu.

### Ein Gruppenreferat

So, so. Sie haben wirklich Pech gehabt! Haben Sie sich überhaupt für ein Thema entschieden?

Ja. Haben wir das nicht angemeldet?

Ich kann mich jedenfalls nicht daran erinnern. Wie heißt Ihr Thema noch mal?

„Kulturmanagement: Koordinierung vom Spielplan"

Schön. Das ist ein wirklich aktuelles Thema. Wie lange wird das Referat dauern?

Das wissen wir noch nicht so genau.

Vergessen Sie nicht: Sie haben maximal fünfundvierzig Minuten. Konzentrieren Sie sich auf das Wichtigste.

Wird es einen Overheadprojektor im Seminarraum geben? Wir haben nämlich viele Folien.

Ich werde einen Overheadprojektor für Sie bestellen.

Und haben Sie zusätzlich auch Handouts?

Ja, natürlich, natürlich. Die haben wir schon vorbereitet und kopiert.

Fein. Ich freue mich schon auf Ihr Referat.

Ja, danke. Auf Wiedersehen, bis nächste Woche.

Na, Karl, wie war's? Was hast du ihr gesagt?

Ach, Stefan, wir müssen unser Referat schon nächste Woche halten. Das werden wir bis nächste Woche nie schaffen. Ich fühle mich jetzt schon krank. Ich muss mich unbedingt hinlegen.

## Rückblick

**4** **Stimmt das?** Stimmen diese Aussagen zum Text oder nicht? Wenn nicht, was stimmt?

| | Ja, das stimmt. | Nein, das stimmt nicht. |
|---|---|---|
| 1. Karl und Stefan sind Partner in einer Arbeitsgruppe. | ☐ | ☐ |
| 2. Stefan sagt, er hat sich erkältet. | ☐ | ☐ |
| 3. Karl und Stefan haben Glück gehabt. | ☐ | ☐ |
| 4. Frau Dr. Osswald kann sich nicht an das Thema für Karls Arbeitsgruppe erinnern. | ☐ | ☐ |
| 5. Das Thema für das Referat ist „Kulturmanagement: Koordinierung vom Spielplan". | ☐ | ☐ |
| 6. Karl weiß noch nicht, wie lange das Referat dauern wird. | ☐ | ☐ |
| 7. Die Arbeitsgruppe soll sich auf die Details konzentrieren. | ☐ | ☐ |
| 8. Karl wird einen Overheadprojektor bestellen. | ☐ | ☐ |
| 9. Dr. Osswald freut sich auf das Referat. | ☐ | ☐ |
| 10. Stefan und Karl haben das Referat schon geschrieben. | ☐ | ☐ |

> Complete the **Ergänzen Sie** activity in your workbook for this text before doing the next activity.

> **Kurz gefragt.** A **Dozent/ Dozentin** is a tenured university professor with a Ph.D. who is not yet a full professor (**Professor/ Professorin**). The number of professors is limited in Germany to the number of positions determined for the country.

**5** **Kurz gefragt.** Beantworten Sie die Fragen auf Deutsch.

1. Welche Probleme haben Karl und Stefan angeblich° gehabt?
2. Was ist das Thema von ihrem Gruppenreferat?
3. Warum gefällt der Dozentin das Thema?
4. Warum will die Dozentin wissen, wie lange das Referat dauern wird?
5. Warum will Karl wissen, ob es einen Overheadprojektor im Seminarraum gibt?
6. Wie wird die Dozentin Karls Arbeitsgruppe helfen?
7. Was haben Karl und Stefan angeblich schon für das Referat vorbereitet?
8. Warum fühlt sich Karl nach dem Gespräch krank?

*supposedly*

**6** **Unsere Universität.** Diskutieren Sie die folgenden Sätze in kleinen Gruppen, bis Sie alle dieselbe Meinung haben. Teilen° andere Gruppen Ihre Meinung?

*share*

1. An dieser Universität muss man _____ schreiben.
   a. sehr viel          b. viel          c. nicht sehr viel
2. Dozenten/Dozentinnen an dieser Universität verbringen viel Zeit _____.
   a. mit Studenten      b. beim Forschen°      c. im Unterricht

*research*

3. Es ist _____, mit Lehrkräften° auf diesem Campus zu sprechen.
   a. leicht          b. schwierig          c. undenkbar°
4. Der beste Fachbereich° auf diesem Campus ist _____.
5. In diesem Deutschkurs müssen wir viel _____.
   a. sprechen          c. lesen          e. schreiben
   b. zuhören           d. Grammatik lernen

*instructors*

*unthinkable*

*department*

6. In diesem Kurs müssen wir zu viele _____.
   a. Hausaufgaben machen    b. Prüfungen schreiben    c. Referate halten

7. Unsere Bibliotheken sind _____.
   a. nicht besonders gut        b. recht gut              c. ausgezeichnet

8. Wer° hier abends im Studentenwohnheim lernen will, _____.  *Whoever*
   a. muss sich sehr intensiv konzentrieren
   b. muss extrem unfreundlich sein
   c. wird keine Probleme haben

9. Assistenten (und nicht Professoren) unterrichten bei uns _____.
   a. nie                b. nicht sehr oft          c. oft

10. Wer hier Schwierigkeiten° in einem Kurs hat, _____.  ***Probleme***
    a. hat einfach Pech°  *bad luck*
    b. muss selber Hilfe suchen
    c. kann ohne Probleme Hilfe bekommen

11. Studenten hier meinen, Pflichtkurse° sind _____.  *required courses*
    a. nervig°            b. akzeptabel        c. wertvoll  *irritating*

**7  Ausreden bewerten°.** Sie sind der Dozent/die Dozentin. Ein  *evaluate*
Student/Eine Studentin kann heute sein/ihr Referat nicht halten. Hier sind einige
typische Ausreden. Bewerten Sie die Ausreden als **sehr glaubhaft, akzeptabel**
oder **Unsinn.**

|  | **Sehr glaubhaft** | **Akzeptabel** | **Unsinn** | |
|---|---|---|---|---|
| 1. Mein Hund hat mein Referat gefressen°. | ☐ | ☐ | ☐ | *ate (for animals)* |
| 2. Ich habe es zu Hause vergessen. | ☐ | ☐ | ☐ | |
| 3. Der Bus hat Verspätung° gehabt. | ☐ | ☐ | ☐ | *late* |
| 4. Ich habe verschlafen. Mein Wecker ist kaputt. | ☐ | ☐ | ☐ | |
| 5. Ich kann nicht zur Uni kommen. Mein Auto ist kaputt. | ☐ | ☐ | ☐ | |
| 6. Ich habe mir das Bein gebrochen. | ☐ | ☐ | ☐ | |
| 7. Ich habe Probleme mit meinem Drucker gehabt. | ☐ | ☐ | ☐ | |
| 8. Meine Oma ist gestorben. | ☐ | ☐ | ☐ | |

## Freie Kommunikation

**Rollenspiel: Ausreden.** Spielen Sie die folgende Situation mit einem
Partner/einer Partnerin.

S1: Sie sind in einer Arbeitsgruppe, aber Sie haben gar nichts gemacht. Sie
müssen heute mit den anderen Studierenden in der Arbeitsgruppe sprechen.
Besprechen Sie mit ihnen so viele Ausreden wie möglich°.  ***so … :** as many excuses as possible*

S2: Sie sind auch in der Arbeitsgruppe. Stellen Sie viele Fragen über diese
Ausreden und versuchen° Sie eine gute Lösung° zu finden.  *try / solution*

## BRENNPUNKT KULTUR

### Universitätskurse

*Eine Physikvorlesung an der Uni Potsdam: Im Hörsaal gibt es kaum noch Sitzplätze.*

A lecture course (**die Vorlesung**), literally "reading to someone," is open to the public and may have as many as 600 students—most of them beginning students. In a **Vorlesung** a professor lectures on a specific topic, with a discussion section (**die Übung**) scheduled at a different time from the **Vorlesung.** In most **Vorlesungen** the professor reads aloud, either from notes or from books, and the students take notes or sometimes purchase the notes (**Skripten**) in a bookstore. There is little opportunity for interaction between students and teacher.

German students are introduced to the specifics of an academic discipline in an introductory seminar (**das Proseminar**), where they often form study groups (**Arbeitsgruppen**) and work together outside of class to prepare a group research paper for oral presentation in class (**das Gruppenreferat**). Completion of a **Vorlesung, Übung,** or a **Seminar** is verified by a graded certificate of completion (**der Schein**) and is recorded in a personal transcript book (**das Studienbuch**). After accumulating enough **Scheine** during their **Grundstudium,** students are admitted to the **Hauptstudium,** where they take advanced-level **Hauptseminare,** which concentrate on specific themes and topics. A seminar is intended for a small group of 15–25 students and allows for closer student-teacher interaction. However, in reality many seminars may have from 25 to 60 participants, more like a lecture.

■ **Kulturkreuzung** Haben Sie viele Vorlesungen? Wie finden Sie das, wenn der Professor oder die Professorin wortwörtlich° aus seinen oder ihren Notizen vorliest? Was machen viele Studierende? Welcher Kurs hat die meisten Studierenden? Wie viele sind das? Wo lernen Sie besser – in einer großen Vorlesung oder in einem kleinen Kurs? Warum?

*word for word*

---

**Proseminare 1**
**Dramen der frühen Goethezeit**                                    *G. Willems*
Proseminar zur Vorlesung „Einführung in die Literatur der Goethezeit"
Fr. 10.15 – 11.45 Uhr
C.-Zeiss-Str., SR 4.119

**Erzählprosa der Moderne**                                         *A. Urban*
Seminar zur Vorlesung „Klassische Moderne". Im Mittelpunkt stehen Erzählungen von Hofmannsthal, Heym, Döblin, Kafka, Benn, Robert Walser, Musil und Brecht.
Mi. 16.15 – 17.45 Uhr
C.-Zeiss-Str., SR 208

This information is from a typical university **Vorlesungsverzeichnis.**

## Strukturen und Vokabeln

### I  Talking about activities we do for ourselves

Reflexive verbs with accusative reflexive pronouns

#### A. Reflexive and non-reflexive usage of verbs

In both German and English, many action verbs may be followed by a direct object that refers to another person, animal, or object.

> Ich wasche **das Kind.**    *I wash/am washing the child.*

The direct object may also refer back to the subject of the sentence.

> Ich wasche **mich.**    *I wash/am washing myself.*

To describe activities people do for themselves, German speakers use a verb with a reflexive pronoun **(das Reflexivpronomen).** The reflexive pronoun refers back to the subject of the sentence, which is performing the action indicated by the verb. A verb that has a reflexive pronoun as the direct object is called a *reflexive verb* **(das Reflexivverb).** Many German verbs require a reflexive pronoun where in English the reflexive pronoun *self/selves* is never required.

> Ich ziehe **mich** an.    *I get/am getting (myself) dressed.*
> Karl rasiert **sich.**    *Karl shaves/is shaving (himself).*
> Ich fühle **mich** jetzt schon krank.    *I feel/am feeling sick already.*

Here are some more reflexive verbs from the previous **Anlauftext.**

> **sich erinnern** an *(to remember)*
>   Ich kann **mich** nicht daran **erinnern.**    *I can't remember it.*
> **sich entscheiden** für *(to decide on)*
>   Für welches Thema haben Sie **sich**
>   **entschieden?**    *Which topic did you decide on?*
> **sich fühlen** *(to feel)*
>   Ich **fühle mich** jetzt schon krank.    *I feel/am feeling sick already.*
> **sich hinlegen** *(to lie down)*
>   Ich muss **mich** unbedingt **hinlegen.**    *I absolutely have to lie down.*
> **sich melden** *(to report, get in touch)*
>   Schön, dass Sie **sich** endlich **melden.**    *It's good that you're finally getting in touch.*

Here are the accusative forms of the reflexive pronouns. Note that the only new reflexive pronoun you need to learn is **sich**.

| | Singular | | | | | | Plural | | | |
|---|---|---|---|---|---|---|---|---|---|---|
| | **1st** | **2nd** | | **3rd** | | | **1st** | | **2nd** | **3rd** |
| **Nom.** | ich | du | Sie | er | es | sie | wir | ihr | Sie | sie |
| **Acc.** | **mich** | **dich** | **sich** | **sich** | **sich** | **sich** | **uns** | **euch** | **sich** | **sich** |
| | *myself* | *yourself* | *yourself* | *himself/itself* | *itself* | *herself/itself* | *ourselves* | *yourselves* | *yourselves* | *themselves* |

## B. Verbs that always require a reflexive pronoun

At the beginning of this section you learned that some German verbs may or may not be used with a reflexive pronoun (e.g., **waschen** vs. **sich waschen**). Some German verbs and verb + preposition expressions always require a reflexive pronoun and cannot be used without one. You have already encountered a few of these reflexive verbs in this and earlier chapters.

| | |
|---|---|
| sich beeilen | *to hurry* |
| sich freuen auf | *to look forward to* |
| sich freuen über | *to be happy about* |
| sich konzentrieren auf | *to concentrate on* |
| sich verlieben in | *to fall in love with* |
| sich verloben mit | *to get engaged to* |
| sich trennen von | *to break up with, separate from* |

> Note that the reflexive pronouns look like direct object pronouns (**mich, dich**) except in the singular and plural forms of the 3rd person, and the 2nd person formal (**sich**).

> Verbs that require a reflexive pronoun appear in the *Vorsprung* vocabulary lists and glossary preceded by the reflexive pronoun **sich** (e.g., **sich beeilen**). In commercial dictionaries, these reflexive verbs are followed by the abbreviation *vr* (e.g., **beeilen** *vr*).

## C. Word order in sentences with reflexive pronouns

### 1. Statements
In main clauses, the reflexive pronoun follows the conjugated verb. When the noun subject and verb are transposed, the reflexive pronoun tends to precede the noun subject, but always follows a pronoun subject.

| | |
|---|---|
| Dr. Osswald <u>freut</u> **sich** auf das Referat. | *Dr. Osswald is looking forward to the oral presentation.* |
| Natürlich <u>freut</u> **sich** Dr. Osswald auf das Referat. | *Of course Dr. Osswald is looking forward to the oral presentation.* |
| Natürlich <u>freut</u> sie **sich** auf das Referat. | *Of course she is looking forward to the oral presentation.* |

In subordinate clauses, it precedes a noun subject but follows a pronoun subject.

| | |
|---|---|
| Ich glaube, dass **sich** <u>Dr. Osswald</u> auf das Referat freut. | *I believe that Dr. Osswald is looking forward to the oral presentation.* |
| Ich glaube, dass <u>sie</u> **sich** auf das Referat freut. | *I believe that she is looking forward to the oral presentation.* |

### 2. Questions
In questions, the reflexive pronoun can precede or follow a noun subject. If the subject is a pronoun, the reflexive pronoun must follow it immediately.

| | |
|---|---|
| Beeilt **sich** <u>Inge</u>? | *Is Inge hurrying up?* |
| Beeilt <u>Inge</u> **sich**? | *Is Inge hurrying up?* |
| Beeilt <u>sie</u> **sich**? | *Is she hurrying up?* |

**8** **In der Sprechstunde.** Barbara spricht mit ihrem Professor in seiner Sprechstunde. Schreiben Sie die richtigen Reflexivpronomen in die Lücken°.

*blanks*

PROFESSOR: Guten Tag, Frau Müller. Setzen Sie *sich* !

BARBARA: Danke schön.

PROFESSOR: Was kann ich für Sie tun?

BARBARA: Ich habe *mich* für das Examen im Dezember angemeldet und ich habe einige Fragen.

PROFESSOR: Dezember? Das überlegen° wir *uns* besser. Warum beeilen Sie *sich* so? Ist das nicht etwas früh?

*consider*

BARBARA: Ich glaube nicht. Ich habe *mich* schon für meine Schwerpunkte° entschieden.

*major topics*

PROFESSOR: Ja, wenn Sie meinen. Aber ich rate° Ihnen, konzentrieren Sie *sich* auf das Wichtigste, ja?

*advise*

BARBARA: Ja, natürlich. Ich freue *mich* eigentlich schon auf das Examen.

## Wissenswerte Vokabeln: die tägliche Routine
### Talking about your daily routine and personal hygiene

Volker bereitet sich auf den Tag vor.

Ich ziehe mich aus und dusche (mich).

Ich trockne mich ab.

Ich rasiere mich.

Ich ziehe mich an und beeile mich.

Sabine bereitet sich auf den Abend vor.

Sie badet.

Sie wäscht sich.

Sie trocknet sich ab.

Sie zieht sich an.

Sie schminkt sich.

Was machst du morgens?

**In der Sprechstunde.** Students at German universities sign up for graduation exams in their majors once they feel they are fully prepared. Depending on the degree they take and on the individual professor, they are often allowed to choose the topic of the exams.

**W. Vok.** Remember that the reflexive form (**mich**) refers back to the subject (**ich**) of the verb.

Remember that **waschen** is a stem-vowel changing verb.

**9**   **Am Morgen.**  In welcher Reihenfolge machen Sie diese Aktivitäten? Benutzen Sie die Zahlen 1 bis 7.

   ____ Ich trockne mich ab.
   ____ Ich ziehe mich an.
   ____ Ich dusche mich.
   ____ Ich stehe auf.
   ____ Ich beeile mich.
   ____ Ich rasiere mich.
   ____ Ich schminke mich.

**10**   **Was hast du heute schon gemacht?**  Sagen Sie, was Sie heute schon gemacht haben, und fragen Sie dann einen Partner/eine Partnerin.

   S1: *Ich habe mich heute schon rasiert. Und du?*
   S2: *Ich habe mich heute auch schon rasiert.* (oder)
       *Ich habe mich heute noch nicht rasiert.*

angezogen • ausgezogen • gebadet • geduscht • geschminkt • gewaschen • abgetrocknet • rasiert • beeilt • hingelegt • gesetzt

**11**   **Minidialog.**  Ingo wohnt in einer Wohngemeinschaft mit fünf anderen Studenten. Er ist gerade° aufgestanden und ist jetzt im Badezimmer.   *just*
Holger wohnt auch in der Wohngemeinschaft und möchte auch ins Badezimmer. Schreiben Sie das richtige Reflexivpronomen (**dich, mich**) in die Lücken. Lesen Sie dann den Dialog mit einem Partner/einer Partnerin.
   (Holger klopft an die Tür zum Badezimmer.)

      HOLGER:  Ingo, bist du's?
      INGO:  Ja.
      HOLGER:  Kannst du ____ beeilen? Ich muss ____ rasieren.
      INGO:  Du, zieh ____ erstmal an. Ich habe ____ gerade geduscht. Ich muss ____ noch abtrocknen.
      HOLGER:  Ich habe ____ schon angezogen. Ich muss ____ schnell waschen, denn ich muss in die Stadt.
      INGO:  Gut. Ich bin gleich fertig.

## *Wissenswerte Vokabeln: im Badezimmer*
### *Talking about bathroom objects*

**W. Vok.** Beware! There may not be a **Toilette** in the **Badezimmer.** If German speakers need to go to the bathroom, they say: **Ich muss auf die Toilette gehen.** In a more informal setting they may say: **Ich muss aufs Klo.**

| | | |
|---|---|---|
| Wo machst du das? | *Ich trockne mich im Badezimmer ab.* | |
| Womit° machst du das? | *Ich trockne mich mit dem Badetuch ab.* | *With what* |

**12**   **Was wollen sie machen?**  Erklären Sie, was Karl und Inge mit diesen Gegenständen im Badezimmer machen.

S1: *Was will Karl machen, wenn er den Rasierapparat hat?*
S2: *Er will sich rasieren.*

Was will Karl machen,

1. wenn er den Rasierapparat hat?
2. wenn er das Badetuch nimmt?
3. wenn er die Seife hält?
4. wenn er unter die Dusche geht?

Was will Inge machen,

5. wenn sie in den Spiegel schaut?
6. wenn sie in die Badewanne steigt?
7. wenn sie eine frische Bluse holt?

**13**   **Wo und womit macht man das?**  Erklären Sie, wo oder mit welchem Gegenstand im Badezimmer man diese Aktivitäten machen kann.

S1: *Wo kann man baden?*
S2: *In der Badewanne. Womit kann man sich waschen?*
S1: *Mit Seife.*

1. Wo kann man baden?
2. Wo kann man sich duschen?
3. Wo kann man sich rasieren?
4. Wo kann man Wasser trinken?
5. Wo kann man sich abtrocknen?
6. Wo kann man sich waschen?

## II Talking about daily hygiene routines

### Reflexive verbs with dative reflexive pronouns

You have already learned some of the reflexive verbs that German speakers use to talk about personal hygiene activities (e.g., **sich waschen, sich duschen, sich rasieren, sich anziehen, sich ausziehen**).

| | |
|---|---|
| Ich rasiere **mich.** | *I'm shaving.* |
| Hast du **dich** gewaschen? | *Did you wash (yourself)?* |
| Er zieht **sich** an. | *He's getting dressed.* |

When a part of the body (teeth, hair, legs, etc.) or an article of clothing (shirt, socks, coat, etc.) is specified, the reflexive pronoun is in the dative case and the direct object (the part of the body or clothing) is in the accusative case.

|   | *Dative* | | |
|---|---|---|---|
| Ich rasiere | **mir** | die Beine. | *I'm shaving my legs.* |
| Hast du | **dir** | die Hände gewaschen? | *Did you wash your hands?* |
| Er zieht | **sich** | die Jacke an. | *He's putting his jacket on.* |

Wir putzen **uns**
die Zähne.

Du rasierst **dir**
die Beine.

Sie wäscht **sich**
die Haare.

Er föhnt **sich**
die Haare.

Kämmst du **dir**
die Haare?

Habt ihr **euch** die
Haare gebürstet?

English speakers say *I'm combing my hair.* German avoids using possessive pronouns. Instead it uses the definite article along with a dative reflexive object: **Ich kämme *mir die Haare.***

A dative case reflexive pronoun may also designate the beneficiary of actions other than grooming.

| | |
|---|---|
| Ich backe **mir** einen Kuchen. | *I'm baking a cake for myself.* |
| Er hat **sich** einen BMW gekauft. | *He bought himself a BMW.* |
| Mach **dir** keine Sorgen. | *Don't worry (yourself).* |

Here are the dative forms of the reflexive pronouns.

| | Singular | | | | | | Plural | | | |
| --- | --- | --- | --- | --- | --- | --- | --- | --- | --- | --- |
| | **1st** | **2nd** | | **3rd** | | | **1st** | **2nd** | | **3rd** |
| **Nom.** | ich | du | Sie | er | es | sie | wir | ihr | Sie | sie |
| **Acc.** | mich | dich | sich | sich | sich | sich | uns | euch | sich | sich |
| **Dat.** | **mir** | **dir** | **sich** | **sich** | **sich** | **sich** | **uns** | **euch** | **sich** | **sich** |
| | *myself* | *yourself* | *yourself* | *himself/itself* | *itself* | *herself/itself* | *ourselves* | *yourselves* | *yourselves* | *themselves* |

**14** **Am Morgen.** In welcher Reihenfolge machen Sie diese Aktivitäten? Benutzen Sie die Zahlen 1 bis 10.

____ Ich kämme (bürste) mir die Haare.
____ Ich stehe auf.
____ Ich putze mir die Zähne.
____ Ich ziehe mich an.
____ Ich föhne mir die Haare.
____ Ich gehe aufs Klo.
____ Ich setze mich hin und frühstücke.
____ Ich rasiere mich. (Ich schminke mich.)
____ Ich wasche mir die Haare.
____ Ich dusche (bade).

> Note that the only dative reflexive forms that are different from the accusative forms are those for **ich** (**mich** vs. **mir**) and **du** (**dich** vs. **dir**). All other reflexive pronouns are identical in the accusative and dative.

**15** **Was haben Sie heute gemacht?** Sagen Sie, was Sie heute gemacht haben, und fragen Sie dann einen Partner/eine Partnerin.

S1: *Ich habe mir heute die Zähne geputzt. Und du?*
S2: *Ja, ich habe mir heute auch die Zähne geputzt.* (oder)
    *Nein, ich habe mir die Zähne noch nicht geputzt.*

die Zähne geputzt • geduscht • die Haare gewaschen • die Haare geföhnt •
die Haare gekämmt • die Haare gebürstet • die Beine rasiert • die Hände
gewaschen • (eine lange Hose) angezogen

**16** **Barbaras Morgen.** Barbara macht jeden Morgen immer dasselbe! Schreiben Sie die richtigen Reflexivpronomen (**mich** oder **mir**) in die Lücken.

Ich stehe jeden Morgen um 7.00 Uhr auf. Zuerst gehe ich auf die Toilette. Dann
ziehe ich _____ aus und steige in die Dusche. Heute ist Freitag und ich wasche
_____ die Haare. Dann trockne ich _____ ab und föhne _____ die Haare. Dann
ziehe ich _____ an. Meistens° ziehe ich _____ Jeans und ein T-Shirt an. Dann    *most of the time*
kämme ich _____ die Haare und ich putze _____ die Zähne. Jetzt muss ich _____
beeilen. Schließlich° gehe ich in die Küche und mache _____ schnell Frühstück.    *finally*

**17    Wie oft machst du das?** Kreuzen Sie mit **x** an, wie oft Sie diese Aktivitäten machen. Fragen Sie dann einen Partner/eine Partnerin, wie oft er/sie das macht, und markieren Sie das mit einem Haken (✓). Benutzen Sie diese Informationen in der **Schreibecke** auf Seite 299.

■ sich die Haare waschen

S1: *Wie oft wäschst du dir die Haare?*
S2: *Ich wasche mir einmal am Tag die Haare.*

| | Zweimal am Tag | Einmal am Tag | Alle zwei Tage | Einmal die Woche | Nie |
|---|---|---|---|---|---|
| 1. sich die Haare waschen | ☐☐ | ☐☐ | ☐☐ | ☐☐ | ☐☐ |
| 2. sich die Haare föhnen | ☐☐ | ☐☐ | ☐☐ | ☐☐ | ☐☐ |
| 3. sich anziehen | ☐☐ | ☐☐ | ☐☐ | ☐☐ | ☐☐ |
| 4. sich ausziehen | ☐☐ | ☐☐ | ☐☐ | ☐☐ | ☐☐ |
| 5. sich die Zähne putzen | ☐☐ | ☐☐ | ☐☐ | ☐☐ | ☐☐ |
| 6. sich duschen | ☐☐ | ☐☐ | ☐☐ | ☐☐ | ☐☐ |
| 7. baden | ☐☐ | ☐☐ | ☐☐ | ☐☐ | ☐☐ |
| 8. sich die Haare bürsten | ☐☐ | ☐☐ | ☐☐ | ☐☐ | ☐☐ |
| 9. sich die Haare kämmen | ☐☐ | ☐☐ | ☐☐ | ☐☐ | ☐☐ |
| 10. sich rasieren | ☐☐ | ☐☐ | ☐☐ | ☐☐ | ☐☐ |
| 11. sich schminken | ☐☐ | ☐☐ | ☐☐ | ☐☐ | ☐☐ |

**18    Ja, aber was brauche ich?** Sie sind im Badezimmer. Sie wissen, was Sie wollen, aber Sie haben nicht den Gegenstand, den Sie brauchen. Ihr Partner/Ihre Partnerin hilft Ihnen mit einer Frage.

■ sich das Gesicht waschen

S1: *Ich will mir das Gesicht waschen.*
S2: *Brauchst du die Seife?*
S1: *Ja, bitte.*

1. sich das Gesicht waschen
2. sich abtrocknen
3. sich die Haare trocknen
4. sich rasieren
5. sich die Hände waschen
6. sich die Zähne putzen
7. sich die Haare waschen
8. sich die Haare bürsten

Hair dryers and electric razors sold in North America may not work in Europe, where the plugs are different and the circuits are 220 volts and not 120 volts. A voltage converter and an adapter plug are needed to use a North American appliance in Europe.

**19    Was wollen sie damit machen?** Bilden Sie Sätze mit einem Reflexivverb.

■ Inge / den Föhn in der Hand halten

S1: *Inge hält den Föhn in der Hand. Was will sie damit machen?*
S2: *Sie will sich die Haare föhnen.*

1. Inge / den Föhn in der Hand halten
2. Oliver / den Kamm in der Hand halten
3. Annegret / die Zahnbürste haben
4. Michael / den Rasierapparat haben
5. Gudrun / das Shampoo haben
6. Werner / die Seife halten
7. Monika / den Rasierapparat haben

8. Torsten / das Badetuch haben
9. Liselotte / den Taschenspiegel und den Lippenstift in der Hand halten
10. Jens / die Haarbürste haben

  **F r e i e   K o m m u n i k a t i o n**

**Rollenspiel: Ein Badezimmer teilen.**  Sie wohnen mit vier Personen in einem Haus mit nur einem Badezimmer. Zu viele Leute wollen das Badezimmer zur gleichen Zeit benutzen. Formulieren Sie einen Plan für die Benutzung des Badezimmers. Benutzen Sie Ausdrücke aus der Liste.

Um wie viel Uhr? • Wann? • Von wann bis wann? • Wie oft? • Wie lange? • baden • duschen • sich die Haare waschen • sich die Zähne putzen • sich rasieren • sich die Haare föhnen • sich schminken

  **S c h r e i b e c k e**

**Studenten am Morgen.**  Schreiben Sie mit den Informationen, die Sie in Aktivität 17 gesammelt haben, einen kurzen Absatz° über das Morgenritual von Ihrem Partner/Ihrer Partnerin. Benutzen Sie den Text in Aktivität 16 als Beispiel.

*paragraph*

## *Wissenswerte Vokabeln: krank sein*
### *Talking about illnesses*

Ich habe Fieber. Meine Temperatur ist über 38 Grad.

Ich habe mich in den Finger geschnitten. Ich brauche ein Heftpflaster.

Ich habe mir das Bein gebrochen. Ich habe einen Gips.

Ich lege mich hin. Ich liege im Bett. Ich ruhe mich aus. Ich erhole mich.

Ich fühle mich nicht wohl.

Ich muss mich übergeben.

Ich habe Durchfall.

Ich habe (einen) Muskelkater.

**Freie Kommunikation.** A useful reflexive verb for conversation is **sich etwas vorstellen** (*to imagine something*): **Das kann ich mir nicht vorstellen.** (*I can't imagine that.*) Don't confuse this with **sich vorstellen** (*to introduce oneself*): **Darf ich mich vorstellen? Mein Name ist (Müller).**

**Schreibecke.** To prepare for this writing assignment, ask your partner about his/her daily habits and find out in what order your partner does them: **Was machst du zuerst? Und dann?**

36.6°C is considered normal body temperature.

**W. Vok. Ich muss mich erbrechen.** (*I have to throw up.*) **Ich muss kotzen.** (*I have to throw up.*) (*vulgar*)

Ich habe Zahn-
schmerzen. Mein
Zahn tut mir weh.

Ich habe Hals-
schmerzen. Mein
Hals tut mir weh.

Ich habe Kopf-
schmerzen. Mein
Kopf tut mir weh.

Ich nehme
Schmerztabletten.

Ich habe mich erkältet. Ich habe eine
Erkältung. Ich habe (einen) Schnupfen.

Wie geht's dir? – Mir geht es so lala.
Wie fühlst du dich? – Mir ist/geht es
ziemlich schlecht. – Gute Besserung!

■ Wie geht es dir?    *Ich habe eine Erkältung.*

**20** **Ursache° und Wirkung.°** Bilden Sie Sätze, die Ursache und    *cause / effect*
Wirkung beschreiben.

1. Wer Zahnschmerzen hat,
2. Wer Kopfschmerzen hat,
3. Wer zu viel Sport treibt,
4. Wer sich in den Finger schneidet,
5. Wer im Winter im Meer schwimmen geht,
6. Wer zu viel Alkohol trinkt,

   a. bekommt am nächsten Tag
     einen Muskelkater.
   b. braucht ein Heftpflaster.
   c. muss sich übergeben.
   d. soll eine Schmerztablette
     nehmen.
   e. soll zum Zahnarzt° gehen.    *dentist*
   f. wird sich erkälten.

**21** **Studentenkrankheiten.** Kann ein Deutschstudium krank
machen? Diese Studenten/Studentinnen behaupten° es jedenfalls°. Besprechen Sie    *claim / in any case*
mit einem Partner/einer Partnerin, wie sich die Kommilitonen und
Kommilitoninnen fühlen. Dann erklären Sie, was sie jetzt machen sollen.

   Augenschmerzen • Bauchschmerzen • Handgelenkschmerzen° •    ***das Handgelenk:*** *wrist*
   Kopfschmerzen • Ohrenschmerzen

■ S1: *John hat die ganze Nacht ohne viel Licht sein Deutschbuch gelesen.*
   S2: *Und wie fühlt er sich jetzt?*
   S1: *Er hat Augenschmerzen. Ihm tun die Augen weh. Jetzt legt er sich hin und
      ruht sich aus.*

1. John hat die ganze Nacht ohne viel Licht sein Deutschbuch gelesen.
2. Susie hat das ganze Wochenende intensiv gelernt. Jetzt ist ihr ganz heiß und sie kann sich nicht konzentrieren. Sie nimmt Aspirin.
3. Daniel war den ganzen Samstag im Sprachlabor° und hat sich Deutsch-CDs angehört, bis er nicht mehr konnte°.
4. Philip hat morgen ein Referat und ist ziemlich nervös. Er kaut° an seinen Fingernägeln, isst Chips, Salzstangen° und Nüsse° und trinkt viel.
5. Joan hat die Nacht beim Tippen° am Computer durchgemacht und hat gerade ihr Referat mit 30 Seiten abgegeben.

*language laboratory*

*nicht ... : couldn't any more / chews*

*pretzel sticks / nuts*

*typing*

**22** **Was ist passiert?** Ein Freund/Eine Freundin beklagt sich°. Was ist wahrscheinlich passiert? Stellen Sie Fragen. Wechseln Sie sich ab°.

*beklagt sich: is complaining*

*Wechseln ... : Switch roles*

S1: *Ich habe Schmerztabletten genommen.*
S2: *Hast du Kopfschmerzen gehabt?*
S1: *Ja, ich habe Kopfschmerzen gehabt.*

sich den Arm gebrochen • sich in den Finger geschnitten • Durchfall/ Kopfschmerzen/Zahnschmerzen/einen Muskelkater gehabt • sich erkältet • sich ausgeruht

1. Ich habe Schmerztabletten genommen.
2. Ich habe jetzt einen Gips am Arm.
3. Ich trage jetzt ein Heftpflaster am Finger.
4. Ich komme von der Massage zurück und fühle mich nicht mehr so steif°.
5. Ich komme von der Toilette zurück, aber der Bauch tut mir noch weh.
6. Der Zahnarzt hat mir einen Weisheitszahn° gezogen.
7. Ich brauche ein Taschentuch°.
8. Ich bin nicht mehr müde.

*stiff*

*wisdom tooth*
*tissue*

**23** **Wie fühlst du dich, wenn...?** Wann fühlen Sie sich nicht wohl? Kreuzen Sie Ihre Antworten an. Fragen Sie dann einen Partner/eine Partnerin.

S1: *Ich fühle mich nicht wohl, wenn ich zu viel Alkohol trinke. Und du?*
S2: *Ich fühle mich auch nicht wohl, wenn ich zu viel Alkohol trinke.* (oder) *Ich fühle mich nicht wohl, wenn ich zu viel esse. Wie fühlst du dich, wenn du zu viel isst?*

| | Ich | Partner(in) |
|---|---|---|
| Ich fühle mich nicht wohl, | | |
| 1. wenn ich zu viel Alkohol trinke. | ☐ | ☐ |
| 2. wenn ich zu viel esse. | ☐ | ☐ |
| 3. wenn ich eine Prüfung in Physik habe. | ☐ | ☐ |
| 4. wenn ich sehr früh° aufstehen muss. | ☐ | ☐ |
| 5. wenn ich mit meinem Professor sprechen muss. | ☐ | ☐ |
| 6. wenn ich am Telefon Deutsch sprechen muss. | ☐ | ☐ |
| 7. wenn ich täglich das Essen in der Mensa essen muss. | ☐ | ☐ |
| 8. wenn ich ... | ☐ | ☐ |

*early*

### Freie Kommunikation

**Rollenspiel: Den Notarzt° anrufen.**  Spielen Sie die folgende Situation mit einem Partner/einer Partnerin.                    *emergency room doctor*

S1:  Sie sind sehr krank. Es ist Samstag. Rufen Sie Dr. Meiser, den Notarzt/die Notärztin, an und beschreiben Sie ihm/ihr Ihre Symptome. Sagen Sie auch, was Sie gemacht haben, bevor Sie diese Symptome bekommen haben.

S2:  Sie sind Dr. Meiser. Ein Patient/Eine Patientin ruft an. Es ist Samstag und Sie wollen heute nicht ins Büro kommen. Er/Sie ist sehr krank. Fragen Sie, wie er/sie sich fühlt, was er/sie gemacht hat und warum er/sie diese Symptome hat. Geben Sie auch ein paar Tipps. Beginnen Sie das Telefongespräch wie folgt.

> DR. MEISER:  *Dr. Meiser. Guten Tag.*
> PATIENT(IN):  *Guten Tag. Hier ist ...*

### Schreibecke

**Eine Entschuldigung.**  Schreiben Sie eine Entschuldigung° an Ihren    *excuse*
Dozenten/Ihre Dozentin. Sie sollen heute ein Referat halten, aber es ist noch nicht fertig. Schreiben Sie, dass Sie sehr krank sind und nicht kommen können. Beschreiben Sie drei Symptome und warum Sie diese Symptome haben.

## Absprungtext     Die beste Uni für mich

Wer in Deutschland studieren will, muss zuerst auf dem Gymnasium° ein großes     *college preparatory high*
Examen, das Abitur, schriftlich sowie mündlich ablegen°. Die Noten auf dem „Abi"     *school / pass*
bestimmen, was und wo man studieren darf. Nach dem Abi kann man sich an verschiedenen Unis bewerben°.                                                  *sich bewerben: to apply*

Für manche jungen Leute sind das Furcht erregende° Fragen: Was will ich     *Furcht ...: frightening*
studieren? Wo soll ich studieren? College-Berater wie in den USA gibt es nicht. Man muss allein Informationen sammeln° und hoffen, man hat die richtige Universität     *gather*
und das richtige Fach ausgewählt°. Wie trifft man so eine wichtige Entscheidung°?     *chosen / decision*
Im folgenden Text erzählt Jessie, eine junge Abiturientin°, von ihrer Reise durch die     **ein Mädchen, das das**
deutsche Uni-Landschaft.                                                             **Abitur ablegen muss**

## *Vorschau*

**24** **Thematische Fragen.** Beantworten Sie die folgenden Fragen auf Deutsch.

1. An wie vielen Universitäten (Colleges) haben Sie sich beworben?
2. Warum studieren Sie an dieser Universität? Nennen Sie drei wichtige Faktoren.
3. Haben Sie ein Hauptfach? Wenn ja, wann haben Sie gewusst, dass Sie sich für dieses Fach interessieren? im ersten Jahr? später?
4. Wie früh sollen Studierende ihr Hauptfach wählen: in der Schule? im ersten Jahr an der Uni? später?
5. Wie sind die Professoren/Professorinnen und die Studierenden an Ihrer Uni?
6. Ist Ihre Unistadt für Studierende interessant? Was kann man da in der Freizeit machen?

**25** **Meine ideale Universität.** Wie wichtig waren Ihnen die folgenden Faktoren, als Sie eine Universität oder ein College gesucht haben?

|  | *Sehr wichtig* | *Mittelwichtig* | *Unwichtig* | |
|---|---|---|---|---|
| 1. ein gutes Ranking in meinem Fach | ☐ | ☐ | ☐ | |
| 2. niedrige Studiengebühren° | ☐ | ☐ | ☐ | *niedrige ...: low tuition* |
| 3. die Stadt | ☐ | ☐ | ☐ | |
| 4. eine gute Bibliothek | ☐ | ☐ | ☐ | |
| 5. gute und nette Professoren | ☐ | ☐ | ☐ | |
| 6. zufriedene Studierende | ☐ | ☐ | ☐ | |
| 7. leichte Vorlesungen und Seminare | ☐ | ☐ | ☐ | |
| 8. ein interessantes Sozialleben auf dem Campus | ☐ | ☐ | ☐ | |
| 9. eine gute Mensa | ☐ | ☐ | ☐ | |
| 10. bequeme° und moderne Wohnheime | ☐ | ☐ | ☐ | *comfortable* |
| 11. die Sportmannschaften | ☐ | ☐ | ☐ | |
| 12. Multikulturalismus | ☐ | ☐ | ☐ | |

---

**Sprache im Alltag:  Studieren vs. lernen**

German distinguishes clearly between **Schule** (*primary or secondary school*) and **Universität** (*post-secondary*) and between **Schüler/Schülerin** (*school pupil*) and **Student/Studentin** (*university/college student*). In recent years it has become commonplace to refer to college students as **der/die Studierende** in the singular, and **Studierende/die Studierenden** in the plural, thus avoiding the necessity to specify masculine or feminine in the plural. North American *high school* is called **Oberschule** in German, while German **Hochschule** refers to a post-secondary institution and not *high school.*

   The German verb **studieren** refers to university and college studies only and never secondary studies. **Lernen** refers to the acquisition of skills, e.g., **Ich lerne Deutsch** (*I'm studying German* [*for a test tomorrow, in high school, in preparation for my trip to Germany, etc*]). The statement **Ich studiere Deutsch** implies a much more advanced study of the German language, literature, and culture and usually implies that one is majoring in the field.

BRENNPUNKT KULTUR

## GESAMTWERTUNG

**Rangplätze in den Einzelfächern**
● Spitzengruppe  ● Mittelfeld  ● Schlussgruppe

Legend for cells below: **G** = Spitzengruppe (grün), **M** = Mittelfeld (gelb), **S** = Schlussgruppe (rot)

| GESAMTERGEBNIS RANG | UNIVERSITÄT | PUNKTZAHL | Betriebswirtschaft | Chemie | Germanistik | Informatik | Maschinenbau | Medizin | Politologie | Psychologie |
|---|---|---|---|---|---|---|---|---|---|---|
| 1 | München, TU | 3,0 | G | G | | | G | G | | |
| 2 | Freiburg, U | 2,9 | | G | G | G | | G | G | G |
| 3 | Leipzig, U | 2,7 | M | G | | | | G | G | G |
| 4 | Berlin, Humboldt-U | 2,6 | M | S | G | M | | G | G | M |
| 4 | Konstanz, U | 2,6 | | G | G | M | | | G | G |
| 4 | München, U | 2,6 | G | G | G | G | | G | G | M |
| 7 | Heidelberg, U | 2,5 | | G | G | G | | G | M | M |
| 7 | Stuttgart, U | 2,5 | G | M | S | G | G | | M | |
| 7 | Tübingen, U | 2,5 | M | G | M | M | | G | M | S |
| 10 | Augsburg, U | 2,4 | G | | M | | | | S | |
| 10 | Mannheim, U | 2,4 | G | | | S | | | M | |
| 12 | Kaiserslautern, TU | 2,3 | G | M | | M | G | | | |
| 12 | Würzburg, U | 2,3 | M | G | | M | | M | M | M |
| 14 | Jena, U | 2,2 | G | G | G | G | | M | M | M |
| 14 | Münster, U | 2,2 | G | G | G | G | | G | M | M |
| 16 | Berlin, FU | 2,1 | S | M | M | M | | G | G | M |
| 16 | Bonn, U | 2,1 | M | M | M | G | | G | M | M |
| 16 | Darmstadt, TU | 2,1 | | M | M | G | G | | | |
| 16 | Dresden, TU | 2,1 | M | M | M | M | M | S | M | |
| 16 | Marburg, U | 2,1 | M | G | M | M | | M | S | S |
| 16 | Regensburg, U | 2,1 | M | M | M | | | M | S | M |
| 16 | Saarbrücken, U | 2,1 | S | G | | M | | M | M | S |
| 23 | Chemnitz, TU | 2,0 | G | | | M | | | M | M |
| 24 | Erlangen-Nürnberg, U | 1,9 | G | S | M | M | | S | S | M |
| 25 | Göttingen, U | 1,8 | M | S | M | | | M | M | M |
| 25 | Köln, U | 1,8 | M | S | M | | | M | M | M |
| 25 | Mainz, U | 1,8 | M | M | M | | | M | M | M |
| 25 | Trier, U | 1,8 | M | | M | S | | G | M | |
| 29 | Aachen, TH | 1,6 | M | S | S | M | S | | | M |
| 29 | Bremen, U | 1,6 | M | S | M | S | | | M | |
| 29 | Kiel, U | 1,6 | M | S | M | M | | M | M | S |
| 32 | Berlin, TU | 1,5 | M | S | M | S | S | | | S |
| 32 | Braunschweig, TU | 1,5 | M | S | M | S | M | | S | |
| 32 | Frankfurt a. M., U | 1,5 | S | M | M | M | | M | S | S |
| 32 | Hamburg, U | 1,5 | S | S | G | M | | S | G | S |

*Im Ranking von **Spiegel-Special** gilt die Technische Universität München als die beste Universität Deutschlands.*

## Das deutsche Universitätssystem

The well-respected German system of higher education is undergoing change as more and more **Abiturienten** enter the university. To limit the number of students to the number of university places (**Studienplätze**) available, the universities have established maximum enrollments (**Numerus clausus**, literally *closed number*) in many high-demand subject areas, such as business, medicine, dentistry, and biology. Selection for these spots depends on grade point average (**der Notendurchschnitt**), exam grade on the **Abitur** (**das Abiturergebnis**), recommendations, interviews, and even lotteries. Applicants submit their credentials to a central clearing-house, **die Zentralstelle für die Vergabe von Studienplätzen (ZVS)** in Dortmund, which assesses their academic record. Those who are denied admission to a **Numerus clausus** program may be redirected to a different major or sometimes to available places in that same major at another university. Some universities do accept a few students directly, without involvement of the **ZVS**.

Passing the **Abitur** signals the completion of a German student's liberal arts education. By and large, there are no general education requirements at German universities. First-year students typically begin taking classes in their majors—for example, business administration, law, medicine—in their first semester at college. Once students have taken the required courses and feel prepared, they can sign up for qualifying exams in their subject, often collaborating with the instructor to determine examination topics. The average German student spends 12 semesters (6 years) at the university. Students are discouraged from exceeding the maximum study time by means of a hefty penalty fee. Students can earn a master's degree (**Magister**), a **Diplom** in an area of specialization, or the **Staatsexamen**, which qualifies the graduate for employment in public service, for example in teaching or in law practice. Thereafter, students may continue their studies through the doctoral and even post-doctoral level.

Globalization and the need for standardization within the European Union have prompted German universities to introduce 3- to 4-year bachelor's-degree programs and an internationally recognized master's-degree program by 2010. However, these programs have met with resistance from some professors, who feel they downgrade education. Ultimately, these degrees should provide German students with more career options internationally.

■ **Kulturkreuzung** Deutsche Studierende müssen keine allgemeinbildenden° Kurse belegen, denn sie haben das meiste schon in der Schule gehabt. Wie finden Sie das? Möchten Sie an der Uni nur Kurse in Ihrem Hauptfach machen und dafür schon an der *High School* schwierige allgemeinbildende Kurse machen? Welches System finden Sie besser? Warum?

*general education*

## Lesestrategien: „Die beste Uni für mich"

Benutzen Sie die Lesestrategien aus **Kapitel 7,** um den Text „Die beste Uni für mich" zu verstehen.

**26  Den Kontext verstehen.** Finden Sie im Text Antworten auf die folgenden Fragen.

1. Was sind die Namen von drei Universitätsstädten in Deutschland?
2. Woher kommt Jessie?
3. Wie alt ist Jessie?
4. Was möchte sie studieren – Soziologie, Psychologie oder Englisch?

**27  Neue Wörter lernen: Erster Versuch.** „Die beste Uni für mich" handelt von Jessie, einer Schülerin, die eine Universität auswählen muss. Können Sie die Bedeutung von den folgenden Ausdrücken erraten°?

*guess*

1. die Abiturientin
2. das Fachwissen
3. der Lehrstuhl
4. das Praktikum (*pl.* Praktika)
5. die Studiendauer
6. sich einschreiben
7. Professoren und Studenten empfehlen die Uni.

**28    Neue Wörter lernen: Drei Strategien.** Erraten Sie die fett gedruckten Wörter mit Hilfe von den drei folgenden Strategien. Beantworten Sie die Fragen.

*Weltwissen*

1. „Nur noch wenige Monate bis zur **Einschreibung.** Der Countdown läuft.“

   Neue Studierende an einer Universität müssen sich einschreiben, bevor sie offiziell studieren dürfen. Was ist wohl die **Einschreibung**?

2. „Professoren und Studenten empfehlen die Uni, die **Studiendauer** ist kurz und die **Ausstattung** top.“

   • Die **Studiendauer** kann lang oder kurz sein. Was kann lang oder kurz sein: Geld? Zeit? Fächer?
   • Eine Universität braucht gute und neue Gegenstände im Labor, im Hörsaal und im Wohnheim. Was gehört wohl zur **Ausstattung**: die Professoren oder die Zimmer?

3. „Nicht nur Jessie reist mit dem Ranking im Rucksack. Immer mehr Abiturienten orientieren sich an den **Ergebnissen**.“

   Jessie, wie viele Abiturienten/Abiturientinnen, wählt ihre Universität mit Hilfe vom Ranking in der Zeitschrift *stern*. Sind Ergebnisse Resultate oder Geschenke?

4. „Wie gut ist die **Betreuung** durch die Professoren?“

   Professoren unterrichten und halten Vorlesungen, aber sie sprechen auch mit Studierenden und helfen ihnen. Sie geben ihnen Tipps, Informationen und Ratschläge. Was heißt **Betreuung**?

5. „Welche Spezialisierungen gibt es am **Lehrstuhl**?“

   Deutsche Universitäten haben Lehrstühle. Das sind keine richtigen Sitzplätze. Wer besitzt° einen Lehrstuhl an einer Uni: ein Professor oder ein Student?    *has*

*Wortformen*

1. „Die 20-Jährige hat sich nach dem Abi ein Jahr **Auszeit** genommen um nachzudenken.“

   Nach dreizehn Jahren Schule ist man oft müde. **Auszeit** = **aus** + **Zeit.** Was hat Jessie wahrscheinlich ein Jahr lang nach der Schule gemacht? Warum?

2. „Eigentlich hatte Jessie gar **keine große Lust ...**“

   Das Wort **Lust** im Deutschen ist neutral und nicht stigmatisiert wie im Englischen. Hat Jessie viel oder wenig Interesse?

3. „ Ein Studium ist keine **Einbahnstraße.** “

   Städte haben Einbahnstraßen (**ein** + **Bahn** + **Straße**), d.h. alle Autos fahren in die gleiche Richtung°. Wie ist das Studium für viele Leute? Kann man die Richtung wechseln°?    *direction*
   *change*

4. „Und oft sind **Praktika** viel wichtiger für den **Berufseinstieg** als irgend-welches **Fachwissen**."

- Ein Universitätsstudium kann sehr theoretisch sein. Das, was man studiert, heißt „Fach". Ist Fachwissen (**Fach** + **wissen**) spezialisiertes oder generelles Wissen?

- Viele Studierende arbeiten im Sommer, um Geld zu verdienen, aber nicht jede Sommerarbeit ist ein Praktikum. Was bedeutet wohl ein **Praktikum**?

- Nach dem Studium muss man sicher praktisch sein und Geld verdienen. Ist der **Berufseinstieg** der Beginn von einem neuen Job oder der Beginn von Freizeit?

*Kontext*

1. „Nur noch wenige Monate bis zur Einschreibung. Der Countdown läuft. Bald **geht** das Leben richtig **los,** bald kommt die große Freiheit."

   Schüler meinen oft, dass sie kein richtiges Leben haben, wenn sie bei ihren Eltern wohnen. Meint Jessie, dass ihr Leben erst mit dem Studium anfängt oder endet? Was bedeutet **losgehen**?

2. „Nach zwölf oder dreizehn vorgezeichneten° Jahren sollen sie plötzlich **selbst entscheiden,** was zu ihnen passt. Von der Schule dürfen sie dabei keine Hilfe erwarten."    *geplant, unflexibel*

   Auf der Schule sagen die Eltern und die Lehrer, was ein Kind machen soll. Wer sagt, was man machen soll, wenn man an die Uni geht? Was heißt **selbst entscheiden**?

3. „Ich will mit so vielen Menschen wie möglich reden, um mir am Ende aus vielen Meinungen und Ansichten die eigene Wahrheit zu **basteln**."

   Was heißt **basteln**: finden? machen? vergessen?

4. „Weiter nach Jena. In der thüringischen Stadt fühlt sich Jessie gleich **wohl**. Jessie ist **beeindruckt** von der Vielfalt° des Faches Psychologie."    *great variety*

   - Hat das Fach Psychologie einen positiven oder negativen Einfluss° auf    *influence*
     Jessie? Was heißt **beeindruckt**?
   - Ist Jessie zufrieden oder nicht in Jena? Was heißt **wohl**?

5. „Berlin ist Jessies Lieblingsstadt; Passau und Jena haben im Ranking **gut abgeschnitten**. "

   Wenn eine Uni unter anderen Unis **gut abschneidet**, hält man sie für eine gute oder eine nicht so gute Uni?

FRIEDRICH-SCHILLER-UNIVERSITÄT JENA
Akademisches Auslandsamt
Fürstengraben 1
D-07743 JENA

**29** **Wichtige Wörter finden: Deutsche Umgangssprache°.** Erraten Sie die Bedeutung von den folgenden Wörtern in den Ausdrücken von jungen Studierenden.

*slang, colloquial language*

1. Der **Countdown** läuft.
   a. die letzte Phase
   b. die erste Phase

2. Nie mehr **büffeln**, was der Lehrplan vorschreibt°.
   a. kurz vor einer Prüfung intensiv lernen
   b. durch das ganze Semester diszipliniert lernen

   *stipulates*

3. Passau ist **ein Flop**.
   a. sehr gut
   b. sehr schlecht

4. Das Essen schmeckt **fade**.
   a. sehr interessant
   b. sehr uninteressant

5. Den Leuten fehlt° der **Pep**.
   a. die Energie
   b. die Müdigkeit

   *is lacking*

6. Sie findet es hier **spießig**.
   a. zu progressiv
   b. zu konservativ

7. Sie findet die Hauptstadt **klasse**.
   a. sehr gut
   b. sehr schlecht

## Absprungtext
### Die beste Uni für mich

Lesen Sie jetzt den Text.

Nur noch wenige Monate bis zur Einschreibung. Der Countdown läuft. Bald geht das Leben richtig los, bald kommt die große Freiheit. Ausziehen, weggehen, sich jeden Tag neu erfinden°! Nie mehr büffeln, was der Lehrplan vorschreibt – endlich lesen, denken, ausprobieren°, was einen wirklich interessiert. Jessie, Abiturientin aus München, freut sich auf „wilde Diskussionen und neue Lebenswelten". Sie möchte „was mit Menschen machen". Sicher weiß sie nur eins: Sie will studieren. Die große Freiheit – für viele Abiturienten ist sie erst mal eine große Zumutung°. Nach zwölf oder dreizehn vorgezeichneten Jahren sollen sie plötzlich selbst entscheiden, was zu ihnen passt. Von der Schule dürfen sie dabei keine Hilfe erwarten.

*sich neu erfinden: to reinvent oneself / to try out*

*burden*

> **Lieblingsstadt.** The prefix **Lieblings-** may be attached to any noun and means *favorite*: **meine Lieblingsstadt** *my favorite city*, **mein Lieblingsbuch** *my favorite book.*

„Ich will mit so vielen Menschen wie möglich reden, um mir am Ende aus vielen Meinungen und Ansichten die eigene Wahrheit zu basteln", sagt Jessie. Die 20-Jährige hat sich nach dem Abi ein Jahr Auszeit genommen, um nachzudenken. Eine Uni-Hopping-Tour soll Klarheit bringen. Passau, Jena, Berlin: Die Route bestimmen° Jessies Studienwünsche – und das Hochschulranking von *stern* und CHE (Centrum für Hochschulentwicklung), das größte und fundierteste Ranking, das jemals in Deutschland erhoben wurde°. Berlin ist Jessies Lieblingsstadt; Passau und Jena haben im Ranking gut abgeschnitten°. Jessie will sich in Vorlesungen und Seminare setzen, Professoren und Studenten befragen und natürlich auch Mensa und Nachtleben testen.

*determine*

*jemals erhoben wurde: was ever conducted / haben gut abgeschnitten: fared well*

Passau ist ein Flop. Beim Ranking im Fach Betriebswirtschaft schneidet die Passauer Uni gut ab°: zufriedene Studenten, schnelles Studium. Dafür steht man an der Mensa lange an°, das Essen schmeckt fade, und auch den Leuten fehlt der

*gut abschneiden: to place well*

*steht ... an: stand in line*

*Am Haupteingang der Humboldt-Universität zu Berlin*

Pep, findet Jessie. Die Jungs da drüben tragen alle rosa Hemden. Und die Mädchen neben ihnen, mit Stöckelschuhen° und Seidentüchern° – wie ihre eigenen Großmütter. Jessie schüttelt sich°. Irgendwie findet sie es hier eng°, spießig, konservativ.

*high-heel shoes*
*silk scarves*
***schüttelt ... :*** *shakes herself*
*narrow*

Weiter nach Jena. In der thüringischen Stadt fühlt sich Jessie gleich wohl. Jessie ist beeindruckt von der Vielfalt des Faches Psychologie. Und von den netten Dozenten: „Ich will Sie verfüüühren° – zum Studium der Psychologie!", ruft Professor Rainer Silbereisen und sieht ihr tief in die Augen. Jessie blinkert zurück: „Ich bin auf einmal sehr sicher, dass Psychologie richtig sein könnte° für mich", sagt sie.

***verführen:*** *to entice, tempt*

*could*

Eigentlich hatte Jessie gar keine große Lust, nach Jena zu kommen, erst das gute Abschneiden des Fachbereichs Psychologie im Hochschulranking hat sie überzeugt°: Professoren und Studenten empfehlen die Uni, die Studiendauer ist kurz und die Ausstattung top. Nicht nur Jessie reist mit dem Ranking im Rucksack. Immer mehr Abiturienten orientieren sich an den Ergebnissen.

***positiv beeinflusst***

Wenn Jessie das Ranking verfassen würde°, würde sie zusätzliche Kriterien einführen: die besten Cafés, die besten Bars, die besten Clubs am Studienort.

***verfassen ... :*** *were to write*

Mag ja sein, dass die Humboldt-Uni im Fachbereich Psychologie nicht immer in der Spitzengruppe landet – aber Berlin macht vieles wett°. Nicht nur Jessie findet die Hauptstadt klasse: Weil alle nach Berlin wollen, ist der Numerus clausus für Psychologie hier besonders hoch. Zwischen 1,2 und 1,5 lag er in den letzten Semestern. Trotzdem ist sie zufrieden mit ihrer Uni-Tour: „Die Reise hat mir super geholfen. Ich weiß jetzt, worauf ich achten muss: Wie gut ist die Betreuung durch die Professoren? Gibt es Möglichkeiten, ins Ausland zu gehen? Welche Spezialisierungen gibt es am Lehrstuhl? Fühle ich mich in der Stadt und unter den Mitstudenten wohl?" Vor allem eins ist ihr klar geworden: Ein Studium ist keine Einbahnstraße. Man ist nicht auf eine Richtung festgelegt, sondern kann ganz unterschiedliche Schwerpunkte setzen. Und oft sind Praktika viel wichtiger für den Berufseinstieg als irgendwelches Fachwissen. Wer zum Beispiel später Manager auf Auslandseinsätze vorbereiten° will, kann das mit einem Psychologiestudium machen – oder mit einem Wirtschaftsstudium. Nichts ist planbar°: Jessies Vater hat Literatur studiert – heute betreibt er einen Holzhandel°. Ihre Mutter wollte Kunstlehrerin werden – als sie das erste Mal vor einer Klasse stand, merkte sie: „Ich kann das nicht!" Heute ist sie Kunsttherapeutin°.

***macht ... :*** *makes up for that*

German grades range from 1 (very good) to 6 (insufficient): **1 = sehr gut; 2 = gut; 3 = befriedigend; 4 = ausreichend; 5 = mangelhaft; 6 = ungenügend**

*prepare*
*capable of being planned*
*lumber business*

*art therapist*

*von Nikola Sellmair in* **stern**, *16/2002.*

## Rückblick

**30** **Stimmt das?** Stimmen diese Aussagen zum Text oder nicht? Wenn nicht, was stimmt?

|  | Ja, das stimmt. | Nein, das stimmt nicht. |
|---|---|---|
| 1. Jessie will studieren, und sie weiß, was und wo sie studieren will. | ☐ | ☐ |
| 2. Nicht alle Abiturienten/Abiturientinnen freuen sich, alles selbst zu entscheiden. | ☐ | ☐ |
| 3. Jessie will direkt vom Gymnasium zur Uni gehen und ihr Studium beginnen. | ☐ | ☐ |
| 4. Jessie will die Unis in Passau und in Jena besuchen, weil sie im Ranking weit oben liegen. | ☐ | ☐ |
| 5. Das Ranking vom Fachbereich Psychologie in Jena hat Jessie sehr interessiert. | ☐ | ☐ |
| 6. Passau gefällt Jessie, weil das Mensa-Essen prima° schmeckt und die Studierenden so ambitioniert sind. | ☐ | ☐ |
| 7. Jena findet Jessie langweilig und die Professoren im Fachbereich Psychologie aggressiv. | ☐ | ☐ |
| 8. Die Humboldt-Universität in Berlin gefällt Jessie, weil der Fachbereich Psychologie zu den Besten gehört. | ☐ | ☐ |
| 9. Für Jessie ist ein Programm mit Möglichkeiten für Praktika und Auslandsstudium wichtig. | ☐ | ☐ |

*top-notch*

Complete the **Ergänzen Sie** activity in your workbook for this text before doing the next activity.

**31** **Kriterien.** Welche „typischen" und welche persönlichen Kriterien sind für Jessie wichtig, wenn sie eine Universität wählt?

1. eine Stadt, wo sie sich „wohl" fühlt
2. die Ausstattung der Universität
3. Studenten, die „modern" sind
4. Spezialisierungen am Lehrstuhl
5. Professoren, die berühmt° sind
6. billige Wohnmöglichkeiten
7. Möglichkeit, im Ausland zu studieren
8. Betreuung durch die Professoren
9. gutes Essen
10. gut im Fach Psychologie
11. kurze Studiendauer
12. viel Sport an der Uni
13. Cafés, Bars, Clubs
14. Studenten mit Energie
15. Möglichkeit für Praktika
16. in der Nähe von München

*famous*

**32** **Kurz gefragt.** Beantworten Sie diese Fragen kurz auf Deutsch.

1. Was finden viele Abiturienten so schwierig?
2. Wie will Jessie die beste Entscheidung treffen?
3. Für welche drei Unis interessiert sich Jessie am Anfang? Warum?
4. Was gefällt Jessie an Berlin und was ist eigentlich nicht so gut für Jessies Pläne°?
5. Wie wichtig findet Jessie ihr Studium für ihre Zukunft°?
6. Welche Beispiele kennt Jessie persönlich, warum man sich nicht immer auf einen Beruf vorbereiten kann ?

*plans*
*future*

In June 2000 the education ministers approved a non-binding recommendation that partial tuition be charged for students who exceed the allotted time to complete a degree (14 semesters) and for those in their second degree program. A nominal tuition fee of approximately 500 Euros per semester for students varies from state to state.

## BRENNPUNKT KULTUR

### Wie Studierende ihr Studium finanzieren

*Diese Studentin verdient relativ viel Geld als Kellnerin.*

University study in Germany has traditionally been tuition-free. Students are only required to pay a modest registration fee of 30€ or more per semester, depending on their university. However, recently a 500-Euro tuition fee for all German universities has been proposed and has met with considerable resistance from students. Students pay for their own living expenses, books, and supplies. Residence halls and meals in the university cafeteria are subsidized by the government. Students can receive financial aid through a loan system known as **BAföG (Bundesausbildungsförderungsgesetz)**, named after the law that provides for it. The federal government provides this loan interest-free to students of families with low and middle incomes. The maximum amount allowed is 583 Euros per month.

Because of the relatively low cost of education, German students historically did not need to hold part-time jobs during the academic year. However, student habits are changing. Students typically work during the two semester breaks **(Semesterferien)** to finance a trip or a major purchase. Whereas only six percent of German university students financed their education by working in 1995, now roughly 58 percent of students work while attending college.

■ **Kulturkreuzung** In Europa kostet ein Universitätsstudium weniger Geld als in den USA oder Kanada. In Europa meint man, dass alle Bürger von guten Universitäten profitieren, nicht nur die Studierenden selbst. Darum zahlt der Staat die meisten Kosten und die Studierenden zahlen keine oder niedrige Studiengebühren. In den USA und Kanada sind die meisten Universitäten und Colleges ziemlich teuer. Finden Sie das akzeptabel? Was sind die Vorteile und Nachteile vom deutschen System? Von dem amerikanischen oder kanadischen System?

**33** **Zum Überlegen.** Denken Sie über die folgenden Fragen nach. *Achtung*: Sie können sie nicht direkt aus dem Text beantworten.

1. Welche von Jessies Ranking-Kriterien finden Sie auch wichtig?
2. Jessie scheint° geographisch sehr flexibel zu sein. Glauben Sie, dass auch andere Schüler so flexibel sind? Warum? Warum nicht?   *seems*
3. Wo möchten Sie eventuell° in Deutschland studieren? Warum?   *perhaps*
4. Wie wichtig sind Praktika, Erfahrung im Ausland oder Fremdsprachen für Ihren zukünftigen Beruf?
5. Wir wissen, dass Jessie 20 Jahre alt ist. Wie stellen Sie sich Jessie sonst noch vor? Wie sieht sie aus? Welche Kleidung trägt sie gern? Welche Musik hört sie gern? Was macht sie in ihrer Freizeit? Arbeitet sie? Hat sie Geschwister° – und wenn ja, ist sie die Älteste oder vielleicht die Jüngste? Wird sie eine gute Studentin sein? Begründen Sie Ihre Antworten.   ***Brüder oder Schwestern***

**34**  **Die Vor- und Nachteile von meinem Studium.** Welche Aspekte von Ihrem Studium finden Sie positiv? Welche negativ? Vergleichen Sie Ihre Liste mit der Liste von einem Partner/einer Partnerin.

|  | Positiv | Negativ |
|---|---|---|
| 1. die Dozenten und Professoren | ☐ | ☐ |
| 2. die Kontaktmöglichkeiten | ☐ | ☐ |
| 3. die Kurse | ☐ | ☐ |
| 4. meine Kommilitonen/Kommilitoninnen | ☐ | ☐ |
| 5. die Arbeitsatmosphäre | ☐ | ☐ |
| 6. die Bibliothek | ☐ | ☐ |
| 7. die Arbeitsmöglichkeiten | ☐ | ☐ |
| 8. die Studienberatung° | ☐ | ☐ |

> Due to several influences, e.g., the European Union, widespread use of the English language, and the growth of international business, Germany has seen an increase in prestigious private universities to 50 accredited institutions. Austria has nine accredited institutions. Tuition for some fields of study may be as much as 30,000 Euros per year.

**Studienberatung:** *academic advising*

**35**  **Interview: Mein Studentenleben.** Beantworten Sie die folgenden Fragen zuerst für sich. Stellen Sie sie dann einem Partner/einer Partnerin.

|  | Ich | Partner(in) |
|---|---|---|
| 1. Was studierst du? | _____ | _____ |
| 2. Welche Kurse belegst° du? | _____ | _____ |
| 3. Wie viele Kurse hast du mit Lehrassistenten°? | _____ | _____ |
| 4. Wo lernst du normalerweise? In der Bibliothek? Zu Hause? | _____ | _____ |
| 5. Wie viele Stunden lernst du jeden Tag? | _____ | _____ |
| 6. Wie viele Stunden verbringst du pro Woche in der Bibliothek? | _____ | _____ |
| 7. Wie viele Referate schreibst du dieses Semester? | _____ | _____ |
| 8. Wie oft schreibst du eine Prüfung? | _____ | _____ |
| 9. Hast du einen Job? | _____ | _____ |
| 10. Hast du noch Zeit für Sport oder andere Hobbys? | _____ | _____ |

*are taking*
*teaching assistants*

**36**  **Wie es bei uns ist.** Das Studium in den USA und in Kanada ist in vielen Aspekten ganz anders als das Studium in deutschsprachigen Ländern. Wie unterscheidet° sich Ihr Studium von einem mitteleuropäischen Studium? Besprechen Sie diese Fragen in einer kleinen Gruppe von drei bis fünf Personen. Berichten Sie dann der Klasse Ihre Ergebnisse.

*differ*

1. Haben Sie auch eine Uni-Hopping-Tour gemacht und viele Unis besucht? Welche Unis haben Sie besucht?
2. Besuchen die meisten Studenten hier im ersten Jahr Vorlesungen?
3. Gibt es auch hier wie in Deutschland keine Diskussionen und keine Prüfungen in Vorlesungen?
4. Was ist einem Proseminar äquivalent?
5. Haben Sie je° in einer organisierten Arbeitsgruppe gearbeitet? Woran°?
6. Halten Sie lieber ein Referat oder schreiben Sie lieber eine Prüfung? Warum?
7. Was sind die Vor- und Nachteile von Gruppenreferaten oder Einzelreferaten?
8. Ist es hier typisch, Dozenten/Dozentinnen in der Sprechstunde zu besuchen? Warum?
9. Kann man hier leicht ein Praktikum außerhalb der Uni machen? Ist das hier populär? Wollen Sie selbst ein Praktikum machen? Was für eins?
10. Was bekommen Studenten an Ihrer Uni anstelle von° Scheinen? Was finden Sie besser?

*ever / about what*

**anstelle von:** *instead of*

## *Strukturen und Vokabeln*

### III Talking about future events

Future time

#### A. The present tense with a time expression

You have already learned that German speakers commonly express the future with a present tense verb and a future time expression, such as **morgen, nächste Woche, im Sommer.**

| | |
|---|---|
| Morgen fliege ich nach Berlin. | *I'm going to fly to Berlin tomorrow.* |

Time expressions (**Zeitausdrücke**) frequently begin German sentences. This helps organize the sequence of events chronologically in a narrative. Once a future time expression establishes the time frame, other future time expressions are not necessary in subsequent sentences.

> The acronym **TRuMP** helps remember the sequence of adverbs:
> **T**ime – **R**eason – **M**anner – **P**lace.

| | |
|---|---|
| Morgen um 7.00 Uhr stehe ich auf. | *I'll get up at 7 A.M. tomorrow.* |
| (Morgen) Um 8.00 Uhr fahre ich zum Flughafen. | *I'll drive to the airport at 8 A.M. (tomorrow).* |
| (Morgen) Um 10.15 Uhr komme ich in Frankfurt an. | *I'll arrive in Frankfurt at 10:15 A.M. (tomorrow).* |

Remember that expressions of time always precede expressions of place.

>     *verb*   *time*    *place*
> Ich <u>fliege</u> <u>morgen</u> <u>nach Berlin</u>.   *I'm going to fly to Berlin tomorrow.*

Here are some time expressions German speakers frequently use. All of them can be used to talk about the future. Some of them will already be familiar to you.

| | |
|---|---|
| heute | *today* |
| heute Morgen (Nachmittag, Abend) | *this morning (afternoon, evening/tonight)* |
| morgen | *tomorrow* |
| morgen früh (Nachmittag, Abend) | *tomorrow morning (afternoon, evening)* |
| übermorgen | *the day after tomorrow* |
| später | *later* |
| am Wochenende (am Freitag, am Abend) | *on the weekend (on Friday, in the evening/ at night)* |
| im Sommer (im Juli) | *in the summer (in July)* |
| in zwei Tagen (Wochen, Monaten, Jahren) | *in two days (weeks, months, years)* |
| diese Woche (dieses Wochenende, diesen Freitag) | *this week (this weekend, this Friday)* |
| nächste Woche (nächstes Wochenende, nächsten Freitag) | *next week (next weekend, next Friday)* |
| jede Woche (jedes Wochenende, jeden Freitag) | *every week (every weekend, every Friday)* |

Time expressions with **an** and **in** occur in the dative case and express specific points in time.

**Am Montag** haben wir Deutsch.      *We have German on Monday.*
**Im Sommer** arbeiten viele Studenten.      *A lot of students work in the summer.*

Time expressions that take the accusative don't need a preposition. They can also express specific points in time.

**Nächsten Freitag** haben wir eine Prüfung.      *We have a test next Friday.*

**37**   **Wann machst du das?** Fragen Sie einen Partner/eine Partnerin, wann diese Situationen in der Zukunft stattfinden°. Benutzen Sie     *take place*
Zeitausdrücke aus der Liste oben.

   S1:   *Wann bringst du die Bücher in die Bibliothek zurück?*
   S2:   *Morgen früh bringe ich die Bücher zurück.*

1. Wann lernst du mit Freunden für die Prüfung?
2. Wann gehst du zu deinem Dozenten/deiner Dozentin in die Sprechstunde?
3. Wann triffst du Freunde in der Mensa?
4. Wann musst du zum Zahnarzt gehen?
5. Wann ist die nächste Deutschprüfung?
6. Wann fährst du nach Hause?
7. Wann treibst du Sport?
8. Wann gehst du in die Bibliothek?
9. Wann putzt du dir die Zähne?
10. Wann beginnen die Semesterferien?

## B. The future tense: *werden* + infinitive

Besides using the present tense with a future time expression, German speakers also use the future tense (**das Futur**) to describe events in the future. The **Futur** consists of the auxiliary or helping verb **werden** with an infinitive at the end of the clause. The **Futur** may be used with or without a future time adverbial.

> The word **Futur** is only a grammatical term and is not used in conversation to refer to the future (**die Zukunft**).

Wie lange **wird** das Referat **dauern?**      *How long will the presentation last?*

**Wird** es einen Overheadprojektor im Seminarraum **geben?**      *Will there be an overhead projector in the seminar room?*

Bei diesem Wetter **wirst** du dich **erkälten!**      *You'll catch a cold in this weather!*

Note the spelling changes in the verb **werden:** e > i in the 2nd, informal, and 3rd persons (**wirst, wird**) and the loss of **d** in the 2nd, informal person (**wirst**).

> With a reflexive verb in the future tense, the reflexive pronoun occurs immediately after **werden** or after the subject if it is positioned mid-sentence: **Du wirst dich bei diesem Wetter erkälten.**

| **werden bauen:** *will (be going to) build* | | | |
|---|---|---|---|
| **Singular** | | **Plural** | |
| ich | **werde** bauen | wir | **werden** bauen |
| du | **wirst** bauen | ihr | **werdet** bauen |
| Sie | **werden** bauen | Sie | **werden** bauen |
| er/sie/es | **wird** bauen | sie | **werden** bauen |

When used with the first-person pronouns, the future tense with **werden** can express a mild promise if directed toward another person.

> Ich **werde** einen Overheadprojektor     *I will/am going to order an*
>   für Sie **bestellen.**                          *overhead projector for you.*

Be careful not to confuse the modal verb **wollen** (*to want to*) with English *will*.

> Ich **will** nach Deutschland fliegen.     *I **want to** fly to Germany.*
> Ich **werde** nach Deutschland fliegen.   *I **will** fly to Germany.*

**38**   **Meine Pläne nach dem Studium.**   Kreuzen Sie zuerst an, was für Sie stimmt. Fragen Sie dann einen Partner/eine Partnerin.

S1: *Ich werde mein Diplom mit Auszeichnung° machen. Wirst du auch dein*      *distinction*
    *Diplom mit Auszeichnung machen?*
S2: *Ja, ich werde auch mein Diplom mit Auszeichnung machen.* (oder)
    *Nein, ich werde es nicht mit Auszeichnung machen.*

| | Ich | Partner(in) | |
|---|---|---|---|
| Ich werde: | | | |
| 1. mein Diplom mit Auszeichnung machen. | ☐ | ☐ | |
| 2. andere Kontinente sehen, bevor ich mir meine erste Arbeitsstelle suche. | ☐ | ☐ | |
| 3. in einer neuen, unbekannten Großstadt leben. | ☐ | ☐ | |
| 4. in meine Heimatstadt zurückkehren°. | ☐ | ☐ | *in ...: go back to my home-town* |
| 5. meinen Doktor machen. | ☐ | ☐ | |
| 6. ein Haus kaufen. | ☐ | ☐ | |
| 7. Präsident/Präsidentin von den USA werden. | ☐ | ☐ | |
| 8. eine Familie mit vielen Kindern haben. | ☐ | ☐ | |
| 9. mich auf meine Karriere° konzentrieren und keine Kinder haben. | ☐ | ☐ | *career* |
| 10. in einem Hollywoodfilm mitspielen. | ☐ | ☐ | |
| 11. eine Firma gründen°. | ☐ | ☐ | *start* |
| 12. ökologisch° (politisch, sozial) aktiv sein. | ☐ | ☐ | *environmentally* |

**39**   **Feste Termine machen.**   Ein Freund/Eine Freundin fragt, ob Sie oder andere diese Dinge machen werden. Antworten Sie affirmativ mit **werden** und geben Sie eine Zeit an. Benutzen Sie Zeitausdrücke wie **heute, heute Abend, später, morgen, nächste Woche, nächstes Jahr,** usw.

S1: *Kannst du mir bei den Hausaufgaben helfen?*
S2: *Ja, sicher. Morgen werde ich dir bei den Hausaufgaben helfen.*

1. Kannst du mir bei den Hausaufgaben helfen?
2. Schreibt dein Freund deine Seminararbeit?
3. Kannst du mit mir in die Sprechstunde gehen?
4. Möchtest du meine Vorlesung in Betriebswirtschaft besuchen?
5. Kannst du mit uns ins Seminar gehen?
6. Gibt uns der Professor die Folien?
7. Kannst du mir deinen Computer leihen?
8. Können deine Freunde mit in die Bibliothek gehen?
9. Möchtest du mit uns in einer Arbeitsgruppe sein?

**40   Ja, ich verspreche° es!** Bevor Sie nach Deutschland reisen, *promise*
müssen Sie Ihren Eltern versprechen, dort verantwortungsvoll° zu handeln°. *responsibly / act*
Sagen Sie, was Sie machen und was Sie nicht machen werden.

S1 (VATER/MUTTER): *Wirst du immer in die Vorlesung gehen?*
S2 (TOCHTER/SOHN): *Ja, ich verspreche es, ich werde immer in die Vorlesung*
*gehen.* (oder)
*Nein, ich werde nicht immer in die Vorlesung gehen.*

1. immer in die Vorlesung gehen
2. viel Zeit in der Bibliothek verbringen
3. jeden Abend ausgehen
4. viele Parties besuchen
5. keinen Alkohol trinken
6. jedes Wochenende nach Paris fahren
7. einen deutschen Freund/eine deutsche Freundin finden und gleich heiraten
8. ins Museum, ins Konzert und in die Oper gehen
9. am Schreibtisch sitzen und sich auf Seminare vorbereiten
10. nie kochen und immer in guten Restaurants essen

## IV  Expressing probability

### The verb **werden** + **wohl**

When used with the adverb **wohl** (*probably*) and an infinitive, **werden** expresses probability.

Er **wird wohl** krank sein.         *He is probably sick.*
Er **wird wohl** ein Motorrad kaufen.   *He'll probably buy a motorcycle.*

You have now learned these three uses of the verb **werden:**

1. As a main verb, meaning *to become, get.*

   Ich **werde** müde.     *I am getting tired.*

2. As an auxiliary verb that, together with an infinitive, designates future tense.

   Das Referat **wird** 45 Minuten **dauern.**     *The presentation will last 45 minutes.*

3. As an auxiliary verb that, together with the adverb **wohl** and an infinitive, expresses probability in the present tense.

   Stefan **wird wohl** nach Moskau fahren.     *Stefan is probably going to Moscow.*

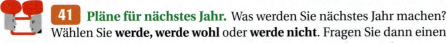

**41   Pläne für nächstes Jahr.** Was werden Sie nächstes Jahr machen?
Wählen Sie **werde, werde wohl** oder **werde nicht.** Fragen Sie dann einen
Partner/eine Partnerin, was er/sie nächstes Jahr bestimmt machen wird, was
er/sie wohl machen wird und was er/sie bestimmt nicht machen wird.

S1: *Wirst du dir nächstes Jahr einen Teilzeitjob suchen?*
S2: *Ja, ich werde mir wohl einen Teilzeitjob suchen.* (oder)
   *Nein, ich werde keinen Teilzeitjob suchen.*

| | Werde | Werde wohl | Werde nicht |
|---|:---:|:---:|:---:|
| 1. sich einen Teilzeitjob suchen | ☐ | ☐ | ☐ |
| 2. viele Seminararbeiten schreiben | ☐ | ☐ | ☐ |
| 3. viel Zeit in der Bibliothek verbringen | ☐ | ☐ | ☐ |
| 4. jeden Abend ausgehen | ☐ | ☐ | ☐ |
| 5. oft in die Sprechstunde gehen | ☐ | ☐ | ☐ |
| 6. neue Freunde kennen lernen | ☐ | ☐ | ☐ |
| 7. sich ein Praktikum suchen | ☐ | ☐ | ☐ |
| 8. jedes Wochenende intensiv lernen | ☐ | ☐ | ☐ |
| 9. mein Studium zu Ende machen | ☐ | ☐ | ☐ |
| 10. so weit wie möglich von hier weggehen | ☐ | ☐ | ☐ |

**42** **Interview: Pläne für die nähere Zukunft.** Stellen Sie einem Partner/einer Partnerin die folgenden Fragen.

S1: *Was wirst du heute nach dem Deutschkurs machen?*
S2: *Ich werde wohl (in die Mensa gehen).*

1. Was wirst du heute nach dem Deutschkurs machen?
2. Was wirst du heute Abend machen?
3. Was wirst du morgen früh machen?
4. Was wirst du übermorgen machen?
5. Wohin wirst du am Wochenende fahren?
6. Wann wirst du mit Freunden ausgehen?
7. Was wirst du im Sommer machen?
8. Wo wirst du nächstes Jahr wohnen?

**43** **Julia wird wohl in den Kindergarten gehen.** Was werden diese Leute wohl nächstes Jahr machen? Wählen Sie eine Antwort von der Liste.

auf die Fachschule gehen • auf die Grundschule gehen •
aufs Gymnasium gehen • auf die Hauptschule gehen • in den Kindergarten gehen • die Matura machen • auf die Musikhochschule gehen •
auf die Realschule gehen

Julia wird im Juli fünf Jahre alt.
*Sie wird wohl im September in den Kindergarten gehen.*

1. Julia wird im Juli fünf Jahre alt.
2. Florian ist im Kindergarten.
3. Thomas ist in der vierten Klasse. Er will später nicht auf die Universität gehen. Er will eine Lehre machen°.
4. Monika interessiert sich für Musik und möchte nach dem Gymnasium weiter studieren.
5. Golo hat die Mittlere Reife gemacht.
6. Claudia ist in der sechsten Klasse und möchte auf die Universität gehen.
7. Gabriele ist Schülerin an einem Gymnasium in Wien.
8. Frank ist in der Hauptschule und möchte eine Kfz°-Mechaniker-Lehre machen.

*eine Lehre machen: to do an apprenticeship*

*Kfz (Kraftfahrzeug): automotive*

BRENNPUNKT KULTUR

## Das deutsche Schulsystem

Germany and Switzerland have similar public school systems that are centrally administered, in Germany by each state Ministry of Education and the Arts (**das Kultusministerium**) and in Switzerland by the individual Cantonal Ministries. The Federal Ministry of Education in Austria oversees educational policy there. These ministries initiate the educational curricula that schools will follow. This guaranees greater educational uniformity.

In Germany 80% of all three- to six-year-olds attend a private preschool (**der Kindergarten**). Thereafter, children enter the public school system (or a private school), where they attend primary school (**die Grundschule**) through the fourth grade. In the third and fourth grades, teachers assess each pupil's abilities and then recommend that they attend **die Hauptschule, die Realschule,** or **das Gymnasium.** During the fifth and sixth grades, called **die Orientierungsstufe,** students can change their minds and switch to a more appropriate school. All German students are required by law to attend school at least on a part-time basis through the age of 18 (**die Schulpflicht**).

Roughly 20% of all German students are **Hauptschüler,** learning a trade at a technical-vocational high school (**die Hauptschule**). They attend school through the 9th grade and thereafter enter the workforce as an apprentice (**der Lehrling** or **der/die Auszubildende [Azubi]**). Students continue with part-time classroom work for three more years at a vocational school (**die Berufsschule**) while acquiring on-the-job skills through their apprenticeship (**die Lehre**).

About 40% of all German students attend **die Realschule. Realschüler** follow a middle-track educational path with a more demanding academic program that concludes with examinations at the end of the 10th grade. An intermediate diploma (**die Mittlere Reife**) is awarded upon successful completion of their training. This diploma qualifies students to attend specialized training colleges (e.g., **die Fachschule** or **Fachoberschule**) and receive training in areas such as engineering, administration, and business. In Austria, this type of school does not exist.

**Gymnasiasten,** making up the final 40% of German high school students, pursue the traditional college preparatory track that customarily lasted through the 13th grade. Recently, a number of **Länder** have introduced laws to expedite gradution from **das Gymnasium** to the end of 12th grade. These students usually take courses in German, math, chemistry, physics, biology, English, a second foreign language, social studies, sports, and the arts. In the 11th through 13th grades, students choose two major areas of academic specialization for their **Leistungskurse** and several minor subjects for their **Grundkurse.** Before graduating from a **Gymnasium,** students must have completed coursework in at least nine subjects. The two major subjects are tested in depth when students face the comprehensive exams required for graduation (**das Abitur,** called **die Matura** in Austria, and **die Reifeprüfung** in Switzerland). With this diploma, the student is qualified to attend a university or any other post-secondary educational institution, such as a **Musikhochschule, Kunsthochschule,** or a **Fachhochschule** specializing in engineering or the sciences.

A fourth type of German school, **die Gesamtschule,** modeled on the comprehensive American high school, was a product of the reform movement of the 1960s. It incorporates the curricula of all three traditional German secondary schools, giving students a broad choice of programs and courses. While hailed by some as more progressive and democratic schools, **Gesamtschulen** have been criticized by others for lowering standards. They remain controversial but are growing in number.

By federal law, administration of national education is a federal responsibility, but it is shared between the federal government and the individual **Länder,** each of which maintains local control of the schools. Educators, politicians, and parents were shocked with the publication of the first PISA Study (Programme for International Student Assessment) in 2000, which ranked Germany's secondary schools in the bottom third internationally. For a nation that has traditionally considered itself a nation of poets and thinkers (**das Land der Dichter und Denker**) with a superior educational system, this ranking came as a huge blow to the national self-image. Partial improvements in mathematics and science were reported in the second PISA study in 2004.

■ **Kulturkreuzung** Nicht alle Schüler müssen oder wollen auf die Universität gehen. Das deutsche Schulsystem gibt Schülern die Möglichkeit, einen guten Beruf zu erlernen, ohne zur Universität zu gehen. Das Schulsystem in den USA dagegen hat ein Universitätsstudium immer als Ziel im Auge. Was sind die Vorteile und Nachteile von beiden Systemen?

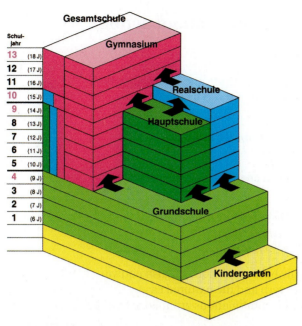

 **F r e i e   K o m m u n i k a t i o n**

**Rollenspiel: Das Gruppenreferat.** Spielen Sie mit einem Partner/einer Partnerin die folgende Situation.

S1: Sie sind Professor/Professorin. Sie halten jetzt Ihre Sprechstunde und wollen mit Repräsentanten von jeder Arbeitsgruppe über das Gruppenreferat sprechen. Fragen Sie nach dem Thema, nach den Vorbereitungen und nach den anderen Studenten/Studentinnen in der Arbeitsgruppe.

S2: Sie sind Student/Studentin und gehen in die Sprechstunde von Ihrem Professor/Ihrer Professorin. Ihre Arbeitsgruppe hat noch kein Thema für das Referat, aber das dürfen Sie dem Professor/der Professorin nicht sagen.

**Rollenspiel: Die Sommerreise.** Spielen Sie mit einem Partner/einer Partnerin die folgende Situation.

S1: Sie sind der Sohn/die Tochter. Sie haben eine Sommerreise geplant und möchten mit einem Rucksack nach Europa fliegen. Sie haben nicht sehr viel Geld aber viele Ideen. Erklären Sie Ihren Eltern, was Sie machen möchten.

S2: Sie sind der Vater/die Mutter. Ihr Sohn/Ihre Tochter erzählt Ihnen, dass er/sie nach Europa fliegen möchte. Sie machen sich Sorgen, denn er/sie hat nicht viel Geld. Stellen Sie viele Fragen (z. B. **Wo wirst du schlafen? Was wirst du alles machen?**).

**S c h r e i b e c k e**

**Ein Brief an Jessie.** Sie werden zwei Semester an der Universität in Jena studieren. Jessie hat schon ein Jahr in Jena studiert. Schreiben Sie einen Brief an Jessie. Stellen Sie sich vor° und beschreiben Sie Ihre Pläne für das Jahr in Deutschland. Stellen Sie Jessie ein paar Fragen über Wohnen, Arbeiten und Studieren in Jena.

*sich vorstellen: to introduce onself*

# V Specifying additional information about actions

## A. Using verbs with prepositional objects

Some German verbs may be accompanied by a preposition and its object, which offer more specific information about the activity expressed by the verb.

| | |
|---|---|
| **Konzentrieren** Sie **sich.** | *Concentrate.* |
| **Konzentrieren** Sie **sich auf** das Wichtigste. | ***Concentrate on** the most important things.* |

The meaning of a verb + prepositional object can change when the preposition changes.

| | |
|---|---|
| Wir freuen uns **auf** die Reise nach Spanien. | *We're looking forward to the trip to Spain.* |
| Wir freuen uns **über** die Universität. | *We're happy about the university.* |

The German preposition does not necessarily have an obvious English equivalent. It needs to be learned together with the verb and the required case.

Here are some important verb-preposition combinations grouped according to case and preposition.

**Da haben alle drauf gewartet.**

**1. Preposition + accusative case**

**an** + *accusative*

| | |
|---|---|
| denken an (hat gedacht) | *to think of* |
| sich erinnern an (hat sich erinnert) | *to remember* |
| glauben an (hat geglaubt) | *to believe in* |

**auf** + *accusative*

| | |
|---|---|
| achten auf (hat geachtet) | *to pay attention to* |
| sich freuen auf (hat sich gefreut) | *to look forward to* |
| gespannt sein auf (ist gespannt gewesen) | *to be excited about* |
| sich konzentrieren auf (hat sich konzentriert) | *to concentrate on* |
| sich vor·bereiten auf (hat sich vorbereitet) | *to prepare for, get ready for* |
| warten auf (hat gewartet) | *to wait for* |

**für** + *accusative*

| | |
|---|---|
| danken für (hat gedankt) | *to thank for* |
| sich entscheiden für (hat sich entschieden) | *to decide on, in favor of* |
| halten für (hält, hat gehalten) | *to consider/think (someone) is (something)* |

**sich entscheiden gegen** means *to decide against*

**in** +*accusative*

| | |
|---|---|
| sich verlieben in (hat sich verliebt) | *to fall in love with* |

**über** + *accusative*

| | |
|---|---|
| sich freuen über (hat sich gefreut) | *to be happy about* |
| reden/sprechen über (redet/spricht, hat geredet/gesprochen) | *to talk about* |
| sich ärgern über (hat sich geärgert) | *to get angry about* |

**um** + *accusative*

| | |
|---|---|
| bitten um (hat gebeten) | *to ask for, request* |

2. **Preposition + dative case**
   **nach** + *dative*
   | | |
   |---|---|
   | fragen nach (hat gefragt) | *to ask about* |

   **von** + *dative*
   | | |
   |---|---|
   | erwarten von (hat erwartet) | *to expect of* |
   | erzählen von (hat erzählt) | *to tell a story about, talk about* |
   | halten von (hält, hat gehalten) | *to think of, about* |
   | handeln von (hat gehandelt) | *to be about* |
   | sich trennen von (hat sich getrennt) | *to break up with, separate from* |
   | etwas verstehen von (hat verstanden) | *to know something about* |
   | wissen von (weiß, hat gewusst) | *to know about* |

   **vor** + *dative*
   | | |
   |---|---|
   | Angst haben vor (hat Angst gehabt) | *to be afraid of* |

   **zu** + *dative*
   | | |
   |---|---|
   | passen zu (hat gepasst) | *to fit, go with* |

> **Handeln von** is used to talk about plots in stories, e.g., **Die Geschichte handelt von einem alten Mann.**

**44** **Annas Jahr in Deutschland.** Ergänzen Sie die Sätze mit der richtigen Präposition **(an, auf, für, in, über, um, von, vor)**.

Anna Adler verbringt jetzt das Jahr an der Universität in Tübingen. Am Anfang war sie sich nicht sicher, ob sie in Hamburg oder Tübingen studieren sollte°. Sie war natürlich gespannt _____ das Jahr in Deutschland.    *should*

 Sie hat mit ihren Eltern und mit ihrer Deutschlehrerin in Ft. Wayne _____ die Vorteile und die Nachteile von beiden Unis gesprochen. Ihre Eltern haben sehr viel Positives _____ Hamburg erzählt. Sie hat auch ihre Deutschlehrerin gefragt, was sie _____ Tübingen weiß. Dann hat sie sich _____ Tübingen entschieden. Sie hält Tübingen _____ die bessere Alternative.

 Anna hat sich gut _____ das Jahr vorbereitet und profitiert sehr von der Erfahrung. Sie freut sich täglich _____ ihre Entscheidung, in Tübingen zu studieren, obwohl° sie sich deshalb° für eine Zeit lang _____ ihrer Familie und ihren Freunden trennen musste°. Bald ist das Jahr aber zu Ende und sie denkt wieder _____ ihre Freunde und Familie in den USA. Jetzt freut sie sich natürlich auch _____ ihre Heimkehr im Sommer.    *even though / for that reason had to*

## B. Using **da**- and **wo**-compounds

The prefix **da** is used with a preposition when the object of that preposition is a pronoun, e.g., **dafür, damit.** This **da**-compound only refers to objects that are things and not people.

| | |
|---|---|
| Was verstehen Sie von diesem Thema? | *What do you know about this topic?* |
| —Ich verstehe nichts **davon.** | *—I don't know anything about it.* |
| | |
| Haben Sie etwas gegen dieses Thema? | *Do you object to this topic?* |
| —Nein, ich habe nichts **dagegen.** | *—No, I don't object to it.* |
| | |
| Haben Sie etwas gegen Carlos? | *Do you have something against Carlos?* |
| —Nein, Ich habe nichts **gegen ihn.** | *—No, I don't have anything against him.* |

Prepositions beginning with a vowel require that an **r** be inserted between **da** and the preposition, e.g., **da** + **r** + **an**.

| | |
|---|---|
| Ich kann mich nicht **daran** erinnern. | *I don't remember that.* |
| Er hat sich wochenlang **darauf** vorbereitet. | *He prepared himself for it for weeks.* |
| Ist schon Milch und Zucker **darin?** | *Is there already milk and sugar in it?* |
| Sie haben lange **darüber** geredet. | *They talked about it for a long time.* |

The prefix **wo-** is used with a preposition to form a question when the object is inanimate. Prepositions beginning with a vowel require that an **r** be inserted between **wo** and the preposition.

| | |
|---|---|
| **Wofür** hat er sich entschieden? | *What did he decide on?* |
| **Worauf** freut ihr euch? | *What are you looking forward to?* |

To refer to people, speakers use a preposition with **wen** (accusative) or **wem** (dative).

| | |
|---|---|
| **Woran** erinnern Sie sich? | *What do you remember?* |
| **An wen** erinnern Sie sich? | *Whom do you remember?* |
| **Wovon** handelt das Buch? | *What is the book about?* |
| **Von wem** handelt das Buch? | *Whom is the book about?* |

*wenden sich: turn to*

## AN WEN WENDEN SICH° STUDIERENDE?

| Aufgabenbereich | Auskunftgebende Stelle |
|---|---|
| Anerkennung von Reifezeugnissen | Studentenabteilung Wilhelmstr. 11, T. 29-68 41 |
| Anrechnung von Studienzeiten | zuständiges Prüfungsamt bzw. Prüfungsausschuß |
| Arbeitsvermittlung für Akademiker, Werk- und Gelegenheitsarbeit | Dienststelle Tübingen des Arbeitsamts Reutlingen und Außenstelle Universität Wilhelmstr. 26, T. 29-35 61 |
| Auslandsstipendien/Auslandsstudium | Akademisches Auslandsamt Nauklerstr. 14, T. 29-64 48 |
| BAföG | Studentenwerk Tübingen AöR Karlstr. 11, T. 29-38 52 |
| Beglaubigung von Urkunden und Zeugnissen | Bürgermeisteramt Tübingen – Amt für öffentliche Ordnung – |
| Beratung in Fragen der Krankenversicherung | Studentenabteilung Wilhelmstr. 11, T. 29-25 19 |

 **45** **Worauf wartet Anna?** Beantworten Sie die folgenden Fragen.

Anna steht an der Bushaltestelle. Worauf wartet sie?
*Sie wartet auf den Bus.*

1. Anna steht an der Bushaltestelle. Worauf wartet sie?
2. Sie braucht Auskunft, wann der Bus abfährt. Worum bittet sie?

3. Im Bus muss sie eine dumme Hausaufgabe für Deutsch schreiben. Worüber ärgert sie sich?
4. Claudia will nächstes Jahr aufs Gymnasium gehen. Wofür hat sie sich entschieden?
5. Karl und Stefan haben heute eine Prüfung. Worauf bereiten sie sich vor?
6. Am Wochenende gibt Barbara eine Party. Worauf freut sie sich?
7. Karl hat seine Bücher vergessen. Woran hat er sich nicht erinnert?
8. Stefan versteht das Thema in Physik kaum. Wovon versteht er nicht viel?
9. Stefan muss einen Bericht für Physik schreiben. Wovor hat er Angst?
10. Nächste Woche hat Stefan zwei Prüfungen. Woran denkt er?
11. Anna ärgert sich über ihren Bruder Jeff und meint, er ist dumm. Wofür hält sie Jeff?

**46** **Was macht Karl?** Stellen Sie einem Partner/einer Partnerin eine Frage mit **wo(r)-** oder **wen/wem.**

Karl hat sich in Inge verliebt.

S1: *In wen hat er sich verliebt?*
S2: *Er hat sich in Inge verliebt.*

1. Karl hat sich in Inge verliebt.
2. Inge hat sich an Karls Geburtstag erinnert.
3. Karl ist gespannt auf die Party heute Abend.
4. Karl und Inge warten auf die Gäste.
5. Die Gäste reden über Karl.
6. Karl hält nicht viel von Rapmusik.
7. Die Gäste freuen sich über das leckere° Essen.    *delicious*
8. Inge hat auch an alkoholfreie Getränke gedacht.
9. Anna erzählt von ihrer Reise nach Mainz.
10. Karl achtet nicht auf die Zeit.

**47** **Gespräch über das Studentenleben.** Stellen Sie einem Partner/einer Partnerin diese Fragen über das Studentenleben. Berichten Sie dann der Klasse von Ihrem Partner/Ihrer Partnerin.

1. Warum hast du dich für Deutsch als Fremdsprache entschieden?
2. Wie lange bereitest du dich auf Deutschprüfungen vor?
3. Worauf freust du dich am meisten im Herbst? Im Winter? Im Frühling?
4. Vor welchen Kursen (oder Professoren/Professorinnen) hast du Angst?
5. Auf welche Kurse (Professoren/Professorinnen) bist du gespannt?
6. Was hält man von den Professoren/Professorinnen und den Kursen in deinem Hauptfach?
7. Worüber hast du dich in der letzten Zeit geärgert?
8. Wovon verstehst du wirklich absolut nichts?
9. Wovon handelt dein Lieblingsfilm?
10. Über welche aktuellen Themen redet man auf diesem Campus?
11. In was für einen Mann/In was für eine Frau möchtest du dich verlieben? Beschreib ihn/sie.

**Freie Kommunikation**

**Rollenspiel: Gespräch mit dem Studienberater°.** Spielen Sie die folgende    *academic advisor*
Situation mit einem Partner/einer Partnerin.

S1:  Sie sind Student/Studentin. Ihre Noten sind dieses Semester schrecklich°    *awfully*
schlecht, Sie haben Pech mit Ihrem Mitbewohner/Ihrer Mitbewohnerin und
Sie haben Ihren Job verloren. Sie sind gerne an der Uni, aber dieses Semester
klappt einfach nichts°, und Sie sind frustriert.    ***klappt …:** nothing is*
Sie überlegen sich, ob Sie mit dem Studium aufhören sollen. Sie melden sich    *working out*
bei Ihrem Berater und reden darüber.

S2:  Sie sind Berater/Beraterin. Sie halten diesen Studenten/diese Studentin für
sehr talentiert, aber Sie verstehen auch die Frustration. Geben Sie ihm/ihr
Rat. Stellen Sie Fragen, sagen Sie Ihre Meinung, machen Sie Vorschläge und
helfen Sie dem Studenten/der Studentin, sich richtig zu entscheiden.

  **Schreibecke**

**Interviews mit Prominenten.** Sie schreiben einen Zeitungsartikel über eine
prominente Person. Nächste Woche machen Sie ein Interview mit dieser Person.
Überlegen Sie sich jetzt schon, welche Fragen Sie stellen möchten. Schreiben Sie
sieben bis zehn Fragen auf. Benutzen Sie die Ausdrücke aus der Liste.

> Angst haben vor • glauben an • fragen nach • erzählen von • sich ärgern
> über • sich vorbereiten auf • warten auf • sich erinnern an • sich freuen
> auf • halten von • bitten um • erwarten von • passen zu • wissen von
> • gespannt sein auf

| *Zieltext* | **Gespräch auf einer Party** |

Karl und Inge nehmen Anna und Barbara mit auf eine Party im Wohnheim. Bald
sehen Inge und Karl eine Studentin aus einem Seminar, aber sie können sich an
ihren Namen nicht erinnern. Die Studentin kommt vorbei, stellt sich vor und
lernt dabei Anna kennen. Sie kommen ins Gespräch und diskutieren die Probleme an der Universität.

## Vorschau

**48** **Partybenehmen°.** Wie benehmen Sie sich auf einer Party? Was    *party behavior*
machen Sie? Lesen Sie Fragen 1 und 2 und wählen Sie eine passende Antwort.

1. Wie oft machen Sie so etwas auf Partys?

| | *Nie* *0%* | *Selten* *20%* | *Oft* *60%* | *Sehr oft* *80%* | *Immer* *100%* |
|---|---|---|---|---|---|
| mit Freunden/Bekannten sprechen | ☐ | ☐ | ☐ | ☐ | ☐ |
| neue Leute ansprechen | ☐ | ☐ | ☐ | ☐ | ☐ |
| etwas essen | ☐ | ☐ | ☐ | ☐ | ☐ |
| Alkohol trinken | ☐ | ☐ | ☐ | ☐ | ☐ |
| zu viel Alkohol trinken | ☐ | ☐ | ☐ | ☐ | ☐ |
| alkoholfreie Getränke trinken | ☐ | ☐ | ☐ | ☐ | ☐ |
| tanzen | ☐ | ☐ | ☐ | ☐ | ☐ |
| Musik hören | ☐ | ☐ | ☐ | ☐ | ☐ |
| Musik spielen | ☐ | ☐ | ☐ | ☐ | ☐ |
| singen | ☐ | ☐ | ☐ | ☐ | ☐ |

2. Mit wem sprechen Sie über diese Themen auf einer Party?

| | *Mit meinem Freund / meiner Freundin* | *Mit meinen Kumpeln°* | *Mit Bekannten* | *Mit Niemandem* | |
|---|---|---|---|---|---|
| Liebesprobleme | ☐ | ☐ | ☐ | ☐ | *buddies* |
| Vorlesungen und Seminare | ☐ | ☐ | ☐ | ☐ | |
| Dozenten und Professoren | ☐ | ☐ | ☐ | ☐ | |
| Freunde | ☐ | ☐ | ☐ | ☐ | |
| die Musik auf der Party | ☐ | ☐ | ☐ | ☐ | |
| Politik | ☐ | ☐ | ☐ | ☐ | |
| das Essen auf der Party | ☐ | ☐ | ☐ | ☐ | |
| die Getränke auf der Party | ☐ | ☐ | ☐ | ☐ | |
| die Familie | ☐ | ☐ | ☐ | ☐ | |
| Sport | ☐ | ☐ | ☐ | ☐ | |
| Skandale | ☐ | ☐ | ☐ | ☐ | |
| die Kleidung von Leuten auf der Party | ☐ | ☐ | ☐ | ☐ | |

**49** **Satzdetektiv.** Welche Sätze bedeuten ungefähr das Gleiche?

1. Die Musik ist ein bisschen **lahm**. Die könnte ein bisschen **peppiger** sein.
2. Wollen wir einfach so 'ne Weile **plaudern?**
3. Ja, die [Studentin] **kommt** mir **bekannt vor.**
4. Mir gefällt der Kurs, weil die Dozentin so **gute Bücher ausgewählt hat.**
5. Der **Inhalt** ist gut.

a. Der Kurs ist gut. Die Dozentin hat interessante Bücher gefunden.
b. Ich denke, ich kenne die Studentin.
c. Die Musik ist etwas langsam und nicht so toll.
d. Sprechen wir ein bisschen?
e. Die Themen im Kurs sind interessant.

6. Zwanzig Leute stehen in der **Schlange.**
7. Habt ihr schon **probiert,** mit der Dozentin zu sprechen?
8. Das **passt** so gar nicht **zu ihr.**
9. Im Kurs **klingt** sie immer so **studentenfreundlich.**
10. Sie hat halt **wenig Zeit.**

f. Habt ihr schon versucht, mit der Dozentin zu sprechen?
g. Zwanzig Studenten warten auf die Dozentin.
h. Sie hat einfach nicht genug Zeit.
i. Das ist untypisch für sie.
j. Wenn sie im Kurs spricht, hat man den Eindruck, dass sie Studenten mag.

## *Zieltext*
### *Gespräch auf einer Party*

 Hören Sie gut zu.

Kommt nächste Woche wieder.

## *Rückblick*

**50** **Stimmt das?** Stimmen diese Aussagen zum Text oder nicht? Wenn nicht, was stimmt?

|  | Ja, das stimmt. | Nein, das stimmt nicht. |
|---|:---:|:---:|
| 1. Karl findet die Musik auf der Party toll. | ☐ | ☐ |
| 2. Karl und Inge treffen eine Studentin aus ihrem Seminar. Die Studentin heißt Martina. | ☐ | ☐ |
| 3. Der Kurs soll ein Seminar sein, aber er ist mehr wie eine Vorlesung. | ☐ | ☐ |
| 4. Dem Karl gefällt der Kurs nicht. | ☐ | ☐ |
| 5. Es ist leicht, mit der Dozentin in ihrer Sprechstunde zu sprechen. | ☐ | ☐ |
| 6. Die Dozentin scheint im Seminar studentenfreundlich zu sein. | ☐ | ☐ |

**51** **Der Kurs ist gut.** Wie wichtig sind Ihnen diese Faktoren für einen guten Kurs? Wählen Sie eine passende Kategorie.

|  | Nicht wichtig | Wichtig | Sehr wichtig |
|---|:---:|:---:|:---:|
| 1. ein interessantes Thema | ☐ | ☐ | ☐ |
| 2. ein netter Dozent/eine nette Dozentin | ☐ | ☐ | ☐ |
| 3. hochintelligente Professoren | ☐ | ☐ | ☐ |
| 4. motivierte Studenten | ☐ | ☐ | ☐ |

> **Der Kurs ist gut.** Be prepared to state your opinion to the class: **Ich finde es wichtig, dass das Thema interessant ist. Ich meine, es ist nicht so wichtig, dass der Dozent/die Dozentin nett ist. Meiner Meinung nach sind die Bücher zu teuer.**

|  | Nicht wichtig | Wichtig | Sehr wichtig |  |
|---|---|---|---|---|
| 5. hohes akademisches Niveau° | ☐ | ☐ | ☐ | *level* |
| 6. gute Bücher | ☐ | ☐ | ☐ |  |
| 7. teure Bücher | ☐ | ☐ | ☐ |  |
| 8. Diskussionen im Kurs | ☐ | ☐ | ☐ |  |
| 9. Sprechstunden | ☐ | ☐ | ☐ |  |
| 10. andere Medien: Video, Computer, DVDs, Film | ☐ | ☐ | ☐ |  |
| 11. nicht zu früh am Tag | ☐ | ☐ | ☐ |  |
| 12. praktische Information | ☐ | ☐ | ☐ |  |
| 13. wenige Studenten | ☐ | ☐ | ☐ |  |

 **52** **Probleme an der Uni.** Welche Probleme an einer Uni finden Sie besonders schlimm? Arbeiten Sie in einer Gruppe von drei Personen und ordnen Sie diese Probleme nach ihrer Wichtigkeit. Benutzen Sie die Zahlen 1 (am schlimmsten°) bis 10 (am wenigsten schlimm°).

> **Probleme an der Uni.** Be prepared to state your opinion: **Ich meine, es ist wirklich schlimm, wenn zu viele Studenten in einem Kurs sind.**

*am schlimmsten: the worst /
am ... schlimm: the least
bad*

___ Zu viele Studenten sind in einem Kurs.

___ Die Dozenten und Professoren haben zu wenige Sprechstunden.

___ Die Kurse sind zu schwierig.

___ Die Kurse sind nicht interessant.

___ Die Professoren sind zu spießig.

___ Die Hörsäle sind schmutzig°.

*dirty*

___ Man muss im Kurs zu viel arbeiten.

___ Die Kommilitonen sind unfreundlich.

___ Das Studium kostet zu viel.

___ Es gibt nicht genug Praktika.

 **Freie Kommunikation**

**Rollenspiel: Wie sind die Dozenten bei euch?** Spielen Sie die folgende Situation mit einem Partner/einer Partnerin.

S1: Sie sind Dozent/Dozentin. Sie sprechen mit einem Studenten/einer Studentin aus Österreich. Er/Sie hat gehört, dass die Dozenten in den USA sehr studenten**un**freundlich sind. Was sagen Sie zu ihm/ihr?

S2: Sie sind der Student/die Studentin aus Österreich. Sie wollen wissen, ob amerikanische Dozenten/Dozentinnen viele Aufgaben aufgeben, ob sie oft Sprechstunden haben, ob sie hilfreich oder distanziert sind, usw.

**Rollenspiel: Wie sind die Studenten bei euch?** Spielen Sie die folgende Situation mit einem Partner/einer Partnerin.

S1: Sie sind Student/Studentin aus Zürich; Sie waren noch nie in Amerika. Sie sprechen mit einem Amerikaner/einer Amerikanerin auf einer Party und erzählen, was Sie so von amerikanischen Studenten hören: Sie lernen nicht viel, sie brauchen nicht viel zu arbeiten, sie haben am Ende keine Examen, aber viele Parties, und die Diplome sind wertlos°. Sie fragen, ob das wirklich stimmt.

*worthless*

S2: Sie sind Amerikaner/Amerikanerin. Beantworten Sie die Fragen und beschreiben Sie das US-Bildungssystem und das Studentenleben.

**Schreibecke**

**Der ideale Kurs der Zukunft.** Wie wird wohl der ideale Universitätskurs im Jahre 2030 sein? Was wird wohl anders sein, was wird dasselbe sein? Besprechen Sie den Inhalt, die Prüfungen, die Lehrkräfte, die Medien usw. in einem solchen Kurs.

**Ein Brief an die Günthers.** Barbara hat Anna den folgenden Brief von ihrer Freundin aus Dresden gezeigt. Anna will auch so einen Brief an die Günthers in Weinheim schreiben. Benutzen Sie den Brief von Barbaras Freundin Caroline als Beispiel für Annas Brief an die Günthers.

> Meißener Straße 27
> 01069 Dresden
> Dienstag, den 2. November
>
> Liebe Barbara,
>     es tut mir Leid, dass ich nicht geschrieben habe. Ich habe mich erkältet und war eine Woche lang krank. Jetzt geht's mir besser.
>     Wie geht es dir an der Uni in Tübingen? Mir gefällt die Uni hier in Dresden sehr gut. Ich habe in diesem Semester einen Kurs in Biologie. Er gefällt mir sehr, denn der Professor ist ausgezeichnet. Er ist sehr studentenfreundlich. Nur sind seine Sprechstunden immer überfüllt. Ich habe mich auch entschieden Medizin zu studieren. Ich warte jetzt nur noch auf einen Studienplatz.
>     Mir gefallen auch meine Vorlesungen hier. Sie sind nicht so voll, und ich habe andere Studenten kennen gelernt.
>     Wie sind deine Kurse? Stimmt es, was man über Tübingen hört? Die Uni ist überfüllt und Kontakt mit Professoren hat man kaum°. Schreib doch mal wieder!
>     Ich werde wohl nächste Woche mehr Zeit haben. Dann kann ich dich eventuell besuchen. Ich würde mich auf eine Antwort per E-Mail oder einen Anruf von dir sehr freuen.
>                     Alles Liebe
>                     deine Caroline

*hardly*

## Wortschatz

### Universität und Schule

**das Abitur, -e (das Abi, -s)** *high school exit examination*

**der Abiturient, [-en], -en / die Abiturientin, -nen** *high school senior, soon-to-be graduate*

**der/die Auszubildende, -n (der/die Azubi, -s)** *apprentice, trainee*

**das Diplom, -e** *diploma*

**der Dozent, [-en], -en / die Dozentin, -nen** *assistant professor, lecturer*

**das Ergebnis, -se** *result*

**das Gymnasium,** *pl.* **Gymnasien** *college preparatory high school*

**die Hauptschule, -n** *technical-vocational secondary school*

**die Hochschule, -n** *college, university, post-secondary school*

**der Kindergarten, ˸** *preschool*

**der Kommilitone, [-n], -n / die Kommilitonin, -nen** *fellow student, classmate*

**die Lust** *desire*

**Lust haben** *to have desire, to be interested in*

**das Praktikum,** *pl.* **Praktika** *internship*

**die Realschule, -n** *middle-track secondary school (through 10th grade)*

**die Schule, -n** *school*

**die Semesterferien** *(pl.) semester break, holiday*

**das Seminar, -e** *seminar*

**der/die Studierende, -n** *(university level) student*

**die Vorlesung, -en** *lecture*

**gut ab·schneiden (hat abgeschnitten)** *to place well, do well*

**sich ein·schreiben (hat sich eingeschrieben)** *to register, enroll*

**tippen (hat getippt)** *to type*

**mündlich** *oral(ly)*

**schriftlich** *in writing*

### Die Gruppenarbeit

**die Arbeitsgruppe, -n** *study group*

**die Folie, -n** *overhead transparency*

**das Handout, -s** *handout*

**der Inhalt, -e** *content*

**das Referat, -e** *(seminar) presentation*

**die Seminararbeit, -en** *seminar project, paper*

**die Sprechstunde, -n** *office hour*

**das Thema,** *pl.* **Themen** *topic; theme*

### Die tägliche Routine

**sich ab·trocknen (hat sich abgetrocknet)** *to dry oneself off*

**sich an·ziehen (hat sich angezogen)** *to get dressed*

**sich (eine Jacke) an·ziehen** *to put on (a jacket)*

**sich aus·ziehen (hat sich ausgezogen)** *to get undressed*

**baden (hat gebadet)** *to bathe*

**sich beeilen (hat sich beeilt)** *to hurry*

**sich die Haare bürsten (hat sich die Haare gebürstet)** *to brush one's hair*

**(sich) duschen (hat [sich] geduscht)** *to take a shower*

**sich die Haare föhnen (hat sich die Haare geföhnt)** *to blow-dry one's hair*

**sich die Haare kämmen (hat sich die Haare gekämmt)** *to comb one's hair*

**sich die Zähne putzen (hat sich die Zähne geputzt)** *to clean/brush one's teeth*

**sich rasieren (hat sich rasiert)** *to shave*

**sich die Beine rasieren** *to shave one's legs*

**sich schminken (hat sich geschminkt)** *to put on make-up*

**sich waschen (wäscht sich, hat sich gewaschen)** *to wash oneself*

**sich die Haare waschen** *to wash one's hair*

**sich die Hände waschen** *to wash one's hands*

### Im Badezimmer und auf der Toilette

**das Badetuch, ˸er** *bath towel*

**die Badewanne, -n** *bathtub*

**der Becher, -** *cup*

**der Föhn, -e** *blow dryer*

**der Haken, -** *hook*

**der Rasierapparat, -e** *electric razor*

**die Seife, -n** *soap*

**das Shampoo, -s** *shampoo*

*Noch einmal:* **das Badezimmer, die Bürste, die Dusche, der Kamm, der Lippenstift, der Spiegel, die Steckdose, die Toilette, das Waschbecken, die Zahnbürste, die Zahnpasta**

### Krank sein

**der Arzt, ˸e / die Ärztin, -nen** *doctor*

**der Durchfall** *diarrhea*

**Durchfall haben** *to have diarrhea*

**die Erkältung, -en** *head cold; chill*

**das Fieber** *fever*

**Fieber haben** *to have a fever*

**der Gips** *cast*

**das Heftpflaster, -** *adhesive bandage*

**der Muskelkater, -** *sore muscle*

**der Schmerz, -en** *pain*

**Zahnschmerzen (Halsschmerzen, Kopfschmerzen) haben** *to have a toothache (sore throat, headache)*

**die Schmerztablette, -n** *painkiller*

**der Schnupfen, -** *head cold, sniffles*

**sich aus·ruhen (hat sich ausgeruht)** *to rest*

**sich (das Bein) brechen (bricht sich, hat sich gebrochen)** *to break one's (leg)*

**sich erholen (hat sich erholt)** *to recuperate, get well*

**sich erkälten (hat sich erkältet)** *to catch a cold*

**sich fühlen (hat sich gefühlt)** *to feel*

**sich nicht wohl fühlen** *to feel unwell*

**sich hin·legen (hat sich hingelegt)** *to lie down*

**sich in den Finger schneiden (hat sich geschnitten)** *to cut one's finger*

**sich melden (hat sich gemeldet)** *to report, show up*

**sich übergeben (übergibt sich, hat sich übergeben)** *to vomit*

**weh·tun (hat wehgetan) + *dat.* *to hurt, be painful (to someone)*

　**sich wehtun** *to hurt oneself*

**krank** *sick*

**wohl** *fine, healthy; probably, in all likelihood*

**Gute Besserung!** *Get well!*

**Mir geht es so lala.** *I'm so so.*

**Mir geht es ziemlich schlecht.** *I'm feeling pretty bad.*

**Wie fühlst du dich?** *How are you feeling?*

*Noch einmal:* **Wie geht's dir?**

### Zeitausdrücke

**der Morgen, -** *morning*
**der Nachmittag, -e** *afternoon*
**der Abend, -e** *evening*

**früh** *early*
**in zwei Tagen (Wochen, Monaten)** *in two days (weeks, months)*
**jeden Tag** *every day*
**morgen früh** *tomorrow morning*
**nächste Woche** *next week*
**nächsten Samstag** *next Saturday*
**nächsten Sommer** *next summer*
**nächstes Jahr** *next year*
**übermorgen** *the day after tomorrow*

*Noch einmal:* **heute, morgen, später**

### Verben mit präpositionalem Objekt

**achten auf + *acc.* (hat geachtet)** *to pay attention to*
**Angst haben vor + *dat.* (hat Angst gehabt)** *to be afraid of*
**sich ärgern über + *acc.* (hat sich geärgert)** *to be angry about*
**bitten um + *acc.* (hat gebeten)** *to ask for, request*
**sich entscheiden für/gegen + *acc.* (hat sich entschieden)** *to decide for/against*

**sich erinnern an + *acc.* (hat sich erinnert)** *to remember*
**erwarten von + *dat.* (hat erwartet)** *to expect of*
**sich freuen auf + *acc.* (hat sich gefreut)** *to look forward to*
**sich freuen über + *acc.* (hat sich gefreut)** *to be happy about*
**gespannt sein auf + *acc.* (ist gespannt gewesen)** *to be excited about*
**halten für + *acc.* (hält, hat gehalten)** *to consider/think (someone) is (something)*
**handeln von + *dat.* (hat gehandelt)** *to be about*
**sich konzentrieren auf + *acc.* (hat sich konzentriert)** *to concentrate on*
**passen zu + *dat.* (hat gepasst)** *to suit, fit*
**sprechen über + *acc.* (spricht, hat gesprochen)** *to talk about, discuss*
**sich trennen von + *dat.* (hat sich getrennt)** *to break up with, separate from*
**sich verlieben in + *acc.* (hat sich verliebt)** *to fall in love with*
**sich verloben mit + *dat.* (hat sich verlobt)** *to get engaged to*
**sich vor·bereiten auf + *acc.* (hat sich vorbereitet)** *to prepare (oneself) for, get ready for*

*Noch einmal:* **danken für + *acc.*, denken an + *acc.*, erzählen von + *dat.*, fragen nach + *dat.*, glauben an + *acc.*, halten von + *dat.*, reden über + *acc.*, etwas verstehen von + *dat.*, warten auf + *acc.*, wissen von + *dat.***

### Andere Verben

**bestellen (hat bestellt)** *to order*
**dauern (hat gedauert)** *to last*
**ein Referat halten (hält; hat gehalten)** *to give an oral report*
**klingen (hat geklungen)** *to ring; to sound*
　**Das klingt gut.** *That sounds good.*
　**Sie klingt freundlich.** *She sounds friendly.*
**kopieren (hat kopiert)** *to copy*
**probieren (hat probiert)** *to try*
**schaffen (hat geschafft)** *to succeed, get done*

**statt·finden (hat stattgefunden)** *to take place*
**versuchen (hat versucht)** *to try*
**sich vor·stellen (hat sich vorgestellt)** *to introduce oneself*
　**Darf ich mich vorstellen?** *Allow me to introduce myself.*
**wählen (hat gewählt)** *to choose*
**wechseln (hat gewechselt)** *to change*
*Noch einmal:* **empfehlen, leihen, scheinen, steigen, vergessen**

### Adjektive und Adverbien

**aktuell** *current(ly)*
**anders** *different(ly)*
**bekannt** *familiar; famous*
**berühmt** *famous*
**gemeinsam** *shared, communal*
**genau** *exact(ly)*
**kaum** *hardly*
**meistens** *mostly*
**natürlich** *natural(ly)*
**plötzlich** *suddenly*
**schließlich** *finally*
**schmutzig** *dirty*
**schrecklich** *awful(ly) terrible; terribly*
**selbst** *oneself*
**verschieden** *different*
**zusätzlich** *additionally*

### Andere Wörter

**die Geschwister** *(pl.) siblings*
**die Lösung, -en** *solution*
**die Schwierigkeit, -en** *difficulty; problem*
**die Freiheit, -en** *freedom, liberty*
**die Wahrheit, -en** *truth*

### Andere Ausdrücke

**deswegen** *that's why*
**ein paar** *a few*
**Herein (bitte).** *Come in (please).*
**klasse** *great, cool*
**noch mal** *(once) again*
**Pech haben** *to have bad luck*

### Meine eigenen Wörter

_____

_____

# Ein Praktikum in Wien

In this chapter you will continue to learn how to describe people, objects, and activities. You will talk and read about professions, job interviews, and job qualifications.

## Kommunikative Funktionen

- Providing additional information about people and topics
- Proposing activities, making suggestions
- Describing people and things
- Expressing the city of origin
- Comparing people and things

## Strukturen

- Nominative, accusative, and dative case relative pronouns
- Present tense subjunctive with **würde, hätte, wäre**
- Endings on adjectives after **ein**-words, **der**-words, or neither
- Forming adjectives from city names
- Comparative and superlative forms of adjectives and adverbs

## Vokabeln

- Berufe
- Eigenschaften von guten Bewerbern
- Österreichs Leute und Länder

## Kulturelles

- Wien
- Berufswahl und Berufsausbildung in den deutschsprachigen Ländern
- Österreich

 In einem Wiener Kaffeehaus kann man gemütlich einen Mokka trinken.

**Online Study Center**

Go to the *Vorsprung* Website at *http://college.hmco.com/pic/vorsprung2e.*

# Karl hat ein Vorstellungsgespräch° bei der Wiener Staatsoper

Anna und Stefan freuen sich für Karl: Karl hat gute Chancen, ein Praktikum im Kulturmanagement an der weltberühmten° Wiener Staatsoper zu bekommen. In einer Woche muss er nach Wien zum Vorstellungsgespräch reisen. Anna und Stefan wünschen° Karl viel Glück, aber dann beginnt Karl wirklich nervös zu werden. Ist er wirklich für die Stelle qualifiziert? Kann er in der Praxis alles benutzen, was er an der Universität gelernt hat? Wird er Fragen beantworten können, die man ihm im Interview stellt? Anna und Stefan helfen Karl, sich auf das Vorstellungsgespräch vorzubereiten.

**Vorstellungsgespräch:** *job interview*

*world-famous*

*wish*

## *Vorschau*

 **1**   **Thematische Fragen.**  Beantworten Sie die folgenden Fragen auf Deutsch.

1. Was versteht man als typische Studentenjobs an Ihrer Uni? Sagen Sie für jeden Job, ob er als Studentenjob typisch oder untypisch ist.
   a. Assistent/in im Studentenwohnheim
   b. Aushilfe° im Kopiergeschäft
   c. Babysitter/in
   d. Forschungsassistent/in°
   e. Kellner/in
   f. Mitarbeiter/in an der Uni-Bibliothek
   g. Pizzazusteller/in
   h. Reinemachefrau°/Hausmeister°
   i. Tellerwäscher/in in der Mensa
   j. Barkeeper/in in einer Kneipe

*part-time worker*

*research assistant*

*housekeeper / apartment manager*

2. Arbeiten Sie jetzt auf dem Campus oder in der Stadt? Als was? Gefällt Ihnen die Arbeit?

3. Was für Jobs haben Sie schon gehabt? Wie viele Stunden in der Woche haben Sie gearbeitet? Wie viel Geld haben Sie verdient?

4. Ein Praktikum ist praktische Arbeit, die man als Teil des Studiums macht, zum Beispiel, ein Ingenieurstudent arbeitet im Sommer bei Ford oder GM. Müssen Sie für Ihr Hauptfach ein Praktikum machen? Halten Sie das für gut oder nicht? Warum?

**2** **Autogrammspiel: Arbeiten und Geld verdienen.** Finden Sie für jede Frage eine Person, die die Frage mit **Ja** beantworten kann. Bitten Sie die Person um ihre Unterschrift.

Wer arbeitet nur in den Sommerferien? \_\_\_\_\_

S1: *Arbeitest du nur in den Sommerferien?*
S2: *Nein, ich arbeite auch während° des Semesters.*          *during*
S1: *Arbeitest du nur in den Sommerferien?*
S3: *Ja, das stimmt, ich arbeite nur in den Sommerferien.*
S1: *OK, danke. Unterschreib bitte hier.*

1. Wer arbeitet nur in den Sommerferien?     \_\_\_\_\_
2. Wer arbeitet während des Semesters?      \_\_\_\_\_
3. Wer arbeitet nur abends?                 \_\_\_\_\_
4. Wer arbeitet nur am Wochenende?          \_\_\_\_\_
5. Wer arbeitet das ganze Jahr durch?       \_\_\_\_\_
6. Wer muss gar nicht arbeiten?             \_\_\_\_\_

**3** **Satzdetektiv.** Welche Sätze bedeuten ungefähr das Gleiche?

1. Gute **Nachrichten** von der Wiener Staatsoper.
2. Ich habe eine Einladung zum **Vorstellungsgespräch** in Wien!
3. **Hast du dich** um ein Praktikum **beworben**?
4. Das ist eine **großartige Stelle** in der **Betriebsleitung**.
5. Ich habe noch **keinen festen Termin**.
6. Das ist eine **einmalige Gelegenheit** für dich.

a. Es ist ein fantastischer Job in der Geschäftsführung°.          *business office*
b. Ich weiß noch nicht genau, wann mein Interview ist.
c. Ich fahre nach Wien für ein Interview!
d. Du hast nur einmal im Leben eine solche° Chance.          *such a*
e. Ich habe eine positive Antwort aus Wien bekommen.
f. Hast du die Papiere für eine Praktikantenstelle eingereicht?

7. Ich **drücke dir** ganz fest **die Daumen**!
8. Wie soll ich **mich** bloß im Vorstellungsgespräch **verhalten**, und was soll ich tragen?
9. **Wie wäre es** mit einem Rollenspiel?
10. Aber was soll ich sagen, wenn sie fragen, welche **Arbeitserfahrung** ich schon habe?
11. **Beruhige dich** doch, Karl.
12. Warum **würdest du** sie nicht **beeindrucken**?

g. Warum sollst du keinen positiven Eindruck° auf die Leute machen?          *impression*
h. Sei nicht so nervös, Karl.
i. Ich wünsche dir viel Glück!
j. Was hältst du davon, wenn wir ein Rollenspiel machen?
k. Wie antworte ich, wenn sie fragen, ob ich schon im Kulturmanagement gearbeitet habe?
l. Was soll ich im Interview sagen und tun und was soll ich anziehen?

## *Anlauftext*

 Hören Sie gut zu.

### Karl hat ein Vorstellungsgespräch bei der Wiener Staatsoper

Anna, Stefan! Gute Nachrichten von der Wiener Staatsoper.

Ich habe eine Einladung zum Vorstellungsgespräch in Wien!

In der Tat? Für das Praktikum, um das du dich beworben hast?

Ja, für die Stelle im Kulturmanagement, die ich im Internet gefunden habe.

Was für eine Stelle soll das sein?

Das ist ja wahnsinnig!

Das ist eine großartige Stelle in der Betriebsleitung.

Fantastisch! Fährst du gleich nach Wien?

Nee, das hat keinen Zweck. Ich habe noch keinen festen Termin.

Trotzdem, das ist eine einmalige Gelegenheit für dich. Ich drücke dir ganz fest die Daumen!

Aber was mache ich nun? Ich bin schon ganz nervös und aufgeregt.

Wie soll ich mich bloß im Vorstellungsgespräch verhalten, und was soll ich tragen?

## *Rückblick*

**4** **Stimmt das?** Stimmen diese Aussagen zum Text oder nicht? Wenn nicht, was stimmt?

|  | Ja, das stimmt. | Nein, das stimmt nicht. |
|---|---|---|
| 1. Karl hat einen permanenten Job an der Wiener Staatsoper bekommen. | ☐ | ☐ |
| 2. Karl hat sich um ein Praktikum im Kulturmanagement beworben. | ☐ | ☐ |
| 3. Karl muss schon heute nach Wien zum Vorstellungsgespräch fahren. | ☐ | ☐ |
| 4. Karls Praktikum ist als Sänger im Chor von der Staatsoper. | ☐ | ☐ |
| 5. Karl meint, er wird die Stelle sicher bekommen. | ☐ | ☐ |
| 6. Stefan bringt Karl zum Friseur für einen anständigen° Haarschnitt. | ☐ | ☐ |
| 7. Der neue Anzug soll einen guten Eindruck machen. | ☐ | ☐ |
| 8. Anna schlägt vor, ein Rollenspiel mit Karl zu machen. | ☐ | ☐ |
| 9. Karl hat Angst, dass er für diese Stelle nicht genug im Kulturmanagement gearbeitet hat und nicht genug weiß. | ☐ | ☐ |
| 10. Anna erinnert Karl daran, dass er mit fast allen Menschen arbeiten kann. | ☐ | ☐ |
| 11. Karl gibt zu, dass er gern Theater spielt. | ☐ | ☐ |

*decent* (next to item 6)

Complete the **Ergänzen Sie** activity in your workbook for this text before doing the next activity.

---

**Sprache im Alltag: Wishing someone luck**

There are several expressions for wishing people luck in German:

| | |
|---|---|
| **Ich drücke dir ganz fest die Daumen!** | *I'm crossing my fingers for you!* |
| **Hals- und Beinbruch!** | *Break a leg!* |
| **Ich wünsch' dir 'was!** | *I'm hoping for you!* |
| **Toi, toi, toi!** | *Lots of luck!* |

Instead of crossing their fingers, German speakers make a clenched fist enclosing the thumb on the left hand to gesture that they're wishing someone good luck.

**Toi, toi, toi** (pronounced just like English *toy*) is used primarily in the context of performances, including job interviews.

---

**5** **Kurz gefragt.** Beantworten Sie die folgenden Fragen auf Deutsch.

1. In welcher Abteilung° von der Wiener Staatsoper soll Karl sein Praktikum machen?   *department*
2. Warum ist Karl nervös und aufgeregt?
3. Wie reagieren Anna und Stefan auf Karls Situation?
4. Warum muss Karl nicht sofort° nach Wien reisen?   *right away*
5. Was schlagen Anna und Stefan vor, um Karl zu helfen?
6. Was sind Karls Vorteile?

## Wien

Vienna (**Wien**) is the capital of modern Austria and the former capital of the Austro-Hungarian Empire (**Österreich-Ungarn**), which comprised portions of Bulgaria, Czechoslovakia, Italy, Poland, Romania, Slovenia, Ukraine, and Yugoslavia, as well as Austria and Hungary. In the 19th century, Austro-Hungary was ruled by the Hapsburgs, and Vienna was home to the emperor or empress (**der Kaiser/die Kaiserin**) and his/her court. As such, Vienna was the showplace of the empire. Absorbing and assimilating peoples of diverse nationalities and their customs, art forms, language, and tastes, Vienna developed an atmosphere conducive to intellectual and artistic creativity. Over the centuries, Vienna has been home to such well-known figures as the psychoanalyst Sigmund Freud, the composers Haydn, Mozart, Beethoven, Schubert, Brahms, and Strauß, the filmmakers Otto Preminger and Billy Wilder, and the painters Friedensreich Hundertwasser and Gustav Klimt.

Vienna is also closely associated with numerous writers, e.g., the playwrights Franz Grillparzer (1791–1872) and Arthur Schnitzler (1862–1931) as well as Ingeborg Bachman (1926–1973), Peter Handke (b. 1942), and Elfriede Jelinek (b. 1946).

*In der Hofburg erkennt man die Größe und die Schönheit vom kaiserlichen und königlichen Österreich-Ungarn.*

Downtown Vienna is a compelling mix of the historic and the modern. The inner city (**die Innenstadt**) is Vienna's oldest part. At its heart is **der Stephansdom**, the seat of the cardinal of Austria and Austria's national cathedral, dating back to 1147 with distinctly Gothic influences from the early 14th century. **Die Ringstraße,** with buildings dating to the mid–19th century, surrounds the **Innenstadt** and reflects the glory days of the Hapsburg empire. One particular building, **das Secessionsgebäude** or **die Secession**, for short, was completed in 1898. It served as the home base of the artistic movement of the same name, led by the painter Gustav Klimt, most well known for his painting **Der Kuss.** The impact of the Hapsburg emperors is seen in their former residences, the **Hofburg**, as well as **der Burggarten, der Heldenplatz, die Österreichische Nationalbibliothek**, and **die Spanische Reitschule** with its famous Lipizzaner horses. In the summer the royal family retreated to its country residence, **Schloss Schönbrunn**, a spectacular rococo palace with 1,441 rooms and expansive baroque gardens, fountains, and a zoo, which lies within the confines of the modern city today.

Visitors to the Vienna of today will find a mix of provincial old-world elegance and international engagement with the contemporary world. In a Viennese **Kaffeehaus**, visitors can savor a rich cup of coffee or enjoy a world-famous Viennese pastry such as **Sachertorte.** Tourists and locals enjoy visiting **der Prater,** the world's oldest amusement park, and riding its gigantic Ferris wheel (**das Riesenrad**). On the other hand, Vienna is also home to institutions such as OPEC, as well as to **UNO-City**, the site of the United Nations headquarters.

## ■ Kulturkreuzung

1. Welche Länder in und außerhalb von Europa haben noch einen König oder eine Königin?

2. Sind diese Monarchien auch Demokratien?

3. Was ist die Funktion von einem König oder einer Königin in einer modernen Demokratie? Was meinen Sie? Hat das Königtum heute noch einen Wert und eine wichtige Funktion?

4. Vergleichen Sie den historischen österreichischen Begriff von Multikulturalismus mit dem heutigen Begriff davon in Ihrem Land. Was sind die Ähnlichkeiten? Was sind die Unterschiede?

**6    Interview: Stundentenjobs und Praktika.** Stellen Sie einem Partner/einer Partnerin die folgenden Fragen.

1. Hast du im Moment einen Job? Ist er gut? Warum, oder warum nicht?
2. Welche Studentenjobs hältst du für gut? Welche hältst du für nicht gut? Warum?
3. Warum arbeiten viele Studierende? Hältst du das für gut oder schlecht?
4. Was findest du besser — ein interessantes Praktikum zu machen oder im Praktikum viel zu verdienen?
5. Wie kann man als Studierender/Studierende sehr viel Geld verdienen?
6. Wie können Studierende deiner Meinung nach° von einem unbezahlten° Praktikum profitieren?
7. Würdest du ein unbezahltes Praktikum machen oder nicht? Warum?

> **Interview.** Jot down notes as your partner answers each of these questions and be prepared to report your findings to the class.

*in your opinion / unpaid*

## Strukturen und Vokabeln

### I    Providing additional information about topics

Nominative, accusative, and dative case relative pronouns

#### A. Nominative case relative pronouns

A relative clause (**der Relativsatz**) allows writers and speakers to provide additional information about something mentioned in the main clause without the awkward repetition of a noun. It is formed from two independent sentences that share a common noun.

> Ich spiele **die Dame. Die Dame** interviewt dich.
> *I'll play the lady. The lady is interviewing you.*

> Ich spiele **die Dame,** die dich interviewt.
> *I'll play the lady who is interviewing you.*

A relative clause always has a relative pronoun (**das Relativpronomen**) at or near its beginning. The relative pronoun (e.g., **die**) refers back to a preceding noun in the sentence (e.g., **die Dame**). This noun is known as the antecedent (**das Bezugswort**). The gender and number of the relative pronoun are determined by the gender and number of the antecedent.

> *masculine, singular*
> Ich spiele **den Betriebsleiter. Der Betriebsleiter** wird dein neuer Chef.
> *I'll play the executive officer. The executive officer will be your new boss.*

> Ich spiele **den Betriebsleiter, der** dein neuer Chef wird.
> *I'll play the executive officer who'll be your new boss.*

> In English, relative clauses are formed with *which*, *who, whom*, or *that*, although sometimes the relative pronoun is omitted: *The job* (*that*) *I found is in Vienna. The person* (*whom*) *I met yesterday comes from Austria.*

The case is determined by the relative pronoun's use in the relative clause. When the relative pronoun is the subject of the relative clause, it occurs in the nominative case (**der, das, die** for singular, and **die** for plural).

| | |
|---|---|
| Du brauchst *einen Anzug,* **der** einen guten Eindruck macht. | *You need a suit that makes a good impression.* |
| Ich suche *ein Auto,* **das** nicht zu teuer ist. | *I'm looking for a car that is not too expensive.* |
| Das ist *eine Gelegenheit,* **die** nur einmal im Leben kommt. | *That is an opportunity that only occurs once in a lifetime.* |
| *Die* anderen *Bewerber,* **die** die Stelle wollen, haben nicht mehr Erfahrung als du. | *The other applicants who want the position don't have any more experience than you.* |

In written German, commas set off the relative clause from the main clause, and since a relative clause is a subordinate clause (**der Nebensatz**), the verb occurs at the end of the subordinate clause.

| | |
|---|---|
| Die Stelle, die ich im Internet gefunden habe, ist in Wien. | *The job that I found on the Internet is in Vienna.* |

> All relative clauses in German are set off with commas. In English only nonrestrictive relative clauses, e.g., those that can be eliminated, have commas: *Barbara, whom everybody knows, was elected president of the class.*

**7**  **Definitionen.**  Definieren Sie die fett gedruckten Wörter. Verbinden Sie jeden Hauptsatz in der linken Spalte° mit einem passenden Relativsatz in der rechten Spalte.  *column*

1. Eine **Praktikumsstelle** ist eine Stelle,
2. Ein **Vorstellungsgespräch** ist ein Gespräch,
3. Ein **Betriebsleiter** ist ein Mann,
4. Eine **Seminararbeit** ist eine Arbeit,
5. Ein **Tellerwäscher** ist ein Mann,

a. das zwischen einem Bewerber° und einem Interviewer ist.  *applicant*
b. die für Studierende gedacht° ist.  *intended*
c. der im Restaurant in der Küche arbeitet.
d. der der Chef von der ganzen Firma ist.
e. die Studierende in einem Proseminar schreiben.

**8**  **Was für ein Job ist das?**  Beschreiben Sie die Jobs der folgenden Personen mit Hilfe der Informationen in der rechten Spalte.

| | | |
|---|---|---|
| 1. Ich habe einen Job, | | mir/ihm/ihr Spaß macht. |
| 2. Ich möchte eine Stelle haben, | der | hart ist. |
| 3. Ich suche ein Praktikum, | das | langweilig ist. |
| 4. Mein(e) Freund(in) hat eine Arbeit, | die | interessant ist. |
| 5. Mein Vater/Meine Mutter hat einen Job, | | Initiative verlangt°.  *requires* |
| | | viel Flexibilität hat.  *offers* |

## Wissenswerte Vokabeln: Berufe
### Talking about occupations

der Apotheker
die Apothekerin

der Automechaniker
die Automechanikerin

der Bäcker
die Bäckerin

der Chef
die Chefin

der Fleischer
die Fleischerin
der Metzger
die Metzgerin

der Friseur
die Friseurin

der Geschäftsmann
die Geschäftsfrau

der Ingenieur
die Ingenieurin

der Kaufmann
die Kauffrau

der Koch
die Köchin

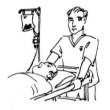

der Krankenpfleger
die Krankenschwester

der Makler
die Maklerin

der Programmierer
die Programmiererin

der Rechtsanwalt
die Rechtsanwältin

der Schauspieler
die Schauspielerin

der Schriftsteller
die Schriftstellerin

der Tierarzt
die Tierärztin

der Verkäufer
die Verkäuferin

der Wissenschaftler
die Wissenschaftlerin

der Zahnarzt
die Zahnärztin

### Andere Berufe

| | | |
|---|---|---|
| der Arbeiter | die Arbeiterin | *worker; laborer, blue-collar worker* |
| der Architekt | die Architektin | *architect* |
| der Arzt | die Ärztin | *physician* |
| der Bauer | die Bäuerin | *farmer* |
| der Beamte | die Beamtin | *civil servant* |

*Andere Berufe*

| | | |
|---|---|---|
| der Berater | die Beraterin | *advisor; consultant* |
| der Dichter | die Dichterin | *poet* |
| der Dirigent | die Dirigentin | *orchestra or chorus conductor* |
| der Filmemacher | die Filmemacherin | *filmmaker* |
| der Journalist | die Journalistin | *journalist* |
| der Kellner | die Kellnerin | *waiter/waitress* |
| der Komponist | die Komponistin | *composer* |
| der Künstler | die Künstlerin | *artist* |
| der Lehrer | die Lehrerin | *school teacher* |
| der Musiker | die Musikerin | *musician* |
| der Politiker | die Politikerin | *politician* |
| der Regisseur | die Regisseurin | *film or play director* |
| der Sänger | die Sängerin | *singer* |
| der Sekretär | die Sekretärin | *secretary* |

> When naming a person's profession, German speakers omit the indefinite article **ein/eine**, e.g., **Er ist Arzt.** (*He's a doctor.*). When describing specifics about a person's professional skills, they use an article before the adjective, e.g., **Er ist mein neuer Arzt.** (*He's my new doctor.*).

■ Wer unterrichtet Deutsch?  *Der Lehrer oder die Lehrerin.*

 **9** **Berufe.** Was ist z. B. ein Kellner? Geben Sie zusammen mit einem Partner/einer Partnerin Definitionen für die folgenden Berufe.

eine Rolle im Theaterstück spielen • Brot und Brötchen backen • Häuser verkaufen • etwas im Geschäft verkaufen • im Krankenhaus arbeiten • im Restaurant das Essen servieren • in einer Schule unterrichten • kranke Tiere behandeln • Romane und Krimis schreiben • Pläne für Häuser zeichnen

■ S1: *Was ist ein Kellner?*
S2: *Ein Kellner ist ein Mann, der im Restaurant das Essen serviert.*

1. Kellner
2. Lehrerin
3. Bäcker
4. Schauspielerin
5. Ärztin
6. Maklerin
7. Schriftstellerin
8. Architekt
9. Tierarzt
10. Verkäuferin

**10** **Autogrammspiel: Was möchten Sie werden?** Finden Sie für jede Frage eine Person, die mit **Ja** antwortet. Bitten Sie die Person um ihre Unterschrift.

■ Lehrer/Lehrerin _____

S1: *Möchtest du Lehrerin werden?*
S2: *Ja. Ich möchte Lehrerin werden.*
S1: *Unterschreib hier bitte.*

1. Lehrer/Lehrerin _____
2. Architekt/Architektin _____
3. Arzt/Ärztin _____
4. Ingenieur/Ingenieurin _____
5. Geschäftsmann/Geschäftsfrau _____
6. Kaufmann/Kauffrau _____
7. Krankenpfleger/Krankenschwester _____
8. Rechtsanwalt/Rechtsanwältin _____
9. Programmierer/Programmiererin _____
10. Künstler/Künstlerin _____

**GÖTTER IN WEISS**

Bei der Frage, vor welchem Beruf die Deutschen die meiste Achtung haben, lagen die Ärzte mit Abstand an der Spitze.

| Berufe mit Prestige | Angaben in Prozent |
|---|---|
| 1. Arzt | 72 |
| 2. Pfarrer, Geistlicher | 39 |
| 3. Hochschulprofessor | 30 |
| 4. Unternehmer | 30 |
| 5. Rechtsanwalt | 29 |
| 6. Grundschullehrer | 27 |
| 7. Ingenieur | 26 |
| 8. Apotheker | 26 |
| 9. Botschafter, Diplomat | 25 |
| 10. Schriftsteller | 22 |

*Pfarrer: minister*

## B. Accusative case relative pronouns

In the preceding activities, you practiced the use of the relative pronoun in the nominative case, when it functions as the subject of the relative clause.

> Ein Mann, **der** Brot bäckt, ist ein Bäcker.

When a relative pronoun functions as a direct object, it is in the accusative case.

> **Der Mann** kommt aus Algerien. Barbara hat **den Mann** in der Arbeit kennen gelernt.
> *The man is from Algeria. Barbara met the man at work.*

> **Der Mann, den** Barbara bei der Arbeit kennen gelernt hat, kommt aus Algerien.
> *The man, whom Barbara met at work, is from Algeria.*

## C. Dative case relative pronouns

A relative pronoun may also replace a noun in the dative case. Frequently the relative pronoun functions as the indirect object of the relative clause.

> Der Mann ist Herr Kronemeyer. Wir geben **dem Mann** die Pläne.
> *The man is Mr. Kronemeyer. We are giving the plans to the man.*

> Der Mann, **dem** wir die Pläne geben, ist Herr Kronemeyer.
> *The man to whom we are giving the plans is Mr. Kronemeyer.*   OR
> *The man we are giving the plans to is Mr. Kronemeyer.*

This is a summary chart of the relative pronouns.

|  | Masculine | Neuter | Feminine | Plural |
|---|---|---|---|---|
| **Nominative** | der | das | die | die |
| **Accusative** | den | das | die | die |
| **Dative** | dem | dem | der | denen |

You should primarily be able to recognize the use of relative pronouns in the accusative and dative cases. Some activities will require you to practice producing them.

Note that most forms of the relative pronouns are identical to the forms of the definite articles. Like the definite articles, all relative pronouns begin with the letter **d.**

**11   Im Büro.** Verbinden Sie einen Hauptsatz in der linken Spalte mit einem passenden Relativsatz in der rechten Spalte.

◻ *Ist das der neue Kollege, den wir gestern in der Kantine getroffen haben?*

1. Ist das der neue Kollege, f
2. Wo ist der neue Computer, A
3. Herr Diehl, haben Sie das Inserat° geschrieben, B
4. Frau Albrecht, hier sind die Papiere, C
5. Frau Anders, geben Sie mir bitte den Brief, E
6. Ich suche das kurze Fax, D
7. Ach, Herr Siegebert. Wie heißt denn dieser Mann in Bad Godesberg, G

a. den Herr Tingelmann gestern bei Siemens gekauft hat?
b. das wir in die Zeitung setzen wollen?   *classified ad*
c. die wir heute losschicken müssen.
d. das gerade aus New York angekommen ist.
e. den Sie gestern getippt haben.
f. den wir gestern in der Kantine getroffen haben?
g. dem wir den Auftrag° für die Fotokopierer gegeben haben?   *contract, order*

## D. Relative pronouns after prepositions

You have learned that a relative pronoun can function as a subject, a direct object, or an indirect object in a relative clause. A relative pronoun can also replace a noun after a preposition and then appears in the case required by that preposition.

*Accusative prepositions* (**durch, für, gegen, ohne, um**):

Ist es für das Praktikum, **um das** du dich beworben hast?
*Is it for the internship that you applied for?*

*Dative prepositions* (**aus, außer, bei, mit, nach, seit, von, zu**):

Klein und Co. ist die Firma, **bei der** er früher gearbeitet hat.
*Klein & Co. is the company that he used to work for.*

Das sind die Leute, **mit denen** Karl arbeiten soll.
*Those are the people with whom Karl is supposed to work.*

*Two-case prepositions* (**an, auf, hinter, in, neben, über, unter, vor, zwischen**):

Das ist ein Job, **in dem** man viel Trinkgeld bekommt.
*That's a job in which one gets a lot of tips.*

Das ist eine Karriere, **an die** ich gedacht habe.
*That's a career (that) I've thought about.*

The interrogative **wo** often replaces the preposition **in** and the relative pronoun in spoken German.

Das ist ein Job, **in dem** man viel Trinkgeld bekommt.
Das ist ein Job, **wo** man viel Trinkgeld bekommt.

> Note that in German the preposition and the relative pronoun must always appear together at the beginning of the relative clause and can never be separated as they might be in English: **Heidelberg ist eine Stadt, <u>von der</u> man viel hört.** (*Heidelberg is a city* that *one hears a lot about.*)

**12**  **Richtig bewerben.**  Hier sind vier Anzeigen aus einer Zeitschrift. Identifizieren Sie das Relativpronomen und das Bezugswort.

■ Der einzige Arztroman, bei dem
das Publikum mitbestimmen kann.
Relativpronomen: *dem*
Bezugswort: *Arztroman*

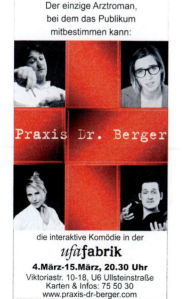

1. Relativpronomen: _____
Bezugswort: _____

2. Relativpronomen: _____
   Bezugswort: _____

3. Relativpronomen: _____
   Bezugswort: _____

**13 Definitionen.** Definieren Sie die fett gedruckten Wörter. Verbinden Sie jeden Hauptsatz in der linken Spalte mit einem passenden Relativsatz in der rechten Spalte.

1. Ein **Vorstellungsgespräch** ist ein Gespräch,
2. Ein **Bäcker** ist ein Mann,
3. Wien ist eine **Stadt**,
4. Kulturmanagement ist ein **Beruf**,
5. Eine Tierärztin ist eine **Frau**,
6. Ein Studienberater ist eine **Person**,

a. bei dem man Brot kauft.
b. in dem man Schauspieler kennen lernen kann.
c. in dem man sich bei einer Firma vorstellt.
d. in der man viel Kultur erleben kann.
e. mit der Studierende sprechen, wenn sie Fragen haben.
f. zu der wir unseren Hund bringen, wenn er krank ist.

## II Proposing activities, making suggestions

### Present tense subjunctive with **würde, hätte, wäre**

The *mood* (**der Modus**) of a verb expresses the speaker's attitude toward what is being said, e.g., certainty, doubt, probability, impossibility, politeness, or hypothetical state. Mood is reflected in the form of the verb.

Factual statements use the indicative mood (**der Indikativ**).

Ich **habe** eine Einladung zum Vorstellungsgespräch.     *I have an invitation for an interview.*

Commands use the imperative mood (**der Imperativ**).

**Sei** schnell!    *Be quick! (Hurry up!)*

To express possibility, hypothetical situations, and politeness, German speakers can use the subjunctive mood (**der Konjunktiv**).

## A. The present subjunctive of *werden*

The most common way to express the present subjunctive in speaking is to use the auxiliary verb **würde** (*would*) with an infinitive. The infinitive occurs at the end of the main clause.

Was **würdest** du **tun**?    *What would you do?*

Here are the forms of **würde** combined with the infinitive **sagen.**

| **würde** sagen: *would say* | | |
|---|---|---|
| **Singular** | | **Plural** |
| ich **würde** sagen | wir | **würden** sagen |
| du **würdest** sagen | ihr | **würdet** sagen |
| Sie **würden** sagen | Sie | **würden** sagen |
| er/sie/es **würde** sagen | sie | **würden** sagen |

> **Würde** is the subjunctive form of the verb **werden**.

**14**  **Das Vorstellungsgespräch.** Was würden Sie in einem Vorstellungsgespräch tun oder nicht tun? Markieren Sie die relevanten Punkte und fragen Sie dann einen Partner/eine Partnerin.

□ einen Anzug tragen

S1: *Würdest du einen Anzug tragen?*
S2: *Ja, ich würde einen Anzug tragen. Und du?*
S1: *Nein, ich würde keinen Anzug tragen.* (oder)
    *Ja, ich würde auch einen Anzug tragen.*

| | Ich | Mein Partner / Meine Partnerin |
|---|---|---|
| 1. einen Anzug tragen | _____ | _____ |
| 2. vorher zum Friseur gehen | _____ | _____ |
| 3. alte Turnschuhe tragen | _____ | _____ |
| 4. über Religion sprechen | _____ | _____ |
| 5. spät zum Vorstellungsgespräch kommen | _____ | _____ |
| 6. über meine (deine) Probleme sprechen | _____ | _____ |
| 7. meine (deine) Dokumente mitbringen | _____ | _____ |
| 8. fragen, wie viel man verdient | _____ | _____ |

## B. The present subjunctive of *haben* and *sein*

The present subjunctive of **haben** (**hätte**) and **sein** (**wäre**) can be used to express possibility.

**Hättest** du jetzt schon Zeit?    *Would you have time now?*
Ja, das **wäre** gut.    *Yes, that would be good.*

The expression **Wie wäre es mit …?** is used to make a suggestion.

**Wie wäre es mit** einem Kaffee?     *How about a cup of coffee?*
**Wie wäre es mit** einem Rollenspiel?  *How would it be if we did a role play?*

The expressions **Das wäre interessant** (**klasse, prima, schön, super, toll,** etc.)
and **Ich hätte Lust dazu** (**Interesse daran,** etc.) are used to respond positively to
suggestions.

Here are the forms of **hätte** and **wäre.**

| **hätte:** *would have* | | |
|---|---|---|
| **Singular** | | **Plural** |
| ich **hätte** | | wir **hätten** |
| du **hättest** | | ihr **hättet** |
| Sie **hätten** | | Sie **hätten** |
| er/sie/es **hätte** | | sie **hätten** |

| **wäre:** *would be* | | |
|---|---|---|
| **Singular** | | **Plural** |
| ich **wäre** | | wir **wären** |
| du **wärest** | | ihr **wäret** |
| Sie **wären** | | Sie **wären** |
| er/sie/es **wäre** | | sie **wären** |

In conversation, many speakers glide over the **-e-** in the **du-** and **ihr**-forms of **wäre,** so that those forms sound like **du wärst** and **ihr wärt.**

**15** **Die Einladung.** Stefan möchte Anna einladen. Spielen Sie in
Paaren, was Stefan und Anna sagen. Bilden Sie Fragen nach dem Beispiel.
Benutzen Sie Ausdrücke aus der Liste.

interessant sein • klasse sein • schön sein • super sein • toll sein
Geld dafür haben • Interesse daran haben • Lust dazu haben • Zeit dazu
haben

▢ heute Abend ins Kino gehen

S1 (STEFAN):  *Ich gehe heute Abend mit Barbara und Karl ins Kino. Hättest
du Zeit?*

S2 (ANNA):  *Au, ja! Das wäre sehr interessant.* (oder)
*Au, ja! Ich hätte schon Interesse.*

1. heute Abend ins Kino gehen
2. morgen Abend essen gehen
3. am Wochenende nach Heidelberg fahren
4. später auf eine Party gehen
5. zusammen eine Pizza kaufen
6. mit Karl und Barbara in die Kneipe gehen

## Freie Kommunikation

**Jeopardy.** Teilen Sie die Klasse in zwei Gruppen auf. Jede Person in der Gruppe
spielt abwechselnd° für die Gruppe. Der Dozent/Die Dozentin sagt ein
Kompositum°, und ein Spieler aus jeder Gruppe meldet sich, wenn er/sie das
Kompositum mit einem Relativsatz definieren kann. Die richtige Antwort muss
eine Frage sein.

*alternatingly*
*compound noun*

▢ LEHRER(IN):  *Tageszeitung*
S1:  *Wie heißt eine Zeitung, die man jeden Tag liest?*

 **S c h r e i b e c k e**

**Die Übersetzung°.** Sie arbeiten als Englischübersetzer/-übersetzerin in einer Werbeagentur°. Ihr Kollege Herr Neumeier hat Sie gebeten, die folgenden englischen Ausdrücke auf Deutsch zu erklären. Schreiben Sie ihm eine Mitteilung°, in der Sie kurze, einfache Definitionen geben.

*translation*
*advertising agency*
*memo*

An: Herrn Neumeier
Anbei sind die Definitionen der englischen Ausdrücke, die Sie mir gestern geschickt haben.

■ *desktop computer:* Das ist ein Computer, der …

| | |
|---|---|
| *desktop computer:* (der Computer) | *high-speed modem:* (das Modem) |
| *freeware:* (die Software) | *computer nerd:* (die Person) |
| *color monitor:* (der Monitor) | *help line:* (die Telefonnummer) |

---

**Absprungtext**    **Wien: Treffen Sie den guten Ton!**

Bevor Karl nach Wien zum Vorstellungsgespräch abreist, will er sich schnell über die Wiener Musikszene informieren. Online gibt es jede Menge° Infos auf der Website vom Wiener Fremdenverkehrsverein.

*jede Menge: a large amount*

## *Vorschau*

**16**  **Thematische Fragen.** Beantworten Sie die folgenden Fragen auf Deutsch.

1. Welche österreichischen Städte kennen Sie? Was assoziieren Sie mit Österreich? Wen assoziieren Sie mit Österreich?
2. Gibt es Stereotypen über Österreich oder Österreicher? Wissen Sie mehr über das historische oder mehr über das moderne Österreich? Warum vielleicht?
3. Wien ist sehr bekannt für Musik. Welche berühmten Komponisten haben in Wien gelebt?
4. Gehen Sie gern in die Oper? ins Konzert? Würden Sie in Wien in die Oper oder ins Konzert gehen? Würden Sie ein Ballett sehen? Warum? Warum nicht?
5. Interessieren Sie sich für Architektur? Haben Sie jemals von den folgenden Stilen gehört? vom Barock? vom Jugendstil? vom Biedermeier?

Das Dreimädlerhaus: Ein Beispiel vom Wiener Biedermeier-Stil.

Das Schloss Belvedere: Ein Beispiel vom Wiener Barock.

Die Secession: Ein Beispiel vom Wiener Jugendstil.

## *Lesestrategien: Wien: Treffen Sie den guten Ton!*

Benutzen Sie die folgenden Lesestrategien, um den Absprungtext über Wien zu verstehen.

**17  Den Kontext verstehen.** Finden Sie im Absprungtext Antworten auf die folgenden Fragen.

1. Für welche Gruppe hat man diesen Text geschrieben? Für Menschen aus Wien? Für Touristen in Wien? Für Kinder? Für Studierende aus den USA?
2. Welche Menschen erwähnt° der Text?  *mentions*
3. Welche Gebäude° erwähnt der Text?  *buildings*
4. Wie ist der Text organisiert? nach der Zeit (chronologisch)? nach Themen? nach Lokalitäten? nach Personen?

**18  Neue Wörter lernen: Erster Versuch.** Manchmal benutzen Autoren viele ähnliche Wörter, um ein Thema zu besprechen. Bei diesen Wörtern geht es um dasselbe Thema.

die Aufführung     das Programm     die Vorstellung
die Inszenierung     die Veranstaltung

Ist das Thema Botanik, Europa oder Musiktheater?

**19  Neue Wörter lernen: Drei Strategien.** Erraten° Sie die fett    *guess* gedruckten Wörter mit Hilfe der drei folgenden Strategien. Beantworten Sie die Fragen.

*Weltwissen*

1. „Die Wiener Staatsoper ist eines der Top-Opernhäuser der Welt° und die    *world* **Bühne** der internationalen Opern-**Elite**."

   • Im Theater steht die Bühne vorne, wo die Schauspieler singen, tanzen und sprechen. Was heißt **Bühne**?
   • Es ist wichtig im Text, den Ton und Stil zu erkennen. Ist der Ton im Satz kritisch, lustig oder enthusiastisch? Ist die Wiener Staatsoper eine gute oder eine schlechte Bühne?

2. „… wo neben Opern auch schwungvolle Operetten und Musicals sowie erstklassige Ballett-**Aufführungen** inszeniert werden."

   Im Theater oder in der Konzerthalle findet die Aufführung auf der Bühne statt. Was führt man auf – ein Drama oder eine Party?

3. „Auf den **Spuren** weltberühmter Musiker"

   Wenn man im Sand geht, sieht man leicht die Spuren im Sand. Weltberühmte Musiker lassen auch Spuren zurück, aber nicht im Sand. Sie haben einen Einfluss auf spätere Generationen. Was für Spuren haben Beethoven und Mozart hinterlassen? politische Spuren? musikalische Spuren? philosophische Spuren?

4. „…, in der er [Mozart] *Figaros Hochzeit* **komponierte**"
   „…, wo er [Haydn] *Die Jahreszeiten* und die heutige deutsche Hymne **schuf**"
   „… Ludwig van Beethoven, der unter anderem die europäische Hymne **schrieb** …"

Sie kennen sicherlich die Namen Mozart, Haydn und Beethoven. Sie wissen schon, dass Mozart, Haydn und Beethoven Musik geschrieben haben. Was bedeutet wohl „Mozart komponierte *Figaros Hochzeit*"? Was bedeutet „Haydn schuf die deutsche Hymne"? Was bedeutet „Beethoven schrieb die europäische Hymne"?

5. „Millionen Musikfreunde auf der ganzen Welt kennen den Wiener Musikverein als **traditionsreichen Veranstaltungsort** klassischer Musik."

Ein Ort ist ein Synonym für Stelle oder Platz. Was ist wohl ein **traditionsreicher Veranstaltungsort**?

6. „Ein weiterer Mittelpunkt des internationalen Konzertlebens ist das Wiener Konzerthaus im **stimmungsvollen** Jugendstil-**Ambiente**."

- Es gibt ein englisches Wort wie **Ambiente**. Was ist das?
- Ein Ambiente kann stimmungsvoll oder nicht sehr interessant sein. Was bedeutet **stimmungsvoll**?

7. „… aus seinem **Goldenen Saal** wird alljährlich das Neujahrskonzert der Wiener Philharmoniker international im Fernsehen **übertragen**."

- Ist der Goldene Saal in Wien ein Hörsaal an der Universität oder eine Konzerthalle?
- Was bedeutet wohl im Fernsehen **übertragen**?

*Wortformen*
„Ein **abwechslungsreiches** Programm bietet auch die Wiener Volksoper, …"

- Die deutsche Sprache bildet oft Wortkombinationen (Komposita) wie **Spielplan** (**Spiel** + **Plan**). Schauen Sie jetzt das Wort **abwechslungsreich** an. Das Wort **abwechslungsreich** = **Abwechslung** + **reich**. Sie wissen schon die Bedeutung von **wechseln**. Sie wissen auch, dass Bill Gates ein sehr **reicher** Mann ist. Hat ein **abwechslungsreiches** Programm viele verschiedene Aufführungen oder nur zwei oder drei im Jahr?
- Woraus bestehen die folgenden Wörter? Was bedeuten sie?

  die Ruhestätte • der Mittelpunkt • erstklassig • zahlreich

*Kontext*
Manchmal kann man erraten, was Wörter im Satz bedeuten, wenn man darüber nachdenkt, was zuerst und dann später kommt.

1. „… Seine musikalische Bandbreite umfasst nicht nur das klassische Repertoire, sondern **reicht** vom **Mittelalter** bis zu progressivsten Tönen der **Gegenwart**."

- Ist die **Gegenwart** die Zeit jetzt oder die Zeit früher?
- Ist das **Mittelalter** die Zeit jetzt oder die Zeit früher?
- Was heißt wohl das Verb **reicht von … bis …**?

Man findet oft Synonyme im Text.

2. „Im Stadtpark befindet sich Europas meist fotografiertes **Denkmal** — die goldene Johann-Strauß-**Statue**."

Ist ein Denkmal eine Person, ein Gebäude oder ein Monument?

3. „ … seine [Mozarts] **letzte Ruhestätte** auf dem romantischen Biedermeier-**Friedhof** St. Marx.“

Männer und Frauen finden am Ende des Leben ihre letzte Ruhestätte. Was findet man in einem Friedhof – tote oder lebende Menschen?

4. „**Das Geburtshaus** … [von] Franz Schubert ist heute ebenso ein Museum, wie [das] **Domizil** von Joseph Haydn.“

- Am Anfang des Lebens wird man geboren°. Was bedeutet **Geburtshaus** (**Geburt + Haus**)?
- Ist ein **Domizil** ein Lied, ein Haus oder ein Museum?

*wird … geboren: is born*

5. „**Raritäten** des Musiktheaters setzt die Wiener Kammeroper in Szene: selten gezeigte Operetten, Musicals und Singspiele sowie barocke und moderne Opern.“

Raritäten werden selten gezeigt°. Sieht man Raritäten oft oder nicht sehr oft?

*werden … gezeigt: are shown*

 **20  Satzdetektiv.** Verbinden Sie die Sätze mit der besten Bedeutung.

1. „ … zahlreich sind hier auch die **Gedenkstätten**, an denen man Leben und Werk der Meister **nachspüren** kann.“

2. „Im Stadtpark befindet sich Europas meist fotografiertes Denkmal – die goldene Johann-Strauß-Statue, **gewidmet** dem **Schöpfer** des Donauwalzers und der *Fledermaus*.“

3. „Im Sommer bietet sie **schwungvolle** Aufführungen populärer Operetten im Schönbrunner Schlosstheater.“

a. Im Park sieht man das Monument für Johann Strauß, der die Donauwalzer und *Die Fledermaus* komponiert hat.

b. Es gibt hier viele Monumente, bei denen man ein Gefühl für das Leben und die Arbeit von Haydn, Beethoven usw. bekommen kann.

c. Sie präsentieren unterhaltsame Produktionen von musikalischen Theaterstücken im Schlosstheater von Schönbrunn.

## *Absprungtext*
### *Wien: Treffen Sie den guten Ton!*

Lesen Sie jetzt den Text.

### Opernhäuser

Die Wiener Staatsoper ist eines der Top-Opern-häuser der Welt und die Bühne der internationalen Opern-Elite. Hier genießen° Sie Abwechslung auf höchstem Niveau°: Man führt rund 50 Opern und 20 Ballettwerke an 300 Tagen im Jahr auf und zwar bei täglich wechselnden Vorstellungen.

Ein abwechslungsreiches Programm bietet auch die Wiener Volksoper, wo neben Opern auch schwungvolle Operetten und Musicals sowie erstklassige Ballett-Aufführungen inszeniert werden.

*enjoy*
*höchstem … : highest level*

Neuverheiratete besuchen gern die goldene Statue vom Walzerkönig Johann Strauß.

Die Wiener Staatsoper: Eines der Top-Opernhäuser der Welt.

Die Wiener Philharmoniker spielen das Neujahrskonzert im Goldenen Saal des Wiener Musikvereins.

Raritäten des Musiktheaters setzt die Wiener Kammeroper in Szene: selten gezeigte Operetten, Musicals und Singspiele sowie barocke und moderne Opern. Im Sommer bietet sie schwungvolle Aufführungen populärer Operetten im Schönbrunner Schlosstheater.

## Konzertsäle°

Millionen Musikfreunde auf der ganzen Welt kennen den Wiener Musikverein als traditionsreichen Veranstaltungsort klassischer Musik. Denn aus seinem Goldenen Saal wird alljährlich das Neujahrskonzert der Wiener Philharmoniker international im Fernsehen übertragen.

Ein weiterer Mittelpunkt des internationalen Konzertlebens ist das Wiener Konzerthaus im stimmungsvollen Jugendstil-Ambiente. Seine musikalische Bandbreite° umfasst nicht nur das klassische Repertoire, sondern reicht vom Mittelalter bis zu progressivsten Tönen der Gegenwart.

## Auf den Spuren weltberühmter Musiker

In keiner anderen Stadt lebten so viele weltberühmte Komponisten wie in Wien. Entsprechend° zahlreich sind hier auch die Gedenkstätten, an denen man Leben und Werk der Meister nachspüren kann:

Johann-Strauß-Denkmal: Im Stadtpark befindet sich Europas meist fotografiertes Denkmal – die goldene Johann-Strauß-Statue, gewidmet dem Schöpfer des Donauwalzers und der *Fledermaus*.

Im Burggarten hingegen können Sie das Denkmal von W. A. Mozart bewundern. Oder besuchen Sie jene Wohnung inmitten der Wiener Altstadt, in der er *Figaros Hochzeit* komponierte, sowie seine letzte Ruhestätte auf dem romantischen Biedermeier-Friedhof St. Marx.

Das Geburtshaus des Liederfürsten° Franz Schubert ist heute ebenso ein Museum wie jenes Domizil von Joseph Haydn, wo er *Die Jahreszeiten* und die heutige deutsche Hymne schuf. Eine weitere Spur führt nach Grinzing, wo Ludwig van Beethoven, der unter anderem° die europäische Hymne schrieb, eine Zeit lang lebte.

*concert halls*

*range*

*correspondingly*

*prince of songs*

**unter anderem:** *among other things*

*Rückblick*

 **21   Stimmt das?** Stimmen die folgenden Aussagen zum Text oder nicht? Wenn nicht, was stimmt?

|  | Ja, das stimmt. | Nein, das stimmt nicht. |
|---|:---:|:---:|
| 1. Die Wiener Staatsoper ist eine kleine, unbekannte Bühne. | ☐ | ☐ |
| 2. An fast 300 Tagen im Jahr kann man Oper oder Ballett in der Wiener Staatsoper besuchen. | ☐ | ☐ |
| 3. Wer sich mehr für Operetten und Musicals interessiert, geht am besten in die Volksoper. | ☐ | ☐ |
| 4. In der Wiener Kammeroper kann man weniger bekannte Stücke sehen. | ☐ | ☐ |
| 5. Zu Neujahr kann man das Konzert von den Wiener Philharmonikern überall im Fernsehen hören. | ☐ | ☐ |
| 6. Das Wiener Konzerthaus ist im Barockstil gebaut°. | ☐ | ☐ |
| 7. Johann Strauß ist der Komponist, den man als den Liederfürsten kennt. | ☐ | ☐ |
| 8. Im Stadtpark steht eine Statue von Johann Strauß. | ☐ | ☐ |
| 9. Ludwig van Beethoven hat die deutsche Hymne komponiert. | ☐ | ☐ |
| 10. Franz Schubert ist der einzige große Komponist, der in Wien geboren wurde. | ☐ | ☐ |
| 11. Wolfgang Amadeus Mozart hat in der Wiener Altstadt seine Oper *Figaros Hochzeit* komponiert. | ☐ | ☐ |

*built* (for item 6)

> Complete the **Ergänzen Sie** activity in your workbook for this text before doing the next activity.

**22   Kurz gefragt.** Beantworten Sie die folgenden Fragen auf Deutsch.

1. Welches von den drei Wiener Opernhäusern möchten Sie besuchen? Warum?
2. Haben Sie Lieblingskomponisten? Haben sie klassische Musik, Jazz oder Rock komponiert?
3. Warum hat eine Stadt wie Wien wohl drei Opernhäuser? Haben Sie eine Oper in Ihrer Stadt? Haben Sie sie besucht? Was halten Sie und Ihre Freunde von der Oper?
4. Haben Sie jemals das Geburtshaus oder die Wohnung von einem Komponisten, Schriftsteller oder Künstler besucht? Warum oder warum nicht?
5. Kennen Sie die deutsche oder die europäische Hymne? Können Sie die amerikanische oder die kanadische Hymne singen?

**Klassiker-Tour von Wien.** Sie arbeiten bei einer Firma in Wien, die sich auf Musikfreunde spezialisiert und Sondertouren° von Wien anbietet. Sie wollen einen einminutigen° Werbe-Spot° für Ihre deutschsprachigen Kunden machen. Beschreiben Sie die Attraktionen von Ihrer Tour für Fans von Ludwig van Beethoven, Josef Haydn, Gustav Mahler, Wolfgang Amadeus Mozart, Franz Schubert und Johann Strauß.

*specialty tours*
*one minute / commercial*

### Freie Kommunikation

**Sondertouren für Musikfreunde.** Rufen Sie diese Firma in Wien an und fragen Sie, ob sie Sondertouren für Musikfreunde von Mozart, Strauß oder Haydn haben. Fragen Sie, wann die Führung ist, wie lange sie dauert, wo man beginnt und was man sieht.

## BRENNPUNKT KULTUR

### Berufswahl und Berufsausbildung in deutschsprachigen Ländern

*Ein Azubi bei der Ausbildung*

Students in Germany, Austria, and Switzerland are trained in a profession that they will most likely have for life. Occupational choices come early in school. During the third and fourth grades in Germany, parents and teachers decide if students will go to **die Hauptschule, die Realschule,** or **das Gymnasium.**

German businesses, government, and schools collaborate closely to provide thorough vocational and academic training for **Hauptschüler,** who will learn manual trades, or for **Realschüler,** who seek administrative positions. This close collaboration ensures a skilled workforce and streamlines the vocational education that students receive.

In an on-the-job apprenticeship (**die Lehre** or **die Ausbildung**) an apprentice from the **Hauptschule (der Lehrling** or **der/die Auszubildende, Azubi**) learns his or her trade in three years. Only about one-third of all apprentices are placed in their first choice of fields, while many others must pursue careers in other fields. During this time apprentices are paid a trainee wage that increases annually. They must also attend academic classes at a school (**die Berufsschule**) one or two days a week. There they take courses in their specialty along with courses in German, history, economics, and other subjects. The training ends when the apprentice passes an exam given by a board of teachers, employer-trainers, and representatives of the appropriate trade guild.

Students who are interested in technical professions or careers in business, administration, or civil service attend **die Realschule** for six years and participate in short-term internships (**die Praktikantenstellen** or **Praktika**). Upon passing **die Mittlere Reife** at the end of the 10th grade, these students may start an apprenticeship in areas such as banking, business, or office administration or attend a technical college (**die Fachschule**) or a special school (**die Fachoberschule**). Increasingly, graduates from a **Gymnasium** who do not go on to college compete with **Realschüler** for apprenticeships and often win out.

■ **Kulturkreuzung** Wissen Sie schon, was Sie später beruflich machen werden? Haben Sie das schon gewusst, als Sie zehn Jahre alt waren? Wie lernt man in Ihrem Land, Mechaniker, Bäcker oder Krankenpfleger zu werden? Was sind die Vorteile und Nachteile vom deutschen Bildungssystem?

## Strukturen und Vokabeln

### III  Describing people and things (I)

Endings on adjectives after **ein**-words, **der**-words, or neither

### A. Endings on adjectives after ein-words: nominative case

Adjectives are words that describe the nature or quality of nouns and occur in one of two positions in a sentence:

1. as a predicate adjective after the verbs **sein, werden,** or **bleiben**

   Der Job ist **toll**.     *The job is great.*

2. before a noun

   Das ist ein **toller** Job!     *That's a great job!*

In German, only adjectives that occur before a noun have an ending. When an adjective follows an **ein**-word, the ending reflects the gender, the number, and the case of the noun that the adjective precedes. Remember that the **ein**-words include the possessive adjectives **mein, dein, sein, ihr, unser, euer, ihr,** and **Ihr,** as well as the negative article **kein.**

> Remember that **ein** (*a, an*) cannot be used with plural nouns.

| | |
|---|---|
| Er ist **ein** sehr nett**er** Typ. | *He's a really nice guy.* |
| **Mein** neu**er** Job is ganz toll. | *My new job is really great.* |
| Das ist **kein** gut**es** Praktikum. | *That's not a good internship.* |
| **Ihre** neu**e** Stelle ist an der Staatsoper. | *Her new position is at the State Opera.* |
| **Unsere** neu**en** Opern sind sehr populär. | *Our new operas are very popular.* |
| Das sind **keine** gut**en** Computer. | *Those are not good computers.* |

In the nominative case, the adjective following the **ein**-word has one of these endings.

> Notice that the last letter on the singular definite article for a word is the same as the last letter on the adjective following the **ein**-word: *masc. sing.* **de** → ein nett**er** Typ; *neut. sing.* **das** → ein gut**es** Praktikum; *fem. sing.* di**e** → eine toll**e** Stelle.

| Gender | | Nominative singular adjective endings | | | Nominative plural adjective endings | | |
|---|---|---|---|---|---|---|---|
| *Masc.* | der Typ | **-er** | ein nett**er** Typ | *a nice guy* | **-en** | keine nett**en** Typen | *no nice guys* |
| *Neut.* | das Praktikum | **-es** | ein gut**es** Praktikum | *a good internship* | **-en** | keine gut**en** Praktika | *no good internships* |
| *Fem.* | die Stelle | **-e** | eine toll**e** Stelle | *a great job* | **-en** | keine toll**en** Stellen | *no good jobs* |

Adjectives that end in **-el** and many that end in **-er** drop the internal **e** when an ending is added.

| | | |
|---|---|---|
| miserabel: | Das ist ein **miserabler** Job. | *That is a terrible job.* |
| teuer: | Ein **teures** Auto ist nicht | *An expensive car is not* |
| | unbedingt ein gutes Auto. | *necessarily a good car.* |

The adjective **hoch** (*high, tall*) has a special form, **hoh-**, to which endings are added.

| | |
|---|---|
| Das Gebäude ist **hoch.** | *The building is tall.* |
| Das ist ein **hohes** Gebäude. | *That is a tall building.* |

**23** **Was ist das?** Erklären Sie einem Partner/einer Partnerin, was diese Begriffe° bedeuten.

*terms*

S1: *Was ist die Volkswagen AG°?*
S2: *Das ist eine deutsche Autofirma.*

*Aktiengesellschaft: corporation*

| | |
|---|---|
| 1. die Volkswagen AG | a.  Das ist eine deutsche Chemiefirma. |
| 2. ein BMW | b.  Das ist eine deutsche Stadt. |
| 3. Dresden | c.  Das ist ein deutsches Auto. |
| 4. der Neckar | d.  Das ist ein deutscher Express-Zug. |
| 5. Bayern | e.  Das ist ein deutscher Fluss. |
| 6. BASF | f.  Das ist ein deutsches Bundesland. |
| 7. der Intercity/ICE | g.  Das ist eine deutsche Autofirma. |

**24** **Was für eine Arbeit ist das?** Wählen Sie für jeden Beruf ein passendes Adjektiv und schreiben Sie es auf. Geben Sie dann Ihre Meinung zu den folgenden Berufen.

> **Was für eine Arbeit ist das?** The words **relativ** and **ziemlich** are adverbs modifying **gut** and do not have adjective endings.

Kellner/Kellnerin
*Das ist eine gute Arbeit (ein guter Beruf, ein gutes Leben).*

| + | +/– | – | |
|---|---|---|---|
| gut | relativ gut | schlecht | |
| fantastisch | ziemlich gut | blöd° | *dumb* |
| interessant | anständig | langweilig | |
| toll | | hart | |
| | | stressig | |
| | | dreckig° | *dirty* |

| | Die Arbeit | Der Beruf | Das Leben |
|---|---|---|---|
| 1. Kellner/Kellnerin | _____ | _____ | _____ |
| 2. Taxifahrer/Taxifahrerin | _____ | _____ | _____ |
| 3. Professor/Professorin | _____ | _____ | _____ |
| 4. Automechaniker/Automechanikerin | _____ | _____ | _____ |
| 5. Pilot/Pilotin | _____ | _____ | _____ |
| 6. Tellerwäscher/Tellerwäscherin | _____ | _____ | _____ |
| 7. Schauspieler/Schauspielerin | _____ | _____ | _____ |
| 8. Rechtsanwalt/Rechtsanwältin | _____ | _____ | _____ |

**25** **Ein Spiel: Trivialwissen.** Was wissen Sie über Deutschland und Österreich? Bilden Sie zwei Teams und stellen Sie einander Fragen. Antworten Sie in ganzen Sätzen.

◻ eine / österreichisch- / Stadt

> S1 (TEAM 1):  *Nennen Sie eine österreichische Stadt.*
> S2 (TEAM 2):  *Salzburg ist eine österreichische Stadt.*

*Team 1*
1. eine / österreichisch- / Stadt
2. ein / deutsch- / Basketballspieler in der NBA
3. eine / deutsch- / Stadt im Osten Deutschlands
4. ein / deutsch- / Bundesland im Norden Deutschlands
5. ein(e) / österreichisch- / Schauspieler(in) und Politiker(in) in den USA
6. ?

*Team 2*
1. eine / deutsch- / Autofirma in München
2. ein(e) / österreichisch- / Musiker(in) aus Salzburg
3. ein(e) / deutsch- / Komponist(in) aus Bonn
4. ein / deutsch- / Fluss in Bayern
5. ein(e) / deutsch- / Politiker(in)
6. ?

## *Wissenswerte Vokabeln: Eigenschaften von guten Bewerbern*
### *Talking about characteristics of good job applicants*

analytisch

begabt *talented*

diszipliniert

dynamisch

gründlich *thorough*

kollegial *cooperative*

kontaktfreudig *sociable*

motiviert

pünktlich

qualifiziert

selbstständig *independent*

zuverlässig *reliable*

🔶 Soll ein Bäcker analytisch sein?    *Nein, er soll (zuverlässig) sein.*

**26    Stellensuche: Beschreibung in einem Inserat.** Wenn man eine Stelle sucht, liest man die Anzeigen in der Zeitung. Die Anzeigen beschreiben die gewünschte Person mit besonderen Adjektiven, wie „dynamisch". Welche von den folgenden Adjektiven findet man wahrscheinlich in einem Jobinserat, welche nicht?

kontaktfreudig • intelligent • dynamisch • faul • langsam • selbstständig • interessiert • unpünktlich • flexibel • passiv • zuverlässig • schüchtern • aggressiv • begabt • desorganisiert

| *In einem Inserat* | | *Nicht in einem Inserat* | |
|---|---|---|---|
| _____ | _____ | _____ | _____ |
| _____ | _____ | _____ | _____ |
| _____ | _____ | _____ | _____ |

> **2. Einkommen:**
> bis zu 1.200 Euro pro Monat, durch seriöse Nebentätigkeit (Büro). Hervorragende Zukunfts-Perspektiven.

**27    Wie heißt eine Person, die…?** Stellen Sie einem Partner / einer Partnerin Fragen über die folgenden Personen und ihre Eigenschaften. Benutzen Sie die Adjektive.

🔶 Eine Person, die gern neue Leute kennen lernt, ist eine …

S1:  *Wie nennt man eine Person, die gern neue Leute kennen lernt?*
S2:  *Eine Person, die gern neue Leute kennen lernt, ist eine kontaktfreudige Person.*

kollegial • kontaktfreudig • pünktlich • qualifiziert • selbstständig

1. Eine Person, die gern neue Leute kennen lernt, ist eine …
2. Ein Arbeiter, der allein gut arbeiten kann, ist ein …
3. Eine Ärztin, die nie zu spät kommt, ist eine …
4. Ein Friseur, der gern mit Kollegen arbeitet, ist ein …
5. Eine Lehrerin, die gute Qualifikationen hat, ist eine …

begabt • diszipliniert • dynamisch • gründlich • motiviert

6. Ein Sekretär, der viel Talent hat, ist ein …
7. Ein Kaufmann, der hohe Motivation hat, ist ein …
8. Eine Architektin, die an alle Details denkt, ist eine …
9. Ein Rechtsanwalt, der viel Energie hat, ist ein …
10. Eine Person, die viel Disziplin bei der Arbeit zeigt, ist eine …

## B. Endings on adjectives after **ein**-words: accusative and dative case

These are the nominative, accusative, and dative case adjective endings following an **ein**-word.

|  | Masculine | Neuter | Feminine | Plural (all genders) |
|---|---|---|---|---|
| **Nominative** | ein nett**er** Mann | ein neu**es** Inserat | eine gut**e** Idee | keine gut**en** Ideen |
| **Accusative** | einen nett**en** Mann | ein neu**es** Inserat | eine gut**e** Idee | keine gut**en** Ideen |
| **Dative** | mit einem nett**en** Mann | in einem neu**en** Inserat | von einer gut**en** Idee | keinen gut**en** **Ideen** |

|  | *Accusative* | *Dative* |
|---|---|---|
| *Masculine:* | Sie hat einen neu**en** Job. | Sie ist glücklich mit ihrem neu**en** Job. |
| *Neuter:* | Sie verkauft ihr alt**es** Auto. | Sie fährt in unserem alt**en** Auto nach München. |
| *Feminine:* | Sie hat eine neu**e** Mitarbeiterin. | Sie gibt ihrer neu**en** Mitarbeiterin einen Brief. |
| *Plural:* | Die Firma hat keine frei**en** Stellen. | Man spricht heute mit keinen neu**en** Bewerbern. |

**28** **Interview mit einem jungen Filmstar.** Sie interviewen einen neuen Filmstar für eine Jugendzeitschrift. Die Leser von dieser Zeitschrift interessieren sich hauptsächlich für die persönliche Information vom Filmstar.

1. Kommen Sie aus einer kleinen Stadt?
2. Haben Sie einen festen° Freund/eine feste Freundin?                    *steady*
3. Wohnen Sie mit einem guten Freund/einer guten Freundin zusammen?
4. Haben Sie eine gute Karriere?
5. Haben Sie ein teures Auto? Was für eins?
6. Würden Sie lieber einen neuen Film machen oder im Theater spielen?
7. Möchten Sie in einer modernen Oper singen?
8. Halten Sie Ihren letzten Film für einen großen Erfolg?

**29** **Was für einen Job hast du?** Barbara und Stefan haben beide einen neuen Job gefunden und sprechen jetzt über ihre neue Arbeit. Barbara ist immer sehr positiv, aber Stefans Situation ist nicht so rosig.

■ S1 (BARBARA): *Ich habe einen guten Job. Und du?*
  S2 (STEFAN): *Ich habe einen schlechten Job.*

|  | *Barbara* | *Stefan* |  |
|---|---|---|---|
| 1. einen … Job | gut | schlecht |  |
| 2. von meinem … Chef viel gelernt | neu | ehemalig° | *former* |
| 3. heute eine … Aufgabe gehabt | interessant | langweilig |  |
| 4. heute einen … Auftrag° erfüllt° | wichtig | unwichtig | *assignment / completed* |
| 5. ein … Interview für eine Beförderung° | leicht | stressig | *promotion* |
| 6. eine … Sporthalle in der Firma | herrlich | furchtbar |  |
| 7. einen … Tag gehabt | fantastisch | miserabel |  |
| 8. einen … Computer bekommen | nagelneu° | uralt° | *sehr neu / sehr alt* |
| 9. eine … Kantine in der Firma | preiswert | teuer |  |
| 10. mit einem … Mitarbeiter gesprochen | sympathisch | unsympathisch |  |

# IV Describing people and things (II)

Endings on adjectives after definite articles

## A. Adjectives preceded by a definite article: nominative, accusative, and dative case endings

Like adjectives that follow **ein**-words, adjectives that follow the definite article also take endings that change according to the gender, the number, and the case of the noun that follows. Here are the nominative, accusative, and dative endings of adjectives that follow **der**-words.

|  | Masculine | Neuter | Feminine | Plural |
|---|---|---|---|---|
| **Nominative** | der neue Beruf | das neue Büro | die neue Stelle | die neuen Berufe/Büros/Stellen |
| **Accusative** | den neuen Beruf | das neue Büro | die neue Stelle | die neuen Berufe/Büros/Stellen |
| **Dative** | dem neuen Beruf | dem neuen Büro | der neuen Stelle | den neuen Berufen/Büros/Stellen |

Speakers use these adjective endings with any of the **der**-words (e.g., **dieser, jeder,** and **welcher**).

> All plural and dative endings are -**en**. All nominative singular endings are -**e**.

| | |
|---|---|
| Nominative: | Dieser neue Computer hat kein Kabel. |
| Accusative: | Angelika findet jedes neue Gesprächsthema langweilig. |
| Dative: | Welchem jungen Mann haben Sie den Schlüssel gegeben? |

If you compare the adjective endings that occur after **der/das/die** with the endings used after **ein**-words, you will note that adjectives following a **der**-word have only one of two endings: **-e** or **-en.** The ending in the plural is always -**en.**

|  | Mascuilne | Neuter | Feminine | Plural |
|---|---|---|---|---|
| **Nominative** | ein neuer Chef | ein neues Büro | eine neue Stelle | meine neuen Kollegen |
|  | der neue Chef | das neue Büro | die neue Stelle | die neuen Kollegen |
| **Accusative** | einen neuen Chef | ein neues Büro | eine neue Stelle | meine neuen Kollegen |
|  | den neuen Chef | das neue Büro | die neue Stelle | die neuen Kollegen |
| **Dative** | einem neuen Chef | einem neuen Büro | einer neuen Stelle | meinen neuen Kollegen |
|  | dem neuen Chef | dem neuen Büro | der neuen Stelle | den neuen Kollegen |

**Studenten wollen nur das eine**

Männer bevorzugen den klassischen **Firmenwagen** (53 Prozent), Frauen eher **Weiterbildungsangebote** (49 Prozent). Dies ist das Ergebnis einer Umfrage des Internet-Portals Jobpilot.de unter 602 Hochschulabsolventen zwischen 25 und 36 Jahren zum Thema Lohnzusatzleistungen.

**30** **Das neue Praktikum.** Karl beginnt ein neues Praktikum. Er beantwortet die Fragen, die seine Freundin stellt. Spielen Sie die Rollen. Wechseln Sie sich ab.

🔸 das Praktikum / interessant

> S1: *Sag mal, Karl, wie gefällt dir das Praktikum? Ist es interessant?*
> S2: *Ja, mir gefällt das interessante Praktikum sehr!*

| | | |
|---|---|---|
| 1. das Praktikum / interessant | 6. das Gehalt° / schön | *salary* |
| 2. der Chef / tolerant | 7. der Firmenwagen / komfortabel | |
| 3. das Büro / groß | 8. das Handy / neu | |
| 4. die Praktikantin / freundlich | 9. der Computer / schnell | |
| 5. die Sekretärin / hilfreich | 10. das Arbeitsklima° in der Staatsoper / kollegial | *Arbeitsatmosphäre* |

**31** **Wie kann Karl das machen?** Verbinden Sie ein Element in der linken Spalte mit einer Funktion in der rechten Spalte.

1. Mit dem schnellen Computer
2. Mit dem komfortablen Firmenwagen
3. Mit dem toleranten Chef
4. Mit der freundlichen Praktikantin
5. Von der hilfreichen Sekretärin
6. Mit dem schönen Gehalt
7. Mit dem großen Büro
8. Mit dem neuen Handy

a. kann Karl effektiv zusammenarbeiten.
b. kann Karl schnell rechnen°.    *compute*
c. hat Karl Platz für einen großen Schreibtisch.
d. kann Karl Schauspieler am Wiener Flughafen abholen.
e. kann Karl Geld für sein Studium verdienen.
f. kann Karl billig telefonieren.
g. kann Karl über Studentenprobleme sprechen.
h. kann Karl wichtige Informationen über das Praktikum online bekommen.

**32** **Was macht Karl lieber?** Beantworten Sie die folgenden Fragen zusammen mit einem Partner/einer Partnerin.

■ mit dem fleißigen/faulen Mitarbeiter arbeiten

S1: *Arbeitet Karl lieber mit dem fleißigen oder mit dem faulen Mitarbeiter?*
S2: *Er arbeitet lieber mit dem fleißigen Mitarbeiter.*
S1: *Und du?*
S2: *Ich arbeite (auch) lieber mit einem fleißigen Mitarbeiter.*

1. mit dem fleißigen/faulen Mitarbeiter arbeiten
2. den neuen/alten Wagen fahren
3. mit dem schnellen/langsamen Computer schreiben
4. mit der kollegialen/unfreundlichen Praktikantin zusammenarbeiten
5. den schweren/leichten Laptop tragen
6. in der bekannten/unbekannten Oper arbeiten

## B. Endings on unpreceded adjectives

An adjective that is preceded by neither an **ein**-word nor a **der**-word has the same ending as a **der**-word.

| | |
|---|---|
| Unser Chef trinkt ungern kalt**en** Kaffee. | *Our boss doesn't like to drink cold coffee.* |
| Die Volksoper bietet schwungvoll**e** Operetten. | *The **Volksoper** offers lively operettas.* |
| Wir haben schön**es** Wetter. | *We're having nice weather.* |
| Nett**e** Mitarbeiter sind wichtig. | *Nice co-workers are important.* |

**33** **Persönliches Profil.** Sie bewerben sich um eine Stelle in diesen Berufen. Sie machen ein Vorstellungsgespräch. Beantworten Sie diese Fragen für jeden von diesen Berufen in der Liste.

Geschäftsperson • Künstler(in) • Professor(in) • Verkäufer(in)

■ S1: *Was für Kleidung tragen Sie normalerweise am Arbeitsplatz?*
S2 (GESCHÄFTSPERSON): *Ich trage normalerweise formelle Kleidung.*

1. Was für Kleidung tragen Sie normalerweise am Arbeitsplatz? (formell / informell / schick / modisch)
2. Was für Essen bestellen Sie bei einem Geschäftstreffen°? (deutsch / chinesisch / französisch / exotisch / vegetarisch)    *business meeting*
3. Was für Bier trinken Sie auf einer Geschäftsparty? (alkoholfrei / bayerisch / deutsch / dunkel)
4. Was für Computerkenntnisse° haben Sie? (gut / mäßig° / schlecht)    *computer skills / moderate*
5. Mit was für Leuten arbeiten Sie gern? (tolerant / kreativ / intelligent / interessant)

## V Expressing the city of origin

### Forming adjectives from city names

German speakers form adjectives from city names by adding the ending **-er**.
Unlike other adjective forms that reflect the case, the number, and the gender,
this adjective form never changes.

| | |
|---|---|
| Die **Wiener** Staatsoper ist ein Top-Opernhaus. | *The Viennese State Opera is a top opera house.* |
| Meine Tochter isst gern **Frankfurter** Würstchen. | *My daughter likes to eat frankfurters.* |

Adjectives that derive from city names like **Dresden, Bremen, München,** and
**Zürich** drop the last internal **e, i,** or **en.**

| | | | |
|---|---|---|---|
| Dresden | → | Dresdner: | die **Dresdner** Zeitung |
| München | → | Münchner: | das **Münchner** Oktoberfest |
| Zürich | → | Zürcher: | das **Zürcher** Schauspielhaus |
| Bremen | → | Bremer: | die **Bremer** Stadtmusikanten |

 **34** **Ihre Urlaubsziele.** Beantworten Sie die folgenden Fragen.

1. Welches Fest schließt die Mozartwoche ein°?
2. Was müssen Sie in München besuchen?
3. In welcher Stadt ist das Riesenrad?
4. Welche Stadt hat ein Fest im September?
5. Was kann man in Erfurt besuchen?
6. Wie heißt die neue Oper?

*ein·schließen: to include*

## Österreich

Austria (**Österreich**), which is about the size of the state of Iowa, is bordered by Germany, the Czech Republic, Slovakia, Hungary, Slovenia, Italy, Switzerland, and Liechtenstein. Its rich history and geographic location in Europe have produced a true multicultural and cosmopolitan society. Austria first became a democracy with the resignation of the Hapsburg **Karl der Erste** on November 11, 1918 after the close of World War I (**der Erste Weltkrieg**). In 1938 Hitler annexed Austria in an action known as **der Anschluss**. After the defeat of Nazi Germany in World War II, the Allies divided Austria into four occupation zones (**Besatzungszonen**), and democracy returned to Austria in 1945. Its constitution requires Austria to be a neutral nation. In 1995 Austria became the second German-speaking country to join the European Union (**die Europäische Union**).

The Danube River (**die Donau**) flows eastward in the north through Linz and Vienna. The Alpine regions in the west and south, which make up about 62% of the total land area, have given Austria its reputation as a country of high mountains.

Although the economy of Austria suffered greatly during and after World War II, it is strong and vibrant today, with a very low unemployment rate.

In addition to the capital Vienna (**Wien**), Austria's major cities include **Graz**, **Innsbruck**, and **Salzburg**. **Graz**, the second largest city, is an industrial center producing chemicals, iron and steel products, mathematical instruments, and more. It has a university dating from 1586. **Innsbruck** is a rail and marketing center, as well as a historic resort town known more recently for hosting the 1964 and 1976 Winter Olympics. **Salzburg**, the birthplace of Wolfgang Amadeus Mozart, holds world-famous music and theater festivals every year.

*In der Getreidegasse in Salzburg findet man viel Charme und viele Menschen.*

■ **Kulturkreuzung** Städte oder Länder zwischen zwei Welten spielen eine besondere Rolle. Die Städte New York, Miami oder Los Angeles, zum Beispiel, integrieren Einwanderer in die USA. Welche Rolle, glauben Sie, spielt das Land Österreich für Menschen aus Osteuropa und welche Rolle für Menschen aus westeuropäischen Ländern?

## *Wissenswerte Vokabeln: Österreichs Leute und Länder*
### *Talking about Austria*

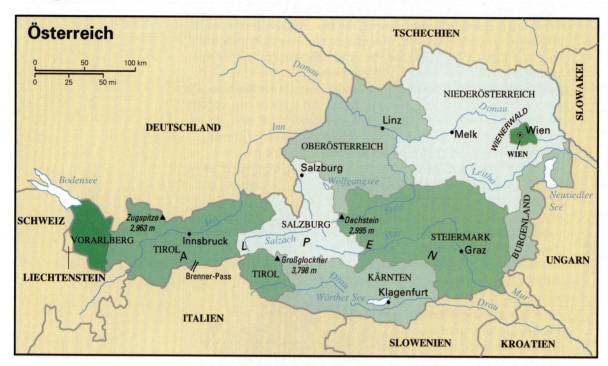

| Fläche | Bevölkerung | Hauptstadt |
|---|---|---|
| 83 855 km² | rund 8,2 Millionen | Wien |

| Geburtsrate | Sterberate |
|---|---|
| 8,9 / 1 000 Personen | 9,56 / 1 000 Personen |

**Sprachzugehörigkeit**
88,5% deutsch
*andere:* slowenisch, kroatisch, ungarisch, tschechisch

**neue Immigranten**
10% aus der Türkei, Bosnien, Serbien, Kroatien

**Religionszugehörigkeit**
73,6% römisch-katholisch 4,7% protestantisch 4,2% Muslime 17,4% keine Religion

**35** **Fragen über Österreich.** Stellen Sie einem Partner/einer Partnerin die folgenden Fragen über Österreich.

1. Wie viele Bundesländer hat Österreich?
2. Wie viele Einwohner hat Österreich? Ist das mehr oder weniger als Deutschland?
3. Findet man wohl mehr Priester oder Pastoren in Österreich? Warum?
4. Welche Sprachen hört man in Österreich außer Deutsch?

5. Ist das Land Österreich so groß wie Kalifornien oder wie Iowa?
6. Welches Bundesland ist gleichzeitig die Hauptstadt von Österreich?
7. Was unterscheidet wahrscheinlich Oberösterreich von Niederösterreich? Was meinst du?
8. Welches Bundesland möchtest du am liebsten besuchen? Warum?

# VI  Comparing people and things

Comparative and superlative forms of adjectives and adverbs

## A. Comparative forms

### 1. Regular adjectives and adverbs

To compare two or more people, objects, animals, or activities, German speakers use the comparative form (**der Komparativ**) of an adjective (**das Adjektiv**) or adverb (**das Adverb**). Adjectives modify nouns; adverbs modify verbs.

| | |
|---|---|
| Das klingt schon **besser.** | *That sounds better.* |
| Eine Meile ist **länger** als ein Kilometer. | *A mile is longer than a kilometer.* |

Most adjectives and adverbs with an **e** or **i** in the stem form the comparative by adding **-er**. To express inequality, speakers use a comparative form with **als.**

| | | |
|---|---|---|
| Adjective: | Ein VW ist **schnell.** | *A VW is fast.* |
| Comparative: | Ein BMW ist **schneller als** ein VW. | *A BMW is faster than a VW.* |
| Adverb: | Ein VW fährt **schnell.** | *A VW goes fast.* |
| Comparative: | Ein BMW fährt **schneller als** ein VW. | *A BMW goes faster than a VW.* |

> Most German adjectives and adverbs are identical in form, unlike English, where many adverbs are identifiable by the ending -*ly* (e.g., *happy, happily*).

To express equality in a comparison, German speakers use the construction **so ... wie** (*as ... as*).

Ein Porsche ist **so** teuer **wie** ein Mercedes.    *A Porsche is as expensive as a Mercedes.*

Here are the base and comparative forms of some regular adjectives and adverbs.

| Base | Comparative | Base | Comparative |
|---|---|---|---|
| bekannt | **bekannter** | schlecht | **schlechter** |
| billig | **billiger** | schnell | **schneller** |
| intelligent | **intelligenter** | schön | **schöner** |
| interessant | **interessanter** | schwer | **schwerer** |
| neu | **neuer** | wenig | **weniger** |

Adjectives that end in **-el** and many that end in **-er** drop the last internal **e** in the comparative form.

| | | |
|---|---|---|
| teuer: | Das Benzin wird jedes Jahr **teurer.** | *Gasoline gets more expensive every year.* |
| flexibel: | Ihre Arbeitszeit ist **flexibler** als meine. | *Her work hours are more flexible than mine.* |

**36** **Frau Günthers VW und Herrn Günthers BMW.** Frau Günther möchte ein neues Auto kaufen. Sie hat mit Herrn Günther diese Informationen über ihre Autos aufgeschrieben. Vergleichen° Sie ihre Autos.

*compare*

🟧 billig sein

S1: *Frau Günthers VW ist billiger als Herrn Günthers BMW.*
S2: *Herrn Günthers BMW ist …*

| | *Frau Günthers VW Golf* | *Herrn Günthers BMW 530:* |
|---|---|---|
| billig (teuer) sein: | 25 000 € | 70 000 € |
| neu sein: | 2005 | 2008 |
| schnell fahren: | 140 km/h° | 220 km/h |
| schwer sein: | 1 740 kg° | 2 055 kg |
| schön sein: | ? | ? |
| Prestige haben: | ? | ? |
| Platz haben: | ? | ? |
| Benzin verbrauchen: | ? | ? |

*Stundenkilometer*
*Kilogramm*

> Use your own ideas for sentences where you see a question mark; e.g., **Herrn Günthers BMW hat mehr Prestige als Frau Günthers VW.**

## 2. Adjectives and adverbs that add an umlaut

Many one-syllable adjectives and adverbs with an **a, o,** or **u** in the stem add an umlaut in the comparative form.

Ich bin **älter** als mein Bruder.     *I am older than my brother.*

Here are some adjectives and adverbs that add an umlaut in the comparative form.

| | Base | Comparative | | Base | Comparative |
|---|---|---|---|---|---|
| **a > ä** | alt | **älter** | **o > ö** | groß | **größer** |
| | hart | **härter** | | oft | **öfter** |
| | kalt | **kälter** | | | |
| | lang | **länger** | **u > ü** | jung | **jünger** |
| | stark | **stärker** | | klug | **klüger** |
| | warm | **wärmer** | | kurz | **kürzer** |

## 3. Irregular adjectives and adverbs

Some adjectives and adverbs are irregular in German. Remember that **hoch** drops the **c** in the comparative.

| Positive | Comparative | Examples | |
|---|---|---|---|
| gut | **besser** | Siehst du jetzt **besser?** | *Do you see better now?* |
| hoch | **höher** | Dieses Gebäude ist **höher.** | *This building is taller.* |
| viel | **mehr** | Wir verdienen jetzt **mehr** Geld. | *We're earning more money now.* |
| gern | **lieber** | Ich gehe **lieber** ins Kino. | *I prefer to go to the movies.* |

## 4. Using comparative adjectives

Like all adjectives, comparative adjectives can be placed before a noun (attributive position) or after the verb **sein** or **bleiben** (predicate adjectives).

- Like any adjective, comparative adjectives that precede a noun must also have an ending that shows the gender, number, and case of the noun.

| | | |
|---|---|---|
| der älter**e** Bruder | das schneller**e** Auto | die lustiger**e** Dame |
| mein älter**er** Bruder | mein schneller**es** Auto | eine lustiger**e** Dame |

- Predicate adjectives after **sein** and adverbs that modify the verb do not require any additional ending.

Ein BMW ist **schneller** als ein VW.
Ein BMW fährt **schneller** als ein VW.

 **37** **Freiburg ist kleiner als Berlin.** Stellen Sie Vergleiche an.

Freiburg(–) / Berlin(+) / klein
*Freiburg ist kleiner als Berlin.* (oder: *Freiburg ist die kleinere Stadt.*)

Dresden(+) / Tübingen(+) / groß
*Dresden ist so groß wie Tübingen.*

1. Freiburg(–) / Berlin(+) / klein
2. Dresden(+) / Tübingen(+) / groß
3. Die Uni in Tübingen(+) / die Uni in Bochum(–) / alt
4. Garmisch-Partenkirchen(+) / Stuttgart(–) / hoch liegen
5. Der Mercedes 500 SL(+) / der VW Golf(–) / teuer
6. Ein Motorrad(+) / ein Fahrrad(–) / schnell
7. Norddeutschland im Winter(–) / Süddeutschland im Winter(+) / viel Schnee haben
8. Der deutsche Weißwein(+) / der deutsche Rotwein(+) / gut
9. Bockbier(+) / Exportbier(–) / stark
10. Der Nürnberger Christkindlesmarkt(+) / der Bremer Weihnachtsmarkt(–) / bekannt

 **38** **Interview.** Stellen Sie einem Partner/einer Partnerin die folgenden Fragen.

1. Wer ist kontaktfreudiger, dein Vater oder deine Mutter?
2. Ist deine Mutter älter oder jünger als dein Vater?
3. Verdient deine Mutter mehr als dein Vater?
4. Wer arbeitet länger, deine Mutter oder dein Vater?
5. Wer ist intelligenter, du oder deine Schwester (dein Bruder, dein Cousin)?
6. Bist du stärker als dein Bruder (deine Schwester, dein Cousin)?
7. Wer ist selbstständiger, du oder dein bester Freund / deine beste Freundin?
8. Wer ist sportlicher, du oder dein bester Freund / deine beste Freundin?
9. Wer studiert disziplinierter, du oder dein bester Freund / deine beste Freundin?
10. Wer ist zuverlässiger, du oder dein bester Freund / deine beste Freundin?

## B. Superlative forms

### 1. Regular adjectives and adverbs

German speakers form the superlative by adding **-st** to the adjective or adverb stem and adding the appropriate adjective ending.

- Like all adjectives, superlative adjectives that precede a noun must have an ending that reflects the gender, number, and case of the noun (e.g., **das schnellste Auto, sein schnellstes Auto**).
- Superlative adjectives in the predicate after **sein** and superlative adverbs that modify the verb are expressed with the construction **am** + adjective/adverb + **-sten** (e.g., **am schnellsten**).

| | |
|---|---|
| Der Porsche ist sein **schnellstes** Auto. | *The Porsche is his fastest car.* |
| Ein Porsche ist **am schnellsten.** | *A Porsche is the fastest (of all).* |
| Ein Porsche fährt **am schnellsten.** | *A Porsche goes the fastest (of all).* |
| Ein Porsche ist das **schnellste** Auto. | *A Porsche is the fastest car (of all).* |
| Wir haben einen **älteren** Wagen gekauft. | *We bought an older car.* |
| Ich studiere an der **ältesten** Universität Deutschlands. | *I'm studying at the oldest university in Germany.* |

Stems that end in **-t** and **-z** form the superlative with **-est.** Many one-syllable adjectives and adverbs with an **-a**, **-o**, or **-u** in the stem add an umlaut in the superlative forms.

| | |
|---|---|
| In dem großen Konzerthaus war es **am lautesten.** | *It was the loudest in the big concert hall.* |
| Herr Müller ist unser **ältester** Mitarbeiter. | *Mr. Müller is our oldest co-worker.* |
| Das Stück in der Volksoper ist **am kürzesten.** | *The piece in the **Volksoper** is the shortest.* |

Here are the superlative forms of some regular adjectives and adverbs.

| Base | Predicate superlative | Attributive superlative (nominative case) |
|---|---|---|
| bekannt | **am bekanntesten** | das **bekannteste** Schloss in Deutschland |
| billig | **am billigsten** | der **billigste** Käse |
| dunkel | **am dunkelsten** | der **dunkelste** Tag |
| flexibel | **am flexibelsten** | die **flexibelsten** Menschen |
| intelligent | **am intelligentesten** | die **intelligentesten** Studenten |
| interessant | **am interessantesten** | der **interessanteste** Kurs |
| miserabel | **am miserabelsten** | das **miserabelste** Wetter |
| neu | **am neuesten** | die **neuesten** Musicals |
| schlecht | **am schlechtesten** | der **schlechteste** Tag |
| schnell | **am schnellsten** | die **schnellste** Mitarbeiterin |
| schön | **am schönsten** | das **schönste** Geschenk |
| schwer | **am schwersten** | die **schwersten** Fragen |
| teuer | **am teuersten** | die **teuersten** Autos |
| wenig | **am wenigsten** | die **wenigsten** Leute |

## 2. Adjectives and adverbs with an umlaut

These are some adjectives and adverbs that add an umlaut in the superlative form. Stems that end in **-ss, -ß, -t,** or **-z** also insert an **-e-** before the **-st.**

| | Base | Superlative | | Base | Superlative |
|---|---|---|---|---|---|
| **a > ä** | alt | **am ältesten** | **o > ö** | groß | **am größten** |
| | hart | **am härtesten** | | oft | **am öftesten** |
| | kalt | **am kältesten** | | | |
| | lang | **am längsten** | **u > ü** | jung | **am jüngsten** |
| | stark | **am stärksten** | | klug | **am klügsten** |
| | warm | **am wärmsten** | | kurz | **am kürzesten** |

Note that **groß/größten** does not add an **-e** but that **heiß/heißesten** and **süß/süßesten** do.

## 3. Irregular adjectives and adverbs

Here are the superlative forms of some common irregular adjectives and adverbs.

| Base | Comparative | Superlative | Examples |
|---|---|---|---|
| gut | besser | **best-** | **Der beste** Weißwein kommt aus Deutschland. |
| | | **am besten** | Alle sind gute Weißweine, aber dieser ist **am besten.** |
| hoch | höher | **höchst-** | **Der höchste** Berg heißt Everest. |
| | | **am höchsten** | Viele Berge sind hoch, aber Everest ist **am höchsten.** |
| viel | mehr | **meist-** | **Die meisten** Kinder spielen Fußball. |
| | | **am meisten** | Henning spielt Fußball, aber er spielt **am meisten** Tennis. |
| gern | lieber | **Lieblings-** | Sein **Lieblings**essen ist Brot. |
| | | **am liebsten** | Er isst **am liebsten** Brot. |

Notice that the superlative of **gern** (**liebst-**) is not typically used as an adjective. Instead, the term **Lieblings-** (*favorite*) is added to the beginning of the noun to form a compound noun: **Lieblingssport, Lieblingsfilm,** etc.

## 4. Using superlative adjectives

German speakers most frequently use the superlative forms with the definite articles **der, das,** and **die.**

| | |
|---|---|
| Herr Wimmer ist **der beste** Chef. | *Mr. Wimmer is the best boss.* |
| Ich habe **das schönste** Büro. | *I have the nicest office.* |
| Er bewirbt sich um **die neueste** Stelle. | *He is applying for the newest position.* |
| **Die höchsten** Gebäude stehen im Stadtzentrum. | *The highest buildings are downtown.* |

Some attributive adjectives form an independent expression by omitting the noun.

| | | |
|---|---|---|
| das Richtige | *the right thing* | Er tut immer **das Richtige.** |
| | | *He always does the right thing.* |
| das Beste | *the best thing* | Sie will nur **das Beste** kaufen. |
| | | *She only wants to buy the best.* |

**39** **Studienzeiten.** Beantworten Sie die folgenden Fragen mit Informationen aus der Tabelle.

**STUDIENZEITEN**
Alter beim ersten Universitätsabschluß

Großbritannien **22,8 Jahre**   Japan **23,3**   USA **24**   Frankreich **26,2**   Italien **27,2**   Schweden **27,5**   Niederlande **27,5**   Deutschland **27,9**

**WUNSCHPROFIL**
Was Unternehmer von Akademikern erwarten.

1 Flexibilität
2 Fremdsprachenkenntnisse
3 Praktische Berufserfahrung
4 Studiendauer
5 Informatik-Kenntnisse
6 Note des Examens
7 Auslandsaufenthalt
8 Hochschulort
9 Promotion°
10 Studium im Ausland
11 Ausländischer Hochschulabschluß

**Promotion:** *to obtain a doctorate*

1. Wo sind die Studenten am jüngsten, wenn sie mit dem Studium fertig sind?
2. Wo sind die Studenten am ältesten?
3. Sind Studenten in den USA jünger oder älter als Studenten in Frankreich?
4. In welchem Land sind die Studenten so alt wie in den Niederlanden?
5. In welchen zwei Ländern sind die Studenten fast so alt wie in Deutschland?

**40** **Fakten über Deutschland.** Sie arbeiten im Fremdenverkehrsamt in Frankfurt und müssen eine Tourismusbroschüre über Deutschland schreiben. Bilden Sie Aussagen im Superlativ.

**Fakten ...** Remember that any adjective following **der/das/die** must have the proper adjective ending **-e** or **-en.**

◻ die Gebäude / hoch = in Frankfurt
  *Die höchsten Gebäude sind in Frankfurt.*

1. die Gebäude / hoch = in Frankfurt
2. der römische° Bau / bekannt = die Porta Nigra in Trier      *Roman*
3. der Fluss / lang = der Rhein
4. die Universität / alt = in Heidelberg
5. der Kirchturm° / hoch = in Ulm      *church steeple*
6. die Bierbrauereien / viel = in Bayern
7. die Autos / schnell = Porsche und BMW
8. die Stadt in Deutschland / nördlich = Flensburg
9. das Bundesland / klein = die Hansestadt Bremen

## Freie Kommunikation

**Verkäufer/in gesucht.** Hier sind drei Personen, die sich für die Stelle bei Foto-Kirsch interessieren. Lesen Sie die Informationen über jede Person und besprechen Sie, wer für die Stelle besser (am besten) geeignet ist.

| | Fabian | Carlos | Jutta |
|---|---|---|---|
| Alter | 20 Jahre | 19 Jahre | 18 Jahre |
| selbstständig | + + + | + + + | + + + |
| dynamisch | + | + + | + + |
| kollegial | + + | + + | + + |
| zuverlässig | + + + | + + | + |
| flexibel | + | + + + | + + |
| motiviert | + + | + | + + + |

Junge(r), dynamische(r) Verkäufer(in)
mit Führerschein für unsere Filiale in Seemarn gesucht.
(Gewerbegebiet B 93).
Sie sollten selbstständig arbeiten können und Spaß am Umgang mit Menschen haben.
Bewerbungen mit Bild an
**Foto-Kirsch**
Arnoldstraße 13
09702 Seltz, Telefon 03941-14 79

## Schreibecke

**Ein Stellengesuch-Inserat schreiben.** Sie suchen eine neue Stelle. Schreiben Sie ein Stellengesuch-Inserat. Sie dürfen maximal 50 Wörter benutzen. Nennen Sie mindestens zwei Eigenschaften. Benutzen Sie die folgenden Inserate als Beispiele.

**Sekretärin (21)** zuverlässig und flexibel, sucht dringend neuen Wirkungskreis im Raum FG/BED, PC-Kenntnisse und Führerschein Klasse 3 vorhanden.

**Einsatzfreudiger** junger Mann, 36 Jahre, sucht Tätigkeit als Kraftfahrer im Fern- oder Nahverkehr, FS Kl. 1 bis 5 vorhanden.

*Zieltext*

# Das Vorstellungsgespräch an der Wiener Staatsoper

Karl kommt, wie bestellt, zur richtigen Zeit für das Vorstellungsgespräch in Wien an. Die Interviewerin ist Frau Eichendorff, die das Praktikantenprogramm an der Wiener Staatsoper führt und alle Bewerber für das Programm interviewt. Im Vorstellungsgespräch weiß Karl relativ schnell, dass er einen wirklich positiven Eindruck° auf Frau Eichendorff macht: er hat gute theoretische Kenntnisse°, er hat praktische Erfahrung, und er findet gute Antworten auf ihre Fragen. Am Ende sieht die Lage° recht positiv aus … aber Karl muss noch eine Weile auf die Nachricht warten, ob er nach Wien zurückkommen darf.

*impression / knowledge*

*situation*

## Vorschau

 **41** **Thematische Fragen.** Beantworten Sie die folgenden Fragen.

1. Welche Dokumente würden Sie wahrscheinlich einem Arbeitgeber° zuschicken, bevor Sie zu einem Vorstellungsgespräch reisen würden?

   einen Bewerbungsbrief° • einen Lebenslauf (eine einseitige Biografie) • Empfehlungen° von Professoren und ehemaligen Arbeitgebern • Kontaktinformationen von ehemaligen° Arbeitgebern • Kurs-Transkript von Ihrem bisherigen Studium • Noten von der Schulzeit

2. Was würden Sie zu einem Interview anziehen? Was für einen visuellen Eindruck wollen Sie machen? Warum ist ein visueller Eindruck wichtig für Arbeitgeber?

3. Wie würden Sie sich über den Arbeitgeber informieren, bevor Sie zum Vorstellungsgespräch fahren würden?

   das Gebäude vorher anschauen • die Website vom Arbeitgeber anschauen • mit anderen Angestellten° sprechen • Broschüren vom Arbeitgeber lesen • andere Mögichkeiten?

4. Was für Fragen hätten Sie für den Interviewer? Warum ist es wichtig, in einem Interview gute Fragen zu stellen?

*employer*

*application letter*
*recommendations*
*former*

*employees*

> Questions that are strictly forbidden in a U.S. job interview are not always illegal in Europe.

 **42** **Interviewthemen.** Beantworten Sie die folgenden Fragen.

1. Welche Themen werden Frau Eichendorff, die Interviewerin, wohl interessieren?

   die Gründe für Karls Interesse am Kulturmanagement • Karls Alter • Karls Berufserfahrung (wo er bisher im Kulturmanagement gearbeitet hat) • Karls früheres Gehalt • Karls Gesundheit • Karls Hobbys in der Freizeit • Karls Kenntnisse von der Opernliteratur • Karls Religion • Karls Schulausbildung (wo er zur Schule gegangen ist) • Karls sexuelle Neigungen° • Karls Studium und theoretische Vorbereitung • Karls Wünsche und Erwartungen vom Praktikum

*preferences, inclinations*

2. Welche Themen würden wohl Karl als Praktikant interessieren?

die Dauer vom Praktikum • seine Funktion in der Betriebsleitung • das Gehalt • die Öffnungszeiten der Theaterkasse° • Parkmöglichkeiten in der Nähe von der Staatsoper • die Zahl von Kollegen in der Betriebsleitung

*box office*

3. Was würden Sie am Ende von einem Vorstellungsgespräch erwarten?

eine feste° Zusage° • ein Gehalt • ein Händeschütteln • einen Termin für ein zweites Interview • einen Vertrag°

*firm / commitment*
*contract*

 **43** **Satzdetektiv.** Welche Sätze bedeuten ungefähr das Gleiche?

1. Aus Ihren **Unterlagen** geht hervor, dass Sie sich hier um eine Praktikumsstelle bewerben.
2. Ich hab' da gemerkt, öh, dass es finanziell immer wieder **hapert**.
3. Also, ich hab' da meistens den organisatorischen Teil **übernommen**.
4. Ich hab' da auch gemerkt, was es da alles zu organisieren gibt, und ich habe gedacht, das wäre **eine klasse Gelegenheit**, das zusammenzubringen.

a. Ich habe gesehen, dass es einfach nie genug Geld gibt.
b. Ich hatte gewöhnlich° Verantwortung° für die Organisation von meiner Schauspielgruppe.
c. Es ist mir aufgefallen, wie viel man organisieren muss, und ich meine, das ist eine gute Chance, alle meine Interessen zu koordinieren.
d. Aus diesen Dokumenten sehe ich, Sie möchten hier ein Praktikum machen.

*usually*
*responsibility*

5. Ich würde mich, glaube ich, erstmal mit der **Geschäftsführung** zusammensetzen und fragen, was die finanziellen Mittel sind …,
6. **Falls**, öh, das dann schwierig werden würde, würde ich **mich** dann gerne dafür **einsetzen**, Sponsoring zu machen.
7. Welcher **Bereich** würde Ihnen da zusagen für Ihren Praktikumsplatz jetzt? Weil es sind da **verschiedene Bereiche**, die wir da abdecken können.
8. Es würde mir auch sehr viel Spaß machen, mit dem **Intendanten**, der dann den Spielplan aufsetzt, zu schauen, welche Stücke auch gut wären …

e. Ich möchte mit der Betriebsleitung diskutieren, wie viel Geld da ist.
f. Es würde mir gefallen, mit dem kreativen Direktor von der Oper zu diskutieren, welche Opern in den Spielplan kommen sollen.
g. In welcher Abteilung möchten Sie am liebsten Ihr Praktikum machen? Denn wir haben viele Möglichkeiten für Sie da.
h. Wenn das problematisch wäre, könnte ich persönlich Sponsoren für die Oper suchen.

## Zieltext

### Das Vorstellungsgespräch an der Wiener Staatsoper

 Hören Sie gut zu.

## Rückblick

 **44   Stimmt das?** Stimmen diese Aussagen zum Text oder nicht? Wenn nicht, was stimmt?

| | *Ja, das stimmt.* | *Nein, das stimmt nicht.* | |
|---|:---:|:---:|---|
| 1. Frau Eichendorff bittet Karl, während des ganzen Vorstellungsgesprächs zu stehen. | ☐ | ☐ | |
| 2. Frau Eichendorff hat Karls Dokumente nicht gelesen und improvisiert das ganze Interview. | ☐ | ☐ | |
| 3. Karl erzählt, dass er immer für die Organisation seiner Theatergruppe zuständig° war. | ☐ | ☐ | *responsible* |
| 4. Für Karl ist die Idee neu, dass auch Museen und Theater viel Hilfe mit der Organisierung brauchen. | ☐ | ☐ | |
| 5. Karl hat gute Ideen, wie die Betriebsleitung von der Oper ihre Arbeit mit der kreativen Intendanz koordinieren kann. | ☐ | ☐ | |
| 6. Karl hat keine feste Vorstellung von einem idealen Job an der Oper. | ☐ | ☐ | |
| 7. Karl hat gute Chancen, in mehr als einem Bereich zu arbeiten. | ☐ | ☐ | |
| 8. Frau Eichendorff will Karl noch heute ihr endgültiges° Ja oder Nein geben. | ☐ | ☐ | *final* |
| 9. Das Praktikum soll höchstens vier Wochen dauern. | ☐ | ☐ | |
| 10. Frau Eichendorff wünscht Karl mehrmals viel Glück. | ☐ | ☐ | |

**45** **Kurz gefragt.** Beantworten Sie die folgenden Fragen auf Deutsch.

1. Sucht Karl an der Wiener Staatsoper eine feste Stelle oder ein Praktikum?
2. Wie weiß Frau Eichendorff, dass Karl Kulturmanagement studiert?
3. Wie hat Karl sein Interesse an Kulturmanagement entdeckt?
4. Was war Karls Funktion in seiner Theatergruppe?
5. In welchen zwei Bereichen von der Oper möchte Karl sein Praktikum machen?
6. Was hält Karl wohl für die interessanteste Aufgabe im Kulturmanagement an der Oper?
7. Darf Karl mit Erfahrung in mehr als zwei Bereichen rechnen°? Warum?      *rechnen mit: to count on*
8. Wer trifft die endgültige Entscheidung über Karls Bewerbung? Wie lange muss Karl auf die Nachricht warten?

**46** **Eine Au-pair-Stelle.** Sie und ein Partner/eine Partnerin sind Herr und Frau Langer, die Eltern von zwei Kindern: ein Kind ist fünf Jahre, das andere ist acht Jahre alt und geht zur Schule. Sie suchen eine Au-pair-Person, die sich um die Kinder kümmern soll. Eine Vermittlungsagentur zeigt Ihnen die Akten von zwei Kandidaten. Diskutieren und entscheiden Sie, wen Sie für die Stelle gut finden. Hier sind die Akten. Geben Sie drei Gründe für Ihre Entscheidung.      *sich kümmern um: to look after*

---

Junge Familie
sucht

# AU-PAIR

für zwei Kinder (Willi, 5 und Julianna, 8) in Freiburg-Littenweiler.

Tätigkeiten: 2 Mahlzeiten kochen, mit den Kindern spielen, leichte Hausarbeit machen, den Kindern mit den Hausaufgaben helfen.

Bewerbungsbrief mit Foto an:
Frau Beate Langer
Schulweg 7a
78012 Freiburg

---

Amelie Eisner
21 Jahre alt
hat einen dreijährigen Bruder und eine vierzehnjährige Schwester
ist sehr kreativ und dynamisch
ist eine erfahrene Köchin
ist nicht immer pünktlich
studiert Kunst
wird manchmal ungeduldig

---

Anton Dunkel
18 Jahre alt
hat eine Schwester, die 8 Jahre alt ist
mag Kinder
ist ein durchschnittlicher Schüler
ist selbstständig und zuverlässig
kocht, aber nicht besonders gut
macht zu Hause nicht gern sauber
hat einen Führerschein
hat keine Erfahrung als Au-pair

 **Schreibecke**

**Ein Brief von Frau Langer.** Schreiben Sie einen Brief an Anton Dunkel oder Amelie Eisner. Schreiben Sie, warum Sie ihm/ihr die Stelle (nicht) geben. Beginnen Sie Ihren Brief mit **Lieber Herr … / Liebe Frau …**

**Mein Bewerbungsbrief.** Schreiben Sie einen Bewerbungsbrief für eine Stelle als Buchhalter/Buchhalterin°. Sie können den Bewerbungsbrief von Andrea Wallner als Beispiel benutzen. Beantworten Sie in Ihrem Brief diese Fragen.  *accountant*

1. Wie und wo haben Sie von der Stelle gehört?
2. Welche Berufserfahrung haben Sie?
3. Wie beschreiben Sie Ihre Persönlichkeit?
4. Warum sind Sie für die Stelle gut qualifiziert?

---

Weinheim, den 21. April

Sehr geehrte Damen und Herren,

ich habe Ihre Anzeige für einen Chefbuchhalter/eine Chefbuchhalterin in der „Mannheimer-Post" gesehen. Ich habe mein Wirtschaftsstudium an der Universität Trier abgeschlossen. Ich habe drei Sommer als Praktikantin bei der Firma Müller gearbeitet. Ich habe die Buchhaltung in der Verkaufs-abteilung° gemacht.  *sales department*

    Ich bin freundlich und kollegial. Ich kann selbstständig arbeiten und ich bin sehr zuverlässig und pünktlich. Weil ich Erfahrung als Buchhalterin und viel Interesse an Teamarbeit habe und immer zuverlässig bin, bin ich die richtige Kandidatin für diese Stelle. Ich hoffe, dass Sie sich für ein näheres Gespräch mit mir interessieren, und ich freue mich darauf, bald von Ihnen zu hören.

Hochachtungsvoll°  *Respectfully*

*Andrea Wallner*

Andrea Wallner

---

  **Freie Kommunikation**

**Das Vorstellungsgespräch.** Geben Sie einem anderen Studenten/einer anderen Studentin Ihren Bewerbungsbrief. Er/Sie führt mit Ihnen ein Vorstellungsge-spräch für diese Stelle. Werden Sie die Stelle bekommen? Besprechen Sie auch, wie viel Geld und wie viel Urlaub Sie bekommen werden.

## Wortschatz

### Die Ausbildung

**die Ausbildung, -en** *education; apprenticeship*

**der Praktikant, [-en], -en / die Praktikantin, -nen** *intern, apprentice*

*Noch einmal:* **der/die Auszubildende (Azubi), das Gymnasium, das Praktikum**

### Das Vorstellungsgespräch

**der Anzug, ¨-e** *suit*

**die Arbeitserfahrung, -en** *work experience*

**der Bewerber, - / die Bewerberin, -nen** *applicant*

**der Bewerbungsbrief** *letter of application*

**der Eindruck, ¨-e** *impression*

**die Empfehlung, -en** *recommendation*

**das Formular, -e** *form (to be filled out)*

**die Gelegenheit, -en** *opportunity*

**die Kenntnis, -se** *knowledge; skill*

**der Lebenslauf, ¨-e** *résumé, CV*

**die Nachricht, -en** *news*

**die Praxis, -en** *practice, doctor's office*

**die Stelle, -n** *position, job*

**der Termin, -e** *appointment*

**die Theorie, -n** *theory*

**die Vorstellung, -en** *introduction; image, idea*

**das Vorstellungsgespräch, -e** *interview*

**beeindrucken (hat beeindruckt)** *to impress*

**sich bewerben (bewirbt sich, hat sich beworben) um/für** + *acc.* *to apply for*

**sich verhalten (verhält sich, hat sich verhalten)** *to behave, act*

*Noch einmal:* **die Erfahrung, sich vor·bereiten, sich vor·stellen**

**Hochachtungsvoll** *Respectfully (at end of a letter)*

**unbezahlt** *unpaid*

### Eigenschaften von guten Bewerbern

**analytisch** *analytical*

**anständig** *decent, respectable*

**begabt** *talented*

**diszipliniert** *disciplined*

**dynamisch** *dynamic*

**flexibel** *flexible*

**gründlich** *thorough, detail-oriented*

**kollegial** *cooperative*

**kontaktfreudig** *sociable*

**motiviert** *motivated*

**pünktlich** *punctual*

**qualifiziert** *qualified*

**selbstständig** *self-reliant, independent*

**zuständig** *responsible*

**zuverlässig** *reliable*

### Die Arbeit

**die Aushilfe** *part-time worker*

**das Gehalt, ¨-er** *salary*

**der Kollege, [-n], -n / die Kollegin, -nen** *colleague, co-worker*

**der Termin, -e** *meeting, appointment*

*Noch einmal:* **die Aufgabe**

**führen (hat geführt)** *to lead, direct*

**gut aus·kommen (ist gut ausgekommen) mit** + *dat.* *to get along with*

### Berufe

**der Beruf, -e** *occupation*

**der Apotheker, - / die Apothekerin, -nen** *pharmacist*

**der Arbeiter, - / die Arbeiterin, -nen** *worker; laborer, blue-collar worker*

**der Bäcker, - / die Bäckerin, -nen** *baker*

**der Chef, -s / die Chefin, -nen** *boss*

**der Fleischer, - / die Fleischerin, -nen** *butcher*

**der Friseur, -e / die Friseurin, -nen** *hairdresser, barber*

**der Geschäftsmann, ¨-er / die Geschäftsfrau, -en** *businessman / -woman*

**der Kaufmann, ¨-er / die Kauffrau, -en** *dealer, merchant*

**der Komponist, [-en], -en / die Komponistin, -nen** *composer*

**der Krankenpfleger, - / die Krankenschwester, -n** *nurse, orderly*

**der Lehrer, - / die Lehrerin, -nen** *school teacher*

**der Makler, - / die Maklerin, -nen** *real estate agent*

**der Metzger, - / die Metzgerin, -nen** *butcher*

**der Musiker, - / die Musikerin, -nen** *musician*

**der Rechtsanwalt, ¨-e / die Rechtsanwältin, -nen** *lawyer, attorney*

**der Schauspieler, - / die Schauspielerin, -nen** *actor / actress*

**der Schriftsteller, - / die Schriftstellerin, -nen** *author*

**der Tierarzt, ¨-e / die Tierärztin, -nen** *veterinarian*

**der Verkäufer, - / die Verkäuferin, -nen** *salesman / woman*

**der Wissenschaftler, - / die Wissenschaftlerin, -nen** *scientist*

**der Zahnarzt, ¨-e / die Zahnärztin, -nen** *dentist*

*Kognate:* **der Architekt / die Architektin, der Automechaniker / die Automechanikerin, der Babysitter / die Babysitterin, der Filmemacher / die Filmemacherin, der Ingenieur / die Ingenieurin, der Journalist / die Journalistin, der Koch / die Köchin, der Politiker / die Politikerin, der Programmierer / die Programmiererin, der Sänger / die Sängerin, der Sekretär / die Sekretärin**

*Noch einmal:* **der Arzt / die Ärztin, der Kellner / die Kellnerin**

### Kultur und Architektur

die Aufführung, -en *performance*
das Ballett, -e *ballet*
die Bühne, -n *stage*
das Denkmal, *pl.* Denkmäler
  *monument*
der Friedhof, ̈e *cemetery*
das Gebäude, - *building*
das Geburtshaus, -häuser *birthplace*
die Gegenwart *present*
der Konzertsaal, -säle *concert hall*
das Mittelalter *Middle Ages*
das Musical, -s *musical*
das Programm, -e *program*
die Vorstellung, -en *presentation,
  performance*
*Noch einmal:* die Oper, das Stück

bauen (hat gebaut) *to build*
komponieren (hat komponiert) *to
  compose*
schaffen (hat geschaffen) *to create*
schaffen (hat geschafft) *to
  accomplish*
üben (hat geübt) *to practice,
  rehearse*

klassisch *classical*
kulturell *cultural*
schwungvoll *lively*
stimmungsvoll *full of atmosphere*
weltberühmt *world-famous*

### Komparative und Superlative

gern / lieber / Lieblings-, am liebsten *with eagerness / preferably /
  favorite, most preferably*
gut / besser / best-, am besten *good,
  well / better / best*
hoch / höher / höchst-, am höchsten
  *high / higher / highest; tall / taller /
  tallest*
höchstens *at the most*
viel / mehr / meist-, am meisten
  *much, many / more / most*
*Noch einmal:* meistens

### Relativpronomen

der/den/dem; das/das/dem;
  die/die/der; die/die/denen
  *relative pronouns*

### Andere Verben

sich beruhigen (hat sich beruhigt)
  *to calm down*
bieten (bietet, hat geboten) *to offer*
merken (hat gemerkt) *to notice*
Recht haben (hat Recht gehabt) *to
  be right*
reichen (hat gereicht) von ... bis *to
  stretch from . . . to*
widmen (hat gewidmet) *to dedicate*
wünschen (hat gewünscht) *to wish*

### Andere Substantive

die Hochzeit, en *wedding ceremony*
der Typ, -en *guy*
die Welt, -en *world*
*Noch einmal:* das Beispiel, die Einladung, die Leute

### Andere Adjektive

andere *other*
aufgeregt *excited, agitated, anxious*
einmalig *unique*
einzig *only*
fest *firm, solid, fixed; steady*
fremd *foreign, strange*
großartig *great, fabulous, fantastic*
hart *hard*
klasse *cool, great*
letzt *last*
möglich *possible*
nett *nice*
stark *strong*
toll *great*
wahnsinnig *crazy, insane*
weitere *further; additional*
*Noch einmal:* nervös, schwierig

### Andere Wörter

als *as; than*
gewöhnlich *usually*
niemals *never*
nun *now*
trotzdem *nevertheless*
*Noch einmal:* gleich, sicher, trotzdem

### Andere Ausdrücke

Das hat keinen Zweck. *There's no
  point in it.*
Hals- und Beinbruch! *Break a leg!*
heute in acht Tagen *a week from
  today*
Ich drücke dir (Ihnen) ganz fest die
  Daumen! *I'll really be crossing my
  fingers for you.*
ich hätte *I would have*
ich wäre *I would be*
Ich wünsch' dir was! *I'm hoping for
  you! Good luck!*
ich würde *I would*
Toi, toi, toi! *Lots of luck!*
was für ein(e)? *what kind of?*
Wie wäre es mit ... ? *How would ...
  be? How about ... ?*
*Noch einmal:* und so weiter (usw.),
  zum Beispiel (z. B.)

### Meine eigenen Wörter

_____
_____
_____
_____
_____
_____

The Internet is a valuable resource for locating job opportunities. Stefan went to *www.monster.de* to find a part-time job that would take advantage of his studies and his English-speaking abilities. He found a job entitled **Praktikum Event Management.**

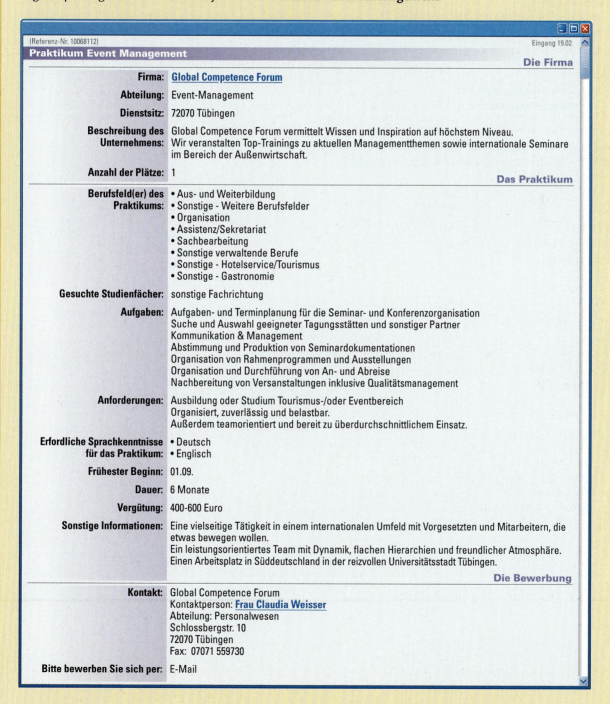

(Referenz-Nr. 10068112)                                                                    Eingang 19.02

**Praktikum Event Management**

**Die Firma**

| | |
|---|---|
| **Firma:** | **Global Competence Forum** |
| **Abteilung:** | Event-Management |
| **Dienstsitz:** | 72070 Tübingen |
| **Beschreibung des Unternehmens:** | Global Competence Forum vermittelt Wissen und Inspiration auf höchstem Niveau. Wir veranstalten Top-Trainings zu aktuellen Managementthemen sowie internationale Seminare im Bereich der Außenwirtschaft. |
| **Anzahl der Plätze:** | 1 |

**Das Praktikum**

| | |
|---|---|
| **Berufsfeld(er) des Praktikums:** | • Aus- und Weiterbildung<br>• Sonstige - Weitere Berufsfelder<br>• Organisation<br>• Assistenz/Sekretariat<br>• Sachbearbeitung<br>• Sonstige verwaltende Berufe<br>• Sonstige - Hotelservice/Tourismus<br>• Sonstige - Gastronomie |
| **Gesuchte Studienfächer:** | sonstige Fachrichtung |
| **Aufgaben:** | Aufgaben- und Terminplanung für die Seminar- und Konferenzorganisation<br>Suche und Auswahl geeigneter Tagungsstätten und sonstiger Partner<br>Kommunikation & Management<br>Abstimmung und Produktion von Seminardokumentationen<br>Organisation von Rahmenprogrammen und Ausstellungen<br>Organisation und Durchführung von An- und Abreise<br>Nachbereitung von Versanstaltungen inklusive Qualitätsmanagement |
| **Anforderungen:** | Ausbildung oder Studium Tourismus-/oder Eventbereich<br>Organisiert, zuverlässig und belastbar.<br>Außerdem teamorientiert und bereit zu überdurchschnittlichem Einsatz. |
| **Erfordliche Sprachkenntnisse für das Praktikum:** | • Deutsch<br>• Englisch |
| **Frühester Beginn:** | 01.09. |
| **Dauer:** | 6 Monate |
| **Vergütung:** | 400-600 Euro |
| **Sonstige Informationen:** | Eine vielseitige Tätigkeit in einem internationalen Umfeld mit Vorgesetzten und Mitarbeitern, die etwas bewegen wollen.<br>Ein leistungsorientiertes Team mit Dynamik, flachen Hierarchien und freundlicher Atmosphäre.<br>Einen Arbeitsplatz in Süddeutschland in der reizvollen Universitätsstadt Tübingen. |

**Die Bewerbung**

| | |
|---|---|
| **Kontakt:** | Global Competence Forum<br>Kontaktperson: **Frau Claudia Weisser**<br>Abteilung: Personalwesen<br>Schlossbergstr. 10<br>72070 Tübingen<br>Fax: 07071 559730 |
| **Bitte bewerben Sie sich per:** | E-Mail |

Beantworten Sie die folgenden Fragen zum Inserat von Global Competence Forum.

### Die Firma

1. In welcher Stadt ist die Firma?
2. Wie viele Personen sucht die Firma?

### Das Praktikum

3. Was sind drei Berufsfelder des Praktikums?
4. Welche Sprachen sind wichtig?
5. Wie viel Geld verdient man?

### Die Bewerbung

6. Wie heißt die Kontaktperson?
7. Wie soll man sich bewerben?

Sie suchen eine Stelle bei der Firma Global Competence Forum. Schreiben Sie eine kurze E-Mail an die Kontaktperson und stellen Sie sich vor. Stellen Sie auch einige Fragen über das Team, die Arbeitsatmosphäre und den Arbeitsplatz.

# Feste, Feiertage und Ferien

In this chapter you will continue to learn how to relate events in the past. You will read and discuss fairy tales and compare holidays and vacation spots in Germany, Austria, and Switzerland.

## Kommunikative Funktionen

- Narrating past events
- Talking about consecutive events in the past
- Talking about concurrent events in the past
- Saying when events occur
- Expressing ownership

## Strukturen

- The narrative past
- The past perfect
- Word order in sentences beginning with a subordinate clause
- The subordinating conjunctions **als, nachdem, ob, wann,** and **wenn**
- The genitive case
- Genitive prepositions

## Vokabeln

- Märchen
- Die Schweiz: geographische Daten

## Kulturelles

- Die Brüder Grimm und ihre **Kinder- und Hausmärchen**
- Karneval, Fasching, Fastnacht
- Die Schweiz
- Fest- und Feiertage

■ Der Karneval in Mainz beginnt für diese Kinder am 11.11. um 11.11. Uhr.

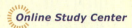

Go to the *Vorsprung* Website at *http://college.hmco.com/pic/vorsprung2e.*

## Anlauftext    Aschenputtel°

**Aschenputtel:** *Cinderella*

**(Ein Märchen nach den Brüdern Grimm)**

Anna und ihre Freunde wollen zum Karneval ein langes Wochenende in Köln verbringen. Tagsüber gibt es viele kostümierte Narren° auf den Straßen und endlose
Umzüge°. Und abends können sie auf einen Karnevalsball gehen, wo man bis
spät in die Nacht tanzt und trinkt … und sich vielleicht verliebt. Wer weiß? Vielleicht lernt Anna dort ihren Prinzen kennen, wie Aschenputtel …

*fools, carnival participants*
*parades*

### *Vorschau*

### *Wissenswerte Vokabeln: Märchen*
### *Talking about fairy tales*

„Es war einmal ein König …"

Did you enjoy reading fairy
tales as a child? Why or why
not? Which ones were your
favorites?

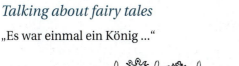

der Königssohn, die Königin, der König, die Königstochter    die Stiefmutter    der Jäger
der Prinz                                    die Prinzessin

der Wald

die Hexe

ein giftiger Apfel

der Zwerg

die gute Fee

der Frosch

der Zauberer

der Spiegel

„… und wenn sie nicht gestorben sind, dann leben sie noch heute."

Was gibt die alte Hexe Schneewittchen?

**1    Schneewittchen.** „Schneewittchen" ist ein sehr bekanntes Märchen von den Brüdern Grimm. Lesen Sie die Sätze und setzen Sie die richtigen Wörter ein.

1. Eine böse _Hexe_ will ihre Stieftochter Schneewittchen von einem _Jäger_ erschießen lassen°.

2. Er erschießt Schneewittchen nicht und sie läuft allein weg in den dunklen _Wald_ hinein.

3. Schneewittchen wohnt bei sieben _Zwerg_en.

4. Die Königin schaut jeden Tag in einen _Spiegel_ und findet heraus, dass sie nicht die Schönste ist.

5. Die Königin verkleidet° sich als _eine Hexe_.

6. Die Königin gibt Schneewittchen einen giftigen _Apfel_ und Schneewittchen scheint zu sterben.

7. Die Zwerge legen Schneewittchen in einen Glassarg°. Ein _Prinz_ bekommt Schneewittchens Glassarg von den Zwergen und auf dem Heimweg fällt der Apfel aus ihrem Hals. Sie wird wieder lebendig.

8. Er heiratet Schneewittchen und sie wird schließlich die neue _Königin_.

*erschießen lassen: have shot to death*

*disguises*

*glass coffin*

„Zum letzten Mal: Haut ab!° Ich bin nicht eure Schneewittchen!"

*Scram!, Get lost!*

> **Märchen** are tales in which a hero/heroine survives an ordeal or injustice but is rewarded for perseverance, hope, and faith, where good triumphs over evil, and where there is often retribution for the evil-doer. Irrational forces play a significant role—animals talk, the forest hides witches and dwarves, and princes become enchanted frogs— but the hero/heroine, subjected to endless trial, learns to trust innate abilities and soon overcomes these evil forces to reach a happy ending.

**2    Thematische Fragen.** Beantworten Sie die folgenden Fragen auf Deutsch.

1. Was passiert in der Version von „Aschenputtel", die wir in Nordamerika kennen? Lebt die Mutter noch? Lebt der Vater noch?

2. Wie ist das Leben für Aschenputtel? Was muss sie alles machen?

3. Wer hilft Aschenputtel, eine Fee, ein Zauberer oder zwei Vögel?

4. Hat Aschenputtel Stiefbrüder oder Stiefschwestern? Wie sind sie?

5. Wohin geht Aschenputtel?

6. Was verliert Aschenputtel auf dem Ball?

> **Märchen.** On the surface **Märchen** are fantastic and antiquated tales, but they speak to the unarticulated, unsophisticated fears of children with vivid imagery and a clear delineation between good and evil, helping them process their worries in a productive manner.

**3** **Zeitdetektiv.** Hier sind siebzehn Sätze im Präteritum°. Welche Sätze im Präsens bedeuten ungefähr das Gleiche?

*narrative past*

> **Zeitdetektiv.** You will learn about the narrative past (**Präteritum**) in this chapter.

1. Aschenputtels Mutter **starb.**
2. Eine schlimme Zeit **begann.**
3. Der König **lud** zu einem Fest° **ein.**
4. Der Königssohn **hielt** Aschenputtel für eine fremde Königstochter.

a. Der Königssohn hält Aschenputtel für eine fremde Königstochter.
b. Der König lädt zu einem Fest ein.
c. Aschenputtels Mutter stirbt.
d. Eine schlimme Zeit beginnt.

*party, celebration*

*Aschenputtels Vater ...*

5. ... **heiratete** eine neue Frau.
6. ... **sollte** für Aschenputtel einen Zweig zurückbringen.
7. ... **brachte** für Aschenputtel einen Haselzweig°.

*Aschenputtels Vater ...*

e. ... heiratet wieder.
f. ... bringt für Aschenputtel einen Haselzweig.
g. ... soll für Aschenputtel einen Haselzweig zurückbringen.

> **Aschenputtel.** The Disney animation *Cinderella* is based on Charles Perrault's French version of the tale.

*hazelnut branch*

*Aschenputtel ...*

8. ... **sah** schmutzig **aus.**
9. ... **ging** jeden Tag zum Baum und **weinte.**
10. ... **zog** das Kleid **an.**
11. ... **rannte** schnell davon.
12. ... **verlor** auf der Treppe ihren linken Schuh.
13. ... **wollte** auch zum Tanz mitgehen.

*Aschenputtel ...*

h. ... rennt° schnell davon.
i. ... will auch zum Tanz mitgehen.
j. ... zieht das Kleid an.
k. ... geht jeden Tag zum Baum und weint°.
l. ... verliert auf der Treppe ihren linken Schuh.
m. ... sieht schmutzig aus.

*runs*

*cries*

*Die Stiefschwestern ...*

14. ... **nannten** sie Aschenputtel.
15. ... **riefen** Aschenputtel **zu:** „Wir gehen auf das Schloss des Königs."
16. ... **erkannten** Aschenputtel nicht.
17. ...**schnitten** sich die Zehe und die Ferse **ab.**

*Die Stiefschwestern ...*

n. ... erkennen° Aschenputtel nicht.
o. ... nennen° sie Aschenputtel.
p. ... schneiden sich die Zehe und die Ferse ab.
q. ... rufen Aschenputtel zu: „Wir gehen auf das Schloss des Königs."

*recognize*
*name*

**4** **Wortfelder.** Welches Wort gehört zum gleichen Wortfeld wie das Wort in der linken Spalte? Unterstreichen Sie es.

| das Messer: | schneiden | schwer arbeiten | tanzen |
|---|---|---|---|
| 1. das Messer: | schneiden | schwer arbeiten | tanzen |
| 2. der Herd: | waschen | kochen | schlafen |
| 3. die Asche: | schön | weiß | schmutzig |
| 4. Edelsteine: | Diamanten | Kleider | Essen |
| 5. der Baum: | passen | bringen | pflanzen |
| 6. der liebe Gott: | beten° | schwer arbeiten | studieren |
| 7. das Vögelchen: | fliegen | schwimmen | heiraten |
| 8. der Ball: | arbeiten | tanzen | studieren |
| 9. der Schuh: | weinen | anprobieren | trinken |
| 10. der Fuß: | das Haar | die Zehe | die Nase |

*to pray*

> Although long sometimes, **Märchen** generally contain many recurring expressions.

## Anlauftext
### Aschenputtel

Lesen Sie eine deutsche Version von „Aschenputtel".

**E**s war einmal ein hübsches Mädchen, dessen[1] Mutter krank wurde. Als die Frau fühlte, dass sie sterben musste, rief sie ihre Tochter zu sich: „Liebes Kind, bleib fromm[2] und gut, so wird dir der liebe Gott immer helfen, und ich will vom Himmel auf dich herabblicken." Dann starb die Frau.

5   Nach einem Jahr heiratete der reiche Vater eine neue Frau, die zwei Töchter mit ins Haus brachte. Diese Schwestern waren schön von Gesicht aber böse von Herzen. Nun musste das Mädchen von morgens bis abends schwer arbeiten. Abends musste sie sich neben den Herd in die Asche legen. Und weil sie darum immer
10  schmutzig aussah, nannten die Stiefschwestern sie Aschenputtel.

Eines Tages machte der Vater eine Reise. Er fragte, was er den
15  Mädchen mitbringen sollte. „Schöne Kleider!", „Perlen und Edelsteine", sagten die Stiefschwestern. Aber Aschenputtel sagte: „Vater, bring mir
20  einfach den ersten Zweig von einem Baum, den du auf dem Heimweg findest."

Der Vater brachte Kleider und Edelsteine für die Stiefschwestern und einen Haselzweig für Aschenputtel. Aschenputtel dankte ihm und pflanzte den Zweig auf dem Grab ihrer Mutter. Er wuchs zu einem schönen Haselnuss-
25  baum. Aschenputtel ging jeden Tag dreimal darunter, weinte und betete. Jedes Mal kam ein weißes Vögelchen auf den Baum und gab dem Mädchen alles, was es sich wünschte.

Eines Tages lud der König alle Mädchen im Land zu
30  einem Fest ein. Der Königssohn suchte eine Braut. Die zwei Stiefschwestern riefen Aschenputtel zu: „Wir gehen auf das Schloss des Königs." Aschenputtel wollte auch gern zum Tanz mitgehen. Die Stiefmutter aber erlaubte es nicht: „Du hast keine Kleider und Schuhe und willst tanzen? Du
35  kommst nicht mit!" Darauf ging sie mit ihren beiden Töchtern fort.

---

[1] *whose*

[2] *pious, devout*

Line 27: **Es = das Mädchen = Aschenputtel**

Aschenputtel ging zum Grab ihrer Mutter unter den Haselbaum und rief:
„Bäumchen, rüttel° dich und schüttel° dich – wirf Gold und Silber über mich! " Da     *shake / shiver*
warf ihr der Vogel ein Kleid aus Gold und Silber herunter. Aschenputtel zog das
40 Kleid an und ging zum Fest. Ihre Schwestern und Stiefmutter erkannten sie nicht.
Der Königssohn hielt sie für eine fremde Königstocher und tanzte nur mit ihr. Als
Aschenputtel nach Hause gehen wollte, sprach der Königssohn: „Ich begleite°     *accompany*
dich!“ Aber Aschenputtel lief schnell fort.

Am zweiten Tag
45    wiederholte sich alles. Am
dritten Tag brachte das
Vögelchen ein glänzendes
Kleid und Schuhe aus Gold.
Wieder tanzte der Königssohn
50    nur mit ihr, wieder lief
Aschenputtel schnell fort.
Aber diesmal verlor sie auf der
Treppe ihren linken Schuh.

Der Königssohn proklamierte: „Die Frau, deren° Fuß in diesen Schuh passt,     *whose*
55 soll meine Braut werden!“ Da freuten sich die Schwestern. Die älteste
Stiefschwester nahm den Schuh mit in ihr Zimmer und probierte ihn an. Aber
der Schuh war zu klein. Da sagte ihr die Mutter: „Schneid die Zehe ab! Wenn du
Königin bist, so brauchst du nicht mehr zu Fuß zu gehen.“ Da schnitt die
Schwester die Zehe ab.

60    Der Königssohn nahm sie als seine Braut aufs Pferd. Als sie am Grab von
Aschenputtels Mutter vorbeiritten°, riefen zwei Täubchen° vom Haselbaum:     *rode past / little doves*
„Rucke di guh, rucke di guh, Blut ist im Schuh. Der Schuh ist zu klein. Die rechte
Braut sitzt noch daheim°.“ Da sah der Königssohn das Blut und brachte sie     *at home*
zurück.

65    Da probierte die andere Schwester den Schuh an, aber
die Ferse° war zu groß. Da nahm sie ein Messer und schnitt
die Ferse ab. Die Schwester und der Königssohn ritten am
Grab vorbei und wieder riefen die Täubchen: „Rucke di guh,
rucke di guh, Blut ist im Schuh ..." Da brachte der Königssohn
70 die falsche Braut wieder nach Hause zurück.

**Ferse:** *heel*

    Er fragte den Vater: „Haben
Sie noch eine andere Tochter?"
„Nein", sagte der, „nur das
schmutzige Aschenputtel. Sie
75 kann nicht die Richtige sein."
Der Königssohn wollte sie aber
sehen. So probierte
Aschenputtel den goldenen
Schuh an, und er passte wie
80 angegossen°. Dann nahm der        *poured on*
Königssohn Aschenputtel aufs
Pferd und ritt mit ihr fort.
Diesmal riefen die Täubchen:
„Rucke di guh, rucke di guh,
85 kein Blut ist im Schuh. Der
Schuh ist nicht zu klein, die
rechte Braut, die führt er heim."
Dann flogen die beiden
Täubchen auf Aschenputtels
90 Schultern, eines rechts, das
andere links.

## *Rückblick*

  **5**  **Stimmt das?** Stimmen diese Aussagen zum Text oder nicht? Wenn nicht, was stimmt?

|  | Ja, das stimmt. | Nein, das stimmt nicht. |
|---|---|---|
| 1. Aschenputtels Vater war krank und starb. | ☐ | ☐ |
| 2. Aschenputtel musste in der Küche schwer arbeiten und in der Asche neben dem Herd schlafen. | ☐ | ☐ |
| 3. Aschenputtels Vater brachte ihr Perlen und Edelsteine von seiner Reise zurück. | ☐ | ☐ |
| 4. Der König lud alle Mädchen im Land zu einem Fest ein, weil sein Sohn eine Braut suchte. | ☐ | ☐ |
| 5. Die Stiefmutter nahm Aschenputtel zum Ball mit. | ☐ | ☐ |
| 6. Aschenputtel rannte zum Grab von ihrer Mutter und rief zum Haselbaum: „Rüttel dich und  schüttel dich, wirf Gold und Silber über mich!" | ☐ | ☐ |
| 7. Am dritten Abend brachte der Vogel Aschenputtel das schönste Kleid und Schuhe aus Glas. | ☐ | ☐ |
| 8. Aschenputtel verlor einen Schuh beim Tanzen. | ☐ | ☐ |
| 9. Der Königssohn wollte die Frau heiraten, deren Fuß in den goldenen Schuh passte. | ☐ | ☐ |
| 10. Aschenputtel musste sich die Ferse und die Zehe abschneiden, damit der Schuh passte. | ☐ | ☐ |
| 11. Die Stiefmutter und die Stiefschwestern freuten sich, dass der Königssohn Aschenputtel als seine Braut erkannte. | ☐ | ☐ |

> Complete the **Ergänzen Sie** activity in your workbook for this text before doing the next activity.

**6**  **Kurz gefragt.** Beantworten Sie diese Fragen auf Deutsch.

1. Was sagte Aschenputtels Mutter zu ihrer Tochter, bevor sie starb?
2. Wie änderte sich° Aschenputtels Leben, nachdem ihre Mutter starb?
3. Warum nannten die Stiefschwestern das Mädchen „Aschenputtel"?
4. Was für ein Andenken wünschte sich Aschenputtel von ihrem Vater und was machte sie damit?
5. Warum hielt der König ein Fest?
6. Warum wollten die Stiefschwestern (und auch Aschenputtel) zum Fest gehen?
7. Was machte das Vögelchen, als Aschenputtel zum Grab ging?
8. Wen nahm die Stiefmutter mit zum Fest?
9. Wie fand der Königssohn Aschenputtel wieder?
10. Wie wusste der Königssohn, dass Aschenputtel wirklich die richtige Braut war?

> **Kurz gefragt.** These questions are in the simple past.
>
> *sich ändern: to change*

**7** **Kurz interpretiert.** Beantworten Sie diese Fragen auf Deutsch.

1. In vielen Märchen hat die Zahl 3 eine symbolische Funktion. Zählen Sie alle Elemente in „Aschenputtel", die in Dreiergruppen passieren. Was symbolisieren sie wohl?

2. Aschenputtels Liebe zu ihrer Mutter ist sehr wichtig. Wie zeigt Aschenputtel diese Liebe? Hält die verstorbene Mutter ihr Versprechen ein, und passt sie auf Aschenputtel auf? Wie?

3. Welche Zauberelemente oder unwahrscheinlichen Episoden gibt es in diesem Märchen? Was sind sie und warum sind sie wichtig?

4. In dieser Geschichte spielt Aschenputtels Vater praktisch keine Rolle. Warum ist die Figur des Vaters so neutral aber die Figuren der Stiefmutter und Stiefschwestern so böse und negativ?

  **Freie Kommunikation**

**Rollenspiel: Der Prinz und Aschenputtel.** S1 ist der Prinz und S2 ist seine Mutter, die Königin. Sprechen Sie miteinander über Aschenputtel. Was haben Sie auf dem Fest gemacht? Wie war Aschenputtel? Was möchten Sie jetzt machen?

**8** **Berühmte Märchensprüche.** Welches Zitat stammt aus welchem Märchen?

Aschenputtel • Die Bremer Stadtmusikanten • Hänsel und Gretel • Rapunzel • Rumpelstilzchen • Rotkäppchen • Schneewittchen

1. „Ei, Großmutter, was hast du für ein entsetzlich großes Maul!"
   —„Dass ich dich besser fressen kann!"

2. „Heute back ich, morgen brau ich, übermorgen hol ich der Königin ihr Kind; ach, wie gut, dass niemand weiß, dass ich _____ heiß!"

3. „Zieh lieber mit uns fort, wir gehen nach Bremen; etwas Besseres als den Tod° findest du überall."                                                    *death*

4. „Rüttel dich und schüttel dich, wirf Gold und Silber über mich."

5. „Rapunzel, Rapunzel, lass dein Haar herunter."

6. „Spieglein, Spieglein an der Wand, wer ist die Schönste im ganzen Land?"

7. „Knusper, knusper, kneischen, wer knuspert an meinem Häuschen?"
   —„Der Wind, der Wind, das himmlische Kind."

Rotkäppchen                                    Hänsel und Gretel

## Die Brüder Grimm und ihre Kinder- und Hausmärchen

There has been no single work of children's literature more important to Western culture than the **Kinder- und Hausmärchen,** an anthology of folk (fairy) tales (**Volksmärchen**) published by the Brothers Grimm, Jacob (1785–1863) and Wilhelm (1786–1859). The Brothers Grimm spent many years collecting these **Märchen,** which were, by tradition and practice, a form of oral literature. The texts existed only in the memory of the many people who told and retold them. Many of these tales were native to specific regions and were told in dialect; others were more universal and spread to other nations and languages, often developing interesting plot twists in traveling abroad. The Grimms did not write the fairy tales themselves, but instead sought out talented storytellers, recording and editing the tales they were told. The Brothers Grimm published the first volume of their anthology in 1812; a second volume, including contributions from other collectors of folk tales, was printed in 1814. They followed with an anthology of Germanic myths, **Deutsche Sagen,** in 1816–18. Because of their research and their fascination with the German language, the Grimm brothers are regarded as the founders of modern German studies (**Germanistik**). This reputation was enhanced by Jacob Grimm's **Deutsche Grammatik** and by their efforts to publish the first comprehensive **Deutsches Wörterbuch,** a project that lasted from 1852 to its completion in 1961.

■ **Kulturkreuzung** Haben Sie als kleines Kind gern gelesen? Was für Geschichten haben Sie am liebsten gehört oder gelesen? Hatten Sie eine Heldenfigur, die Sie verehrt° haben? Warum hatten Sie diese Figur so gern? Welche Märchen haben Ihnen besonders gut gefallen? Gibt es Unterschiede zwischen Märchenfiguren, die Jungen und Mädchen am besten gefallen?

*cherished*

**9**  **Interview: Märchen.** Stellen Sie einem Partner / einer Partnerin die folgenden Fragen.

*Märchen: singular and plural form*

1. Hast du als Kind „Aschenputtel" gelesen? Was war damals deine Reaktion?
2. Was sollen Kinder von „Aschenputtel" lernen?
3. Welche Märchen machte das Disney-Studio als Zeichentrickfilme bekannt?
4. Welche Märchen findest du sexistisch? Warum?
5. Hast du als Kind gern Märchen gelesen? Hast du sie immer noch gern?
6. Welche sind deine Lieblingsmärchen? Beschreib die Hauptfiguren in deinen Lieblingsmärchen.
7. Beschreib den Feind° in deinen Lieblingsmärchen.

*adversary*

8. In den meisten Märchen passiert ein großes Unglück. Was ist das Unglück in deinen Lieblingsmärchen?
9. Welche Zauberkräfte helfen der Hauptfigur in deinen Lieblingsmärchen?
10. Welche Märchen aus anderen Ländern, Kontinenten und Kulturen kennst du?

## Strukturen und Vokabeln

### I  Narrating past events

The narrative past

In **Kapitel 5** you learned that the conversational past tense **(das Perfekt)** is used in informal contexts, in speaking, and in letter writing to talk about events in the past.

Tante Uschi **hat** als Kellnerin **gearbeitet.**

German speakers use the narrative past **(das Präteritum),** also called the simple past, to recount past events in written texts, such as novels, stories, news articles, and occasionally in speaking, especially when telling a long, uninterrupted story. Some of these forms look very much like the English simple past forms and should present few problems in reading.

Da **begann** eine schlimme Zeit.  *With that began a difficult time.*
Jedesmal **kam** ein weißes  *A little white bird came to the tree every*
    Vögelchen auf den Baum.      *time.*

> Many North German speakers prefer the narrative past over the conversational past in conversation.

### A. Narrative past: regular (weak) verbs

Regular (weak) verbs **(schwache Verben)** add a **-te** as a narrative past tense marker. All forms except the **ich-** and **er/sie/es-**forms add the same endings as in the present tense (e.g., **-st, -t,** or **-n**).

| machen: *to do, make* | |
|---|---|
| **Singular** | **Plural** |
| ich mach**te** | wir mach**ten** |
| du mach**test** | ihr mach**tet** |
| Sie mach**ten** | Sie mach**ten** |
| er/sie/es mach**te** | sie mach**ten** |

> Notice that the **ich-**form and the **er/sie/es-**forms of the narrative past are identical, as are the **wir-** and **sie/Sie-**forms.

Regular verbs with a stem ending in **-t, -d, -fn, -gn** (e.g., **regnen**), **-chn** (e.g., **rechnen**), or **-kn** (e.g., **trocknen**) insert an additional **e** before the narrative past tense marker **-te** to facilitate pronunciation.

Aschenputtel weinte und bet**e**te.  *Cinderella cried and prayed.*

> In general, regular (weak) verbs in English form the past tense with **-ed.** However, the **-ed** can sound like d (e.g., **he cried, she prayed, it rained**), or t (e.g., **they walked, he skipped, we worked**), or **-id** (e.g., **she batted, I swatted, we landed**).

These are the narrative past forms of **arbeiten.**

| arbeiten: *to work* | | |
|---|---|---|
| **Singular** | | **Plural** |
| ich arbeit**ete** | | wir arbeit**eten** |
| du arbeit**etest** | | ihr arbeit**etet** |
| Sie arbeit**eten** | | Sie arbeit**eten** |
| er/sie/es arbeit**ete** | | sie arbeit**eten** |

> Verbs with stems ending in **-t, -d,** and **-fn** include **arbeiten, beten, reden,** and **öffnen.**

As in the present tense, regular verbs with separable prefixes place the prefix at the end of the sentence, leaving the conjugated narrative past form of the verb in the second position.

> **an·probieren**
>
> Aschenputtel **probierte** den   *Cinderella tried on the golden slipper.*
> goldenen Schuh **an.**

Remember that regular (weak) verbs have a letter **-t** in both the narrative past tense and the conversational past tense.

| *Infinitive* | *Present* | *Narrative past* | *Conversational past* |
|---|---|---|---|
| sagen | ich sage | ich sag**te** | ich habe gesag**t** |

⟲ **10** **Meine eigene Verbtabelle.** Füllen Sie diese Verbtabelle mit den richtigen Verbformen aus.

> **Meine eigene Verbtabelle.** These are all regular (weak) verbs. You may add other verbs to this list.

| *Infinitiv* | *Präteritum* | *Perfekt* | |
|---|---|---|---|
| 1. lachen | _____ | _____ | |
| 2. _____ | wohnte | _____ | |
| 3. fragen | _____ | _____ | |
| 4. legen | _____ | _____ | |
| 5. _____ | _____ | hat getanzt | |
| 6. feiern° | _____ | _____ | *to celebrate* |
| 7. _____ | bedeutete | _____ | |
| 8. _____ | _____ | hat gefühlt | |
| 9. setzen | _____ | _____ | |
| 10. _____ | _____ | hat sich gefreut | |
| 11. _____ | _____ | hat gekauft | |
| 12. _____ | küsste | _____ | |
| 13. _____ | _____ | hat geregnet | |
| 14. _____ | erzählte | _____ | |
| 15. heiraten | _____ | _____ | |
| 16. _____ | _____ | hat gemacht | |
| 17. _____ | wartete | _____ | |
| 18. kosten | _____ | _____ | |
| 19. _____ | dauerte | _____ | |
| 20. _____ | _____ | hat sich verliebt | |

**11** **Hannelores Kindheit° in Deutschland.** Annas Mutter Hannelore erlebte° die 60er Jahre in Deutschland. Erzählen Sie ihre Geschichte im Präteritum mit den angegebenen schwachen Verben.

*childhood*
*experienced*

**Hannelore**
1. in Weinheim leben
2. oft auf der Straße spielen
3. 1965 ihren fünften Geburtstag feiern
4. mit ihren Eltern im Wald Pilze° suchen
5. von amerikanischen Soldaten Englisch lernen

*mushrooms*

**Oma Kunz**
6. jeden Tag einkaufen
7. für die ganze Familie kochen
8. Opa heiraten
9. in der Stadt arbeiten
10. jeden Sonntag in der Kirche beten

**Ihre Nachbarn**
11. einen Tante-Emma-Laden° gründen°
12. Brot, Käse und Wurst verkaufen
13. den Laden morgens um halb sieben aufmachen
14. den Laden abends um sechs zumachen
15. ein gutes Einkommen verdienen

*family-run shop / establish*

**12** **Verliebt, verlobt, verheiratet.** Erzählen Sie die Liebesgeschichte von Hannelore und Bob Adler mit den angegebenen schwachen Verben im Präteritum.

**Hannelore**
1. die Universität in Heidelberg wählen
2. zu Hause bei den Eltern wohnen und Geld sparen°
3. mit dem Zug von Weinheim nach Heidelberg pendeln°
4. Englisch und Volkswirtschaft studieren
5. mit Nachhilfestunden° in Deutsch und Englisch Taschengeld verdienen
6. mit Schülern und mit amerikanischen Soldaten arbeiten
7. eines Tages einen deutschsprechenden GI namens Bob Adler kennen lernen

*to save*
*commute*

*tutoring*

**Bob**
8. der Hannelore lustige Witze° erzählen
9. einen guten Eindruck auf sie machen
10. als Ingenieur in der Armee dienen°
11. sich auf die Wochenenden in Heidelberg freuen
12. die Studentin nach ihrer Telefonnummer fragen
13. sich schnell in die Hannelore verlieben
14. eine Weile warten und sich dann den Eltern in Weinheim vorstellen
15. sich nach einem romantischen Jahr in Heidelberg mit der Hannelore verloben
16. im Juli 1982 die Hannelore heiraten

*jokes*

*serve*

## Karneval, Fasching, Fastnacht

The "crazy" days (**Die tollen Tage**) of the **Karneval** season are some of the most popular holidays of the calendar in German-speaking countries. The name changes with location—**Karneval** in the Rhineland, **Fasching** in Bavaria and Austria, **Fastnacht** in Southwestern Germany, and **Fasnacht** in Switzerland—as do customs and actual dates, but it is generally regarded as the high point of the winter season. These are the days of revelry and merrymaking that precede the beginning of Lent (**die Fastenzeit**), the period in which Catholics have been traditionally required to fast in preparation for Easter.

In the Rhineland, the **Karneval** season always opens on November 11th at 11:11 A.M., while in the south the season traditionally begins on Epiphany, January 6 (**Dreikönigstag**). The season heats up on the last Thursday before Ash Wednesday (**Fetter Donnerstag**, or **Altweiberfastnacht**), when women customarily chase men with scissors and try to cut off a piece of their neckties. This marks the start of the six-day celebration: social taboos are relaxed, romances blossom, and the partying begins. Schools either go on vacation or suspend classes, while students hold costumed dance parties and small towns and city neighborhoods put on their own parades. In and around the Rhineland, special "fools' guilds" (**Narrengesellschaften**) hold balls and "roasts" (**Kappensitzungen**) presided over by a **Narrenkönig** and **Narrenkönigin**. On **Rosenmontag**, two days before Ash Wednesday, Cologne and Mainz host their famous parades with marching bands, costumed participants, dancing spectators, and decorated floats, some with humorous political themes, others from which candy and favors are tossed to the crowds. On **Karnevalsdienstag** final parades, parties, and costume balls signal the conclusion of the holiday season, which traditionally ends with a fish dinner and a ritualistic "funeral of the **Karneval**" on Ash Wednesday (**Aschermittwoch**).

Am Rosenmontag zieht der Narrenzug durch die Kölner Innenstadt.

**Kulturkreuzung** Viele Kulturen haben einen Feiertag, an dem die Menschen ein Kostüm oder eine Verkleidung tragen. An welchem Tag ist das in den USA und in Kanada? Welche religiöse oder nicht-religiöse Funktion haben die Kostüme an diesem Feiertag? Feiert man in den USA und Kanada Karneval? Wo?

## B. Narrative past: irregular (strong) verbs

Strong verbs (**starke Verben**) show a vowel change from the infinitive to the narrative (simple) past. In English these verbs are referred to as *irregular verbs* (e.g., *see > saw, eat > ate*). You should learn to recognize these forms in German texts.

> sehen > sah
> Da **sah** der Königssohn das Blut.     *Then the king's son saw the blood.*

Some verbs change consonants as well as the vowel in the narrative past.

> **geh**en > g**ing**
> Aschenputtel **ging** zum Grab ihrer     *Cinderella went to her mother's*
> Mutter.                                   *grave.*

As in the present tense, verbs with separable prefixes in the narrative past position the prefix at the end of the sentence, leaving the conjugated narrative past form of the verb in the second position.

> an·**zieh**en > zo**g** an
> Aschenputtel **zog** das Kleid **an.**     *Cinderella put the dress on.*
> ab·schn**eid**en > schn**itt** ab
> Da nahm sie ein Messer und                *So she took a knife and cut off her heel.*
> **schnitt** die Ferse **ab.**

Irregular verbs have no ending in the **ich-** and the **er/sie/es**-forms. The endings of all other forms are the same as the present tense endings.

| sehen: *to see* | | |
|---|---|---|
| **Singular** | | **Plural** |
| ich sah | | wir sah**en** |
| du sah**st** | | ihr sah**t** |
| Sie sah**en** | | Sie sah**en** |
| er/sie/es sah | | sie sah**en** |

Strong verbs with stems ending in **-t** or **-d** generally insert an additional **e** in the narrative past forms for **du** and **ihr** (e.g., **du schnittest, ihr schnittet**). Those with stems ending in an **s**-sound generally insert an **e** for **du** (e.g., **du lasest, du aßest**).

Here are some of the most common strong verbs in the narrative and conversational past.

| Infinitive | Narrative past | Present perfect | |
|---|---|---|---|
| | ich/er/sie/es | er/sie/es | |
| an·**fang**en | f**ing** an | hat angefangen | *began* |
| beg**inn**en | beg**ann** | hat begonnen | *began* |
| bek**omm**en | bek**am** | hat bekommen | *received* |
| b**itt**en | b**at** | hat gebeten | *requested, asked for* |
| bl**eib**en | bl**ieb** | ist geblieben | *stayed* |
| ein·**lad**en | l**ud** ein | hat eingeladen | *invited* |
| **ess**en | **aß** | hat gegessen | *ate* |

Use your knowledge of English irregular verbs to aid you in remembering some of the German forms (e.g., *sing/sang, eat/ate, swim/swam*).

| Infinitive | Narrative past | Present perfect | |
|---|---|---|---|
| fahren | fuhr | ist gefahren | *drove* |
| fangen | fing | hat gefangen | *caught* |
| finden | fand | hat gefunden | *found* |
| fliegen | flog | ist geflogen | *flew* |
| geben | gab | hat gegeben | *gave* |
| gehen | ging | ist gegangen | *went* |
| halten | hielt | hat gehalten | *held* |
| helfen | half | hat geholfen | *helped* |
| kommen | kam | ist gekommen | *came* |
| laufen | lief | ist gelaufen | *ran* |
| lesen | las | hat gelesen | *read* |
| nehmen | nahm | hat genommen | *took* |
| reiten | ritt | ist geritten | *rode* |
| rufen | rief | hat gerufen | *called* |
| schlafen | schlief | hat geschlafen | *slept* |
| schneiden | schnitt | hat geschnitten | *cut* |
| schreiben | schrieb | hat geschrieben | *wrote* |
| schwimmen | schwamm | ist geschwommen | *swam* |
| sehen | sah | hat gesehen | *saw* |
| singen | sang | hat gesungen | *sang* |
| sitzen | saß | hat gesessen | *sat* |
| sprechen | sprach | hat gesprochen | *spoke* |
| stehen | stand | hat gestanden | *stood* |
| steigen | stieg | ist gestiegen | *climbed* |
| sterben | starb | ist gestorben | *died* |
| tragen | trug | hat getragen | *wore, carried* |
| treffen | traf | hat getroffen | *met, hit* |
| trinken | trank | hat getrunken | *drank* |
| werfen | warf | hat geworfen | *threw, tossed* |
| ziehen | zog | hat gezogen | *pulled* |

**13** **Der gestiefelte Kater°.** Kennen Sie das Märchen vom gestiefelten Kater? Ein Müller° hatte drei Söhne. Der Müller starb, und der jüngste (und auch dümmste) Sohn bekam kein Geld, sondern nur einen Kater. Dieser Kater war aber sehr intelligent und half dem Sohn, reich zu werden. Schreiben Sie das richtige Verb in die Lücken und erzählen Sie das Märchen vom gestiefelten Kater nach.

*Puss-in-Boots*
*miller*

aß • bat • begann • bekam • trug

**D**er jüngste Müllerssohn _____ nach dem Tod seines Vaters nichts als einen Kater. Doch plötzlich _____ dieser Kater zu sprechen und bat den Müllerssohn um ein Paar Stiefel. Bald _____ der Kater wunderbare° rote Stiefel. Dann jagte° er Rebhühner°, brachte° sie zu dem König und sagte: „Die hat Ihnen mein Herr, der Graf°, geschickt!" Das freute den König sehr, weil er sehr gern Rebhühner _____, und er schenkte dem Kater einen Sack voll Gold. Der Müllerssohn war erstaunt°, als ihm der Kater das Gold brachte und ihn _____: „Tu, was ich dir sage, und so wirst du reich!"

*wonderful / hunted*
*partridges / brought*
*count*
*astounded*

fuhr • hörte • lief • lud ... ein • saß • schenkte • schwamm

Ein paar Tage später _____ der Müllerssohn im Fluss und der Kater versteckte° seine Kleider. Als der König in seiner Kutsche° vorbei _____, rief der Kater: „Hilfe, jemand° hat meinem Herrn, dem Grafen, die Kleider gestohlen!!!" Der König _____ dem Müllerssohn schöne Kleider und _____ ihn _____ mitzufahren. In der Kutsche _____ die schöne Tochter des Königs, die Prinzessin. Der Kater _____ voraus und befahl° den Leuten in den Feldern: „Gleich wird der König vorbeifahren. Wenn er fragt, so sagt, das ganze Land gehört dem Grafen!" Als der König dies _____, meinte er, der Müllerssohn sei ein reicher Edelmann°.

*hid*
*coach*
*someone*

*ordered*

*nobleman*

ankam • fragte • fraß° • bekam • kam • sprang

Bald _____ der Kater ins Schloss des großen Zauberers. Der Kater _____: „Also, Zauberer, kannst du dich in jedes Tier verwandeln°?" „Ja, natürlich," sagte er! Kaum hatte der Zauberer sich in eine Maus verwandelt, _____ der Kater auf und _____ sie. So wurde der Müllerssohn der Besitzer° des großen Schlosses. Als die Kutsche am Schloss _____, begrüßte der Kater den König: „Willkommen im Schloss meines Herrn!" Der arme° Müllerssohn _____ die Prinzessin zur Frau und wurde selbst König.

*devoured (as an animal
   eats)*

*transform*

*owner*

*poor*

**14** **Der Mann im Smoking°.** Helene Dornhuber ist in Tübingen auf einen Fastnachtsball gegangen. Dort hat sie einen „Prinzen" im Smoking getroffen, aber leider hat ihr „Märchen" kein Happyend. Ergänzen Sie die Geschichte mit der richtigen Präteritumform.

*tuxedo*

| an·kommen | an·rufen | auf·schreiben | beginnen | essen | finden |
|---|---|---|---|---|---|
| sagen | sitzen | sprechen | tragen | treffen | trinken |

Gestern Abend ging Helene auf einen Fastnachtsball in der Tübinger Stadthalle. Der Ball _____ um 20.00 Uhr, aber sie _____ erst um 21.00 Uhr an. Dort _____ sie einen jungen Mann. Er _____ einen eleganten Smoking. Sie _____ lange zusammen, _____ ein Glas Wein und tanzten. Sie _____ auch Pizza und Kuchen. Um 24.00 Uhr _____ sie, dass sie gehen musste. Er _____ ihre Adresse auf. Am nächsten Tag _____ er ihre Adresse nicht mehr und war sehr traurig darüber. Helene _____ den ganzen Tag in ihrem Zimmer und wartete auf den Mann im Smoking, aber er _____ sie nicht an.

## C. Narrative past: *sein, haben, and the modal verbs*

German speakers frequently use the auxiliary verbs **haben** and **sein** in the narrative (simple) past—in speaking as well as in writing. These are their forms.

| sein: *to be* | | | |
|---|---|---|---|
| **Singular** | | **Plural** | |
| ich | **war** | wir | **waren** |
| du | **warst** | ihr | **wart** |
| Sie | **waren** | Sie | **waren** |
| er/sie/es | **war** | sie | **waren** |

| haben: *to have* | | | |
|---|---|---|---|
| **Singular** | | **Plural** | |
| ich | **hatte** | wir | **hatten** |
| du | **hattest** | ihr | **hattet** |
| Sie | **hatten** | Sie | **hatten** |
| er/sie/es | **hatte** | sie | **hatten** |

The modal verbs form their past tense like the regular (weak) verbs with the **-te** past tense marker. In the narrative past the umlaut is dropped.

| Infinitive | Narrative past | Meaning |
|---|---|---|
| dürfen | durfte | *was allowed to* |
| können | konnte | *was able to, could* |
| mögen | mochte | *liked* |
| müssen | musste | *had to* |
| sollen | sollte | *was supposed to* |
| wollen | wollte | *wanted to* |

Note that the **g** in **mögen** changes to **ch** in the narrative past.

**15** **Als Kind durfte ich nicht rauchen.** Was durften (konnten usw.) Sie als Kind nicht machen? Beantworten Sie die folgenden Fragen mit einem Partner/einer Partnerin. Benutzen Sie das passende Modalverb im Präteritum.

S1: *Was durftest du als Kind nicht machen?*
S2: *Als Kind durfte ich nicht rauchen.*

| weit zur Schule fahren | mein Zimmer sauber° machen | Sport treiben | *clean* |
| Gemüse essen | schnell laufen | spät ins Kino gehen | |
| früh aufstehen | (sich) baden | rauchen | |
| Auto fahren | in die Schule gehen | Schlittschuh° laufen | *ice skate* |
| Alkohol trinken | Deutsch sprechen | Klavier üben | |

1. Was durftest du als Kind nicht machen?
2. Was konntest du als Kind nicht machen?
3. Was musstest du als Kind nicht machen?
4. Was wolltest du als Kind nicht machen?
5. Was solltest du als Kind zu Hause nicht machen?

**16**　**Was wollte Aschenputtel?** Beschreiben Sie mit Hilfe von den Modalverben alles, was Aschenputtel **wollte, sollte, musste, konnte** oder **durfte.**

■　fromm und gut bleiben　*Aschenputtel sollte fromm und gut bleiben.*

1. fromm und gut bleiben
2. nicht mehr in einem Bett schlafen
3. neben dem Herd in der Asche schlafen
4. einen Zweig als Andenken von ihrem Vater bekommen
5. auch zum Fest des Königs mitgehen
6. ohne Kleid und Schuhe nicht zum Fest mitgehen
7. allein zu Hause bleiben
8. allein mit dem Königssohn tanzen
9. nur als die Letzte den Schuh anprobieren

## D. Narrative past: mixed verbs

Mixed verbs (**gemischte Verben**) combine the past tense marker **-te** that is added to the stem of regular (weak) verbs with the vowel change of irregular (strong) verbs when forming the narrative (simple) past.

> Infinitive: **denken**
> Der Vater **dachte:** „Kann das　　*The father thought: "Can that be*
> 　Aschenputtel sein?"　　　*Cinderella?"*

Here are some of the most common mixed verbs.

> Remember: **ich durfte nicht** = *I wasn't allowed to, was forbidden to*; **ich musste nicht** = *I didn't have to*; **ich sollte nicht** = *I wasn't supposed to.*

> The English verbs *bring/brought, think/thought* are mixed verb forms from an older form of English.

> The consonant clusters **nk** and **ng** in the infinitive change to **ch** in the narrative past.

| | Infinitive | Narrative past | Conversational past | |
|---|---|---|---|---|
| **e > a** | bren**n**en | bra**nnte** | hat gebrannt | *burned* |
| | den**k**en | da**chte** | hat gedacht | *thought* |
| | erken**n**en | erka**nnte** | hat erkannt | *recognized* |
| | ken**n**en | ka**nnte** | hat gekannt | *knew (person or place)* |
| | nen**n**en | na**nnte** | hat genannt | *named* |
| | ren**n**en | ra**nnte** | ist gerannt | *ran* |
| **i > a** | brin**g**en | bra**chte** | hat gebracht | *brought* |
| | verbrin**g**en | verbra**chte** | hat verbracht | *spent time* |

Similarly, the verbs **wissen** and **werden** also mix both strong and weak verb narrative past tense markers. Note that **werden** has a **-d** instead of a **-t**.

| Infinitive | Narrative past | Conversational past | |
|------------|----------------|---------------------|---|
| wissen | wus**ste** | hat gewusst | *knew (a fact)* |
| werden | wur**de** | ist geworden | *became* |

  **17** **Aus „Aschenputtel".** Ergänzen Sie die folgenden Sätze aus „Aschenputtel" mit einer passenden Verbform aus der Liste.

| | | | |
|---|---|---|---|
| brachte (3x) | hatte | rannte | waren |
| erkannten | nannten | war | wurde |

1. Es war einmal ein hübsches Mädchen, dessen Mutter krank _____ und starb.
2. Nach einem Jahr nahm sich der Mann eine neue Frau, die zwei Töchter mit ins Haus _____.
3. Diese Schwestern _____ schön von Gesicht aber böse von Herzen.
4. Selbst ein Bett _____ das Mädchen nicht mehr, es musste neben dem Herd in der Asche liegen.
5. Und weil sie darum immer schmutzig aussah, _____ die Stiefschwestern sie „Aschenputtel".
6. Als der Vater zurückkam, _____ er Kleider und Edelsteine für die Stiefschwestern.
7. Ihre Schwestern und Stiefmutter _____ Aschenputtel nicht auf dem Fest.
8. Das Vögelchen _____ ihr ein noch viel schöneres Kleid.
9. Wieder _____ Aschenputtel schnell davon.
10. Da ging die andere Schwester in das Zimmer und probierte den Schuh an, aber die Ferse _____ zu groß.

## Freie Kommunikation

**Ein tolles Fest!** Erzählen Sie einem Partner/einer Partnerin im Präteritum von einem Fest. Geben Sie zehn Details an. Davon sind drei falsch. Der Partner/Die Partnerin soll herausfinden, welche drei Details falsch sind.

**Ein erlebnisvoller°Abend.** Erzählen Sie einer Gruppe von drei bis vier Studenten von einem erlebnisvollen Abend auf einem Fest, einer Hochzeit oder einem anderen Tanzabend (z.B. *senior prom*). Was passierte dort? Was machten Sie? Beschreiben Sie fünf bis sechs Details im Präteritum (z.B. **Ich ging/aß/trank/tanzte** ...).

*eventful*

**Das ist zu grausam°!** Lesen Sie die folgende Schlussszene aus der ursprünglichen° Grimmschen Version von „Aschenputtel". Mehrere Eltern in der Schule halten diese Version für zu brutal für Kinder. Teilen Sie die Klasse in drei Gruppen auf: **Pro, Kontra** und **Revisionisten.** Die Kontra-Gruppe will diese Schlussszene verbieten°. Die Revisionisten finden die Schlussszene auch unakzeptabel und schlagen Änderungen vor. Die Pro-Gruppe argumentiert gegen

*gruesome, cruel*
*original*

*ban, prohibit*

eine Zensur°. Die Mitglieder von allen Gruppen erklären, warum sie für oder gegen die Schlussszene sind. Ihr Dozent/Ihre Dozentin spielt den Schuldirektor/die Schuldirektorin und entscheidet, wie das Märchen enden soll.

*censorship*

**A**ls die Brautleute zur Kirche gingen, war die ältere Schwester zur rechten Seite und die jüngere zur linken Seite der Braut. Da pickten die Tauben° einer jeden° ein Auge aus. Danach, als sie aus der Kirche kamen, war die jüngere Schwester zur rechten Seite und die ältere zur linken Seite der Braut. Da pickten die Tauben einer jeden das andere Auge aus. So war Blindheit die Strafe° für ihre Bosheit° und Falschheit.

*pigeons / **einer jeden:** from each one*

*punishment / mean-spiritedness*

  **S c h r e i b e c k e**

**Ein neues Märchen.**  Schreiben Sie Ihr eigenes Märchen mit Hilfe der Sätze unten.

1. Es war einmal … ein Prinz/eine Prinzessin • ein Student/eine Studentin • ein Zauberer/eine Hexe • ein Deutschlehrer/eine Deutschlehrerin

2. Er/Sie war sehr … schön/hässlich • intelligent/dumm • gut/böse

3. Er/Sie lebte … auf einem Schloss • in einem Wald • an der Uni

4. Dort hatte er/sie … viele Freunde/Feinde • Bücher • wilde Tiere • giftige Äpfel • Edelsteine

5. Er/Sie wollte …

6. Da kam ein/eine …

7. Der/Die war …

8. Und wenn sie nicht gestorben sind, dann …

**Absprungtext**

# Braunwald autofrei: Ein Wintermärchen ... hoch über dem Alltag

Anna und ihre Freunde haben von Mitte Februar bis Mitte April Semesterferien und planen seit Wochen einen Skiurlaub°. Sie haben Broschüren von bekannten Wintersportorten bestellt und jetzt diskutieren sie alle Möglichkeiten. Für Anna klingt Braunwald in der Schweiz wirklich ideal: viel Schnee und viele Pisten° zum Skilaufen in den Alpen und keine Autos! Die Gruppe muss sich entscheiden, ob sie sich einen Skiurlaub in der Schweiz leisten° kann oder ob er einfach zu teuer ist.

*skiing vacation*

*ski runs*

*afford*

---

### Sprache im Alltag: Urlaub oder Ferien?

German has two separate words for vacation, **der Urlaub** and **die Ferien** *(pl)*. **Ferien** are school-free vacation days that are scheduled into a school year and observed by students and teachers alike **(Schulferien, Semesterferien, Weihnachtsferien)**. German university students have two long vacation breaks: **Winterferien** from mid-February to mid-April and **Sommerferien** from mid-July to mid-October. **Urlaub,** on the other hand, is active vacation time taken to relax and recuperate from work, and in most instances, to travel. The average German employee gets 24 paid vacation days, or roughly five weeks.

## *Vorschau*

 **18** **Thematische Fragen.** Beantworten Sie die folgenden Fragen auf Deutsch.

1. Wann machen Sie lieber Urlaub: im Winter, Frühling, Sommer oder Herbst?
2. Wann haben Sie als Kind meistens mit der Familie Urlaub gemacht: im Winter, Frühling, Sommer oder Herbst?
3. Sind Sie als Kind weit gefahren oder sind Sie in der Nähe geblieben?
4. Was wollten Ihre Eltern damals° im Urlaub erleben und was sind heute Ihre Ziele für den Urlaub? Kreuzen Sie die passenden Antworten an.   *at that time*

|  | Meine Eltern damals | Ich heute |
|---|---|---|
| a. viele Sehenswürdigkeiten sehen | ☐ | ☐ |
| b. Tiere und Natur erleben | ☐ | ☐ |
| c. Verwandte besuchen | ☐ | ☐ |
| d. Ruhe und Entspannung° haben | ☐ | ☐ *relaxation* |
| e. viel Aktivität haben | ☐ | ☐ |
| f. eine fremde Kultur und Sprache kennen lernen | ☐ | ☐ |
| g. so wenig Geld wie möglich ausgeben | ☐ | ☐ |
| h. viel Geld ausgeben und tolle Andenken kaufen | ☐ | ☐ |
| i. viel Zeit mit Freunden verbringen | ☐ | ☐ |
| j. gut essen und trinken | ☐ | ☐ |

5. Mit wem reisen Sie jetzt am liebsten, wenn Sie Urlaub machen? Oder fahren Sie lieber allein?
6. Was ist Ihr Traum-Urlaubsland? Warum? Was möchten Sie dort machen, sehen, hören, lernen? Wann wollen Sie dorthin reisen?

## *Lesestrategien: Braunwald autofrei: Ein Wintermärchen.*

Benutzen Sie die folgenden Strategien, um den Text „Braunwald autofrei" zu verstehen.

 **19** **Den Kontext verstehen.** Suchen Sie im Text die Information unten.

1. Wie heißt der Ort?
2. Welche Jahreszeit (Sommer, Herbst usw.) sieht man in der Broschüre dargestellt?
3. Warum kommen Menschen dahin? Was kann man dort machen?
4. Schauen Sie sich die Bilder an. Suchen Sie die Wörter **einen Schlitten, schlittelnde Kinder, Millionen von Menschen, die Autos.**

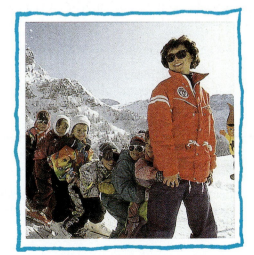

**20** **Neue Wörter lernen: erster Versuch.** Erraten Sie die Bedeutung von den Ausdrücken aus dem Kontext.

1. „Glauben Sie, dass es die kleinen **Winterferienwunder** noch gibt?"

Was sind die drei Wörter im Kompositum? Welche Stimmung° sieht man in den Bildern? Ist ein Wunder etwas Normales?

*Atmosphäre*

2. „Unten sind **gestresste Stadtmenschen** eingestiegen, oben steigen **gutgelaunte Ferienmenschen** aus."

Welcher Kontrast zwischen Menschen sieht man hier im Satz? Können Sie den Unterschied° zwischen dem Alltagsleben in der Stadt und dem Leben in den Ferien erklären?

*difference*

3. „Gutgelaunte Spaziergänger in einer echten **Postkartenlandschaft.**"

Die Landschaft bedeutet die Geographie des Landes. Wie ist die Landschaft in Braunwald? Was hat das mit einer Postkarte zu tun?

4. „Ein Schlittelparadies, eine **Langlaufloipe** und eine Schweizer Skischule … **Pisten** für Anfänger und Fortgeschrittene und auch **Pisten** zum gemütlichen Bergrestaurant."

Es gibt zwei Arten von Skifahren – Alpin und Langlauf. Welcher ist schneller? Für Alpin braucht man Pisten. Was braucht man für Langlauf?

5. „Nach der Schussfahrt auf der Piste, Aufwärmen auf der **Sonnenterrasse** der **Bergwirtschaft** oder beim Kaffeefertig unten **im Dorf.**"

In einer Wirtschaft kauft man etwas zu essen und trinken. Wo sind die zwei Wirtschaften in diesem Satz? Wo kann man sitzen, wenn man draußen im Freien etwas trinken will?

6. „Eine herzliche, unkomplizierte **Gastfreundschaft.** Ein gutes Gefühl, **Gast** in einem **gastlichen** Haus zu sein."

Ein Gast ist eine Person, die zu Besuch kommt und kurze Zeit bleibt. Gäste will man besonders nett und freundlich behandeln°. Was bietet man als Gastgeber dem Gast an? Wie verhalten sich gute Gäste? Schlechte Gäste?

*treat*

7. „Abendliches Wintermärchen Braunwald: **Zauberstimmung.**"

Ein Zauberer ist ein Mann, der Magie macht. Wie ist die Stimmung am Abend in Braunwald? Was hat das mit Magie zu tun? Was ist die Verbindung zwischen Märchen, Zauber und Stimmung?

**21** **Neue Wörter lernen: Drei Strategien.** Erraten Sie die fett gedruckten Wörter mit Hilfe der drei Strategien. Wählen Sie die korrekte Antwort.

*Weltwissen*

1. „Hier bringt der **Postbote** … auf seinem Schlitten gerade die Morgenzeitung."
   □ Der Briefträger bringt die Zeitung.     □ Ein Boot bringt die Zeitung.

2. „**Gutgelaunte** Spaziergänger in einer echten Postkartenlandschaft.“
☐ in schlechter Stimmung        ☐ in guter Stimmung

3. „Was für ein Spass, im Pferdeschlitten durch das **verschneite** Wintermärchenland zu fahren!“
☐ eine Landschaft ohne Schnee        ☐ eine Landschaft mit viel Schnee

4. „Nach der Schussfahrt auf der **Piste ...**“
☐ Man fährt Ski auf einer Piste.        ☐ Man fährt Auto auf einer Piste.

5. „Pisten für Anfänger und **Fortgeschrittene** ...“
☐ für Leute, die schon sehr gut Ski        ☐ für Leute, die nicht gut Ski
laufen.        laufen.

> Note that in this Swiss text ss is used instead of standard German ß following long vowels, e.g., **Spaß-Spass, Fuß-Fuss, Straße-Strasse, Genießer-Geniesser.**

### Kontext

1. „Eben Leute von heute. Gestresst, überarbeitet und **ferienreif.**“
☐ Leute, die Ferien brauchen        ☐ Leute, die mehr Arbeit brauchen

2. „Es [das Bähnli] **rüttelt und schüttelt sich** und **klettert** durch den Schnee
hinauf auf die Sonnenterrasse.“
☐ Es fährt sehr schnell hinauf.        ☐ Es fährt langsam und mit Mühe°        *effort*
hinauf.

3. „Das Wunder des Wandels **findet** im Bähnli **statt ...** Unten sind gestresste
Stadtmenschen eingestiegen, oben steigen gutgelaunte Ferienmenschen aus.“
☐ Etwas Wunderbares passiert im        ☐ Man findet die Stadt im Bähnli.
Bähnli.

4. „Einfach keine Autos! Da **fehlt das Dröhnen** der Motoren.“
☐ Man hört keine Motoren.        ☐ Man hört laute Motoren.

5. „Braunwald ist nichts für die Massen, sondern für **echte Geniesser.**“
☐ Menschen, die Braunwald kennen und gut finden.
☐ Menschen, die Braunwald uninteressant finden.

### Wortformen im „Schwyzerdüütsch“ (Schweizerdeutsch-Dialekt)

1. „**Wach' uf, liäbs Bruuwald.**“
☐ Wasch auf, liebe Brunhilde.        ☐ Wach auf, liebes Braunwald.

2. „Das **Bähnli** führt in die Zukunft.“
☐ die kleine Eisenbahn°        ☐ ein Mann namens Bähnli        *railroad*

3. „Man sagt **‚Grüezi‘**, wenn man sich begegnet.“
☐ Grüß Sie!        ☐ Gute Zeit!

---

### Sprache im Alltag: Diminutives

The Swiss German dialects form diminutives by adding the suffix **-li** to nouns instead of the standard German **-chen** and **-lein**.

| *Standard* | *Schweizerdeutsch* |
|---|---|
| das Bähnchen | das Bähnli |
| das Bähnlein | |

These diminutives change the gender of the noun to **das**, and add an umlaut
(e.g., **die Bahn** > **das Bähnli**).

*Absprungtext*
*Braunwald autofrei:*
*Ein Wintermärchen ... hoch über dem Alltag*

Lesen Sie jetzt den Text.

## Wach' uf liäbs Bruuwald

### Das Bähnliwunder im Wunderbähnli

Glauben Sie, dass es die kleinen Winterferienwunder noch gibt? Wir aus Braunwald glauben daran, denn Winter für Winter erleben wir eine seltsame Geschichte ...

Nach Braunwald führt keine Strasse – nur ein Bähnli in die Zukunft. In dieses Bähnli steigen unten im Tal täglich Menschen aus dem Unterland. Müde vom Alltag, den grauen Wolken und langen Nebeltagen. Eben Leute von heute. Gestresst, überarbeitet und ferienreif.

Dann setzt sich das rote Bähnli in Bewegung°. Es rüttelt und schüttelt sich und klettert durch den Schnee hinauf auf die Sonnenterrasse.

Das Bähnli steigt und steigt. Jetzt noch der kleine Tunnel und schon ist das alltägliche Bähnliwunder von Braunwald perfekt.

Das Wunder des Wandels findet im Bähnli statt. Ob Millionär oder Tellerwäscher – am Bähnli kommt keiner vorbei. Unten sind gestresste Stadtmenschen eingestiegen, oben steigen gutgelaunte Ferienmenschen aus. Jeden Winter täglich neu: das kleine Bähnliwunder von Braunwald.

***Bewegung:*** *motion*

# Guätä Morgä liäbs Bruuwald

**G**ut geschlafen, lieber Gast? Hier bringt der Postbote – den wir in Braunwald „Pöschtler" nennen – auf seinem Schlitten gerade die Morgenzeitung. Der "Pöschtler" geht zu Fuss, weil er kein Auto hat.

**D**as ist normal hier oben. Denn in Braunwald gibt es keine Autos. Braunwald ist autofrei. Zuerst ist es ein richtiger Schock. Einfach keine Autos! Da fehlt das Dröhnen der Motoren. An die saubere Luft muss man sich zuerst gewöhnen. Hier ist eben schon alles etwas anders als

anderswo. Gast bedeutet nicht nur Gastfreundschaft. GAST heisst auch Gemeinschaft Autofreier Schweizer Tourismusorte.

*Persönlichkeit ist alles –*
*Prestige ist gar nichts.*
*Eine herzliche, unkomplizierte*
*Gastfreundschaft. Ein gutes*
*Gefühl, Gast in einem*
*gastlichen Haus zu sein.*

**G**utgelaunte Spaziergänger in einer echten Postkartenlandschaft. Schlittelnde Kinder, die keine Angst vor Autos haben. Hier sagt man sich noch „Grüezi", wenn man sich begegnet. Man kennt sich eben in Braunwald.

# Guätä Tag liäbs Bruuwald

**D**er sanfte° Tourismus findet auch im Winter statt. Auch wer nicht Ski fährt, ist hier Erstklassgast. Was für ein Spass, im Pferdeschlitten durch das verschneite Wintermärchenland zu fahren!

Was den Winter attraktiv und sportlich macht, ist in Braunwald zu finden. Ein Schlittelparadies, eine

Langlaufloipe und eine Schweizer Skischule.

**D**as Skifahren ist noch Spass und weniger aggressiv als anderswo. Pisten für Anfänger und Fortgeschrittene und auch Pisten zum gemütlichen Bergrestaurant. Sonnige Pisten auf der Südseite und Pulverschnee an den Nordhängen.

Für die ehemaligen Skistars und die ewigen Anfänger, die gar nie Pistenraser° werden wollen.

**N**ach der Schussfahrt auf der Piste, Aufwärmen auf der Sonnenterrasse der Bergwirtschaft oder beim Kaffeefertig unten im Dorf. Eine ehrliche Gastronomie der kleinen Familienbetriebe.

# Guät Nacht liäbs Bruuwald

**A**bendliches Wintermärchen Braunwald: Zauberstimmung. Was ist schon Glück? Vielleicht die Stille eines Bergabends, eine nächtliche Schlittelfahrt, ein Kinoabend oder ein Schlummertrunk° an einer Hotelbar? „Hoch über dem Alltag"

finden Sie noch Naturschönheit, Herzlichkeit und Lebensfreude. Millionen von Menschen kommen Gott sei Dank gar nie nach Braunwald.

**B**raunwald ist nichts für die Massen, sondern für echte Geniesser. Braunwald ist etwas ganz Besonderes. Die wesentlichen° Dinge sind in Braunwald sichtbar° – mit den Augen und dem Herzen.

**sanfte:** *relaxing*
**Schlummertrunk:** *nightcap*

**Pistenraser:** *speed demon*
**wesentlichen:** *essential*
**sichtbar:** *visible*

## Rückblick

**22** **Stimmt das?** Stimmen die folgenden Aussagen zum Text oder nicht? Wenn nicht, was stimmt?

|  | Ja, das stimmt. | Nein, das stimmt nicht. |
|---|---|---|
| 1. Nur mit dem „Bähnli" kommt man nach Braunwald, weil keine Straße dahin führt. | ☐ | ☐ |
| 2. Es kann tagelang dauern, bis man in Braunwald gutgelaunt und in Ferienstimmung ist. | ☐ | ☐ |
| 3. Im Winter bringt der Postbote die Post mit seinem Fahrrad. | ☐ | ☐ |
| 4. Es ist ein Schock, dass man in Braunwald keine Motoren hört. | ☐ | ☐ |
| 5. Die Leute in Braunwald sagen „Grüezi", wenn sie einander treffen. | ☐ | ☐ |
| 6. Wer gern Ski läuft, kann hier Alpin und Langlauf machen, zur Skischule gehen und Pisten für Anfänger oder Fortgeschrittene finden. | ☐ | ☐ |
| 7. Für die Nicht-Skifahrer gibt es in Braunwald nichts zu tun. | ☐ | ☐ |
| 8. Essen kann man oben auf dem Berg in der Bergwirtschaft. | ☐ | ☐ |
| 9. Abends gibt es wilde Après-Ski-Partys°, laute Diskomusik und viel Bier. | ☐ | ☐ |
| 10. Braunwald ist nicht für jedermann°, sondern nur für echte Genießer. | ☐ | ☐ |

> Complete the **Ergänzen Sie** activity in your workbook for this text before doing the next activity.

*after-ski parties*

*everyone*

**23** **Kurz interpretiert.** Beantworten Sie die folgenden Fragen auf Deutsch.

1. Was für eine Stimmung oder Atmosphäre will diese Broschüre erzeugen°? Warum?    *create*
2. Was assoziiert der Normalmensch mit dem Wort „Märchen"? Ist das für einen Tourismusort positiv?
3. Welche Assoziationen mit einem Märchen hat man, wenn man die Broschüre liest? Erklären Sie die Wörter **Wunder, rüttelt und schüttelt, Postkartenlandschaft.**
4. In welcher Hinsicht° ist Braunwald märchenhaft?    *way, respect*
5. Wie ist das Skifahren in Braunwald in der Broschüre beschrieben? Klingt das langweilig, normal, attraktiv?
6. Welche Attraktionen gibt es in Braunwald für Leute, die nicht Alpinski fahren?
7. Wie ist die Stimmung des Nachtlebens in Braunwald? Welche Aktivitäten nennt man hier? Welchen Ton will man mit dieser Beschreibung erzeugen?

### Die Schweiz

Switzerland (**die Schweiz,** officially **Confœderatio Helvetica**) is a small, multilingual nation of approximately 7 million people located in the heart of central Europe. Bordered by Germany, France, Italy, Austria, and Liechtenstein, the country has four national languages: German, the native language of nearly two-thirds (63.7%) of all Swiss, French (spoken by 20.4% of the population), Italian (6.5%), and Rhaeto-Romanic (0.5%). Each of these languages is spoken in regional dialects. Important German-speaking cities are Bern, the capital of Switzerland; Zürich, the business and banking center; and Basel, the center of the Swiss chemical and pharmaceutical industry. Geneva (called **Genf** in German and Genève in French), the chief French-speaking city, is headquarters for the International Red Cross and one of two European headquarters for the United Nations.

Switzerland is one of Europe's oldest democracies, dating from an alliance signed in 1291 by the cantons of Uri, Schwyz, and Unterwalden that guaranteed the traditional autonomy of the communes and their citizens. This loose confederation was later replaced with a federation of 26 individual Swiss states **(Kantone).** Since then, the Swiss have maintained a reputation of tolerance and respect for the rights and autonomy of individuals, although ironically, Swiss women did not acquire the right to vote until 1971. Switzerland has maintained a policy of diplomatic neutrality and does not belong to NATO or to the European Union. Switzerland also does not use the Euro.

Although the country has relatively few natural resources and nearly 70% of its land mass is covered by the Alps and Jura Mountains, the Swiss economy is robust and its service industries are world-famous. In banking, insurance, and tourism, Switzerland has few peers. In addition, Swiss industries such as chemicals, pharmaceuticals, watchmaking, textiles, and metal-, machine-, and instrument-making have helped establish a per capita income that surpasses that of Germany, France, the U.S.A., Canada, and Sweden.

■ **Kulturkreuzung** Spricht man mehrere Sprachen in Ihrer Stadt? in Ihrem Staat oder Ihrer Provinz? in Ihrem Land? Welche Sprachen? Sind diese Sprachen offizielle Sprachen? Warum hat Kanada zwei offizielle Sprachen? Warum haben die USA keine offizielle Sprache?

Der Zytglogge-Turm (Zeitglocken-turm) in der Hauptstadt der Schweiz – Bern

**24   Die Schweiz.** Was assoziieren Sie *nicht* mit der Schweiz?
Streichen Sie in jeder Zeile einen Begriff durch°.

1. die Schokolade, der Käse, das Wiener Schnitzel, das Müesli
2. der Atlantik, die Alpen, der Genfer See, der Rhein
3. Deutsch, Spanisch, Italienisch, Französisch, Rätoromanisch
4. das Rote Kreuz, die chemische Industrie, Banken, Popmusik
5. die Demokratie, die Diktatur, die Neutralität
6. Wandern, Surfen, Bergsteigen, Ski laufen

**durchstreichen:** *to cross out*

Basel-Land

Jura

Zürich

Schaffhausen

## *Wissenswerte Vokabeln: die Schweiz – geographische Daten*
### *Talking about Switzerland*

The island of Mainau belongs to Germany, not to Switzerland.

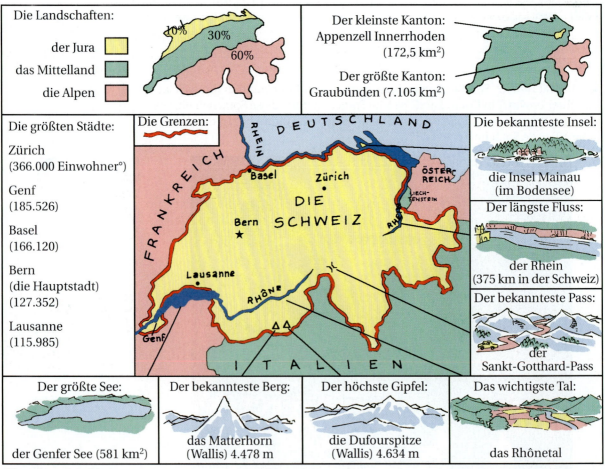

Die Landschaften:

der Jura
das Mittelland
die Alpen

10%   30%   60%

Der kleinste Kanton:
Appenzell Innerrhoden
(172,5 km²)

Der größte Kanton:
Graubünden (7.105 km²)

Die größten Städte:

Zürich
(366.000 Einwohner°)

Genf
(185.526)

Basel
(166.120)

Bern
(die Hauptstadt)
(127.352)

Lausanne
(115.985)

Die Grenzen:

DEUTSCHLAND
FRANKREICH
RHEIN
Basel   Zürich
ÖSTER-REICH
LIECH-TENSTEIN
DIE SCHWEIZ
Bern ★
RHEIN
Lausanne
RHÔNE
Genf
ITALIEN

Die bekannteste Insel:

die Insel Mainau
(im Bodensee)

Der längste Fluss:

der Rhein
(375 km in der Schweiz)

Der bekannteste Pass:

der
Sankt-Gotthard-Pass

Der größte See:

der Genfer See (581 km²)

Der bekannteste Berg:

das Matterhorn
(Wallis) 4.478 m

Der höchste Gipfel:

die Dufourspitze
(Wallis) 4.634 m

Das wichtigste Tal:

das Rhônetal

*Einwohner: inhabitants*

Wie heißt der längste Fluss in der Schweiz?

**25** **Geographie-Jeopardy.** Sie wissen die Antwort schon, aber wie heißt die Frage? Fragen Sie nach Superlativen in der Schweiz.

 S1: *Zürich*
S2: *Was ist die größte Stadt in der Schweiz?*

1. Zürich
2. Dufourspitze
3. Appenzell Innerrhoden
4. Graubünden

5. die Alpen
6. das Rhônetal
7. Mainau

8. der Sankt-Gotthard
9. der Rhein
10. der Genfer See

 **Freie Kommunikation**

**Rollenspiel: Braunwald besuchen.**

S1: Sie planen eine Winterreise und suchen Informationen im Reisebüro. Sie fahren nicht so gern Ski, sind aber gern draußen im Winter, mögen Massentourismus nicht so gern und sind etwas snobbistisch.

S2: Sie arbeiten im Reisebüro. Sie sind gerade vom Winterurlaub in Braunwald zurückgekommen und erzählen, was Sie alles dort gemacht haben und warum Braunwald Touristen so gut gefällt oder was Touristen dort ärgert. Versuchen Sie den Kunden/die Kundin (S1) zu überzeugen, auch mal in Braunwald Urlaub zu machen oder Braunwald fernzubleiben° und einen besseren Urlaubsort zu finden.    *stay away from*

 **Schreibecke**

**Reisetagebuch.** Sie haben in Braunwald eine Woche Urlaub gemacht. Schreiben Sie ein Reisetagebuch im Präteritum. Machen Sie für jeden Tag einen Eintrag°, in dem Sie beschreiben, was Sie machten und sahen. Vergessen Sie nicht das Datum: Zuerst kommt der Tag, dann der Monat und zuletzt das Jahr, z. B. Montag, den 6. März 2010.    *entry*

## *Strukturen und Vokabeln*

## **II** **Talking about consecutive events in the past**

### The past perfect

*Using the conjunction **nachdem** with the past perfect*

German speakers use the past perfect tense (**das Plusquamperfekt**) to refer to the earlier of two or more events that occurred in the past. It frequently occurs

with the subordinating conjunction **nachdem** (*after*). The past perfect consists of a form of **haben** or **sein** in the narrative past and a past participle.

> Nachdem Aschenputtels Vater ihr den Haselzweig **gebracht hatte,** pflanzte sie ihn auf dem Grab ihrer Mutter.
>
> *After Cinderella's father had brought her the hazelnut branch, she planted it on her mother's grave.*

> Just as in English, the German narrative past tense is frequently substituted for the past perfect in spoken German.

In colloquial speech Germans frequently prefer to use the conversational past instead of the past perfect. In these cases, the subordinating conjunction **nachdem** alone serves to signal the sequence of events.

> Wohin bist du gegangen, nachdem wir uns **gesehen haben**?
>
> *Where did you go after we saw each other?*

## Word order in sentences beginning with a subordinate clause

A German complex sentence frequently begins with a subordinate clause. It is followed by a main clause, which begins with the verb and is followed by the subject. This sequence results in two conjugated verbs appearing side by side. The subordinate clause is always separated from the main clause by a comma.

> Nachdem Aschenputtel zum Grab ihrer Mutter **gegangen war, bekam** sie ein schönes Kleid von dem Vögelchen.
>
> *After Cinderella had gone to her mother's grave, she received a beautiful dress from the little bird.*

**26    Was passierte den Märchenfiguren nachher?**  Finden Sie für jeden Hauptsatz den Nebensatz, der erklärt, was im Märchen später passierte.

☐ *Nachdem Aschenputtel die kranke Mutter besucht hatte, starb die Mutter.*

1. Nachdem Aschenputtel die kranke Mutter besucht hatte,
2. Nachdem der Wolf Rotkäppchen gefressen hatte,
3. Nachdem der gestiefelte Kater die Kleider seines Herrn genommen hatte,
4. Nachdem Schneewittchen in den vergifteten Apfel gebissen hatte,
5. Nachdem Schneewittchen eingeschlafen war,
6. Nachdem die böse Hexe Hänsel und Gretel ins Pfefferkuchenhaus eingeladen hatte,
7. Nachdem die Hexe ein Feuer im Ofen gemacht hatte,

a. ging er zum König und sagte, dass Diebe die Kleider gestohlen hatten.
b. schloss sie Hänsel in einen Käfig° ein.    *cage*
c. schob Gretel die Hexe in den Ofen und sie verbrannte.
d. fiel sie wie tot um.
e. starb die Mutter.
f. legten die sieben Zwerge sie in einen Glassarg.
g. kam der Jäger, schnitt dem Wolf den Bauch auf und rettete Rotkäppchen.

**27   Was passierte zuerst?** Bilden Sie Nebensätze im Plusquamperfekt und Hauptsätze im Präteritum, die die richtige Reihenfolge wiedergeben.

▢ Aschenputtels Mutter: krank werden / sterben
*Nachdem Aschenputtels Mutter krank geworden war, starb sie.*

1. Aschenputtels Mutter: krank werden / sterben
2. Aschenputtels Vater: eine neue Frau heiraten / eine schlimme Zeit für Aschenputtel beginnen
3. Aschenputtel: schwer arbeiten / sich in die Asche legen müssen
4. Aschenputtels Vater: den Haselzweig für Aschenputtel bringen / Aschenputtel: jeden Tag zum Baum gehen
5. Aschenputtel: sich etwas wünschen / ihren Wunsch erfüllt° bekommen          *fulfilled*
6. der Königssohn: alle schönen Jungfrauen zum Ball einladen / die Stiefschwestern: zum Ball gehen wollen
7. Aschenputtel: zum Grab laufen / der Vogel: Aschenputtel ein Kleid geben
8. Aschenputtel: nach Hause gehen / der Königssohn: ihren Schuh finden
9. die ältere Stiefschwester: den Schuh anprobieren / die Zehe abschneiden
10. der Königssohn: die Vögel am Grab hören / die falsche Braut zurückbringen
11. Aschenputtel: den Schuh anprobieren / der Königssohn: das Mädchen vom Fest erkennen
12. der Königssohn: Aschenputtel finden / sie heiraten

**28   Meine Zeittafel°.** Unten ist Annas Zeittafel. Schreiben Sie Ihre eigene Zeittafel. Stellen Sie sich dann mit einem Partner/einer Partnerin gegenseitig Fragen über Ihre Zeittafel. Beginnen Sie mit der Frage über die Schule.          *time line*

▢ S1: *Was hast du gemacht, nachdem du die Schule angefangen hattest?*
   S2: *Nachdem ich die Schule angefangen hatte, lernte ich schwimmen.*

> **Meine Zeittafel.** The most commonly used narrative past forms in speaking are **war, hatte, ging, kam,** and the modal verbs (**konnte, wollte, musste, sollte, durfte, mochte**).

| *Anna Adler* | | *Ich* |
|---|---|---|
| 1987 | in Fort Wayne geboren | _____ |
| 1992 | die Schule anfangen | _____ |
| 1997 | eine Reise nach Florida machen | _____ |
| 1999 | nach Kanada fahren | _____ |
| 2001 | im Softballtournier in San Diego spielen | _____ |
| 2004 | die Uni in Michigan beginnen | _____ |
| 2006 | nach Deutschland fliegen | _____ |

## III  Talking about concurrent events in the past
### Using the conjunction **als**

German speakers use the subordinating conjunction **als** (*when*) with the narrative (simple) past or the conversational past to talk about two or more past events that happened at the same time.

**Als** sie am Grab von Aschenputtels **Mutter** vorbeiritten, riefen zwei Täubchen vom Haselbaum.

*When they rode past the grave of Cinderella's mother, two doves called out from the hazelnut tree.*

**29** **Als Kind in Deutschland oder in den USA.** Was machte Barbara in Dresden, als Anna in den USA Kind war? Stellen Sie einem Partner/einer Partnerin mit Hilfe der Tabellen Fragen.

🟨 S1: *Was machte Anna, als Barbara Fußball spielte?*
S2: *Als Barbara Fußball spielte, spielte Anna Softball.*

**Tabelle A (S1):**

| Anna | Barbara |
|---|---|
| ? | Fußball spielen |
| Orangensaft zum Frühstück trinken | ? |
| jeden Sonntag in die Kirche gehen | ? |
| bis spät nachmittags in der Schule bleiben | ? |
| ? | den Nachmittag frei haben |
| ? | am Samstag die Schule besuchen |
| ? | nach Italien fahren wollen |
| eine Reise durch Kanada machen | ? |

**Tabelle B (S2):**

| Anna | Barbara |
|---|---|
| Softball spielen | ? |
| ? | Kaffee zum Frühstück trinken |
| ? | jeden Sonntag spazieren gehen |
| ? | um 13.00 Uhr nach Hause gehen |
| täglich nach der Schule Sport haben | ? |
| am Samstag keine Schule haben | ? |
| alle Länder besuchen können | ? |
| ? | eine Reise nach Polen machen |

**30** **Autogrammspiel: Als ich zehn Jahre alt war, ...** Bilden Sie Fragen im Präteritum. Finden Sie für jede Frage eine Person, die mit **Ja** antwortet. Bitten Sie dann die Person um ihre Unterschrift.

🟨 S1: *Hattest du schon lange Haare, als du zehn Jahre alt warst?*
S2: *Ja. Als ich zehn Jahre alt war, hatte ich schon lange Haare.*
S1: *Unterschreib hier bitte.*

1. 10 Jahre alt: lange Haare haben _____
2. 11 Jahre alt: groß sein _____
3. 12 Jahre alt: ein Instrument
   (z. B. Klavier) spielen können _____
4. 13 Jahre alt: Hausarbeit machen müssen _____

5. 14 Jahre alt: einen Computer haben    _____
6. 15 Jahre alt: Deutsch sprechen können    _____
7. 16 Jahre alt: Auto fahren dürfen    _____
8. 17 Jahre alt: zur Uni gehen wollen    _____

## IV Saying when events occur

### Using **wenn** vs. **wann** vs. **ob**

The subordinating conjunction **wenn** (*whenever, if*) points to an event that occurs (or occured) repeatedly. It may be used with the present tense or any past tense. German speakers often use it in the expression **immer wenn** (*always when, whenever*).

| | |
|---|---|
| Hier sagt man sich noch „Grüezi", **wenn** man sich begegnet. | *Here, people still greet each other with "Grüezi" whenever they meet.* |
| **Immer wenn** ich nachmittags nach Hause komme, habe ich Hunger. | *Whenever I come home in the afternoon, I'm hungry.* |

The interrogative pronoun **wann** (*when*) occurs in questions about when something happened or will happen. It establishes a specific point of time.

| | |
|---|---|
| **Wann** ist der Winterball? | *When is the winter ball?* |

**Wann** can also be embedded into a sentence as an indirect question. In this case, the conjugated verb moves to the end of the subordinate clause.

| | |
|---|---|
| Sie weiß nicht, **wann** der Ball stattfindet. | *She doesn't know when the ball is taking place.* |

In complex sentences, embedded yes/no questions start with the subordinating conjunction **ob** (*if, whether*).

| | |
|---|---|
| Sie weiß nicht, **ob** der Ball stattfindet. | *She doesn't know if the ball will take place.* |

You can always determine whether you should use **wenn, wann,** or **ob** by reconstructing the original question or statement.

| *Statement* | *Question* |
|---|---|
| Der Ball findet um 20.00 Uhr statt. | **Wann** findet der Ball statt? (*correct answer:* **um 20.00 Uhr**) |

| *Question* | *Statement* |
|---|---|
| Findet der Ball Sonnabend statt? | Sie möchte wissen, **wann** der Ball stattfindet. (*correct answer:* am **Sonnabend**) |
| | Sie möchte wissen, **ob** der Ball Sonnabend stattfindet. (*correct answer:* **ja**) |

> As you learned in **Kapitel 6**, **wenn** (*if*) also expresses a condition. The presence of **so** or **dann** in the second clause often signals that, e.g., „**... und** *wenn* **sie nicht gestorben sind,** *dann* **leben sie noch heute.** ("*... and if they haven't died, then they are still living today.*"); *Wenn* **du Königin bist,** *so* **brauchst du nicht mehr zu Fuß zu gehen.** (*If you are the queen, you do not need to go on foot anymore.*)

**31  Als, wenn, wann oder ob?** Ergänzen Sie die Sätze mit **als, wenn, wann** oder **ob.**

1. ANNA: _____ kommst du morgen Abend vorbei? Um 19.00 Uhr?
   BARBARA: _____ ich Zeit habe, komme ich kurz vor 19.00 Uhr bei dir vorbei.

2. KARL: Weißt du, _____ der Film beginnt?
   STEFAN: Nein. Aber sag mir doch bitte, _____ du's herausfindest.
   KARL: Ich weiß nicht, _____ ich die Zeit dazu habe. Mal sehen.

3. ANNA: Immer _____ ich müde bin, bekomme ich Hunger.
   BARBARA: _____ ich Hunger habe, will ich schlafen.
   ANNA: _____ hast du zuletzt gegessen?
   BARBARA: _____ ich an der Uni war.

4. ANNA: _____ ist meine Mutter in die USA gegangen?
   OMA: _____ sie 23 Jahre alt war.
   OPA: Damals haben wir nicht gewusst, _____ wir die Hannelore je wiedersehen.
   OMA: Aber natürlich ist sie dann immer gekommen, _____ sie die Familie sehen wollte.
   ANNA: Und _____ kommt ihr endlich zum Besuch nach Fort Wayne?
   OPA: Ach, Anna! Vielleicht, _____ ich endlich Englisch verstehen kann.

5. KARL: _____ bist du heute morgen zur Uni gegangen?
   INGE: Um halb acht. Warum? Hast du mich gehört?
   KARL: Ja, _____ die Tür zuknallte°, wachte ich auf.          *slammed shut*
   INGE: Ich habe mich schon gefragt, _____ du das hörst. Ich werde vorsichtiger mit der Tür sein, _____ ich rausgehe.

6. STEFAN: Du, Anna, _____ macht die Mensa heute auf?
   ANNA: Um halb elf, glaube ich. Willst du heute dort zu Mittag essen?
   STEFAN: Nur, _____ es warmes vegetarisches Essen gibt.
   ANNA: Gibt es. Das habe ich gelesen, _____ ich gestern in der Mensa war. Denn ich wollte herausfinden, _____ sie auch an Feiertagen geöffnet war.
   STEFAN: Ja, Gott sei Dank. Denn du weißt ja, ich koche nur, _____ ich absolut muss.

**32  Interview: Fest- und Feiertage.** Stellen Sie einem Partner/einer Partnerin die folgenden Fragen.

1. Auf welchen Feiertag hast du dich am meisten gefreut, als du ein Kind warst? Warum? Und jetzt?
2. Kannst du dich an einen besonderen Feiertag aus deiner Kindheit erinnern?
3. Welche Feiertage feierst du, wenn du bei deiner Familie zu Hause bist?
4. Welche Feiertage feierst du mit Freunden?
5. Welche Feiertage feierst du gar nicht? Warum?
6. Wie feierst du deinen Geburtstag am liebsten?
7. Was hast du als Kind zu Halloween gemacht?
8. Welche deutschen Feiertage kennt man in Amerika und Kanada nicht?

## Fest- und Feiertage

Germans celebrate numerous holidays (**Fest- und Feiertage**) throughout the year. New Year's Eve (**Silvester**) is celebrated with parties, dances, and fireworks, and New Year's Day (**Neujahr**) is celebrated with a festive dinner. **Karneval** season precedes the beginning of Lent in February. On Easter Sunday (**Ostern**), many children hunt for chocolates and colored eggs hidden by the Easter bunny (**der Osterhase**). Trade unions organize public rallies on May 1st, International Labor Day (**Tag der Arbeit**). Throughout the summer, cities and towns stage local fairs and festivals (**der Jahrmarkt, die Kirmes**) that feature parades, rides, food and drink booths, contests, concerts, and dancing.

During the fall season, Germans observe the Day of German Unity (**Tag der deutschen Einheit**) on October 3rd as their national holiday. It commemorates the date in 1990 when the German Democratic Republic was dissolved and officially united with the Federal Republic of Germany. Muslims celebrate the month-long **Ramadan** fast period, during which they abstain from eating or drinking during daylight hours. The month ends with a three-day **Ramadanfest.**

Jewish citizens celebrate **Chanukka** for eight days late in the year. Candles are lit on the menorah, festive holiday foods are enjoyed, children receive **Chanukkageld** as a reward for good deeds. Open-air Christmas markets (**Weihnachtsmärkte**) are held in many cities in December. Families bake seasonal treats such as gingerbread (**der Lebkuchen**) and fruit cakes called **Christstollen. Sankt Nikolaus** comes on December 6th and puts candy in children's shoes. On Christmas Eve (**der Heilige Abend**), parents decorate the Christmas tree, often with real candles, and Christmas presents are placed under the tree by the Christ Child (**das Christkind**) or by **der Weihnachtsmann.** Families exchange gifts on Christmas Eve. Christmas Day (**Weihnachten**) is a holiday and is generally spent quietly, visiting with relatives and friends. The day after Christmas is also an official holiday.

Sometimes **Sankt Nikolaus** comes in person with his assistant, **Knecht Ruprecht,** who threatens to punish the bad children.

**Kulturkreuzung** Hat Ihre Familie religiöse Feste gefeiert, als Sie ein Kind waren? Welche? Welche Feste sind Familienfeste und welche nicht? Kommen Familien immer am Feiertag zusammen? Warum? Warum nicht?

Der berühmte ChristkIndlesmarkt in Nürnberg

## V　Expressing ownership

### The genitive case

The primary function of the genitive case (**der Genitiv**) is to show ownership.

> Wir gehen auf das Schloss **des Königs.**　　*We are going to the king's castle.*

The genitive is also used to express a relationship between things that is indicated by *of* in English.

> Das Wunder **des Wandels** findet im Bähnli statt.
> *The miracle of transformation takes place in the little train.*
> Da fehlt das Dröhnen **der Motoren.**
> *The roar of engines is missing.*
> ... die Stille **eines Bergabends**
> *. . . the quiet calm of a mountain evening*

The genitive case frequently occurs in answers to the question **wessen?** (*whose?*).

> *Question*
> **Wessen** Auto ist das?　　*Whose car is that?*
>
> *Answer*
> Das ist das Auto **der Studentin.**　　*That is the student's car (car of the student).*

Note the word order: In German, the person who possesses something follows the object being possessed. In English, the possessor precedes the item possessed.

> das Auto **der Studentin**　　*the student's car*

> English speakers express ownership by adding *'s* to the person who possesses the object or who is related to the person mentioned: *Is that really **your friend's** car? Of* can also be used: *What's the name **of** that French restaurant?*

> The genitive is also used for indefinite time phrases, such as **eines Tages** (*one day*), **eines Abends** (*one evening*), **eines Morgens** (*one morning*), and **eines Nachts** (*one night*).

### A. Masculine and neuter nouns

Articles that precede masculine and neuter nouns in the genitive case end in **-es** (e.g., **des, eines**). The masculine and neuter nouns themselves also add **-s** or **-es** in the genitive singular.

- Most nouns of one syllable add **-es** (e.g., **eines Tages, des Buches**).
- Most nouns of more than one syllable add **-s** (e.g., **des Königs, meines Professors**).
- Nouns ending in **-s, -ss, -ß, -tsch, -tz, -x, -z,** and **-zt** add **-es** (e.g., **des Schlosses, meines Arztes**).

### B. Feminine and plural nouns

Articles that precede all feminine and plural nouns in the genitive case end in **-er** (e.g., **meiner Mutter**). The feminine and plural nouns themselves have no special genitive endings.

### C. Masculine N-nouns

Nouns like **der Student, der Herr, der Mensch** that add **-(e)n** in the accusative and dative singular also have the ending **-(e)n** instead of **-(e)s** in the genitive singular (e.g., **des Studenten, des Herrn, des Prinzen**) and in the genitive plural (e.g., **der Studenten**).

## D. Adjective endings

The ending on adjectives used with genitive nouns preceded by any article or possessive is always **-en.**

| Eine ehrliche Gastronomie der klein**en** Familienbetriebe. | *An honest catering trade of small family businesses.* |

These are the genitive case forms.

| Masculine | Neuter | Feminine | Plural |
|---|---|---|---|
| **des** Königs | des Zimmers | **der** Person | **der** Könige/Zimmer/Personen |
| ein**es** Tag**es** | ein**es** Märchens | ein**er** Frau | kein**er** Tage/Märchen/Frauen |
| sein**es** Professors | sein**es** Buches | sein**er** Tochter | sein**er** Professoren/Bücher/Töchter |
| dies**es** Herr**n** | dies**es** Schloss**es** | dies**er** Stadt | dies**er** Herren/Schlösser/Städte |

## E. Proper names

Proper names of people and countries simply add an **-s** without an apostrophe to show possession.

| Er übernachtet in **Roberts** Ferienwohnung. | *He's staying overnight in Robert's vacation home.* |
| Die Schweiz liegt im Herzen **Mitteleuropas.** | *Switzerland is located in the heart of central Europe.* |

However, when additional descriptive information is present, the genitive case is required.

| Er übernachtet in der Ferienwohnung **meines Freundes Robert.** | *He's staying overnight in my friend Robert's vacation home.* |

## F. The dative preposition *von*

As you learned in **Kapitel 6,** German speakers frequently express ownership with the preposition **von** + *dative.* The word **von** is increasingly replacing the genitive case in spoken German.

| Was ist die Adresse **deines Hotels?** Was ist die Adresse **von deinem Hotel?** | *What's the address of your hotel?* |
| Mich interessieren die Bücher **dieser italienischen Journalistin** sehr. Mich interessieren die Bücher **von dieser italienischen Journalistin** sehr. | *I am very interested in the books by this Italian journalist.* |

**33**    **Wessen Sachen sind das?** Ihre Freunde fragen dauernd°, wessen    *continuously*
Sachen Sie benutzen. Antworten Sie mit den passenden Genitivformulierungen.

S1:   *Wessen Wagen fährst du in der Schweiz? (mein Freund Tom)*
S2:   *Ich fahre den Wagen meines Freundes Tom.*

1.  In wessen Haus hast du übernachtet? (meine Freunde Willi und Maria)
2.  Wessen Skier hast du benutzt? (Willi)
3.  Wessen Gastfreundschaft hast du genossen°? (mein guter Freund Willi)    *enjoy*
4.  Wessen Sonnenbrille hast du getragen? (meine gute Freundin Maria)
5.  Wessen Anorak° hast du zum Skilaufen getragen? (Maria)    *parka*
6.  In wessen Sauna hast du den Nachmittag verbracht? (meine neue Bekannte Jutta)
7.  Wessen Bier hast du getrunken? (mein lieber alter Freund Jörg)
8.  Wessen Weingläser hast du eben kaputt gemacht? (meine lieben Freunde)

**34**    **Was ist der Preis?** Anna und Barbara haben vor, in den Semesterferien mit einer Gruppe von Freunden Ski fahren zu gehen. Sie beschließen, Anfang März nach Braunwald in der Schweiz zu fahren, aber jetzt müssen sie für die Gruppe eine preiswerte Unterkunft finden. Die Schweiz ist ja bekanntlich teuer. Was sollen sie nehmen: Halbpension° in einem Hotel, ein    *two meals per day*
Doppel- oder Einzelzimmer in einer Pension oder einen billigen Schlafplatz in einem Mehrbettzimmer? Hauptsache, der Preis stimmt! Lesen Sie die Anzeigen auf Seite 421.

S1 (ANNA):   Was ist der Preis von einem Doppelzimmer mit Bad und Halbpension für eine Woche im Märchenhotel Bellevue?
S2 (BARBARA):   Der Preis eines Doppelzimmers im Hotel Bellevue am Anfang März liegt zwischen 2 240 und 2 780 Franken.
S1 (ANNA):   Oje, das ist viel zu teuer für uns! Was ist der Preis von … ?

> **Fr. = Franken; 350.–/T = 350 Franken pro Tag; 2 100.–/W = 2 100 Franken pro Woche**

1.  ein Doppelzimmer mit Bad und Halbpension für eine Woche im Märchenhotel Bellevue
2.  ein Einzelzimmer mit Bad und Halbpension für eine Woche im Märchenhotel Bellevue
3.  eine Übernachtung im 3er/4er Zimmer mit Bad im Berggasthaus Gumen
4.  eine Übernachtung im 8er Zimmer mit Bad im Berggasthaus Gumen
5.  ein Schlafplatz im Bänningerhaus
6.  ein Doppelzimmer mit Bad ohne WC in Pension Ahorn
7.  ein Doppelzimmer ohne Bad in Pension Ahorn
8.  die Übernachtung pro Person in dem adrenalin backpackers hostel
9.  ein einfaches Frühstück in dem adrenalin backpackers hostel
10. die Bettwäsche in dem adrenalin backpackers hostel

## Märchenhotel Bellevue ★★★★

Familie Lydia und Martin Vogel-Curty
CH-8784 Braunwald

**Nr. / Planquadrat: 12 / F5**

Tel.: 055 653 71 71
Fax: 055 643 10 00
info@maerchenhotel.ch; www.maerchenhotel.ch

Z 54  ⊨ 100  ♂ 6-10/12-4

Geniessen Sie den Komfort des einzigen 4-Stern-Hotels in der Region. Geschmackvolle Designer- und Familienzimmer. Kinder erwartet viel Spass und Abenteuer mit oder ohne Betreuung. Luftschloss, Hallenbad mit Tarzankletterparcours, Rutschbahn von

| | | | 18.05.-23.10. | 11.12.-25.12. 01.01.-29.01. 26.02.-03.04. | 25.12.-01.01. 29.02.-26.02. |
|---|---|---|---|---|---|
| ♀♀ | | 330.- bis 350.-/T 1960.- bis 2100.-/W | 2240.- bis 2780.-/W | 3240.- bis 3360.-/W |
| ♀ | | 165.- bis 175.-/T 980.- bis 1050.-/W | 1120.- bis 1390.-/W | 1610.- bis 1680.-/W |

☺ Kinderermässigung im Zimmer der Eltern
bis 6J.: gratis, 6 - 9J.: 70%, 9 - 12J.: 50%, 12 - 16J.: 30%
max. 1 Reduktion pro vollzahlende Erw.

🍽 inkl.    ☾ inkl.

Stock zu Stock. Spielplatz. Die all-abendliche Märchenstunde mit dem Märchenonkel ist nicht wegzudenken. Erwachsene schätzen die Relax-Oase "Wellness on the top", die hervorragende Küche und den Charme des stilvoll renovierten Grand Hôtels. Speisesaal mit einer traumhaften Aussicht und elegante Bar.

## Berggasthaus Gumen ★    1'904m.ü.M.

Nica u. Nico / Altra Management AG
CH-8784 Braunwald

**Nr. / Planquadrat: 30 / B1**

Tel.: 055 643 13 24
Fax: 055 653 10 25
Für Zimmerreservationen:
Tel.: 055 647 40 20; Fax: 055 647 40 39
e-mail@truempi-ag.ch; www.gumen.ch

Z 5 8-er und 3 3/4-er  ⊨ 50  ♂ 6-10/12-3

Das 1999 vollständig renovierte Berggasthaus mit einmaliger Aussicht auf die Glarner Alpen. Sonnenterrasse. Am Start der

| | | Sommer 29.05.-07.11. | Winter 18.12.-03.04. |
|---|---|---|---|
| | im 3/4-er-Zimmer | 70.- / Person | 70.- / Person |
| bis 12J. | im 3/4-er-Zimmer | 55.- / Person | 55.- / Person |
| | im 8-er-Zimmer | 47.- / Person | 47.- / Person |
| | im 8-er-Zimmer | 35.- / Person | 35.- / Person |
| mit Bettwäsche | | | |
| Zuschlag Einzelzimmer in 3-er | | 50.- | 50.- |

🍽 inkl    ☾ 18.-/15.-

Pisten und am Ausgangspunkt für Wanderungen, dem "Zwäarg Baartli"-Märchenweg und die Begehung der Klettersteige. Die Zimmer sind zweckmässig eingerichtet. 2 Waschräume für 8-er Mehrbettzimmer. Ski- und Schuhraum. Selbstbedienungsrestaurant (tagsüber) und gemütliche Gaststube (abends) mit guter Küche. Kleines Stübli für Sitzungen.

## Bänningerhaus    1'375m.ü.M.

Strick
CH-8784 Braunwald

**Nr. / Planquadrat: 33 / J3**

Vermietung:
Claudio Keller; 8755 Ennenda
Tel.: 055 645 41 51; Fax: 055 645 41 52

Total 20-25 Schlafplätze:
- 1 x 3, 1 x 8-12, 1 x 12-14

| | | Sommer | Winter |
|---|---|---|---|
| Schlafplatz | Sa/So | 27.-/Person | 27.-/Person |
| | Mo-Sa | 15.- | 15.- |
| exkl. Kur- und Beherbergungstaxen = 1.15 p.P. ab 16J. | | | |

Für Schulen und Familien Spezialpreise!

Renoviertes Haus an schöner Lage. 2 Duschen, Wasch- und Trockenraum. Gut ausgestattete Küche für Selbstskocher. Essraum, Aufenthaltsraum. Ideal für Familien! Fixleintücher und Kopfkissen vorhanden. Eine gemütliche und günstige Unterkunft für Ferien in Braunwald.

## Pension Ahorn ★★

Ursula und Fredy Hutter
CH-8784 Braunwald

**Nr. / Planquadrat: 18 / H3**

Tel.: 055 643 15 37
Fax: 055 643 17 35
ahorn-braunwald@bluewin.ch; www.ahorn-braunwald.ch

Z 10  ⊨ 21  ♂ 6-10/12-3

Gemütliche familienfreundliche Pension an aussichtsreicher Lage im oberen Dorfteil Schwettiberg auf 1'400 m.ü.M. Gutbürgerliche Küche mit diversen Spezialitäten. Spielzimmer für Kinder. Seminarraum (bis 12 Pers.) mit guter Infrastruktur (Beamer).

| | | 19.06.-01.11. 18.12.-03.04. |
|---|---|---|
| ♀♀ | | 170.- |
| ♀♀ | o. WC | 150.- |
| ♀♀ | | 130.- |
| ♀ | o. WC | 80.- |
| ♀ | | 70.- |

🍽 inkl    ☾ 30.-

**Sommeraktivitäten:** Ausgangspunkt für Wanderungen und Biketouren. Geheiztes Freibad. Sauna. **Winteraktivitäten:** Schneesportschule vor dem Haus, 2 Min. zum Skilift Mattwald. Sportgeschäft. Am Schlittelweg Grotzenbüel-Dorf. Ideal gelegen für Schneeschuhtouren.

## adrenalin backpackers hostel ★

Fam. Brigitte u. Markus
Zweifel-Schumacher CH-8784 Braunwald

**Nr. / Planquadrat: 24 / E6**

Tel.: 079 347 29 05
Fax: 055 643 36 44
buchen@adrenalin.gl; www.adrenalin.gl

Z 28  ⊨ 60  ♂ 1-12

nur Bargeld

Das zentral gelegene Hostel verfolgt folgende Philosophie: Low-Budget-Tourismusangebot für Junge und junggebliebene Gäste, denen Erlebnis und das Knüpfen von Kontakten wichtiger ist, als Komfort und Luxus. Kleine sehr einfach eingerichtete Zimmer. Bar/Dorfbeiz täglich ab 16.00 Uhr geöffnet mit Billard, Airhockey

| | | 01.01.-31.12. |
|---|---|---|
| ♀/♀♀ | | 35.- / Person |
| 4-er / 6-er | | auf Anfrage |
| Zuschläge: | | |
| Bettwäsche | | 5.- |
| einfaches Frühstück | | 8.- |
| Frottierwäsche | | 5.- |
| Frottierw. / tägl. Roomservice | | 10.- |
| nur 1 Nacht: | | 20.- / Zimmer |
| Keine Kinderermässigungen | | |
| Ab 4. Nacht: 10% Ermässigung auf Totalpreis | | |

und anderen Spieltischen. Frühstückservice. Keine Küche. Zum Essen haben die Gäste die Möglichkeit, individuell die Vielfalt der Braunwalder Gastronomiebetriebe zu geniessen.

# Infos A–Z
Hoch über dem Alltag

**Apotheke**
RehaClinic Braunwald. Montag – Freitag, 9.00 – 12.00 und 13.00 – 17.00 Uhr. Nur Medikamente, keine Drogerieartikel; telefonische Vorabklärung wird empfohlen (055 643 22 55).

**Braunwaldbahnen**
Schalteröffnungszeiten Berg- und Talstation:
jeweils 10 Minuten vor Abfahrt
SBB-Schalter: 7.00 – 19.00 Uhr

**Fundbüro**
Braunwald Tourismus, Tel. 055 653 65 85.

**Hallenbad**
Jeden Mittwochnachmittag von 14.00 bis 16.00 Uhr (übrige Zeit auf Anfrage) öffentliches Hallenbad im Panorama-Hotel Waldhaus. Eintritt Erwachsene CHF 8.–, Kinder 6 bis 16 Jahre CHF 5.– und Kinder bis 5 Jahre CHF 2.–.

**Internet-Ecke und Internet-Café**
Internet-Ecke für jedermann in der Bibliothek der RehaClinic Braunwald. Öffnungszeiten wie Bibliothek, CHF 4.–/Stunde. Internet-Café mit Public Wireless LAN-Access im Hotel Alpenblick. Öffnungszeiten auf Anfrage, Tel. 055 643 15 44.

**Kino**
Jeden Mittwoch um 21.15 Uhr im Saalkino des Hotels Alpenblick. Topaktuelles Filmangebot. Hotel Alpenblick, Tel. 055 643 15 44.

**Langlauf**
Langlaufloipe auf dem Grotzenbüel bis zu vier Kilometer je nach Schneeverhältnissen.   Mittelschwere Strecke (Klassisch und Skating gespurt). Umkleidekabine und Dusche bei der Bergstation der Gondelbahn.
Weitere Loipen in der Umgebung: «Töditritt» entlang der Talsohle zwischen Schwanden und Linthal, Langlaufloipe «Gulispur» auf dem Urnerboden.

**Ski- und Snowboardmiete, Service**
Vermietung von Sportausrüstungen im Dorf bei Kessler Sport, Tel. 055 643 22 22, und im Schwettiberg bei Ahorn Sport, Tel. 055 643 35 69.

**Wäscherei**
Wäscherei im Dorf, Tel. 055 643 14 68; Wäscherei Schwettiberg, Tel. 055 643 10 86.

**Zahnarzt**
Med. dent. F. Christensen, Linthal, Tel. 055 643 18 55

| | |
|---|---|
| Montag – Dienstag | 8.00 – 12.00 und 13.30 – 17.30 Uhr |
| Mittwoch | 8.00 – 12.00 Uhr, Nachmittag geschlossen |
| Donnerstag | 8.00 – 12.00 und 13.30 – 17.30 Uhr |
| Freitag | 8.00 – 15.00 Uhr durchgehend |

---

**35  Allwissende° Anna.**  Die Gruppe ist schon in Braunwald *all-knowing*
angekommen. Anna muss die Fragen ihrer Freunde mit Hilfe der Broschüre beantworten. Spielen Sie die Rollen von Anna und ihren Freunden. Anna benutzt den Genitiv und ihre Freunde benutzen **von.** Wechseln Sie die Rollen.

S1 (FREUND/FREUNDIN):  *Sag mal, Anna. Was sind die Ruhetage von der Apotheke?*

S2 (ANNA):  *Die Ruhetage der Apotheke sind Samstag und Sonntag.*

1. die Ruhetage / die Apotheke
2. der Name / der einzige Zahnarzt im Dorf
3. die Telefonnummer / das Fundbüro
4. der Name / ein Ski- und Snowboardvermieter
5. die Länge / die Langlaufloipe
6. die Spielzeit / das Kino im Hotel Alpenblick
7. der Preis / eine Stunde in der Internet-Ecke von der RehaClinic
8. die Öffnungszeiten / das Hallenbad
9. die Telefonnummer / eine Wäscherei im Dorf
10. die Öffnungszeiten / der Braunwaldbahnen-Schalter

## G. Genitive prepositions

German speakers also use the genitive case after certain prepositions.

| | |
|---|---|
| **(an)statt** | *instead of* |
| **außerhalb** | *outside of* |
| **innerhalb** | *inside of* |
| **trotz** | *in spite of, despite* |
| **während** | *during* |
| **wegen** | *on account of, because of* |

| | |
|---|---|
| **Trotz ihrer Stiefmutter** ist Aschenputtel zum Ball gegangen. | *In spite of her stepmother, Cinderella went to the ball.* |
| **Während des Balls** hat der Prinz mit Aschenputtel viel getanzt. | *During the ball, the prince danced a lot with Cinderella.* |

---

### Sprache im Alltag: Replacing the genitive in spoken German

While the genitive case is used in written texts, it is increasingly being replaced by the dative case in conversation.

**Written German**

| | |
|---|---|
| Trotz **des** Regen**s** sind wir zu Fuß hingegangen. | *Despite the rain, we walked there.* |

**Spoken German**

Trotz **dem** Regen sind wir zu Fuß hingegangen.

---

**36    Wo übernachten Anna und Barbara während ihrer Semesterferien?** Wählen Sie für jeden Satz die richtige Genitivpräposition.

außerhalb • innerhalb • trotz • (an)statt • während • wegen

1. _____ der Semesterferien wollen Anna und Barbara in die Schweiz fahren.
2. _____ der hohen Preise in der Schweiz möchten sie in Braunwald Urlaub machen.
3. _____ eines Jugendhotels buchen sie Zimmer in einem Familien-Hotel.
4. _____ der besseren Preise buchen sie Zimmer im Bänningerhaus und nicht im teuren Bellevue.
5. _____ des Dorfes gibt es wenige Schlafmöglichkeiten.
6. _____ der sagenhaften Preise im Bänningerhaus können sie ein paar Tage länger bleiben.
7. _____ der Woche wollen sie Ski fahren und snowboarden gehen.
8. _____ der zwei Sterne ist die Pension Ahorn relativ preiswert.
9. _____ der RehaClinic kann man eine Internet-Ecke finden.

**37**  **Interview: Das Leben eines Studenten/einer Studentin.**
Stellen Sie einem Partner/einer Partnerin die folgenden Fragen und beantworten
Sie sie dann selber. Benutzen Sie den Genitiv.

S1:  *Mit wessen Geld finanzierst du dein Studium?*
S2:  *Ich finanziere mein Studium mit dem Geld meiner Eltern.*

1. Mit wessen Geld finanzierst du dein Studium?
2. In wessen Zimmer verbringst du mehr Zeit: in deinem eigenen Zimmer oder
   im Zimmer deiner Freundin (deines Freundes)?
3. Mit wessen Computer arbeitest du auf dem Campus? Zu Hause?
4. Was ist der Titel deines Lieblingskurses?
5. Wessen Auto leihst du dir für eine Verabredung?
6. Wessen Geld hast du geborgt°?                                              *borrowed*
7. Wessen Job möchtest du eines Tages haben? Warum?

  **F r e i e   K o m m u n i k a t i o n**

**Rollenspiel: Italien oder die Schweiz?**  Es ist März und Sie können zwei Wochen
Urlaub machen. Fahren Sie lieber nach Italien oder in die Schweiz? Besprechen
Sie mit einem Partner/einer Partnerin die zwei Reisemöglichkeiten. Versuchen Sie,
die andere Person mit Argumenten aus den folgenden Listen zu überzeugen°. S1       *convince*
fährt gern im Auto, möchte in der Sonne liegen und etwas Exotisches erleben.
S2 ist sehr aktiv, fährt gern mit dem Zug und hat Massentourismus nicht gern.

| *Italien* | *die Schweiz* |
|---|---|
| die Sonne genießen | Ski fahren |
| schwimmen gehen | eine Bergwanderung machen |
| relativ billig | relativ teuer |
| weit fahren | nicht so weit fahren |
| mit dem Auto fahren | mit dem Auto/Zug fahren |
| Italienisch hören | Deutsch, Französisch oder Italienisch sprechen |
| viele Touristen | wenige Touristen |
| viele Sehenswürdigkeiten besuchen | aktiv sein, Sport treiben |
| gutes Essen | gutes Bier, guter Käse |

  **S c h r e i b e c k e**

**Schönen Gruß aus der Schweiz!**  Sie kommen gerade vom Skilaufen zurück und
haben ein paar Minuten Zeit. Schreiben Sie Ihren Freunden/Freundinnen oder
Ihrer Familie zu Hause, wie Ihnen der Winterurlaub in der Schweiz gefällt.
Erzählen Sie im Präteritum, was Sie schon alles gemacht haben. Dann
adressieren Sie die Postkarte an den Empfänger/die Empfängerin°. Die folgende       *recipient*
Liste enthält° ein paar Ideen.                                                      *contains*

Ski laufen • Schlitten fahren • Gastfreundschaft • Spaß machen
• autofrei • Postkartenlandschaft • märchenhafte Landschaft
• Zauberstimmung • fehlen° • gute Pisten • hoch über dem Alltag             *to be missing, lacking*
• Spaziergänger • Touristen • Grüezi!

**Puddingschlacht:** *pudding*
  *fight*

*tour guide*
*adult*

## Stefans Puddingschlacht°

An Urlaubserlebnisse erinnert man sich das ganze Leben lang – besonders, wenn sie lustig oder schlecht gewesen sind. Hier erzählt Stefan von seinen Erfahrungen in Frankreich als Reiseleiter° einer deutschen Touristengruppe und was passieren kann, wenn erwachsene° Menschen mit dem Essen herumspielen.

## Vorschau

 **38** **Thematische Fragen.** Beantworten Sie die Fragen auf Deutsch.

1. Wohin fahren Sie am liebsten? Warum haben Sie es dort so gern?
2. Was gefällt Ihnen am meisten am Reisen?
3. Was missfällt° Ihnen am meisten, wenn Sie verreisen und unterwegs sind?    *displeases*
4. Wo übernachten Sie meistens, wenn Sie unterwegs sind: in Hotels? In Motels? In Pensionen? Bei Freunden? Im Zelt? In Jugendherbergen°?    *youth hostels*
5. Haben Sie mal eine Gruppenreise gemacht? Wann? Wohin? Mit wem? Was hat Ihnen daran gefallen/nicht gefallen?
6. Wenn Sie im Ausland (oder im ausländischen Restaurant) sind, können Sie alles essen? Haben Sie besonders gute oder schlechte Erfahrungen mit der Küche gemacht?

**39** **Satzdetektiv.** Welche Sätze passen zu welchem Bild? Schreiben Sie die passende Bildnummer neben jeden Satz.

**Bild Nr.**

\_\_\_\_\_ Wirf doch mal den Pudding rüber ... Das kam zu einer richtigen Puddingschlacht im Speisesaal.

\_\_1\_\_ Ich habe meine Ferien in Nordfrankreich verbracht.

\_\_\_\_\_ Es war mehr eine Kulturreise und Pudding gehört dann auch zur Kultur.

\_\_\_\_\_ Nein, es waren zwei Betreuer°, und wir mussten dann ein Programm    *group guides*
zusammenstellen für insgesamt° zwei Wochen.    *in total*

\_\_\_\_\_ Aber das Aufräumen° hat keinen Spaß gemacht.    **sauber machen**

\_\_\_\_\_ Aber sie waren alle in so einem Jugendhotel oder in einer Jugendherberge
untergebracht°.    **geschlafen**

## Stefans Puddingschlacht

## Zieltext

### Stefans Puddingschlacht

 Hören Sie gut zu und schauen Sie sich die Bilder oben an.

## *Rückblick*

**40**  **Stimmt das?** Stimmen die folgenden Aussagen zum Text oder nicht? Wenn nicht, was stimmt?

|   | Ja, das stimmt. | Nein, das stimmt nicht. |   |
|---|---|---|---|
| 1. Stefan ist allein nach Frankreich in Urlaub gefahren. | ☐ | ☐ | |
| 2. Stefan hat eine Gruppe von Schülern, Studenten und auch älteren Leuten betreut°. | ☐ | ☐ | *took care of* |
| 3. Es war keine Sprachreise, sondern mehr eine Kulturreise für die Touristen. | ☐ | ☐ | |
| 4. Sie waren in einem Luxushotel untergebracht. | ☐ | ☐ | |
| 5. Sie schliefen alle in Mehrbettzimmern und hatten nicht immer gutes Essen. | ☐ | ☐ | |
| 6. Eines Tages beim Mittagessen gab es zum Nachtisch einen schönen Schokoladenpudding. | ☐ | ☐ | |
| 7. Der Pudding hat allen gut geschmeckt, und sie wollten immer mehr davon haben. | ☐ | ☐ | |
| 8. Einer aus der Gruppe rief zu einem Freund: „Wirf doch mal den Pudding 'rüber!" | ☐ | ☐ | |
| 9. Der Freund warf den Pudding, und so kam es zu einer richtigen Puddingschlacht im Speisesaal. | ☐ | ☐ | |
| 10. Als die Puddingschlacht begann, gab es nur zwei Möglichkeiten: sich unter dem Tisch verstecken oder mitmachen. | ☐ | ☐ | |
| 11. Das Aufräumen und Saubermachen nach der Puddingschlacht hat viel Spaß gemacht. | ☐ | ☐ | |
| 12. Stefan hatte mit einer zweiten Person zusammen die ganze Tour geplant – Anreise, Abreise, Kulturprogramm – und auch betreut. | ☐ | ☐ | |

**41**  **Kurz gefragt.** Beantworten Sie die folgenden Fragen auf Deutsch.

1. Warum war Stefan in Nordfrankreich?
2. Musste er dort allein arbeiten?
3. Wer gehörte zu der Gruppe?
4. Wo waren die Touristen untergebracht?
5. Wie fing die Puddingschlacht an?
6. Was waren die zwei Möglichkeiten, nachdem die Schlacht begonnen hatte?
7. Warum machte das Stefan keinen Spaß?
8. Was waren seine Aufgaben als Reiseleiter?
9. Was gehörte alles zu der Planung für die Reise?
10. Für wen arbeiteten die Betreuer eigentlich?

## Freie Kommunikation

**Ein altes Märchen erzählen.** Bilden Sie eine Gruppe von fünf Personen und erzählen Sie der Gruppe Ihr Lieblingsmärchen. Wenn Sie möchten, benutzen Sie beim Sprechen das Perfekt (z. B. **hat gewohnt, hat geheiratet**). Die anderen Studenten/Studentinnen müssen den Titel Ihres Märchens erraten. Geben Sie Ihrem Märchen einen typischen Anfang und ein typisches Ende.

▪ SIE: *Es war einmal ein(e) …*

*…*

*… Und wenn sie nicht gestorben sind, dann leben sie noch heute.*

**Ein modernes Märchen erzählen.** Bilden Sie eine Gruppe von drei bis vier Personen und erzählen Sie ein modernes Märchen aus Ihrem Leben. Geben Sie einige wahre und ein paar erfundene° Details an. Die anderen Studenten/Studentinnen raten, was falsch ist.

*made up*

**Ein Märchen gemeinsam erzählen.** Bilden Sie eine Gruppe von sechs bis sieben Personen. Bilden Sie mit Ihren Stühlen einen Kreis. S1 beginnt die Erzählung mit einem Satz. Der nächste Student/Die nächste Studentin im Kreis erfindet den nächsten Satz usw., bis alle Personen einen Satz gesagt haben.

## Schreibecke

**Anekdoten aus dem Urlaub.** Jeder von uns hat komische oder traurige Erinnerungen an den Urlaub. Was ist Ihnen mal im Urlaub passiert, das Sie in einer kurzen Geschichte erzählen können? Schreiben Sie eine kleine Erzählung von mindestens zehn Sätzen im Präteritum. Beschreiben Sie, wo Sie waren, mit wem Sie da waren, was Sie machen wollten und was dann passierte.

**Ein Märchen schreiben.** Schreiben Sie die Handlung° Ihres Lieblingsmärchens nach. Es kann auch ein amerikanisches Märchen sein, wie z. B. „Paul Bunyan", „Pecos Bill", „Johnny Appleseed" usw. Vergessen Sie nicht, das Präteritum zu benutzen (z. B. **war, gab, kam, wohnte**). Hier sind einige bekannte Märchen zur Auswahl°.

*plot*

*choice*

| | | |
|---|---|---|
| Hänsel und Gretel | Dornröschen | Die kleine Meerjungfrau |
| Der Froschkönig | Schneewittchen | Der Wolf und die sieben jungen |
| Das hässliche Entlein | Rotkäppchen | Geißlein |
| Die goldene Gans | Rumpelstilzchen | Des Kaisers neue Kleider |
| Rapunzel | | Die Bremer Stadtmusikanten |

## Wortschatz

### Märchen

**Es war einmal ein …** *Once upon a time there was a …; There once was a …*
**eines Tages (Morgens, Abends, Nachts)** *one day (morning, evening, night)*
**Und wenn sie nicht gestorben sind, dann leben sie noch heute.** *And they lived happily ever after.*

**die Asche, -n** *ash*
**der Ball, ⸚e** *ball, dance*
**der Baum, ⸚e** *tree*
**das Blut** *blood*
**die Braut, ⸚e** *bride*
**der Edelstein, -e** *jewel*
**die Fee, -n** *fairy*
**die Ferse, -n** *heel*
**der Frosch, ⸚e** *frog*
**der giftige Apfel, ⸚** *poison apple*
**das Gold** *gold*
**das Grab, ⸚e** *grave*
**die Handlung, -en** *plot (of a story)*
**der Herd, -e** *stove, hearth*
**die Hexe, -n** *witch*
**der Himmel** *heaven*
**der Jäger, -** *hunter*
**der König, -e** *king*
**die Königin, -nen** *queen*
**der Königssohn, ⸚e** *prince*
**die Königstochter, ⸚** *princess*
**das Messer, -** *knife*
**der Prinz, [-en], -en** *prince*
**die Prinzessin, -nen** *princess*
**das Silber** *silver*
**die Stiefmutter, ⸚** *stepmother*
**die Stieftochter, ⸚** *stepdaughter*
**die Treppe, -n** *stair*
**der Wald, ⸚er** *forest, woods*
**der Zauberer, -** *sorcerer, magician*
**die Zehe -n** *toe*
**der Zweig, -e** *branch*
**der Zwerg, -e** *dwarf*

*Noch einmal:* **das Märchen, der Spiegel, das Tier**

**arm** *poor*
**fromm** *religious, faithful*
**grausam** *gruesome; cruel*
**hässlich** *ugly*
**schmutzig** *dirty*

**ab·schneiden (schnitt ab, hat abgeschnitten)** *to cut off*
**erlauben (hat erlaubt)** *to allow*
**passen (hat gepasst)** *to fit*
**pflanzen (hat gepflanzt)** *to plant*
**sterben (stirbt, starb, ist gestorben)** *to die*
**suchen (hat gesucht)** *to seek, look for*
**sich verkleiden (hat sich verkleidet)** *to disguise oneself*
**verlieren (verlor, hat verloren)** *to lose*
**verstecken (hat versteckt)** *to hide, conceal*
**wachsen (wächst, wuchs, ist gewachsen)** *to grow*

### Die Schweiz

**der Anfänger, -** *beginner*
**der Berg, -e** *mountain*
**der/die Fortgeschrittene, [-n], -n** *advanced student*
**der Gast, ⸚e** *guest*
**der Geniesser, -** *connoisseur, fan*
**der Gipfel, -** *peak*
**die Grenze, -n** *border*
**die Hauptstadt, ⸚e** *capital city*
**die Insel, -n** *island*
**der Kanton, -e** *canton (Swiss state)*
**die Landschaft, -en** *landscape*
**der Pass, ⸚e** *pass (through a mountain)*
**der Postbote, [-n], -n** *mail carrier*
**der See, -n** *lake*
**die Stimmung, -en** *mood*
**das Tal, ⸚er** *valley*

*Noch einmal:* **der Fluss, die Stadt**

**der Wandel** *change, transformation*
**die Wirtschaft, -en** *tavern*
**das Wunder, -** *miracle*
**die Zukunft** *future*

**ehemalig** *former*
**seltsam** *strange, odd, unusual*
**verschneit** *snowy*

**sich gewöhnen (hat sich gewöhnt) an+** *acc. to get used to*
**steigen (stieg, ist gestiegen)** *to rise, climb*
  **ein·steigen (stieg ein, ist eingestiegen)** *to get on*
  **aus·stiegen (stieg aus, ist ausgestiegen)** *to get off*

### Urlaub, Ferien und Festtage

**das Andenken, -** *souvenir*
**die Entspannung** *relaxation*
**der Feiertag, -e** *holiday*
**das Fest, -e** *party, celebration, festival, feast*
**der Festtag, -e** *holiday*
**das Hotel, -s** *hotel*
**die Jugendherberge, -n** *youth hostel*
**der Reiseleiter, - / die Reiseleiterin, -nen** *tour guide*
**die Sehenswürdigkeit, -en** *sightseeing attraction*
**der Umzug, ⸚e** *parade*
**der Urlaub, -e** *vacation taken by a person to relax (often involves travel)*

*Noch einmal:* **die Erfahrung, die Ferien** *(pl.)*, **die Pension**

**Chanukka** *Chanukkah*
**Karneval, Fasching, Fastnacht** *celebration before Lent, Mardi Gras*
**das Neujahr** *New Year's Day*
**Ostern** *Easter*
**Ramadan** *Ramadan*
**Silvester** *New Year's Eve*
**Weihnachten** *Christmas*

**erleben (hat erlebt)**  *to experience*
**feiern (hat gefeiert)**  *to celebrate, have a party*
**genießen (genoss, hat genossen)**  *to enjoy*
**Schlittschuh laufen (läuft, lief, ist gelaufen)**  *to ice-skate*
**verreisen (ist verreist)**  *to take a trip*

*Noch einmal:* **verbringen**

**gestresst**  *stressed*
**gut gelaunt**  *easy-going*
**preiswert**  *reasonably priced, well worth the money*

*Noch einmal:* **fremd, wunderbar**

## Skiurlaub

**der Anorak, -s**  *parka*
**das Dorf, ¨er**  *village*
**die Piste, -n**  *(downhill) ski run, ski slope; track*

## Andere Verben

**an·probieren (hat anprobiert)**  *to try on*
**beten (hat gebetet)**  *to pray*
**brennen (brannte, hat gebrannt)**  *to burn*
**erkennen (erkannte, hat erkannt)**  *to recognize*
**fangen (fängt, fing, hat gefangen)**  *to catch*
**fehlen (hat gefehlt)**  *to be missing, lacking*

**kosten (hat gekostet)**  *to cost*
**nennen (nannte, hat genannt)**  *to name, call (someone something)*
**rennen (rannte, ist gerannt)**  *to run*
**rufen (rief, hat gerufen)**  *to call*
**sparen (hat gespart)**  *to save (money)*
**überzeugen (hat überzeugt)**  *to convince*
**verbieten (verbat, hat verboten)**  *to ban, prohibit*
**weinen (hat geweint)**  *to cry*
**werfen (wirft, warf, hat geworfen)**  *to throw*
**ziehen (zog, hat gezogen)**  *to pull*

*Noch einmal:* **schneiden, statt·finden, wünschen**

## Andere Substantive

**die Art, -en**  *type, kind*
**der Feind, -e**  *enemy, adversary*
**die Kindheit**  *childhood*
**der Unterschied, -e**  *difference*
**der Witz, -e**  *joke*

## Andere Adjektive

**echt**  *true, real*
**eigene**  *own*
**erstaunt**  *astounded*
**erwachsen**  *grown-up, adult*
**sauber**  *clean*
**ursprünglich**  *original*

## Andere Adverbien

**damals**  *at that time, then*
**insgesamt**  *all in all*

## Andere Wörter

**wessen?**  *whose?*
**dessen/dessen/deren**  *whose*
**jedermann**  *everyone*
**jemand**  *someone*

**als**  *when*
**nachdem**  *after*
**ob**  *if, whether*
**von + dat.**  *of (possession)*
**wann**  *when*
**wenn**  *whenever; if*
  **immer wenn**  *always when, whenever*

## Andere Ausdrücke

**Haut ab!**  *Get lost!, Scram!*
**ohne es zu sagen**  *without telling*

## Meine eigenen Wörter

_____

_____

_____

_____

_____

_____

# Geschichte und Geographie Deutschlands

**In this chapter you will learn to talk about what you might do, make polite suggestions and requests, describe actions as a process, and state what you could or should have done.**

## Kommunikative Funktionen

- Speculating about activities, making suggestions
- Talking about unreal situations
- Talking about actions as a process

## Strukturen

- The subjunctive mood
- Role reversal statements (*If I were you, . . .*)
- The double-infinitive construction
- **Wenn**-clauses for unreal conditions
- The passive voice

## Vokabeln

- Sehenswürdigkeiten in Berlin
- Die Landeskunde Deutschlands

## Kulturelles

- Deutschland: von der Monarchie zur Demokratie (I, II, III)
- Freistaat Sachsen: Leipzig und Dresden

■ Das Brandenburger Tor ist seit 1990 wieder das Zentrum der Stadt „Bärlin".

**Online Study Center**

Go to the *Vorsprung* Website at *http://college.hmco.com/pic/vorsprung2e.*

## Anlauftext    Was würdest du dann vorschlagen?

In den Ferien fährt Anna nach Berlin, wo sie ihren Onkel Werner besucht. Beim Abendessen erzählt Anna ihrem Onkel Werner von ihrem ersten Tag in Berlin. Anna wollte den Reichstag und die Mauer sehen. Aber zu viele Leute haben vor dem Reichstag Schlange gestanden° und später konnte sie Reste von der Mauer nirgendwo° finden. Anna und Onkel Werner machen Pläne für die nächsten Tage und besprechen, was Anna sehen möchte und was sie zusammen machen könnten. Heute Abend gehen sie ins Konzert, und nachher will Anna noch jemanden treffen.

*Schlange stehen: to stand in line / nowhere*

Five museums in the heart of Berlin-Mitte form the nucleus of Berlin's art exhibition space: **(1) die Alte Nationalgalerie,** with German art of the 19th and 20th centuries; **(2) das Bodemuseum,** with collections ranging from Egyptian and Byzantine art to sculpture;

*city bus tour*
*walking tour*
*slide show*

**(3) das Pergamonmuseum** with its famous Greek Pergamon altar and collections of Near Eastern and Islamic art; **(4) Altes Museum,** with a program of special exhibits; and **(5) Neues Museum,** opened in 1859 and housing art work of Berlin Classicism.

### Vorschau

 **1    Thematische Fragen.**  Beantworten Sie die folgenden Fragen auf Deutsch.

1. Wie lernen Sie am ersten Tag eine neue Stadt kennen?
   - a. auf einer Stadtrundfahrt°
   - b. auf einer Führung°
   - c. durch einen Ton-Dia-Vortrag°
   - d. allein
   - e. mit Freunden
   - f. durch ein Video

2. Wo informieren Sie sich über eine neue Stadt?
   - a. bei Freunden
   - b. bei Verwandten
   - c. bei jungen Leuten
   - d. beim Verkehrsbüro
   - e. beim Fremdenführer/bei der Fremdenführerin
   - f. beim Telefondienst
   - g. im World Wide Web

3. Was möchten Sie als Tourist/Touristin als erstes in Berlin erleben?
   - a. die Museen
   - b. die Disko- und Clubszene
   - c. die Architektur
   - d. die tollen Parks und Seen
   - e. die Musikszene
   - f. die Kunstszene

### Wissenswerte Vokabeln: Sehenswürdigkeiten in Berlin
*Talking about sights in and around Berlin*

der Kurfürstendamm (Kudamm)  die Kaiser-Wilhelms-Gedächtniskirche  die Philharmonie  die Museumsinsel  der Potsdamer Platz

Unter den Linden

das Brandenburger Tor

der Alexanderplatz

das Schloss Charlottenburg

die Humboldt-Universität

Berlin-Mitte

der Reichstag

die Spree

die Mauer

das neue Regierungsviertel

der Prenzlauer Berg

🔲 Was würdest du in Berlin machen?    *Ich würde gern die Mauer besichtigen°.*    visit, look at

**2    Lernen Sie Berlin kennen.** Wählen Sie die beste Beschreibung für jede Sehenswürdigkeit in **Wissenswerte Vokabeln.**

1. Hier spielt das berühmteste Orchester Deutschlands. *die Philharmonie*
2. Diese Kirche – im Krieg bombardiert – steht heute noch als Ruine. *die K.-W.- Gedächtniskirche*
3. Das ist der große Einkaufsplatz im ehemaligen Ostberlin, mit der Internationalen Weltzeituhr. *der Alexanderplatz*
4. Das ist eine lebendige Einkaufsstraße° im westlichen Teil Berlins mit dem Warenhaus Ka-De-We: Kaufhaus des Westens. *der Kudamm*    *shopping street*
5. Hier ist der Sitz des deutschen Bundestages ab 1999. *der Reichstag*
6. Diese neuen Gebäude stehen in Berlin-Mitte um den Reichstag und sind für die Ministerien. *das neue Regierungsviertel*
7. Hier findet man den Stadtteil, der bei jungen Leuten „in" ist, mit vielen Szene-Clubs und Kneipen. *der Prenzlauer Berg*
8. Diese Barriere stand als Symbol des Kalten Krieges zwischen Ost und West. Sie existiert nicht mehr als Ganzes. *die Mauer*
9. Das ist ein Sommerpalast mitten in Berlin, der für die Frau von König Friedrich I, Sophie Charlotte, gebaut wurde. *das Schloss Charlottenburg*
10. Das ist die elegante Hauptstraße im östlichen Teil Berlins. *Unter den Linden*
11. Dies ist das Wahrzeichen Berlins und steht am Anfang von Unter den Linden. *das B. Tor*
12. Das ist der berühmteste Fluss Berlins. *die Spree*
13. Hier gibt es fünf Museen: die Alte Nationalgalerie, das Bodemuseum, das Pergamonmuseum, das Alte Museum und das Neue Museum. *die Museumsinsel*
14. Hier ist der historische Mittelpunkt Berlins. *Berlin-Mitte*
15. Dieser Platz mit dem Sony Center ist ein architektonisches Wunder.
16. Das ist die älteste Universität Berlins. *die Humboldt-Universität*

**The Kurfürstendamm,** West Berlin's main boulevard and shopping street, has its name because it was originally constructed by Berlin's electors (**Kurfürsten**).

The **Humboldt-Universität** was founded in 1809 and named for Wilhelm von Humboldt (1767–1835) and his brother Alexander (1769–1859).

**3    Würdest du das machen?** Was würden Sie als Tourist/Touristin in einer fremden Stadt machen? Kreuzen Sie die Aktivitäten an. Fragen Sie dann einen Partner/eine Partnerin, was er/sie machen würde.

S1:  *Würdest du in ein Konzert gehen?*
S2:  *Ja, das würde ich machen.* (oder)
      *Nein, das würde ich nicht machen.*

After doing this activity, determine which things both of you find interesting and report to the class what you could do together (e.g., **Wir könnten zusammen in ein Konzert gehen.**).

|  | Ich | | Mein(e) Partner(in) | |
|---|:---:|:---:|:---:|:---:|
|  | Ja | Nein | Ja | Nein |
| 1. in ein Konzert gehen | ☐ | ☐ | ☐ | ☐ |
| 2. historische Denkmäler° anschauen | ☐ | ☐ | ☐ | ☐ |
| 3. eine historische Kirche oder einen Dom° ansehen | ☐ | ☐ | ☐ | ☐ |
| 4. einen Park oder einen Platz im Freien° besuchen | ☐ | ☐ | ☐ | ☐ |
| 5. eine berühmte Sehenswürdigkeit anschauen | ☐ | ☐ | ☐ | ☐ |
| 6. durch die Altstadt bummeln° | ☐ | ☐ | ☐ | ☐ |
| 7. ein Museum besuchen | ☐ | ☐ | ☐ | ☐ |
| 8. die Clubszene ausprobieren | ☐ | ☐ | ☐ | ☐ |
| 9. durch Geschäfte bummeln | ☐ | ☐ | ☐ | ☐ |
| 10. eine berühmte Universität besichtigen | ☐ | ☐ | ☐ | ☐ |

*monuments*

*cathedral*

*outdoors*

*stroll*

Seit der Vereinigung ist der Potsdamer Platz ein Symbol für das neue Berlin geworden.

## Anlauftext

 Hören Sie gut zu.

**Was würdest du dann vorschlagen?**

1. Grüß dich, Onkel Werner. Entschuldige die Verspätung.

   Komm, erzähl mal von deinem ersten Tag in Berlin.

2. Haben wir Zeit?

   Klar. Die Philharmonie fängt erst um 20 Uhr an. Wir essen erst eine Kleinigkeit.

3. Also, es war recht interessant, aber frustrierend. Ich wollte als erstes die Kuppel des Reichstags besichtigen, aber ich hätte stundenlang anstehen müssen.

   Ja, der Reichstag ist zum Touristenziel Nummer 1 geworden.

   Und dann bin ich zum Brandenburger Tor gelaufen, weil ich die Mauer sehen wollte, aber da war nichts. Und ich hätte sie so gern gesehen!

4. Oje, ich hätte dich warnen sollen! In Berlin-Mitte sind Mauerreste kaum noch zu finden. Wir könnten ja morgen oder übermorgen zur East Side Gallery oder zur Bernauerstraße gehen. Dort stehen noch Mauerreste.

   Gut. Das würde mich schon interessieren.

5. Abgemacht. Und was hast du für morgen vor?

   Tja, ich würde gern Potsdam sehen. Vielleicht morgen Nachmittag …

6. Nee, nee pass mal auf. Allein für den Park Sanssouci braucht man einen ganzen Tag! Wir sollten damit bis Samstag warten. Dann habe ich mehr Zeit.

7. Klingt gut. Aber was würdest du dann für morgen vorschlagen?

## *Rückblick*

**4** **Stimmt das?** Stimmen die folgenden Aussagen zum Text oder nicht? Wenn nicht, was stimmt?

|  | Ja, das stimmt. | Nein, das stimmt nicht. |
|---|:---:|:---:|
| 1. Annas erster Tag in Berlin war frustrierend. | ☒ | ☐ |
| 2. Der Reichstag war geschlossen. | ☐ | ☒ |
| 3. Anna hat das Brandenburger Tor gesehen, aber die Mauer hat sie nicht finden können. | ☒ | ☐ |
| 4. Für morgen hat Anna keine Pläne. | ☐ | ☒ |
| 5. Werner meint, dass man für Potsdam und den Park Sanssouci nur ein paar Stunden braucht. | ☐ | ☒ |
| 6. Werner schlägt Anna vor, dass sie am Vormittag den Kurfürstendamm allein besuchen soll. | ☒ | ☒ |
| 7. Am Nachmittag könnten sie zusammen eine Schifffahrt auf der Spree machen. | ☐ | ☒ |
| 8. Heute Abend gehen sie zusammen in ein Rockkonzert. | ☐ | ☒ |
| 9. Nachher will Anna in den Prenzlauer Berg fahren. | ☒ | ☐ |
| 10. Werner versteht endlich, dass Anna noch heute mit einem jungen Mann im Prenzlauer Berg verabredet ist. | ☒ | ☐ |

> (See page 436, #9.) After years of intense debate, the memorial for the Jewish victims of the Holocaust (**das Mahnmal für die ermordeten Juden Europas**) was opened in 2005 on a site just a short walk from the **Brandenburger Tor.**

> Complete the **Ergänzen Sie** activity in your workbook for this text before doing the next activity.

**5** **Kurz gesagt.** Vervollständigen Sie diese Sätze. Benutzen Sie Ihre eigenen Worte.

1. Werner und Anna haben heute Abend Eile°, weil …
2. Anna soll noch eine Kleinigkeit essen, bevor …
3. Anna hat die Kuppel vom Reichstag nicht besichtigt, weil …
4. Werner meint, er hätte Anna warnen sollen, dass …
5. Werner schlägt Anna vor, morgen nicht nach Potsdam zu fahren, weil …
6. Werner sagt, dass er an Annas Stelle morgen Vormittag …
7. Am Nachmittag meint Werner, dass …
8. Anna möchte in den Prenzlauer Berg fahren, weil …

> **haben … Eile:** *are in a hurry*

---

**Sprache im Alltag: Confirming what someone said**

In informal conversation, the expressions below are used for the following purposes.

- to seek confirmation: **nicht wahr?, na?**
- to give confirmation: **fantastisch, fein, klar, Das wäre schön, Das klingt gut, Das hört sich gut an.** Sometimes **das** is abbreviated or dropped in these expressions: **'S wäre schön, Klingt gut, Hört sich gut an.**
- to agree with an opinion: **Du hast vollkommen Recht.**
- to agree with or accept a proposal: **Abgemacht!**
- to express hesitation: **aha, ach so, naja**

**6** **Was möchtest du in Berlin sehen?** Sie verbringen ein paar Tage in Berlin. Was möchten Sie machen? Planen Sie mit einem Partner/einer Partnerin den ersten Tag. Benutzen Sie die Sehenswürdigkeiten in **Wissenswerte Vokabeln: Sehenswürdigkeiten in Berlin.**

S1: *Was möchtest du in Berlin machen?*
S2: *Ich möchte den Ku-Damm sehen, und du?*
S1: *Ich möchte gern den Ku-Damm sehen.* (oder)
    *Naja, ich möchte lieber in den Prenzlauer Berg gehen.*
S2: *(Das) Klingt gut!*

## BRENNPUNKT KULTUR

## Deutschland: von der Monarchie zur Demokratie (I)

*Kaiser Wilhelm I im Gespräch mit Kanzler Otto von Bismarck*

Germany's evolution to a peaceful democratic republic has been slow and painful. Until the early 19th century, the German landscape was divided into a number of separate principalities. It took until 1871 to unify Germany as a nation (**das Deutsche Reich**). The Prussian king became Emperor (**Kaiser**) Wilhelm I, and Otto von Bismarck was his chancellor (**Kanzler**).

After the defeat of the Germans in World War I (**der Erste Weltkrieg**) in 1918, Germany formed a democracy, the Weimar Republic (**die Weimarer Republik**). Radical forces on both the left and the right, most notably the Nazi party, officially known as **die Nationalsozialistische Deutsche Arbeiterpartei (NSDAP)**, did not support it, however. The stability of the Weimar government was further undermined by immense war reparations to France, the post-war occupation of German territory by foreign troops, large-scale unemployment, astronomical inflation, and the stock market crash and world economic crisis of 1929.

The Nazi party promised to create jobs, fix social chaos and economic misery, and eliminate the purported root causes of these problems, which they blamed on world Jewry. By 1933, Adolf Hitler (referred to as **der Führer**, *the leader*) and the Nazi party had assumed power and established a one-party dictatorship. Establishment of the Third Reich (**das Dritte Reich**) followed shortly thereafter. The Nazis broke up trade unions, repressed the freedom of the press, and abolished most human and civil rights. Jews and other minority groups were denied their German citizenship and basic protection under the law and were forced into labor camps and concentration camps. Although open dissent was eliminated, there were still pockets of resistance (**der Widerstand**) in Germany that were always in grave danger and therefore operated in secrecy. Meanwhile, the German military set its sights on new territories throughout Europe and northern Africa. Hitler's 1939 attack on Poland signaled the beginning of World War II (**der Zweite Weltkrieg**), which would last over five years, engulf the continent in war, and lead to the Holocaust during which Jews and others were systematically killed by the Nazis. The war in total claimed an estimated 55 million lives.

*Adolf Hitler auf dem Parteitag der NSDAP in Nürnberg*

■ **Kulturkreuzung** Die Nazizeit ist eine sehr problematische Epoche für die Deutschen heute. Wie war es möglich, dass mitten in Europa im zwanzigsten Jahrhundert eine Diktatur entstehen konnte? Besteht diese Gefahr noch heute in der Welt, oder ist der Mensch dafür zu intelligent und tolerant geworden?

## *Strukturen und Vokabeln*

## I  Speculating about activities, making suggestions

### The subjunctive mood

In **Kapitel 9,** you learned how to propose activities and make polite requests and suggestions using the present subjunctive of **werden (würde), haben (hätte),** and **sein (wäre).**

**7**  **Anna würde gern alles sehen.** Anna hofft, alles in Berlin zu sehen, aber in der kurzen Zeit ist das unmöglich. Fragen Sie einen Partner/eine Partnerin, was Anna und ihr Onkel sehen möchten. Fragen Sie dann, was Ihr Partner/Ihre Partnerin gern sehen möchte.

■ S1: *Würde Anna die Mauer gern sehen?*
   S2: *Ja. Sie würde gern die Mauer sehen. Und du? Würdest du die Mauer auch gern sehen?*
   S1: *Ja (Nein), ich würde die Mauer (nicht) gern sehen.*

**Tabelle A (S1):**

|  | Anna | Onkel Werner | Partner(in) |
|---|---|---|---|
| das neue Regierungsviertel sehen | ? | Ja | _____ |
| die Mauerreste fotografieren | Ja | ? | _____ |
| den Reichstag besichtigen | Ja | ? | _____ |
| zum Potsdamer Platz fahren | Ja | ? | _____ |
| das Museum am Checkpoint Charlie besuchen | ? | Nein | _____ |
| in Kreuzberg türkisch essen | ? | Ja | _____ |
| am Alexanderplatz einkaufen gehen | Ja | ? | _____ |
| ins Ägyptische Museum gehen | ? | Ja | _____ |
| ins Olympiastadion gehen | Nein | ? | _____ |
| die Gedächtniskirche anschauen | ? | Nein | _____ |

Placing **nicht gern** towards the end of the sentence gives it special emphasis.

**Anna würde gern alles sehen.** Checkpoint Charlie was the most famous border crossing from the American to the Soviet sector of Berlin and the site of heroic escape attempts and confrontations between American and Soviet diplomats and soldiers.

**Kreuzberg,** a district of Berlin, is known for its countercultural ambiance and its large Turkish population.

**Das Olympiastadion,** where Hitler refused to shake gold-medalist Jesse Owens' hand, was renovated in 2004 to host the Berlin games of the 2006 **Fußballweltmeisterschaft.**

**Tabelle B (S2):**

| | Anna | Onkel Werner | Partner(in) |
|---|---|---|---|
| das neue Regierungsviertel sehen | Ja | ? | ——— |
| die Mauerreste fotografieren | ? | Nein | ——— |
| den Reichstag besichtigen | ? | Nein | ——— |
| zum Potsdamer Platz fahren | Ja | ? | ——— |
| das Museum am Checkpoint Charlie besuchen | ? | Nein | ——— |
| in Kreuzberg türkisch essen | Nein | ? | ——— |
| am Alexanderplatz einkaufen gehen | ? | Nein | ——— |
| ins Ägyptische Museum gehen | Ja | ? | ——— |
| ins Olympiastadion gehen | ? | Nein | ——— |
| die Gedächtniskirche anschauen | Ja | ? | ——— |

**8** **Das wäre wirklich interessant!** Ihr Freund hat viele Vorschläge für heute Abend in Berlin. Reagieren Sie auf seine Vorschläge mit einer passenden Antwort aus der Liste.

S1 (IHR FREUND):   *Ich habe eine Idee: Gehen wir heute Abend ins Konzert!*
S2 (SIE):   *Das wäre aber wirklich langweilig.*

**Positiv:**   Das wäre … (ganz toll / prima / echt spitze / super gut!)
Ich hätte schon … (Lust° dazu / Interesse daran.)

**Negativ:**   Das wäre aber … (wirklich langweilig / zu gefährlich / viel zu teuer.)
Nein, ich hätte … (gar keine Lust dazu / überhaupt kein Interesse daran.)

*Lust zu etwas haben: to want to do something, to feel like doing something*

1. heute Abend ins Konzert gehen
2. einen Kaffee trinken
3. in die Nationalgalerie gehen
4. in die Disko gehen
5. die Punkerszene suchen
6. zum Konzentrationslager Sachsenhausen fahren
7. die Clubszene im Prenzlauer Berg erleben
8. das neue Regierungsviertel besuchen
9. mit der U-Bahn zum Olympiastadion fahren
10. die Neue Synagoge in der Oranienburger Straße besuchen

## A. The present subjunctive of **können** and the other modal verbs

To express the possibility or the potential of an action, German speakers frequently use the present subjunctive of modal verbs, such as **können.** The infinitive appears at the end of the main clause.

**Könnten** wir nach der Philharmonie in den Prenzlauer Berg **fahren?**

*Could we go to Prenzlauer Berg after the concert at the Philharmonie?*

These are the present subjunctive forms of **können.**

| **könnte:** *could* | | |
|---|---|---|
| **Singular** | | **Plural** |
| ich **könnte** | | wir **könnten** |
| du **könntest** | | ihr **könntet** |
| Sie **könnten** | | Sie **könnten** |
| er/sie/es **könnte** | | sie **könnten** |

The other modal verbs follow the same pattern as **können/könnte** in the present subjunctive. Modals with an umlaut in the infinitive (e.g., **müssen**) lose the umlaut in the narrative past (e.g., **musste**) but regain it in the subjunctive (e.g., **müsste**). The narrative past and the present subjunctive of modals without an umlaut in the infinitive (e.g., **sollen, wollen**) are identical (e.g., **sollte, wollte**).

| **Infinitive** | **Subjunctive** | |
|---|---|---|
| mögen | ich **möchte** | *I would like to* |
| dürfen | ich **dürfte** | *I would be allowed to* |
| müssen | ich **müsste** | *I would have to* |
| sollen *(no umlaut)* | ich **sollte** *(no umlaut)* | *I should, ought to* |
| wollen *(no umlaut)* | ich **wollte** *(no umlaut)* | *I would want to* |

 **9** **Das könntest du machen!** Anna hilft Onkel Werner eine Party zu planen. Was sagt Anna?

◻ S1 (ONKEL WERNER): *Tanja hat viele CDs.*
　　　 S2 (ANNA): *Sie könnte die Musik organisieren.*

1. Tanja hat viele CDs.
2. Margit und Waltraud haben ein Auto.
3. Andreas kennt die Nachbarn relativ gut.
4. Ich habe heute Geld bekommen.
5. Klaus-Peter arbeitet im Supermarkt.
6. Karl und ich kochen gern.
7. Claudia möchte helfen, aber sie hat vor der Party überhaupt keine Zeit.
8. Wir haben morgen relativ viel Zeit.

a. zwei Kästen° Bier mitbringen
b. nachher abwaschen
c. die anderen anrufen
d. auch die Nachbarn einladen
e. alles bezahlen
f. die Musik organisieren
g. Brot und Käse mitbringen
h. Obstsalat machen

*cases*

**Kästen** = northern German;
**Kasten** = southern German

**10    Aber ich könnte das machen!** Onkel Werner sieht immer Probleme. Anna hat immer eine Lösung. Benutzen Sie den Konjunktiv von **können** in Annas Antwort.

S1 (WERNER): *Ich kann nicht mit dem Hund spazieren gehen. (die Nachbarin)*
　　S2 (ANNA): *Die Nachbarin könnte mit dem Hund spazieren gehen.*

1. Ich kann nicht mit dem Hund spazieren gehen. (die Nachbarin)
2. Wir können heute nicht in die Neue Nationalgalerie. (wir / übermorgen)
3. Ich will morgen frische Brötchen vom Bäcker holen. (ich / noch heute)
4. Wir können keine Theaterkarten für Freitagabend kriegen. (du / zwei / für Sonnabend am Telefon reservieren)
5. Wir können erst nächste Woche zu Erich und Veronika hinausfahren. (sie / diese Woche zu uns kommen)
6. Du darfst nicht alleine in die Clubs gehen! (ich / mit dem Typ vom Prenzlauer Berg gehen)
7. Ich möchte meinen Chef heute Abend einladen, aber ich habe keine Zeit. (du / nächste Woche)
8. Ich soll dir das neue Jüdische Museum von Daniel Libeskind zeigen, aber mein Auto ist in der Reparatur. (wir / mit dem Bus fahren)

## B. Making polite requests and suggestions

To make polite requests and suggestions (**höfliche Bitten und Vorschläge**), German speakers often use the present subjunctive. The subjunctive makes a request or suggestion sound less explicit or demanding than the indicative or imperative. Compare the tone in the following statements.

| *Imperative (Commands)* | *Subjunctive (Requests, Suggestions)* |
|---|---|
| **Bringen** Sie mir bitte die Speisekarte! | **Könnten (Würden)** Sie mir bitte die Speisekarte **bringen?** |
| **Kauf** nicht bei Müller ein! | Du **solltest** nicht bei Müller **einkaufen.** |

| *Indicative (Neutral)* | *Subjunctive (Polite)* |
|---|---|
| **Haben** Sie einen Tisch frei? | **Hätten** Sie einen Tisch frei? |
| Ich **will** ein Bier trinken. | Ich **würde gern** ein Bier trinken. |
| Ich **will** bezahlen. | Ich **wollte gern** bezahlen. |
| **Können** Sie mir sagen, wo die U-Bahn-Haltestelle ist? | **Könnten** Sie mir sagen, wo die U-Bahn-Haltestelle ist? |

**11**   **Annas zweite Reaktion.**   Onkel Werner hat viele Vorschläge für Anna. Anna sagt nicht direkt, was sie denkt, denn sie will eine höfliche Antwort geben. Was sagt Anna?

□ Werner sagt: Wir könnten ins Ägyptische Museum gehen.
Anna denkt: Das finde ich nicht so interessant.
Anna sagt: *Das würde ich nicht so interessant finden.*

• Das könnte sehr schön sein • Das wäre eine großartige Idee. • Das würde ich nicht so interessant finden. • Das würde schon Spaß machen. • Dazu hätte ich nicht so viel Lust. • Ich hätte wirklich kein Interesse daran.

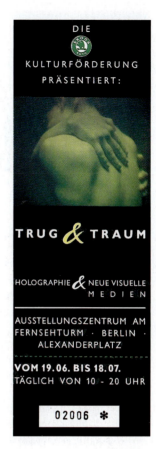

1. Werner sagt: Wir könnten ins Ägyptische Museum gehen.
Anna denkt: Das finde ich nicht so interessant.
Anna sagt: _____
2. Werner sagt: Wir könnten Kaffee bei meinen Nachbarn trinken.
Anna denkt: Dazu habe ich nicht so viel Lust.
Anna sagt: _____
3. Werner sagt: Wir könnten Checkpoint Charlie besuchen.
Anna denkt: Das ist eine großartige Idee.
Anna sagt: _____
4. Werner sagt: Wir könnten die alternative Kunstszene aufsuchen.
Anna denkt: Das macht schon Spaß.
Anna sagt: _____
5. Werner sagt: Wir könnten einfach zu Hause fernsehen.
Anna denkt: Ich habe wirklich kein Interesse daran.
Anna sagt: _____
6. Werner sagt: Wir könnten eine Stadtrundfahrt machen.
Anna denkt: Das kann sehr schön sein.
Anna sagt: _____

**12**   **Nicht so direkt!**   Sie sitzen in einem Café und haben großen Hunger und Durst. Formulieren Sie Ihre Gedanken höflicher. Benutzen Sie **hätte gern** oder **würde gern** + Infinitiv.

□ Ich will ein Bier haben.     *Ich hätte gern ein Bier.*
□ Wir wollen jetzt bestellen.     *Wir würden jetzt gern bestellen.*

1. Ich will ein Bier haben.
2. Ich will die Speisekarte sehen.
3. Wir wollen jetzt bestellen.
4. Bringen Sie uns sofort die Vorspeisen!
5. Wir wollen eine Pizza mit Salami essen.
6. Wir wollen auch gleich zahlen.

BRENNPUNKT KULTUR

## Deutschland: von der Monarchie zur Demokratie (II)

*Elf Monate lang versorgten die Alliierten ganz West-Berlin durch die Luftbrücke.*

After the unconditional surrender of Nazi Germany on May 8, 1945 to the Allies, the U.S., Great Britain, France, and the Soviet Union agreed to disarm, demilitarize, and denazify Germany and divide the country into four occupation zones (**Besatzungszonen**) under their control. Berlin was located in the Soviet zone but was itself divided into four occupation zones as well. Tensions immediately grew between the western Allies and the Soviets, leading to the Cold War (**der Kalte Krieg**).

The Soviets established hegemony throughout eastern Europe and allowed formation of Soviet-leaning political parties in their zones in 1945. This led to a pro-Communist regime ruled by the Socialist Unity Party (**Sozialistische Einheitspartei, SED**) in their zone. Wanting to respond with strong western political and economic systems and western values, the Allies pursued common political and economic structures in the three West German Zones. This essentially resulted in the formation of two separate Germanys, which lasted for forty years.

In 1948, in response to a currency reform that introduced a new **Deutschmark** in place of the old **Reichsmark** in the west, the Soviets attempted to gain control of all of Berlin by blockading all roads from western Germany to West Berlin. The Allies responded with a massive air transport of goods to West Berlin (**die Luftbrücke**) that lasted eleven months. It saved West Berlin and forced the Soviets to back down.

In 1949 the Federal Republic of Germany (**die Bundesrepublik Deutschland**), with its provisional capital in Bonn, drew up its Constitution (**das Grundgesetz**) for the territories of the three western zones. Shortly thereafter, the **SED** established a government in the Soviet zone, and the German Democratic Republic or GDR (**die Deutsche Demokratische Republik, die DDR**) came into being. Two completely different economic and political systems now existed: one a Western-oriented, capitalist-leaning, social-market economy in an elective democracy; the other a centrally planned economy in a one-party Marxist society. Berlin remained divided as well, West Berlin becoming a de facto state of the Federal Republic, while East Berlin became the capital of the **DDR**. American, British, French, and Russian troops remained stationed in Germany and Berlin for the next forty years.

*Zu DDR-Zeiten war diese Gedenkstätte ein Mahnmal für die Opfer des Faschismus.*

■ **Kulturkreuzung** Vierzig Jahre lang gab es zwei deutsche Staaten. Familien durften einander nicht besuchen. Das war sehr traumatisch für die Menschen. Hat es irgendwann in der US-Geschichte eine ähnliche Spaltung° zwischen Familien gegeben? Hat das noch heute Folgen in den USA?     *separation*

## C. Making role-reversal statements with **an deiner** (**Ihrer,** etc.) **Stelle** ... and the present subjunctive

A common expression to introduce a hypothetical suggestion in German is

> **An deiner Stelle würde ich ...  / An Ihrer Stelle würde ich ...**
> (*In your position, I would . . . / If I were you, I'd...*).

**13   An deiner Stelle würde ich ...**  Ihr Partner/Ihre Partnerin hat Probleme. Geben Sie ihm/ihr Rat.

S1: *Du, ich habe ein Problem. Ich muss morgen mein Referat abgeben°,*     *hand in*
    *aber ich bin damit noch nicht fertig.*
S2: *An deiner Stelle würde ich mich auf die Arbeit konzentrieren und sie*
    *schnell zu Ende schreiben.*

1. Ich muss morgen mein Referat abgeben, aber ich bin noch nicht fertig.
2. Ich möchte morgen Abend ins Brecht-Theater gehen und „Die Dreigroschenoper" sehen.
3. Ich muss einen Brief per Express nach New York schicken.
4. Ich weiß nicht, was ich meiner Mutter zum Geburtstag schenken soll.
5. Ich habe meine Miete nicht bezahlt, und die Vermieterin will mich auf die Straße setzen.

a. die Theaterkasse anrufen und Karten bestellen
b. schnell die Miete° zahlen und der Vermieterin Blumen bringen     *rent*
c. einen Expressdienst anrufen und den Brief abholen lassen°     **abholen lassen:** *have picked up*
d. einfach fragen, was sie zum Geburtstag möchte
e. mich auf die Arbeit konzentrieren und sie schnell zu Ende schreiben

**14   An seiner Stelle würde ich ...**  Besprechen Sie mit einem Partner/einer Partnerin, was diese Personen in Annas Studentenwohnheim machen sollen. Was würden Sie an ihrer Stelle machen?

S1: *Tina trinkt zu viel Kaffee und kann nachts nicht schlafen.*
S2: *An ihrer Stelle würde ich nicht so viel Kaffee trinken.*

1. Tina trinkt zu viel Kaffee und kann nachts nicht schlafen.
2. Jennifer fährt übers Wochenende nach Berlin. Was soll sie dort machen?
3. Johnny und Dagmar haben zu viele Hausaufgaben.
4. Katja ist mit ihrem Job nicht zufrieden.
5. Sascha hat Karten für die Philharmonie, aber er will nicht hingehen.
6. Ulf braucht einen neuen Computer, aber er hat nicht genug Geld.
7. Ingo hat einen Monat Urlaub, aber er möchte wenig Geld ausgeben.
8. Karin hat neue Arbeitsangebote° in München und in Basel bekommen.     *job offers*

## D. The past-time subjunctive

The past-time subjunctive (**der Vergangenheitskonjunktiv**) expresses events that might have taken place in the past. The past-time subjunctive is formed with **hätte** or **wäre** + past participle.

Anna **hätte** die Mauer **gesehen.**     *Anna would have seen the Wall.*
Ich **hätte** die Antwort **gewusst.**     *I would have known the answer.*
Wir **wären** nach Potsdam **gefahren.**     *We would have gone to Potsdam.*

The past-time subjunctive looks like the past perfect, except for the umlaut on **hätte** and **wäre** and the **-e** ending on **wäre.**

| Infinitive | Past perfect | Past-time subjunctive |
|---|---|---|
| sehen | hatte gesehen | hätte gesehen |
| fahren | war gefahren | wäre gefahren |

The past-time subjunctive is used for all three past tense forms used in the indicative.

*Conversational past*
Er **hat** das **gewusst.**
Er **ist** nach Hause **gefahren.**

*Narrative past*
Er **wusste** das.　　　　　　　　Er **hätte** das **gewusst.**
Er **fuhr** nach Hause.　　　　　　Er **wäre** nach Hause **gefahren.**

*Past perfect*
Er **hatte** das **gewusst.**
Er **war** nach Hause **gefahren.**

**15** **Ich hätte es anders gemacht.** Ein reicher Freund/Eine reiche Freundin erzählt von einer luxuriösen Europareise. Sie haben nicht so viel Geld. Was hätten Sie anders gemacht? Benutzen Sie den Vergangenheitskonjunktiv.

S1 (FREUND/IN): *Ich habe überall in Luxushotels gewohnt.*
　　S2 (SIE): *Ich hätte in Jugendherbergen übernachtet.*

1. in Luxushotels gewohnt
2. jeden Abend in die Oper gegangen
3. ein Auto gemietet°
4. in den besten Restaurants gegessen
5. tagsüber in Museen und alte Kirchen gegangen
6. nach Baden-Baden in die Casinos gefahren

a. in Jugendherbergen übernachtet
b. das Essen im Lebensmittelgeschäft gekauft
c. an die Nordsee an den Strand gefahren
d. mit dem Zug gefahren
e. auf dem Land oder im Wald wandern gegangen
f. den Abend mit jungen Leuten in der Stadt verbracht

*rented*

## E. The double-infinitive construction

Sometimes German speakers use a special construction called the *double infinitive* (**der Doppelinfinitiv**) to express the past time in statements with a modal verb. The term *double infinitive* refers to the presence of two infinitives (verb + modal) at the end of the clause that replace the past participle and may occur in the indicative or subjunctive.

Wir haben die Mauer **sehen wollen.**　　*We wanted to see the Wall.*

To express the past-time subjunctive, **hätte** (never **wäre**) is always used with a double-infinitive construction.

Oje, Anna, ich **hätte** dich **warnen**　　*Oh, Anna, I should have warned*
　**sollen.**　　　　　　　　　　　　　　*you.*
Ich **hätte** es gleich **ahnen sollen.**　　*I should have guessed it right away.*

> The double-infinitive construction (in the subjunctive) can be used with any modal verb, e.g., **hätte machen können (dürfen, müssen, sollen, wollen)** = *could have (would have been allowed to, would have had to, should have, would have wanted to) done/do.*

In subordinate clauses following **weil, dass,** etc., **hätte** occurs <u>before</u> the double infinitive, not at the end of the clause.

Onkel Werner hat gesagt, dass er es **hätte ahnen sollen.**

**16** **Wir hätten das machen sollen!** Onkel Werner und Anna sprechen über ihren gemeinsamen Tag. Anna sagt, was (nicht) passiert ist, und Onkel Werner sagt, was (nicht) hätte passieren sollen. Drücken Sie seine Gedanken im Vergangenheitskonjunktiv mit einem Doppelinfinitiv aus.

S1 (ANNA): *Wir sind nicht ins Schloss Charlottenburg gegangen.*
S2 (ONKEL WERNER): *Wir hätten ins Schloss Charlottenburg gehen sollen.*

1. Wir sind nicht ins Schloss Charlottenburg gegangen. (Wir …)
2. Ich habe die Kaiser-Wilhelms-Gedächtniskirche vergessen. (Du …) *hättest die KWG nicht vergessen sollen.*
3. Wir haben die Aufführung von Brechts „Dreigroschenoper" verpasst. (Wir …)
4. Wir sind einfach am Brandenburger Tor vorbeigelaufen. (Wir …)
5. Wir sind in Kreuzberg nicht türkisch essen gegangen. (Wir …)
6. Du hast deine Kamera vergessen. (Ich …)
7. Ich habe meinen Studentenausweis vergessen. (Du …)
8. Wir sind nicht nach Potsdam gefahren. (Wir …)
9. Du hast mir das neue Regierungsviertel nicht gezeigt. (Ich …)
10. Wir haben den Reichstag nicht besichtigt. (Wir …)

## II Talking about unreal situations

In Section I you used the subjunctive mood to propose activities, to make polite requests and suggestions, and to express possibility and potential. This subjunctive form is called the subjunctive II (**Konjunktiv II**).

### A. Expressing unreal conditions: *Wenn-clauses*

A conditional sentence (**der Konditionalsatz**) may express a hypothetical, unreal speculative, or contrary-to-fact situation (**irrealer Konditionalsatz**). In this case the subjunctive II is always used.

| | |
|---|---|
| Anna **würde** mehr machen, wenn sie mehr Zeit **hätte.** | *Anna would do more if she had more time. (But she has no time, so she can't do more.)* |
| Was **könnten** wir machen, wenn wir mehr Zeit **hätten?** | *What could we do if we had more time?* |

The **wenn**-clause with the conjugated verb in final position frequently introduces the conditional sentence. The main clause, with the conjugated verb in the first position, follows the **wenn**-clause. This results in two conjugated verbs occurring side by side.

> Wenn er netter **wäre, würde**    *If he were nicer, I would call him more often.*
>   ich ihn öfter anrufen.          *(But he's not nice, so I won't call him.)*

Informal German allows the use of **würde** in **wenn**-clauses while more formal German requires the single subjunctive II verb form.

> *Formal German:* Das wäre toll, wenn    *That would be great if you visited us.*
>   du uns **besuchtest.**
> *Informal German:* Es wäre toll,        *It would be great if you*
>   wenn du uns **besuchen würdest.**        *visited us.*

In formal English, too, it is considered improper to use *would* in an *if*-clause, but it is very common in speech (e.g., If she would come to Austria . . .).

To express hypothetical past-time events, German uses the past tense of the subjunctive II.

> Wenn Anna nicht nach Tübingen **gekommen wäre, hätte** sie Stefan nicht
>   **kennen gelernt.**
> *If Anna had not come to Tübingen, she would not have met Stefan.*
>   *(But she came to Tübingen and she met him.)*

## B. Subjunctive II forms of regular, irregular, and mixed verbs

In **Kapitel 9** you learned that the subjunctive II forms for **haben, sein,** and **werden** are formed by adding an umlaut to the narrative past form.

German has another subjunctive form, the subjunctive I (**Konjunktiv I**). Speakers use it primarily for indirect speech, but since the subjunctive II frequently replaces the subjunctive I in indirect speech, it is not discussed in this book. The most common form is **sei** (< **sein**).

| Infinitive | Narrative past | Subjunctive II |
|------------|----------------|----------------|
| haben      | ich hatte      | ich hätte      |
| sein       | ich war        | ich wäre       |
| werden     | ich wurde      | ich würde      |

In speech, German speakers mostly use **würde** with an infinitive when expressing hypothetical situations in the present tense.

### 1. Regular (weak) verbs

Regular (weak) verbs look identical in the narrative past and in the subjunctive II. To form the subjunctive II, add **-te** to the present tense stem, followed by the endings **-st, -t,** or **-n.** These are the subjective II forms of **machen.**

Due to the similarity of the subjunctive II and the narrative past indicative of weak verbs and to the fact that native speakers do not often use these forms, only the **würde**-form will be practiced for production.

| machen: *to do; to make* | |
|---------|---------|
| **Singular** | **Plural** |
| ich mach**te** | wir mach**ten** |
| du mach**test** | ihr mach**tet** |
| Sie mach**ten** | Sie mach**ten** |
| er/sie/es mach**te** | sie mach**ten** |

Because the narrative past and subjunctive II forms of regular verbs are identical, German speakers prefer to use **würde** + infinitive in the present tense subjunctive II.

> Wenn ich Zeit **hätte, machte** ich einen Bummel auf dem Kurfürstendamm.
> Wenn ich Zeit **hätte, würde** ich einen Bummel auf dem Kurfürstendamm **machen.**
> *If I had time, I would go for a stroll on the Kurfürstendamm.*

**17    Was würde Stefan (Anna) machen, wenn …?**  Fragen Sie einen Partner/eine Partnerin, was Anna oder Stefan in den folgenden Situationen machen würde. Fragen Sie dann, was Ihr Partner/Ihre Partnerin machen würde. Benutzen Sie **würde** + Infinitiv.

> S1: *Was würde Stefan machen, wenn er mehr Geld hätte?*
> S2: *Wenn Stefan mehr Geld hätte, würde er eine Reise machen.*
> S1: *Was würdest du machen, wenn du mehr Geld hättest?*
> S2: *Ich würde (ins Ausland reisen).*

> **Was würde Stefan (Anna) machen, wenn …** You should recognize the verbs in both **Tabellen** as the subjunctive II forms of common weak verbs.

**Tabelle A (S1):**

| Wenn er/sie … | Stefan | Anna | Partner(in) |
|---|---|---|---|
| mehr Geld hätte | ? | kaufte sie ein neues Auto | _____ |
| mehr Zeit hätte | besuchte er seine Eltern | ? | _____ |
| Lust hätte | schickte er Anna Blumen | ? | _____ |
| Freunde in Berlin hätte | ? | wohnte sie ein Jahr lang dort | _____ |
| die Unterlagen hätte | schickte er sie ein | ? | _____ |
| mit dem Studium fertig wäre | ? | bezahlte sie nichts mehr dafür | _____ |

**Tabelle B (S2):**

| Wenn er/sie ... | Stefan | Anna | Partner(in) |
|---|---|---|---|
| mehr Geld hätte | machte er eine Reise | ? | _____ |
| mehr Zeit hätte | ? | besuchte sie die Günthers | |
| Lust hätte | ? | lernte sie Spanisch | _____ |
| Freunde in Berlin hätte | hörte er auf, in Tübingen zu studieren | ? | _____ |
| die Unterlagen hätte | ? | reichte sie die Unterlagen ein | |
| mit dem Studium fertig wäre | arbeitete er im Ausland | ? | _____ |

## 2. Irregular (strong) verbs

The subjunctive II forms of irregular (strong) verbs add the endings **-e, -est, -en,** or **-et** to the stem of the narrative past verb (**Präteritum**). Stems with **a, o,** and **u** also add an umlaut.

| *Infinitive* | *Narrative past* | *Subjunctive II* | *Meaning* |
|---|---|---|---|
| kommen | er kam | er k**ä**m**e** | (*if*) *he came/would come* |

These are the subjunctive II forms of **kommen.**

| **kommen:** *to come* | |
|---|---|
| **Singular** | **Plural** |
| ich **käme** | wir **kämen** |
| du **kämest** | ihr **kämet** |
| Sie **kämen** | Sie **kämen** |
| er/sie/es **käme** | sie **kämen** |

The following chart lists the most frequently used irregular (strong) verbs in the subjunctive II.

| Infinitive | Subjunctive II | Infinitive | Subjunctive II |
|---|---|---|---|
| bleiben | ich **bliebe** | kommen | ich **käme** |
| fahren | ich **führe** | nehmen | ich **nähme** |
| finden | ich **fände** | sprechen | ich **spräche** |
| geben | ich **gäbe** | stehen | ich **stünde** |
| gehen | ich **ginge** | tun | ich **täte** |

| | |
|---|---|
| Wenn es etwas zu essen **gäbe, bliebe** ich hier. | *If there were something to eat, I would stay here.* |
| Es **ginge** mir besser, wenn wir nicht so weit **führen.** | *I would feel better if we weren't driving so far.* |

There are many other subjunctive II forms of irregular verbs that German speakers generally avoid in speech because they are archaic, (e.g., **hülfe**), or because they sound like non-subjunctive forms (e.g., **nähme** vs. **nehme**).

## 3. Mixed verbs

Mixed verbs add **-t** plus the endings **-e, -st, -t,** or **-n** to the stem like regular verbs. Some have a vowel change like irregular verbs in the subjunctive II, and others do not. The only mixed verb that is used with any frequency is **wüsste.** The others almost always occur with **würde,** e.g., **würde bringen, würde denken.**

| Infinitive | Subjunctive II |
|------------|----------------|
| bringen | br**ä**chte |
| denken | d**ä**chte |
| kennen | kennte |
| nennen | nennte |
| rennen | rennte |
| wissen | w**ü**sste |

> The verb **brauchen** frequently forms its subjunctive II like a mixed verb, **bräuchte.**

  **18**   **Annas Besuch in Berlin.**  Sprechen Sie über Annas Besuch in Berlin. Verbinden Sie die richtigen Satzteile.

1. Wenn es nicht zu viel zu tun gäbe,
2. Wenn es nicht so viele Touristen gäbe,
3. Wenn es ihr besser ginge,
4. Wenn sie mehr Zeit hätte,
5. Wenn die Autofahrer nicht so schnell führen,
6. Wenn die Berliner nicht so schnell sprächen,

a. könnte Anna länger unterwegs sein, aber sie muss zum Arzt.

b. könnte Anna sie besser verstehen.

c. müsste Anna nicht so schnell überall hinfahren.

d. bliebe Anna länger in Berlin, aber sie muss zurück nach Tübingen.

e. wäre die Schlange nicht so lang.

f. würde Anna auch gern in Berlin Auto fahren, aber sie hat Angst.

## Freie Kommunikation

**Rollenspiel: Besuch aus Deutschland.**  Sie haben einen Besucher/eine Besucherin aus Deutschland und Sie möchten ihm/ihr Ihre Stadt zeigen. Besprechen Sie, was Sie zusammen in Ihrer Stadt unternehmen können. Was würde diese Person interessieren? Stellen Sie Fragen und machen Sie Vorschläge.

S1 (SIE):  *Wir könnten zusammen in den Zoo gehen.*
S2 (BESUCHER/IN):  *Das wäre O.K., aber ich würde lieber schwimmen gehen.*
S1:  *Schwimmen wäre auch möglich. Wir könnten auch zu einem amerikanischen Footballspiel gehen.*
S2:  *Das wäre …*

zum Strand fahren • wandern • ins Rockkonzert gehen • zum Rodeo gehen • zu einem amerikanischen Footballspiel  gehen
• Sehenswürdigkeiten ansehen • klettern° • ins Museum gehen          *climbing*

**Ihre Sorgen. Mein Rat.**  Frau Maria Burg schreibt für eine Zeitung und beantwortet Fragen der Leser/Leserinnen. Sie bekommt viele Briefe von Frauen und
Männern, die Antworten auf ihre Probleme suchen. Lesen Sie die Probleme der
folgenden Personen und schreiben Sie Frau Burgs Antwortbrief(e). Benutzen Sie
den Konjunktiv (z. B. **An Ihrer Stelle hätte ich …; Ich würde das …**).

> This is a summary of
> authentic letters seeking
> advice from Maria Burg.

**Lutz F.:**
Sucht eine Partnerin, bisher ohne Erfolg. Er schreibt, dass Frauen in seinem Alter
(53) nur Sex und Geld suchen. Sein Hund ist sein bester Freund.

**Anna G.:**
Ihre Tochter Peggy hat keinen Mann. Jetzt schreibt Peggy intensiv an ihrer Dok-
torarbeit. Die Chancen, einen Mann zu finden, werden immer schlechter. Anna
möchte, dass ihre Tochter Peggy heiratet.

---

**Absprungtext**    **Die Geschichte Berlins**

## Vorschau

Berlin hat in der deutschen Geschichte eine wichtige Rolle gespielt. Zu verschiedenen Zeiten war Berlin Hauptstadt, Regierungssitz°, Kulturzentrum und
auch das Hauptquartier Adolf Hitlers. Später wurde Berlin Brennpunkt° des
Kalten Krieges und die Hauptstadt der Deutschen Demokratischen Republik,
bevor es die Hauptstadt des vereinten Deutschlands wurde. In der Geschichte
Berlins spiegelt sich die politische Geschichte Deutschlands wider°.

*seat of government*
*focal point*

**spiegelt sich wider:** *is reflected*

**19  Was ist das?**  Finden Sie für jede Definition in der linken Spalte den passenden Begriff oder Namen in der rechten Spalte.

| | |
|---|---|
| 1. das deutsche Parlament | a. das Dritte Reich |
| 2. moderner deutscher Regierungschef (wie z. B. der Premierminister in Kanada) | b. der Bundestag |
| | c. die Republik |
| 3. der Führer | d. das Grundgesetz |
| 4. moderne Staatsform in Deutschland | e. der Bundeskanzler |
| 5. der deutsche Monarch von früher | f. Adolf Hitler |
| 6. das zeremonielle Oberhaupt° Deutschlands (wie z. B. die Königin in Großbritannien) | g. der Kaiser    *head of state* |
| | h. die Weimarer Republik |
| 7. die erste deutsche Republik (1918–1933) | i. der Bundespräsident |
| 8. die Verfassung° der Bundesrepublik | *constitution* |
| 9. nationalsozialistische Diktatur | |

**20  Zeittafel: Was wissen Sie schon?**  Welche Daten gehören zu welchen Ereignissen°?    *events*

| Daten | Ereignisse |
|---|---|
| 1. 1918 | a. Ex-DDR wird Teil der Bundesrepublik Deutschland. |
| 2. 1933 | b. Die DDR baut die Mauer um West-Berlin. |
| 3. 1945 | c. Der 1. Weltkrieg endet. |
| 4. 1961 | d. Der 2. Weltkrieg endet. |
| 5. 1989 | e. Die Berliner Mauer fällt. DDR-Bürger dürfen in den Westen. |
| 6. 1990 | f. Hitler und die Nazis kommen an die Macht. |

9. NOVEMBER 1989 FRIEDLICHER AUFBRUCH ZUR DEUTSCHEN EINHEIT

GRÜNES BERLIN

Britzer Garten *Neukölln*
Pfaueninsel *Zehlendorf*
Erholungspark Marzahn *Marzahn*
Gärten im Luisenstädtischen Kanal *Kreuzberg*
Tiergarten *Tiergarten*
Viktoriapark *Kreuzberg*

Unter den Linden

**21  Thematische Fragen.**  Beantworten Sie die folgenden Fragen auf Deutsch.

1. Berlin ist jetzt die Hauptstadt Deutschlands. Wie hieß die Hauptstadt der Bundesrepublik im Jahre 1989?
2. Was assoziieren Sie mit Berlin?
3. Warum spielt Berlin so eine wichtige Rolle in der Weltgeschichte?
4. Kennen Sie den Namen Bismarck? Warum ist er eine wichtige Persönlichkeit der deutschen Geschichte?

---

**Sprache im Alltag: Special meanings of Wende**

The verb **wenden** means *to turn,* and the noun **die Wende** can refer to any significant turn of events or change. Today it generally refers to 1990, the time when East Germany was formally reunited with West Germany, the most profound change in postwar German history.

BRENNPUNKT KULTUR

## Deutschland: von der Monarchie zur Demokratie (III)

Throughout the Cold War (**der Kalte Krieg**), the tensions between East and West were nowhere more obvious than in Berlin. West Berlin became everything that East Berlin was not: affluent, colorful, free-spirited, and western. East Berlin and East Germany, in contrast, became a Marxist worker's state and socialist economy that was a model to Eastern Bloc countries.

As a so-called worker's state, where pro-communist, anti-fascist sentiment found a home, the **DDR** developed a strong economy and guaranteed full employment, inexpensive housing, universal health care, child care, and free education for all its citizens. Nevertheless, dissatisfaction with socialism existed at grassroots levels in the **DDR**. In 1953, workers in East Berlin staged a spontaneous revolt against productivity quotas and price hikes but were crushed by Soviet forces. As life in East Germany became more and more repressive and borders became harder to cross, many (20,000 per day by the late 1950s) attempted to flee to the West via Berlin, where movement between the different parts of the city was basically unrestricted. To end the drain on its workforce, the **DDR** began to construct a wall around West Berlin during the night of August 13, 1961. It became known to the rest of the world as "The Wall" (**die Mauer**). Even though the Berlin Wall encircled West Berlin, it was the East Berliners and East Germans who were truly locked in.

*(a) Der Deutsche Bundestag hat seinen Sitz im renovierten Reichstagsgebäude mit der neuen Glaskuppel.*

*(b) Berlin nach dem Zweiten Weltkrieg.*

In 1989, the brave citizens of Leipzig in the **DDR** started weekly demonstrations against the East German state. That summer, East Germans vacationing in Czechoslovakia and Hungary stormed embassies and borders demanding access to the West. On November 9, 1989, fearing another mass flight of refugees to the West, East German authorities opened borders to the West for the first time in 28 years. The wall in Berlin came down, dismantled in part by jubilant Germans in the streets. This was the beginning of the end for the **DDR**: within a year, the East German People's Parliament (**Volkskammer**) voted the socialist state out of existence (**die Wende**, *the Turning Point*). On October 3, 1990, the reunification of Germany (**die Wiedervereinigung**) was completed. As stipulated by the German Constitution, the capital of unified Germany returned to Berlin. In 1999 the parliament building (**der Reichstag**) was rededicated as the seat of the German Parliament (**der Bundestag**) in Berlin.

In national elections, voters select the political party of their choice. The majority party wins the election and its leader becomes the federal chancellor (**der Bundeskanzler**). If

there is no clear majority, the leading party forms a coalition government with another political party and shares power. The president (**der Bundespräsident**) is the ceremonial head of the German state.

*Eine Sitzung des Bundestags im renovierten Reichstagsgebäude.*

*Good Bye Lenin!* (2003) is a hugely popular film set in 1990. It deals with a son's extraordinary efforts to keep the collapse of the **DDR** from his terminally ill mother. This reflected a nationwide period of nostalgia for the East called **Ostalgie.**

■ **Kulturkreuzung** Manche Menschen haben Konflikte mit ihrem Staat. Wann würden Sie Ihre Heimat verlassen, wie die Menschen in der ehemaligen DDR? Wann haben Sie das letzte Mal wegen Ihrer Nation ein Gefühl von Euphorie oder Schock gehabt?

## Lesestrategien: Die Geschichte Berlins

Benutzen Sie die folgenden Strategien, um den Text zu verstehen.

**22** **Den Kontext herstellen.** Finden Sie im **Absprungtext** Antworten auf die folgenden Fragen.

1. Welche drei wichtigen Persönlichkeiten werden hier genannt?
2. In welchem Jahr sind die folgenden Ereignisse passiert?

- die nationalsozialistische Machtergreifung (das Dritte Reich)
- die Gründung° der Bundesrepublik Deutschland          *founding*
- die Gründung der Weimarer Republik
- die Gründung des Zweiten Deutschen Reiches
- der Beitritt der DDR zur Bundesrepublik Deutschland
- die Gründung der Deutschen Demokratischen Republik

**23** **Strategien verwenden.** Können Sie diese neuen Wörter ungefähr verstehen? Versuchen Sie, die fett gedruckten Wörter zu erraten. Benutzen Sie die Strategien, die Sie gelernt haben.

*Strategie 1: Weltwissen*

1. **die Machtergreifung:** Hitler ist auf legale Weise Reichskanzler geworden. Der Kanzler hat die **Macht** zu regieren. Hitler hat dann sehr schnell auf illegale Weise mehr Macht genommen oder ergriffen. Spricht man in den USA von einer Machtergreifung bei der Präsidentenwahl? Haben die Bolschewiken in Russland die Macht bekommen oder ergriffen?

2. **statt·finden:** Alle vier Jahre finden in den USA die Wahlen für die Präsidentschaft statt. Alle vier Jahre finden die Olympischen Spiele statt. Wie oft findet ein Test im Deutschkurs statt?

3. **besetzen:** Wenn man die Toilette nicht benutzen kann, weil jemand anders sie benutzt, sagt man: *Die Toilette ist besetzt.* Im militärischen Kontext ist ein Land besetzt, wenn ein ausländisches Militär die Macht hat. Welche Länder haben die Nazis im Krieg besetzt?

4. **Siegermächte:** Das sind die Mächte oder Länder, die einen Krieg gewinnen. Wer war im Jahr 1945 eine Siegermacht – die USA oder Nazi-Deutschland?

5. **verwalten:** Die Verwaltung ist der Staatsapparat oder die Bürokratie. Wer hat Deutschland nach dem Krieg verwaltet?

6. **das Abkommen:** Wenn zwei Staaten zu einem Verständnis kommen, dokumentieren sie das Verständnis in einem **Abkommen.** Haben die USA Abkommen mit Kanada oder Kuba?

> **die Abkommen** = plural form

*Strategie 2: Kontext*

1. **zerstören:** Wenn man etwas **zerstört,** macht man es kaputt. Die Nazis haben viele jüdische° Geschäfte in der Kristallnacht zerstört. Welchen Teil eines Hauses oder eines Geschäftes kann man leicht mit einem Stock° zerstören?

2. **vollenden:** Etwas ist nur dann **vollendet,** wenn man alle Ziele erreicht° und vielleicht sogar perfektioniert hat. Dann hat man nicht nur das Ende erreicht, man hat etwas **vollendet.** Hat Hitler seine Pläne für ein Drittes Reich vollendet?

3. **bei·treten** (+ *dat.*): Wenn man Mitglied bei einem Klub, einer Organisation oder einer Partei wird, tritt man der Organisation bei. Was bedeutet wohl **beitreten?**

4. **um·siedeln:** Wenn man von einer Stadt zu einer anderen Stadt umzieht, siedelt man um. Ist der deutsche Regierungssitz 1999 von oder nach Bonn umgesiedelt?

> *Jewish*
> *stick*
> *has reached*

*Strategie 3: Wortformen*

1. **erobern:** Sowjetische Soldaten kamen als erste nach Berlin. Die Sowjets hatten die Kontrolle. Die Nazis kapitulierten, und die Sowjets hatten Berlin erobert. Welches Land hat Japan im Zweiten Weltkrieg erobert?

2. **die Arbeitsnorm:** Eine Norm ist ein Standard oder eine Quote. Was für Normen hat man am Arbeitsplatz?

3. **erhöhen:** Von welchem Adjektiv ist **höher** die Komparativform? Das Präfix **er-** findet man auch in **erhärten (hart werden)** und **erstarken (stark werden).** Was bedeutet wohl das Verb **erhöhen?**

4. **der Aufstand:** Von welchem Verb stammt dieses Nomen? Stellen Sie sich die Bewegung im Verb **auf·stehen** vor: ist sie aktiv oder passiv? Nun stellen Sie sich diese Aktion als politische Aktion vor: ist sie freundlich oder aggressiv? Was wäre ein gutes Synonym für das Wort **Aufstand?**

5. **der Widerstand:** Wenn man aktiv gegen eine politische Struktur kämpft, die man für unmenschlich hält, leistet° man politischen **Widerstand.** Wogegen hat Dr. Martin Luther King Widerstand geleistet?

*leisten: to undertake, put up*

## Absprungtext
### Die Geschichte Berlins, 1740–2002

Lesen Sie jetzt den Text.

**1740**  Friedrich II. (Friedrich der Große) wird König von Preußen. Berlin gewinnt als Hauptstadt Preußens europäischen Rang°.

*status*

**1871**  Gründung des Deutschen Reiches. Berlin wird Residenz des deutschen Kaisers (Wilhelm I.) und Reichshauptstadt.

**1918**  (9. November) Vom Balkon des Reichstages in Berlin ruft der Sozialdemokrat Philipp Scheidemann die „Deutsche Republik" aus°. Berlin ist Hauptstadt der Weimarer Republik.

*ausrufen: proklamieren*

**1933**  Machtergreifung der Nationalsozialisten. Hitler wird Reichskanzler. Berlin wird Zentrum der nationalsozialistischen Diktatur, aber auch des Widerstandes.

**1936**  Die XI. Olympischen Sommerspiele finden in Berlin statt.

**1938**  (9. November) Reichspogromnacht („Kristallnacht"). Jüdische Geschäfte werden von den Nazis zerstört.

**1945**  Berlin wird durch die Rote Armee erobert. Berlin wird von den vier Siegermächten (USA, UdSSR, Großbritannien, Frankreich) besetzt und verwaltet.

**1948/49** Die Blockade Berlins: Die Stadt wird politisch geteilt. Die westlichen Alliierten reagieren mit der „Luftbrücke", dem größten Lufttransportunternehmen der Geschichte.

**1949**  Aus den westdeutschen Besatzungszonen wird die Bundesrepublik Deutschland mit Hauptstadt Bonn gegründet. Aus der sowjetischen Besatzungszone entsteht die Deutsche Demokratische Republik mit Hauptstadt Berlin (Ost).

**1953**  (17. Juni) Die Arbeitsnormen und auch die Preise für Lebensmittel werden in Ost-Berlin erhöht. Es kommt zum Aufstand Ost-Berliner Arbeiter.

**1961**  (13. August) Die Stadt wird durch den Bau der Mauer geteilt.

**1963**  Berlin wird vom amerikanischen Präsidenten Kennedy besucht. („Ich bin ein Berliner.")

In his famous 1963 speech, President Kennedy expressed the West's unflinching support for West Berlin by stating in German: **Ich bin ein Berliner.** Kennedy's visit to Berlin as the Cold War escalated demonstrated Allied resolve to keep West Berlin free.

**1972**    Das Vier-Mächte-Abkommen regelt den Transit sowie Reisen und Besuche in die DDR. *treaty*

**1989**    (9. November) Die Mauer fällt: Die Grenzen zu West-Berlin und zur
Bundesrepublik Deutschland werden von der DDR geöffnet.

**1990**    (3. Oktober) Die DDR tritt der Bundesrepublik Deutschland nach Artikel 23 des Grundgesetzes bei. Die deutsche Einheit ist vollendet.

**1999**    Die Regierung siedelt offiziell nach Berlin um.

**2002**    (3. Oktober) Die zentralen Feierlichkeiten der Bundesrepublik zum Tag
der Deutschen Einheit finden am restaurierten Brandenburger Tor statt.
*renoviert*

Die deutsche Wiedervereinigung
wird am Brandenburger Tor
gefeiert.

## *Rückblick*

 **24**   **Was wissen Sie jetzt von Berlin?** Wählen Sie die richtige Antwort.

1. Zur Zeit Friedrichs des Großen war Berlin die Hauptstadt von \_\_\_\_\_.
   a. Preußen        b. Weimar        c. der Bundesrepublik Deutschland

2. Der Reichstag steht \_\_\_\_\_.
   a. in Weimar      b. in Berlin      c. in Bonn

3. Berlin war die Hauptstadt der ersten deutschen Republik von \_\_\_\_\_.
   a. 1871–1918    b. 1918–1933    c. 1933–1945

4. Von 1949 bis 1989 war Berlin (Ost) die Hauptstadt von \_\_\_\_\_.
   a. der Deutschen Demokratischen Republik
   b. der Bundesrepublik Deutschland
   c. dem Freistaat Bayern

5. Der afro-amerikanische Sportler Jesse Owens hat 1936 in Berlin an \_\_\_\_\_
   teilgenommen.
   a. den Olympischen Spielen
   b. der Kristallnacht
   c. der Eroberung Berlins

6. Die Luftbrücke \_\_\_\_\_.
   a. ist eine Brücke über die Spree in Berlin-Mitte
   b. war der Transport von Gütern und Lebensmitteln für West-Berliner per
      Flugzeug
   c. war 1953 in Ost-Berlin

7. Präsident Kennedy hat in Berlin _____.
   a. Urlaub gemacht
   b. studiert
   c. eine sehr wichtige Rede während des Kalten Krieges gehalten

8. 1961 baute die DDR eine Mauer _____.
   a. um West-Berlin
   b. durch die Mitte Ost-Berlins
   c. um Ost-Berlin

9. Während des Kalten Krieges waren in Berlin Truppen von _____ stationiert.
   a. den USA, Frankreich, Großbritannien und der UdSSR
   b. den USA und der UdSSR
   c. der UNO

> Complete the **Ergänzen Sie** activity in your workbook for this text before doing the next activity.

**25  Kurz gefragt/Kurz interpretiert.** Beantworten Sie diese Fragen auf Deutsch.

1. Schauen Sie sich eine Karte von Deutschland an. Wo liegt Berlin: im Nordwesten, im Nordosten oder im Südwesten von Deutschland?
2. Welchen Einfluss hat Berlins geographische Lage auf seine politische Rolle?
3. Für viele Ausländer ist Berlin das Symbol von Nazi-Deutschland. Ist dieses Image gerechtfertigt°? Was meinen Sie?
4. Welche symbolische Rolle spielte Berlin zur Zeit des Kalten Krieges für die Siegermächte? Für die Ostdeutschen? Für die Westdeutschen?
5. Berlin hat eine negative und eine tragische Geschichte. Wie sehen Sie die Rolle Berlins in der Zukunft?

*justified*

## Strukturen und Vokabeln

## III  Talking about actions as a process

### The passive voice

#### A. *The passive voice: present tense*

In most sentences the grammatical subject performs the action described by the verb. This subject is called the *agent,* and it is the focus of the sentence. The verb in these sentences uses the form of the active voice.

    *subject and agent*                     *direct subject*
    <u>Philipp Scheidemann</u> ruft die „<u>Deutsche Republik</u>" aus.
    *Philipp Scheidemann proclaims the "German Republic."*

**Philipp Scheidemann** is the grammatical subject as well as the agent in this sentence.

> The present passive in German is the equivalent of two possible tenses in English—the simple present and the present continuous. For example, **Bücher werden jeden Tag in der Bibliothek gelesen.** (*Books **are read** every day in the library.*) and **Das Museum wird momentan renoviert.** (*The museum **is** currently **being renovated.***)

Sometimes, however, it is important to focus on the process (**Vorgang**) and not on the agent. This occurs when the agent or performer of the action is not known at all or may simply not be as important as the action itself. In these sentences the passive voice (**das Passiv**) is used. Frequently the agent is not even mentioned in the passive. When it is included, it appears after the verb **werden** in a dative case **von** phrase.

> The passive voice is often used in newspaper articles, instructions, and instances where there is reason not to mention the agent.

| | |
|---|---|
| Die Deutsche Republik **wird** (von Philipp Scheidemann) **ausgerufen**. | *The German Republic is proclaimed (by Philipp Scheidemann).* |
| Jüdische Geschäfte **werden** (von den Nazis) **zerstört**. | *Jewish businesses are being destroyed (by the Nazis).* |

Notice that the present tense of the passive voice (**das Passiv Präsens**) is formed with a conjugated form of the verb **werden** and a past participle, which expresses the meaning of the action. The grammatical subject is not the agent in a passive sentence. In main clauses, the conjugated form of **werden** occurs in the second position and the past participle comes last in the clause.

| **geliebt werden:** *to be loved* | | | |
|---|---|---|---|
| **Singular** | | **Plural** | |
| ich **werde geliebt** | *I am loved* | wir **werden geliebt** | *we are loved* |
| du **wirst geliebt** | *you are loved* | ihr **werdet geliebt** | *you are loved* |
| Sie **werden geliebt** | *you are loved* | Sie **werden geliebt** | *you are loved* |
| er/sie/es **wird geliebt** | *he/she/it is loved* | sie **werden geliebt** | *they are loved* |

**26** **Was wird hier gemacht?** Verbinden Sie eine Sehenswürdigkeit in Berlin mit einer passenden Passiv-Konstruktion.

■ in der Bibliothek an der Humboldt-Universität

> S1: *Was wird in der Bibliothek an der Humboldt-Universität gemacht?*
> S2: *Hier werden viele Bücher gelesen.*

1. in der Bibliothek an der Humboldt-Universität
2. am Brandenburger Tor
3. auf dem Kurfürstendamm
4. in der Clubszene im Prenzlauer Berg
5. in den Cafés am Alexanderplatz
6. im Reichstag

a. Andenken von Berlin werden verkauft und gekauft.
b. Viele Bücher werden gelesen.
c. Neue Gesetze° werden gemacht.          *laws*
d. Musik wird gemacht.
e. Viele Fotos werden gemacht.
f. Kaffee wird getrunken.

**27** **Das geht leider nicht.** Onkel Werner und Anna besprechen, was sie machen können. Leider können sie nicht alles machen, was sie machen wollen. Viele Sehenswürdigkeiten sind gerade geschlossen.

S1 (ANNA): *Wie wäre es mit dem Pergamonmuseum?*
S2 (WERNER): *Tja, das geht leider nicht. Das Pergamonmuseum wird momentan renoviert.*

1. das Pergamonmuseum / momentan renovieren
2. die Philharmonie / wegen Regenschaden° reparieren
3. das Schloss Charlottenburg / von oben bis unten putzen
4. die Gedächtniskirche / heute wegen einer Veranstaltung° schließen
5. das Museum für deutsche Geschichte / neu organisieren
6. das Neue Museum auf der Museumsinsel / renovieren
7. die Kongresshalle / für die nächste Konferenz sauber machen
8. das Schloss Sanssouci / außen und innen putzen

*wegen Regenschaden:*
 *because of rain damage*

*event*

## B. The passive voice: narrative and conversational past

### 1. Narrative past tense

The narrative past tense of the passive voice (**das Passiv Präteritum**) is formed with the narrative past tense forms of **werden** and a participle at the end of the clause.

Die Grenzen zu West-Berlin **wurden**      *The borders to West Berlin were*
 1989 **geöffnet.**                                  *opened in 1989.*

| **wurde angerufen:** *was called* | | | |
|---|---|---|---|
| **Singular** | | **Plural** | |
| ich **wurde angerufen** | *I was called* | wir **wurden angerufen** | *we were called* |
| du **wurdest angerufen** | *you were called* | ihr **wurdet angerufen** | *you were called* |
| Sie **wurden angerufen** | *you were called* | Sie **wurden angerufen** | *you were called* |
| er/sie/es **wurde angerufen** | *he/she/it was called* | sie **wurden angerufen** | *they were called* |

### 2. Conversational past and past perfect of the passive

The conversational past of the passive voice (**das Passiv Perfekt**) is formed with the past participle of the verb expressing the action and the conversational past of the verb **werden**. The conversational past of the verb **werden** consists of a conjugated form of **sein** and the shortened past participle **worden.**

Ich **bin** vor einer Stunde **angerufen worden**.   *I was/got called one hour ago.*

The past perfect passive (**das Passiv Plusquamperfekt**) is formed with the past participle of the verb expressing the action and a form of the past perfect of the verb **werden.**

Ich **war** schon **angerufen worden.**   *I had already been called.*

The past perfect passive is for recognition only.

The passive is frequently formed in informal English with the verb *get*, e.g., *The car got hit by a bus.*

The conversational past passive and the past perfect passive always consist of three verbs:

1. a conjugated form of **sein** (e.g., **bin** in the conversational past or **war** in the past perfect)
2. the past participle of the verb expressing the action (e.g., **angerufen**)
3. **worden** (a shortened form of the past participle of **werden**). In the past perfect passive the past participle is followed by **worden** and comes last in main clauses.

Here is the conjugation of **an·rufen** in the conversational past passive.

| **angerufen worden:** *was/have been called* | | |
|---|---|---|
| **Singular** | **Plural** | |
| ich **bin angerufen worden** | wir **sind angerufen worden** | |
| du **bist angerufen worden** | ihr **seid angerufen worden** | |
| Sie **sind angerufen worden** | Sie **sind angerufen worden** | |
| er/sie/es **ist angerufen worden** | sie **sind angerufen worden** | |

Here is a summary chart of tenses in the passive voice.

| **Present** | Er **wird angerufen.** | *He is (being) called.* |
|---|---|---|
| **Narrative past** | Er **wurde angerufen.** | *He was called.* |
| **Conversational past** | Er **ist angerufen worden.** | *He was/has been called.* |
| **Past perfect** | Er **war angerufen worden.** | *He had been called.* |

**28**   **Wann ist das gemacht worden?**  Beschreiben Sie diese Ereignisse aus der deutschen Geschichte. Benutzen Sie das Passiv.

▪ die Mauer / abreißen°                                                           *tear down*

   S1:  *Wann ist die Mauer abgerissen worden?*
   S2:  *Die Mauer ist 1990 abgerissen worden.*

   1918      1938      1949      1953      1961      1972      1989      2002

1. die Mauer / öffnen 1989
2. die Bundesrepublik Deutschland und die DDR / gründen 1949
3. die deutsche Einheit / am neuen Brandenburger Tor / feiern 2002
4. die Mauer / bauen 1961
5. die Arbeitsnormen in Ost-Berlin / erhöhen 1953
6. die Weimarer Republik / ausrufen 1918
7. jüdische Geschäfte in der „Kristallnacht" / zerstören 1938
8. der Transit zwischen Ost und West / regeln 1972

**29**  **Eine Zeittafel für Ihre Heimatstadt.**  Schreiben Sie eine Zeittafel für Ihre Heimatstadt mit mindestens fünf wichtigen Ereignissen. Die folgende Liste enthält einige Ideen.

- das neue Schwimmbad  *Das neue Schwimmbad ist 1994 gebaut worden.*

| | | | | |
|---|---|---|---|---|
| das Schwimmbad | ist | gegründet | worden | |
| das Einkaufszentrum° | | erweitert° | | *mall / expanded* |
| die Schule | | gebaut | | |
| unser Haus | | abgerissen | | |
| die Autobahn | | zerstört | | |
| das Autokino | | renoviert | | |
| die Innenstadt | | geschlossen | | |
| das Sportstadion | | wieder aufgebaut | | |
| die Kirche | | | | |

**30**  **Das 20. Jahrhundert.**  Stellen Sie einem Partner / einer Partnerin Fragen mit **von**. Beantworten Sie die Fragen mit einem Passiv-Satz. Wechseln Sie sich ab.

- die Deutsche Republik ausrufen

    S1:  *Von wem ist die Deutsche Republik ausgerufen worden?*
    S2:  *Die Deutsche Republik ist von Philipp Scheidemann ausgerufen worden.*

    die DDR • Philipp Scheidemann • der deutsche Kaiser • die Siegermächte • die Alliierten • John F. Kennedy • die Nazis • Adolf Hitler

1. die Deutsche Republik ausrufen
2. die jüdischen Geschäfte und Synagogen zerstören
3. Deutschland nach dem Krieg besetzen
4. die Mauer bauen
5. die Macht ergreifen
6. Berlin im Jahre 1963 besuchen
7. die Luftbrücke organisieren
8. Preußen regieren

## C. The impersonal passive

Both English and German allow passive sentences to be formed from an active sentence with a direct object.

**Active**

|  |  |
|---|---|
| *direct object* | *direct object* |
| Die DDR hat **die Grenze** geöffnet. | *The GDR opened **the border**.* |

**Passive**

|  |  |
|---|---|
| **Die Grenze** ist von der DDR geöffnet worden. | ***The border** was opened by the GDR.* |

Unlike English, however, German has passive constructions with no corresponding direct object in the active sentence. These expressions have only approximate equivalents in English. There are two frequently occurring types of passive sentences, formed with a dative or intransitive verb, that do not specify who is performing the action.

1. Intransitive verbs (e.g., **schwimmen, singen, sprechen, tanzen**)

   Es wird getanzt.          *There is dancing going on. (People are dancing.)*
   Es wird laut gesungen.    *Loud singing is going on. (People are singing loudly.)*

2. Dative verbs (e.g., **helfen, danken**)

   Dem Mann ist nicht geholfen worden.    *The man was not (being) helped.*
   Der Frau wird gedankt.                 *The woman is (being) thanked.*

Since intransitive verbs and dative verbs do not have direct objects in the active voice, they cannot have a subject in the passive voice and are therefore termed *impersonal passive* or *subjectless passive*.

An impersonal passive construction frequently begins with **es**. This **es** is a placeholder, or dummy subject, and drops out whenever another element such as an adverb of location (e.g., **hier**), begins the sentence.

**Es** wird hier getanzt. ⎫  *Dancing goes/is going on here.*
**Hier** wird getanzt. ⎭   *(People dance/are dancing here.)*

The corresponding active sentence uses **man**.

   **Man** tanzt hier.    *One dances here.*

Dependent clauses that begin with a subordinate conjunction, such as **weil, als, dass, wenn,** also omit the placeholder **es** in the passive.

   **Es** wird heute gegrillt.            *There's barbecuing going on today.*
   Wir hören, **dass** heute gegrillt wird.    *We hear that there's barbecuing today.*

For impersonal passives, the verb is always in the third-person singular, because the subject of the sentence is **es**. The corresponding English sentence may have a plural verb.

   Dem Mann **wird** (es) geholfen.       *The man **is** being helped.*
   Den Männern **wird** (es) geholfen.    *The men **are** being helped.*

**31    Was wird hier gemacht?** Beschreiben Sie, was an jedem Ort gemacht wird.

🟨 in der Diskothek    *In der Diskothek wird getanzt.*

1. in der Diskothek     a.  arbeiten
2. in der Oper          b.  auftanken
3. im Lesesaal          c.  einkaufen
4. im Kaufhaus          d.  lernen
5. im Büro              e.  schwimmen
6. im Deutschkurs       f.  singen
7. im Schwimmbad        g.  Deutsch sprechen
8. an der Tankstelle    h.  tanzen

Schleswig-Holstein
Landeshauptstadt:  Kiel
Fläche:            15.761 km²
Einwohner:         2,804 Millionen

Bremen
Landeshauptstadt:  Bremen
Fläche:            404 km²
Einwohner:         0,660 Millionen

Niedersachsen
Landeshauptstadt:  Hannover
Fläche:            47.616 km²
Einwohner:         7,956 Millionen

Nordrhein-Westfalen
Landeshauptstadt:  Düsseldorf
Fläche:            34.082 km²
Einwohner:         18,052 Millionen

Hessen
Landeshauptstadt:  Wiesbaden
Fläche:            21.114 km²
Einwohner:         6,078 Millionen

Rheinland-Pfalz
Landeshauptstadt:  Mainz
Fläche:            19.847 km²
Einwohner:         4,049 Millionen

Saarland
Landeshauptstadt:  Saarbrücken
Fläche:            2.569 km²
Einwohner:         1,066 Millionen

Baden-Württemberg
Landeshauptstadt:  Stuttgart
Fläche:            35.752 km²
Einwohner:         10,601 Millionen

Stand 2002

*Wissenswerte Vokabeln: Die Landeskunde Deutschlands*
*Talking about geographic landmarks in Germany*

Bundesrepublik Deutschland
| | |
|---|---|
| Hauptstadt: | Berlin |
| Fläche: | 357.023 km² |
| Einwohner: | 82,6 Millionen |

# Bundesländer

Mecklenburg-Vorpommern
| | |
|---|---|
| Landeshauptstadt: | Schwerin |
| Fläche: | 23.173 km² |
| Einwohner: | 1,760 Millionen |

Hamburg
| | |
|---|---|
| Landeshauptstadt: | Hamburg |
| Fläche: | 755 km² |
| Einwohner: | 1,726 Millionen |

Brandenburg
| | |
|---|---|
| Landeshauptstadt: | Potsdam |
| Fläche: | 29.476 km² |
| Einwohner: | 2,593 Millionen |

Berlin
| | |
|---|---|
| Landeshauptstadt: | Berlin |
| Fläche: | 892 km² |
| Einwohner: | 3,388 Millionen |

Sachsen-Anhalt
| | |
|---|---|
| Landeshauptstadt: | Magdeburg |
| Fläche: | 20.447 km² |
| Einwohner: | 2,581 Millionen |

Sachsen
| | |
|---|---|
| Landeshauptstadt: | Dresden |
| Fläche: | 18.413 km² |
| Einwohner: | 4,384 Millionen |

Thüringen
| | |
|---|---|
| Landeshauptstadt: | Erfurt |
| Fläche: | 16.172 km² |
| Einwohner: | 2,411 Millionen |

Bayern
| | |
|---|---|
| Landeshauptstadt: | München |
| Fläche: | 70.549 km² |
| Einwohner: | 12,330 Millionen |

**Deutschland – politisch**
Maßstab 1 : 3 500 000
- Staatsgrenze
- Ländergrenze
- Hauptstadt eines Staates
- Bundesstadt
- Landeshauptstadt
- Verwaltungssitz eines Regierungsbezirkes

Wie heißt das kleinste Bundesland?    *Es heißt Bremen.*
Wie heißt der bekannteste Fluss?    *Er heißt der Rhein.*

**32** **Land und Leute kennen lernen.** Beantworten Sie die folgenden Fragen mit Hilfe der Länderkarte und der Informationen aus **Wissenswerte Vokabeln**.

1. Welche drei Großstädte sind auch Bundesländer?
2. Welche drei Bundesländer haben die meisten Einwohner?
3. Welche drei Bundesländer haben die wenigsten Einwohner?
4. Welches Bundesland hat die größte Landfläche?
5. Welche drei Bundesländer grenzen an die Nord- und/oder Ostsee?
6. Welche drei Bundesländer grenzen an Frankreich?
7. Durch welche Bundesländer fließt der Rhein?
8. Für welche Bundesländer bilden die Oder und die Neiße eine Grenze mit Polen?
9. Durch welche Bundesländer fließt die Elbe?
10. Wie heißt die Hauptstadt von Rheinland-Pfalz?

**Eine Seite aus dem Tagebuch.** Sie haben einen Wirbelsturm° in einem Keller überlebt°. Schreiben Sie in Ihr Tagebuch, was Sie während des Wirbelsturms erlebt haben. War es während des Tages oder der Nacht? Haben Sie die Sirenen gehört? Haben Sie Angst gehabt? Mit wem sind Sie in den Keller gegangen? Was ist im Keller passiert? Wie lange sind Sie im Keller gewesen? Wie sind Sie aus dem Keller gekommen? Wurde das Haus zerstört? Haben Sie alle Hausgegenstände gefunden? Was hätten Sie anders machen sollen? Würden Sie das nächste Mal etwas anders machen?

*tornado*
*survived*

**Zieltext** | **Wie lange hab' ich das nicht mehr gegessen!**

Hier spricht Anna mit Karl und Stefan über ihre Erfahrungen mit Verwandten und Freunden aus der ehemaligen DDR. Karl spricht über eine Reise vor 1989 nach Halle. Stefan erzählt von der Schwester seiner Oma, die in Dresden wohnte. Beide versuchen das Leben zu DDR-Zeiten und das Leben nach der Wende in Berlin objektiv und neutral zu beschreiben.

## *Vorschau*

**33** **Thematische Fragen.** Beantworten Sie die folgenden Fragen auf Deutsch.

1. Wie alt waren Sie, als die Mauer im Jahr 1989 gefallen ist, oder waren Sie noch nicht geboren?
2. Was, wenn überhaupt etwas, assoziieren Sie mit der Mauer oder mit Ostdeutschland oder mit der Deutschen Demokratischen Republik (DDR)?

3. Welche Bundesländer sind die „neuen Bundesländer"? In welchem Bundesland liegt die Stadt Halle? Wo liegt Dresden? Wo liegt Weimar?

4. Wann wurde die Mauer gebaut? Warum konnte ein Kind in Westdeutschland im Jahre 1989 eine Oma mit einer Schwester in der DDR haben?

5. „Konsumorientiert" bedeutet, man kauft gern Produkte. Wer war vielleicht mehr konsumorientiert – die Westdeutschen oder die Ostdeutschen? Halten Sie es für gut, schlecht oder neutral, wenn Leute konsumorientiert sind? Warum?

6. Glauben Sie, dass das Leben für alle Menschen in Ostdeutschland gleich war, oder hatten einige mehr als andere? Erklären Sie Ihre Meinung.

 **34** **Satzdetektiv.** Welche Sätze bedeuten ungefähr das Gleiche?

1. Ich kann mich noch dran erinnern, ja, und dass wir denen öfter mal **Sachen geschickt hatten,** über die sie sich sehr gefreut haben.

2. Ab und zu **klappte** das dann.

3. Die hat zum Beispiel erzählt, dass sie nichts dergleichen **entbehrt** hat.

4. Vielleicht **kam's auf die Familien an – oder auf den Wohnort** – kann ich mir auch vorstellen.

a. Dann und wann haben wir Glück gehabt.

b. Das hat wahrscheinlich damit zu tun, wer die Leute waren und wo sie gewohnt haben. Das kann ich mir denken.

c. Sie hat gesagt, dass sie nicht ohne viele Sachen existieren musste.

d. Ich weiß noch, dass wir ihnen Konsumwaren per Post verschickt haben, und sie waren sehr zufrieden damit.

5. Also einerseits hat das auch **was Schönes,** dass sie manchmal da nicht so ganz so konsumorientiert sind.

6. Aber jetzt **merk'** ich immer mehr, dass man's nicht unbedingt **merkt.**

7. Also, das **hat** sich ziemlich alles **ausgeglichen**?

8. Ja, also, in der Schule gleich nachdem die Mauer offen war, **ist es mir aufgefallen**.

e. Auf der einen Seite ist es gut, dass die Leute im Osten nicht immer so viel Wert auf Konsumwaren legen.

f. Gleich nach dem Mauerfall habe ich es in der Schule gemerkt.

g. Heute sehe ich immer öfter, dass man es nicht sieht.

h. Ist jetzt die Situation in beiden Teilen Deutschlands gleich geworden?

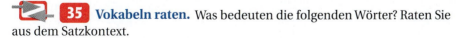 **35** **Vokabeln raten.** Was bedeuten die folgenden Wörter? Raten Sie aus dem Satzkontext.

1. „Was hattet ihr überhaupt für **eine Vorstellung**?"
   a. eine Idee                    b. eine Antwort          c. ein Theater

2. „Ich kann mich noch erinnern, … das alles so grau war und so 'n bisschen **drückende Stimmung**."
   a. deprimierende° Atmosphäre       b. leichte Situation    c. billige Stadt       *depressing*

3. „Meine Oma hatte **Früchte aufgedeckt und Wurstsorten und Käsesorten**."
   a. Mittagessen gekocht
   b. im Supermarkt viel eingekauft
   c. gutes oder besonderes Obst und Delikatessen auf den Tisch gestellt

4. „Ich merke doch, dass es [das Leben im Osten] **schlichter** ist."
   a. schöner          b. einfacher          c. schneller

5. „[Die Leute im Osten kennen] noch so **Hausmittel** bei Krankheiten."
   a. medizinisches Personal
   b. ein Krankenhaus
   c. Medizin aus natürlichen Substanzen wie Honig oder Milch

6. „Man merkt so gewisse° **Einstellungen**."          *certain*
   a. wie man denkt      b. wie man isst    c. wie man aussieht

7. „Da **spürt** man es schon, glaube ich."
   a. denkt               b. macht               c. fühlt

 **36**  **Im Osten oder im Westen?** Wo ist das wohl passiert: im ehemaligen Westdeutschland oder im ehemaligen Ostdeutschland oder in beiden?

| *Was ist passiert?* | *In Westdeutschland?* | *In Ostdeutschland?* |
|---|---|---|
| 1. zur Konfirmation gehen | ☐ | ☐ |
| 2. Grenzsoldaten an der Mauer sehen | ☐ | ☐ |
| 3. die Schwester „auf der anderen Seite" besuchen | ☐ | ☐ |
| 4. Früchte, Wurst- und Käsesorten aufdecken | ☐ | ☐ |
| 5. keine Luxusartikeln haben | ☐ | ☐ |
| 6. schlicht und einfach leben | ☐ | ☐ |
| 7. Hausmittel kennen und verwenden° | ☐ | ☐ | *use* |
| 8. konsumorientiert leben | ☐ | ☐ |

Religious practices and religiously-affiliated political parties were officially tolerated in the GDR. However, those who chose to practice their religion, like those who chose not to join the official party, faced many obstacles in life. Because the churches offered a sanctuary for the relatively free expression of ideas, they became a major force in the disintegration of the GDR in the final year of its existence.

## Zieltext

*Wie lange hab' ich das nicht mehr gegessen!*

Hören Sie gut zu.

## *Rückblick*

 **37  Stimmt das?** Stimmen die folgenden Aussagen zum Text oder nicht? Wenn nicht, was stimmt?

|  | Ja, das stimmt. | Nein, das stimmt nicht. |
|---|---|---|
| 1. Sowohl Karl wie auch Stefan haben die DDR besucht. | ☐ | ☐ |
| 2. Karl hat die DDR sehr gut gefallen. | ☐ | ☐ |
| 3. Karls Familie hatte Freunde in der DDR. | ☐ | ☐ |
| 4. Stefans Oma hat in der DDR gelebt. | ☐ | ☐ |
| 5. Stefans Oma hat Früchte, Wurst und Käse für ihre Schwester gekauft. | ☐ | ☐ |
| 6. Stefan glaubt, dass alles in der DDR besser war. | ☐ | ☐ |
| 7. Karl glaubt, dass das Leben in der DDR einfacher und nicht so konsumorientiert war. | ☐ | ☐ |
| 8. Karl findet, dass die Unterschiede zwischen West- und Ostdeutschland immer größer werden. | ☐ | ☐ |
| 9. Stefan sagt, dass es ihm nicht so wichtig ist, wer aus Ostdeutschland und wer aus Westdeutschland kommt. | ☐ | ☐ |

> Complete the **Ergänzen Sie** activity in your workbook for this text before doing the next activity.

 **38  Kurz gefragt.** Beantworten Sie die folgenden Fragen auf Deutsch.

1. Warum war Karl in der DDR? Was hat er dort gemacht?
2. Wie beschreibt Karl die DDR?
3. Welche Verwandten von Stefan haben in der DDR gewohnt?
4. Wie sind die Erfahrungen von der Schwester von Stefans Oma anders als die Erfahrungen von der Freundin von Stefans Bruder?
5. Gibt Karl eine klare Antwort auf die Frage, ob es auch heute noch Unterschiede zwischen dem Ostteil und dem Westteil von Berlin gibt? Was sagt er zuerst und was sagt er ein paar Sätze später?
6. Wie beantwortet Stefan die gleiche Frage?

**39  Kurz interpretiert.** Beantworten Sie die folgenden Fragen auf Deutsch.

1. Warum wurden die DDR-Bürger – Ihrer Meinung nach – mit ihrem sozialistischen Staat unzufrieden?
2. Was halten Sie von dem ehemaligen sozialistischen System in der DDR?
3. Sind Sie der Meinung, dass die Unterschiede zwischen Westdeutschland und Ostdeutschland noch lange existieren werden? Warum? Warum nicht?

**BRENNPUNKT KULTUR**

## Freistaat Sachsen: Leipzig und Dresden

Barbara's hometown, Dresden, is in the Free State of Saxony (**der Freistaat Sachsen**), which borders Poland and the Czech Republic. With a population of 4.5 million and a rapidly improving infrastructure, Saxony is well positioned to compete economically. It is also the home of two of the most important and vibrant cities in eastern Germany, Leipzig and Dresden.

Leipzig, with 438,000 inhabitants, is located at the intersection of two important medieval trade routes, making it a natural center for the exchange of ideas and for East-West trade. Leipzig is also home to Germany's second oldest university.

Johann Sebastian Bach served the city of Leipzig as choirmaster (**Kantor**) from 1723 until his death in 1750, directing the famous boys' choir, **der Thomanerchor**, at the **Thomaskirche**, and playing the organ at the Church of St. Nicholas (**die Nikolaikirche**). In 1989, the **Nikolaikirche** was the site of the "Monday demonstrations" which ultimately brought down the German Democratic Republic and led to unification with then West Germany.

Der Zwinger in Dresden

Dresden (pop. 480,000), the capital of Saxony (**Sachsen**), is located on the banks of the Elbe River and is known as **das deutsche Florenz** for the beauty of its art collections and architectural treasures. On February 13–14, 1945, Dresden was the target of Allied firebombing attacks. The bombing left more than 35,000 civilians dead and completely destroyed large parts of the city. In the decades after WWII, the East German government slowly reconstructed such architectural masterpieces as the Semper Opera House (**die Semperoper**), **die Brühlsche Terrasse** along the Elbe River, and **der Zwinger**, an elaborate complex of baroque pavilions, galleries, and gardens built by Saxony's ruler **August der Starke** (1670–1733). Today the Zwinger is home to many art treasures and exhibits of the world-famous **Meißner Porzellan**. The ruins of the **Frauenkirche** served as a reminder of WWII for many years. The church has now been reconstructed.

■ **Kulturkreuzung** Die Stadt Leipzig verliert Einwohner. Kennen Sie Städte in Ihrem Land, die auch Menschen verlieren? Woran liegt das? Dresden hat eine bekannte kulturelle Tradition aber auch eine traurige Geschichte vom Krieg. Kennen Sie Städte in Ihrem Land, die auch eine traurige Geschichte haben?

> Companies such as Audi, Zeiss, and Melitta Coffee, and inventions such as the washing machine, the tea bag, the coffee filter, and toothpaste all hail from Saxony.

**40  Der Tag nach der Maueröffnung.** Nehmen wir an°, Sie wohnen in Ost-Berlin. Es ist der 9. November 1989, und die Mauer ist gerade „gefallen", d.h. die Grenzen zum Westen sind geöffnet worden. Was hätten Sie zuerst gemacht? Was hätten Sie danach gemacht? Fragen Sie dann Ihren Partner/Ihre Partnerin.

*Nehmen ... an: Let us assume*

- S1: *Hättest du Freunde oder Verwandte im Westen besucht?*
- S2: *Ja, das hätte ich gemacht.* (oder)
  *Nein, das hätte ich nicht gemacht.*
- S1: *Was hättest du zuerst gemacht? Und als zweites?*

1. Freunde oder Verwandte im Westen besuchen
2. im Westen einkaufen gehen
3. im Westen bummeln gehen
4. Freunde in der DDR anrufen und mit ihnen feiern
5. zu Hause bleiben und nichts Besonderes machen
6. an eine westdeutsche Uni schreiben: vielleicht dort studieren
7. eine große Reise ins Ausland planen
8. eine Umsiedlung in die Bundesrepublik planen
9. vielleicht ins Ausland ziehen
10. ganz laut und offen die politische Meinung ausdrücken
11. Souvenirs sammeln: ein Stück Mauer holen, eine Tageszeitung kaufen usw.
12. im Westen ins Kino gehen und West-Filme anschauen

  **Freie Kommunikation**

**Konsumgesellschaft oder nicht? Eine Diskussion.**  Man könnte sagen, dass Kanada, die USA und die deutschsprachigen Länder Konsumgesellschaften sind. Besprechen Sie die Vorteile und die Nachteile davon mit anderen Studenten. Was brauchen Sie persönlich, um zufrieden zu sein?

  **Schreibecke**

**Was ich in Mitteleuropa unbedingt sehen müsste.**  Hier finden Sie eine Liste von wichtigen Städten, Flüssen und Sehenswürdigkeiten, die in *Vorsprung* erwähnt worden sind. Was würden Sie auf einer Europareise unbedingt sehen wollen? Schreiben Sie einen kurzen Aufsatz und erklären Sie, warum es für Sie wichtig wäre, diesen Ort zu besuchen.

| | |
|---|---|
| Bad Krozingen | das Münchner Rathaus |
| die Berliner Mauer | die Nikolaikirche in Leipzig |
| Bismarcks Grab | Prenzlauer Berg |
| das Brandenburger Tor | die Quadratenstadt Mannheim |
| Braunwald in der Schweiz | der Reichstag |
| der Dresdner Zwinger | der Rhein |
| die Elbe | die Romantische Straße |
| ein Fußballspiel von TSV 1860 | St. Pauli in Hamburg |
| Genf | das Schloss Sanssouci in Potsdam |
| die Geburtsstadt von Arnold Schwarzenegger | Schloss Schönbrunn in Wien |
| das Goethehaus in Frankfurt/Main | der Stefansdom in Wien |
| das Heidelberger Schloss | Stuttgart |
| der Kölner Dom | die Universität in Tübingen |
| ein Konzentrationslager | Waldhäuser-Ost in Tübingen |
| das Matterhorn | Weinheim |
| Mozarts Geburtshaus in Salzburg | die Wiener Staatsoper |
| | Zürich in der Schweiz |

Famous graduates of Leipzig's university include the philosopher and mathematician Baron Gottfried Wilhelm von Leibnitz, the writer Gotthold Ephraim Lessing, and the philosopher Friedrich Nietzsche.

Creative genius has always thrived in Dresden. The composers Carl Maria von Weber, Robert Schumann, and Richard Wagner were born there, as was the German Romantic painter Caspar David Friedrich. *Die Brücke,* the art movement (German Expressionist) was started here in 1905 by Ernst Ludwig Kirchner, Karl Schmidt-Rottluff, Fritz Bleyl, and Erich Heckel.

## Wortschatz

### Eine Stadt erleben / Tourist sein

**der Bummel, -**  *leisurely stroll, walk*
**der Dom, -e**  *cathedral*
**das Erlebnis, -se**  *experience*
**das Zentrum,** *pl.* **Zentren** *center*
   **das Einkaufszentrum** *mall*

### Berlin

**die (Kaiser-Wilhelms-) Gedächt-niskirche** (*Kaiser Wilhelm*) *Memorial Church*
**der Kurfürstendamm (Ku-damm)** *a main street of Berlin*
**das Mahnmal, ̈er** *memorial*
**die Mauer, -n** *the Wall* (*in Berlin*); (*exterior*) *wall*
**die Mitte, -n** *middle*
   **Berlin-Mitte** *center of Berlin*
   **die Museumsinsel** *museum district of Berlin*
**das Olympiastadion** *Olympic Stadium*
**die Philharmonie** (*Berlin*) *Philharmonic Orchestra*
**der Platz, ̈e** *place, square*
**der Reichstag** *parliament building*
**die Spree** *river through Berlin*
**die Stelle, -n** *spot, place*
**das Tor, -e** *gate*
   **das Brandenburger Tor** *Brandenburg Gate*
**das Viertel, -** *quarter, district, neighborhood*
   **das neue Regierungsviertel** *new government district*
**der Wunsch, ̈e** *wish*
**das Ziel, -e** *goal, target, destination*

### Regierung und Politik

**der Bundeskanzler, - / Bundeskanz-lerin, -nen** *Federal Chancellor*
**das Bundesland, ̈er** *federal state*

**der Bundespräsident, [-en], -en / die Bundespräsidentin -nen** *Federal President*
**die Bundesrepublik Deutschland** *Federal Republic of Germany*
**der Bundestag** *Federal Parliament*
**das Gesetz, -e** *law*
   **das Grundgesetz** *basic law, constitution*

### Die Landeskunde Deutschlands

**die Fläche, -n** *land area*
**der Fluss, ̈e** *river*
**die Landeskunde** *geography*
**die See, -n** *sea*
   **die Nordsee** *North Sea*
   **die Ostsee** *Baltic Sea*
*Noch einmal:* **der Einwohner / die Einwohnerin, die Grenze, die Hauptstadt**

### Die Geschichte Deutschlands

**das Abkommen, -** *treaty; agreement*
**die Alliierten** (*pl.*) *the Allies* (*in World War II*)
**die Armee, -n** *army*
**der Aufstand, ̈e** *uprising, revolt*
**die Besatzungszone, -n** *occupation zone*
**die Blockade, -n** *blockade*
**die Deutsche Demokratische Republik (DDR)** *German Democratic Republic* (*GDR*)
**die Einheit** *unity*
**der Führer, -** *leader* (*of Nazi Party*)
**die Grenze, -n** *border*
**die Gründung** *foundation*
**der Kaiser, - / die Kaiserin, -nen** *emperor / empress*
**der Kanzler, - / die Kanzlerin, -nen** *chancellor*
**der Krieg, -e** *war*
   **der Erste (Zweite) Weltkrieg** *First (Second) World War*
   **der Kalte Krieg** *Cold War*

**die Luftbrücke** *airlift*
**die Macht, ̈e** *power, strength*
**die Machtergreifung, -en** *coup, seizure of power*
**die Monarchie, -n** *monarchy*
**die Partei, -en** *political party*
**das Reich, -e** *empire; realm*
   **das Deutsche Reich** *German Empire*
   **das Dritte Reich** *Third Reich*
**die Republik, -en** *republic*
   **die Weimarer Republik** *Weimar Republic*
**die Siegermacht, ̈e** *victor, conquering power*
**der Tag der Deutschen Einheit** *German Unity Day*
**die Vereinigung, -en** *unification, union*
   **die Wiedervereinigung** *reunification*
**die Wende** *turning point*
**der Widerstand** *resistance*
*Noch einmal:* **das Schloss**

**jüdisch** *Jewish*

### Positive Antworten

**Abgemacht!** *Agreed! It's a deal!*
**Ach so.** *Oh.*
**Aha.** *Oh.*
**Das hört sich gut an.** *That sounds good.*
**Das klingt gut.** *That sounds good.*
**Das wäre schön.** *That would be nice.*
**Du hast vollkommen Recht.** *You're absolutely right.*
**fantastisch** *fantastic*
**fein** *fine*
**klar** *of course*
**na?** *well?*
**nicht wahr?** *right? no?*
*Noch einmal:* **na ja**

## Die Stimmung

**die Einstellung, -en** *attitude*
**das Gefühl, -e** *feeling*
**die Stimmung, -en,** *atmosphere*

**deprimierend** *depressing*
**drückend** *depressing*
**frustrierend** *frustrating*
**lebendig** *lively, alive*
**schlicht** *simple*
**überraschend** *surprising(ly)*

## Substantive

**der Eindruck, ̈e** *impression*
**die Frucht, ̈e** *fruit*
**das Hausmittel, -** *home remedy*
**der Kasten, ̈** *case*
**die Kleinigkeit, -en** *trifle, little something; detail*
**die Miete, -n** *rent*
**der Rest, -e** *rest, remainder*
**das Sommerhäuschen, -** *summer cottage*
**das Unternehmen, -** *undertaking, project, operation*
**der Wohnort, -e** *home town, place of residence*
**die Vorstellung, -en** *impression, image*

## Adjektive und Adverbien

**ausgeglichen** *similar, balanced*
**ehemalig** *former*
**gemeinsam** *in partnership, together*
**gewiss** *certain*
**konsumorientiert** *materialistic, consumer-oriented*
**manche** *several, some*
**neulich** *recently*
**nirgendwo** *nowhere*
**stundenlang** *for hours*
**unbedingt** *clearly*
**vollkommen** *completely*

## Verben

**ahnen (hat geahnt)** *to guess, suspect, sense*
  **Das hätte ich ahnen sollen.**
    *I should have guessed.*
**an·kommen (kam an, ist angekommen) auf** + *acc.* *to depend on*
**auf·decken (hat aufgedeckt)** *to reveal*
**auf·fallen (fällt auf, fiel auf, ist aufgefallen)** + *dat.* *to occur to s.o.*
  **Das fällt mir auf.** *It occurs to me.*
**auf·wachsen (wächst auf, wuchs auf, ist aufgewachsen)** *to grow up*
**aus·rufen (rief aus, hat ausgerufen)** *to proclaim, declare*
**bei·treten (tritt bei, trat bei, ist beigetreten)** + *dat.* *to join*
**besetzen (hat besetzt)** *to occupy*
**besichtigen (hat besichtigt)** *to visit, look at*
**bummeln (ist gebummelt)** *to stroll*
**entschuldigen (hat entschuldigt)** *to excuse, pardon*
  **Entschuldige die Verspätung.**
    *Sorry I'm late.*
**erobern (hat erobert)** *to defeat, conquer*
**erreichen (hat erreicht)** *to reach*
**gewinnen (gewann, hat gewonnen)** *to win*
**gründen (hat gegründet)** *to found, establish*
**interessieren (hat interessiert)** *to interest*
**klappen (hat geklappt)** *to work out, happen as planned*
**merken (hat gemerkt)** *to notice*
**reagieren (hat reagiert)** *to react*
**Recht haben** *to be right, correct*
**regeln (hat geregelt)** *to regulate*
**renovieren (hat renoviert)** *to renovate, remodel*
**Schlange stehen (stand, hat gestanden)** *stand in line*
**spalten (hat gespalten)** *to separate*
**spüren (hat gespürt)** *to feel, sense*

**teilen (hat geteilt)** *to divide*
**sich verabreden (hat sich verabredet) mit** + *dat.* *to make a date with*
**verwenden (hat verwendet)** *to use*
**vor·haben (hatte vor, hat vorgehabt)** *to plan, have planned*
  **Was hast du vor?** *What have you got planned?*
**vor·schlagen (schlägt vor, schlug vor, hat vorgeschlagen)** *to suggest*
**warnen (hat gewarnt)** *to warn*
**wenden (hat gewendet)** *to turn*
**zerstören (hat zerstört)** *to destroy*
*Noch einmal:* **statt·finden**

## ↱ Andere Wörter und Ausdrücke

**ab und zu** *now and then*
**an deiner (Ihrer) Stelle würde ich …**
  *in your place, I would …, if I were you, I'd …*
**deswegen** *therefore*
**einerseits** *on the one hand*
**Es spielt gar keine Rolle** *It plays no role. It's not at all important.*
**Ich hätte dich warnen sollen.**
  *I should have warned you.*
**Ich kann mich noch erinnern.** *I can still remember.*
**im Freien** *outdoors*
**im Grunde** *basically*
**nicht unbedingt** *not necessarily*
**Pass mal auf!** *Look here! Now listen up!; Pay attention!*
**und so** *and stuff like that*

## Meine eigenen Wörter

_____
_____
_____
_____
_____
_____

# Ende gut, alles gut!

In this chapter you will review Anna Adler's year in Germany. You will also learn about the importance of learning German, why many people choose to learn German, and how you might be able to use German in the future.

## Strukturen

- Review of high-frequency structures, e.g., the conversational past, modal verbs, and the subjunctive.

## Kulturelles

- Amerikaner und amerikanische Kultur im deutschsprachigen Mitteleuropa
- Der Einfluss der englischen und der deutschen Sprache aufeinander
- Deutsche und österreichische Einflüsse auf Amerikas Kultur

■ Hurra! Ende gut, alles gut!

Go to the *Vorsprung* Website at *http:// college.hmco.com/pic/ vorsprung2e.*

*Anlauftext*

## Oh, Stefan, wenn du nur wüsstest!

Anna sitzt am Laptop in ihrem Zimmer und denkt über einiges nach: über einen Bericht über das Jahr in Tübingen, den sie schreiben soll, und über die Leute, die sie in Tübingen kennen gelernt hat und besonders über Stefan, von dem sie sich bald verabschieden° muss.

*sich verabschieden: say good-bye to*

### Vorschau

  **1   Thematische Fragen.**  Beantworten Sie die folgenden Fragen auf Deutsch.

1. Warum studieren Sie Deutsch oder andere Fremdsprachen? Haben Sie auch eine andere Fremdsprache gelernt?
2. Wenn Studierende im Ausland studieren, machen sie viele verschiedene Erfahrungen°, sowohl in ihrem Studium wie auch in ihrem Privatleben. Was, denken Sie, könnte ein ausländischer Student oder eine ausländische Studentin in Deutschland (oder in Österreich oder in der Schweiz) erleben und lernen?
3. Wer von Annas deutschen Freunden hat vielleicht ein romantisches Interesse an Anna? Glauben Sie, dass das die richtige Person für Anna ist? Was könnte in der Zukunft passieren?
4. Welche Erfahrungen in Deutschland, glauben Sie, waren für Anna besonders interessant? wichtig? stressig? Glauben Sie, dass das Studium in Deutschland Annas Leben verändert° hat? verändern wird? Wie?
5. Würden Sie gern im Ausland studieren? Wo? Wie lange? Was würden Sie lernen oder erfahren wollen?

*experiences*

*verändern: to alter*

**2   Ratespiel.**  Was denken Sie: Wie steht es mit Deutsch als Fremdsprache° auf der Welt? Raten Sie.

*foreign language*

1. Wie viele Menschen auf der Welt lernen Deutsch als Fremdsprache?
   a. 1 Million
   b. 10 Millionen
   c. mehr als 15 Millionen

2. Wie viele Universitätsstudenten auf der Welt lernen jedes Jahr Deutsch?
   a. 200 000
   b. 2 Millionen
   c. 20 Millionen

3. Wie viele Universitätsstudenten außerhalb Deutschlands haben Deutsch als Hauptfach?
   a. 7 200
   b. 72 000
   c. 720 000

> You will find the answers to these questions in the **Anlauftext**.

**3**   **Satzdetektiv.** Welche Sätze bedeuten ungefähr das Gleiche?

1. Wenn du nur **wüsstest**!
2. Oh, Entschuldigung, **störe** ich?
3. Ich **hätte** gern mal mit dir **was besprochen**.
4. Du wirst **mir fehlen**.
5. Mensch, bin ich aber **in einer Stimmung**!
6. Das hat mich **total umgeworfen**.

a. Wenn du nur eine Ahnung° hättest!    *idea*
b. Ich werde dich sehr vermissen.
c. Pardon, unterbreche ich dich?
d. Ich möchte mit dir über etwas sprechen.
e. Das hat mich völlig überrascht.
f. Mensch, ich bin so verwirrt!

7. Ich habe **gar nicht damit gerechnet**, dass …
8. Das ist **ja Unsinn**!
9. Wir haben **uns** von Anfang an **sehr gut verstanden**.
10. Ich **kämpfe mit dem Gedanken**, dass …
11. Das kann ich einfach nicht **ertragen**.
12. Wir **passen** wirklich prima **zusammen**.

g. Das ist ja verrückt!
h. Ich habe es nicht erwartet, dass …
i. Ich werde traurig, wenn ich daran denke, dass …,
j. Das kann ich gar nicht akzeptieren.
k. Wir sind ein gutes Paar.
l. Wir haben uns von Anfang an gern gehabt.

## Anlauftext

 Hören Sie gut zu.

Und was schreibst du denn genau?

Einen Bericht über mein Jahr in Tübingen. Im ersten Teil soll ich über die Rolle der deutschen Sprache weltweit schreiben – wie viele Menschen zum Beispiel Deutsch lernen – und auch noch, was ich in meiner Zukunft mit Deutsch anfangen soll.

Hast du zum Beispiel gewusst, dass weltweit 15 bis 18 Millionen Menschen Deutsch als Fremdsprache lernen? Davon sind mehr als 2 Millionen Universitätsstudenten, und über 720 000 haben Deutsch sogar als Hauptfach. Wahnsinn!

Aber was soll ich sonst noch schreiben? Mensch, bin ich aber in einer Stimmung!

Ja, ja, ganz interessant …

Im zweiten Teil soll ich dann über meine persönlichen Erfahrungen in Tübingen berichten, und das macht mich echt traurig. Ich werde euch so sehr <u>vermissen</u>, Barbara und Karl und auch dich Stefan. Ihr wart alle so nett zu mir und ihr habt mir so geholfen. Das hat mich total umgeworfen. Ich habe gar nicht damit gerechnet, dass es so schwierig sein würde, mich von euch zu verabschieden.

Wie wäre es, wenn ich ein Kapitel nur über meine Erfahrungen mit Stefan schreiben würde?

Du hast uns, hmm, mich auch sehr …

Wie bitte?

Ja, Anna. Du hast mich mit deiner Spontaneität und deinem Humor einfach umgeworfen. Und ich werde dich vermissen, Anna. Du und ich, wir haben uns von Anfang an sehr gut verstanden, ich habe dich schon immer gemocht, und du mich auch, nicht wahr?

Will er mir endlich etwas Persönliches sagen? Aber nein, das ist ja Unsinn.

Nach all den Monaten vom Nichtssagen und gerade jetzt, wo ich wieder nach Hause muss?

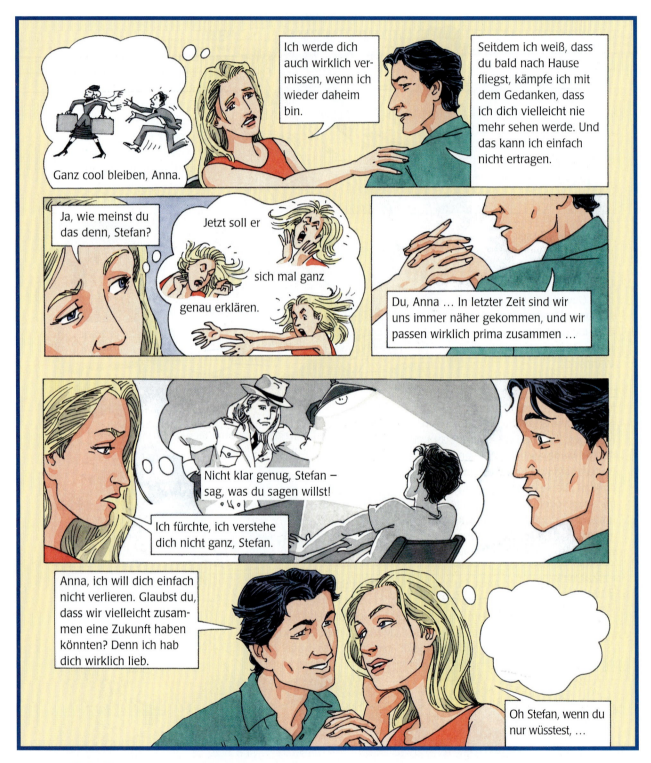

## *Rückblick*

**4** **Stimmt das?** Stimmen die Aussagen auf Seite 479 zum Text oder nicht? Wenn nicht, was stimmt?

|  | Ja, das stimmt. | Nein, das stimmt nicht. |
|---|---|---|
| 1. Anna muss noch eine Seminararbeit fertig schreiben. | ☐ | ☐ |
| 2. Anna will mit Stefan gar nicht sprechen. | ☐ | ☐ |
| 3. Stefan will Anna mit der Arbeit helfen. | ☐ | ☐ |
| 4. Stefan ist in Anna verliebt. | ☐ | ☐ |
| 5. Anna versteht, worüber Stefan mit ihr sprechen will. | ☐ | ☐ |
| 6. In ihrem Bericht muss Anna über Deutschlernen weltweit schreiben. | ☐ | ☐ |
| 7. Anna wird ein bisschen ungeduldig° mit Stefan. | ☐ | ☐ |
| 8. Anna ist dankbar dafür, dass sie gute Freunde wie Barbara, Karl und Stefan kennen gelernt hat. | ☐ | ☐ |
| 9. Stefan hat Schwierigkeiten die richtigen Worte zu finden. | ☐ | ☐ |
| 10. Anna erklärt Stefan, dass sie ihn liebt. | ☐ | ☐ |

*impatient*

> Complete the **Ergänzen Sie** activity in your workbook for this text before doing the next activity.

**5**    **Kurz gefragt.** Beantworten Sie die folgenden Fragen auf Deutsch.

1. Was haben Stefan und Anna vorher nicht klar gewusst? Warum haben sie das nicht gewusst?
2. Wie kann man die Beziehung zwischen Stefan und Anna beschreiben? Wie sehen Sie die Zukunft von Stefan und Anna?
3. Welche Fragen aus dem Ratespiel haben Sie richtig, welche falsch beantwortet? Haben Sie Zahlen unter- oder überschätzt°?
4. Glauben Sie, dass man in einem deutschsprachigen Land studieren oder arbeiten muss, um die Sprache gut zu° lernen und besser über die Kultur Bescheid zu wissen?
5. Was würde Sie an einem Studium oder einem Praktikum in einem deutschsprachigen Land interessieren?

***unter ... :*** *under- or overestimated*

***um ... zu:*** *in order to*

**6**    **Interview.** Stellen Sie einem Partner/einer Partnerin die folgenden Fragen. Lassen Sie sich genug Zeit, Gedanken miteinander auszutauschen.

1. Warum  hast du beschlossen, dieses Jahr Deutsch zu lernen?
2. Hat dir das Studium der deutschen Sprache gefallen? Warum? Warum nicht?
3. Was hast du besonders toll gefunden?
4. Was hast du besonders schwierig gefunden?
5. Willst du dein Studium der deutschen Sprache nächstes Jahr fortsetzen? In welchem Kurs? Wie lange willst du noch Deutsch studieren?
6. Würdest du gern ein Semester oder ein Jahr im Ausland studieren? Wie viele deiner Freunde und Klassenkameraden haben solche Pläne? Was erwartest du davon? Was erwarten deine Freunde und Klassenkameraden davon?
7. Findest du es wichtig, eine andere Sprache zu lernen? Hast du deine Meinung geändert? Erkläre deine Antwort.
8. Möchtest du noch mehr Sprachen lernen? Welche? Warum würdest du diese Sprache(n) lernen wollen?
9. Kannst du dich vorstellen, dass du deine Sprachkenntnisse in deinem zukünftigen Beruf oder Privatleben benutzen könntest? Erkläre deine Antwort.

**7    Rollenspiel: Das Gespräch zwischen Anna und Stefan.** Spielen Sie Annas und Stefans Gespräch weiter. Anna will ihre Gefühle für Stefan klar ausdrücken und Stefan will Anna überzeugen, dass er es ernst meint und sie wirklich lieb hat.

## BRENNPUNKT KULTUR

### Der Einfluss der englischen und der deutschen Sprache aufeinander

The German and English languages share many common features due to their common origin as Germanic languages. Some words are easily recognized as cognates, that is, words with similar forms and meanings, such as **Haus – house, Morgen – morning, Wasser – water, Apfel – apple**, or **Haar – hair**. Many others, however, have undergone sound changes that make them less transparent and more fascinating, for example, **Zaun** (*fence*) **– town, Zimmer – timber, gestern – yester(day), Garten – garden/yard** or **Weib – wife**.

*Englisch ist in deutschen Werbetexten überall zu finden.*

Over the years the impact of German scholarship has contributed many words to English, such as **Gesellschaft, Gemeinschaft** (in the field of sociology), **Angst, Gestalt** (in the field of psychology), **Kindergarten**, and of course many military terms from World War II, for example, **Blitzkrieg, Luftwaffe**, and **Flak** (acronym of **Flugzeug-abwehr-kanone**).

In modern times English has been the source of many new words in German. In the realm of information technology, for example, English terms are everywhere in German (**downloaden, klicken, dumpen, der Laptop, das Modem, die Software**, and so on) and are usually adapted to follow German grammar rules. Marketers exploit the attraction of English in their advertising campaigns based on key English terms (**Leasing, DriverLounge, Wellness, Shirts**). Since American movies are well-known worldwide, English expressions—often with a slightly different meaning (**Mister, Kids**)—have been borrowed into colloquial German, especially by the youth culture, and have had an impact on German culture.

**Kulturkreuzung** Können Sie einige „deutsche" Wörter im Englischen nennen? Aus welchen Gebieten (z.B. Politik, Psychologie, Erziehung usw.) kommen diese Wörter? Kennen Sie auch einige Wörter aus dem Jiddischen, das von einem deutschen Dialekt abstammt°? Nicht alle Deutschsprechenden finden den Einfluss der englischen/amerikanischen Sprache auf ihre Sprache so gut. Warum wohl?

*stems from*

**8    Rollenspiel: Anna und ihr Enkelkind.** In **Kapitel 5** haben Sie die Geschichte von Tante Uschi und Onkel Hannes gelesen. Jetzt ist es dreißig Jahre her, seit Anna in Tübingen studiert hat. Spielen Sie die Rollen von Anna und ihrem Enkelkind mit einem Partner oder einer Partnerin. Das Enkelkind stellt Fragen über Annas Geschichte, die Anna beantwortet. Anna versucht, das

Kind zu überzeugen, Deutsch zu lernen. Sprechen Sie nicht nur über Annas Zeit in Tübingen, sondern auch darüber, was später passiert ist, wo und wie sie gelebt hat und wie sie ihr Deutsch benutzt hat. Bevor Sie beginnen, besprechen Sie mit Ihrem Partner/mit Ihrer Partnerin, worüber Sie genau sprechen wollen.

### Schreibecke

**Einen schwierigen Brief schreiben.** Im Gespräch haben Anna and Stefan Schwierigkeiten gehabt, die richtigen Worte zu finden. Es ist leichter für sie, ihre Gefühle in einem Brief zu beschreiben. Schreiben Sie Annas Brief an Stefan oder Stefans Brief an Anna. Erklären Sie Ihre Gefühle aus der Perspektive von Anna oder Stefan, und wie Sie sich die Zukunft ohne oder mit einander vorstellen.

**Meine Erfahrungen in Deutschland.** Schreiben Sie einen kurzen Bericht über Annas Erfahrungen in Deutschland. Was hat sie erlebt? Was hat sie gelernt? Wie hat es ihr gefallen? War es insgesamt eine gute oder eine schlechte Erfahrung? Welche Tipps kann Anna Studenten geben, die auch in Deutschland studieren wollen. Schreiben Sie zirka 100 Worte.

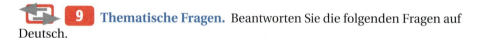

**Absprungtext**    **Warum Deutsch lernen?**

Das *Sprachinstitut Treffpunkt* in Bamberg stellt die Frage „Warum Deutsch lernen?" auf seiner Website und stützt sich auf mehrere wissenschaftlichen Arbeiten. Viele Menschen lernen Deutsch als Hobby, fürs Reisen, für Beruf und Karriere und noch mehr. Die folgende Internetseite gibt eine ausführliche Antwort auf die Frage: „Warum Deutsch lernen?"

## *Vorschau*

**9** **Thematische Fragen.** Beantworten Sie die folgenden Fragen auf Deutsch.

1. Haben Sie schon einmal mit einer Person aus Deutschland, Österreich oder der Schweiz gesprochen? Welche Sprache haben Sie verwendet? Konnten Sie gut miteinander kommunizieren?
2. Wie lange müssen Sie wahrscheinlich noch Deutsch lernen, bis Sie fließend°    *fluent*
Deutsch können?
3. Glauben Sie, dass man eine fremde Sprache nur auf der Uni oder in der Schule lernen kann, oder muss man auch im Ausland leben oder studieren, um die Sprache gut zu lernen?
4. Was ist für Sie am wichtigsten: auf Deutsch gut hören, lesen, sprechen oder schreiben können? Warum?
5. Warum hat das *Sprachinstitut Treffpunkt* wahrscheinlich eine Seite im Internet?

## BRENNPUNKT KULTUR

### Amerikaner und amerikanische Kultur im deutschsprachigen Mitteleuropa

*In Deutschland sowie in den USA war Elvis Presley ein großer Star.*

Central Europe's interest in the United States started with the American Revolution and lasted through the 20th century, ultimately drawing wave after wave of immigrants from Germany, Austria, Switzerland, and other German-speaking areas well into the 1950s. But with the occupation of Germany and Austria after World War II, the American presence and its influence on German-speaking central European culture grew exponentially. In postwar Germany of the 50's, American GIs spent much-needed dollars in the community, bought their German-speaking friends cheap American cigarettes at the PX, and spread interest in American popular culture, especially jazz and jitterbug music.

Broadcasting in English for U.S. forces stationed in Germany in the 1960s and 1970s, the American Forces Network (AFN) played the latest and most progressive forms of pop music, creating huge interest in American stars and their music in Germany as well as Austria. Serving his stint in the U.S. Army in Friedberg, Germany, in 1958, Elvis Presley made German girls swoon just as much as he had the girls back home. German kids became aficionados of everything from soul, funk, hip-hop and rap music to gospel and country music, and gradually adapted the musical styles to songs sung and performed in German. German hip-hop artists S.M.U.D.O. and Thomas D. spent half a year honing their craft in the U.S. before launching their band, **Die fantastischen Vier,** back home in Stuttgart. Others such as the heavy metal band the Scorpions, and John Kay of Steppenwolf, have made careers singing in English to a broader international fan base. American diva Tina Turner has taken up residence in Switzerland.

Many American sports have taken hold in Europe, including American football, basketball, hockey, and golf. Even baseball and softball are gaining popularity.

Texan theater director Robert Wilson became the darling of German theaters for his avant garde productions and novel use of color and light. American film and television have had a profound impact on German cinema and television programming, resulting in TV spin-offs that mirror the very latest in American TV programming.

In the classical music world, the availability of jobs in European cities has drawn many talented American musicians, conductors, and dancers to the government-supported theaters of central Europe. Brilliant young Americans became star players in groups such as **Concentus musicus Wien.** James Levine regularly worked as guest conductor of the **Wiener Philarmoniker, Berliner Philharmoniker** and the **Dresdner Staatskapelle,** and at summer festivals in Salzburg, Austria; Bayreuth, Germany; and Verbier, Switzerland before becoming chief conductor of the **Münchner Philharmoniker** in 1999 and later chief conductor of the Metropolitan Opera and the Boston Symphony Orchestra.

■ **Kulturkreuzung** Warum, glauben Sie, hat die amerikanische Kultur einen so starken Einfluss auf Europa und die ganze Welt? Sehen Sie das positiv oder negativ?

**10** **Meine Gründe° für das Deutschlernen.** Warum haben Sie sich          *reasons* für Deutsch als Fremdsprache entschieden? Bewerten Sie jeden Grund mit einer Zahl: 0 = kein Grund; 1 = ein nicht so wichtiger Grund; oder 2 = ein wichtiger Grund. Vergleichen Sie Ihre Antworten mit anderen Studenten in der Klasse. Kann man sagen, dass es Gründe gibt, die viele Studenten wichtig finden?

| *Der Grund* | *Die Wichtigkeit* |
| --- | --- |
| 1. Deutsch ist eine schöne Sprache. | _____ |
| 2. Man kann im Deutschkurs leicht eine gute Note bekommen. | _____ |

| *Der Grund* | *Die Wichtigkeit* |
|---|---|
| 3. Ich habe Verwandte aus/in einem deutschsprachigen Land. | _____ |
| 4. Deutschkenntnisse sind wichtig für meinen Beruf. | _____ |
| 5. Die Kultur und Geschichte der deutschsprachigen Länder sind interessant. | _____ |
| 6. Ich möchte so viele Sprachen wie möglich lernen. | _____ |
| 7. Deutsch ist eine wichtige Sprache in Europa. | _____ |
| 8. Das Deutschprogramm an meiner Uni ist sehr gut. | _____ |
| 9. Ich möchte in einem deutschsprachigen Land studieren oder arbeiten. | _____ |
| 10. Meine Freunde oder Verwandten lernen auch Deutsch. | _____ |

**11** **Satzdetektiv.** Welche Sätze bedeuten ungefähr das Gleiche?

1. Persönliche **Vorlieben** und Hobbys beinhalten ein weites Feld verschiedenster Themen, zu denen Kenntnisse in Deutsch **eine große Bereicherung** sein können.

2. Viele **wissenschaftliche Abhandlungen** werden nach wie vor° zuerst in Deutsch veröffentlicht.

3. Nicht wenige Menschen erzielen° einen **Informationsvorsprung**, indem sie **Originaltexte** auf Deutsch lesen.

4. **Erschließen° Sie sich** die berühmtesten Operetten und Opern neu, indem Sie die Originaltexte verstehen können.

a. Wenn Sie Deutsch verstehen, können Sie deutsche Operetten und Opern ganz neu interpretieren.

b. Viele Personen sind besser informiert, weil sie deutsche Texte in der Originalsprache lesen können.

c. Deutsch zu sprechen kann helfen, die eigenen Interessen und Hobbys noch interessanter zu machen.

d. Manche Wissenschaftsstudien erscheinen° zuerst auf Deutsch.

*nach ... : still*

*strive for*

*appear*
*figure out, understand*

5. **Je dominanter** die englische Sprache ... **desto wichtiger°** ist es, für die **Englisch-Muttersprachler** eine fremde Sprache zu lernen.

6. So werden Sie an den europäischen Urlaubsorten ... sich häufig° besser auf Deutsch **verständlich machen** können als auf Englisch.

7. Nicht zuletzt verdeutlicht° auch **die bedeutende Anzahl** von deutschsprachigen Nobelpreisträgern den Stellenwert° der deutschen Sprache in der wissenschaftlich-kulturellen Welt.

8. Viele der Nachfahren° interessieren sich heute für **den Lebensraum** und **die Kultur** ihrer Großväter und Urgroßväter.

e. In vielen europäischen Ländern versteht man Deutsch besser als Englisch.

f. Viele Leute möchten sich über das Land und die Kultur ihrer Vorfahren° informieren.

g. Weil Englisch ... die wichtigste Weltsprache ist, ist es noch wichtiger für Englischsprechende eine Fremdsprache zu lernen.

h. Die hohe Anzahl von deutschsprachigen Nobelpreisträgern zeigt, dass Deutsch in der Wissenschaft und in der Kultur sehr wichtig ist.

*je ... wichtiger: the more dominant the English language, the more important*

*ancestors*
**oft**

*clarifies*

**der Status**

*descendants*

## Absprungtext
### Warum Deutsch lernen?

**I. Deutschlernen macht einfach Spaß**

Deutsch ist eine lebendige Sprache – Deutsch lernen „aus Spaß an der Freude" und aus kulturellem, wirtschaftlichem und politischem Interesse! Persönliche Vorlieben und Hobbys beinhalten ein weites Feld verschiedenster Themen, zu denen Kenntnisse in Deutsch eine große Bereicherung sein können:

- Geschichte: Entdecken Sie die faszinierende Welt 2000-jähriger deutscher Geschichte von den Germanen über das Deutsche Reich bis in die jüngste Geschichte der Bundesrepublik Deutschland.

- Wissenschaft: Viele wissenschaftliche Abhandlungen werden nach wie vor zuerst in Deutsch veröffentlicht. Man betrachte dazu zum Beispiel auch die Publikationen im Internet: Deutsch ist die zweitwichtigste Sprache im Internet und nicht wenige Menschen erzielen einen Informationsvorsprung, indem sie Originaltexte auf Deutsch lesen.

- Literatur: Die deutschsprachige Literatur ist berühmt und sehr reichhaltig. Viele der weltbekanntesten Autoren, wie Goethe, Kafka, Luther, Hegel, Nietzsche, Marx, Freud und die Nobelpreisträger/trägerinnen Thomas Mann (1929), Hermann Hesse (1946), Heinrich Böll (1972) Günter Grass (1999) und Elfriede Jelinek (2004), schreiben auf Deutsch.

- Popmusik: Musik von Falco, Kraftwerk, Nina Hagen, Nena, Herbert Grönemeyer oder Rammstein – um nur einige Namen zu nennen – stehen auch international ganz oben auf den Hitlisten.

- Klassische Musik: Mit Komponisten wie Bach, Beethoven, Mahler, Mozart, Strauß und Wagner nehmen die deutschsprachigen Komponisten eine dominierende Stellung innerhalb dieser Musikrichtung ein. Erschließen Sie sich die berühmtesten Operetten und Opern neu, indem Sie die Originaltexte verstehen können.

- Sprache und Kultur: Je dominanter die englische Sprache – nicht nur durch den vielschichtigen weltweiten Einfluss der Supermacht Amerika, sondern auch durch die Verbreitung des Internets – desto wichtiger ist es, für die Englisch-Muttersprachler, eine fremde Sprache zu lernen. In vielen Bereichen ist die deutsche Sprache besonders bedeutend: Architektur, Literatur, Malerei, Musik, Philosophie, Wissenschaft und Business. Sie werden erstaunt sein, wie viele der weltgeschichtlich bedeutendsten Werke im Original in deutscher Sprache verfasst sind.

**Hermann Hesse** (1877–1962), Nobel Prize for Literature in 1946; **Franz Kafka** (1883–1924), German author; **Martin Luther** (1483–1546), translator of the Bible and founder of the Protestant Reformation; **Georg Wilhelm Friedrich Hegel** (1770–1831), German philosopher; **Friedrich Nietzsche** (1844–1900), philosopher, psychologist, and philologist; **Karl Marx** (1818–1883), philosopher, political economist, and revolutionary; **Sigmund Freud** (1856–1939), psychiatrist and founder of psychoanalysis; **Günter Grass** (1927–), Nobel Prize for Literature in 1999; **Thomas Mann** (1875–1955), Nobel Prize for Literature in 1929; **Heinrich Böll** (1917–1985), Nobel Prize for Literature in 1972; **Elfriede Jelinek** (1946–), Austrian, Nobel Prize for Literature in 2004.

FREUDE AM SCHAUEN UND BEGREIFEN IST DIE SCHÖNSTE GABE DER NATUR.

## II. Deutschlernen für das Reisen

Lernen Sie Deutsch, um Ihre Reise durch Mitteleuropa zu einem intensiven, persönlichen Erlebnis zu machen.

Deutsch ist die in Europa am häufigsten und weit verbreitesten gesprochene Sprache. Mit Kenntnissen der deutschen Sprache gestaltet sich das Reisen in Europa viel einfacher. So werden Sie an den europäischen Urlaubsorten in Italien, Frankreich, Spanien, Portugal, der Türkei oder Griechenland sich häufig besser auf Deutsch verständlich machen können als auf Englisch. Dazu trägt bei, dass viele Südeuropäer in den 60er und 70er Jahren als Gastarbeiter in Deutschland, der Schweiz oder Österreich tätig waren und dass die Deutschsprachigen als eifrige „Mittelmeertouristen" eine lange Tradition haben.

## III. Deutschlernen zur Verbesserung der Berufs- and Karrierechancen

„Deutsch" ist die Muttersprache für mehr Europäer als etwa Englisch, Französisch, Spanisch oder Italienisch. In den Bereichen Wirtschaft, Tourismus und Diplomatie ist Deutsch – nach Englisch – heute die weltweit zweitwichtigste Sprache. In Mittel- und Osteuropa ist Deutsch die wichtigste Fremdsprache.

Mit Deutsch als Fremdsprache können Sie Ihre Berufschancen entscheidend verbessern. Besonders in den Bereichen Biologie, Diplomatie, Finanzen, Elektrotechnik, Maschinenbau, Chemie, Pharmazie, Sport, Fahrzeugbau, Tourismus und dem gesamten Bildungsbereich ist Deutsch – nach Englisch – die wichtigste Sprache zur Qualifikation junger Menschen weltweit.

Weltweit geben etwa 130 Millionen Menschen Deutsch als ihre Muttersprache an und etwa 15 –18 Millionen lernen Deutsch.

Gemäß einer Studie, die 1994 im Auftrag des German American Chamber of Commerce durchgeführt wurde, gaben rund 65% aller befragten Firmen an, dass bei der Suche nach neuen Mitarbeitern speziell bilinguale Fähigkeiten in Englisch und Deutsch ein wichtiges Auswahlkriterium sind.

Deutsch ist die wichtigste Wirtschaftssprache in der Europäischen Union und eine Brücke zu den aufstrebenden Nationen Osteuropas.

Innerhalb der europäischen Union sind die Deutschsprachigen mit rund 1/3 die größten Handelspartner.

Auch spielt die deutsche Sprache bei Wirtschaftskontakten in den aufstrebenden Märkten Osteuropas oftmals eine größere Rolle als Englisch: In vielen Gebieten Polens, Ungarns, Rumäniens, Russlands, der Ukraine und in den baltischen Staaten und der Tschechischen Republik ist Deutsch eine wichtige Sprache.

Nicht zuletzt verdeutlicht auch die bedeutende Anzahl von deutschsprachigen Nobelpreisträgern den Stellenwert der deutschen Sprache in der wissenschaftlich-kulturellen Welt: 30 Nobelpreise in Chemie, 25 in Medizin, 21 in Physik, 10 in Literatur und 8 Friedenspreise.

## IV. Deutschlernen, um die Geschichte der Vorfahren kennen zu lernen

Während der letzten vier Jahrhunderte sind aus Mitteleuropa besonders viele Menschen nach Nord- und Südamerika und auch nach Australien ausgewandert. Viele der Nachfahren interessieren sich heute für den Lebensraum und die Kultur ihrer Großväter und Urgroßväter. Wer dazu die alte Heimat besucht und wirklich kennen lernen will, kommt kaum daran vorbei, Deutsch zu lernen.

## *Rückblick*

**12** **Stimmt das?** Stimmen die folgenden Aussagen zum Text oder nicht? Wenn nicht, was stimmt?

| | Ja, das stimmt. | Nein, das stimmt nicht. |
|---|---|---|
| 1. Viele Studenten lernen Deutsch, weil es einfach Spaß macht. | ☐ | ☐ |
| 2. Alle wissenschaftlichen Publikationen erscheinen heute nur auf Englisch. | ☐ | ☐ |
| 3. Die deutsche Literatur spielt eine große Rolle in der Weltliteratur. | ☐ | ☐ |
| 4. Elfriede Jelinek aus Österreich hat den Nobelpreis für Literatur im Jahre 2004 gewonnen. | ☐ | ☐ |
| 5. Es gibt keine gute Popmusik in Deutschland und schon gar keine Gruppe, die weltweit bekannt ist. | ☐ | ☐ |
| 6. Deutsche haben eine große Rolle in der klassischen Musik gespielt. | ☐ | ☐ |
| 7. Im Zeitalter von Englisch ist es nicht wichtig, die deutsche Kultur und Sprache zu verstehen. | ☐ | ☐ |
| 8. Deutschkenntnisse helfen, wenn man in Südeuropa Urlaub macht. | ☐ | ☐ |
| 9. Deutsch ist in der Wirtschaft, im Tourismus und in der Diplomatie wichtiger als Englisch. | ☐ | ☐ |
| 10. Es gibt mehr Leute, die Deutsch als Fremdsprache lernen als Leute, die Deutsch als Muttersprache sprechen. | ☐ | ☐ |
| 11. Für weniger als die Hälfte aller befragten Firmen in den USA ist es wichtig, dass ihre Mitarbeiter nicht nur Englisch, sondern auch Deutsch sprechen. | ☐ | ☐ |
| 12. Deutsch ist die wichtigste Wirtschaftssprache Europas. | ☐ | ☐ |
| 13. In Osteuropa versteht und spricht man mehr Englisch als Deutsch. | ☐ | ☐ |
| 14. Viele Leute in Nord- und Südamerika und in Australien haben deutsche Vorfahren. | ☐ | ☐ |

> Complete the **Ergänzen Sie** activity in your workbook for this text before doing the next activity.

**13** **Kurz gefragt.** Beantworten Sie die folgenden Fragen auf Deutsch.

1. Aus welchen Gründen sollte man Deutsch lernen? Nennen Sie wenigstens zwei Gründe.
2. Welche Fakten und Zahlen haben Sie überrascht°? Warum? — *surprised*
3. In welchen Branchen und in welchen geographischen Gebieten° ist Deutsch besonders wichtig? — *areas*
4. Glauben Sie, dass Sie Deutsch in Ihrem Beruf und/oder Privatleben verwenden werden? Müssen Sie Ihr Deutsch dafür noch verbessern?
5. Kennen Sie deutsche Popmusikgruppen, die international bekannt sind? Warum sind sie wohl international bekannt? Was für Musik spielen sie?

6. Waren Sie schon einmal in einem deutschsprachigen Land? Wenn ja, erzählen Sie von Ihren Erfahrungen.

7. Sehen Sie Verbindungen mit Deutschkursen und Ihren anderen Kursen? Erklären Sie Ihre Antwort.

8. Warum sollte man Deutsch lernen, auch wenn viele deutschsprachige Leute Englisch können?

**14** **Warum Deutsch lernen?** Schreiben Sie die fehlende Information aus dem Text in die Grafik.

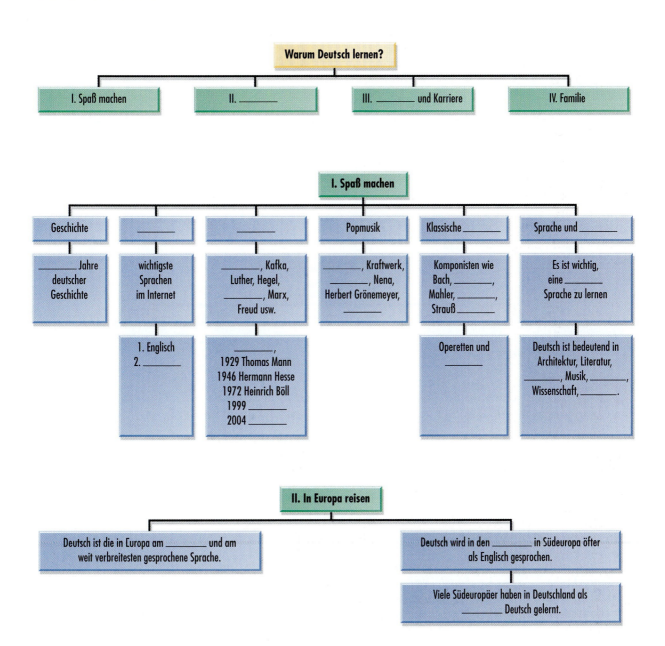

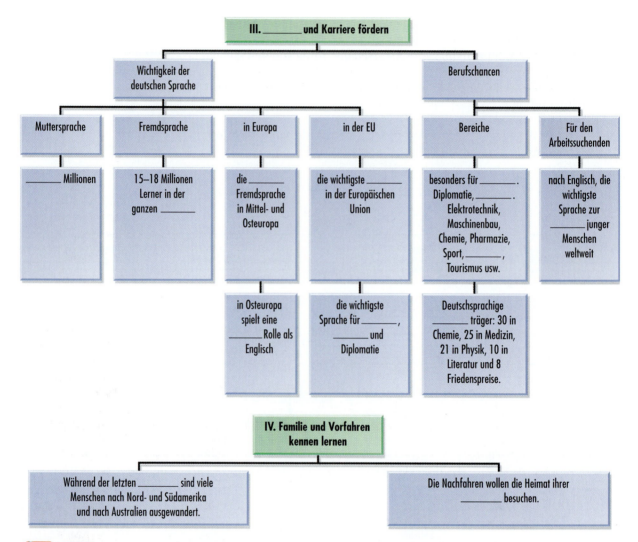

**III. _____ und Karriere fördern**

**Wichtigkeit der deutschen Sprache**

**Berufschancen**

**Muttersprache**

_____ Millionen

**Fremdsprache**

15–18 Millionen Lerner in der ganzen _____

**in Europa**

die _____ Fremdsprache in Mittel- und Osteuropa

in Osteuropa spielt eine _____ Rolle als Englisch

**in der EU**

die wichtigste _____ in der Europäischen Union

die wichtigste Sprache für _____, _____ und Diplomatie

**Bereiche**

besonders für _____. Diplomatie, _____. Elektrotechnik, Maschinenbau, Chemie, Pharmazie, Sport, _____, Tourismus usw.

Deutschsprachige _____ träger: 30 in Chemie, 25 in Medizin, 21 in Physik, 10 in Literatur und 8 Friedenspreise.

**Für den Arbeitssuchenden**

nach Englisch, die wichtigste Sprache zur _____ junger Menschen weltweit

**IV. Familie und Vorfahren kennen lernen**

Während der letzten _____ sind viele Menschen nach Nord- und Südamerika und nach Australien ausgewandert.

Die Nachfahren wollen die Heimat ihrer _____ besuchen.

---

**15   Deutsche Autoren.** Wer hat was geschrieben? Verbinden Sie einen berühmten Autor/eine berühmte Autorin mit den passenden Buchtiteln.

1. Heinrich Böll
2. Sigmund Freud
3. Johann Wolfgang von Goethe
4. Günter Grass
5. Georg Wilhelm Friedrich Hegel
6. Hermann Hesse
7. Elfriede Jelinek
8. Franz Kafka
9. Martin Luther
10. Thomas Mann
11. Karl Marx
12. Friedrich Nietzsche
13. Christa Wolf

a. _Also sprach Zarathustra, Jenseits von Gut und Böse_
b. _Billard um halb zehn, Gruppenbild mit Dame_
c. _Das Ich und das Es, Die Traumdeutung_
d. _Das Kapital, Das Kommunistische Manifest_
e. _Der Große und der Kleine Katechismus_
f. _Der Zauberberg, Buddenbrooks, Der Tod in Venedig_
g. _Der geteilte Himmel, Nachdenken über Christa T_
h. _Die Klavierspielerin, Die Kinder der Toten_
i. _Die Verwandlung, Der Prozess, Das Schloss, Amerika_
j. _Faust, Die Leiden des jungen Werther_
k. _Phänomenologie des Geistes_
l. _Steppenwolf, Das Glasperlenspiel_
m. _Die Blechtrommel, Katz und Maus_

**16**  **Rollenspiel: Studienberater.**  Finden Sie einen Partner oder eine Partnerin. Eine Person ist ein Student oder eine Studentin und will wissen, warum er/sie Deutsch lernen soll. Diese Person meint, dass es gut genug ist, wenn man Englisch sprechen kann. Die andere Person ist ein Studienberater oder eine Studienberaterin und erklärt, warum es wichtig ist, Deutsch zu lernen.

## BRENNPUNKT KULTUR

### Deutsche und österreichische Einflüsse auf Amerikas Kultur

In the tumult of 20th century history, the immigration of countless German-speaking Europeans had a profound impact on American life, letters, science, culture, and business. The Nazi ban on Jewish artists, authors, and academics and their sympathizers forced a whole generation of creative talent to leave Germany for the U.S. and other countries offering asylum. In 1933 the 20th century's most brilliant physicist, **Albert Einstein,** left Germany for the U.S., where he continued his work at the Institute for Advanced Study at Princeton University. The Nobel Prize laureate **Thomas Mann** spent the war years in exile in California. Theater revolutionary and author of the famous *Dreigroschenoper,* **Bertolt Brecht,** also moved to California, hoping to find work as a screenwriter. He only worked on one movie but spent his time completing his most important plays. Several German and Austrian actors left their mark in Hollywood: **Marlene Dietrich,** a fierce opponent of Hitler, became the romantic lead in numerous Hollywood films. The Austrian actress **Hedy Lamarr,** known as the "most beautiful woman in the world", became a Hollywood legend in the 30's and 40's. **Peter Lorre,** born in the Austro-Hungarian Empire, became a successful character actor and **Billy Wilder** made familiar Hollywood movies from the 30's into the 90's. Brecht collaborator **Kurl Weill** made a successful transition to Broadway, later penning memorable songs and musicals in English. After the war, German rocket scientist **Wernher von Braun** came to the U.S. and became the leading figure of NASA, leading the way to manned space flight.

*Der Film „Lola rennt" mit Franke Potente war ein weltweiter Filmerfolg*

In American pop music, German-singing performers have scored the occasional novelty hit: **Falco**'s "Der Kommissar" (made popular by the band After the Fire) and "Rock Me Amadeus," **Nena**'s "99 Luftballons," and **Rammstein**'s "Du hast mich." The German impact in Hollywood was more profound. After gaining worldwide attention for his groundbreaking film, *Das Boot,* German director **Wolfgang Petersen** moved on to Hollywood, directing films as diverse as *The NeverEnding Story* to *Troy* (2004). Director **Roland Emmerich**'s experience with special effects made him a natural choice to direct Will Smith in *Independence Day.* Actress **Franka Potente,** originally famous for running through Berlin as the punk Lola in *Lola rennt,* has made a name for herself in Hollywood, starring in movies with Matt Damon and Johnny Depp. Actor **Daniel Brühl,** star of *Good Bye Lenin!,* is also expanding into an international career with English-language movies *Ladies in Lavender* and *Cargo.* The aspirations and successes of Austrian bodybuilder-actor-politician, **Arnold Schwarzenegger,** moved from being the "Terminator" to becoming the governor of California. German models from **Claudia Schiffer** to **Heidi Klum** keep images of vivacious Germanic beauty alive for the world, while Austrian chef and actor **Wolfgang Puck** has built a dining dynasty in the U.S.

**Kulturkreuzung**  Zur Kultur gehört auch der Sport. Welche Sportarten werden mehr in den deutschsprachigen Ländern und welche werden mehr in den USA gespielt? Warum, glauben Sie, ist das so? Welche „amerikanischen" Sportarten spielt man aber jetzt auch in den deutschsprachigen Ländern, und umgekehrt, welche Sportarten, die typisch für die deutschsprachigen Länder sind, spielt man jetzt auch in den USA? Kennen Sie amerikanische Sportler, die in Deutschland leben?

### Schreibecke

**Annas Bericht.** Schreiben Sie die erste Fassung° von Annas Bericht über das      *draft*
Deutschlernen weltweit und die Gründe, warum das Deutschlernen wichtig ist.
Identifizieren Sie drei persönliche Gründe. Schreiben Sie 250–300 Worte.

**17  Internetprojekt.** Gehen Sie zur Website von dem *Sprachinstitut Treffpunkt* in Bamberg (*http://www.deutschkurse.com*) und finden Sie Antworten zu den folgenden Fragen.

1. Unter *Unsere Deutschkurse/Unser Angebot im Überblick:* Wie viele Teilnehmer sind im Durchschnitt in einem Kurs?
2. Unter *Preise und Konditionen:* Wie viel kostet ein 20-stündiger Kurs für eine Woche? Finden Sie das preiswert?
3. Unter *Lernmaterial/Deutschtest online:* Schreiben Sie den Deutschtest online. Wenn Sie Ihre Resultate haben möchten, schicken Sie den Test ab!
4. Unter *Bamberg/Stadtinformationen:* Wie sieht Bamberg aus? Möchten Sie dort Deutsch lernen? Nennen Sie drei interessante Fakten über Bamberg.

**18  Posterprojekt: Warum Deutsch lernen?** Sie sollen eine Präsentation über Deutschlernen machen. Das Ziel ist es, viele Studenten/Studentinnen zum Deutschlernen zu motivieren. Machen Sie ein Poster mit Bildern und Überschriften und zeigen Sie es den anderen Studenten/Studentinnen.

**19  Annas Tipps für Deutsch.** Anna fragt sich, wie sie zu Hause in den USA noch mit Deutsch in Kontakt bleiben kann. Markieren Sie alle Aussagen, die Sie auch relevant finden.

*Annas Tipps für Deutsch*                                                           **Meine Tipps**

1. Ich kann ab und zu einen deutschsprachigen Film anschauen. ☐
2. Ich kann E-Mails an meine Freunde in Deutschland schicken. ☐
3. Ich kann an meine Verwandten in Deutschland schreiben. ☐
4. Ich kann deutschsprachige Nachrichten im Internet lesen. ☐
5. Ich kann deutschsprachige Nachrichten im Radio oder im Fernsehen hören. ☐
6. Ich kann deutschsprachige Menschen in meiner Stadt finden und mit ihnen sprechen. ☐
7. Ich kann an meiner Uni zur Kaffeestunde oder zum Deutschklub gehen. ☐
8. Ich kann Städte in meiner Region besuchen, die deutschsprachige Einwohner haben. ☐
9. Ich kann das nächste Goethe Institut besuchen. ☐
10. Ich kann in meinen Uni-Kursen deutsch-relevante Themen identifizieren. ☐
11. Ich kann Beethoven-Konzerte besuchen. ☐

> Visit the Goethe Institut at *www.goethe.de*. Visit the Website of the American Association of Teachers of German at *www.aatg.org*.

**Zieltext**

## Ich möchte mein Deutsch benutzen in meinem Beruf.

Es stimmt: Um gut Deutsch zu lernen, muss man geduldig sein, hart arbeiten und gute Strategien entwickeln. Aber man kann es schaffen. Drei erfolgreiche° *successful* Personen erzählen Ihnen hier von ihren Erfahrungen mit ihrem Deutschlernen. Hoffentlich können Sie etwas davon lernen oder sich damit identifizieren.

### Vorschau

**20    Thematische Fragen.** Beantworten Sie die folgenden Fragen auf Deutsch.

1. Kennen Sie Studenten/Studentinnen, die im Ausland studiert haben? Was erzählen sie davon? Wo haben sie studiert? Was sind einige Vorteile vom Auslandsstudium?
2. Welche Fächerkombinationen mit Deutsch sind üblich?
3. Ist es wichtig, dass man vorher etwas Deutsch kann, bevor man in Deutschland, Österreich oder in der Schweiz studiert? Warum? Warum nicht?
4. Welche Sprachen sind in der heutigen Zeit wichtig? Welche Rolle spielt Deutsch als Sprache in der Welt?

**21    Interviewfragen.** Welche Fragen sind plausible Fragen in einem Interview mit Studenten über ihr Deutschstudium?

|  | Plausibel | Nicht plausibel |
|---|---|---|
| 1. Könnt ihr euch kurz vorstellen? | ☐ | ☐ |
| 2. Was studiert ihr? | ☐ | ☐ |
| 3. Habt ihr heute gut geschlafen? | ☐ | ☐ |
| 4. Habt ihr im Ausland studiert? | ☐ | ☐ |
| 5. Wie findet ihr meinen Pullover? | ☐ | ☐ |
| 6. Seht ihr Vorteile in einem Auslandsstudium? | ☐ | ☐ |
| 7. Kann man eine Sprache gut lernen, ohne im Ausland zu wohnen? | ☐ | ☐ |
| 8. Welche Sprache ist besser – Deutsch oder Englisch? | ☐ | ☐ |
| 9. Wie werdet ihr Deutsch später im Beruf benutzen? | ☐ | ☐ |
| 10. Warum habt ihr Deutsch gewählt? | ☐ | ☐ |

### Zieltext

#### Ich möchte mein Deutsch benutzen in meinem Beruf.

Hier sprechen drei Studierende über ihre Erfahrungen mit Deutschlernen und ihre Pläne für die Zukunft. Alle drei haben im Ausland studiert und möchten ihr Deutsch später im Beruf benutzen. Nate war ein Jahr lang Student an der Universität in Freiburg; Bob war ein Semester lang Student an der Uni in Jena und Minna hat an einem Sommerprogramm in Mayen in der Eifel teilgenommen.

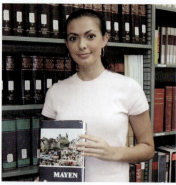

Bob, Nate und Minna: Es macht viel Spaß in Deutschland zu studieren und man lernt sehr viel.

 Hören Sie gut zu.

## *Rückblick*

 **22** **Wer hat das gesagt?** Markieren Sie die richtige Person für die folgenden Aussagen. Es können alle drei Personen sein oder auch niemand.

|  | Bob | Minna | Nate | Niemand |
|---|---|---|---|---|
| 1. kommt aus Deutschland | ☐ | ☐ | ☐ | ☐ |
| 2. schreibt gern Kurzgeschichten | ☐ | ☐ | ☐ | ☐ |
| 3. studiert Pflanzenbiologie | ☐ | ☐ | ☐ | ☐ |
| 4. hat zu Hause Deutsch gesprochen | ☐ | ☐ | ☐ | ☐ |
| 5. war im Sommer in Mayen | ☐ | ☐ | ☐ | ☐ |
| 6. hat in Frankfurt studiert | ☐ | ☐ | ☐ | ☐ |
| 7. sieht die Vorteile von einem Auslandsstudium | ☐ | ☐ | ☐ | ☐ |
| 8. möchte später osteuropäische Geschichte studieren | ☐ | ☐ | ☐ | ☐ |
| 9. hat mit Pflanzen in Deutschland gesprochen | ☐ | ☐ | ☐ | ☐ |
| 10. hat auch etwas Spanisch gelernt | ☐ | ☐ | ☐ | ☐ |

**23** **Kurz gefragt.** Beantworten Sie die folgenden Fragen auf Deutsch.

1. Wann hat Nate angefangen, Deutsch zu lernen?
2. Wer studiert nur Deutsch?
3. Wo liegen Mayen, Jena und Freiburg?
4. Welches von den drei Programmen scheint am interessantesten für Sie persönlich? Warum?
5. Warum ist es wichtig im Ausland zu sein, wenn man Deutsch lernen will?
6. Wie werden die drei Leute später ihr Deutsch benutzen?

**24** **Jeder macht Fehler.** Bob, Minna und Nate sprechen schon gut Deutsch, aber sie machen auch grammatische Fehler. Jeder Satz enthält einen grammatischen Fehler. Können Sie in Sätzen 1–4 einen Fehler mit der Endung identifizieren? Können Sie in Satz 5 einen Fehler oder ein Problem in der Wortstellung identifizieren?

1. „Ich habe fünf Jahren Deutsch gehabt."
2. „Auf jeden Fall, ich würde sagen, es gibt Vorteile auf viele Ebene."

> These sentences exhibit various errors of German.

3. „Es gibt viel Forschung über Pflanzen, die in Deutschland gemacht worden sind.“
4. „Als ich mit Deutsch angefangen habe, …“
5. „Als ich 13 war, es gab zu viele Leute in de[n] Spanischkursen.“

  **25** **Gesprochenes Deutsch.** Sprecher verwenden unter anderem diese fünf Strategien, wenn sie sprechen.

A. Sie sagen Dinge früher im Satz, als man sie laut Grammatik sagen sollte – damit sie diese Dinge nicht vergessen.
B. Sie korrigieren sich selbst.
C. Sie geben Beispiele, um etwas näher zu erklären.
D. Sie lassen Information aus, die der Hörer sich selbst denken kann.
E. Sie lassen Laute° am Ende eines Wortes aus.    *sounds*

Können Sie die richtige Strategie (A–E) in jedem Satz identifizieren?

1. Ich habe in Jena studiert, an der Friedrich Schiller Universität.
2. Andererseits ist auch gut, dass, em, ja man lernt die Kultur kennen.
3. Ich möchte mein Deutsch benutzen in meinem Beruf.
4. Es gibt 'n Vorteil.
5. Ich hab, ich bin mit Spanisch weitergegangen.
6. Ich wollte mehr Aufmerksamkeit von den, von der Lehrerin, also wählte ich Deutsch und [ich] bin auch ursprünglich deutsch.

  **F r e i e   K o m m u n i k a t i o n**

**Deutsch Dauersprechen.** Bilden Sie Paare und sprechen Sie mit Ihrem Partner/Ihrer Partnerin ohne Unterbrechung° über diese Frage auf Deutsch. Welches Paar kann am längsten ununterbrochen sprechen, ohne ein englisches Wort zu verwenden?    *interruption*

**Frage:** Wie war Ihr Deutschkurs anders und besser als andere Kurse oder Vorlesungen in diesem Semester?

**S c h r e i b e c k e**

**Meine Kompetenzenliste.** Machen Sie eine lange und konkrete Liste von allen Dingen, die Sie jetzt auf Deutsch machen können. Zum Beispiel, schreiben Sie: **Ich kann jetzt auf Deutsch Lebensmittel einkaufen gehen. Ich kann jemandem auf Deutsch erklären, wie mein Zimmer aussieht. Ich kann jetzt auf Deutsch sagen, warum ich meine Hausaufgabe nicht abgegeben habe.** Vergleichen Sie Ihre Liste mit anderen Studenten/Studentinnen im Kurs. Wer kann mehr sagen?

**Ein Gedicht über Deutsch.** Schreiben Sie ein Gedicht über Ihre Erfahrungen mit dem Deutschlernen.

## Wortschatz

### Persönliche Beziehungen

**die Beziehung, -en** *relationship*
**das Gefühl, -e** *feeling*
**der Humor** *humor*
**die Spontaneität** *spontaneity*
**die Stimmung, -en** *mood*
  **in einer Stimmung sein** *to be upset*
**der Tipp, -s** *tip, suggestion*
**die Vergangenheit** *past*
**die Zukunft** *future*
*Noch einmal:* **die Erfahrung**

**berichten (hat berichtet)** *to report*
**besprechen (bespricht, besprach, hat besprochen)** *to discuss*
**erfahren (erfährt, erfuhr, hat erfahren)** *to learn, find out, experience*
**erklären (hat erklärt)** *to explain*
**erleben (hat erlebt)** *to experience*
**ertragen (erträgt, ertrug, hat ertragen)** *to tolerate, bear*
**fehlen (hat gefehlt)** + *dat.* *to be missing, lacking*
**fort·setzen (hat fortgesetzt)** *to continue*
**nach·denken (dachte nach, hat nachgedacht)** + *acc.* *to consider something, think something over*
**passieren (ist passiert)** *to happen*
**rechnen (hat gerechnet)** *to count*
  **mit etwas rechnen** *to count on something*
**stören (hat gestört)** *to disturb*
**überzeugen (hat überzeugt)** *to convince*
**um·werfen (wirft um, warf um, hat umgeworfen)** *to knock over*
**(sich) verabschieden (hat [sich] verabschiedet) von** + *dat.* *to say good-bye (to someone)*
**verändern (hat verändert)** *to change*
**vermissen (hat vermisst)** *to miss (a person)*

**(sich) verstehen (verstand, hat [sich] verstanden)** *to understand (one another)*
  **Wir haben uns sehr gut verstanden.** *We got along very well with each other.*
**zusammen·passen (hat zusammengepasst)** *to fit together, belong together*

**echt** *(with an adjective)* *really*
**nett** *nice*
  **echt nett** *really nice*
**stressig** *stressful*
**toll** *great*
  **Ich finde es toll.** *I think it's great.*
**traurig** *sad(ly)*

### Ausdrücke

**auf der Welt** *in the world*
**Das hat mich total umgeworfen!** *That completely surprised me!*
**Das ist ja Unsinn!** *That's just nonsense!*
**Das kann ich nicht ertragen.** *I can't bear that.*
**etwas Persönliches** *something personal*
**Ganz cool bleiben!** *Keep cool! Stay calm!*
**ich fürchte** *I'm afraid*
**mit dem Gedanken kämpfen** *to struggle with the thought*
**von Anfang an** *from the very beginning*
**was ich damit anfangen soll** *what I should do with that*
**Wenn du nur wüsstest!** *If you only knew!*

### Deutschlernen

**der Aspekt, -e** *aspect*
**der Bereich, -e** *area, region*
**der Bericht, -e** *report*

**Deutsch als Fremdsprache** *German as a foreign language*
**der Dialekt, -e** *dialect*
**das Erlebnis, -se** *experience*
**die Fähigkeit, -en** *ability*
**das Gebiet, -e** *area*
**die Heimat, -en** *home*
**das Hobby, -s** *hobby*
**der Informationsvorsprung** *information advantage*
**das Institut, -e** *institute*
  **das Sprachinstitut, -e** *language institute*
**die Internetseite, -n** *Internet page*
**der Kurs, -e** *course*
**der Kursteilnehmer, - / die Kursteilnehmerin, -nen** *course participant*
**der Lebensraum, -räume** *habitat, living space*
**der Nobelpreisträger, - / Nobelpreisträgerin, -nen** *Nobel Prize winner*
**die Note, -n** *grade in a course*
**der Originaltext, -e** *original text*
**die Sprachkenntnis, -se** *linguistic competence*
**der Stellenwert, -e** *value, status*
**die Stellung, -en** *position, rank*
**der Übersetzer, - / die Übersetzerin, -nen** *translator*
**der Urgroßvater, -väter** *great grandfather*
**der Vorfahr, [-en], -en / die Vorfahrin, -nen** *forefathers, ancestors*
**die Website, -s** *Website*
**der Zusammenhang, ̈-e** *connection*
*Noch einmal:* **die Kenntnis, der Komponist, der Laptop, die Seminararbeit**

**aus·wandern (ist ausgewandert)** *to emigrate*

**sich bedanken für (hat sich bedankt)** + *acc.* *to thank for (something), express gratitude for (something)*

**berichten (hat berichtet)** *to report*

**unterrichten (hat unterrichtet)** *to teach*

**verbessern (hat verbessert)** *to improve*

**veröffentlichen (hat veröffentlicht)** *to publish*

**sich verständlich machen (hat sich verständlich gemacht)** *to make oneself understood*

**ausführlich** *detailed*

**erfolgreich** *successful(ly)*

**fließend** *fluent(ly)*

**lebendig** *alive, lively*

**tätig sein** *to be active, working*

**wissenschaftlich** *scientific, scholarly*

## Ausdrücke

**ab und zu** *now and then*

**aus Spaß** *for fun*

**indem** *(sub. conj.)* *by (doing something)*

**je dominanter, desto wichtiger** *the more dominant, the more important*

**ohne im Ausland zu wohnen** *without living abroad*

## Meine eigenen Wörter

_____

_____

_____

_____

_____

_____

## Literarisches Deutsch: Zwei Gedichte

### Gedicht 1

### In der Frühe
*Theodor Storm, 1817–1888*

Theodor Storm was born on September 14, 1817, in Husum (now North Germany), as a citizen of Denmark. He studied law and as a young married man, he fell violently in love with a 19-year old, whom he married after the death of his first wife. After his law career had taken him to Berlin for some time, he returned to Husum, where he died on July 4, 1888, of stomach cancer.

*Theodor Storm*

**Der poetische Student/die poetische Studentin.** Welche Wörter und Symbole würden Sie verwenden, wenn Sie ein Gedicht über den Morgen schreiben würden? Machen Sie eine Liste.

| | | |
|---|---|---|
| das Auto | ein Kaffee | schießen |
| das Bett | der Klang | der Sonnenschein |
| das Dach | krähen | sterben |
| die Goldstrahlen | der Mondschein | die Sterne |
| der Hahn | nun | ein Schwein |
| horchen° | der Ort | wach |

Notice that the **e** is missing in **krähen** (line 2). This reflects a colloquial variety of language as well as an attempt by Storm to maintain the meter or rhythm of the poem.

*listen, eavesdrop*

### In der Frühe

1  Goldstrahlen schießen übers Dach,
2  Die Hähne krähn den Morgen wach;
3  Nun einer hier, nun einer dort,
4  So kräht es nun von Ort zu Ort.
5  Und in der Ferne° stirbt der Klang —
6  Ich höre nichts, ich horche lang.
7  Ihr wackern° Hähne, krähet doch!
8  Sie schlafen immer, immer noch.

*distance*

*valiant*

**Die poetische Werkzeugkiste°.** Hier ist eine Liste von möglichen poetischen Werkzeugen°. Welche von diesen Werkzeugen findet man in dem Gedicht „In der Frühe"? Und in welcher Zeile oder in welchen Zeilen im Gedicht?

*toolbox*
*tools*

| | Im Gedicht? | Wo? | |
|---|---|---|---|
| 1. Symbolik | _____ | _____ | |
| 2. Wörter, die für den Kontext ungewöhnlich sind | _____ | _____ | |
| 3. Rhythmus | _____ | _____ | |
| 4. Reim | _____ | _____ | |
| 5. Wiederholung° von ähnlichen Wörtern | _____ | _____ | *repetition* |
| 6. Wörter, die Gegenteile° bedeuten | _____ | _____ | *opposites* |

**Das Gedicht in einem Satz.** Welcher von den fünf Sätzen unten fasst das Gedicht am besten zusammen°? Es gibt keine einzige richtige Antwort. Diskutieren Sie.

*zusammenfassen: to summarize*

1. Es wird Morgen.
2. Die Tiere sind laut.
3. Die Menschen sind faul.
4. Ein schöner Tag fängt an.
5. Die Tiere begrüßen den Morgen.

## Gedicht 2

### Zum Einschlafen zu sagen
*Rainer Maria Rilke, 1875–1926*

René Karl Wilhelm Johann Josef Maria Rilke was born on December 4, 1875, in Prague. Educated at an Austrian military school, he later studied philosophy at the University of Munich (1896–1899). There, he met an older married woman, with whom he traveled to Russia (1899–1900). He later married and then divorced a sculptor, through whom he met the famous French sculptor Rodin. Rilke traveled throughout Europe and lived in Paris from 1904–1914. After World War I, he moved to Switzerland. After the collapse of the Austrian-Hungarian Empire in 1920, he obtained Czech citizenship. He died of leukemia in a Swiss sanatorium on December 29, 1926.

*Rainer Maria Rilke*

**Der poetische Student/die poetische Studentin.** Welche Wörter und Symbole würden Sie verwenden, wenn Sie ein Gedicht über das Einschlafen° schreiben würden? Machen Sie eine Liste.

*falling asleep*

| | | |
|---|---|---|
| die Augen | der Mondschein | eine Uhr |
| ein Bett | die Nacht | der Wein |
| das Dunkel | die Sterne | die Zeit |
| ein Hund | die Stille | |

### Zum Einschlafen zu sagen

1 Ich möchte jemanden einsingen,
2 bei jemandem sitzen und sein.
3 Ich möchte dich wiegen° und kleinsingen — *to rock*
4 und begleiten° schlafaus und schlafein. — *to accompany*
5 Ich möchte der Einzige sein im Haus,
6 der wüsste°: die Nacht war kalt. — *would know*
7 Und möchte horchen herein und hinaus
8 in dich, in die Welt, in den Wald.
9 Die Uhren rufen sich schlagend° an, — *chiming*
10 und man sieht der Zeit auf den Grund.
11 Und unten geht noch ein fremder Mann
12 und stört einen fremden Hund.
13 Dahinter wird Stille. Ich habe groß
14 die Augen auf dich gelegt;
15 und sie halten dich sanft° und lassen dich los, — *gently*
16 wenn ein Ding sich im Dunkel bewegt°. — *stirs, moves*

**Der poetische Wortdetektiv.** Welche Ausdrücke und Sätze aus dem Gedicht von Rilke bedeuten ungefähr das Gleiche? Rilke hat selbst viele Wörter erfunden° und anderen eine neue Bedeutung gegeben. Spielen Sie mit der Sprache wie ein Poet und raten Sie.

*invented*

1. jemanden einsingen
2. jemanden kleinsingen
3. schlafaus und schlafein
4. herein horchen und hinaus horchen
5. der Zeit auf den Grund sehen
6. die Augen groß auf jemanden legen

a. in den Schlaf und aus dem Schlaf
b. bis ans Ende der Zeit sehen
c. für jemanden wie für ein kleines Kind singen
d. jemanden ganz genau anschauen
e. für jemanden singen, bis er/sie einschläft
f. ganz genau zuhören

**Fragen zum Gedicht.** Beantworten Sie die folgenden Fragen.

1. Ein Gedicht hat Strophen° und Zeilen°. Die Zeilen in einer Strophe folgen oft einem Reimschema. Dieses Gedicht hat vier Strophen. Was ist das Reimschema – abba? abab? aabb?

*stanzas / lines*

2. Das Gedicht hat das Wort „jemanden" in der ersten und der zweiten Zeile und geht mit „dich" in Zeile 3 weiter. Wie könnte man das erklären?

3. An wen ist das Gedicht geschrieben – an sich selbst? an ein Kind? an einen Geliebten/eine Geliebte°? an einen Hund? an _____?

*lover*

4. Welche Stimmung oder welches Gefühl drückt das Gedicht Ihrer Meinung nach aus – Liebe? Freundschaft? Melancholie? Müdigkeit? etwas anderes?

# Reference

# Appendix

## 1. Personal pronouns

| Nominative | Accusative | Accusative reflexive | Dative | Dative reflexive |
|---|---|---|---|---|
| ich | mich | mich | mir | mir |
| du | dich | dich | dir | dir |
| Sie | Sie | sich | Ihnen | sich |
| er | ihn | sich | ihm | sich |
| es | es | sich | ihm | sich |
| sie | sie | sich | ihr | sich |
| wir | uns | uns | uns | uns |
| ihr | euch | euch | euch | euch |
| Sie | Sie | sich | Ihnen | sich |
| sie | sie | sich | ihnen | sich |

## 2. Interrogative pronouns

| | | |
|---|---|---|
| **Nominative** | wer | was |
| **Accusative** | wen | was |
| **Dative** | wem | |
| **Genitive** | wessen | |

## 3. Relative pronouns

| | Masculine | Neuter | Feminine | Plural |
|---|---|---|---|---|
| **Nominative** | der | das | die | die |
| **Accusative** | den | das | die | die |
| **Dative** | dem | dem | der | denen |
| **Genitive** | dessen | dessen | deren | deren |

## 4. Definite articles and *der*-words

| | Masculine | Neuter | Feminine | Plural |
|---|---|---|---|---|
| **Nominative** | der | das | die | die |
| | dieser | dieses | diese | diese |
| **Accusative** | den | das | die | die |
| | diesen | dieses | diese | diese |
| **Dative** | dem | dem | der | den |
| | diesem | diesem | dieser | diesen |
| **Genitive** | des | des | der | der |
| | dieses | dieses | dieser | dieser |

Common **der**-words are **dieser, jeder, mancher, solcher,** and **welcher.**

## 5. Indefinite articles and *ein*-words

|  | Masculine | Neuter | Feminine | Plural |
|---|---|---|---|---|
| **Nominative** | ein | ein | eine | — |
|  | kein | kein | keine | keine |
|  | mein | mein | meine | meine |
| **Accusative** | einen | ein | eine | — |
|  | keinen | kein | keine | keine |
|  | meinen | mein | meine | meine |
| **Dative** | einem | einem | einer | — |
|  | keinem | keinem | keiner | keinen |
|  | meinem | meinem | meiner | meinen |
| **Genitive** | eines | eines | einer | — |
|  | keines | keines | keiner | keiner |
|  | meines | meines | meiner | meiner |

The **ein**-words include **kein** and the possessive adjectives **mein, dein, sein, ihr, unser, euer, ihr,** and **Ihr.**

## 6. Plural of nouns

| Type | Plural signal | Singular | Plural | Notes |
|---|---|---|---|---|
| 1 | (no change) | das Zimmer | **die Zimmer** | Masculine and neuter nouns |
|  | ¨(umlaut) | der Garten | **die Gärten** | ending in **-el, -en, -er** |
| 2 | -e | der Tisch | **die Tische** | |
|  | ¨e | der Stuhl | **die Stühle** | |
| 3 | -er | das Bild | **die Bilder** | Stem vowel **e, i** takes no umlaut |
|  | ¨er | das Buch | **die Bücher** | Stem vowel **a, o, u** takes umlaut |
| 4 | -en | die Uhr | **die Uhren** | |
|  | -n | die Lampe | **die Lampen** | |
| 5 | -nen | die Freundin | **die Freundinnen** | |
|  | -s | das Radio | **die Radios** | Mostly foreign words |

## 7. Masculine *N*-nouns

|  | Singular | Plural |
|---|---|---|
| **Nominative** | der Herr | die Herren |
| **Accusative** | den Herrn | die Herren |
| **Dative** | dem Herrn | den Herren |
| **Genitive** | des Herrn | der Herren |

Some other masculine *N*-nouns are **der Journalist, der Junge, der Kollege, der Komponist, der Kunde, der Mensch, der Nachbar, der Neffe, der Pilot, der Poet, der Präsident, der Praktikant, der Prinz, der Soldat, der Student, der Tourist.**

A few masculine *N*-nouns add **-ns** in the genitive: **der Name** → **des Namens.**

## 8. Preceded adjectives

|  | Masculine | Neuter | Feminine | Plural |
|---|---|---|---|---|
| Nominative | der **alte** Tisch<br>ein **alter** Tisch | das **alte** Buch<br>ein **altes** Buch | die **alte** Uhr<br>eine **alte** Uhr | die **alten** Bilder<br>keine **alten** Bilder |
| Accusative | den **alten** Tisch<br>einen **alten** Tisch | das **alte** Buch<br>ein **altes** Buch | die **alte** Uhr<br>eine **alte** Uhr | die **alten** Bilder<br>keine **alten** Bilder |
| Dative | dem **alten** Tisch<br>einem **alten** Tisch | dem **alten** Buch<br>einem **alten** Buch | der **alten** Uhr<br>einer **alten** Uhr | den **alten** Bildern<br>keinen **alten** Bildern |
| Genitive | des **alten** Tisches<br>eines **alten** Tisches | des **alten** Buches<br>eines **alten** Buches | der **alten** Uhr<br>einer **alten** Uhr | der **alten** Bilder<br>keiner **alten** Bilder |

## 9. Unpreceded adjectives

|  | Masculine | Neuter | Feminine | Plural |
|---|---|---|---|---|
| Nominative | kalt**er** Wein | kalt**es** Bier | kalt**e** Milch | alt**e** Leute |
| Accusative | kalt**en** Wein | kalt**es** Bier | kalt**e** Milch | alt**e** Leute |
| Dative | kalt**em** Wein | kalt**em** Bier | kalt**er** Milch | alt**en** Leuten |
| Genitive | kalt**en** Weines | kalt**en** Bieres | kalt**er** Milch | alt**er** Leute |

## 10. Nouns declined like adjectives

• *Nouns preceded by definite articles or* **der**-*words*

|  | Masculine | Neuter | Feminine | Plural |
|---|---|---|---|---|
| Nominative | der Deutsch**e** | das Gut**e** | die Deutsch**e** | die Deutsch**en** |
| Accusative | den Deutsch**en** | das Gut**e** | die Deutsch**e** | die Deutsch**en** |
| Dative | dem Deutsch**en** | dem Gut**en** | der Deutsch**en** | den Deutsch**en** |
| Genitive | des Deutsch**en** | des Gut**en** | der Deutsch**en** | der Deutsch**en** |

• *Nouns preceded by indefinite articles or* **ein**-*words*

|  | Masculine | Neuter | Feminine | Plural |
|---|---|---|---|---|
| Nominative | ein Deutsch**er** | ein Gut**es** | eine Deutsch**e** | keine Deutsch**en** |
| Accusative | einen Deutsch**en** | ein Gut**es** | eine Deutsch**e** | keine Deutsch**en** |
| Dative | einem Deutsch**en** | einem Gut**en** | einer Deutsch**en** | keinen Deutsch**en** |
| Genitive | eines Deutsch**en** | — | einer Deutsch**en** | keiner Deutsch**en** |

Other nouns declined like adjectives are **der/die Angestellte, Bekannte, Erwach-sene, Fremde, Jugendliche, Studierende, Verwandte.**

## 11. Irregular comparatives and superlatives

| Base form | bald | gern | gut | hoch | nah | viel |
|---|---|---|---|---|---|---|
| Comparative | eher | lieber | besser | höher | näher | mehr |
| Superlative | ehest- | liebst- | best- | höchst- | nächst - | meist- |

## 12. Adjectives and adverbs taking umlauts in the comparative and superlative

| | | | |
|---|---|---|---|
| alt | gesund (gesünder *or* gesunder) | kurz | schwach |
| arm | groß | lang | schwarz |
| blass (blasser or blässer) | jung | nass (nässer *or* nasser) | stark |
| dumm | kalt | oft | warm |
| fromm (frömmer *or* frommer) | krank | rot | |

## 13. Prepositions

| With accusative | With dative | With either accusative or dative | With genitive |
|---|---|---|---|
| durch | aus | an | (an)statt |
| für | außer | auf | außerhalb |
| gegen | bei | hinter | innerhalb |
| ohne | mit | in | trotz |
| um | nach | neben | während |
| | seit | über | wegen |
| | von | unter | |
| | zu | vor | |
| | gegenüber (von) | zwischen | |

## 14. Verbs and prepositions with special meanings

**Accusative**

| | | | |
|---|---|---|---|
| achten auf | *to pay attention to* | hoffen auf | *to hope for* |
| bitten um | *to ask for* | lachen über | *to laugh about* |
| böse sein auf | *to be mad at* | reden über | *to talk about* |
| danken für | *to thank (s.o.) for* | schreiben an | *to write to* |
| denken an | *to think about* | schreiben über | *to write about* |
| erinnern an | *to remind (s.o.) of* | sprechen über | *to talk about* |
| gespannt sein auf | *to be excited about* | warten auf | *to wait for* |
| glauben an | *to believe in* | wissen über | *to know about* |
| halten für | *to think (s.o.) is* | | |

**sich + Accusative**

| | | | |
|---|---|---|---|
| sich ärgern über | to be angry about | sich interessieren für | to be interested in |
| sich bewerben um | to apply for | sich konzentrieren auf | to concentrate on |
| sich entscheiden für/gegen | to decide on/against | sich unterhalten über | to converse about |
| sich erinnern an | to remember | sich verabreden mit | to make a date with |
| sich freuen auf | to look forward to | sich verlieben in | to fall in love with |
| sich freuen über | to be happy about | sich vor·bereiten auf | to prepare for |

**Dative**

| | | | |
|---|---|---|---|
| an·fangen mit | to begin with | handeln von | to be about |
| Angst haben vor | to be afraid of | sprechen mit | to talk to |
| arbeiten bei | to work at (the business of) | sprechen von | to talk of |
| beginnen mit | to begin with | suchen nach | to look for |
| erzählen von | to tell about | träumen von | to dream of |
| fahren mit | to go/travel by | etwas verstehen von | to know something about |
| fertig werden mit | to come to grips with, accept | wissen von | to know about |
| fragen nach | to ask about | wohnen bei | to live at the home of |
| halten von | to think of; to value | | |

**sich + Dative**

| | | | |
|---|---|---|---|
| sich beschäftigen mit | to keep busy with | sich verabreden mit | to make a date with |
| sich trennen von | to break up with | sich versöhnen mit | to reconcile with, make up with |

## 15. Dative verbs

| | | |
|---|---|---|
| antworten | gehören | passen |
| danken | glauben (*dat.* of person) | passieren |
| fehlen | gratulieren | schaden |
| folgen | helfen | schmecken |
| gefallen | Leid tun | weh·tun |

The verb **glauben** may take an impersonal accusative object: **ich glaube es.**

## 16. Guidelines for the position of *nicht*

1. **Nicht** always *follows* the finite verb.

   Hannes **arbeitet nicht.**
   Anna **kann nicht** gehen.

2. **Nicht** always *follows*:
   a. noun objects
   b. pronouns used as objects
   c. specific adverbs of time

   Ich glaube **Hannes nicht.**
   Ich glaube **es nicht.**
   Anna geht **heute nicht** mit.

3. **Nicht** *precedes* most other elements:
   a. predicate adjectives
   b. predicate nouns
   c. adverbs
   d. adverbs of general time
   e. prepositional phrases

   Dieter ist **nicht freundlich.**
   Dieter ist **nicht mein Freund.**
   Katrin spielt **nicht gern** Tennis.
   Katrin spielt **nicht oft** Tennis.
   Oliver geht **nicht ins Kino.**

4. If several of the elements that are preceded by **nicht** occur in a sentence, **nicht** usually *precedes* the first one.

   Ich gehe **nicht oft** ins Kino.

## 17. Verb conjugation

| | | Present | Narrative past | Subjunctive | Conversational past |
|---|---|---|---|---|---|
| **Irregular (Strong)** | *ich* | komme | kam | käme | bin gekommen |
| | *du* | kommst | kamst | kämest | bist gekommen |
| | *er/sie/es* | kommt | kam | käme | ist gekommen |
| | *wir* | kommen | kamen | kämen | sind gekommen |
| | *ihr* | kommt | kamt | kämet | seid gekommen |
| | *sie, Sie* | kommen | kamen | kämen | sind gekommen |
| **Regular (Weak)** | *ich* | mache | machte | machte | habe gemacht |
| | *du* | machst | machtest | machtest | hast gemacht |
| | *er/sie/es* | macht | machte | machte | hat gemacht |
| | *wir* | machen | machten | machten | haben gemacht |
| | *ihr* | macht | machtet | machtet | habt gemacht |
| | *sie, Sie* | machen | machten | machten | haben gemacht |
| **Mixed** | *ich* | weiß | wusste | wüsste | habe gewusst |
| | *du* | weißt | wusstest | wüsstest | hast gewusst |
| | *er/sie/es* | weiß | wusste | wüsste | hat gewusst |
| | *wir* | wissen | wussten | wüssten | haben gewusst |
| | *ihr* | wisst | wusstet | wüsstet | habt gewusst |
| | *sie, Sie* | wissen | wussten | wüssten | haben gewusst |
| **haben** | *ich* | habe | hatte | hätte | habe gehabt |
| | *du* | hast | hattest | hättest | hast gehabt |
| | *er/sie/es* | hat | hatte | hätte | hat gehabt |
| | *wir* | haben | hatten | hätten | haben gehabt |
| | *ihr* | habt | hattet | hättet | habt gehabt |
| | *sie, Sie* | haben | hatten | hätten | haben gehabt |
| **sein** | *ich* | bin | war | wäre | bin gewesen |
| | *du* | bist | warst | wärst | bist gewesen |
| | *er/sie/es* | ist | war | wäre | ist gewesen |
| | *wir* | sind | waren | wären | sind gewesen |
| | *ihr* | seid | wart | wärt | seid gewesen |
| | *sie, Sie* | sind | waren | wären | sind gewesen |

| | | Present | Narrative past | Subjunctive | Conversational past |
|---|---|---|---|---|---|
| **werden** | *ich* | werde | wurde | würde | bin geworden |
| | *du* | wirst | wurdest | würdest | bist geworden |
| | *er/sie/es* | wlrd | wurde | würde | lst geworden |
| | *wir* | werden | wurden | würden | sind geworden |
| | *ihr* | werdet | wurdet | würdet | seid geworden |
| | *sie, Sie* | werden | wurden | würden | sind geworden |

## 18. Modal auxiliaries

| | dürfen | können | müssen | sollen | wollen | mögen | (möchte) |
|---|---|---|---|---|---|---|---|
| *ich* | darf | kann | muss | soll | will | mag | (möchte) |
| *du* | darfst | kannst | musst | sollst | willst | magst | (möchtest) |
| *er/sie/es* | darf | kann | muss | soll | will | mag | (möchte) |
| *wir* | dürfen | können | müssen | sollen | wollen | mögen | (möchten) |
| *ihr* | dürft | könnt | müsst | sollt | wollt | mögt | (möchtet) |
| *sie, Sie* | dürfen | können | müssen | sollen | wollen | mögen | (möchten) |
| **Narrative past** | durfte | konnte | musste | sollte | wollte | mochte | |
| **Past participle** | gedurft | gekonnt | gemusst | gesollt | gewollt | gemocht | |

## 19. Imperative

| | gehen | sehen | arbeiten | sein | haben |
|---|---|---|---|---|---|
| **Familiar singular** | geh(e) | sieh | arbeite | sei | hab |
| **Familiar plural** | geht | seht | arbeitet | seid | habt |
| **Formal** | gehen Sie | sehen Sie | arbeiten Sie | seien Sie | haben Sie |
| ***Wir*-form** | gehen wir | sehen wir | arbeiten wir | seien wir | haben wir |

## 20. Future

| | | | |
|---|---|---|---|
| *ich* | werde | werde | |
| *du* | wirst | wirst | |
| *er/sie/es* | wird | wird | |
| *wir* | werden | werden | |
| *ihr* | werdet | werdet | |
| *sie, Sie* | werden | werden | |

sehen    gehen

## 21. Passive voice

| | | Present passive | | Conversational past passive | | Past perfect passive | |
|---|---|---|---|---|---|---|---|
| *ich* | werde | | | wurde | | bin | |
| *du* | wirst | | | wurdest | | bist | |
| *er/sie/es* | wird | } gesehen | | wurde | } gesehen | ist | } gesehen worden |
| *wir* | werden | | | wurden | | sind | |
| *ihr* | werdet | | | wurdet | | seid | |
| *sie, Sie* | werden | | | wurden | | sind | |

## 22. Principal parts of irregular (strong) and mixed verbs

The following list contains the principal parts of most of the high-frequency irregular (strong) and mixed verbs that appear in the second edition of **Vorsprung.** Regular (weak) verbs and most other verbs with separable and inseparable prefixes that follow the pattern of corresponding verbs on this list are not included here. Some high-frequency verbs with separable prefixes, whose meanings differ substantially from the base verb, have also been included. All forms given here are in the third-person singular (**er, sie, es**).

| Infinitive | Present | Narrative past | Conversational past | Meaning |
|---|---|---|---|---|
| an·fangen | fängt an | fing an | hat angefangen | *to begin* |
| an·rufen | ruft an | rief an | hat angerufen | *to call up, phone* |
| (sich) an·ziehen | zieht an | zog an | hat angezogen | *to put on, dress* |
| auf·fallen | fällt auf | fiel auf | ist aufgefallen | *to occur to* |
| aus·geben | gibt aus | gab aus | hat ausgegeben | *to spend* |
| (sich) aus·ziehen | zieht aus | zog aus | hat ausgezogen | *to undress, get undressed* |
| befehlen | befiehlt | befahl | hat befohlen | *to command* |
| beginnen | beginnt | begann | hat begonnen | *to start, begin* |
| beschreiben | beschreibt | beschrieb | hat beschrieben | *to describe* |
| sich bewerben | bewirbt sich | bewarb sich | hat sich beworben | *to apply* |
| bieten | bietet | bot | hat geboten | *to offer* |
| bitten | bittet | bat | hat gebeten | *to request, ask for* |
| bleiben | bleibt | blieb | ist geblieben | *to stay, remain* |
| brechen | bricht | brach | hat gebrochen | *to break* |
| brennen | brennt | brannte | hat gebrannt | *to burn* |
| bringen | bringt | brachte | hat gebracht | *to bring* |
| denken | denkt | dachte | hat gedacht | *to think* |
| dürfen | darf | durfte | hat gedurft | *to be allowed to; may* |
| ein·laden | lädt ein | lud ein | hat eingeladen | *to invite* |
| empfehlen | empfiehlt | empfahl | hat empfohlen | *to recommend* |
| sich entscheiden | entscheidet sich | entschied sich | hat sich entschieden | *to decide* |
| erkennen | erkennt | erkannte | hat erkannt | *to recognize* |

| Infinitive | Present | Narrative past | Conversational past | Meaning |
|---|---|---|---|---|
| essen | isst | aß | hat gegessen | *to eat* |
| fahren | fährt | fuhr | ist gefahren | *to drive* |
| fallen | fällt | fiel | ist gefallen | *to fall* |
| fangen | fängt | fing | hat gefangen | *to catch* |
| fern·sehen | sieht fern | sah fern | hat ferngesehen | *to watch TV* |
| finden | findet | fand | hat gefunden | *to find* |
| fliegen | fliegt | flog | ist geflogen | *to fly* |
| geben | gibt | gab | hat gegeben | *to give* |
| gefallen | gefällt | gefiel | hat gefallen | *to please* |
| gehen | geht | ging | ist gegangen | *to go* |
| genießen | genießt | genoss | hat genossen | *to enjoy* |
| gewinnen | gewinnt | gewann | hat gewonnen | *to win* |
| haben | hat | hatte | hat gehabt | *to have to* |
| halten | hält | hielt | hat gehalten | *to stop; to hold* |
| hängen | hängt | hing | hat/ist gehangen | *to be hanging* |
| heben | hebt | hob | hat gehoben | *to lift* |
| heißen | heißt | hieß | hat geheißen | *to be named* |
| helfen | hilft | half | hat geholfen | *to help* |
| kennen | kennt | kannte | hat gekannt | *to know* |
| klingen | klingt | klang | hat geklungen | *to sound* |
| kommen | kommt | kam | ist gekommen | *to come* |
| können | kann | konnte | hat gekonnt | *to be able; can* |
| lassen | lässt | ließ | hat gelassen | *to let; to allow* |
| laufen | läuft | lief | hat gelaufen | *to run* |
| leihen | leiht | lieh | hat geliehen | *to lend* |
| lesen | liest | las | hat gelesen | *to read* |
| liegen | liegt | lag | hat gelegen | *to lie* |
| mögen | mag | mochte | hat gemocht | *to like* |
| müssen | muss | musste | hat gemusst | *to have to; must* |
| nehmen | nimmt | nahm | hat genommen | *to take* |
| nennen | nennt | nannte | hat genannt | *to name* |
| reiten | reitet | ritt | ist geritten | *to ride horseback* |
| rennen | rennt | rannte | ist gerannt | *to run, race* |
| rufen | ruft | rief | hat gerufen | *to call* |
| scheinen | scheint | schien | hat geschienen | *to shine; to seem* |
| schlafen | schläft | schlief | hat geschlafen | *to sleep* |
| schließen | schließt | schloss | hat geschlossen | *to close* |
| schneiden | schneidet | schnitt | hat geschnitten | *to cut* |
| schreiben | schreibt | schrieb | hat geschrieben | *to write* |
| schwimmen | schwimmt | schwamm | ist geschwommen | *to swim* |
| sehen | sieht | sah | hat gesehen | *to see* |

| Infinitive | Present | Narrative past | Conversational past | Meaning |
|---|---|---|---|---|
| sein | ist | war | ist gewesen | *to be* |
| singen | singt | sang | hat gesungen | *to sing* |
| sinken | sinkt | sank | ist gesunken | *to sink* |
| sitzen | sitzt | saß | hat gesessen | *to sit* |
| sollen | soll | sollte | hat gesollt | *to be supposed to; should* |
| sprechen | spricht | sprach | hat gesprochen | *to speak* |
| springen | springt | sprang | ist gesprungen | *to jump* |
| statt·finden | findet statt | fand statt | hat stattgefunden | *to take place, occur* |
| stehen | steht | stand | hat gestanden | *to stand* |
| steigen | steigt | stieg | ist gestiegen | *to climb* |
| sterben | stirbt | starb | ist gestorben | *to die* |
| stinken | stinkt | stank | hat gestunken | *to stink* |
| streiten | streitet | stritt | hat gestritten | *to argue* |
| tragen | trägt | trug | hat getragen | *to wear; to carry* |
| treffen | trifft | traf | hat getroffen | *to meet; to score* |
| treiben | treibt | trieb | hat getrieben | *to engage in* |
| treten | tritt | trat | ist getreten | *to step* |
| trinken | trinkt | trank | hat getrunken | *to drink* |
| tun | tut | tat | hat getan | *to do* |
| verbieten | verbietet | verbot | hat verboten | *to forbid* |
| verbringen | verbringt | verbrachte | hat verbracht | *to spend time* |
| vergessen | vergisst | vergaß | hat vergessen | *to forget* |
| verlieren | verliert | verlor | hat verloren | *to lose* |
| verstehen | versteht | verstand | hat verstanden | *to understand* |
| vor·schlagen | schlägt vor | schlug vor | hat vorgeschlagen | *to suggest* |
| wachsen | wächst | wuchs | ist gewachsen | *to grow* |
| waschen | wäscht | wusch | hat gewaschen | *to wash* |
| werden | wird | wurde | ist geworden | *to become* |
| werfen | wirft | warf | hat geworfen | *to throw* |
| wissen | weiß | wusste | hat gewusst | *to know* |
| wollen | will | wollte | hat gewollt | *to want* |
| ziehen | zieht | zog | hat gezogen | *to pull* |

# German-English Vocabulary

This German-English vocabulary is a comprehensive compilation of all active and receptive vocabulary used in *Vorsprung.* The information in brackets indicates the chapter in which the word was presented as active vocabulary. The symbol ~ represents the key word within an entry.

Nouns are preceded by the definite articles; the plural endings follow after a comma. Weak masculine nouns have the accusative, dative and genitive endings in brackets before the plural ending, e.g., [-en], -en. If the plural form of a noun is rarely or never used, no plural ending is indicated. Adjectives and adverbs that take an umlaut in the comparative and superlative are shown: **alt (ä)**.

Regular (weak) verbs are listed with conversational past tense forms only in parentheses, e.g., **spielen (hat gespielt)**. Irregular (strong or mixed) verbs generally are listed with both the narrative and conversational past tense forms in parentheses, e.g., **ziehen (zog, hat gezogen)**; if there is a present tense vowel change, the present tense will be listed before the other tenses, e.g., **geben (gibt, gab, hat gegeben)**. Separable prefixes are indicated with a raised dot, e.g., **zurück·bringen**. Reflexive verbs are preceded by the reflexive pronoun **sich.**

The glossary uses the following abbreviations:

| | |
|---|---|
| *acc.* | accusative |
| *adj.* | adjective |
| *adv.* | adverb |
| *colloq.* | colloquial |
| *conj.* | conjunction |
| *dat.* | dative |
| *fam.* | familiar |
| *gen.* | genitive |
| *pl.* | plural |
| *sing.* | singular |

## A

**ab und zu**   occasionally [K. 4]

**ab·bauen (hat abgebaut)**   to reduce, decrease

**ab·biegen (bog ab, ist abgebogen)**   to turn; **links/rechts ~**   to turn to the left/right [K. 7]

**die Abbildung, -en**   illustration

**ab·drehen (hat abgedreht)**   to turn off

**der Abend, -e**   evening [K. 3, 8]; **eines Abends**   one evening [K. 10]; **Guten ~!**   Good Evening! [K. 1] **der Heilige ~**   Christmas Eve

**das Abendbrot**   evening meal, supper [K. 3]

**das Abendessen**   evening meal, supper [K. 3]

**abendlich**   evening time

**abends**   in the evening [K. 2]

**der Abenteuerfilm, -e**   adventure film [K. 7]

**aber**   but [K. 2]

**ab·geben (gibt ab, gab ab, hat abgegeben)**   to turn in (a paper)

**Abgemacht!**   Deal! Agreed! [K. 11]

**der/die Abgeordnete, -n**   representative

**abgetragen**   worn out

**ab·hängen (hing ab, hat abgehangen) von + dat.**   to depend on

**ab·hauen (ist abgehauen)**   to take off, scram [K. 10]

**ab·heben (hob ab, hat abgehoben)**   to withdraw money [K. 7]

**ab·holen (hat abgeholt)**   to pick up

**das Abitur**   high school graduation exam [K. 8]

**der Abiturient, [-en], -en/die Abiturientin, -nen**   high school senior, soon-to-be graduate [K. 8]

**das Abkommen, -**   treaty [K. 11]

**ab·lenken (hat abgelenkt)**   to divert

**abnormal**   abnormal, unusual

**die Abreise, -n**   departure

**ab·reißen (riss ab, hat abgerissen)**   to tear down, demolish

**der Absatz, ¨e**   paragraph

**der Abschied**   farewell [K. 1]

**die Abschiedsparty, -s**   bon voyage party

**ab·schießen (schoss ab, hat abgeschossen)**   to shoot down

**ab·schließen (schließt ab, schloss ab, hat abgeschlossen)**   to lock

**der Abschluss, *pl.* Abschlüsse**   completion of program, degree

**ab·schneiden (schnitt ab, hat abgeschnitten)**   to cut off [K. 10]; **gut ~**   to place well, do well [K. 8]

**ab·stammen (hat abgestammt) von + dat.**   to stem from

**die Abstammung**   origin

**ab·stellen (hat abgestellt)**   to turn off

**der Abstellraum, ¨e**   storage room [K. 6]

**das Abteil, -e**   compartment

**die Abteilung, -en**   department

**ab·trocknen (hat abgetrocknet)**   to dry off [K. 8]

**abwechselnd**   alternatingly

**Ach so!**   Oh! I see! I get it! [K. 11]

**acht**   eight [K. 1]

**achten (hat geachtet) auf + *acc.***   to pay attention to, watch for [K. 8]

**achtzehn**   eighteen [K. 1]

**achtzig**   eighty [K. 1]

**das Adjektiv, -e**   adjective

**die Adresse, -n**   address

**das Adressbuch, ¨er**   address book [K. 4]

**der Advent**   Advent

**das Adverb, -(i)en**   adverb

**afrikanisch**   African

**die AG: die Aktiengesellschaft, -en**   corporation

**aggressiv**   aggressive

**Aha.** Oh. [K. 11]

**ahnen (hat geahnt)** to guess, suspect, sense [K. 11]

**ähnlich** similar, resembling

**die Ahnung; -en** foreboding, idea

**die Akte, -n** file

**die Aktiengesellschaft, -en** corporation

**die Aktivität, -en** activity [K. 2]

**aktuell** current, up-to-date [K. 8]

**akzeptabel** acceptable

**der Alarm** alarm

**der Albtraum, ̈e** nightmare [K. 1]

**der Alexanderplatz** Alexander Square *(in Berlin)*

**der Alkohol** alcohol

**alkoholfrei** non-alcoholic

**alle** all, everybody [K. 6]; **aller Art** all kinds of; **vor allem** above all

**allein** alone [K. 6]

**allerdings** nonetheless [AB 8]

**alles** everything, all [K. 6]; **~ Gute** all the best [K. 1]; **~ was du brauchst** everything you need; **~ in Ordnung** everything is in order [K. 6]; **Alles klar!** Okay!, Great! [K. 6]

**die Alliierten** *(pl.)* the Allies (in World War II) [K. 11]

**der Alltag** everyday life, routine; **hoch über dem ~** far beyond the everyday

**allwissend** all-knowing

**die Alpen** *(pl.)* the Alps

**das Alphabet, -e** alphabet

**als** as, than [K. 9]; when [K. 10]

**also** well, all right, OK *(conversation starter);* well . . ., so . . . *(for stalling)*

**alt (ä)** old [K. 1]

**der Altar, ̈e** altar

**das Alter** age

**die Altstadt** historic part of town

**am: ~ ersten Januar** on the first of January [K. 2]; **~ liebsten** most of all, the most; **~ Sonntag** on (this) Sunday [K. 2]; **~ Wochenende** on the weekend [K. 2]

**Amerika** America [K. 11]

**der Amerikaner, -/die Amerikanerin, -nen** American [K. 1]

**amerikanisch** American; **der amerikanische Football** American football [K. 7]

**die Ampel, -n** traffic light [K. 7]

**an** at, on; to [K. 7]

**analytisch** analytical [K. 9]

**an·bieten (bot an, hat angeboten)** to offer

**das Andenken, -** souvenir [K. 10]

**andere** other [K. 9]; **unter anderem** among other things

**andererseits** on the other hand

**ändern (hat geändert)** to change

**anders** different(ly) [K. 8]; **~ als** different from

**anderswo** someplace else

**die Anekdote, -n** anecdote

**der Anfang, ̈e** beginning [K. 12]

**an·fangen (fängt an, fing an, hat angefangen)** to start, begin [K. 5]

**der Anfänger, -/die Anfangerin, -nen** beginner [K. 10]

**angeblich** supposedly

**angegossen: wie ~ passen** to have a perfect fit

**an·gehören (hat angehört)** + *dat.* to belong to

**angeln** to fish [K. 3]

**angenehm** pleasant; **Sehr ~!** Pleased to meet you! [K. 1]

**der/die Angestellte, -n** *(adj. as noun)* employee [K. 9]

**der Anglist, [-en], -en/die Anglistin, -nen** English major

**die Anglistik** English language and literature

**an·glotzen (hat angeglotzt)** to stare at

**die Angst, ̈e** fear, anxiety [K. 2]

**Angst haben (hat, hatte, hat gehabt) vor** + *dat.* to be afraid of [K. 2, 8]

**an·halten (hält an, hielt an, hat angehalten)** to stop

**der Anhänger, -/die Anhängerin, -nen** follower, supporter [K. 7]

**sich an·hören (hat sich angehört)** to sound like [K. 11]

**an·kommen (kam an, ist angekommen)** to arrive [K. 2]; **~ auf** + *acc.* to depend on [K. 11]

**an·kreuzen (hat angekreuzt)** to check (off)

**die Ankunft, ̈e** arrival

**der Anlauftext** start-up text

**an·melden (hat angemeldet)** to announce, register

**die Annonce, -n** want ad

**der Anorak, -s** parka [K. 10]

**an·pöbeln (hat angepöbelt)** to pester

**an·probieren (hat anprobiert)** to try on [K. 10]

**an·reden (hat angeredet)** to address

**die Anreise** arrival

**an·rufen (rief an, hat angerufen)** to phone, call up [K. 2]

**an·schauen (hat angeschaut)** to (take a) look at [K. 6]; **schief ~** to look at (someone) funny [K. 6]

**der Anschluss** *pl.* **Anschlüsse** (train) connection

**die Ansichtskarte, -n** picture postcard

**an·sprechen (spricht an, sprach an, hat angesprochen)** to initiate a conversation [K. 5]

**anspruchsvoll** demanding; sophisticated

**anständig** decent, respectable [K. 9]

**an·starren (hat angestarrt)** to stare at

**anstatt** + *gen.* instead of [K. 8]

**anstelle von** instead of

**die Antwort, -en** answer

**antworten (hat geantwortet)** to answer [K. 1]

**die Anweisung, -en** direction

**die Anzeige, -n** ad

**sich an·ziehen (zog sich an, hat sich angezogen)** to put on clothes, get dressed [K. 8]

**der Anzug, ̈e** suit

**der Apfel, ̈** apple [K. 3]

**die Apfelsine, -n** orange [K. 3]

**die Apotheke, -n** pharmacy, drug store [K. 7]

**der Apotheker, -/die Apothekerin, -nen** pharmacist [K. 9]

**Appetit: Guten ~ !** Bon appetit!, Enjoy your meal! [K. 6]

**der April** April [K. 2]

**das Äquivalent, -e** equivalent

**die Arbeit, -en** work [K. 9]

**arbeiten (hat gearbeitet)** to work [K. 5]

**der Arbeiter, -/die Arbeiterin, -nen** worker [K. 9]

**das Arbeitsamt, ̈er** (un)employment agency

**das Arbeitsangebot, -e** job offer

**das Arbeitsbuch, ̈er** workbook [K. 1]

**die Arbeitserfahrung, -en** work experience [K. 9]

**die Arbeitsgruppe, -n** study group [K. 8]

**das Arbeitsklima**   work environment
**arbeitslos**   unemployed
**die Arbeitsnorm, -en**   work quota/standard
**der Arbeitsplatz, ¨e**   job; place of work
**die Arbeitsvermittlung, -en**   job placement agency
**das Arbeitszimmer, -**   workroom; study
**der Architekt, [-en], -en/die Architektin, -nen**   architect [K. 9]
**der Ärger**   annoyance
**sich ärgern (hat sich geärgert) über +** *acc.*   to be angry about [K. 8]
**der Arm, -e**   arm [K. 6]
**arm(ä)**   poor [K. 10]
**die Armbanduhr, -en**   wristwatch
**die Armee, -n**   army [K. 11]; **die Rote ~**   Red Army
**die Art, -en**   kind, type [K. 10]
**der Artikel, -**   article; **der bestimmte ~**   definite article; **der unbestimmte ~**   indefinite article
**der Arzt, ¨e/die Ärztin, -nen**   physician [K. 8, 9]
**die Asche, -n**   ash, cinder [K. 10]   **Aschenputtel**   Cinderella; **der Aschermittwoch**   Ash Wednesday
**asiatisch**   Asian
**der Aspekt, -e**   aspect [K. 12]
**das Aspirin**   aspirin
**der Assistent, [-en], -en/die Assistentin, -nen**   assistant
**die Astronomie**   astronomy
**attraktiv**   attractive [K. 1]
**auch**   also [K. 2]
**auf**   on, onto [K. 7]; **~ dem Dachboden**   in the attic; **~ Deutsch**   in German
**auf·bleiben (blieb auf, ist aufgeblieben)**   to stay up
**auf·decken (hat aufgedeckt)**   to reveal [K. 11]
**der Aufenthalt, -e**   stay, time spent in a place
**auf·fallen (fällt auf, fiel auf, ist aufgefallen) +** *dat.*   to occur to s.o.
**die Aufführung, -en**   performance [K. 9]
**die Aufgabe, -n**   assignment, task [K. 9]
**auf·geben (gibt auf, gab auf, hat aufgegeben)**   to drop off, post; to give up

**aufgeregt**   excited; tense, nervous [K. 4, 9]
**aufgrund**   on the basis of
**auf·hängen (hat aufgehängt)**   to hang up
**auf·hören (hat aufgehört)**   to stop [K. 2]
**auf·kriegen (hat aufgekriegt)**   to get open (*colloq.*) [K. 6]
**auf·machen (hat aufgemacht)**   to open [K. 1]
**auf·passen (hat aufgepasst) auf +** *acc.*   to watch out for, pay attention to; **Pass mal auf!**   Look here! [K. 11]
**auf·räumen (hat aufgeräumt)**   to pick up, clean up
**aufrecht·erhalten (erhält aufrecht, erhielt aufrecht, hat aufrecht erhalten)**   to maintain, preserve
**sich auf·regen (hat sich aufgeregt)**   to get upset, nervous; to get excited
**die Aufregung -en**   excitement; nervousness
**auf·schauen (hat aufgeschaut)**   to look up
**auf·schließen (hat aufgeschlossen)**   to unlock [K. 6]
**der Aufschnitt**   cold cuts [K. 3]
**auf·schreiben (schrieb auf, hat aufgeschrieben)**   to write down [K. 6]
**der Aufstand, ¨e**   revolt, uprising [K. 11]
**auf·stehen (steht auf, stand auf, ist aufgestanden)**   to get up, get out of bed [K. 2]
**der Auftrag, ¨e**   assignment
**auf·wachen (ist aufgewacht)**   to wake up [K. 2]
**auf·wachsen (wächst auf, wuchs auf, ist aufgewachsen)**   to grow up [K. 11]
**auf·wärmen (hat aufgewärmt)**   to warm up
**das Auge, -n**   eye [K. 1, 6]
**die Augenbraue, -n**   eyebrow
**der August**   August [K. 2]
**aus +** *dat.*   from [K. 6]
**die Ausbildung, -en**   education, job training [K. 9]
**der Ausbildungsleiter, -/die Ausbildungsleiterin, -nen**   head trainer, lead teacher
**der Ausdruck, ¨e**   expression

**aus·fahren (fährt aus, fuhr aus, ist ausgefahren)**   to deliver
**aus·fallen (fällt aus, fiel aus, ist ausgefallen)**   to be canceled
**ausführlich**   detailed [K. 12]
**aus·füllen (hat ausgefüllt)**   to fill out
**aus·geben (gibt aus, gab aus, hat aus·gegeben)**   to spend (money) [K. 4]
**ausgeglichen**   similar, uniform [K. 11]
**aus·gehen (ging aus, ist ausgegangen)**   to go out [K. 5]
**ausgesprochen**   decidedly
**ausgezeichnet**   excellent
**die Aushilfe, -n**   temporary, part-time worker [K. 9]
**sich aus·kennen (hat sich ausgekannt) mit +** *dat.*   to know a lot about
**aus·kommen (kam aus, ist ausgekommen) mit +** *dat.*   to get along with [K. 9]
**das Ausland**   abroad; foreign country [K. 12]
**der Ausländer, -/die Ausländerin, -nen**   foreigner [K. 6]
**die Ausländerfeindlichkeit**   xenophobia [K. 6]
**ausländisch**   foreign [K. 6]
**aus·liegen (lag aus, hat ausgelegen)**   to be displayed
**die Ausnahme, -n**   exception
**die Ausrede, -n**   excuse; **Ausreden machen (hat gemacht)**   to make excuses
**aus·rufen (rief aus, hat ausgerufen)**   to proclaim, announce
**sich aus·ruhen (hat sich ausgeruht)**   to relax [K. 8]
**aus·schreiben (schrieb aus, hat ausgeschrieben)**   to advertise, announce
**die Aussage, -n**   statement
**das Aussehen**   appearance [K. 1]
**aus·sehen (sieht aus, sah aus, hat ausgesehen)**   to appear, look (like) [K. 1, 5]
**der Außenminister, -/die Außenministerin, -nen**   foreign minister
**außer +** *dat.*   except for [K. 5, 6]
**außerdem**   besides, by the way
**außerhalb +** *gen.*   outside of [K. 8]
**die Aussicht, -en**   view [K. 3]; prospect, view

aus·steigen (stieg aus, ist ausgestiegen) to get out of, disembark [K. 10]

der Austausch   exchange; das Austauschprogramm, -e study-abroad exchange program [K. 6]; der Austauschstudent, [-en], -en/die Austauschstudentin, -nen exchange student [K. 6]

aus·tragen (trägt aus, trug aus, hat ausgetragen) to deliver

(das) Australien   Australia [K. 2]

aus·üben (hat ausgeübt): einen Beruf ~ to practice, pursue [a profession]

die Auswahl   selection

aus·wählen (hat ausgewählt) to pick out, select

aus·wandern (ist ausgewandert) to emigrate [K. 12]

das Auswärtstor, -e goal scored at an away-game (soccer)

auswendig   by heart, memorized

die Auszeichnung   award, recognition

sich aus·ziehen (zog sich aus, hat sich ausgezogen) to get undressed [K. 8]

der/die Auszubildende, -n (Azubi) (adj. as noun) apprentice [K. 8, 9]

authentisch   authentic

das Auto, -s automobile, car [K. 4]; ~ fahren to drive a car

die Autobahn, -en autobahn, superhighway [K. 4]

die Autobiographie, -n autobiography [K. 7]

der Autobus, -se bus [K. 4]

autofrei   car-free

das Autogrammspiel, -e autograph game

der Automat, [-en], -en vending machine [K. 6]

der Automechaniker, -/die Automechanikerin, -nen car mechanic [K. 9]

der Autor, -en/die Autorin, -nen author

der Autoschlüssel, - car key

der/die Azubi, -s apprentice

## B

babysitten (hat gebabysittet) to babysit

der Babysitter, -/die Babysitterin, -nen babysitter [K. 9]

der Bach, ⁻e brook

der Bäcker, -/die Bäckerin, -nen baker [K. 9]

die Bäckerei, -en bakery [K. 7]

das Bad, ⁻er bath [K. 6]

der Badeanzug, ⁻e (woman's) bathing suit [K. 4]

die Badehose, -n (man's) bathing suit [K. 4]

sich baden (hat sich gebadet) to bathe [K. 8]

das Badetuch, ⁻er bath towel [K. 8]

die Badewanne, -n bathtub [K. 8]

das Badezimmer, - bathroom [K. 6]

das BAföG federal tuition assistance, financial aid

die Bahn, -en railroad, train [K. 4] mit der ~ fahren to travel by train [K. 4]

die Bahncard   discount rail pass

der Bahnhof, ⁻e train station [K. 3]; ~ verstehen to not have a clue

das Bähnli, -s little train (Swiss dialect)

bald   soon [K. 2]

der Balkon, -s (-e) balcony [K. 6]

der Ball, ⁻e ball [K. 7]; ball, dance [K. 10]

das Ballett, -e ballet [K. 9]

die Banane, -n banana [K. 3]

die Bandbreite   range

die Bank, -en bank [K. 7]

die Bankkarte, -n bank card, ATM card [K. 4, 7]

der Bankkredit, -e bank loan [K. 10]

das Bargeld   cash [K. 7]

das Barock   Baroque

die Barriere, -n barrier

der Baseball   baseball [K. 3]

der Basketball   basketball [K. 3]

der Bauch, ⁻e stomach [K. 6]

bauen (hat gebaut) to construct, build [K. 9]

der Bauer, [-n], -n/die Bäuerin, -nen farmer

der Baum, ⁻e tree [K. 10]

(das) Bayern   Bavaria

beachten (hat beachtet) to observe, pay attention to [K. 4]

der Beamte, [-en] -n/die Beamtin, -nen civil servant, official

der Becher, - cup [K. 8]

sich bedanken (hat sich bedankt) für + acc. to thank for (something) [K. 12]

bedeckt   overcast [K. 5]

bedeuten (hat bedeutet) to mean [K. 4]

das Bedürfnis, -se need

sich beeilen (hat sich beeilt) to hurry [K. 8]

beeindrucken (hat beeindruckt) to impress [K. 9]

beeindruckend   impressive

der Befehl, -e command

befehlen (beflehlt, befahl, hat befohlen) to command

die Beförderung, -en advancement, promotion

begabt   talented [K. 9]

begegnen (ist begegnet) + dat. to meet, run into

begeistert   enthusiastic, excited

beginnen (begann, hat begonnen) to begin [K. 2, 5]

begleiten (hat begleitet) to accompany

begraben   to bury; buried

begrenzt   limited

der Begriff, -e concept, term

behalten (behält, behielt, hat behalten) to keep [K. 7]

behandeln (hat behandelt) to treat

behaupten (hat behauptet) to claim, maintain

beheizt   heated

bei + dat. at, by, near, with [K. 6]

beide   both [K. 5]

beige   beige [K. 1]

das Bein, -e leg [K. 6]

das Beispiel, -e example [K. 2]; zum ~ (z.B.) for example [K. 2]

bei·treten (tritt bei, trat bei, ist beigetreten) + dat. to join, become a member [K. 11]

bekannt   familiar, well-known [K. 8]

der/die Bekannte, -n (adj. as noun) acquaintance [K. 5]

bekannt geben (gibt bekannt, gab bekannt, hat bekannt gegeben) to announce

die Bekanntschaft, -en acquaintanceship

bekommen (bekam, hat bekommen) to get, receive [K. 5]

belegen (hat belegt) to enroll in

(das) Belgien   Belgium

beliebt   popular

bemerkenswert   noteworthy

die Bemerkung, -en  observation

benachrichtigen (hat benachrichtigt) to inform

das Benehmen  behavior

sich benehmen (benimmt sich, benahm sich, hat sich benommen) to behave

benötigen (hat benötigt)  to require, need

benutzen (hat benutzt)  to use [K. 4]

das Benzin  gasoline [K. 4]

bequem  comfortable

der Berater, -/die Beraterin, -nen counselor, advisor

die Beratung  counseling

der Bereich, -e  area, region [K. 12]

bereit  ready

der Berg, -e  mountain [K. 10]

berg·steigen (ist berggestiegen)  to go mountainclimbing

die Bergwirtschaft, -en  mountain restaurant

der Bericht, -e  report [K. 12]

berichten (hat berichtet)  to report [K. 12]

der Beruf, -e  profession, job, occupation [K. 9]

die Berufsschule, -n  technical-vocational high school

sich beruhigen (hat sich beruhigt) to calm down [K. 9]

berühmt  famous [K. 8]

die Besatzungszone, -n  occupation zone [K. 11]

Bescheid bekommen (hat Bescheid bekommen)  to get an answer, be notified

beschreiben (beschrieb, hat beschrieben)  to describe [K. 4]

besetzen (hat besetzt)  to occupy [K. 11]

besichtigen (hat besichtigt)  to visit, look at [K. 11]

besitzen (besaß, hat besessen)  to own, to have

der Besitzer, -/die Besitzerin, -nen owner

besonders  especially [K. 4]

besorgen (hat besorgt)  to acquire, get

besprechen (bespricht, besprach, hat besprochen)  to discuss [K. 12]

die Besprechung, -en  discussion

besser  better [K. 2]

Besserung: Gute ~!  Speedy recovery! [K. 8]

best-  best; am besten  best of all [K. 9]

die Bestandsaufnahme  assessment

das Beste  the best (thing)

bestellen (hat bestellt)  to order [K. 5]

bestimmen (hat bestimmt)  to determine

bestimmt  undoubtedly [K. 3]

bestrafen (hat bestraft)  to punish

der Bestseller, -s  bestseller

besuchen (hat besucht)  to visit [K. 3]

der Besucher, -/die Besucherin, -nen visitor

beten (hat gebetet)  to pray [K. 10]

betrachten (hat betrachtet)  to view

betreuen (hat betreut)  to take care of

der Betreuer, -/die Betreuerin, -nen person in charge

der Betrieb, -e  business

die Betriebswirtschaft  business administration [K. 2]

das Bett, -en  bed [K. 6]

bevor  before [K. 3]

die Bewegung, -en  movement, motion

der Beweis, -e  proof

beweisen (bewies, hat bewiesen)  to prove

sich bewerben (bewirbt sich, bewarb sich, hat sich beworben) an  to apply to [K. 9]; ~ um/für + acc.  to apply for [K. 9]

der Bewerber, -/die Bewerberin, -nen applicant [K.9]

die Bewerbung, -en  application

der Bewerbungsbrief, -e  letter of application [K. 9]

das Bewerbungsformular, -e  application form

bewerkstelligen (hat bewerkstelligt) to manage, take care of

bewerten (hat bewertet)  to evaluate

bewirtet  meals included

bewölkt  cloudy, overcast

bezahlbar  payable

bezahlen (hat bezahlt)  to pay [K. 4]

beziehen (bezog, hat bezogen)  to move in

die Beziehung, -en  contact, relationship, relation [K. 7, 12];

internationale Beziehungen (pl.) international relations [K. 2]

Bezug: in ~ auf  in regard to [K. 12]; auf etwas ~ nehmen  to refer to

das Bezugswort, ¨er  antecedent

die Bibliothek, -en  library [K. 3]

der Bibliothekar, -/die Bibliothekarin, -nen  librarian

das Bibliothekarswesen  library science

das Bier  beer [K. 3]

die Bierbrauerei, -en  brewery

das Bierzelt, -e  beer tent

bieten (bot, hat geboten)  to offer [K. 9]

das Bild, -er  picture [K. 6]

bilden (hat gebildet)  to construct, form

billig  cheap, inexpensive [K. 7]

die Biographie, -n  biography [K. 7]

der Bioladen, ¨  health food store [K. 7]

die Biologie  biology [K. 2]

bis  until, as far as; ~ gleich!  See you soon! [K. 6]; bis zur Ampel  as far as the traffic light [K. 7]

bisschen: ein ~  a little [K. 2]

bitte  please [K. 1], you're welcome; ~ schön!  There you are!

die Bitte, -n  request [K. 2]

bitten (bat, hat gebeten) um + acc. to ask for, request [K. 8]

das Blatt, ¨er  page, sheet

blättern (hat geblättert) in + dat.  to leaf through

blau  blue [K. 1]

bleiben (blieb, ist geblieben)  to stay, remain [K. 2]

der Bleistift, -e  pencil [K. 1]

blitzen (hat geblitzt)  to have lightning [K. 5]

das Blitzlicht, -er  flash (for a camera)

die Blockade, -n  blockade [K. 11]

blond  blond [K. 1]

die Blume, -n  flower [K. 6]

die Bluse, -n  blouse [K. 4]

das Blut  blood [K. 10]

der Boden (pl. Böden)  floor, ground [K. 6]

der Bombenangriff, -e  bombardment, bombing attack

die Bordkarte, -n  boarding pass [K. 4]

die Börse  stock market

**böse**   angry [K. 5]; **~ sein (war, ist gewesen) auf** + *acc.*   to be upset with, mad at
**die Bosheit, -en**   meanspiritedness
**der Boss,** *pl.* **Bosse**   boss
**boxen (hat geboxt)**   to box, hit
**Brandenburg**   Brandenburg
**das Brandenburger Tor**   Brandenburg Gate (in Berlin) [K. 11]
**die Bratwurst, ˝e**   bratwurst, fried sausage
**brauchen (hat gebraucht)**   to need [K. 4]; **ich brauche nicht**   I don't have to [K. 4]
**braun**   brown [K. 1]
**die Braut, ˝e**   bride [K. 10]
**sich etwas brechen (bricht sich, brach sich, hat sich gebrochen)**   to break [K. 8]
**brennen (brannte, hat gebrannt)**   to burn [K. 10]
**Brett: das schwarze ~**   bulletin board [K. 6]
**die Bretzel, -n**   pretzel
**der Brief, -e**   letter [K. 4]
**die Briefmarke, -n**   stamp [K. 7]
**die Brille, -n**   glasses [K. 1]
**bringen (brachte, hat gebracht)**   to bring [K. 5]
**die Brokkoli** *(pl.)*   broccoli
**die Broschüre, -n**   brochure
**das Brot, -e**   bread [K. 3]
**das Brötchen, -**   hard roll [K. 3]; **ein belegtes ~**   roll spread with cold cuts, slice of cheese, etc. [K. 3]
**die Brücke, -n**   bridge
**der Bruder, ˝**   brother [K. 2]
**die Brüderschaft**   brotherhood, fraternity
**brüllen (hat gebrüllt)**   to yell, scream
**die Brust, ˝e**   breast, chest
**das Buch, ˝er**   book, textbook [K. 1]
**das Bücherregal, -e**   bookcase [K. 6]
**der Buchhalter, -/die Buchhalterin, -nen**   accountant
**die Buchhandlung, -en**   bookstore [K. 7]
**buchstabieren (hat buchstabiert)**   to spell
**die Bude, -n**   student room *(colloq.)* [K. 6]
**die Bühne, -n**   stage [K. 9]
**der Bummel, -**   walk, leisurely stroll [K. 11]

**bummeln (ist gebummelt)**   to stroll [K. 11]
**der Bund**   alliance; Federal Government
**der Bundeskanzler, -/die Bundeskanzlerin, -nen**   Federal Chancellor [K. 11]
**das Bundesland, ˝er**   state, province [K. 11]
**der Bundespräsident, (-en), -en/die Bundespräsidentin, -nen**   Federal President [K. 11]
**der Bundesrat**   Federal Council
**die Bundesregierung**   Federal Government
**die Bundesrepublik Deutschland**   Federal Republic of Germany [K. 11]
**der Bundestag**   Federal Parliament [K. 11]
**der Bürger, -/die Bürgerin, -nen**   citizen
**der Bürgermeister, -/die Bürgermeisterin, -nen**   mayor
**das Büro, -s**   office [K. 7]
**die Bürste, -n**   (hair)brush
**sich bürsten (hat sich gebürstet): sich die Haare bürsten**   to brush one's hair [K. 8]
**der Bus, -se**   bus
**die Bushaltestelle, -n**   bus stop
**die Butter**   butter [K. 3]

**das Café, -s**   café [K. 3]
**der Campingplatz, ˝e**   campground
**der Campus**   campus
**die CD, -s**   CD [K. 4]
**der CD-Player, -**   CD player [K. 4]
**Celsius**   Centigrade
**(die) Chanukka**   Chanukkah [K. 10]
**chaotisch**   chaotic
**der Chef, -s/die Chefin, -nen**   boss [K. 9]
**die Chemie**   chemistry [K. 2]
**chinesisch**   Chinese
**der Chor, ˝e**   chorus, choir
**das Christentum**   Christianity
**das Christkind**   Christ child
**die Christlich-Demokratische Union (CDU)**   Christian Democratic Union
**die Christlich-Soziale Union (CSU)**   Christian Social Union
**die Clique, -n**   clique, circle of friends

**der Club, -s**   club
**die Cola, -s**   cola [K. 3]
**der Computer, -**   computer [K. 1, 6]
**das Comicheft, -e**   comic book
**Confoederatio Helvetica**   Switzerland
**die Couch, -s (-en)**   couch [K. 6]
**der Cousin, -s**   male cousin [K. 2]

**D**

**da**   there [K. 1]
**dabei sein**   to participate in something
**der Dachboden, ˝**   attic [K. 6]; **auf dem ~**   in the attic [K. 6]
**dagegen**   against it
**daheim**   at home
**daher**   for that reason, that's why
**damals**   back then [K. 10]
**die Dame, -n**   lady
**damit**   so that [K. 7]
**danach**   afterwards [K. 3]
**(das) Dänemark**   Denmark
**der Dank**   thanks; **Vielen ~!**   Thanks a lot! [K. 6]
**danke**   thanks, thank you [K. 1]; **~ schön!**   Thanks a lot! [K. 1]
**danken (hat gedankt)** + *dat.*   to thank [K. 6]; **~ für** + *acc.*   to thank for
**dann**   then
**darf**   may, be permitted
**darüber**   about it
**das**   the *(neuter)* [K. 1]
**das Datum,** *pl.* **Daten**   date
**dass**   that *(conj.)* [K. 5]
**dauern (hat gedauert)**   to last [K. 6]
**dauernd**   continuously
**die Daumen drücken (hat gedrückt)** + *dat.*   to cross one's finger for [K. 9]
**dazu·kommen (kam dazu, ist dazugekommen)**   to get to; to arrive at
**der Deckel, -**   lid, top
**dein**   your *(fam. sing.)* [K. 3]
**der Dekan, -e**   dean
**die Demokratie, -n**   democracy
**denken (dachte, hat gedacht)**   to think [K. 4]; **~ an** + *acc.*   to think of [K. 4]
**das Denkmal, ˝er**   monument [K. 9]
**denn**   for, because, then [K. 3]
**das Deo**   deodorant [K. 4]
**deprimierend**   depressing [K. 11]

**der**   the *(masc.)* [K. 1]

**deren**   whose [K. 10]

**deshalb**   that's (the reason) why

**dessen**   whose [K. 10]

**deswegen**   that's why, for that reason, therefore [K. 6, 8]

**das Detail, -s**   detail

**der Detektiv, -e**   detective

**(das) Deutsch**   the German language [K. 2]; **auf Deutsch**   in German [K. 2]

**der/die Deutsche, -n** *(adj. as noun)*   German [K. 1]

**die Deutsche Demokratische Republik, (DDR)**   German Democratic Republic (GDR) [K. 11]

**das Deutsche Reich**   German Empire

**der Deutschkurs, -e**   German language course

**(das) Deutschland**   Germany [K. 1]

**die Deutschprüfung, -en**   German test

**der Deutschunterricht**   German class

**der Dezember**   December [K. 2]

**der Dialekt, -e**   dialect [K. 12]

**dich**   you *(informal sing., acc.)* [K. 3]

**der Dichter, -/die Dichterin, -nen**   poet [K. 9]

**die**   the *(fem.)* [K.1]

**die Diele, -n**   entrance hallway [K. 6]

**dienen (hat gedient)**   to serve

**der Dienstag, -e**   Tuesday [K. 2]

**dieser, diese, dieses**   this, that *(pl.* these, that) [K. 6]

**der Diktator, -en**   dictator

**die Diktatur, -en**   dictatorship

**das Ding, -e**   object, thing [K. 6]

**der Dinosaurier, -**   dinosaur

**das Diplom, -e**   diploma [K. 8]

**dir**   (to, for) you *(informal sing., dat.)*

**der Dirigent, [-en], -en/die Dirigentin, -nen**   orchestra conductor

**die Diskothek, -en (die Disko)**   discotheque, disco

**der Diskurs, -e**   discourse

**die Diskussion, -en**   discussion

**diskutieren (hat diskutiert) über** + *acc.*   to discuss [K. 5]

**diszipliniert**   disciplined [K. 9]

**doch**   go ahead and . . . *(persuasive particle)* [K. 2]; Oh, yes it is! *(response to negative statement)*

**der Doktortitel,-**   doctorate, Ph.D.

**der Dokumentarfilm, -e**   documentary film [K. 7]

**der Dom, -e**   cathedral [K. 11]

**dominant**   dominant [K. 12]

**die Donau**   Danube River

**donnern (hat gedonnert)**   to thunder [K. 5]

**der Donnerstag, -e**   Thursday [K. 2]

**doof**   goofy [K. 4]

**das Doppelbett, -en**   double bed

**der Doppelinfinitiv, -e**   double infinitive

**das Dorf, ¨er**   village

**dort**   there; **~ drüben**   over there

**der Dozent, [-en], -en/die Dozentin, -nen**   assistant professor, instructor [K. 8]

**das Drama,** *pl.* **Dramen**   drama, play [K. 7]

**dran sein: Sie sind dran.**   It's your turn.

**der Dreck**   dirt, mud [K. 7]

**drehen (hat gedreht): einen Film ~ über** + *acc.*   to make a movie about

**drei**   three [K. 1]

**dreißig**   thirty [K. 1]

**dreizehn**   thirteen [K. 1]

**dringlich**   urgent, pressing

**drinnen**   inside

**dröhnen (hat gedröhnt)**   to drone

**der Druck**   pressure

**drückend**   depressing [K. 11]

**der Drucker, -**   printer [K. 6]

**drunter (darunter)**   down below

**du**   you *(informal sing.)* [K. 1]; Hey . . . *(used to introduce an utterance)*

**dumm (ü)**   dumb, stupid [K. 4]

**dunkel**   dark [K. 1]

**dunkelgrau**   dark gray [K. 1]

**durch** + *acc.*   through [K. 4]; **~ dick und dünn**   through thick and thin

**durcheinander**   messy

**der Durchfall**   diarrhea [K. 8]

**durch·gucken (hat durchgeguckt)**   to look through, look over

**durch·machen (hat durchgemacht)**   to stay up, get through

**durch·streichen (strich durch, hat durchgestrichen)**   to cross out

**dürfen (darf, durfte, hat gedurft)**   may; to be allowed to, permitted to [K. 4]; **ich darf nicht**   I must not [K. 4]

**der Durst**   thirst; **~ haben**   to be thirsty [K. 4]

**die Dusche, -n**   shower [K. 6]

**(sich) duschen (hat sich geduscht)**   to shower [K. 8]

**der Duschraum, ¨e**   shower room

**die DVD, -s**   DVD

**der DVD-Spieler, -**   DVD player [K. 1]

**dynamisch**   dynamic [K. 9]

**eben**   just

**echt**   authentic, genuine; real(ly) [K. 10]

**die Ecke, -n**   corner; **an der ~**   at the corner; **um die ~**   around the corner [K. 7]

**der Edelmann, ¨er**   nobleman

**der Edelstein, -e**   jewel, precious stone [K. 10]

**egal**   no difference [K. 6]

**ehemalig**   former(ly), previous(ly) [K. 10]

**eher**   rather; sooner

**ehrlich**   honest

**das Ei, -er**   egg [K. 3]; **weich gekochtes ~**   softboiled egg [K. 3]

**eifersüchtig**   jealous

**eigen**   own [K. 10]

**die Eigenschaft, -en**   personal trait, quality, characteristic [K. 4]

**eigentlich**   actually [K. 5]

**die Eile**   hurry; **~ haben**   to be in a hurry

**der Eilzug, ¨e**   fast train

**ein, eine**   a, an [K. 1]

**einander**   one another, each other [K. 5]

**die Einbahnstraße, -n**   one-way street

**der Eindruck, ¨e**   impression [K. 9]

**einerseits**   on the one hand [K. 11]

**einfach**   simple, simply [K. 5]

**die Einfahrt, -en**   entry

**ein·fallen (fällt ein, fiel ein, ist eingefallen)** + *dat.*   to think of something, get an idea, occur to

**einfallslos**   uncreative [K. 4]

**das Einfamilienhaus, ¨er**   single-family house [K. 6]

**der Einfluss,** *pl.* **Einflüsse**   influence

**der Eingang, ¨e**   entrance, front door [K. 6]

**eingestellt: ~ sein auf**   to be geared for, ready for

**die Einheit, -en**   unity [K. 11]

**einige**   a few, several

**ein·kaufen (hat eingekauft)** to shop [K. 2]

**Einkaufs...** *(in compounds)* shopping; **der Einkaufsbummel, -** shopping trip; **der Einkaufskorb, ¨e** shopping basket; **das Einkaufsnetz, -e** mesh shopping bag [K. 7]; **die Einkaufstasche, -n** shopping bag; **die Einkaufstüte, -n** shopping bag; **das Einkaufszentrum,** *pl.* **-zentren** shopping center, mall [K. 11]

**ein·laden (lädt ein, lud ein, hat eingeladen)** to invite; to take out [K. 5]

**die Einladung, -en** invitation [K. 5]

**einmal** once [K. 7]

**einmalig** unique [K. 9]

**einminütig** one-minute

**die Einreise, -n** arrival

**ein·richten (hat eingerichtet)** to set up, institute

**eins** one [K. 1]

**ein·schlafen (schläft ein, schlief ein, ist eingeschlafen)** to fall asleep

**ein·schlagen (schlägt ein, schlug ein, ist eingeschlagen)** to strike, impact

**ein·schließen (schloss ein, hat eingeschlossen)** to include; to lock up

**sich ein·schreiben (schrieb sich ein, hat sich eingeschrieben)** to register, to enroll [K. 8]

**ein·setzen (hat eingesetzt)** to start

**ein·steigen (stieg ein, ist eingestiegen)** to get into a vehicle, board, climb in [K. 10]

**ein·stellen (hat eingestellt)** to hire

**die Einstellung, -en** attitude, outlook [K. 11]

**ein·tauschen (hat eingetauscht)** to exchange

**der Eintopf, ¨e** stew

**der Eintrag, ¨e** entry

**der Einwohner, -/die Einwohnerin, -nen** inhabitant [K. 3]

**ein·zahlen (hat eingezahlt)** to deposit (money) [K. 7]

**das Einzelzimmer, -** single room [K. 6]

**ein·ziehen (zog ein, ist eingezogen)** to move in [K. 5, 6]; to deposit

**einzig** single; only [K. 9]

**einzigartig** unique, singular

**der Einzug** the move into a house/an apartment

**das Eis** ice; ice cream [K. 3]

**die Eisenbahn** railroad, train

**der Eisenbahnzug, ¨e** train

**das Eishockey** ice hockey [K. 7]

**der Eiskunstlauf** figure skating

**der Eiskunstläufer, -/die Eiskunstläuferin, -nen** figure skater

**das Eisstadion,** *pl.* **-stadien** skating rink

**die Elbe** Elbe River

**elegant** elegant

**elf** eleven [K. 1]

**der Ellenbogen, -** elbow

**die Eltern** *(pl.)* parents [K. 2]

**die E-Mail** e-mail (message) [K. 2]

**der Empfänger, -** recipient

**empfehlen (empfiehlt, empfahl, hat empfohlen)** to recommend [K. 7]

**die Empfehlung, -en** recommendation [K. 9]

**sich empören (hat sich empört)** to become indignant

**das Ende, -n** end

**endgültig** final

**endlich** finally [K. 2]

**die „Endlösung"** "final solution"

**eng** narrow

**(das) England** England [K. 1]

**der Engländer, -/die Engländerin, -nen** Englishman/Englishwoman [K. 1]

**(das) Englisch** the English language [K. 2]

**der Enkel, -/die Enkelin, -innen** grandson/granddaughter [K. 2]

**das Enkelkind, -er** grandchild [K. 2]

**entdecken (hat entdeckt)** to discover [K. 7]

**die Entdeckung, -en** discovery

**entfernt** distant [K. 12]

**enthalten (enthält, enthielt, hat enthalten)** to contain

**sich entscheiden (entschied sich, hat sich entschieden) für/gegen +** *acc.* to decide on/against [K. 8]

**die Entscheidung, -en** decision

**entschuldigen (hat entschuldigt)** to excuse, pardon [K. 11]

**die Entschuldigung, -en** excuse **Entschuldigung!** Pardon! Excuse me! [K. 1, 6]

**die Entspannung** relaxation [K. 10]

**entsprechend** appropriate(ly)

**entstehen (entstand, ist entstanden)** to originate; to be built

**enttäuscht** disappointed [K. 5]

**entweder... oder** either . . . or

**entwickeln (hat entwickelt)** to develop

**er** he, it [K. 1]

**erarbeiten (hat erarbeitet)** to acquire, work out

**die Erbse, -n** pea [K. 3]

**das Erdgeschoss, -e** ground floor [K. 6]; **im~** on the ground floor [K. 6]

**die Erdkunde** geography

**das Ereignis, -se** event

**erdrücken (hat erdrückt)** to crush; to overwhelm

**erfahren (erfährt, erfuhr, hat erfahren)** to experience [K. 12]

**die Erfahrung, -en** experience [K. 6]

**erfinden (erfand, hat erfunden)** to invent; **sich neu ~** to reinvent oneself

**erfolgreich** successful [K. 12]

**erfordern (hat erfordert)** to request, demand [K. 5]

**erfüllen (hat erfüllt)** to fulfill, complete [K. 6]

**erfunden** made-up, invented

**ergänzen (hat ergänzt)** to complete

**sich ergeben (ergibt sich, ergab sich, hat sich ergeben)** to materialize, result

**das Ergebnis, -se** result [K. 8]

**erhöhen (hat erhöht)** to raise, increase

**sich erholen (hat sich erholt)** to recuperate [K. 8]

**sich erinnern (hat sich erinnert) an +** *acc.* to remember [K. 8]

**sich erkälten (hat sich erkältet)** to catch cold [K. 8]

**die Erkältung, -en** common cold [K. 8]

**erkennen (erkannte, hat erkannt)** to recognize [K. 10]

**erklären (hat erklärt)** to explain [K. 7, 12]; **~für +** *acc.* to describe

**erlauben (hat erlaubt)** to permit, allow [K. 10]

**erlaubt** allowed, permitted

**erläutern (hat erläutert)** to explain

**erleben (hat erlebt)** to experience [K. 10]

**das Erlebnis, -se** experience [K. 11]

**erlebnisvoll** eventful

**erledigen (hat erledigt)** to take care of, deal with [K. 7]

**ernst** serious [K. 4]

**erobern (hat erobert)** to conquer, capture [K. 11]

**eröffnen (hat eröffnet)** to open; **ein Konto ~** to open an account [K. 7]

**erraten (errät, erriet, hat erraten)** to guess

**erreichen (hat erreicht)** to reach [K. 11]

**erschießen (erschoss, hat erschossen)** to shoot to death

**erschließen (erschloss, hat erschlossen)** to figure out, understand

**erst** not until; first [K. 5]; **erst seit** just since [K. 5]

**erstaunt** astonished [K. 10]

**ertragen (erträgt, ertrug, hat ertragen)** to tolerate, bear [K. 12]

**erträglich** tolerable, manageable

**erwachsen** grown-up, adult [K. 10]

**erwähnen (hat erwähnt)** to mention

**erwarten (hat erwartet) von** + *dat.* to expect of [K. 8]

**die Erwartung, -en** expectation

**erweitern (hat erweitert)** to expand

**erwünscht** desired, sought

**erzählen (hat erzählt) von** + *dat.* to talk/tell a story about [K. 5]

**die Erzählung, -en** story [K. 7]

**erzeugen (hat erzeugt)** to create

**erziehen (erzog, hat erzogen)** to raise (children)

**erzielen (hat erzielt)** to strive for

**es** it [K. 3]

**essen (isst, aß, hat gegessen)** to eat [K. 3]

**das Essen** food

**die Etage, -n** floor; **die erste (zweite) ~** second (third) floor

**etwas** some, somewhat [K. 2]; some(thing) [K. 3]; **~ anderes** something else

**euch** (to, for) you *(informal pl. acc./dat.)* [K. 3, 6]

**euer** your *(fam. pl. )* [K. 3]

**der Euro, -s** Euro *(European currency unit)*

**(das) Europa** Europe

**europäisch** European

**die Europäische Union** European Union

**der Euroscheck, -s** Euro check

**eventuell** perhaps, possibly; eventually [K. 6]

**ewig** eternal

**exotisch** exotic

**der Experte, [-n], -n/die Expertin, -nen** expert

**das Fach, ̈er** academic subject; compartment [K. 6]

**der Fachbereich, -e** academic department

**die Fachhochschule, -n** specialized university [K. 6]

**die Fachoberschule, -n** technical college

**die Fachschule, -n** special school, technical college

**das Fachwerk** half-timbered architecture

**die Fachzeitschrift, -en** professional journal

**die Fähigkeit, -en** ability [K. 12]

**fahren (fährt, fuhr, ist gefahren)** to drive, ride [K. 3], **per Anhalter ~** to hitch-hike [K. 4]

**der Fahrplan, ̈e** schedule of transportation

**die Fahrprüfung, -en** driving test

**das Fahrrad, ̈er** bicycle [K. 4]

**der Fahrradverleih** bicycle rental

**der Fahrschein, -e** public transportation ticket

**die Fahrschule, -n** driving school, driver's education

**die Fahrt, -en** trip, journey

**das Fahrzeug, -e** vehicle

**der Faktor, -en** factor

**der Fall, ̈e** case, situation; **auf jeden ~** at any rate, in any case; **in diesem Fall(e)** in this case

**fallen (fällt, fiel, ist gefallen)** to fall [K. 5]; **~ lassen** to drop

**die Familie, -n** family [K. 2]

**der Familienbetrieb, -e** family-owned business

**der Familienstammbaum, ̈e** family tree

**das Familienverhältnis, -se** family affair

**der Fan, -s** fan [K. 9]

**fangen (fängt, fing, hat gefangen)** to catch [K. 10]

**die Fantasie, -n** fantasy

**fantastisch** fantastic [K. 11]

**die Farbe, -n** color; [K. 1] **Welche Farbe hat... ?** What color is. . .? [K. 1]

**der Fasching** Carnival, Fasching [K. 10]

**das Fass,** *pl.* **Fässer** barrel

**die Fassung, -en** version; **die erste ~** first draft

**fast** almost, practically [K. 5]

**die Fastenzeit** Lent

**die Fastnacht** Carnival, Fasching [K. 10]

**faul** lazy [K. 4]

**das Fax** fax

**der Februar** February [K. 2]

**das Fechten** fencing

**die Fee, -n** fairy [K. 10]

**fehlen (hat gefehlt)** to be missing, be lacking [K. 10]

**feiern (hat gefeiert)** to celebrate [K. 10]

**der Feiertag, -e** holiday [K. 10]

**fein** fine [K. 11]

**der Feind, -e** enemy, adversary

**das Feldhockey** field hockey [K. 7]

**das Fenster -** window [K. 1]

**die Ferien** *(pl.)* (school) vacation [K. 5]

**der Ferienort, -e** resort town

**ferienreif** ready for a vacation

**die Ferienwohnung, -en** vacation home

**fern·bleiben (blieb fern, ist ferngeblieben)** + *dat.* to stay away from

**die Ferne** distance

**fern·sehen (sieht fern, sah fern, hat ferngesehen)** to watch television [K. 3]

**der Fernseher, -** television set [K. 1]

**der Fernsehturm, ̈e** television tower

**die Ferse, -n** heel [K. 10]

**fertig** finished [K. 5]; **~ werden (wird, wurde, ist geworden) mit** + *dat.* to come to grips with, accept [K. 5]

**fest** permanent; firm, solid [K. 9]

**das Fest, -e** festival, feast [K. 10]

**das Festspiel, -e** festival

**fest·stellen (hat festgestellt)** to determine

**der Festtag, -e** holiday [K. 10]

**die Fete, -n** party; **auf eine ~ gehen:** to go to a party [K. 7]

**die Feuerwache, -n** fire station

**das Fieber** fever, temperature [K. 8]

**die Figur, -en** figure; (story) character

**die Filiale, -n** branch office

**der Film, -e** movie, film [K. 7]

**der Filmemacher, -/die Filmemacherin, -nen** filmmaker [K. 9]

**die Finanzen** *(pl.)* finances

**finden (fand, hat gefunden)** to find [K. 2]

**der Finger, -** finger [K. 6]

**der Fingernagel, ⸚** fingernail

**(das) Finnisch** the Finnish language

**(das) Finnland** Finland

**die Firma,** *pl.* **Firmen** firm, company

**der Fisch, -e** fish [K. 3]

**der Fischmarkt, ⸚e** fish market

**das Fitnessstudio, -s** health club [K. 7]

**flach** flat; low

**die Fläche, -n** land area [K. 11]

**die Flak (Flugzeugabwehrkanone)** flak, anti-aircraft weapon

**die Flasche, -n** bottle [K. 3]

**das Fleisch** meat [K. 3]

**der Fleischer, -/die Fleischerin, -nen** butcher [K. 9]

**die Fleischerei, -en** butcher shop [K. 7]

**fleißig** hardworking, industrious; busy [K. 4]

**flexibel** flexible [K. 9]

**fliegen (flog, ist geflogen)** to fly [K. 2, 7]

**fließen (floss, ist geflossen)** to flow

**fließend** fluent(ly) [K. 12]

**flirten (hat geflirtet)** to flirt [K. 5]

**die Flöte, -n** flute [K. 3]

**die Flötenmusik** flute music

**der Flug, ⸚e** flight [K. 4]

**der Flughafen, ⸚** airport [K. 4]

**der Flugschein, -e** plane ticket [K. 4]

**das Flugticket, -s** plane ticket

**das Flugzeug, -e** airplane [K. 4]

**der Flur, -e** hallway, corridor [K. 6]

**der Fluss, ⸚e** river [K. 7, 10]

**die Folie, -n** overhead transparency [K. 8]

**der Föhn, -e** blow dryer [K. 8]

**sich die Haare föhnen (hat sich geföhnt)** to blow-dry one's hair [K. 8]

**die Fontäne, -n** fountain

**das Formular, -e** form (to be filled out) [K. 9]

**die Forschung, -en** research

**der Forschungsassistent, [-en], -en/die Forschungsassistentin, -nen** research assistant

**der/die Fortgeschrittene, -n** *(adj. as noun)* advanced student [K. 10]

**fort-gehen (ging fort, ist fortgegangen)** to go away

**fort·setzen (hat fortgesetzt)** to continue [K. 12]

**das Fotoalbum,** *pl.* **-alben** photo album

**der Fotograf, [-en], -en/die Fotografin, -nen** photographer

**der Fotoapparat, -e** photo camera

**die Frage, -n** question [K. 2]; **Fragen stellen (hat gestellt)** to ask questions [K. 9]

**fragen (hat gefragt)** to ask [K. 2]; **~ nach** + *dat.* to ask about

**das Fragewort, ⸚er** question word, interrogative

**(das) Frankreich** France [K. 1]

**der Franzose, [-n], -n/die Französin, -nen** French man/woman [K. 1]

**(das) Französisch** the French language [K. 2]

**die Frau, -en** woman: Mrs., Ms. [K. 1]; wife, wives [K. 2]

**die Frauenzeitschrift, -en** women's magazine

**das Fräulein, -** Miss [K. 1]

**frei** free, open; allowed [K. 5]; **~ haben** to have time off [K. 2]; **im Freien** outdoors

**die Freie Demokratische Partei (FDP)** Free Democratic Party

**die Freiheit, -en** freedom [K. 8]

**das Frei(schwimm)bad, ⸚er** outdoor swimming pool

**der Freitag, -e** Friday [K. 2]

**freiwillig** voluntarily

**die Freizeit** free time, leisure time

**die Freizeitaktivität, -en** leisure activity [K. 3]

**fremd** foreign [K. 9, 10]

**der/die Fremde, -n** *(adj. as noun)* foreigner

**der Fremdenführer, -/die Fremdenführerin, -nen** tour guide

**der Fremdenhass** xenophobia

**die Fremdsprache, -n** foreign language [K. 12]

**fressen (frisst, fraß, hat gefressen)** to eat *(said of animals)*

**die Freude, -n** joy

**sich freuen (hat sich gefreut)** to be happy; **~ auf** + *acc.* to look forward to [K. 8]; **~ über** + *acc.* to be happy about [K. 8]

**der Freund, -e/die Freundin, -nen** friend, boy/girlfriend [K. 5]; **die Freunde** *(pl.)* a group of friends

**der Freundeskreis, -e** circle of friends; clique [K. 6]

**freundlich** friendly [K. 1]

**die Freundschaft, -en** friendship [K. 5]; **dicke ~** close, intimate friendship [K. 5]; **~ schließen** to make friends [K. 5]

**der Friedhof, ⸚e** cemetery [K. 9]

**der Friseur, -e/die Friseurin, -nen/die Friseuse, -n** hair dresser [K. 9]

**froh** happy [K. 5]

**fromm (ö)** pious, religious [K. 10]

**der Frosch, ⸚e** frog [K. 10]

**die Frucht, ⸚e** fruit [K. 11]

**früh** early [K. 8]

**früher** earlier, in the past [K. 5]

**der Frühling** spring [K. 5]

**das Frühstück** breakfast [K. 3]

**frustrierend** frustrating [K. 11]

**sich fühlen (hat sich gefühlt)** to feel [K. 8]; **sich krank ~** to feel sick; **sich nicht wohl ~** to feel unwell [K. 8]

**führen (hat geführt)** to lead [K. 9]

**der Führer, -** leader (used to refer to Adolf Hitler) [K. 11]

**der Führerschein, -e** driver's license

**die Führung, -en** leadership; tour [K. 11]

**fünf** five [K. 1]

**fünfzehn** fifteen [K. 1]

**fünfzig** fifty [K. 1]

**für** + *acc.* for [AB 4]

**fürchten (hat gefürchtet)** to be afraid of [K. 12]

**furcht erregend** frightening

**das Fürstentum, ⸚er** principality, kingdom

**der Fuß, ⸚e** foot [K. 6]; **zu ~** on foot [K. 7]

**der Fußball** soccer [K. 3]; **~ spielen** to play soccer [K. 3]

**der Fußballplatz, ¨e** soccer field [K. 7]

**der Fußgänger, -/die Fußgängerin, -nen** pedestrian [K. 4]

**der Fußgängerbereich, -e** pedestrian zone

**die Fußgängerzone, -n** pedestrian zone [K. 3]

**der Fußweg, -e** footpath [K. 4]

**füttern (hat gefüttert)** to feed

## G

**die Gabel, -n** fork [K. 6]

**der Gang, ¨e** hall, hallway, corridor

**ganz** really, very; whole [K. 5]; **~ nass** completely wet [K. 5]; **~ schlimm** really bad [K. 5]; **die ganze Zeit** the whole time [K. 5]

**gar nicht** not at all [K. 3]

**die Garage, -n** garage

**die Gardine, -n** curtain(s) [K. 6]

**der Garten, ¨** garden [K. 6]

**der Gast, ¨e** guest [K. 10]

**das Gästezimmer, -** guest room

**die Gastfreundschaft** hospitality

**der Gastgeber, -/die Gastgeberin, -nen** host

**der Gasthof, ¨e** inn [K. 3]

**gastlich** hospitable, friendly [K. 3]

**das Gebäck** pastry

**das Gebäude, -** building [K. 3]

**geben (gibt, gab, hat gegeben)** to give [K. 3]; **es gibt (gab, hat gegeben)** there is, there are [K. 3]; **Was gibt's?** What's up? [K. 3]

**das Gebiet, -e** district, area [K. 12]

**geboren** born [K. 5]

**gebraucht** used

**gebunden** hard-bound

**das Geburtshaus, ¨er** birth place [K. 9]

**der Geburtstag, -e** birthday [K. 2]

**die (Kaiser-Wilhelms) Gedächtniskirche** (Kaiser Wilhelm) Memorial Church [K. 11]

**gedacht sein für** to be intended for

**der Gedanke [-n], -n** thought [K. 12] **auf andere Gedanken kommen** to get one's mind off something

**gedeckt** set

**das Gedicht, -e** poem [K. 7]

**die Geduld** patience

**gefährlich** dangerous [K. 4]

**gefallen (gefällt, gefiel, hat gefallen)** + *dat.* to please; to like [K. 6]

**das Geflügel** poultry, fowl [K. 3]

**der Gefrierpunkt** freezing point [K. 5]

**das Gefühl, -e** feeling [K. 12]

**gegen** + *acc.* against; around *(time)* [K. 4]

**der Gegensatz, ¨e** opposite

**gegenseitig** each other, reciprocal(ly)

**der Gegenstand, ¨e** object [K. 4]

**das Gegenteil, -e** opposite; **im ~** in opposition, contrary to

**gegenüber** + *dat.* in regard to; **~ (von)** + *dat.* across from [K. 7]

**die Gegenwart** present [K. 9]

**der Gegner, -/die Gegnerin, -nen** opponent

**das Gehalt, ¨er** salary, wage [K. 9]

**die Gehaltsvorstellung, -en** salary expectation

**gehen (ging, ist gegangen)** to go [K. 2, 7]; **nach Hause ~** to go home [K. 2]; **unter die Dusche ~** to take a shower; **Wie geht es Ihnen/dir?,** How are you? [K. 6]

**gehören (hat gehört)** + *dat.* to belong to [K. 6]

**geil** way cool *(slang)* [K. 1]

**gelb** yellow

**das Geld** money [K. 4]

**die Gelegenheit, -en** opportunity, [K. 9]

**der/die Geliebte, -n** (*adj. as noun*) lover

**gelten (gilt, galt, hat gegolten) als** to be considered (as) [K. 7]

**gemeinsam** common, shared, in partnership [K. 8]

**die Gemeinschaft, -en** association, group

**das Gemeinschaftsbad, ¨er** shared bathroom, floor bathroom [K. 6]

**die Gemeinschaftsküche, -n** shared kitchen [K. 6]

**gemischt** mixed

**das Gemüse, -** vegetable, vegetables [K. 3]

**gemütlich** cozy

**genau** exactly [K. 8]

**genießen (genoss, hat genossen)** to enjoy

**der Genießer, -/die Genießerin, -nen** connoisseur [K. 10]

**der Genitiv** genitive case

**genug** enough, sufficient [K. 4]

**genügend** sufficient, enough

**das Genus** gender

**das Gepäck** luggage [K. 3]

**gerade** just now; directly [K. 6]

**geradeaus** straight ahead [K. 7]

**das Gericht, -e** dish

**gering** low, small, limited

**die Germanistik** German studies

**gern** + *verb* to like to . . . [K. 2]; **~ geschehen!** Glad to help!, My pleasure! **~ haben** to like [K. 2]

**die Gesamtschule, -n** comprehensive secondary school

**das Geschäft, -e** store, business [K. 3]

**die Geschäftsführung, -en** business office

**der Geschäftsmann, ¨er/die Geschäftsfrau, -en** businessman/-woman [K. 9]

**die Geschäftsreise, -n** business trip

**das Geschäftstreffen, -** business meeting

**das Geschenk, -e** gift, present [K. 4]

**die Geschichte, -n** history [K. 2]; story

**geschieden** divorced

**die Geschirrspülmaschine, -n** dishwasher

**geschlossen** closed

**der Geschmack, ¨e(r)** taste

**die Geschwister** (*pl.*) siblings [K. 8]

**gesellig** gregarious, sociable [K. 4]

**die Gesellschaft, -en** society

**das Gesetz, -e** law [K. 11]

**das Gesicht, -er** face [K. 6]

**gespannt** excited [K. 4]; **~ sein auf** + *acc.* to be excited about [K. 2, 8]

**das Gespräch, -e** conversation [K. 8]; **ins ~ kommen** to strike up a conversation

**gestern** yesterday [K. 5]

**gestresst** stressed [K. 10]

**gesund (ü)** healthy [K. 7]

**die Gesundheit** health [K. 9]

**das Getränk, -e** beverage, drink [K. 3]

**sich getrauen (hat sich getraut)** to venture, dare

**getrennt** separate

**die Gewalt** violence

**gewinnen (gewann, hat gewonnen)** to win [K. 11]

**gewiss** certain [K. 10]

**das Gewitter** thunderstorm [K. 5]

**sich gewöhnen (hat sich gewöhnt) an** + *acc.* to get used to, get accustomed to [K. 10]

**gewöhnlich** usually [K. 9]

**das Ghetto, -s** ghetto

**das Gift, -e** poison

**giftig** poisonous [K. 10]

**der Gipfel, -** mountain peak [K. 10]

**der Gips, -e** cast [K. 8]

**das Girokonto, -konten** checking/debit account [K. 7]

**die Gitarre, -n** guitar [K. 3]

**glänzend** gleaming

**das Glas, ¨er** glass [K. 3]

**der Glassarg, ¨e** glass coffin

**glatt** smooth, straight [K. 1]

**glauben (hat geglaubt)** to believe, think [K. 5]; **~ an** + *acc.* to believe in

**glaubhaft** plausible, believable

**gleich** just, right away [K. 2]; similar, same [K. 4]

**gleichzeitig** simultaneously, at the same time

**das Glück** good luck, fortune

**glücklich** happy [K. 4]

**das Gold** gold [K. 10]

**der Golf** golf [K. 3]

**der Golfschläger, -** golf club

**der Gott, ¨er** God [K. 1]; **~ sei Dank!** Thank God!

**das Grab, ¨er** grave [K. 10]

**der Grad** degree

**der Graf, [-en], -en** count [K. 5]

**das Gramm** gram [K. 3]

**die Grammatik** grammar

**die Graphik, -en** graphics

**grau** gray [K. 1]; **dunkelgrau** dark gray [K. 1]; **hellgrau** light gray [K. 1]

**grausam** gruesome, cruel [K. 10]

**die Grenze, -n** border [K. 10]

**grenzen (hat gegrenzt) an** + *dat.* to border on

**(das) Griechenland** Greece

**grillen (hat gegrillt)** to grill, barbeque

**groß (ö)** large, big, tall [K. 1]

**großartig** great, fantastic [K. 9]

**der Großbuchstabe, -n** capital letter

**die Größe, -n** size [K. 9]

**die Großeltern** (*pl.*) grandparents [K. 2]

**die Großmutter, ¨** grandmother [K. 2]

**die Großstadt,** *pl.* **Großstädte** big city

**der Großvater, ¨** grandfather [K. 2]

**großzügig** generous

**Grüezi!** Hello! (*in Switzerland*)

**grün** green [K. 1]

**der Grund, ¨e** reason [K. 9]; **im Grunde** basically [K. 11]

**gründen (hat gegründet)** to establish [K. 11]

**das Grundgesetz** Basic Law (Germany's constitution) [K. 11]

**gründlich** thorough, careful [K. 9]

**die Grundschule, -n** elementary school

**die Gründung, -en** foundation [K. 11]

**die Grünen** the Green Party

**die Gruppe, -n** group

**der Gruppenleiter, -/die Gruppenleiterin, -nen** group leader

**das Gruppenreferat, -e** group research paper

**die Gruppenunterkunft, ¨e** group lodging

**der Gruß, ¨e** greeting [K. 1]; **Herzliche Grüße** Sincerely yours (*to close a letter*) [K. 2]

**grüßen: Grüßt euch! Grüß dich!** Hi, you (guys)!; **Grüß Gott!** Hello! (*in southern Germany*) [K. 1]

**gucken (hat geguckt)** to look [K. 6]; **Guck mal!** Look! [K. 6]

**gültig** valid

**gut** good [K. 1]; **~ aus·kommen** to get along [K. 9]; **~ aussehend** good looking [K. 1]; **~ gelaunt** in a good mood [K. 10]

**der Gymnasiast, [-en], -en/die Gymnasiastin, -nen** college-track high school student

**das Gymnasium,** *pl.* **Gymnasien** college-track high school

## H

**das Haar, -e** hair [K. 1, 6]

**die Haarbürste, -n** hairbrush [K. 4]

**das Haarwaschmittel, -** shampoo

**haben (hat, hatte, hat gehabt)** to have [K. 2]

**das Hackfleisch** hamburger, chopped meat [K. 3]

**der Hafen, ¨** harbor

**das Hähnchen, -** chicken [K. 3]

**der Haken, -** hook [K. 8]

**halb** half; **~ [zwei]** half past [one] [K. 2]

**das Hallenschwimmbad, ¨er** indoor swimming pool

**Hallo!** Hello! [K. 1]

**der Hals, ¨e** throat [K. 6]; **Hals- und Beinbruch!** Break a leg! [K. 9]

**die Halsschmerzen** (*pl.*) sore throat [K. 8]

**halt** just

**halten (hält, hielt, hat gehalten)** to stop [K. 3]; **~ für** + *acc.* to believe someone to be [K. 8]; **~ von** + *dat.* to think of [K. 3]

**die Haltestelle, -n** bus stop [K. 7]

**das Halteverbot** no stopping (sign)

**der Hamburger, -** hamburger [K. 3]; **~/die Hamburgerin, -nen** resident of Hamburg

**die Hand, ¨e** hand [K. 6]

**das Handgelenk, -e** wrist

**das Handout, -s** handout [K. 8]

**handeln (hat gehandelt) von** + *dat.* to be about [K. 8]

**die Handlung, -en** dramatic action, plot [K. 10]

**der Handschuh, -e** glove, mitten [K. 4]

**die Handtasche, -n** handbag, purse [K. 4]

**das Handy, -s** cell phone [K. 4]

**hängen (hat gehängt)** to hang up [K. 7]

**hängen (hing, hat gehangen)** to be hanging [K. 7]

**hart (ä)** hard [K. 9]

**hässlich** ugly [K. 10]

**der Haufen, -** heap, pile

**häufig** frequent

**Haupt ...** (*in compounds*) main; **der Hauptbahnhof, ¨e** main train station [K. 4]; **das Hauptfach, ¨er** main subject, major [K. 2]; **das Hauptgericht, -e** main course [K. 3]; **der Hauptsatz, ¨e** main clause

**die Hauptschule, -n** equivalent to junior high school, technical-vocational school

**der Hauptschüler, -/die Hauptschülerin, -nen** technical-vocational student

**das Hauptseminar, -e** advanced seminar

**die Hauptstadt, ¨e**   capital city [K. 10]
**die Hauptstraße, -n**   main street [K. 3]
**das Haus, ¨er**   house [K. 6]; **nach Hause**   (to) home [K. 2]; **zu Hause**   at home [K. 2]
**die Hausaufgabe, -n**   homework, assignment; **die Hausaufgaben machen**   to do homework [K. 2]
**der Hauskamerad, [-en], -en/die Hauskameradin, -nen**   housemate
**die Hausleiter, -n**   fire escape
**der Hausmeister, -/die Hausmeisterin, -nen**   custodian, superintendent
**das Hausmittel, -**   home remedy [K. 11]
**der Hauswart, -e**   custodian
**die Haut**   skin [K. 6]
**die Hautfarbe, -n**   skin color [K. 6]
**heben (hob, hat gehoben)**   to lift, raise
**das Heftpflaster, -**   bandage [K. 8]
**die Heiligenfigur, -en**   sacred figure
**der Heilige Geist**   Holy Ghost
**die Heimat**   home, hometown [K. 12]
**die Heimatstadt, ¨e**   hometown
**heim·kommen (kam heim, ist heimgekommen)**   to come home [K. 5]
**das Heimweh**   homesickness
**heiraten (hat geheiratet)**   to get married [K. 5]
**heiß**   hot [K. 5]
**heißen (hieß, hat geheißen)**   to be called [K. 1]; **das heißt (d.h.)**   that is (to say) [K. 4]
**heiter**   funny, cheerful [K. 4]; sunny, clear [K. 5]
**heizen (hat geheizt)**   to heat
**die Heizung, -en**   heating system; heat
**die Hektik**   frenzy, fast pace
**helfen (hilft, half, hat geholfen) + dat.**   to help [K. 4, 6]; **auf die Sprünge ~**   to give a boost to
**hell**   light [K. 1]
**hellgrau**   light gray [K. 1]
**hellwach**   wide awake
**(das) Helvetia**   Switzerland (Latin)
**das Hemd, -en**   shirt [K. 4]
**her**   here (from point of origin) [K. 7]
**herab·blicken (hat herabgeblickt)**   to look down

**heraus·finden (fand heraus, hat herausgefunden)**   to find out, discover
**sich heraus·putzen (hat sich herausgeputzt)**   to dress up, get decked out
**der Herbst**   autumn, fall [K. 5]
**der Herd, -e**   cooking stove [K. 6]
**Herein, bitte!**   Please come in! [K. 8]
**herein·kommen (kam herein) ist hereingekommen)**   to come in
**die Herkunft**   origin [K. 6]
**das Herkunftsland, ¨er**   country of origin, home country
**der Herr, [-n], -en**   (gentle)man; Mr. [K. 1]
**das Herz, -en**   heart [K. 6]; **im Herzen**   in the heart [K. 6]
**der Herzanfall, ¨e**   heart attack
**herzlich**   heartfelt, warm, **~ willkommen in ... !**   Welcome to . . . !
**die Herzlichkeit**   warmth, heartfeltness, sincerity
**Hessen**   Hesse
**heulen (hat geheult)**   to cry; to howl
**heute**   today [K. 2]; **~ Abend**   this evening; **~ in acht Tagen**   a week from today [K. 9]; **~ Morgen**   this morning; **~ Nachmittag**   this afternoon
**die Hexe, -n**   witch [K. 10]
**hier**   here [K. 1]
**die Hilfe, -n**   help, aid [K. 9]
**hilfsbereit**   helpful
**der Himmel**   heaven, sky [K. 10]
**hin**   there (point of destination) [K. 7]; **~ und wieder**   now and then [K. 4]
**hinein**   inside
**hinein·gehen (ging hinein, ist hineingegangen)**   to walk in [K. 1]
**sich hin·legen (hat sich hingelegt)**   to lie down [K. 8]
**die Hinsicht**   respect, regard
**hinten**   behind, in back
**hinter**   behind, in back of [K. 7]
**hinterlassen (hinterlässt, hinterließ, hat hinterlassen)**   to leave behind
**der Hintern, -**   rear
**historisch**   historic
**das Hobby, -s**   hobby [K. 12]
**der Hobbygärtner, -/die Hobbygärtnerin, -nen**   amateur gardener
**der Hobbyraum, ¨e**   hobby room
**hoch**   high, up [K. 9]; **am höchsten**

highest [K. 9]; **höchstens**   at the most [K. 9]
**hochachtungsvoll**   respectfully [K. 7]
**hochaktuell**   very current, very timely [K. 7]
**hoch·laufen (läuft hoch, lief hoch, ist hochgelaufen)**   to walk up (a street)
**die Hochschule, -n**   college, university [K. 8]
**die Hochzeit, -en**   marriage, wedding [K. 9]
**der Hochzeitstag, -e**   wedding anniversary
**hoffen (hat gehofft) auf + acc.**   to hope for [K. 7]
**hoffentlich**   hopefully, one hopes [K. 6]
**höher**   higher [K. 9]
**holen (hat geholt)**   to go get, fetch [K. 7]
**das Holz, ¨er**   wood
**der Holzhandel**   lumber business
**der/die Homosexuelle, -n** (adj. as noun)   homosexual
**der Honig**   honey [K. 3]
**hören (hat gehört)**   to hear, listen to [K. 2]
**das Horoskop, -e**   horoscope
**der Horrorfilm, -e**   horror movie [K. 7]
**der Hörsaal,** pl. **Hörsäle**   lecture hall [K. 1]
**die Hose, -n**   pants [K. 4]
**das Hotel, -s**   hotel [K. 3]
**der Hoteleingang, ¨e**   hotel entrance
**hübsch**   pretty [K. 1]
**der Humor**   humor, sense of humor [K. 12]
**humorvoll**   humorous
**der Hund, -e**   dog [K. 2]
**hundemüde**   dog-tired [AL 6]
**hundert**   hundred [K. 1]
**der Hunger**   hunger; **~ haben**   to be hungry [K. 2]
**der Hypochonder, -**   hypochondriac
**hypochondrisch**   hypochondriac(al)

**I**

**ich**   I [K. 1]
**die Idee, -n**   idea [K. 3]
**sich identifizieren (hat sich identifiziert) mit + dat.**   to identify with
**identisch**   identical

**die Identität** identity
**ihm** (to, for) him/it (*dat.*) [K. 6]
**ihn** him/it (*acc.*) [K. 3]
**Ihnen** (to, for) you (*dat.*) [K. 6]
**ihnen** (to, for) them (*dat.*) [K. 6]
**ihr** her; their [K. 3, 6]; you (*fam. pl.*) [K. 1]
**Ihr** your (*formal*) [K. 1]
**immer** always [K. 3]; ~ **[beliebter]** more and more [popular]
**imstande sein** to be capable of
**in** at, in; into; to [K. 7]
**indem** (*sub. conj.*) by (doing something) [K. 12]
**indes** meantime, meanwhile
**indianisch** Native American
**der Indikativ** indicative mood
**die Industrie, -n** industry
**die Info, -s** information
**die Informatik** computer science [K. 2]
**die Information, -en** information
**der Informationsvorsprung** information advantage [K. 12]
**sich informieren (hat sich informiert) über** + *acc.* to inform oneself, educate oneself about
**der Ingenieur, -e/die Ingenieurin, -nen** engineer [K. 9]
**das Ingenieurwesen** engineering [K. 2]
**der Inhalt, -e** content [K. 8]
**inklusive** inclusive
**innerhalb** + *gen.* inside of [K. 8]
**die Insel, -n** island [K. 10]
**das Inserat, -e** newspaper advertisement
**insgesamt** for a total of [K. 10]
**das Institut, -e** institute [K. 12]
**integriert** integrated
**intelligent** intelligent [K. 4]
**interessant** interesting [K. 4]
**das Interesse, -n** interest
**interessieren (hat interessiert)** to interest [K. 11]
**der Internet-Anschluss, ¨e** Internet connection [K. 6]
**die Internetseite, -n** Internet page [K. 12]
**interpretieren (hat interpretiert)** to interpret
**das Interview, -s** interview
**inwiefern** to what extent

**inzwischen** in the meantime
**irgendwas** something, anything
**(das) Irland** Ireland
**ironisch** ironic
**irritieren (hat irritiert)** to irritate
**irritierend** irritating
**der Islam** Islam
**(das) Island** Iceland
**(das) Italien** Italy
**italienisch** Italian

## J

**ja** yes [K. 1]
**die Jacke, -n** jacket [K. 4]
**jagen (hat gejagt)** to hunt
**der Jäger, -/die Jägerin, -nen** hunter [K. 10]
**das Jahr, -e** year [K. 2]; **schon seit Jahren** for years
**die Jahreszeit, -en** season [K. 5]
**der Jahrmarkt, ¨e** fair
**jammern (hat gejammert)** to whine, cry, lament
**Jänner** (*Austrian*) January
**der Januar** January [K. 2]; **am ersten** ~ on the first of January [K. 2]; **im** ~ in January [K. 2]
**(das) Japan** Japan [K. 1]
**der Japaner, -/die Japanerin, -nen** Japanese [K. 1]
**der Jazzkeller, -** jazz club [K. 7]
**die Jeans, -** jeans [K. 4]
**jedenfalls** anyway, at any rate
**jeder, jedes, jede** each; every [K. 5, 6]
**jedermann** everyone [K. 10]
**jederzeit** anytime
**jedoch** however
**jemand** someone, somebody [K. 10]; **irgend** ~ somebody, anybody
**jetzt** now [K. 5]
**das Jiddisch** Yiddish
**der Job, -s** job
**jobben (hat gejobbt)** to work part-time
**der/das Joghurt** yogurt [K. 3]
**der Journalist, [-en], -en/die Journalistin, -nen** journalist [K. 9]
**jubeln (hat gejubelt)** to cheer [K. 7]
**das Jubiläum,** *pl.* **Jubiläen** anniversary
**der Jude, [-n], -n/die Jüdin, -nen** Jew
**jüdisch** Jewish [K. 11]

**die Jugendherberge, -n** youth hostel [K. 3]
**das Jugendhotel, -s** budget youth hotel
**die Jugendliteratur** youth literature
**der Jugendstil** Art Nouveau
**(das) Jugoslawien** Yugoslavia
**der Juli** July [K. 2]
**jung (ü)** young [K. 1]
**der Junge, [-n], -n** (*adj. as noun*) boy [K. 2, 5]
**die Jungs** (*pl.*) boys, guys (*slang*)
**der Juni** June [K. 2]
**der Jura** Jura Mountains

## K

**der Kaffee** coffee [K. 3]
**das Kaffeehaus, ¨er** coffee house
**die Kaffeemaschine, -n** coffee maker
**der Käfig, -e** cage
**der Kaiser, -/die Kaiserin, -nen** emperor, empress [K. 11]
**Kalifornien** California
**kalt (ä)** cold [K. 5]
**die (digitale) Kamera, -s** (digital) camera [K. 4]
**der Kamin, -e** fireplace
**der Kamm, ¨e** comb [K. 4]
**kämmen (hat gekämmt)** to comb; **sich die Haare** ~ to comb one's hair [K. 8]
**kämpfen (hat gekämpft)** to fight
**(das) Kanada** Canada [K. 1]
**der Kanadier, -/die Kanadierin, -nen** Canadian [K. 1]
**der Kandidat, [-en], -en/die Kandidatin, -nen** candidate
**die Kantine, -n** cafeteria, cantine
**der Kanton, -e** canton, state (*in Switzerland*) [K. 10]
**der Kantor, -en** choirmaster
**der Kanzler, -/die Kanzlerin, -nen** chancellor [K. 11]
**die Kappensitzung, -en** Carnival guild party, "roast"
**der Karfreitag, -e** Good Friday
**der Karneval** Carnival [K. 10]
**die Karotte, -n** carrot [K. 3]
**die Karriere, -n** career
**die Karte, -n** card; **Karten spielen** to play cards [K. 3]

**die Kartoffel, -n**   potato [K. 3]

**der Käse**   cheese [K. 3]

**die Kasse, -n**   checkout counter, cash register [K. 7]

**der Kasten, -, (¨)**   case [K. 11]

**der Katalog, -e**   catalogue

**die Katastrophe, -n**   catastrophe

**der Kater, -**   tomcat; hangover (*slang*); **der gestiefelte ~**   Puss-in-Boots; **einen ~ haben**   to have a hangover [K. 6]

**die Katze, -n**   cat [K. 2]

**kauen (hat gekaut)**   to chew

**kaufen (hat gekauft)**   to buy, purchase [K. 2]

**der Kaufmann, ¨er/die Kauffrau, -en**   clerk [K. 9]

**der Kaugummi, -s**   chewing gum [K. 3]; **~ kauen**   to chew gum

**kaum**   hardly

**kein, keine, *pl.* keine**   no, none, not one [K. 1] **kein ... mehr**   no more

**der Keller, -**   basement, cellar [K. 6]

**der Kellner, -/die Kellnerin, -nen**   waiter/waitress [K. 5]

**kennen (kannte, hat gekannt)**   to know (a city, person) [K. 3]

**kennen lernen (hat kennen gelernt)**   to meet, get to know [K. 2]

**die Kenntnis, -se**   knowledge, skill [K. 9]

**das Kilogramm**   kilogram [K. 3]

**der Kilometer, -**   kilometer [K. 3]

**das Kind, -er**   child, children [K. 2]

**das Kinderbuch, ¨er**   children's book

**der Kindergarten, ¨**   preschool [K. 8]

**das Kinderzimmer, -**   children's room, nursery

**die Kindheit**   childhood [K. 10]

**das Kinn -e**   chin

**das Kino, -s**   movie theater, cinema [K. 7]; **ins ~ gehen**   to go to the movies [K. 3]

**der Kinoabend, -e**   night at the movies

**der Kiosk, -s**   kiosk, stand [K. 7]

**die Kirche, -n**   church [K. 3]

**der Kirchturm, ¨e**   church tower, steeple

**die Kirmes**   fair

**die Kirsche, -n**   cherry [K. 3]

**die Klamotten** *(pl.)*   clothes, duds [K. 6]

**klappen (hat geklappt)**   to work out all right [K. 11]

**klar**   clear; **Klar!**   Sure! All clear! [K. 6]

**klasse**   cool, great [K. 9]

**die Klassengröße, -n**   class size

**das Klassenzimmer, -**   classroom [K. 1]

**klassisch**   classical [K. 9]

**das Klavier, -e**   piano [K. 3]

**das Kleid, -er**   dress [K. 4]

**der Kleiderschrank, ¨e**   armoire, wardrobe [K. 6]

**die Kleidung, -en**   clothing, clothes [K. 4]

**das Kleidungsstück, -e**   piece of clothing

**klein**   short [K. 1]

**das Kleingeld**   pocket change

**die Kleinigkeit, -en**   trifle, a little something; detail [K. 11]

**klettern (ist geklettert)**   to climb

**das Klima, *pl.* Klimen**   climate

**klingen (klang, hat geklungen)**   to sound, ring [K. 8]

**das Klo, -s (das Klosett, -e)**   toilet (*colloq.*) [K. 6]

**klopfen (hat geklopft)**   to knock

**klug (ü)**   smart, intelligent [K. 2]

**knapp**   just barely, almost

**die Kneipe, -n**   bar, pub [K. 5]

**das Knie, -**   knee [K. 6]; **Knie- und Ellenbogenschutz**   knee and elbow pads

**der Koch, ¨e/die Köchin, -nen**   cook, chef [K. 9]

**kochen (hat gekocht**   to cook [K. 3]

**der Koffer, -**   suitcase [K. 4]

**der Kofferraum**   trunk of a car

**der Kognat, -e**   cognate

**die Kohle, -n**   coal

**der Kollege, [-n], -n/die Kollegin, -nen**   colleague, co-worker [K. 9]

**kollegial**   collegial [K. 9]

**der Kölner Dom**   cathedral in Cologne

**kombinieren (hat kombiniert)**   to combine

**kommen (kam, ist gekommen) aus +** *dat.*   to come, be from [K. 2]

**der Kommilitone, [-n], -n/die Kommilitonin, -nen**   fellow student [K. 8]

**die Kommode, -n**   chest of drawers [K. 6]

**der Kommunismus**   communism

**der Kommunist, [-en], -en/die Kommunistin, -nen**   communist

**die Komödie, -n**   comedy [K. 7]

**kompliziert**   complicated

**komponieren (hat komponiert)**   to compose [K. 9]

**der Komponist, [-en], -en/die Komponistin, -nen**   composer [K. 9]

**das Kompositum, *pl.* Komposita**   composite word

**die Konditorei, -en**   pastry shop [K. 7]

**der Konflikt, -e**   conflict

**konfus**   confused

**die Kongresshalle, -n**   convention center

**das Kongresszentrum, *pl.* -zentren**   convention center

**der König, -e/die Königin, -nen**   king/queen [K. 10]

**der Königssohn, ¨e**   prince [K. 10]

**die Königstochter, ¨**   princess [K. 10]

**das Königtum, ¨er**   kingdom

**die Konjunktion, -en**   conjunction

**der Konjunktiv**   subjunctive mood

**konkret**   concrete [K. 6]

**können (kann, konnte, hat gekonnt)**   to be able to; can [K. 3, 4]

**könnte**   could

**konstruieren (hat konstruiert)**   to construct

**konsumorientiert**   consumer-oriented [K. 11]

**der Kontakt, -e**   contact, communication [K. 5]

**kontaktfreudig**   outgoing, sociable [K. 9]

**der Kontext, -e**   context

**das Konto, *pl.* Konten**   bank account [K. 7]

**der Kontrast, -e**   contrast

**kontrollieren (hat kontrolliert)**   to check

**kontrovers**   controversial

**die Konversation, -en**   conversation

**sich konzentrieren (hat sich konzentriert) auf +** *acc.*   to concentrate on [K. 8]

**das Konzept, -e**   concept

**der Konzern, -e**   company

**das Konzert, -e**   concert [K. 3]

**der Konzertsaal, -säle**   concert hall [K. 9]

**der Kopf, ¨e**   head [K. 6]

die **Kopfschmerzen** *(pl.)* headache [K. 8]

**kopieren (hat kopiert)** to copy [K. 8]

der **Kopierer, -** photocopier

der **Kopierladen, ∹** copy shop

der **Körper, -** body

der **Körperteil, -e** body part [K. 6]

der **Korridor, -e** hall, corridor

die **Kost** food

die **Kosten** *(pl.)* expenses, costs

**kosten (hat gekostet)** to cost [K. 10]

**kotzen (hat gekotzt)** to throw up *(slang)*

der **Krach** argument, quarrel, noise [K. 5]; **~ haben** to have a fight, quarrel [K. 5]

**krachen (hat gekracht)** to crash

die **Kraftfahrstraße, -n** road for motorized vehicles

**krank (ä)** sick, ill [K. 8]

das **Krankenhaus, ∹er** hospital

der **Krankenpfleger, -/die Kranken-schwester, -n** orderly, nurse [K. 9]

der **Krankenurlaub** sick leave, sick days

**kraus** tightly curled [K. 1]

die **Krawatte, -n** necktie

**kreativ** creative [K. 4]

die **Kreditkarte, -n** credit card [K. 4]

die **Kreide** chalk [K. 1]

die **Kreuzung, -en** intersection, crossing [K. 7]; **bis zur ~** up to the intersection [K. 7]

der **Krieg, -e** war [K. 11]; **der Kalte ~** Cold War [K. 11]; **der Erste (Zweite) Weltkrieg** First (Second) World War [K. 11]

der **Krimi, -s** detective story

die **Kriminalität** crime, criminal activity

der **Kriminalroman, -e (der Krimi, -s)** detective story [K. 7]

der/die **Kriminelle, -n** *(adj. as noun)* criminal

die **Kriterien** *(pl.)* criteria

**kritisieren (hat kritisiert)** to criticize

**(das) Kroatien** Croatia

die **Küche, -n** kitchen [K. 6]; cuisine, food

der **Kuchen, -** cake [K. 3]

**kühl** cool [K. 5]

der **Kühlschrank, ∹e** refrigerator [K. 6]

der **Kuli, -s** ballpoint pen [K. 1]

die **Kultur, -en** culture; civilization

der **Kulturbeutel, -** shaving kit/cosmetic kit [K. 4]

**kulturell** cultural(ly) [K. 9]

das **Kulturzentrum,** *pl.* **-zentren** arts center, cultural center [AB 3]

das **Kultusministerium,** *pl.* **Ministerien** Ministry of Culture and Education

der **Kunde, [-n], -n/die Kundin, -nen** customer, client [K. 7]

die **Kunst** art [K. 2]

die **Kunsthalle, -n** art museum

die **Kunsthochschule, -n** art and design school

der **Künstler, -/die Künstlerin, -nen** artist

der **Kunstverein, -e** art association

der **Kurfürstendamm (Ku'damm)** *main street of Berlin* [K. 11]

**kurfürstlich** electoral

die **Kurpfalz** Electoral Palatinate (until 1806, princes of the Palatinate region **[Pfalz]** helped select **[Kur]** German emperors)

der **Kurs, -e** course [K. 2]

der **Kursteilnehmer, -/die Kursteilnehmerin, -nen** course participant [K. 12]

**kurz (ü)** short [K. 1]

die **Kurzgeschichte, -n** short story [K. 7]

die **Kusine, -n** female cousin [K. 2]

**küssen (hat geküsst)** to kiss [K. 5]

die **Kutsche, -n** coach, carriage

## L

**lächeln (hat gelächelt)** to smile [K. 3]

**lachen (hat gelacht)** to laugh [K. 1, 7]; **~ über** + *acc.* to laugh about, at

das **Lacrosse** lacrosse [K. 7]

die **Lade, -n** drawer

die **Lage, -n** position, situation

der **Lagerarbeiter, -/die Lagerarbei-terin, -nen** warehouse worker

**lahm** weak, boring, lame [ZT 8]

**lala: (Das) finde ich so ~.** I find (that) so-so. [K. 7]; **Mir geht es so ~.** I'm so-so. [K. 8]

die **Lampe, -n** lamp, light, light fixture [K. 1]

das **Land, ∹er** country [K. 1]

**landen (ist gelandet)** to land

die **Landeshauptstadt, ∹e** state capital

die **Landeskunde** geography [K. 1]

die **Landfläche, -n** land mass

die **Landkarte, -n** map [K. 1]

die **Landschaft, -en** landscape, scenery [K. 10]

**lang (ä)** *(adj.)* long; tall [K. 1]

**lange** *(adv.)* for a long time

die **Länge, -n** length

der **Langlauf** cross-country skiing

die **Langlaufloipe, -n** cross-country ski run [K. 10]

**langsam** slow(ly) [K. 4]

**langweilig** boring [K. 3]

der **Laptop, -s** laptop computer [K. 4]

**lassen (lässt, ließ, hat gelassen)** to let, allow; to leave

**laufen (läuft, lief, ist gelaufen)** to run; to walk [K. 3]

**laut** loud [K. 4]

der **Laut, -e** sound

**leben (hat gelebt)** to live [K. 5]

das **Leben, -** life

**lebendig** alive, lively [K. 11]

die **Lebensfreude** joy of life

der **Lebenslauf, ∹e** resume, CV [K. 9]

die **Lebensmittel** *(pl.)* groceries

das **Lebensmittelgeschäft, -e** grocery store [K. 3]

der **Lebensraum, ∹e** habitat, living space [K. 12]

die **Leberwurst, ∹e** liverwurst, liver sausage

der **Lebkuchen, -** gingerbread

**lecker** delicious

die **Lederhose, -n** lederhosen

**ledig** single [K. 2]

**leer** empty

**legen (hat gelegt)** to lay down, put down [K. 7]

das **Lehrangebot, -e** course offering

der **Lehrassistent, [-en], -en/die Lehrassistentin, -nen** teaching assistant

die **Lehre, -n** apprenticeship

der **Lehrer, -/die Lehrerin, -nen** teacher [K. 9]

die **Lehrkraft, ∹e** instructor

der **Lehrling, -e** apprentice

die **Leiche, -n** corpse

**leicht** easy, light [K. 5]

**Leid tun (tat Leid, hat Leid getan)** + *dat.* to feel sorry for [K. 6]; **Es tut mir Leid** I'm sorry

**leidenschaftlich** passionately

**leider** unfortunately [K. 4]

**leihen (lieh, hat geliehen)** to lend; to borrow [K. 6, 8]

**die Leinwand, ¨e** projection screen [K. 1]

**leise** quiet(ly)

**leisten (hat geleistet)** to achieve, accomplish; **sich ~ (hat sich geleistet)** to afford

**leiten (hat geleitet)** to lead, be in charge of

**lernen (hat gelernt)** to learn; to study [K. 2]

**lesbisch** lesbian

**lesen (liest, las, hat gelesen)** to read [K. 3]

**die Lesestrategie, -n** reading strategy

**letzte** last [K. 9]

**die Leute** (*pl.*) people [K. 2, 5]

**lieb** dear; **Liebe ... /Lieber ...** Dear . . . (*used to begin a letter*)

**die Liebe** love [K. 5]

**lieben (hat geliebt)** to love [K. 5]

**lieber** (*comparative of* **gern**) preferably, rather [K. 9]; **~ als** rather than; **~** + *verb* preferably; [I would] rather . . . [K. 3]

**das Liebesgedicht, -e** love poem

**der Liebeskummer** lovesickness; heartbreak [K. 5]

**der Liebesroman, -e** romance novel [K. 7]

**der Lieblingssport** favorite sport

**liebsten: am ~** most preferably [K. 9]

**Liechtenstein** (principality of) Liechtenstein

**der Liederfürst** prince of songs

**liegen (lag, hat gelegen)** to lie, be located [K. 5, 7]; **es liegt daran, dass ...** that's because . . .

**die Liga,** *pl.* **Ligen** league [K. 7]

**lila** purple [K. 1]

**links** left, on the left [K. 4]

**die Lippe, -n** lip

**der Lippenstift, -e** lipstick [K. 4]

**die List** cunning

**die Liste, -n** list [K. 7]

**der Liter, -** liter [K. 3]

**die Literatur** literature [K. 7]

**locken (hat gelockt)** to entice, attract

**locker** relaxed, cool (*colloq.*) [K. 4]

**der Löffel, -** spoon [K. 6]

**das Lokal, -e** pub [K. 3]

**die Lokalzeitung, -en** local newspaper

**der Lokalzug, ¨e** local commuter train

**los** off, loose; **Was ist ~?** What's the matter? [K. 5]; **Los!** Let's go!

**lösen (hat gelöst)** to solve

**los·fahren (fährt los, fuhr los, ist losgefahren)** to take off, leave, drive away [K. 5]

**die Lösung, -en** solution [K. 8]

**die Lücke, -n** blank

**die Luft, ¨e** air

**die Luftbrücke, -n** airlift [K. 11]

**die Lust** desire [K. 8]; **~ haben** to want, wish, have desire [K. 8]

**lustig** funny, jovial, comical [K. 4, 7]

**(das) Luxemburg** Luxembourg [K. 12]

**die Luxusbude, -n** "luxury" student room (*colloq.*) [K. 6]

## M

**machen (hat gemacht)** to make, do [K. 2]

**die Macht, ¨e** power, strength [K. 11]

**die Machtergreifung** seizure of power [K. 11]

**das Mädchen, -** girl [K. 2, 5]

**das Magazin, -e** magazine

**der Magister, -** Master of Arts

**Mahlzeit!** Good day! (*at lunchtime*), Have a nice lunch! [K. 1]

**das Mahnmal, -e** (*selten:* -mäler) memorial [K. 11]

**der Mai** May [K. 2]

**das Mail** e-mail (the concept) [K. 2]

**mailen (hat gemailt)** to e-mail [K. 5]

**der Makler, -/die Maklerin, -nen** real estate agent [K. 9]

**mal** once (*emphatic particle*) [K. 4]

**das Mal: zum ersten ~** for the first time [K. 5]

**malerisch** scenic

**man (einen, einem)** a person, anybody; you (*impersonal*), one [K. 3]

**der Manager, -/die Managerin, -nen** manager

**manche** several, some [K. 11]

**manchmal** sometimes [K. 6]

**der Mann, ¨er** man; husband [K. 2, 5]

**die Mannschaft, -en** team [K. 7]

**der Mantel, ¨** coat [K. 4]

**das Märchen, -** folk/fairy tale [K. 7]

**das Märchenelement, -e** fairy tale element

**die Märchenfigur, -en** fairy tale character

**markieren (hat markiert)** to mark

**der Markt, ¨e** market [K. 7]

**die Markthalle, -n** market hall, indoor market

**der Marktplatz, ¨e** market square [K. 3]

**die Marmelade, -n** marmelade, preserves [K. 3]

**der Marsmensch, [-en], -en** Martian

**der März** March [K. 2]

**der Maschinenbau** mechanical engineering

**die Maß, -en** one and a half liters; **die ~ Bier** one and a half liters of beer

**die Massage, -n** massage

**die Masse, -n** mass, crowd; **die Massen-Uni, -s** mega-university

**das Material, -ien** material

**die Mathematik (die Mathe)** mathematics [K. 2]

**die Matura** high school graduation exam (*in Austria*)

**die Mauer, -n** exterior wall; the Wall (in Berlin) [K. 11]

**maximal** maximally

**die Medizin** medicine [K. 2]

**das Meer, -e** sea

**mehr** more [K. 3]

**das Mehrbettzimmer, -** room with multiple beds

**mein** my [K. 3]

**meinen (hat gemeint)** to think, have an opinion [K. 2]

**die Meinung, -en** opinion; **meiner ~ nach** in my opinion [K. 6]

**meisten: am ~** most (of all) [K. 9]

**meistens** usually, mostly [K. 8]

**melancholisch** melancholic

**sich melden (hat sich gemeldet)** to report, show up; to get in touch [K. 8]

**die Menge, -n** a bunch of, a lot of; crowd; **jede ~** (a) large amount

**die Mensa**, *pl.* **Mensen**   student dining hall [K. 6]

**das Mensa-Essen**   food in student dining hall

**der Mensch, [-en], -en**   person, human being [K. 3, 6]; **Mensch!** Man!

**merken (hat gemerkt)**   to notice [K. 9]

**das Messer, -**   knife [K. 6]

**der Meter, -**   meter [K. 5]

**der Metzger, -/die Metzgerin, -nen**   butcher [K. 9]

**die Metzgerei, -en**   butcher shop [K. 7]

**der Mexikaner, -/die Mexikanerin, -nen**   Mexican [K. 1]

**(das) Mexiko**   Mexico [K. 1]

**mich**   me *(acc.)* [K. 3]

**mies**   rotten, lousy [K. 5]

**die Miete, -n**   rent [K. 11]

**der Mikrowellenherd, -e**   microwave oven [K. 6]

**die Milch**   milk [K. 3]

**die Million, -en**   million

**die Minderheit, -en**   minority

**mindestens**   at least

**das Mineralwasser, -**   mineral water [K. 3]

**mir**   me *(dat.)* (to, for) [K. 6]

**mischen (hat gemischt)**   to mix

**miserabel**   miserable

**missfallen (missfällt, missfiel, hat missfallen) +** *dat.*   to displease

**das Missverständnis, -se**   misunderstanding

**mit +** *dat.*   with [K. 2, 6]

**der Mitarbeiter, /die Mitarbeiterin, -nen**   co-worker

**der Mitbewohner, -/die Mitbewohnerin, -nen**   roommate [K. 7]

**mit·bringen (brachte mit, hat mitgebracht)**   to bring along, bring back [K. 3]

**miteinander**   with one another

**das Mitglied, -er**   member

**mit·machen (hat mitgemacht)**   to join in, participate [K. 6, 10]

**mit·nehmen (nimmt mit, nahm mit, hat mitgenommen)**   to take along [K. 4]

**der Mittag**   noon [K. 2]

**das Mittagessen, -**   lunch [K. 3]

**die Mitte, -n**   middle [K. 11]; **Berlin-Mitte**   center of Berlin [K. 11]

**die Mitteilung, -en**   memo

**das Mittelalter**   Middle Ages [K. 9]

**(das) Mitteleuropa**   Central Europe

**das Mittelland**   midlands, flatlands

**der Mittelpunkt**   midpoint, center

**die Mitternacht**   midnight [K. 2]

**die Mittlere Reife**   10th grade high school exam

**mittlerweile**   meantime, meanwhile

**der Mittwoch, -e**   Wednesday [K. 2]

**die Möbel** *(pl.)*   furniture [K. 6]

**möchte**   would like to [K. 2, 4]

**der Modus**, *pl.* **Modi**   mood

**mögen (ich/er mag, mochte, hat gemocht)**   to like [K. 4]

**möglich**   possible [K. 9]

**die Möglichkeit, -en**   possibility [K. 6]

**der Mokka**   mocha coffee

**mollig**   chubby, plump [K. 1]

**Moment: ~ mal!**   Wait a minute!

**momentan**   at the moment, momentarily

**die Monarchie, -n**   monarchy [K. 11]

**der Monat, -e**   month [K. 2]

**der Montag, -e**   Monday [K. 2]

**montags**   on Mondays

**der Morgen, -**   morning [K. 8]; **eines Morgens**   one morning [K. 10] **Guten ~!**   Good morning! [K. 1]

**morgen**   tomorrow [K. 5]; **~ Abend (früh, Nachmittag)**   tomorrow evening (morning, afternoon) [K. 8]

**morgens**   in the morning [K. 2]

**die Moschee, -n**   mosque

**das Motiv, -e**   motive

**motiviert**   motivated [K. 9]

**das Motorrad, ̈er**   motorcycle [K. 7]

**müde**   tired [K. 4]

**das Müesli**   muesli, whole grain cereal

**die Mühe, -n**   effort

**mühselig**   with difficulty [K. 11]

**der Müller, -/die Müllerin, -nen**   miller

**der Multikulturalismus**   multiculturalism

**multikulturell**   multicultural [K. 6]

**der Mund, ̈er**   mouth [K. 6]

**mündlich**   oral(ly) [K. 8]

**das Museum**, *pl.* **Museen**   museum [K. 3]

**die Museumsinsel**   "Museum Island" *(in Berlin)* [K. 11]

**das Musical, -s**   musical [K. 9]

**die Musik**   music [K. 2]

**musikalisch**   musical [K. 3]

**der Musikant, [-en], -en/die Musikantin, -nen**   musician

**der Musiker, -/die Musikerin, -nen**   musician [K. 9]

**das Musikgeschäft, -e**   music store [K. 3]

**die Musikhochschule, -n**   music conservatory

**der Muskelkater,-**   sore muscle [K. 8]

**müssen (muss, musste, hat gemusst)**   to have to, must; to be required to [K. 4]: **ich muss nicht**   I don't need to [K. 4]

**mutig**   brave, courageous

**die Mutter, ̈**   mother [K. 2]

**die Muttersprache, -n**   native language

**die Mutti, -s**   mom, ma, mommy

**die Mütze, -n**   cap, hat

## N

**na**   well; **~ ja**   oh, well [K. 6]; **~, wie auch immer ...**   yeah, whatever . . .

**nach +** *dat.*   to *(countries, cities)*; past/after [K. 6]; **~ wie vor**   still

**nachdem** *(conj.)*   after [K. 10]

**nach·denken (dachte nach, hat nachgedacht)**   to consider something, to think something over [K. 12]

**der Nachfahr, -n**   descendant

**nachher** *(adv.)*   afterwards

**die Nachhilfestunde, -n**   tutoring lesson

**das Nachhinein: im ~**   in retrospect

**der Nachmittag**   afternoon [K. 8]

**die Nachricht, -en**   news, message [K. 9]

**das Nachrichtenmagazin, -e**   news magazine

**die Nachspeise, -n**   dessert [K. 3]

**nächst-: nächste Woche**   next week [K. 8]; **nächsten Samstag**   next Saturday [K. 8]

**die Nacht, ̈e**   night [K. 1]; **eines Nachts**   one night [K. 10]; **Gute ~!**   Good night! [K. 1]

**der Nachteil, -e**   disadvantage

**der Nachtisch, -e**   dessert [K. 3]

**nächtlich**   nighttime, nocturnal

**nackt**   naked

**der Nagellack**   nail polish [K. 4]

**nagelneu**   brand-new
**nah (ä)**   near
**die Nähe**   vicinity; **in der ~ von**   in the vicinity of, near [K. 3]
**näher**   nearer, closer [K. 7]
**der Name, [-ns], -n**   name [K. 1]
**namens**   by the name of
**nämlich**   namely, that is
**der Narr, [-en], -en**   fool
**die Narrengesellschaft, -en**   fools' guild
**die Nase, -n**   nose [K. 6]
**nass (a/ä)**   wet, damp [K. 5]
**die Nationalität, -en**   nationality [K. 1]
**der Nationalsozialist, [-en], -en/die Nationalsozialistin, -nen**   National Socialist, Nazi
**die Natur, -en**   nature
**natürlich**   natural(ly) [K. 8]
**die Naturschönheit, -en**   natural beauty
**der Nebel, -**   fog [K. 5]
**neben**   next to, beside [K. 7]
**nebenan**   next door
**nebendran**   adjacent, next to
**nebeneinander**   next to each other
**das Nebenfach, ̈er**   minor *(area of study)* [K. 2]
**nee**   nope, naw
**der Neffe, [-n], -n**   nephew [K. 2]
**nehmen (nimmt, nahm, hat genommen)**   to take [K. 1]; **Platz ~**   to have a seat
**die Neigung, -en**   preference, inclination
**nein**   no [K. 1]
**nennen (nannte, hat genannt)**   to name, call someone something [K. 7]
**der Neo-Nazi, -s**   Neo-Nazi
**nervös**   nervous; irritable [K. 4]
**nett**   nice [K. 6]
**neu**   new [K. 4]
**die Neuauflage, -n**   reprint
**der Neubau, -ten**   new building
**neugierig**   curious, nosy [K. 7]
**das Neujahr**   New Year's Day [K. 10]
**neulich**   recently [K. 11]
**neun**   nine [K. 1]
**neunzehn**   nineteen [K. 1]
**neunzig**   ninety [K. 1]
**die Neutralität**   neutrality
**nicht**   not [K. 1]; **~ sehr**   not very [K. 2]; **~ so**   not so [K. 2]; **gar ~**   not at all; **Ich weiß ~**   I don't know. [K. 1]

**die Nichte, -n**   niece [K. 2]
**nichts**   nothing [K. 1, 3]
**nicken (hat genickt)**   to nod
**nie**   never [K. 4]; **gar ~**   never at all
**nieder·brennen (brannte nieder, hat niedergebrannt)**   to burn down
**die Niederlande** *(pl.)*   the Netherlands
**(das) Niedersachsen**   Lower Saxony
**niemals**   never [K. 9]
**niemand (niemanden, niemandem)**   no one, nobody [K. 4]
**der Nikolaustag**   St. Nicholas Day
**nirgendwo**   nowhere [K. 11]
**das Niveau, -s**   level
**der Nobelpreisträger, -/die Nobelpreisträgerin, -nen**   Nobel Prize winner [K. 12]
**noch**   still; again [K. 4]; **~ (ein)mal**   once again [K. 4]; **Was ~?**   What else? [K. 5]
**(das) Nordamerika**   North America
**der Nordosten**   northeast
**die Nordsee**   North Sea [K. 11]
**der Nordwesten**   northwest
**normalerweise**   normally, usually
**(das) Norwegen**   Norway
**der Notarzt, ̈e**   emergency room physician
**die Note, -n**   grade in course [K. 12]
**der Notendurchschnitt**   grade point average
**die Notiz, -en**   note
**notwendig**   necessary
**das Notwendigste**   bare necessities
**der November**   November [K. 2]
**der Numerus clausus**   restricted enrollment
**null**   zero [K. 1]
**die Nummer, -n**   number
**nun**   now [K. 9]
**nur**   only, just [K. 2]
**die Nuss, ̈e**   nut

## O

**ob**   whether, if [K. 5]
**das Oberhaupt**   head *(of state)*
**das Obst**   fruit, fruits [K. 3]
**oder**   or [K. 2]
**offen**   open [K. 4]
**öffentlich**   public(ly)
**öffnen (hat geöffnet)**   to open [K. 5]
**die Öffnung, -en**   opening

**oft (ö)**   often [K. 4]
**ohne + *acc.***   without [K. 4]; **ohne ... zu**   without . . . -ing
**das Ohr, -en**   ear [K. 6]
**Oje!**   Geez! Oh boy!
**ökologisch**   ecological
**der Oktober**   October [K. 2]
**das Öl, -e**   oil
**das Olympiastadion**   Olympic Stadium in Berlin [K. 11]
**die Olympiade, -n**   Olympic Games
**die Oma, -s**   grandma [K. 2]
**der Onkel, -**   uncle [K. 2]
**der Opa, -s**   grandpa [K. 2]
**die Oper, -n**   opera; opera house [K. 7]
**die Opposition, -en**   opposition
**optimistisch**   optimistic
**orange** *(adj.)*   orange [K. 1]
**die Orange, -n**   orange [K. 3]
**ordnen (hat geordnet)**   to put in order, organize
**die Ordnung**   order; **alles in ~**   everything's in order [K. 6]; **~ schaffen (hat geschafft)**   to tidy up
**die Organisation, -en**   organization
**organisieren (hat organisiert)**   to organize
**die Orientierung, -en**   orientation
**die Orientierungsstufe**   orientation stage (5th and 6th grades)
**der Originaltext, -e**   original text [K. 12]
**der Ort, -e**   place
**örtlich**   local
**der Osterhase, [-n], -n**   Easter bunny
**Ostern**   Easter [K. 10]
**(das) Österreich**   Austria [K. 1]
**der Österreicher, -/die Österreicherin, -nen**   Austrian [K. 1]
**die Ostsee**   Baltic Sea [K. 11]
**der Overheadprojektor, -en**   overhead projector [K. 1]

## P

**paar: ein ~**   a few, some [K. 5, 8]; **das Paar, -e**   pair
**packen (hat gepackt)**   to pack [K. 4]
**die Pädagogik**   pedagogy, education [K. 2]
**das Paket, -e**   package [K. 7]
**die Panik**   panic
**der Papa, -s**   papa, dad

**der Papierkorb, ¨e** wastepaper basket [K. 1]

**das Paradies, -e** paradise

**parken (hat geparkt)** to park

**die Parkgebühr, -en** parking fee

**das Parkhaus, ¨er** parking garage

**der Parkplatz, ¨e** parking space, parking lot

**der Parkschein, -e** parking stub, ticket

**das Parlament, -e** parliament

**die Partei, -en** political party [K. 11];

**die Party, -s** party [K. 6]; **auf eine ~ gehen** to go to a party

**der Pass,** *pl.* **Pässe** passport [K. 4]; mountain/ski pass [K. 10]

**passen (hat gepasst) zu** + *dat.* to suit, fit [K. 8]

**passieren (ist passiert)** + *dat.* to happen [K. 5]

**der Pastor, -en** pastor

**der Patient, [-en], -en/die Patientin, -nen** patient

**die Pause, -n** break, recess

**der Pazifist, [-en], -en/die Pazifistin, -nen** pacifist

**Pech haben (hat Pech gehabt)** to have bad luck [K. 8]

**peinlich** embarrassing

**pendeln (hat gependelt)** to commute

**der Pendler, -/Pendlerin, -nen** commuter

**die Pension, -en** guesthouse [K. 3]

**peppig** peppy

**perfekt** perfect

**das Perfekt** conversational past

**die Perle, -n** pearl, bead

**die Person, -en** person [K. 1]

**die Personalabteilung, -en** personnel department [K. 9]

**der Personalchef, -s/die Personalchefin, -nen** head of the personnel department

**der Personenkraftwagen, -** car

**persönlich** personal; *etwas Persönliches* something personal [K. 12]

**die Persönlichkeit, -en** personality

**pessimistisch** pessimistic

**die Pfanne, -n** pan

**der Pfeffer** pepper [K. 6]

**der Pfennig, -e** pfennig (1/100 of a deutsche mark)

**das Pferd, -e** horse

**der Pferdeschlitten, -** horse-drawn sleigh

**(das) Pfingsten** Pentecost

**die Pflanze, -n** plant [K. 6]

**pflanzen (hat gepflanzt)** to plant [K. 10]

**pflegen (hat gepflegt)** to maintain, keep up

**der Pflichtkurs, -e** required course

**das Pfund, -e** pound [K. 3]

**die Pharmazie** pharmaceutics

**die Philharmonie** (Berlin) Philharmonic Orchestra [K. 11]

**die Philosophie, -n** philosophy [K. 2]

**die Physik** physics [K. 2]

**der Pilz, -e** mushroom

**die Piste, -n** (downhill) ski run, track [K. 10]

**der Pistenraser, -** speed demon

**der PKW, -s (Personenkraftwagen)** car [K. 7]

**der Plan, ¨e** plan

**planbar** capable of being planned

**das Planetarium,** *pl.* **Planetarien** planetarium

**die Planung, -en** plan; planning

**das Plattengeschäft, -e** record store

**der Platz, ¨e** plaza, square [K. 3]; space, room; seat [K. 4]; **~ nehmen** to sit down

**plaudern (hat geplaudert)** to chat

**plötzlich** suddenly [K. 8]

**der Pluspunkt, -e** advantage, plus

**pochen (hat gepocht)** to pound, beat

**der Poet, [-en], -en/die Poetin, -nen** poet [K. 9]

**(das) Polen** Poland [K. 1]

**die Politik** politics

**der Politiker, -/die Politikerin, -nen** politician [K. 9]

**die Politikwissenschaft** political science [K. 2]

**die Popmusik** popular music [K. 2]

**populär** popular

**das Portmonee, -s** wallet [K. 4]

**die Portion, -en** portion

**(das) Portugal** Portugal

**das Porzellan** porcelain, china

**positiv** positive

**die Post** post office [K. 7]

**der Postbote, [-n], -n/die Postbotin,**

**-nen** mailman, letter carrier [K. 10]

**das Poster, -** poster

**das Postfach, ¨er** mailbox, P. O. box [K. 6]

**die Postkarte, -n** postcard [K. 2]

**der Praktikant, [-en], -en/die Praktikantin, -nen** intern, trainee [K. 9]

**das Praktikum,** *pl.* **Praktika** internship [K. 8, 9]

**praktisch** practical(ly) [K. 7]

**praktizieren (hat praktiziert)** to practice (a profession)

**sich präsentieren (hat sich präsentiert)** to present oneself

**das Präteritum** narrative past

**die Praxis,** *pl.* **Praxen** doctor's office; *(no pl.)* practice [K. 9]

**der Preis, -e** price; prize

**preiswert** reasonably priced [K. 10]

**das Prestige** prestige

**(das) Preußen** Prussia

**prima** top-notch

**der Prinz, [-en], -en/die Prinzessin, -nen** prince/princess [K. 10]

**das Privatbad, ¨er** private bath

**die Privatstunde, -n** private lesson

**pro** per

**probieren (hat probiert)** to try [K. 8]

**das Problem, -e** problem [K. 2, 5]

**problemlos** without a problem, hassle-free

**der Professor, -en/die Professorin, -nen** professor [K. 1]

**der Profi, -s** professional [K. 7]

**das Programm, -e** program [K. 9]

**der Programmierer, -/die Programmiererin, -nen** programmer [K. 9]

**das Projekt, -e** project

**proklamieren (hat proklamiert)** to proclaim

**der/die Prominente, -n** *(adj. as noun)* public figure

**das Proseminar, -e** introductory seminar

**die Prüfung, -en** test, **examination** [K. 6]

**die Psychologie** psychology [K. 2]

**der Pudding, -s** pudding

**der Pullover, -** pullover, sweater [K. 4]

**der Pulverschnee** powder snow

**pünktlich** punctual, on time [K. 9]

die Puppe, -n   doll
das Puppenhaus, ¨er   doll house
die Pute, -n   turkey [K. 3]
putzen (hat sich geputzt): sich die
   Zähne ~   to brush one's teeth
   [K. 8]

## Q

das Quadrat, -e   square
qualifiziert   qualified [K. 9]
der Quark   *special German dairy
   spread* [K. 3]
quer   diagonal, across; ~ **gegenüber
   von**   diagonally across from [K. 7]
die Quittung, -en   receipt [K. 7]

## R

der Rabatt, -e   rebate
das Rad, ¨er   bicycle; **Rad fahren
   (fährt Rad, fuhr Rad, ist Rad
   gefahren)**   to bicycle [K. 3]
das Radfahren   bicycle riding
der Radfahrer, -/die Radfahrerin,
   -nen   cyclist, bicycle rider [K. 4];
   ~ **frei**   open to cyclists, bicycles
   allowed
das Radio, -s   radio [K. 6]
der Radweg, -e   bicycle path [K. 4]
der Ramadan   Ramadan [K. 10]
der Rang, ¨e   rank, standing
rar   rare
der Rasierapparat, -e   electric razor,
   shaver [K. 8]
sich rasieren (hat sich rasiert)   to
   shave [K. 8]
der Rat, *pl.* Ratschläge   advice
raten (rät, riet, hat geraten)   to advise
das Ratespiel, -e   guessing game
das Rathaus, *pl.* Rathäuser   city hall
   [K. 3]
(das) Rätoromanisch   the Romansh
   language
der Ratschlag, ¨e   advice, suggestion
das Rätsel, -   puzzle, riddle
der Ratskeller, -   ratskeller, town hall
   basement restaurant
rauchen (hat geraucht)   to smoke
   [K. 6]
der Raum, ¨e   room [K. 6]
raus   out
raus·kommen (kam raus, ist
   rausgekommen)   to come out

raus·springen (sprang raus, ist raus
   gesprungen)   to jump out
reagieren (hat reagiert)   to react
   [K. 11]
die Reaktion, -en   reaction
realistisch   realistic
die Realität, -en   reality
die Realschule, -n   non-college track
   high school
der Realschüler, -/die Realschülerin,
   -nen   high school student
das Rebhuhn, ¨er   partridge
rechnen (hat gerechnet)   to count
   [K. 12]; ~ **mit** + *dat.*   to count on,
   reckon with, expect [K. 12]
der Rechtsanwalt, ¨e/die Rechtsanwältin, -nen   lawyer
Recht haben (hat Recht gehabt)   to
   be right [K. 3]; **Du hast vollkommen
   Recht.**   You are absolutely right.
   [K. 11]
recht sein (ist, war, ist gewesen) + *dat.*
   to be all right with someone; **wenn es
   dir recht ist**   if it's all right with you
rechtfertigen (hat gerechtfertigt)   to
   justify
rechts   right, on the right [K. 4]
der Rechtsanwalt, ¨e/die Rechtsanwältin, -nen   lawyer, attorney [K. 9]
der/die Rechtsradikale, -n *(adj. as
   noun)*   right-wing extremist
der Rechtsradikalismus   right-wing
   extremism
rechtzeitig   on time
das Recycling   recycling
reden (hat geredet) über + *acc.*   to
   talk about [K. 5, 8]
das Referat, -e   seminar paper,
   presentation [K. 8]; **ein ~ halten**   to
   make an oral presentation [K. 8]
das Reformhaus, ¨er   health food
   store [K. 7]
das Regal, -e   shelf, shelving [K. 6]
die Regel, -n   rule, regulation [K. 4]
regeln (hat geregelt)   to regulate
   [K. 11].
der Regen   rain [K. 5]
der Regenmantel, ¨   raincoat
der Regenschaden   rain damage
der Regenschirm, -e   umbrella
der Regierungsantritt, -e   taking
   office
das Regierungsviertel, -   area of
   federal government buildings [K. 11]

der Regisseur, -e/die Regisseurin,
   -nen   film or play director [K. 9]
regnen (hat geregnet)   to rain [K. 5]
das Reich, -e   empire; realm [K. 11];
   **das Deutsche ~**   German Empire
   [K. 11]; **das Dritte ~**   Third Reich
   [K. 11]
reichen (hat gereicht)   to be enough,
   suffice, last; to hand, give; ~ **von . . .
   bis**   to stretch from . . . to [K. 9]
der Reichstag   parliament [K. 11]
   building
die Reifeprüfung, -en   high school
   exam *(Switzerland)*
die Reihenfolge, -n   order, sequence
die Reinemachefrau, -en   cleaning
   lady
rein·stellen (hat reingestellt)   to put
   in
der Reis   rice
die Reise, -n   trip, journey, travel
   [K. 4]
der Reisekoffer, -   suitcase
der Reiseleiter, -/die Reiseleiterin,
   -nen   tour guide, courier, group
   leader [K. 10]
reisen (ist gereist)   to travel [K. 7]
der Reiseplan, ¨e   travel itinerary
das Reisetagebuch, ¨er   travel log,
   diary
das Reiseunternehmen, -   travel
   agency
reißen (hat gerissen): aus den Angeln
   ~   to tear off its hinges
reiten (ritt, ist geritten)   to ride
   horseback [K. 3]
rekonstruieren (hat rekonstruiert)
   to reconstruct
relativ   relative(ly)
das Relativpronomen, -   relative
   pronoun
der Relativsatz, ¨e   relative clause
die Religion, -en   religion
rennen (rannte, ist gerannt)   to run,
   race [K. 10]
renovieren (hat renoviert)   to
   renovate, remodel [K. 11]
die Rente, -n   pension
die Rentenversicherung, -en
   pension insurance, social
   security
die Republik, -en   republic [K. 11]
   **die Weimarer ~**   Weimar
Republic

**der Republikaner, -/die Republi-
kanerin, -nen** member of the
Republican Party

**der Respekt** respect [K. 5]

**respektieren (hat respektiert)** to
respect

**die Ressource, -n** resource

**der Rest, -e** rest, remainder
[K. 11]

**das Restaurant, -s** restaurant
[K. 3]; **im ~** in the restaurant
[K. 3]

**das Resultat, -e** result

**retten (hat gerettet) vor** + *dat.* to
rescue, save from

**der Revisionist, [-en], -en/die
Revisionistin, -nen** revisionist

**die Revolution, -en** revolution

**der Rhein** Rhine

**richtig** right [K. 5]; authentic, really
[K. 5]

**das Richtige** the right thing

**die Richtung, -en** direction
[K. 7]

**das Rindfleisch** beef [K. 3]

**riskant** risky

**riskieren (hat riskiert)** to risk

**der Rock, ̈e** skirt [K. 4]

**der Rocksänger, -/die Rocksängerin,
-nen** rock singer

**rodeln (ist gerodelt)** to sled

**die Rolle, -n** role, part

**die Rollerblades** *(pl.)* in-line skates
[K. 7]

**der Rollladen, ̈** roll-top shutters
[K. 6]

**der Rollschuh, -e** roller skates

**der Roman, -e** novel [K. 7]

**romantisch** romantic [K. 1]

**römisch** Roman

**rosa** pink [K. 1]

**die Rose, -n** rose

**rot (ö)** red [K. 1]

**das Rotkäppchen** Little Red Riding
Hood

**die Routine, -n** routine

**der Rückblick** review

**der Rücken, -** back [K. 6]

**der Rucksack, ̈e** backpack [K. 4]

**der Ruf** reputation

**rufen (rief, hat gerufen)** to call

**ruhig** quiet, peaceful [K. 4]

**das Rumpelstilzchen** Rumpelstiltskin

**rund** approximately, roughly; **~ um**
all around

**die Runde, -n** round

**(das) Russisch** the Russian language
[K. 2]

**rütteln (hat gerüttelt)** to shake

### S

**die Sache, -n** thing, object, item
[K. 4]

**die Sachertorte, -n** Sacher chocolate
layer cake

**(das) Sachsen** Saxony

**der Saft, ̈e** juice [K. 3]

**die Sage, -n** myth, legend

**sagen (hat gesagt)** to say [K. 5]

**die Saison, -s** (travel) season

**der/das Sakko, -s** sport coat [K. 4]

**der Salat, -e** salad; lettuce [K. 3]

**das Salz** salt [K. 6]

**die Salzstange, -n** pretzel stick

**der Samstag, -e** Saturday (*in
Southern Germany*) [K. 2]

**die Sandale, -n** sandal [K. 4]

**sanft** gentle, soft

**der Sänger, -/die Sängerin, -nen**
singer [K. 9]

**der Satz, ̈e** sentence

**sauber** clean [K. 10]

**sauber machen (hat sauber gemacht)**
to clean

**die Sauna, -s** sauna

**sausen (hat gesaust)** to whistle

**schade** to bad, unfortunate [K. 5]

**schaden (hat geschadet)** + *dat.* to
harm, hurt

**schaffen (hat geschaffen)** to create
[K. 9]

**schaffen (hat geschafft)** to accomplish [K. 9]

**der Schal, -s** scarf, shawl [K. 4]

**der Schatz, ̈e** treasure

**schauen (hat geschaut)** to look at, to
watch [K. 7]; **Schau mal!** Look!

**der Schauer, -** shower; shivers [K. 5]

**der Schauspieler, -/die Schauspiele-
rin, -nen** actor/actress [K. 9]

**das Schauspielhaus, ̈er** theater

**der Scheck, -s** check [K. 7]

**die Scheibe, -n** slice [K. 3]

**der Schein, -e** paper money, bill;
course credit certificate

**scheinbar** apparently, seemingly

**scheinen (schien, hat geschienen)**
to shine; to appear to be [K. 5, 8]

**schenken (hat geschenkt)** to give a
gift [K. 6]

**das Scheunenviertel** former Jewish
neighborhood in Berlin [K. 11]

**schicken (hat geschickt)** to send [K. 4]

**schief gehen (ging schief, ist schief
gegangen)** to fail, go wrong

**schießen (schoss, hat geschossen)**
to shoot [K. 7]

**das Schiff, -e** boat [K. 7]

**die Schifffahrt, -en** boat trip

**das Schild, -er** sign

**schildern (hat geschildert)** to
portray, describe (an action)

**der Schirm, -e** umbrella

**die Schlacht, -en** battle, fight

**schlafen (schläft, schlief, hat
geschlafen)** to sleep [K. 2]

**schlafen gehen (ging schlafen, ist
schlafen gegangen)** to go to sleep
[K. 2]

**das Schlafzimmer, -** bedroom [K. 6]

**die Schlange, -n** waiting line; snake;
**[in der] ~ stehen** to stand/wait in
line [K. 11]

**schlank** slim, slender [K. 1]

**schlecht** bad [K. 5]

**der Schleier, -** veil [K. 5]

**schlicht** simple [K. 11]

**schließlich** finally [K. 8]

**schlimm** bad, nasty [K. 5]

**die Schlittelfahrt, -en** toboggan run,
sleighride (*Swiss dialect*)

**schlittelnd** sledding, by sled (*Swiss
dialect*)

**der Schlitten, -** sled, sleigh

**Schlittschuh laufen (läuft, lief, ist
gelaufen)** to skate [K. 10]

**das Schlittschuhlaufen** skating
[K. 10]

**das Schloss,** *pl.* **Schlösser** castle,
palace [K. 3]

**der Schlossgarten, ̈** palace grounds,
castle garden

**der Schlossplatz, ̈e** castle square

**der Schlummertrunk, -e** bedtime
drink, nightcap

**der Schluss, ̈e** conclusion, finish, end

**der Schlüssel, -** key [K. 6]

**schmecken (hat geschmeckt)** + *dat.*
to taste good [K. 6]

**schmächtig** lanky

**der Schmerz, -en**   pain [K. 8]

**die Schmerztablette, -n**   pain killer [K. 8]

**sich schminken (hat sich geschminkt)**   to put on make-up [K. 8]

**schmusen (hat geschmust)**   to cuddle, to make out [K. 5]

**schmutzig**   dirty [K. 8]

**der Schnee**   snow [K. 5]

**das Schneewittchen**   Snow White

**die Schneidemaschine, -n**   slicer

**sich schneiden (schnitt sich, hat sich geschnitten) in + *acc.***   to cut one-self in [K. 8]

**schneien (hat geschneit)**   to snow [K. 5]

**schnell**   fast, quickly [K. 4]

**der Schnupfen**   head cold [K. 8]; **einen ~ haben**   to have a head cold [K. 8]

**der Schock, -s**   shock

**die Schokolade, -n**   chocolate

**schon**   already [K. 5]; **~ seit Jahren**   for years [K. 5]

**schonen (hat geschont)**   to save, preserve

**schön**   pretty, beautiful [K. 1]

**die Schönheit, -en**   beauty

**der Schrank, ̈e**   closet, wardrobe [K. 6]

**schrecklich**   awful(ly), terrible, terri-bly [K. 8]

**schreiben (schrieb, hat geschrieben)**   to write [K. 2, 7]; **~ an + *acc.***   to write to

**die Schreibstube, -n**   office

**der Schreibtisch, -e**   desk [K. 1, 6]

**schreien (schrie, hat geschrien)**   to scream; to cheer

**schriftlich**   in writing [K. 8]

**der Schriftsteller, -/die Schriftstel-lerin, -nen**   author [K. 5]

**der Schritt, -e**   step

**die Schublade, -n**   drawer

**schüchtern**   shy, bashful [K. 4]

**der Schuh, -e**   shoe [K. 4]

**das Schuhgeschäft, -e**   shoe store [K. 3]

**der Schulbereich, -e**   school district

**die Schule, -n**   school [K. 8]

**der Schüler, -/die Schülerin, -nen**   school pupil [K. 7]

**der Schülerausweis, -e**   high school student ID

**die Schulpflicht**   mandatory education

**die Schulter, -n**   shoulder [K. 6]

**die Schulzeit, -en**   school days

**die Schussfahrt, -en**   schussing, a straight downhill ski run *(Swiss dialect)*

**der Schutt**   rubble

**schütteln (hat geschüttelt)**   to shiver, shake

**schütten (hat geschüttet)**   to spill

**schützen (hat geschützt)**   to protect

**das Schützenfest, -e**   marksmen festival

**der Schutzumschlag, ̈e**   dust cover

**(das) Schwaben**   Swabia

**schwach (ä)**   weak

**schwarz (ä)**   black [K. 1]

**schwätzen (hat geschwätzt)**   to talk, blab *(southern German dialect)*

**(das) Schweden**   Sweden

**Schwein haben (hat Schwein gehabt)**   to be lucky [K. 1]

**das Schweinefleisch**   pork [K. 3]

**die Schweiz**   Switzerland [K. 1]

**der Schweizer, -/die Schweizerin, -nen**   Swiss [K. 1]

**schwer**   difficult, hard [K. 6]; heavy

**schwerhörig**   hard-of-hearing

**die Schwester, -n**   sister [K. 2]

**schwierig**   difficult, hard [K. 5]

**die Schwierigkeit, -en**   difficulty, problem [K. 8]

**das Schwimmbad, ̈er**   swimming pool [K. 3]

**schwimmen (schwamm, ist geschwommen)**   to swim [K. 5]

**schwul**   gay, homosexual *(colloq.)*

**schwül**   humid [K. 5]

**schwungvoll**   lively [K. 9]

**sechs**   six [K. 1]

**sechzehn**   sixteen [K. 1]

**sechzig**   sixty [K. 1]

**der See, -n**   lake [K. 10]

**die See, -n**   sea [K. 11]

**segeln (ist gesegelt)**   to sail [K. 3]

**sehen (sieht, sah, hat gesehen)**   to see [K. 2]

**die Sehenswürdigkeit, -en**   sight-seeing attraction [K. 10]

**sehr**   very [K. 2]; **nicht ~**   not very, not much [K. 2]

**das Seidentuch, ̈er**   silk scarf

**die Seife, -n**   soap [K. 8]

**die Seifenoper, -n**   soap opera

**sein**   his, its [K. 3]

**sein (ist, war, ist gewesen)**   to be [K. 1]

**seit + *dat.***   since, for (+ *time phrase*) [K. 5, 6]

**seitdem**   ever since

**die Seite, -n**   page; side

**der Sekretär, -e/die Sekretärin, -nen**   secretary [K. 9]

**die Sekunde, -n**   second

**selber**   self; oneself, myself, etc.

**selbst**   self; (by) oneself, myself, etc. [K. 8]

**selbstständig**   independent, self-reliant [K. 9]

**selbstsicher**   self-assured, self-confident [K. 4]

**selten**   rare, seldom [K. 5]

**seltsam**   strange, unusual [K. 10]

**das Semester, -**   semester [K. 2]

**die Semesterferien (*pl.*)**   semester break [K. 8]

**die Semesterkarte, -n**   semester bus pass

**das Semesterticket, -s**   semester pass *(for city transportation)* [K. 7]

**das Seminar, -e**   seminar; academic department [K. 8]

**die Seminararbeit, -en**   seminar paper [K. 8]

**der Seminarraum, ̈e**   seminar room

**die Semmel, -n**   hard roll *(in southern Germany and Austria)* [K. 3]

**senden (hat gesendet)**   to send

**die Sendepause, -n**   non-broadcast time

**der September**   September [K. 2]

**die Serenade, -n**   serenade

**Servus!**   Hello! *(in Austria)* [K. 1]

**der Sessel, -**   armchair [K. 6]

**setzen (hat gesetzt)**   to set down, put down [K. 7]; **sich ~ (hat sich gesetzt)**   to sit (oneself) down [K. 1]

**die Sexualität**   sexuality [K. 2]

**das Shampoo, -s**   shampoo [K. 8]

**sicher**   certain(ly), sure(ly) [K. 3]

**die Sicherheit, -en**   safety, security

**der Sicherheitshelm, -e**   safety helmet [K. 4]

**sichtbar**   visible, clear to the eye

**sie**   she, it; they [K. 1]; her, it, them *(acc.)* [K. 3]

**Sie**  you *(formal)* [K. 1] *(formal nom. + acc.)* [K. 3]

**sieben**  seven [K. 1]

**siebzehn**  seventeen [K. 1]

**siebzig**  seventy [K. 1]

**siegen (hat gesiegt)**  to win [K. 7]

**die Siegermacht, ̈e**  victor, victorious foreign power [K. 11]

**das Silber**  silver [K. 10]

**das Silvester**  New Year's Eve [K. 10]

**singen (sang, hat gesungen)**  to sing [K. 3]

**sinken (sank, ist gesunken)**  to sink [K. 5]

**sitzen (saß, hat gesessen)**  to be sitting, sit [K. 5, 7]

**der Skandal, -e**  scandal

**Ski laufen (läuft Ski, lief Ski, ist Ski gelaufen)**  to ski [K. 3]

**der Skianorak, -s**  ski parka

**die Skihütte, -n**  ski chalet

**der Skistiefel, -**  ski boot

**die Skizze, -n**  sketch

**das Skript, -en**  lecture notes

**die Slowakei**  Slovakia

**(das) Slowenien**  Slovenia

**der Smoking, -s**  tuxedo

**so**  so; ~ **war das**  that's the way it was

**sobald**  as soon as

**die Socke, -n**  sock [K. 4]

**das Sofa, -s**  sofa

**sofort**  at once

**der Sohn, ̈e**  son

**solange**  as long as [K. 4]

**solche**  such

**sollen (soll, sollte, hat gesollt)**  should, ought to; to be supposed to [K. 4]

**der Sommer, -**  summer [K. 5]

**das Sommerhäuschen, -**  summer cottage [K. 11]

**der Sommerpalast, ̈e**  summer palace

**sondern**  but, rather [K. 3]

**die Sondertour, -en**  specialty tour

**der Sonnabend, -e**  Saturday *(in northern Germany)* [K. 2]

**die Sonne, -n**  sun [K. 5]

**die Sonnenschutzcreme**  suntan lotion

**die Sonnenterrasse, -n**  sunning deck

**sonnig**  sunny [K. 5]

**der Sonntag, -e**  Sunday [K. 2]

**sonntags**  on Sundays [K. 2]

**sonst**  otherwise; ~ **noch etwas?**  Anything else?

**Sonstiges**  other things

**sonst wo (sonst irgendwo)**  somewhere else

**sooft**  whenever

**die Sorge, -n**  worry, concern; **sich Sorgen machen**  to worry [K. 4]

**sortieren (hat sortiert)**  to sort

**die Sowjetunion (UdSSR)**  Soviet Union (USSR)

**die Soziologie**  sociology [K. 2]

**die Spalte, -n**  column

**spalten (hat gespaltet)**  to separate [K. 11]

**(das) Spanien**  Spain

**das Spanisch**  the Spanish language [K. 2]

**spannend**  exciting [K. 7]

**sparen (hat gespart)**  to save [K. 10]

**die Sparkasse, -n**  savings bank [K. 7]

**das Sparkonto, -konten**  savings account [K. 7]

**der Spaß, ̈e**  fun; **aus ~**  for fun [K. 12]; ~ **machen** + *dat.*  to be fun

**spät**  late [K. 4]; **später**  later [K. 5]; **spätestens**  at the latest [K. 4]

**spazieren gehen (ging spazieren, ist spazieren gegangen)**  to go for a walk [K. 2]

**der Spaziergang, ̈e**  walk, stroll

**der Spaziergänger, -/die Spaziergängerin, -nen**  walker, stroller

**der Speisesaal, *pl.* -säle**  hotel dining room

**der Spiegel, -**  mirror [K. 4]

**das Spiel, -e**  game, match [K. 7]

**spielen (hat gespielt)**  to play

**der Spielkamerad, [-en] -en/die Spielkameradin, -nen**  playmate

**der Spielplatz, ̈e**  playground [K. 7]

**die Spielsache, -n**  toy

**das Spielzeug, -e**  toy

**das Spital, ̈er**  hospital *(in Austria)*

**die Spitze, -n**  peak, summit

**spontan**  spontaneous

**die Spontaneität**  spontaneity [K. 12]

**der Sport**  sports, athletics; ~ **treiben (hat Sport getrieben)**  to do sports [K. 7]

**der Sportler, -/die Sportlerin, -nen**  athlete

**sportlich**  athletic [K. 2, 4]

**die Sportstätte, -n**  training field

**die Sprache, -n**  language

**das Sprachinstitut, -e**  language institute [K. 12]

**die Sprachkenntnis, -se**  linguistic competence [K. 12]

**das Sprachlabor, -s (*or* -e)**  language lab

**die Sprachreise, -n**  language study tour

**sprechen (spricht, sprach, hat gesprochen)**  to speak [K. 3]; ~ **für** + *acc.*  to speak for, speak well of; to indicate; ~ **mit** + *dat.*  to talk to; ~ **über** + *acc.*  to talk about [K. 8]

**die Sprechstunde, -n**  office hour [K. 8]

**die Spree**  river through Berlin [K. 11]

**das Sprichwort, ̈er**  proverb

**springen (sprang, ist gesprungen)**  to jump [K. 7]

**das Spülbecken, -**  kitchen sink

**spüren (hat gespürt)**  to feel, to sense [K. 11]

**der Staat, -en**  state, government

**staatlich**  governmental, state-

**das Staatsexamen, -**  state exam; teacher's degree

**die Staatsgalerie, -n**  state gallery

**das Stadion, *pl.* Stadien**  stadium [K. 7]

**die Stadt, ̈e**  city [K. 3]

**der Stadtplan, ̈e**  city map [K. 3]

**der Stadtrand, ̈er**  outskirts of the city

**die Stadtrundfahrt, -en**  city bus tour

**der Stadtteil, -e**  city district

**stark (ä)**  strong [K. 9]

**statistisch**  statistically

**statt** + *gen.*  instead of

**statt·finden (fand statt, hat stattge-funden)**  to take place, occur [K. 8]

**staub·saugen (hat gestaubsaugt; hat staubgesaugt)**  to vacuum

**die Steckdose, -n**  electrical outlet [K. 1]

**stecken (hat gesteckt)**  to stick

**stehen (stand, hat gestanden)**  to stand [K. 7]

**steif**  stiff, ill-at-ease [K. 4]

**steigen (stieg, ist gestiegen)**  to climb; to rise [K. 5, 7]

**die Stelle, -n**  position, job [K. 9]; spot, place [K. 11]; **an deiner ~**  if I were you [K. 11]

**stellen (hat gestellt)**   to stand (something), put [K. 7]

**der Stellenwert, -e**   value, status [K. 12]

**die Stellung, -en**   position, rank [K. 12]

**die Stellungnahme**   opinion

**sterben (stirbt, starb, ist gestorben)**   to die [K. 5]

**die Stereoanlage, -n**   stereo set [K. 6]

**der Stiefbruder, ⸚**   stepbrother

**die Stieftochter, ⸚**   stepdaughter [K. 10]

**der Stiefel, -**   boot [K. 4]

**die Stiefmutter, ⸚**   stepmother [K. 10]

**die Stiefschwester, -n**   stepsister

**der Stift, -e**   pen or pencil

**still**   still, quiet

**die Stille**   quiet, silence

**still·stehen (stand still, hat stillgestanden)**   to stand still

**stimmen (hat gestimmt)**   to be correct [K. 1]

**die Stimmung, -en**   atmosphere, mood [K. 10]; **in einer ~ sein**   to be upset [K. 12]

**stimmungsvoll**   full of atmosphere [K. 9]

**stinken (stank, hat gestunken)**   to stink

**stinklangweilig**   boring as heck

**das Stipendium, *pl.* Stipendien**   scholarship, stipend

**die Stirn, -en**   forehead

**der Stock, ⸚e**   stick

**der Stock, *pl.* Stockwerke**   floor, story [K. 6]; **der erste ~**   second floor [K. 6]; **im zweiten ~**   on the third floor [K. 6]; **einen ~ höher**   one floor up; **einen ~ tiefer**   one floor down

**der Stöckelschuh, -e**   high-heeled shoe

**stolz**   proud [K. 5]

**stören (hat gestört)**   to disturb [K. 12]

**die Strafe, -n**   punishment

**der Strand, ⸚e**   beach

**die Straße, -n**   street; **die ~ entlang**   down the street [K. 7]

**die Straßenbahn, -en**   streetcar [K. 7]

**der Streit**   argument [K. 5]

**sich streiten (streitet, stritt, hat gestritten)**   to argue, quarrel

**stressen (hat gestresst)**   to stress

**stressig**   stressful [K. 12]

**die Strophe, -n**   stanza

**die Struktur, -en**   structure

**die Strumpfhose, -n**   panty hose, stockings [K. 4]

**das Stück, -e**   piece [K. 3]

**der Student, [-en], -en/die Studentin, -nen**   student [K. 1]

**der Studentenausweis, -e**   student ID [K. 7]

**die Studentenermäßigung, -en**   student discount

**die Studentenkneipe, -n**   student bar, pub

**das Studentenleben**   student life

**das Studenten(wohn)heim, -e**   dormitory [K. 6]

**das Studentenzimmer, -**   student room [K. 6]

**der Studienberater, -/die Studienberaterin, -nen**   academic adviser

**das Studienbuch, ⸚er**   ledger of completed courses

**das Studienfach, ⸚er**   academic subject [K. 2]

**die Studiengebühr, -en**   tuition

**der Studienplatz, ⸚e**   place; university admission

**studieren (hat studiert)**   to study [K. 2]

**der/die Studierende, -n**   *(adj. as noun)*   (university-level) student [K. 8]

**das Studium, *pl.* Studien**   studies, college education

**der Stuhl, ⸚e**   chair [K. 1]

**die Stunde, -n**   hour

**stundenlang**   for hours [K. 11]

**der Stundenplan, ⸚e**   schedule

**der Sturm, ⸚e**   storm [K. 5]

**das Subjekt, -e**   subject

**die Suche, -n**   search, hunt

**suchen (hat gesucht)**   to look for; **~ nach** + *dat.*   to search for, seek, look for [K. 7]

**südamerikanisch**   South American

**der Südwesten**   southwest

**südwestlich**   southwestern

**der Supermarkt, ⸚e**   supermarket [K. 3]

**die Suppe, -n**   soup [K. 3]

**surfen (hat gesurft)**   to surf [K. 5, 7]

**die Sympathie**   likeability [K. 5]

**sympathisch**   likeable, pleasant, nice [K. 4]

**das Symptom, -e**   symptom

**die Synagoge, -n**   synagogue [K. 7]

**systematisch**   systematically [K. 7]

**die Szene, -n**   scene, "in-crowd"

**T**

**die Tabelle, -n**   table, chart

**die Tafel, -n**   blackboard [K. 1]

**der Tag, -e**   day [K. 2]; **~ der deutschen Einheit**   Day of German Unity [K. 11]; **eines Tages**   one day [K. 10]; **Guten ~!**   Good day!, Hello! [K. 1]; **in zwei Tagen**   in two days [K. 8]; **jeden ~**   every day [K. 8]

**der Tagesablauf**   plan for the day, day's schedule

**täglich**   daily [K. 5]

**das Tal, ⸚er**   valley [K. 10]

**die Tankstelle, -n**   gas station

**der Tankwart, -e/die Tankwärtin, -nen**   gas station attendant

**die Tante, -n**   aunt [K. 2]

**der Tante-Emma-Laden, ⸚**   family-run shop, "mom-and-pop" store

**tanzen (hat getanzt)**   to dance [K. 2]

**der Tarif, -e**   wage rate

**die Tasche, -n**   bag [K. 4]

**das Taschengeld**   pocket money, allowance

**das Taschentuch, ⸚er**   tissue

**die Tasse, -n**   cup [K. 3]

**tätig**   active, involved

**das Täubchen, -**   pigeon, dove

**tausend**   thousand [K. 1]

**das Taxi, -s**   taxi cab [K. 7]

**der Tee, -s**   tea [K. 3]; **~ kochen**   to make tea

**der Teil, -e**   part, portion [K. 9]

**teilen (hat geteilt)**   to divide [K. 11]; **sich ~ (hat sich geteilt)**   to share; to divide, split (up)

**der Teilzeitjob, -s**   part-time job

**das Telefon, -e**   telephone [K. 6]

**telefonisch**   by telephone

**die Telefonzelle, -n**   telephone booth [K. 6]

**der Teller, -**   plate [K. 6]

**die Temperatur, -en**   temperature [K. 5]; **Die ~ liegt um 10 Grad Celsius.**   The temperature is around 10 degrees Celsius. [K. 5]

**das Tennis**   tennis [K. 3]

**der Tennisball, ⸚e**   tennis ball

**der Tennisschläger, -**  tennis racket

**der Teppich, -e**  carpet, rug [K. 6]

**der Termin, -e**  appointment, date [K. 9]

**der Terrorismus**  terrorism

**teuer**  expensive [K. 2]

**das Theater, -**  theater [K. 3]

**die Theaterkasse, -n**  box office

**das Theaterstück, -e**  play [K. 7]

**das Thema,** *pl.* **Themen**  topic, theme [K. 8]

**thematisch**  topical

**die Theorie, -n**  theory [K. 9]

**(das) Thüringen**  Thuringia

**der Tiefflieger, -**  low-flying (fighter) plane

**das Tier, -e**  animal [K. 9]

**der Tierarzt, ̈e/die Tierärztin, -nen**  veterinarian [K. 9]

**der Tierpark, -s**  zoo

**der Tipp, -s**  suggestion, tip [K. 12]

**tippen (hat getippt)**  to type [K. 8]

**der Tisch, -e**  table [K. 1]

**die Tochter, ̈**  daughter [K. 2]

**der Tod**  death

**todmüde**  dead-tired

**Toi, toi, toi!**  Lots of luck! [K. 9]

**die Toilette, -n**  toilet; bathroom [K. 6]

**der Toilettenartikel, -**  toiletry

**tolerant**  tolerant

**toleriert**  tolerated

**toll**  great, neat, cool [K. 5]

**die Tomate, -n**  tomato [K. 3]

**die Ton-Dia-Vorstellung, -en**  slide show with sound track

**die Tonne, -n**  ton

**der Topf, ̈e**  pot [K. 6]

**das Tor, -e**  gate; goal [K. 7, 11]; **das Brandenburger ~**  Brandenburg Gate [K. 11]

**die Torte, -n**  layer cake

**tot**  dead [K. 4]

**töten (hat getötet)**  to kill

**der Tourismus**  tourism

**der Tourist, [-en], -en/die Touristin, -nen**  tourist [K. 3]

**tragen (trägt, trug, hat getragen)**  to wear; to carry [K. 3]

**die Tragetasche, -n**  bag [K. 7]

**der Trainer, -/die Trainerin, -nen**  coach [K. 7]

**der Transit**  transit

**das Transportunternehmen, -**  transportation company

**die Tratschzeitschrift, -en**  gossip magazine

**die Traube, -n**  grape [K. 3]

**der Traum, ̈e**  dream

**träumen (hat geträumt)**  to dream

**der Traumpartner, -/die Traumpartnerin, -nen**  dream partner

**traurig**  sad [K. 5]

**treffen (trifft, traf, hat getroffen)**  to meet, run into [K. 5]; to score *(in a game)* [K. 7]

**treiben (trieb, hat getrieben)**  to do, play; **Sport ~**  to do sports

**sich trennen (hat sich getrennt) von** + *dat.*  to break up with, separate from [K. 8]

**die Treppe, -n**  stairs, stairway [K. 6]

**das Treppenhaus, ̈er**  stairway

**treten (tritt, trat, hat getreten)**  to kick, step

**treu**  faithful, loyal, true [K. 5]

**die Treue**  loyalty [K. 5]

**der Trimm-dich-Pfad, -e**  exercise course

**trinken (trank, hat getrunken)**  to drink [K. 2]

**das Trinkgeld, -er**  tip, gratuity [K. 5]

**trivial**  trivial

**trocken**  dry [K. 5]

**trotz** + *gen.*  in spite of, despite [K. 8]

**trotzdem**  nevertheless, in spite of that [K. 5, 9]

**(das) Tschechien, die Tschechische Republik**  Czech Republic

**die Tschechoslowakei**  Czechoslovakia

**Tschüss!**  Bye! [K. 1]

**das T-Shirt, -s**  T-shirt [K. 4]

**die Tulpe, -n**  tulip

**tun (tat, hat getan)**  to do; put [K. 3]

**der Tunnel, -s** *or* **-**  tunnel

**die Tür, -en**  door

**der Türke, [-n], -n/die Türkin, -nen**  Turk

**die Türkei**  Turkey

**der Turm, ̈e**  tower

**das Turnier, -e**  tournament

**der Turnschuh, -e**  athletic shoe [K. 3]

**der Turnverein, -e**  athletic club [K. 7]

**die Tüte, -n**  sack, bag [K. 7]

**der Tutor, -en/die Tutorin, -nen**  tutor

**der Typ, -en**  type; guy, fellow *(colloq.)* [K. 9]

**typisch**  typical

**U**

**die U-Bahn, -en**  subway [K. 7]

**üben (hat geübt)**  to practice, rehearse [K. 9]

**über**  above, over [K. 7]

**überarbeitet**  overworked

**überfüllt**  overfilled, oversubscribed

**sich übergeben (übergibt sich, übergab sich, hat sich übergeben)**  to vomit [K. 8]

**überhaupt**  at all [K. 4]; **~ kein**  none at all [K. 2]

**überholen (hat überholt)**  to pass (a vehicle)

**überlegen (hat überlegt)**  to consider, think about; **sich ~ (überlegt sich, hat sich überlegt)**  to think over, consider

**übermäßig**  excessively

**übermorgen**  the day after tomorrow [K. 8]

**überprüfen (hat überprüft)**  to check

**überraschen (hat überrascht)**  to surprise

**überraschend**  surprising(ly) [K. 11]

**überreden (hat überredet)**  to persuade

**überrumpeln (hat überrumpelt)**  to take by surprise

**überschätzen (hat überschätzt)**  to overestimate

**übersehen (übersieht, übersah, hat übersehen)**  to oversee, supervise

**der Übersetzer, -/die Übersetzerin, -nen**  translator, interpreter [K. 12]

**die Übersetzung, -en**  translation

**übertreiben (übertrieb, hat übertrieben)**  to exaggerate

**die Übertreibung, -en**  exaggeration

**überzeugen (hat überzeugt)**  to convince [K. 10]

**üblich**  usual, common

**die Übung, -en**  practice; exercise; discussion section

**die Uhr, -en**  clock, watch [K. 1]; time [K. 2]; **Wie viel ~ ist es?** What time is it? [K. 2]; **um (sechs) ~**  at (six) o'clock [K. 2]

**die Ukraine**  Ukraine

**um** + *acc.*  around; at *(time)* [K. 4]

**umarmen (hat umarmt)**  to embrace, to hug [K. 5]

**die Umbauarbeit, -en**   renovation work, remodeling

**um·bauen (hat umgebaut)**   to renovate

**sich um·drehen (hat sich umgedreht)**   to turn (self) around [K. 2]

**die Umgangssprache, -n**   colloquial language

**die Umgebung, -en**   surroundings, area

**umgekehrt**   the other way around, vice versa

**um·steigen (steigt um, stieg um, ist umgestiegen)**   to change trains

**die Umwelt**   environment

**umweltbewusst**   environmentally aware

**um·werfen (wirft um, warf um, hat umgeworfen)**   to knock over [K. 12]

**der Umzug, ̈e**   parade [K. 10]

**um . . . zu**   in order to

**unattraktiv**   unattractive [K. 1]

**unbedeutend**   unimportant

**unbedingt**   absolutely, really [K. 11]

**unbezahlt**   unpaid [K. 9]

**und**   and [K. 1]; **. . . ~ so**   . . . and stuff like that [K. 11]; **~ so weiter (usw.)**   et cetera (etc.) [K. 5]

**undenkbar**   unthinkable

**unentbehrlich**   indispensable

**der Unfall, ̈e**   accident

**unfreundlich**   unfriendly [K. 4]

**(das) Ungarn**   Hungary

**ungeduldig**   impatient

**ungefähr**   approximately [K. 4]

**unglücklich**   unhappy [K. 4]

**unhöflich**   impolite [K. 7]

**die Uni, -s**   university

**die Universität, -en**   university [K. 1]; **an der ~**   at college, at the university

**unmusikalisch**   unmusical [K. 4]

**die UNO**   United Nations Organization (UN)

**unpersönlich**   impersonal

**uns**   us *(acc., dat.)* [K. 3, 6]

**unser**   our [K. 3]

**unsicher**   unsure, insecure [K. 4]

**der Unsinn**   nonsense [K. 12]

**unsportlich**   unathletic [K. 4]

**unsympathisch**   unlikeable, disagreeable [K. 4]

**unten**   downstairs

**unter**   under, underneath [K. 7]; **~ sich**   among themselves;

**~ Verschluss halten (hält, hielt, hat gehalten)**   to keep under lock and key

**unterbezahlt**   underpaid

**die Unterbrechung, -en**   interruption

**unter·bringen (brachte unter, hat untergebracht)**   to house, put up overnight

**sich unterhalten (unterhält sich, unterhielt sich, hat sich unterhalten) mit** + *dat.*   to converse with, talk to [K. 5]

**unterhaltend**   entertaining K. 7]

**die Unterhaltung, -en**   entertainment; conversation

**unter·kommen (ist untergekommen)**   to find lodging

**die Unterlage, -n**   form, document

**das Unternehmen, -**   business, company; undertaking, project [K. 11]

**der Unternehmer, -/die Unternehmerin, -nen**   entrepreneur, venture capitalist

**unternehmungslustig**   active, eager to participate

**der Unteroffizier, -e**   non-commissioned officer

**der Unterricht**   instruction, lesson, class [K. 6]

**unterrichten (hat unterrichtet)**   to instruct, teach [K. 12]

**unterschätzen (hat unterschätzt)**   to underestimate

**der Unterschied, -e**   difference [K. 10]

**unterstützen (hat unterstützt)**   to support

**der Untertitel, -**   subtitle

**die Unterwäsche**   underwear [K. 4]

**unterwegs**   enroute, underway [K. 4]

**der Urgroßvater, -väter**   great-grandfather [K. 12]

**der Urlaub, -e**   vacation [K. 10]

**der Urlaubsschein, -e**   leave permit, pass

**die Ursache, -n**   cause

**ursprünglich**   originally [K. 10]

**die USA** *(pl.)*   U.S.A. [K. 1]

**usw. (und so weiter)**   etc. (et cetera) [K. 5]

**der Vater, ̈**   father [K. 2]

**der Vati, -s**   dad

**vegetarisch**   vegetarian

**sich verabreden (hat sich verabredet) mit** + *dat.*   to make a date with [K. 11]

**verabredet**   committed; have a date

**die Verabredung, -en**   date

**(sich) verabschieden (hat [sich] verabschiedet) von** + *dat.*   to say good-bye to (to someone) [K. 12]

**verändern (hat verändert)**   to change [K. 12]

**verantwortlich**   responsible

**die Verantwortung, -en**   responsibility

**verantwortungsvoll**   responsible, reponsibly

**verbessern (hat verbessert)**   to improve [K. 12]

**verbieten (verbot, hat verboten)**   to forbid [K. 10]

**das Verbot, -e**   ban, prohibition [K. 4]; **~ für Fahrzeuge aller Art**   closed to all vehicles; **~ für Radfahrer**   no bicycles allowed

**verboten**   forbidden, prohibited [K. 6]

**verbrauchen (hat verbraucht)**   to consume, use

**[Zeit] verbringen (verbrachte, hat verbracht)**   to spend [time] [K. 2, 10]

**verdeutlichen (hat verdeutlicht)**   to clarify

**verdienen (hat verdient)**   to earn [K. 5]

**sich verdoppeln (hat sich verdoppelt)**   to double

**der Verein, -e**   association, organization, club [K. 7]

**die Vereinigten Staaten** *(pl.)*   the United States (of America)

**die Vereinigung, -en**   union, unification [K. 11]

**verfassen (hat verfasst)**   to write

**die Verfassung**   constitution [K. 11]

**verführen (hat verführt)**   to tempt, entice

**die Vergangenheit**   past [K. 12]

**vergessen (vergisst, vergaß, hat vergessen)**   to forget [K. 3]

**vergiften (hat vergiftet)**   to poison

**vergleichen (verglich, hat verglichen)**   to compare

**vergrößern (hat vergrößert)** to enlarge, expand

**sich verhalten (verhält sich, verhielt sich, hat sich verhalten)** to behave, act [K. 9]

**verheiratet** married [K. 2]

**verhüllen (hat verhüllt)** to wrap, conceal

**verkaufen (hat verkauft)** to sell [K. 5]

**der Verkäufer, -/die Verkäuferin, -nen** salesperson [K. 9]

**die Verkaufsabteilung, -en** sales department

**der Verkehr** traffic [K. 4]

**das Verkehrsmittel, -** means of transportation

**die Verkehrsregel, -n** rule of the road, traffic regulation

**das Verkehrsschild, -er** traffic sign

**der Verkehrsverein, -e** tourist office

**das Verkehrszeichen, -** traffic sign [K. 4]

**verkleiden (hat verkleidet)** to disguise [K. 10]

**verlangen (hat verlangt)** to demand, require

**verlassen (verlässt, verließ, hat verlassen)** to leave

**der Verleih, -e** rental company

**verleihen (verlieh, hat verliehen)** to loan out

**sich verletzen (hat sich verletzt)** to hurt oneself, injure oneself

**sich verlieben (hat sich verliebt) in +** acc. to fall in love with [K. 8]

**verliebt sein (ist verliebt gewesen) in** + acc. to be in love with [K. 5]; **über beide Ohren verliebt in** + acc. head over heels in love with

**verlieren (verlor, hat verloren)** to lose [K. 5]

**sich verloben (hat sich verlobt) mit +** dat. to get engaged to [K. 5]

**der/die Verlobte, -n** (adj. as noun) fiancé(e) [K. 5]

**sich vermählen (hat sich vermählt)** to wed

**vermeiden (vermied, hat vermieden)** to avoid

**vermissen (hat vermisst)** to miss [K. 12]

**der Vermieter, -/die Vermieterin, -nen** landlord/landlady

**die Vermittlungsagentur, -en** placement agency

**vernünftig** reasonable, logical

**veröffentlichen (hat veröffentlicht)** to publish [K. 12]

**die Veröffentlichung, -en** publication

**die Verpflegung** food, board

**verreisen (ist verreist)** to go on a trip [K. 10]

**verrückt** crazy

**verschieden** different [K. 8]

**verschlafen (verschläft, verschlief, hat verschlafen)** to oversleep

**sich verschließen (hat sich verschlossen)** to close oneself off

**der Verschluss, ⸚e** lock, clasp

**verschneit** snow-covered [K. 10]

**verschüttet** blocked in

**die Versicherung, -en** insurance

**die Version, -en** version

**sich versöhnen (hat sich versöhnt) mit** + dat. to make up, reconcile with [K. 5]

**die Verspätung, -en** delay, late arrival, tardiness [K. 11]

**versprechen (verspricht, versprach, hat versprochen)** to promise

**die Versprechung, -en** promise

**der Verstand** reason, logic

**sich verständlich machen (hat sich verständlich gemacht)** to make oneself understood [K. 12]

**das Verständnis** understanding, sympathy

**verstecken (hat versteckt)** to hide, conceal [K. 10]

**verstehen (verstand, hat verstanden)** to understand, comprehend; **sich ~** to understand (one another) [K. 12]; **~ von** + dat. to know something (anything) about

**versuchen (hat versucht)** to try, attempt [K. 8]

**der Vertrag, ⸚e** contract

**das Vertrauen** trust [K. 5]

**vervollständigen (hat vervollständigt)** to complete

**verwalten (hat verwaltet)** to administrate

**verwandeln (hat verwandelt)** to transform

**der/die Verwandte, -n** (adj. as noun) relative [K. 2]

**die Verwandtschaft, -en** relatives

**verwenden (hat verwendet)** to apply, use [K. 11]

**verwitwet** widowed

**verwundert** amazed

**der Videofilm, -e** movie on video cassette

**der Videoverleih, -e** video store

**viel** a lot, much [K. 2]; **viele** many [K. 2]; **Vielen Dank!** Thanks a lot! [K. 6]; **zu viele** too many [K. 3]

**die Vielfalt** great variety

**vielleicht** perhaps, maybe [K. 3]

**vier** four [K. 1]

**vierzehn** fourteen [K. 1]

**vierzig** forty [K. 1]

**das Vier-Mächte-Abkommen** Quadropartite Treaty

**das Viertel, -** quarter; district, neighborhood [K. 11]; **~ nach** quarter past [K. 2]; **~ vor zwei** quarter to two [K. 2]; **drei viertel zwei** quarter of two, quarter to two

**der Vogel, ⸚** bird; **Er hat einen ~** He's crazy. He's nuts. [K. 6]; **das Vögelchen, -** little bird

**der Vogelkäfig, -e** bird cage

**die Vokabel, -n** word

**die Völkerverständigung** international understanding [K. 6]

**die Volkskammer** People's Chamber of the GDR Parliament [K. 11]

**der Volkswagen, -** Volkswagen

**die Volkswirtschaft, -en** economics [K. 2]

**vollendet** completed

**der Volleyball** volleyball [K. 3]

**vollkommen** completely [K. 11]

**vollständig** complete(ly)

**von** + dat. of, from, by [K. 6]; **~ da an** from that point on; **~ wem?** from whom? ; **~ ... bis** from . . . until

**vor** + dat. before; in front of; (of time) ago [K. 6, 7]

**vorbei·reiten (ritt vorbei, ist vorbeigeritten)** to ride by, ride past on horseback [K. 10]

**vor·bereiten (hat vorbereitet)** to prepare [K. 8]; **sich ~ (hat sich vorbereitet) auf** + acc. to prepare for, get ready for [K. 8]

**die Vorbereitung, -en** preparation

**vorbildlich** exemplary

**der Vorfahr, [-en], -en/die Vorfahrin, -nen** ancestor [K. 12]

**vor·haben (hat vor, hatte vor, hat vorgehabt)** to plan, have planned [K. 11]

**vorher** before, previously

**vor·kommen (ist vorgekommen) + *dat.*** to appear to be

**vor·lesen (liest vor, las vor, hat vorgelesen)** to read aloud; lecture

**die Vorlesung, -en** lecture [K. 6]

**das Vorlesungsverzeichnis, -se** course catalogue

**vor·machen (macht vor, hat vorgemacht)** to fool, kid, delude

**vormittags** in the morning, A.M.

**vorne** up front [K. 1]; **da~** overthere

**die Vorschau** preview

**der Vorschlag, ̈e** suggestion

**vor·schlagen (schlägt vor, schlug vor, hat vorgeschlagen)** to suggest [K. 7]

**vor·schreiben (schrieb vor, hat vorgeschrieben)** to stipulate

**vorsichtig** careful, cautious [K. 4]

**der/die Vorsitzende, -n** *(adj. as noun)* chairperson

**die Vorspeise, -n** appetizer [K. 3]

**der Vorsprung** lead; advantage

**sich vor·stellen (hat sich vorgestellt)** to imagine; to introduce oneself [K. 8]

**die Vorstellung, -en** presentation, performance; introduction; image [K. 9]

**das Vorstellungsgespräch, -e** job interview [K. 9]

**der Vorteil, -e** advantage

**der Vortrag, ̈e** presentation

**das Vorurteil, -e** prejudice

**vor·ziehen (zog vor, hat vorgezogen) + *dat.*** to prefer to

**der VW, -s** VW, Volkswagen

**W**

**wachsen (wächst, wuchs, ist gewachsen)** to grow [K. 10]

**wackeln (hat gewackelt)** to wobble

**wacker** honest, upright

**wagen (hat gewagt)** to dare, risk

**der Wagen, -** car [K. 4]

**die Wahl, -en** selection, choice; election

**wählen (hat gewählt)** to choose, select; elect [K. 8]

**der Wähler, -/die Wählerin, -nen** voter

**der Wahnsinn** insanity

**wahnsinnig** crazy, insane [K. 9]

**wahr** real, true [K. 5]

**während + *gen.*** during [K. 8]

**die Wahrheit, -en** truth [K. 8]

**wahrscheinlich** probably [K. 3]

**das Wahrzeichen, -** emblem, symbol

**der Wald, ̈er** forest, woods [K. 9, 10]

**die Wand, ̈e** interior wall [K. 1]

**der Wandel, -** change, transformation [K. 10]

**wandern (ist gewandert)** to hike, go hiking [K. 2]

**die Wanderung, -en** hike [K. 4]

**der Wanderweg, -e** hiking path

**wann** when [K. 1]

**warm (ä)** warm [K. 5]

**warnen (hat gewarnt)** to warn [K. 11]

**warten (hat gewartet)** to wait [K. 4]; to service; **~ auf + *acc.*** to wait for

**die Wartezeit, -en** waiting period

**warum** why [K. 1]

**was** what; **Was für ein(e)?** What kind of? [K. 9]; **Was gibt's?** What's up?; **Was tut dir weh?** Where do you hurt?

**das Waschbecken, -** sink [K. 6]

**die Wäsche** laundry

**sich waschen (wäscht sich, wusch sich, hat sich gewaschen)** to wash (oneself) [K. 8]; **sich die Haare -** to shampoo [K. 8]; **sich die Hände ~** to wash one's hands [K. 8]

**die Waschküche, -n** laundry room [K. 6]

**die Waschmaschine, -n** washing machine

**das Wasser** water [K. 3]

**die Wasserflasche, -n** water bottle

**Wasserski fahren (fährt, fuhr, ist gefahren)** to waterski

**das Wasserspiel, -e** trick fountains

**der Wassersport** water sports

**der Wasserturm, ̈e** water tower

**das WC, -s** toilet [K. 6]

**die Website, -s** Website [K. 12]

**wechseln (hat gewechselt)** to change [K. 8]

**der Wecker, -** alarm clock [K. 6]

**weg** away

**der Weg, -e** path [K. 4]; **auf dem ~** on the way

**die Wegbeschreibung, -en** directions

**wegen + *gen.*** because of [K. 8]

**weg·räumen (hat weggeräumt)** to clear away

**weg·ziehen (zog weg, ist weggezogen)** to move away [K. 5]

**weh·tun (tat weh, hat wehgetan) + *dat.*** to hurt (someone) [K. 8]; **sich ~ (tat sich weh, hat sich wehgetan)** to hurt oneself

**das Weihnachten** Christmas [K. 10]

**der Weinachtsmann, ̈er** Santa Claus

**der Weihnachtsmarkt, ̈e** Christmas market

**weil** because [K. 5]

**die Weile** awhile

**der Wein, -e** wine [K. 3]

**der Weinberg, -e** vineyard

**weinen (hat geweint)** to cry [K. 10]

**der Weisheitszahn, ̈e** wisdom tooth

**weiß** white [K. 1]

**weit** far [K. 5]; **~ weg** far away [K. 5]

**weitere** further, additional [K. 9]

**weiter·gehen (geht weiter, ging weiter, ist weitergegangen)** to continue

**welcher, welches, welche** which [K. 1, 6]

**wellig** wavy [K. 1]

**die Welt, -en** world [K. 9]

**weltberühmt** world-famous [K. 9]

**der Weltkrieg, -e** world war [K. 11]

**die Weltmeisterschaft (die WM)** World Cup

**wem** (to) whom *(dat.)* [K. 2, 6]

**wen** whom *(acc.)* [K. 2]

**die Wende** turning point; *time in East Germany before unification* [K. 11]

**wenden (hat gewendet)** to turn [K. 11]

**wenig** little [K. 2]; **wenige** a few [K. 2]; **weniger** fewer, less

**wenigstens** at least [K. 5]

**wenn** if, when [K. 6, 10]; **immer ~** always when, whenever [K. 10]

**wer** who *(nom.)* [K. 1]

**die Werbeagentur, -en** advertising agency

**die Werbebroschüre, -n** advertising brochure

**der Werbespot** commercial

**der Werdegang, ̈e** development; career

**werden (wird, wurde, ist geworden)** to become [K. 3]; will, shall *(future tense)* [K. 8]

**werfen (wirft, warf, hat geworfen)** to throw, toss [K. 10]

**das Werk, -e** (creative) work

**das Werkzeug, -e** tool

**die Werkzeugkiste, -n** toolbox

**wertvoll** valuable

**wesentlich** essential

**wessen** whose [K. 10]

**das Wetter** weather [K. 5]

**der Wetterbericht, -e** weather report

**wett·machen (hat wett gemacht)** to make up for, compensate for

**wichtig** important [K. 4]

**die Wichtigkeit, -en** importance

**das Wichtigste** the most important thing

**wider·spiegeln (hat widergespiegelt)** to reflect

**der Widerstand, ⸚e** resistance [K. 11]

**widmen (hat gewidmet)** to dedicate [K. 9]

**wie** how; what [K. 1]; **~ alt?** how old?; **~ bitte?** Please repeat that. [K. 1]; **~ heißen Sie?** What's your name? [K. 1]; **~ viel** how much [K. 1]; **~ viele** how many [K. 1]

**wieder** again [K. 6]

**wieder·aufbauen (hat wiederaufgebaut)** to reconstruct

**wiederholen (hat wiederholt)** to repeat

**die Wiederholung, -en** repetition

**Wiederhören: Auf ~!** Good-bye! (*on the phone*)

**wieder·kommen (ist wiedergekommen)** to come back, return

**Wiedersehen: Auf ~!** Good-bye! [K. 1]

**die Wiedervereinigung** reunification [K. 11]

**Wien** Vienna

**die Wiese, -n** meadow

**wie viel** how much [K. 1]; **~ Uhr ist es?** What time is it? [K. 2]

**das Willkommen, -** welcome [K. 1]; **Herzlich willkommen in . . .** Welcome to . . .

**der Wind, -e** wind

**windig** windy [K. 5]

**die Windpocken** *(pl.)* chicken pox

**der Winter, -** winter [K. 5]

**wir** we [K. 1]

**der Wirbelsturm, ⸚e** tornado

**wirken (hat gewirkt)** to effect, have an effect, impact

**wirklich** really [K. 5]

**die Wirklichkeit, -en** reality

**die Wirkung, -en** effect

**der Wirt, -e/die Wirtin, -nen** host (in a restaurant or bar)

**die Wirtschaft, -en** tavern [K. 10]; economy

**die Wirtschaftszeitung, -en** business/ economics newspaper

**wissen (weiß, wusste, hat gewusst)** to know (a fact) [K. 3]; **~ von** + *dat.* to know about

**der Wissenschaftler, -/die Wissenschaftlerin, -nen** scientist [K. 9]

**wissenschaftlich** scientific [K. 12]

**wissenswert** worth knowing

**der Witz, -e** joke, wit [K. 10]

**wo** where [K. 1]

**die Woche, -n** week [K. 2]; **nächste ~** next week [K. 8]; **vor einer ~** a week ago [AL 6]

**das Wochenende, -n** weekend [K. 2]; **am ~** on the weekend [K. 2]

**der Wochentag, -e** day of the week [K. 2]

**woher** from where [K. 1]

**wohin** where to [K. 1]

**wohl** in all likelihood, no doubt, probably [K. 3]; well, healthy [K. 8]

**wohnen (hat gewohnt)** to live [K. 2]; **in Untermiete ~** to live in a sublet room

**die Wohngemeinschaft, -en (WG)** shared apartment, cooperative living [K. 6]

**der Wohnort, -e** place of residence [K. 11]

**die Wohnung, -en** apartment [K. 6]

**der Wohnungsmarkt, ⸚e** real estate market

**das Wohnzimmer, -** living room [K. 6]

**die Wolke, -n** cloud [K. 5]

**wolkig** cloudy [K. 5]

**wollen (will, wollte, hat gewollt)** to want to [K. 4]

**womit** with what

**das Wort, ⸚er** word [K. 5]

**das Wörterbuch, ⸚er** dictionary [K. 4]

**wortwörtlich** literally

**das Wunder, -** miracle, wonder [K. 10]

**wunderbar** wonderful

**der Wunsch, ⸚e** wish, request [K. 11]

**wünschen (hat gewünscht)** to wish [K. 9]

**die Wurst, ⸚e** sausage [K. 3]

**die Wut** rage

**x-mal** umpteen times

**die Zahl, -en** number [K. 1]

**zahlen (hat gezahlt)** to pay

**zahllos** innumerable

**zahlreich** multiple, many

**der Zahn, ⸚e** tooth [K. 6]

**der Zahnarzt, ⸚e/die Zahnärztin, -nen** dentist [K. 9]

**die Zahnbürste, -n** toothbrush [K. 4]

**die Zahnpasta,** *pl.* **-pasten** toothpaste [K. 4]

**die Zahnschmerzen** *(pl.)* toothache [K. 8]

**der Zauberer, -** magician, sorcerer [K. 10]

**die Zauberstimmung** magical mood

**der Zeh, -en** *or* **die Zehe, -n** toe [K. 6]

**zehn,** ten [K. 1]

**das Zeichen, ~** sign, marker

**der Zeichenblock, ⸚e** sketch pad

**der Zeichentrickfilm, -e** animated movie, cartoon [K. 7]

**zeichnen (hat gezeichnet)** to draw, sketch

**die Zeichnung, -en** drawing, sketch

**zeigen (hat gezeigt)** to show, point

**die Zeile, -n** line

**die Zeit, -en** time [K. 2]; **die ganze ~** the whole time

**die Zeitschrift, -en** magazine [K. 7]

**die Zeittafel, -n** timetable, time line

**die Zeitung, -en** newspaper [K. 5]

**der Zeitungskiosk, -e** newspaper stand

**der Zeitungsstand, ⸚e** newspaper stand [K. 7]

**das Zelt, -e** tent

**die Zensur, -en** censorship
**das Zentrum,** *pl.* **Zentren** center [K. 11]
**zerbrechlich** fragile, breakable
**zerreißen (zerriss, hat zerrissen)** to rip up, tear up
**zerschlagen** all beat up
**zerschossen** shot up, riddled with bullet holes
**zerstören (hat zerstört)** to destroy [K. 11]
**der Zettel, -** note, scrap of paper
**das Zeug** stuff, things
**ziehen (zog, hat gezogen)** to pull, raise [K. 10]
**das Ziel, -e** goal, target, destination [K. 11]
**ziemlich** rather, pretty . . . [K. 4]
**zigmal** umpteen times [K. 7]
**das Zimmer, -** room [K. 6]; **~ und Verpflegung** room and board; **die ~-und Wohungsvermittlung, -en** housing placement service
**der Zimmerkamerad, [-en], -en/die Zimmerkameradin, -nen** roommate
**die Zimmernummer, -n** room number
**der Zoll, ̈e** customs
**der Zoo, -s** zoo
**zu** + *dat.* to [K. 6]; **~ Hause** at home [K. 6]; **~ zweit** as a couple, in twos [K. 5]; **~** + *inf.* to [K. 5]
**zuerst** first of all [K. 3]
**der Zufall, ̈e** coincidence
**zufrieden** satisfied, content [K. 7]

**der Zug, ̈e** train [K. 4]
**die Zugverbindung, -en** train connection
**zu·hören (hat zugehört)** + *dat.* to listen
**der Zuhörer, -/die Zuhörerin, -nen** listener
**zu·knallen (hat zugeknallt)** to slam shut
**die Zukunft** future [K. 10]
**zuletzt** finally
**zum** to (the); for; **~ ersten Mal** for the first time [K. 5] **~ Spaß** for fun
**zu·machen (hat zugemacht)** to close
**die Zumutung, -en** unreasonable demand
**zunächst** first of all
**die Zunge, -n** tongue
**zu·reden (hat zugeredet)** + *dat.* to talk to
**zurück·bringen (brachte zurück, hat zurückgebracht)** to bring back, return
**zurück·geben (gibt zurück, gab zurück, hat zurückgegeben)** to give back, return
**zurück·gehen (ging zurück, ist zurückgegangen)** to go back
**zurück·kehren (ist zurückgekehrt)** to return
**zurück·kommen (kam zurück, ist zurückgekommen)** to come back, return, get back [K. 2]
**die Zusage, -n** commitment

**zusammen** together [K. 5]
**die Zusammenarbeit, -en** collaboration, joint project
**der Zusammenbruch, ̈e** collapse
**zusammen·fassen (hat zusammengefasst)** to summarize
**der Zusammenhang, ̈e** connection [K. 12]
**zusammen·leben (hat zusammengelebt)** to live together, cohabitate [K. 5]
**zusammen·passen (hat zusammengepasst)** to fit together, belong together [K. 12]
**zusammen·stellen (hat zusammengestellt)** to put together, organize
**zusätzlich** additionally [K. 8]
**der Zuschauer, -/die Zuschauerin, -nen** spectator [K. 7]
**zuständig** responsible [K. 9]
**zu·stimmen (hat zugestimmt)** + *dat.* to agree with someone
**zuverlässig** dependable [K. 3]
**zu viel(e)** too much, too many
**zwanzig** twenty [K. 1]
**zwar** actually, in fact
**der Zweck, -e** purpose, point [K. 9]
**zwei** two [K. 1]
**der Zweig, -e** branch [K. 10]
**zweit** second; by two; **zu ~** as a couple [K. 5]; two at a time, in a pair
**der Zwerg, -e** dwarf [K. 10]
**zwischen** between [K. 5, 7]
**der Zwischenfall, ̈e** incident
**zwölf** twelve [K. 1]

# English-German Vocabulary

The English-German vocabulary focuses on key words (highest frequency words) from the core texts and the **Wissenwerte Vokabeln** sections of the chapters. Definite articles and plural forms are given for nouns. Verbs are listed with their participles. Separable-prefix verbs are marked with a raised dot: **mit·bringen.** For the principal parts of irregular (strong) verbs, refer to pages R-9 through R-11.

## A

**a/an**  ein, eine
**ability**  die Fähigkeit, -en
**able: to be ~ to**  können (hat gekonnt)
**above**  über
**absolutely**  unbedingt
**accident**  der Unfall, ¨e
**achieve**  leisten (hat geleistet)
**accompany**  begleiten (hat begleitet)
**accomplish**  leisten (hat geleistet); schaffen (hat geschafft)
**account: on ~ of**  wegen + *gen.;* **current (bank) ~**  das Girokonten, *pl.* Girokonten
**accountant**  der Buchhalter, -/ die Buchhalterin, -nen
**acquaintance**  der/die Bekannte, -n *(noun decl. like adj.)*
**across from**  gegenüber von
**active**  tätig; aktiv
**activity**  die Aktivität, -en; **leisure ~** die Freizeitaktivität, -en
**actor/actress**  der Schauspieler, - / die Schauspielerin, -nen
**actually**  eigentlich; zwar
**additionally**  zusätzlich
**address book**  das Adressbuch, ¨er
**administer**  verwalten (hat verwaltet)
**admit**  zu·geben (hat zugegeben)
**adult**  erwachsen *(adj.)*
**advanced student**  der/die Fortgeschrittene, -n *(noun decl. like adj.)*
**advantage**  der Pluspunkt, -e; der Vorteil, -e; der Vorsprung; **information ~**  der Informationsvorsprung
**adventure film**  der Abenteuerfilm, -e
**advertisement**  die Annonce, -n; das Inserat, -e; die Anzeige, -n
**advice**  der Rat, *pl.* Ratschläge
**advisor**  der Berater, - / die Beraterin, -nen

**after**  nach + *dat. (prep.)*; nachdem *(conj.)*
**afternoon**  der Nachmittag, -e; **this ~** heute Nachmittag; **Good ~.**  Guten Tag.; Tag.
**afternoons**  nachmittags
**afterwards**  nachher
**afraid: to be ~ of**  Angst haben (hat gehabt) vor + *dat.;* fürchten (hat gefürchtet)
**African**  afrikanisch
**again**  wieder; noch (ein)mal
**against**  gegen + *acc.*
**ago**  vor + *dat.*
**agree**  zu·stimmen (hat zugestimmt) + *dat.;* **Agreed!**  Abgemacht!
**air**  die Luft
**airlift**  die Luftbrücke
**airline ticket**  der Flugschein, -e; das Flugticket, -s
**airplane**  das Flugzeug, -e
**airport**  der Flughafen, ¨
**alarm clock**  der Wecker, -
**alcohol**  der Alkohol
**alcoholic**  alkoholisch; **non- ~** alkoholfrei
**all**  alle; *(noun)* alles, *(pl.)* alle; **at ~** überhaupt; **~ day**  den ganzen Tag; **~ in ~**  insgesamt
**Allies**  die Alliierten *(pl.)*
**allow**  erlauben (hat erlaubt); **~ me to introduce myself.**  Darf ich mich vorstellen?
**allowed: to be ~**  dürfen (hat gedurft)
**almost**  fast; beinahe
**alone**  allein
**Alps**  die Alpen *(pl.)*
**already**  schon
**also**  auch
**although**  obwohl
**always**  immer
**America**  (das) Amerika; **United States of ~**  die Vereinigten Staaten von Amerika

**American**  amerikanisch *(adj.);* der Amerikaner, -/ die Amerikanerin, -nen
**among**  unter + *dat.;* **~ themselves** unter sich
**analytical**  analytisch
**ancestor**  der Vorfahr [e], [-en], -en / die Vorfahrin, -nen
**and**  und; **~ so on**  und so weiter (usw.); **~ stuff like that**  und so; **~ you?**  Und Sie?
**angry**  böse; **to be ~**  sich ärgern (hat sich geärgert) über + *acc.*
**animal**  das Tier, -e
**animated cartoon**  der Zeichentrickfilm, -e
**animation**  der Zeichentrickfilm, -e
**announce**  aus·rufen (hat ausgerufen); bekannt geben (hat bekannt gegeben); aus·schreiben (hat ausgeschrieben)
**answer**  die Antwort, -en; **to ~** antworten + *dat.;* beantworten + *acc.*
**any**  einige; etwas
**anything**  irgendetwas, irgendwas; **~ else?**  Sonst noch etwas?
**anytime**  jederzeit
**anyway**  jedenfalls
**apartment**  die Wohnung, -en
**appear**  scheinen (hat geschienen), erscheinen (ist erschienen); aus· sehen (hat ausgesehen); **to ~ to be** vor·kommen (ist vorgekommen) + *dat.*
**appearance**  das Aussehen
**appetizer**  die Vorspeise, -n
**apple**  der Apfel, ¨; **~ juice**  der Apfelsaft
**applicant**  der Bewerber, - / die Bewerberin, -nen
**application**  die Bewerbung, -en; **~ form**  das Bewerbungsformular, -e; **~ letter**  der Bewerbungsbrief, -e

**apply**   sich bewerben (hat sich beworben) für/um + *acc.*

**appointment**   der Termin, -e

**apprentice**   der Lehrling, -e; der/die Auszubildende, -n *(noun decl. like adj.);* der/die Azubi, -s

**approximately**   ungefähr

**April**   der April

**architect**   der Architekt, [-en], -en/die Architektin, -nen

**area**   die Umgebung; **in the ~**   in der Nähe; in der Umgebung; **land ~**   die Fläche

**area code**   die Vorwahl, -en

**argue**   sich streiten (hat sich gestritten) mit + *dat.*

**argument**   der Krach, ̈e; der Streit

**arm**   der Arm, -e

**armchair**   der Sessel, -

**army**   die Armee, -n

**around**   um + *acc.;* - **[time]** gegen + *acc.*

**arrival**   die Ankunft, ̈e; die Anreise, -n

**arrive**   an·kommen (ist angekommen)

**art**   die Kunst; **~ association**   der Kunstverein, -e; **~ museum**   die Kunsthalle, -n, **~ school**   die Kunsthochschule, -n

**artist**   der Künstler, -/die Künstlerin, -nen

**article**   der Artikel, -

**as**   als; wie; **~ . . . ~** sowie; **~ a couple**   zu zweit; **~ always** wie immer

**Asian**   asiatisch

**ask: to ~ about**   fragen (hat gefragt) nach + *dat.;* **to ~ for**   bitten (hat gebeten) um + *acc.;* **to ~ a question**   eine Frage stellen (hat gestellt)

**aspect**   der Aspekt, -e

**aspirin**   das Aspirin

**assignment**   die Aufgabe, -n

**association**   der Verein, -e; die Gemeinschaft, -en

**astonished**   erstaunt

**at**   an; auf; in; **~ (someone's house)**   bei + *dat.;* **[time]** um + *acc.*

**at all**   überhaupt; **not ~**   gar nicht

**athlete**   der Sportler, -/die Sportlerin, -nen

**athletic**   sportlich

**atmosphere**   die Stimmung, -en; **full of ~**   stimmungsvoll

**attempt**   versuchen (hat versucht)

**attic**   der Dachboden, ̈; **in the ~**   auf dem Dachboden

**attractive**   attraktiv

**August**   der August

**aunt**   die Tante, -n

**Austria**   (das) Österreich

**Austrian**   österreichisch *(adj.);* der Österreicher, -/die Österreicherin, -nen

**authentic**   echt; authentisch; wahr

**author**   der Autor, -en/die Autorin, -nen; der Schriftsteller, -/die Schriftstellerin, -nen

**automobile**   das Auto, -s; der Wagen, -

**autumn**   der Herbst, -e

**away**   weg; ab; fort; **far ~**   weit weg

**awful**   schrecklich

**awhile**   eine Weile

## B

**babysitter**   der Babysitter, -/die Babysitterin, -nen

**back**   der Rücken, -; *(adv.)* zurück

**backpack**   der Rucksack, ̈e

**bad**   schlecht; schlimm; böse; **have ~ luck**   Pech haben; **not ~**   ganz gut, nicht schlecht; **too ~**   schade

**bag**   die Tasche, -n; die Tüte, -n

**baggage**   das Gepäck

**baker**   der Bäcker, -/die Bäckerin, -nen

**bakery**   die Bäckerei, -en; **at the ~**   beim Bäcker; **to the ~**   zum Bäcker in die Bäckerei

**balcony**   der Balkon, -s

**ball**   der Ball, ̈e

**ballet**   das Ballett, -e

**ballpoint pen**   der Kugelschreiber, -; der Kuli, -s *(colloq.)*

**Baltic Sea**   die Ostsee

**ban**   das Verbot, -e; **to ~**   verbieten (hat verboten)

**banana**   die Banane, -n

**band**   die Band, -s

**Band-Aid**   das Heftpflaster, -

**bank**   die Bank, -en; die Sparkasse, -n; **~ account**   das Konto, *pl.* Konten; **~ card (ATM card)**   die Bankkarte, -n

**bar**   die Bar, -s; die Kneipe, -n; das Lokal, -e

**barrel**   das Fass, *pl.* Fässer

**baseball**   der Baseball

**basement**   der Keller, -

**basically**   im Grunde

**basketball**   der Basketball

**bath**   das Bad, ̈er; **~ towel**   das Badetuch, ̈er

**bathe**   baden (hat gebadet)

**bathing suit**   *(man's)* die Badehose, -n; *(woman's)* der Badeanzug, ̈e

**bathroom**   das Badezimmer, -; **to go to the ~**   auf die Toilette (aufs Klo, *colloq.*) gehen

**bathtub**   die Badewanne, -n

**be: to ~**   sein (ist gewesen); **to ~ able to**   können (hat gekonnt); **to ~ about**   handeln (hat gehandelt) von + *dat.;* **to ~ all right with someone**   recht sein (ist gewesen) + *dat.;* **to ~ enough**   reichen (hat gereicht); **to ~ in charge**   leiten (hat geleitet)

**beautiful**   schön

**because**   weil; denn *(conj.);* **~ of**   wegen *(prep.)* + *gen.*

**become**   werden (ist geworden)

**bed**   das Bett, -en; **~room**   das Schlafzimmer, -

**beef**   das Rindfleisch; **ground ~**   das Hackfleisch

**beer**   das Bier

**before**   vor + *dat.;* vorher *(adv.);* bevor *(conj.)*

**begin**   an·fangen (hat angefangen); beginnen (hat begonnen)

**beginner**   der Anfänger, -/die Anfängerin, -nen

**beginning**   der Anfang, ̈e

**behave**   sich verhalten (hat sich verhalten)

**behind**   hinter + *acc./dat.*

**beige**   beige

**believable**   glaubhaft

**believe**   glauben (hat geglaubt); **to ~ in**   glauben an + *acc.*

**belong to**   gehören (hat gehört) + *dat.*

**beside**   bei + *dat.;* neben + *acc./dat.*

**besides**   außerdem; außer + *dat.*

**best**   best; **~ of all**   am besten

**better**   besser

**between**   zwischen + *acc./dat.*

**beverage**   das Getränk, -e

**bicycle**   das Fahrrad, ̈er; das Rad, ̈er; **to ~**   Rad fahren (ist Rad gefahren); **to ride a ~**   mit dem Fahrrad fahren

**bicycle path**   der Radweg, -e

**bicycle rider**   der Radfahrer, -/die Radfahrerin, -nen

**big** groß (ö); **~ city** die Großstadt, ⸚e

**bike** das Rad, ⸚er

**biography** die Biographie, -n

**biology** die Biologie

**bird** der Vogel, ⸚; **little ~** das Vögelchen, -

**birdcage** der Vogelkäfig, -e

**birthday** der Geburtstag, -e; **When is your ~?** Wann hast du Geburtstag?; **for one's ~** zum Geburtstag

**black** schwarz (ä)

**blackboard** die Tafel, -n

**blockade** die Blockade, -n

**blood** das Blut

**blond** blond

**blouse** die Bluse, -n

**blow-dry** föhnen (hat geföhnt)

**blow dryer** der Föhn, -e

**blue** blau

**board** das Brett, -er; **bulletin ~** das schwarze Brett; **chalk ~** die Tafel, -n

**boarding pass** die Bordkarte, -n

**body** der Körper, -; **~ part** der Körperteil, -e

**bombed out** zerbombt

**book** das Buch, ⸚er

**bookcase** das Bücherregal, -e

**bookkeeper** der Buchhalter, -/die Buchhalterin, -nen

**bookstore** die Buchhandlung, -en

**boot** der Stiefel, -

**border** die Grenze, -n

**border on** grenzen (hat gegrenzt) an + acc.

**boring** langweilig; **~ as heck** stinklangweilig

**born** geboren

**borrow** leihen (hat geliehen)

**boss** der Chef, -s/die Chefin, -nen

**both** beide; beides

**bother** stören (hat gestört)

**bottle** die Flasche, -n

**boy** der Junge, [-n], -n; **~friend** der Freund, -e; **boys** die Jungs (slang)

**branch** der Zweig, -e; **~ office** die Filiale, -n

**brave** mutig

**bread** das Brot, -e

**break** brechen (hat gebrochen); **~ a leg! (Good Luck!)** Hals- und Beinbruch!; **to ~ one's (leg)** sich (das Bein) brechen (hat sich gebrochen); **to ~ up with** sich trennen (hat sich getrennt) von + dat.

**breakable** zerbrechlich

**breakfast** das Frühstück; **for ~** zum Frühstück

**brewery** die Bierbrauerei, -en

**brick** der Ziegelstein, -e

**bribe** die Bestechung, -en

**bride** die Braut, ⸚e

**bridge** die Brücke, -n

**bright** hell

**bring** bringen (hat gebracht); **~ along** mit·bringen (hat mitgebracht)

**broken** kaputt; **~ to pieces** zerbrochen

**brother** der Bruder, ⸚; **brothers and sisters** die Geschwister (pl.)

**brown** braun

**brush** die Bürste, -n; **hair ~** die Haarbürste, -n; **tooth ~** die Zahnbürste, -n; **to ~ one's hair** sich die Haare bürsten (hat sich gebürstet); **to ~ one's teeth** sich die Zähne putzen (hat sich geputzt)

**build** bauen (hat gebaut); konstruieren (hat konstruiert)

**building** das Gebäude, -

**bulletin board** das schwarze Brett, -er

**burn** brennen (hat gebrannt)

**bus** der (Auto)bus, -se; **~ stop** die Bushaltestelle, -n

**business** das Geschäft, -e; der Betrieb, -e; **~ administration** die Betriebswirtschaft; **~ trip** die Geschäftsreise, -n

**businessman/businesswoman** der Geschäftsmann, ⸚er/die Geschäftsfrau, -en

**but** aber; sondern

**butcher** der Metzger, -/die Metzgerin, -nen; der Fleischer, -/die Fleischerin, -nen; **~ shop** die Metzgerei, -en; die Fleischerei, -en

**butter** die Butter

**buy** kaufen (hat gekauft)

**by** bei + dat., an + dat., von + dat.; **~ [car]** mit [dem Auto]

---

## C

**café** das Café, -s

**cafeteria** die Mensa, pl. Mensen

**cake** der Kuchen, -; **layer ~** die Torte, -n

**call** rufen (hat gerufen); an·rufen (hat angerufen), telefonieren (hat telefoniert); **to ~ someone something** nennen (hat genannt)

**called: to be ~** heißen (hat geheißen)

**calm** ruhig; **to ~ down** (sich); beruhigen (hat beruhigt)

**camera: digital ~** die digitale Kamera, -s; **movie ~** die Kamera, -s; **still ~** der Fotoapparat, -e

**campground** der Campingplatz, ⸚e

**campus** der Campus

**can (to be able to)** können (hat gekonnt)

**Canada** (das) Kanada

**Canadian** kanadisch (adj.); der Kanadier, -/die Kanadierin, -nen

**candidate** der Kandidat, [-en], -en/die Kandidatin, -nen

**cancelled to be ~** aus·fallen (ist ausgefallen)

**canton** der Kanton, -e

**cap** die Mütze, -n

**capital** die Hauptstadt, ⸚e

**car** das Auto, -s; der Wagen, -; der PKW, -s (Personenkraftwagen, -)

**card** die Karte, -n; **to play cards** Karten spielen (hat Karten gespielt)

**cardboard** die Pappe

**care** die Sorge, -n; **to take ~ of something** erledigen (hat erledigt)

**careful** vorsichtig

**carpet** der Teppich, -e

**carrot** die Karotte, -n

**carry** tragen (hat getragen)

**case** der Fall, ⸚e; **(container)** der Kasten, ⸚

**cash** das Bargeld; **~ register** die Kasse, -n

**cassette** die Kassette, -n

**cast** der Gips

**castle** das Schloss, pl. Schlösser; **~ garden** der Schlossgarten, ⸚; **~ square** der Schlossplatz, ⸚e

**cat** die Katze, -n

**catalogue** der Katalog, -e

**catastrophe** die Katastrophe, -n

**catch** fangen (hat gefangen); **to ~ a cold** sich erkälten (hat sich erkältet)

**cathedral** der Dom, -e

**cause** die Ursache, -n; der Grund, ⸚e

**CD** die CD, -s; **~ player** der CD-Player, -; der CD-Spieler, -

**celebrate**   feiern (hat gefeiert)

**celebration**   die Feier, -n; das Fest, -e; **~ before Lent**   der Karneval, der Fasching, die Fastnacht

**cell phone**   das Handy, -s

**cellar**   der Keller, -

**center**   die Mitte, -n; das Zentrum, *pl.* Zentren

**century**   das Jahrhundert, -e

**cereal (grain)**   das Müesli

**certain(ly)**   bestimmt; gewiss; sicher

**chair**   der Stuhl, ¨e; **easy ~**   der Sessel, -

**chalk**   die Kreide

**chalkboard**   die Tafel, -n

**chancellor**   der Kanzler, -/die Kanzlerin, -nen; **federal ~**   der Bundeskanzler, -/die Bundeskanzlerin, -nen

**change**   der Wandel; **to ~**   wechseln (hat gewechselt) (sich) verändern (hat verändert); **pocket ~**   das Kleingeld

**Chanukkah**   Chanukka

**characteristic**   die Eigenschaft, -en

**chat**   plaudern (hat geplaudert)

**cheap**   billig

**check**   der Scheck, -s; **traveller's ~**   der Reisescheck, -s; **to ~**   kontrollieren (hat kontrolliert)

**check-out counter**   die Kasse, -n

**cheer**   jubeln (hat gejubelt)

**cheerful**   heiter

**cheese**   der Käse

**chemistry**   die Chemie

**cherry**   die Kirsche, -n

**chest: ~ of drawers**   die Kommode, -n; **clothes ~**   der Kleiderschrank, ¨e

**chew**   kauen (hat gekaut); **to ~ gum**   Kaugummi kauen

**chewing gum**   der Kaugummi, -s

**chicken**   das Hähnchen, -

**child**   das Kind, -er; **~ care subsidy**   das Kindergeld

**childhood**   die Kindheit

**children's book**   das Kinderbuch, ¨er

**children's room**   das Kinderzimmer, -

**chin**   das Kinn

**chocolate**   die Schokolade, -n

**choice**   die Wahl, -en

**choose**   wählen (hat gewählt)

**Christianity**   das Christentum

**Christmas**   das Weihnachten; **Merry ~!**   Fröhliche Weihnachten!

**chubby**   mollig

**church**   die Kirche, -n

**cigarette**   die Zigarette, -n

**Cinderella**   Aschenputtel

**circle**   der Kreis, -e

**citizen**   der Bürger, -/die Bürgerin, -nen

**city**   die Stadt, ¨e; **old part of the ~**   die Altstadt; **~ hall**   das Rathaus, ¨er; **~ district**   der Stadtteil, -e; das Stadtviertel; **~ map**   der Stadtplan, ¨e; **~ outskirts**   der Stadtrand, ¨er; **~ bus tour**   die Stadtrundfahrt, -en

**civil servant**   der Beamte *(noun decl. like adj.)* /die Beamtin, -nen

**class**   die Klasse, -n; der Unterricht; **~ size**   die Klassengröße, -n

**classical**   klassisch

**classmate**   der Kommilitone, [-n], -n/die Kommilitonin, -nen

**classroom**   das Klassenzimmer, -

**clean**   sauber; **to ~**   sauber machen (hat sauber gemacht); **to ~ up**   auf·räumen (hat aufgeräumt)

**cleaning lady**   die Reinemachefrau, -en

**clear**   klar; heiter; **to ~ away**   weg·räumen (hat weggeräumt)

**clearly**   unbedingt

**climate**   das Klima

**climb**   klettern (ist geklettert); steigen (ist gestiegen); **to ~ into a train, car, etc.**   ein·steigen (ist eingestiegen); **to ~ out**   aus·steigen (ist ausgestiegen)

**clique**   die Clique, -n; der Freundeskreis, -

**clock**   die Uhr, -en; **alarm ~**   der Wecker, -

**close**   eng; nah(e); **a ~ friendship**   eine dicke Freundschaft; **~ to**   in der Nähe von + *dat.;* **to ~**   schließen (hat geschlossen), zu·machen (hat zugemacht)

**closet**   der Schrank, ¨e

**clothing**   die Kleidung; die Klamotten *(pl.)*

**cloud**   die Wolke, -n

**cloudy**   wolkig

**club**   der Verein, -e; der Klub, -s; **athletic ~**   der Turnverein, -e

**coach**   der Trainer, -/die Trainerin, -nen

**coal**   die Kohle, -n

**coat**   der Mantel, ¨; **rain~**   der Regenmantel, ¨; **sport~**   der/das Sakko, -s

**coffee**   der Kaffee; **~house**   das Kaffeehaus, ¨er; **~maker**   die Kaffeemaschine, -n

**coincidence**   der Zufall, ¨e

**cola**   die Cola, -s

**cold**   kalt (ä) *(adj.);* **~ cuts**   der Aufschnitt, -e; **~ war**   der Kalte Krieg; **~ *(noun)***   die Erkältung, -en; der Schnupfen, -; **to catch a ~**   sich erkälten (hat sich erkältet)

**collaboration**   die Zusammenarbeit, -en

**collapse**   der Zusammenbruch; **to ~**   ein·stürzen (ist eingestürzt)

**collegial**   kollegial

**colleague**   der Kollege, [-n], -n/die Kollegin, -nen

**college**   die Universität, -en; die Hochschule, -n; **to go to ~**   studieren (hat studiert), an die Universität gehen

**color**   die Farbe, -n; **What ~ is ... ?**   Welche Farbe hat. . . ?

**comb**   der Kamm, ¨e; **to ~ one's hair**   sich die Haare kämmen (hat sich gekämmt)

**combine**   kombinieren (hat kombiniert)

**come**   kommen (ist gekommen); **to ~ along**   mit·kommen (ist mitgekommen); **to ~ back**   zurück·kommen (ist zurückgekommen); **to ~ by**   vorbei·kommen (ist vorbeigekommen); **to ~ from**   aus ... kommen; **to ~ home**   heim·kommen (ist heimgekommen); **to ~ out**   raus·kommen (ist rausgekommen); **to ~ to grips (with)**   fertig werden (ist fertig geworden) mit + *dat.;* **~ in!**   Herein!; **Where are you coming from?**   Woher kommst du?

**comedy**   die Komödie, -n

**comical**   lustig, komisch

**command**   befehlen (hat befohlen) + *dat.*

**common**   gemeinsam; **~ bathroom**   das Gemeinschaftsbad, ¨er

**communism**   der Kommunismus

**communist**   der Kommunist, [-en], -en/die Kommunistin, -nen

**commuter**   der Pendler, -

**compact disc**   die CD, -s
**company**   die Gesellschaft, -en;
  die Firma, *pl.* Firmen; der Konzern, -e
**compare**   vergleichen (hat
  verglichen)
**compartment**   das Fach, ¨er
**complete**   ganz; voll; **to ~**   vervollständigen (hat vervollständigt);
  ergänzen (hat ergänzt)
**completed**   vollendet
**completely**   vollkommen; **~ wet**
  ganz nass
**complicated**   kompliziert
**compose**   komponieren (hat
  komponiert)
**composer**   der Komponist, [-en],
  -en/die Komponistin, -nen
**computer**   der Computer, -;
  **~ science**   die Informatik
**concentrate**   sich konzentrieren (hat
  sich konzentriert) auf + *acc.*
**concert**   das Konzert, -e; **~ hall**   der
  Konzertsaal (*pl.* -säle); **to go to a ~**
  ins Konzert gehen
**concierge**   der Hausmeister, -/die
  Hausmeisterin, -nen
**connection**   der Zusammenhang, ¨e
**connoisseur**   der Genießer, -/die
  Genießerin, -nen
**conquer**   erobern (hat erobert)
**consider**   sich überlegen (hat sich
  überlegt); **to be considered as**
  gelten (hat gegolten) als
**constitution**   die Verfassung, -en;
  **German ~**   das Grundgesetz
**consume**   verbrauchen (hat
  verbraucht)
**consumer-oriented**   konsum
  orientiert
**contact**   der Kontakt, -e
**contain**   enthalten (hat enthalten)
**content**   der Inhalt, -e
**continue**   fort·setzen (hat fortgesetzt)/ fort·fahren (ist fortgefahren);
  **~ walking**   weiter·gehen (ist weitergegangen)
**contradictory**   widersprüchlich
**contrary: on the ~**   sondern; doch
**controversial**   kontrovers
**conversation**   das Gespräch, -e; die
  Unterhaltung, -en; **initiate a ~**
  an·sprechen (hat angesprochen)
**converse with**   sich unterhalten (hat
  sich unterhalten) mit + *dat.*

**convince**   überzeugen (hat
  überzeugt)
**cook**   der Koch, ¨e/die Köchin, -nen;
  **to ~**   kochen (hat gekocht)
**cool**   kühl; cool; locker; klasse
**cooperative**   kollegial
**copy**   die Kopie, -n; **~ shop**   der
  Kopierladen, ¨; das Kopiergeschäft,
  -e; **to ~**   kopieren (hat kopiert)
**corner**   die Ecke, -n; **around the ~**
  um die Ecke
**correct**   richtig; **that's ~!**   das
  stimmt!
**corridor**   der Flur, -e; der Gang, ¨e;
  der Korridor, -e
**cosmetic case**   der Kulturbeutel, -
**cost**   kosten (hat gekostet)
**couch**   die Couch, - *or* -s
**could**   könnte
**counsel**   beraten (hat beraten)
**counseling**   die Beratung, -en
**counselor**   der Berater, -/die
  Beraterin, -nen
**count**   zählen (hat gezählt); **to ~ on**
  rechnen (hat gerechnet) mit + *dat.*
**country**   das Land, ¨er; der Staat, -en;
  **in the ~**   auf dem Land(e)
**coup**   die Machtergreifung, -en
**courageous**   mutig
**course**   der Kurs, -e; **~ catalogue**
  das Vorlesungsverzeichnis, -se; **main
  ~**   das Hauptgericht, -e; **of ~**
  natürlich; klar; selbstverständlich;
  **What ~s are you taking?**   Welche
  Fächer haben Sie?
**courtyard**   der Hof, ¨e
**cousin:** *(female)* **~**   die Kusine, -n;
  *(male)* **~**   der Cousin, -s
**co-worker**   der Mitarbeiter, -/die
  Mitarbeiterin, -nen
**cozy**   gemütlich
**cramp**   der Muskelkater, -
**crazy**   wahnsinnig; verrückt; **to be ~**
  einen Vogel haben (*colloq.*)
**create**   schaffen (hat geschaffen)
**creative**   kreativ
**credit card**   die Kreditkarte, -n
**crime**   die Kriminalität
**criminal**   der/die Kriminelle, -n
  *(noun decl. like adj.)*
**criteria**   die Kriterien *(pl.)*
**criticize**   kritisieren (hat kritisiert)
**cross-country skiing**   der Langlauf;
  **~ trail**   die Langlaufloipe, -n

**crossing**   die Kreuzung, -en
**crowd**   die Masse, -n; die Menge, -n
**cruel**   grausam
**cry**   weinen (hat geweint)
**cucumber**   die Gurke, -n
**cuddle**   schmusen (hat geschmust)
**cuisine**   die Küche, -n
**culture**   die Kultur, -en
**cultural**   kulturell; **~ center**   das
  Kulturzentrum, *pl.* Kulturzentren
**cunning**   die List
**cup**   die Tasse, -n; der Becher, -
**curious**   neugierig; gespannt
**curly hair**   krause Haare
**current**   aktuell
**curtain**   die Gardine, -n
**custodian**   der Hauswart, -e
**customer**   der Kunde, [-n], -n/die
  Kundin, -nen
**customs**   der Zoll; **~ agent**   der
  Zöllner, -/die Zöllnerin, -nen
**cut**   schneiden (hat geschnitten); **to ~
  oneself**   sich schneiden in + *acc.;* **to
  ~ back**   kürzen (hat gekürzt); **to ~
  off**   ab·schneiden (hat abgeschnitten)
**cyclist**   der Radfahrer, -/die
  Radfahrerin, -nen

**dad**   der Vati, -s; **grand~**   der Opa, -s
**daily**   täglich
**damp**   nass (a/ä), feucht
**dance**   der Ball, ¨e; **to ~**   tanzen (hat
  getanzt)
**dangerous**   gefährlich
**dare**   wagen (hat gewagt); riskieren
  (hat riskiert)
**dark**   dunkel; **~ gray**   dunkelgrau
**darling**   der Liebling, -e
**data**   die Tatsachen, die Daten *(pl.)*
**date**   das Datum, *pl.* Daten; die
  Verabredung, -en; **to make a ~**   sich
  verabreden (hat sich verabredet) mit
  + *dat.*
**daughter**   die Tochter, ¨
**day**   der Tag, -e; **~ after tomorrow**
  übermorgen; **~ of the week**   der
  Wochentag, -e; **~'s schedule**   der
  Tagesablauf; **all ~**   den ganzen Tag;
  **one ~**   eines Tages; **Good ~.**   Guten
  Tag.; Tag.; **What ~ is today?**   Was ist
  heute?

**dead**  tot; **~tired**  todmüde

**dear**  lieb (-er, -e, -es)

**December**  der Dezember

**decide**  sich entscheiden (hat sich
entschieden); **to ~ on/against**  sich
entscheiden für/gegen + *acc.*

**decidedly**  ausgesprochen

**decision**  die Entscheidung, -en

**declare**  bekannt geben (hat bekannt
gegeben); erklären (hat erklärt) für +
*acc.*

**decorate**  auf·decken (hat
aufgedeckt)

**dedicate**  widmen (hat gewidmet)

**defeat**  erobern (hat erobert)

**degree**  der Abschluss, *pl.*
Abschlüsse; *(temperature)*
der Grad

**delicious**  lecker

**dentist**  der Zahnarzt, ¨e/die
Zahnärztin, -nen

**deodorant**  das Deo, -s

**depart**  ab·fahren (ist abgefahren)

**departure**  die Abreise, -n; die
Abfahrt, -en; der Abflug, ¨e

**department**  die Abteilung, -en;
**academic ~**  der Fachbereich, -e;
**~ store**  das Kaufhaus, ¨er

**deposit**  ein·zahlen (hat eingezahlt)

**depressing**  deprimierend, drückend

**describe**  beschreiben (hat
beschrieben)

**desk**  der Schreibtisch, -e

**dessert**  die Nachspeise, -n; der
Nachtisch, -e

**destination**  das Ziel, -e

**destroy**  zerstören (hat zerstört)

**detail**  die Kleinigkeit, -en; das Detail,
-s; **~-oriented**  gründlich

**detailed**  ausführlich

**detective story**  der Kriminalroman,
-e; der Krimi, -s

**dependable**  zuverlässig

**develop**  entwickeln (hat entwickelt)

**development**  die Entwicklung, -en;
der Werdegang

**diagonally across from**  quer
gegenüber von + *dat.*

**dialect**  der Dialekt, -e

**diarrhea**  der Durchfall

**dictator**  der Diktator, -en

**dictatorship**  die Diktatur, -en

**dictionary**  das Wörterbuch, ¨er

**die**  sterben (ist gestorben)

**difference**  der Unterschied, -e; **no ~**
egal

**different**  verschieden; anders;
**something ~**  etwas anderes

**difficult**  schwer; schwierig

**difficulty**  die Schwierigkeit, -en

**digital**  digital

**dining hall**  die Mensa, *pl.* Mensen

**dining room**  das Esszimmer, -; **hotel
~**  der Speisesaal, *pl.* Speisesäle

**dinner**  das Abendessen, -; **for ~**
zum Abendessen

**diploma**  das Diplom, -e

**direction**  die Richtung, -en

**dirt**  der Dreck

**dirty**  schmutzig

**disappointed**  enttäscht

**disciplined**  diszipliniert

**discotheque**  die Diskothek, -en (die
Disko, -s)

**discover**  entdecken (hat entdeckt)

**discuss**  diskutieren (hat diskutiert)
über + *acc.;* besprechen (hat besprochen); sich unterhalten (hat sich
unterhalten) über + *acc.*

**discussion**  die Diskussion, -en; die
Besprechung, -en

**disguise oneself**  sich verkleiden (hat
sich verkleidet)

**dishes**  das Geschirr

**dishwasher: electric ~**  die
Geschirrspülmaschine, -n

**diskette**  die Diskette, -n

**district**  das Viertel, -; **city ~**  das
Stadviertel, -

**disturb**  stören (hat gestört)

**divide**  teilen; auf·teilen (hat
aufgeteilt) in + *acc.*

**divorced**  geschieden

**do**  machen (hat gemacht); tun (hat
getan); **to ~ homework**  Hausaufgaben machen; **to ~ sports**  Sport
treiben (hat Sport getrieben)

**doctor**  der Arzt, ¨e/die Ärztin,
-nen

**documentary film**  der Dokumentarfilm, -e

**dog**  der Hund, -e

**done**  fertig, erledigt

**door**  die Tür, -en

**dormitory**  das Studentenwohnheim, -e

**doubt: no ~**  wohl

**dove**  das Täubchen, -

**downstairs**  unten; **to go ~**  die
Treppe hinunter·gehen (ist hin-
untergegangen)

**down the street**  die Straße entlang

**drama**  das Drama, *pl.* Dramen

**drawer**  die Schublade, -n

**dream**  der Traum, ¨e; **to ~ of**  träumen (hat geträumt) von + *dat.*

**dress**  das Kleid, -er; **to ~, get dressed**
sich an·ziehen (hat sich angezogen)

**drink**  das Getränk, -e; **to ~**  trinken
(hat getrunken)

**drive**  fahren (ist gefahren); **to ~ away**
weg·fahren (ist weggefahren)

**driver**  der Fahrer, -/die Fahrerin,
-nen

**driver's license**  der Führerschein,
-e

**drug**  die Droge, -n

**dry**  trocken; **to ~ off**  ab·trocknen
(hat abgetrocknet); **to ~ hair**  föhnen (hat geföhnt)

**dumb**  dumm (ü); doof; **something ~**
etwas Dummes

**during**  während + *gen.*

**DVD**  die DVD, -s; **~ player**  der
DVD-Spieler, -

**dwarf**  der Zwerg, -e

**dynamic**  dynamisch

**each**  jed- (-er, -es, -e); **~ other**  einander

**ear**  das Ohr, -en

**earlier**  früher

**early**  früh

**earn**  verdienen (hat verdient)

**east**  der Osten; **~ German**  ostdeutsch

**Easter**  Ostern

**easy**  einfach; leicht; **~ going**  gut
gelaunt

**eat**  essen (hat gegessen); **to ~**  *(said
of animals)*  fressen (hat gefressen)

**economics**  die Volkswirtschaft

**economy**  die Wirtschaft

**educate**  aus·bilden (hat ausgebildet)

**education**  die Erziehung; die Ausbildung; die Pädagogik

**effect**  die Wirkung, -en; **to ~**  wirken
(hat gewirkt)

**effort**  die Mühe

**egg**  das Ei, -er; **soft-boiled ~**  das
weich gekochte Ei

**either . . . or** entweder ... oder
**elbow** der Ellenbogen, -
**election** die Wahl, -en
**electrical: ~ outlet** die Steckdose, -n;
**~ storm** das Gewitter, -
**else; what ~?** was noch?; **something ~?** sonst noch etwas?
**e-mail** die E-Mail, -s; *(concept)* das Mail; **to ~** mailen (hat gemailt)
**emblem** das Wahrzeichen, -
**embrace** umarmen (hat umarmt)
**emperor/empress** der Kaiser, -/die Kaiserin, -nen
**empire** das Reich, -e
**employed** berufstätig
**employee** der/die Angestellte, -n *(noun decl. like adj.)* der Mitarbeiter, -/die Mitarbeiterin, -nen
**employer** der Arbeitgeber, -/die Arbeitgeberin, -nen
**empty** leer
**end** das Ende, -n; **in/at the ~** am Ende
**enemy** der Feind, -e
**energy** die Energie
**engaged** verlobt; **to get ~** sich verloben (hat sich verlobt) mit + *dat.*
**engineer** der Ingenieur, -e/die Ingenieurin, -nen
**engineering** das Ingenieurwesen; **mechanical ~** der Maschinenbau
**England** (das) England
**English** englisch *(adj.);* **~ (language)** (das) Englisch; **~ (person)** der Engländer, -/die Engländerin, -nen
**enjoy** genießen (hat genossen); **~ your meal!** Guten Appetit!
**enjoyment** die Lust; das Vergnügen; der Spaß
**enlarge** vergrößern (hat vergrößert)
**enough** genug; genügend
**entertaining** unterhaltend
**entrance** der Eingang, ̈e; **~ hall** die Diele, -n; der Flur, -e
**entry** *(in a diary)* der Eintrag, ̈e
**environment** die Umwelt
**environmental: ~ protection** der Umweltschutz
**environmentally friendly** umweltfreundlich
**especially** besonders
**et cetera (etc.)** und so weiter (usw.)
**eternal** ewig
**Euro** *(currency unit)* der Euro, -s

**Europe** (das) Europa
**European** europäisch; **~ Union** die Europäische Union
**even** sogar; **~ if** auch wenn
**evening** der Abend, -e; **good ~** Guten Abend., Abend.; **this ~** heute Abend
**evenings** abends
**eventually** schließlich, endlich
**every** jed- (-er, -es, -e)
**everyone** jeder; alle; jedermann
**everything** alles; **~ okay** alles in Ordnung
**exactly** genau
**examination** die Prüfung, -en; das Examen, -; **high school graduation ~** das Abitur
**examine** überprüfen (hat überprüft)
**example** das Beispiel, -e; **for ~** zum Beispiel (z.B.)
**excellent** ausgezeichnet
**except** außer + *dat.*
**exciting** spannend
**excited** aufgeregt; **to be ~ about** gespannt sein auf + *acc.*
**excitement** die Aufregung, -en
**excuse** die Ausrede, -n; die Entschuldigung, -en; **~ me!** Entschuldigung!; **to ~** entschuldigen (hat entschuldigt)
**expand** erweitern (hat erweitert)
**expect** erwarten (hat erwartet)
**expectation** die Erwartung, -en
**expensive** teuer
**experience** die Erfahrung, -en; das Erlebnis, -se; **to ~** erleben (hat erlebt); erfahren (hat erfahren)
**explain** erklären (hat erklärt)
**explanation** die Erklärung, -en
**expression** der Ausdruck, ̈e
**expressway** die Autobahn, -en
**eye** das Auge, -n

**F**

**face** das Gesicht, -er
**fairly** ganz; ziemlich
**fairy** die Fee, -n; **~ tale** das Märchen, -; **~ tale figure** die Märchenfigur, -en
**fall** der Herbst; **to ~** fallen (ist gefallen); **to ~ asleep** ein·schlafen (ist eingeschlafen); **to ~ in love** sich verlieben (hat sich verliebt) in + *acc.*

**false** falsch
**familiar** bekannt
**family** die Familie, -n; **~ owned business** der Familienbetrieb, -e; **~ tree** der Familienstammbaum, ̈e
**famous** bekannt; berühmt; **world-~** weltberühmt
**fan** *(sports)* der Fan, -s; der Anhänger, -
**fantastic** phantastisch; toll; prima; großartig
**far** weit; **~ away** weit weg
**farewell** der Abschied
**farmer** der Bauer, [-n], -n/die Bäuerin, -nen
**fast** schnell
**fat** dick; mollig
**father** der Vater, ̈; **grand~** der Großvater, ̈
**favorite** Lieblings-
**fax** das Fax; **to ~** faxen (hat gefaxt)
**fear** die Angst, ̈e; **to ~** Angst haben (hat gehabt) vor + *dat.*; fürchten (hat gefürchtet)
**feast** das Fest, -e
**February** der Februar
**Federal Republic of Germany** die Bundesrepublik Deutschland
**feel** sich fühlen (hat sich gefühlt); spüren (hat gespürt); **to ~ like** Lust haben; **to ~ unwell** sich nicht wohl fühlen; **I'm ~ing pretty bad.** Mir geht's ziemlich schlecht.
**feeling** das Gefühl, -e
**fetch** holen (hat geholt)
**fever** das Fieber; **to have a ~** Fieber haben
**few** wenig(e); **a ~** ein paar
**fiancé(e)** der/die Verlobte, -n *(noun decl. like adj.)*
**field hockey** das Feldhockey
**fight** sich streiten (hat sich gestritten)
**figure skater** der Eiskunstläufer, -/die Eiskunstläuferin, -nen
**film** der Film, -e; **~ director** der Regisseur, -e/ die Regisseurin, -nen; **~maker** der Filmemacher, /die Filmemacherin, -nen; **documentary ~** der Dokumentarfilm, -e
**finally** endlich, schließlich
**finances** die Finanzen *(pl.)*
**find** finden (hat gefunden); **to ~ out** heraus·finden (hat herausgefunden)

**fine**    fein; gut; **I'm ~.**    Es geht mir gut.

**finger**    der Finger, -; **to cross one's ~s**    ganz fest die Daumen drücken (hat gedrückt)

**finished**    fertig; zu Ende

**fireplace**    der Kamin, -e

**firm**    die Firma, *pl.* Firmen; *(adj.)* fest

**first**    erst; **~ name**    der Vorname, [-n], -n; **~ of all**    zuerst; zunächst; **for the ~ time**    zum ersten Mal

**fish**    der Fisch, -e; **~ market**    der Fischmarkt, ¨e; **to ~**    angeln (hat geangelt)

**fit**    passen (hat gepasst) zu + *dat.*; **to ~ together**    zusammen·passen (hat zusammengepasst)

**flash**    das Blitzlicht, -er

**flexible**    flexibel

**flight**    der Flug, ¨e

**flirt**    flirten (hat geflirtet)

**floor**    der Boden, *pl.* Böden; der Stock, *pl.* Stockwerke; die Etage, -n; **first ~**    das Erdgeschoss; **one ~ down**    einen Stock tiefer

**flow**    fließen (ist geflossen)

**flower**    die Blume, -n

**fluent**    fließend

**fly**    fliegen (ist geflogen)

**flute**    die Flöte, -n

**fog**    der Nebel

**follower**    der Anhänger,-/die Anhängerin, -nen

**food**    das Essen; die Lebensmittel *(pl.)*; die Kost

**foot**    der Fuß, ¨e; **~path**    der Fußweg, -e; **to go on ~**    zu Fuß gehen (ist gegangen); laufen (ist gelaufen)

**football**    *(American)* der amerikanische Football

**for**    für + *acc.*; denn *(conj.)*; **~ (time)**    seit/schon seit + *dat.*; **~ years**    seit Jahren

**forbid**    verbieten (hat verboten)

**forbidden**    verboten

**foreign**    fremd; ausländisch

**foreigner**    der Ausländer, -/die Ausländerin, -nen; der/die Fremde, -n *(noun decl. like adj.)*

**forest**    der Wald, ¨er

**forever**    ewig

**forget**    vergessen (hat vergessen)

**forehead**    die Stirn, -en

**fork**    die Gabel, -n

**form**    die Unterlage, -n; das Formular, -e

**former**    ehemalig

**formerly**    früher

**fragile**    zerbrechlich

**France**    (das) Frankreich

**free**    frei; **~ time**    die Freizeit

**freedom**    die Freiheit

**freeway**    die Autobahn, -en

**freezing point**    der Gefrierpunkt

**French**    französisch *(adj.)*; **~ (language)**    (das) Französisch

**Frenchman**    der Franzose, [-n], -n; **Frenchwoman**    die Französin, -nen

**frequent**    häufig; oft

**Friday**    der Freitag

**friend**    der Freund, -e/die Freundin, -nen

**friendliness**    die Freundlichkeit

**friendly**    freundlich

**friendship**    die Freundschaft, -en **make a ~ official**    eine Freundschaft schließen

**frog**    der Frosch, ¨e

**from**    von + *dat.*; **~ (native of)**    aus + *dat.*; **~ where?**    woher?

**front: up ~**    da vorne; **in ~ of**    vor + *dat.*

**fruit**    das Obst; die Frucht, ¨e; **~ jam, preserves**    die Marmelade

**frustrating**    frustrierend

**full**    voll

**fun**    der Spaß; **That's ~.**    Das macht Spaß. (hat Spaß gemacht)

**funny**    lustig, heiter

**furniture**    die Möbel *(pl.)*

**further**    weiter

**future**    die Zukunft

## G

**game**    das Spiel, -e

**garage**    die Garage, -n

**garden**    der Garten, ¨

**gasoline**    das Benzin

**gate**    das Tor, -e

**generous**    großzügig

**gentle**    sanft

**gentleman**    der Herr, [-n], -en

**genuine**    echt, authentisch

**geography**    die Landeskunde; die Erdkunde

**German**    deutsch *(adj.)*; **~ (person)**    der/die Deutsche *(noun decl. like adj.)*; **~ (language)**    (das) Deutsch; **in ~**    auf Deutsch; **~ studies**    die Germanistik; **~ Democratic Republic**    die Deutsche Demokratische Republik (DDR); **~ Empire**    das Deutsche Reich; **~ Unity Day**    der Tag der Deutschen Einheit

**Germany**    (das) Deutschland; die Bundesrepublik Deutschland

**get**    bekommen (hat bekommen); kriegen (hat gekriegt); besorgen (hat besorgt); **to ~ along with**    gut aus·kommen (ist gut ausgekommen) mit + *dat.*; **~ lost!**    Haut ab!; **~ well!**    Gute Besserung!; **to go ~**    holen (hat geholt); **to ~ through**    durch·machen (hat durchgemacht); **to ~ up**    auf·stehen (ist aufgestanden); **to ~ used to**    sich gewöhnen (hat sich gewöhnt) an + *acc.*; **to ~ to know**    kennen lernen (hat kennen gelernt); **to ~ in touch**    sich melden (hat sich gemeldet)

**gift**    das Geschenk, -e

**girl**    das Mädchen, -

**girlfriend**    die Freundin, -nen

**give**    geben (hat gegeben); **to ~ (as a gift)**    schenken (hat geschenkt); **to ~ up**    auf·geben (hat aufgegeben)

**glad**    froh; **to be ~**    sich freuen (hat sich gefreut)

**glass**    das Glas, ¨er

**glasses**    die Brille, -n

**gladly**    gern

**glove**    der Handschuh, -e

**go**    gehen (ist gegangen); **to ~ along**    mit·gehen (ist mitgegangen); **to ~ by [train]**    mit [dem Zug] fahren (ist gefahren); **to ~ away**    fort·gehen (ist fortgegangen); weg·gehen (ist weggegangen); **to ~ on foot**    zu Fuß gehen; **to ~ out**    aus·gehen (ist ausgegangen); **to ~ to**    auf/in . . . gehen

**goal**    das Tor, -e; das Ziel, -e

**God**    der Gott, ¨er

**gold**    das Gold

**golf**    der Golf; **~club**    der Golfschläger, -

**gone**    weg

**good**    gut, **~-looking**    gut aussehend

**good-bye**   auf Wiedersehen; tschüss *(colloq.)*; **to say ~**   sich verabschieden (hat sich verabschiedet)

**goofy**   doof

**got to**   müssen (hat gemusst)

**government**   die Regierung, -en; der Staat, -en; **~ district**   das Regierungsviertel

**grade**   die Note, -n; **[seventh] ~**   [die siebte] Klasse

**gram**   das Gramm

**grammar**   die Grammatik

**grand**   groß (ö); großartig

**grandchild**   das Enkelkind, -er

**granddaughter**   die Enkelin, -nen

**grandfather**   der Großvater, ̈-; der Opa, -s; **great-~**   der Urgroßvater, -väter/

**grandmother**   die Großmutter, ̈-; die Oma, -s

**grandparents**   die Großeltern *(pl.)*

**grandson**   der Enkel, -

**grape**   die Traube, -n

**grave**   das Grab, ̈-er

**gray**   grau; **dark ~**   dunkelgrau; **light ~**   hellgrau/

**great**   toll, ausgezeichnet, prima, klasse, großartig

**Greece**   (das) Griechenland

**green**   grün

**greeting**   der Gruß, ̈-e

**groceries**   die Lebensmittel *(pl.)*

**grocery store**   das Lebensmittel-geschäft, -e

**ground**   der Boden, ̈-; **~ floor**   das Erdgeschoss; **on the ~ floor**   im Erdgeschoss

**group**   die Gruppe, -n; **~ leader**   der Gruppenleiter; der Betreuer; **~ project**   das Gruppenprojekt, -e; **~ research paper**   das Gruppen-referat, -e; **study ~**   die Arbeits-gruppe, -n

**grow**   wachsen (ist gewachsen); **to ~ up**   auf·wachsen (ist aufgewachsen)

**gruesome**   grausam

**guess**   ahnen

**guest**   der Gast, ̈-e; der Besucher, -/die Besucherin, -nen; **~ room**   das Gästezimmer, -; **~ house**   die Pension, -en; das Gasthaus, ̈-er; der Gasthof, ̈-e

**guitar**   die Gitarre, -n

**guy**   der Typ, -en; **a really nice ~**   ein ganz netter Typ

### H

**habitat**   der Lebensraum

**hair**   das Haar, -e; **~cut**   der Haarschnitt, -e; **straight (tightly curled, wavy) ~**   glatte (krause, wellige) Haare

**hair brush**   die Haarbürste, -n/

**hairdresser**   der Friseur, -e/die Friseurin, -nen/die Friseuse, -n

**half past (one o'clock)**   halb (zwei)

**hallway**   der Flur, -e; der Gang, ̈-e; der Korridor, -e

**hamburger**   der Hamburger, -

**hand**   die Hand, ̈-e; **on the one ~**   einerseits

**handbag**   die Handtasche, -n

**handout**   das Handout, -s

**hang: to ~ up**   hängen (hat gehängt)

**hanging: to be ~**   hängen (hat gehangen)

**hangover: to have a ~**   (einen) Kater haben *(colloq.)*

**happen**   passieren (ist passiert); **What happened to you?**   Was ist dir passiert?

**happily: And they lived ~ ever after.**   Und wenn sie nicht gestorben sind, dann leben sie noch heute.

**happy**   froh, glücklich; **to be ~ about**   sich freuen (hat sich gefreut) über + *acc.*

**harbor**   der Hafen, ̈-

**hard**   hart (ä); schwer

**hardly**   kaum

**hard-working**   fleißig

**harm**   schaden (hat geschadet) + *dat.*

**hatred**   der Hass; **~ of foreigners**   der Ausländerhass; der Fremdennass

**have**   haben (hat gehabt); **to ~ to**   müssen (hat gemusst); **I don't ~ to**   Ich brauche nicht

**he**   er

**head**   der Kopf, ̈-e; **~ cold**   der Schnupfen, die Erkältung

**headache**   die Kopfschmerzen *(pl.)*

**health**   die Gesundheit; **~ club**   das Fitnessstudio, -s; **~ food store**   der Bioladen, ̈-; das Reformhaus, ̈-er

**healthy**   gesund (ü), wohl

**heap**   der Haufen, -

**hear**   hören (hat gehört)

**heart**   das Herz, -en

**hearth**   der Herd, -e

**heaven**   der Himmel, -

**heavy**   schwer

**hello**   Guten Morgen/Tag/Abend; Grüß dich.; Hallo.

**help**   die Hilfe, -n; **to ~**   helfen (hat geholfen) + *dat.*

**her**   *(pronoun)* sie *(acc.)*; ihr *(dat.)*; *(possessive)* ihr

**here**   hier, da; **~** *(toward the speaker)* her; **~ you are**   bitte sehr

**hey!**   du!; he!; Hallo!

**hi!**   Tag! Grüß dich! Servus!

**hide**   verstecken (hat versteckt)

**high (higher, highest)**   hoch (höher, am höchsten)

**high school**   das Gymnasium *(pl.* Gymnasien); **~ exit examination**   das Abitur, -s (Abi); **~ senior**   der Abiturient, [en], -en/die Abitu-rientin, -nen

**hike**   die Wanderung, -en; **to ~**   wandern (ist gewandert)

**him**   ihn *(acc.)*; ihm *(dat.)*

**hire**   ein·stellen (hat eingestellt)

**his**   sein

**history**   die Geschichte

**hitchhike**   per Anhalter fahren (ist gefahren)

**hobby**   das Hobby, -s; **~ room**   der Hobbyraum, ̈-e

**hockey: ice ~**   das Eishockey; **field ~**   das Feldhockey

**hold**   halten (hat gehalten)

**holiday**   der Feiertag, -e, der Festtag, -e

**home: at ~**   zu Hause; daheim; **to come ~**   heim·kommen (ist heimgekommen); **to go ~**   nach Hause gehen (ist gegangen); **~ remedy**   das Hausmittel, -

**homeland**   die Heimat; das Her-kunftsland, ̈-er

**homesickness**   das Heimweh

**hometown**   die Heimatstadt, ̈-e, der Wohnort, -e

**homework**   die Hausaufgaben *(pl.)*; **to do ~**   die Hausaufgaben machen

**homosexual**   der/die Homosexuelle, -n *(noun decl. like adj.)*; schwul

**honest**   ehrlich
**honey**   der Honig
**hook**   der Haken, -
**hope**   hoffen (hat gehofft); **to ~ for**   hoffen auf + *acc.*
**hopefully**   hoffentlich
**horrible**   furchtbar; fürchterlich; schrecklich
**horror movie**   der Horrorfilm, -e; der Gruselfilm, -e
**horse**   das Pferd, -e; **~ -drawn sleigh**   der Pferdeschlitten, -
**hospital**   das Krankenhaus, ⸚er; [*Austrian*] ~   das Spital, ⸚er
**hospitality**   die Gastfreundschaft
**host**   der Gastgeber, -/die Gastgeberin, -nen; (*in a restaurant*) der Wirt, -e/die Wirtin, -nen
**hot**   heiß
**hotel**   das Hotel, -s
**hour**   die Stunde, -n; **for ~s**   stundenlang
**house**   das Haus, ⸚er
**housekeeper**   die Reinemachefrau, -en
**how**   wie; **~ are you?**   Wie geht es Ihnen?/Wie geht's?; **~ are you feeling?**   wie fühlst du dich?; **~ do I get to . . . ?**   Wie komme ich nach/zu ... ?; **~ many?**   wie viele?; **~ much?**   wie viel?; **~ would . . . be?**   Wie wäre es mit ... ?
**hug**   umarmen (hat umarmt)
**human being**   der Mensch, [-en], -en
**humid**   schwül
**hundred**   hundert
**hunger**   der Hunger
**hungry**   hungrig; **to be ~**   Hunger haben (hat gehabt)
**hunter**   der Jäger, -
**hurry**   sich beeilen (hat sich beeilt)
**hurt**   weh·tun (hat wehgetan) + *dat.;* **(My arm) ~s.**   (Der Arm) tut mir weh.
**husband**   der Mann, ⸚er

**I**   ich
**ice**   das Eis; **~ cream**   das Eis; **~ hockey**   das Eishockey
**idea**   die Idee, -n; der Einfall, ⸚e; die Vorstellung, -en

**if**   wenn; ob; **even ~**   wenn auch
**identify: to ~ with**   sich identifizieren (hat sich identifiziert) mit + *dat.*
**identity**   die Identität
**ill**   krank
**illness**   die Krankheit, -en
**image**   das Bild, -er; die Vorstellung, -en
**imagine**   sich vor·stellen (hat sich vorgestellt) + *dat.;* **~ that!**   Stell dir mal vor!
**immediately**   gleich
**impatient**   ungeduldig
**impolite**   unhöflich
**important**   wichtig; **the most ~ thing**   das Wichtigste
**impress**   beeindrucken (hat beeindruckt)
**impression**   der Eindruck, ⸚e
**impressive**   beeindruckend
**improve**   verbessern (hat verbessert)
**in**   in + *acc./dat.;* **~ order to**   um ... zu; **~ spite of**   trotz + *gen.*
**in-line skates**   die Rollerblades (*pl.*)
**increase**   erhöhen (hat erhöht)
**industrious**   fleißig
**industry**   die Industrie, -n
**influence**   der Einfluss, *pl.* Einflüsse; **to ~**   beeinflussen (hat beeinflusst)
**inhabitant**   der Einwohner, -/ die Einwohnerin, -nen
**injure**   verletzen (hat verletzt)
**inn**   der Gasthof, ⸚e
**innumerable**   zahllos
**inquire**   fragen (hat gefragt) nach + *dat.*
**insane**   wahnsinnig
**insecure**   unsicher
**inside**   innerhalb + *gen.*
**instead of**   (an)statt + *gen.*
**instrument**   das Instrument, -e
**insurance**   die Versicherung, -en
**intelligent**   intelligent, klug (ü)
**intend to**   vor·haben (hat vorgehabt)
**interest**   das Interesse, -n; **to ~**   interessieren (hat interessiert)
**interested: to be ~ in**   (sich) interessieren für+ *acc.*
**interesting**   interessant
**intern**   der Praktikant, [-en], -en/die Praktikantin, -nen

**international**   international; **~ relations**   internationale Beziehungen (*pl.*)
**Internet**   das Internet; **~ connection**   der Internet-Anschluss, ⸚e; **~ page**   die Internetseite, -n
**intersection**   die Kreuzung, -en
**internship**   das Praktikum, *pl.* Praktika; die Praktikantenstelle, -n
**interview**   das Interview, -s; das Vorstellungsgespräch, -e
**into**   in + *acc.;* hinein
**introduce**   vor·stellen (hat vorgestellt)
**introduction**   die Vorstellung, -en
**invitation**   die Einladung, -en
**invite**   ein·laden (hat eingeladen)
**irritate**   irritieren (hat irritiert)
**Islam**   der Islam
**is**   ist; **isn't it?**   nicht?; nicht wahr? *(tag question)*
**island**   die Insel, -n
**it**   er/sie/es
**Italian**   italienisch *(adj.);* **~ (language)**   (das) Italienisch

**jacket**   die Jacke, -n
**January**   der Januar
**Japanese**   (das) Japanisch; **~ (person)**   der Japaner, -/die Japanerin, -nen
**jazz**   die Jazzmusik; **~ club**   der Jazzkeller, -
**jeans**   die Jeans *(pl.)*
**Jew**   der Jude, [-n], -n /die Jüdin, -nen
**Jewish**   jüdisch
**job**   der Job, -s; die Stelle, -n; **to have a part-time ~**   jobben (hat gejobbt)
**join**   bei·treten (ist beigetreten) + *dat.;* **to ~ in**   mit·machen (hat mitgemacht)
**joke**   der Witz, -e
**journalist**   der Journalist, [-en], -en/die Journalistin, -nen
**joy**   die Freude, -n
**juice**   der Saft, ⸚e
**July**   der Juli
**jump**   springen (ist gesprungen)
**June**   der Juni
**just**   eben; erst; gerade; halt

## K

**key**   der Schlüssel, -
**kick**   treten (hat getreten); **to ~ (the ball)**   schießen (hat geschossen)
**kilogram**   das Kilo(gramm), -
**kilometer**   der Kilometer, -
**kind**   die Art, -en; **what ~ of . . .?** was für ein . . . ?; *(adj.)* gut; nett
**kindergarten**   der Kindergarten
**king**   der König, -e
**kingdom**   das Königtum, ̈er
**kiss**   der Kuss, *pl.* Küsse; **to ~** küssen (hat geküsst)
**kitchen**   die Küche, -n
**knee**   das Knie, -
**knife**   das Messer, -
**knock over**   um·werfen (hat umgeworfen)
**know: to ~ (a fact)**   wissen (hat gewusst); **to ~ (be acquainted)** kennen (hat gekannt); **to ~ something about**   etwas verstehen (hat verstanden) von + *dat.;* **to get to ~** kennen lernen (hat kennen gelernt)
**knowledge**   die Kenntnis, -se

## L

**lack**   fehlen (hat gefehlt)
**lacrosse**   das Lacrosse
**lake**   der See, -n
**lame**   lahm
**lamp**   die Lampe, -n
**land**   das Land, ̈er
**landscape**   die Landschaft, -en
**language**   die Sprache, -n; **foreign ~** die Fremdsprache, -n; **~ institute** das Sprachinstitut, -e; **~ lab** das Sprachlabor, -s
**laptop computer**   der Laptop, -s
**large**   groß (ö)
**last**   letzt; **~ night**   gestern Abend; **to ~**   dauern (hat gedauert)
**lastly**   zuletzt
**late**   spät
**later**   später; **until ~**   bis später, tschüss, bis dann, bis bald
**latest: at the ~**   spätestens
**laugh**   lachen (hat gelacht); **to ~ about**   lachen über + *acc.*
**laundry room**   die Waschküche, -n
**law**   das Gesetz, -e; **~ (field of study)** Jura *(no article);* **Basic ~** *(German Constitution)*   das Grundgesetz

**lawyer**   der Rechtsanwalt, ̈e/die Rechtsanwältin, -nen
**lay (something down)**   legen (hat gelegt)
**lazy**   faul
**lead**   führen (hat geführt); leiten (hat geleitet)
**leader**   der Führer, -
**league**   die Liga (*pl.* Ligen)
**learn**   lernen (hat gelernt)
**least: at ~**   wenigstens; mindestens
**leave**   lassen (hat gelassen); verlassen (hat verlassen); weg·fahren (ist weggefahren); ab·fahren (ist abgefahren)
**lecture**   die Vorlesung, -en; **~ hall** der Hörsaal, *pl.* Hörsäle; **~ notes** das Skript, -en
**left: on/to the ~**   links
**leg**   das Bein, -e
**leisure activity**   die Freizeitaktivität, -en
**lend**   leihen (hat geliehen)
**lesson**   der Unterricht; die Stunde, -n
**let**   lassen (hat gelassen)
**letter**   der Brief, -e
**lettuce**   der Salat, -e
**librarian**   der Bibliothekar, -e/die Bibliothekarin, -nen
**library**   die Bibliothek, -en
**lie**   liegen (hat gelegen); **to ~ down** (sich) hin·legen (hat sich hingelegt); **to tell a ~**   lügen (hat gelogen)
**life**   das Leben, -; **life-threatening** lebensgefährlich
**light**   das Licht, -er; **traffic ~**   die Ampel, -n; *(adj.)* leicht; **~** *(color)* hell; **~ blue**   hellblau
**lightning: to flash ~**   blitzen (es blitzt, es hat geblitzt)
**likability**   die Sympathie
**likable**   sympathisch
**like**   gern haben (hat gern gehabt); mögen (hat gemocht); gefallen (hat gefallen) + *dat.;* **I ~ to swim.** Ich schwimme gern.; **I (don't) ~ that** Das gefällt mir (nicht).; **I'd ~** ich möchte
**limited**   begrenzt
**line: waiting ~**   die Schlange, -n; **to stand in ~**   [in der] Schlange stehen (hat gestanden)
**lip**   die Lippe, -n
**lipstick**   der Lippenstift, -e
**list**   die Liste, -n

**listen**   zu·hören (hat zugehört) + *dat.;* **to ~ to music**   Musik hören (hat gehört)
**liter**   der Liter, -
**literature**   die Literatur, -en
**little**   klein; wenig; **a ~**   ein bisschen, ein wenig, **Little Red Riding Hood** Rotkäppchen
**live**   leben (hat gelebt); wohnen (hat gewohnt); **to ~ together**   zusammen·leben (hat zusammengelebt); **And they ~d happily ever after.** Und wenn sie nicht gestorben sind, dann leben sie nach heute.
**lively**   lebendig; schwungvoll
**living room**   das Wohnzimmer, -
**located: to be ~**   liegen (hat gelegen)
**lock**   das Schloss, *pl.* Schlösser; **to un~**   auf·schließen (hat aufgeschlossen)
**lodgings: to find ~**   unter·kommen (ist untergekommen)
**logical**   vernünftig
**long**   lang (ä); lange; **for a ~ time** lange
**longer: no ~**   nicht mehr
**look**   schauen (hat geschaut); **to ~ at** sich an·schauen (hat angeschaut); **to ~ like**   aus·sehen (hat ausgesehen) wie; **to ~ down**   herab·blicken (hat herabgeblickt); **to ~ for**   suchen (hat gesucht); **to ~ forward to**   sich freuen (hat sich gefreut) auf + *acc.;* **to ~ funny at someone**   (jemanden) schief an·schauen (hat angeschaut); **to ~ through**   durch·gucken (hat durchgeguckt); **~ !**   Guck mal!
**lose**   verlieren (hat verloren)
**lot: a ~**   viel
**loud**   laut
**lousy**   mies
**love**   die Liebe, -n; **~ poem**   das Liebesgedicht, -e; **to ~**   lieben; **to be in ~ with**   verliebt sein in + *dat.;* **to fall in ~ with**   sich verlieben in + *acc.*
**lovesickness**   der Liebeskummer
**low**   gering; niedrig
**loyal**   treu
**loyalty**   die Treue
**luck**   das Glück; **to have bad ~**   Pech haben; **Lots of ~ !**   Toi, toi, toi!
**lucky: to be ~**   Glück haben (hat gehabt); Schwein haben *(colloq.)*

**lunch**   das Mittagessen; **for ~**   zum Mittagessen; **to have ~**   zu Mittag essen

## M

**machine**   die Maschine, -n
**magazine**   die Zeitschrift, -en
**magician**   der Zauberer, -
**major subject**   das Hauptfach, ¨er
**mail**   die Post; **~box**   das Postfach, ¨er; **~ carrier**   der Briefträger, -/die Briefträgerin, -nen; der Postbote, [-n], -n/die Postbotin, -nen
**main**   Haupt-; **~ course**   das Hauptgericht, -e; **~ street**   die Hauptstraße, -n; **~ street (of Berlin),**   der Kurfürstendamm (Ku'damm); **~ train station**   der Hauptbahnhof, ¨e
**major: college ~**   das Hauptfach, ¨er; **What's your ~?**   Was haben Sie als Hauptfach?
**make**   machen (hat gemacht); **to ~ up with**   sich versöhnen (hat sich versöhnt) mit + *dat.*
**mall**   das Einkaufszentrum, *pl.* -zentren
**man**   der Mann, ¨er; **Man!**   Mensch! Mann!
**manage**   schaffen (hat geschafft); bewerkstelligen (hat bewerkstelligt)
**manner**   die Art
**many**   viele; **how ~**   wie viele; **too ~**   zu viele
**map**   die Landkarte, -n
**March**   der März
**market**   der Markt, ¨e; **indoor ~**   die Markthalle, -n
**marketplace**   der Marktplatz, ¨e
**marmalade**   die Marmelade, -n
**marriage**   die Heirat, -en
**married**   verheiratet
**marry: to ~, get married**   heiraten (hat geheiratet)
**mass**   die Masse, -n
**match**   das Spiel, -e
**materialistic**   konsumorientiert
**math**   die Mathematik; die Mathe
**matter: What's the ~?**   Was ist los?
**May**   der Mai
**may**   dürfen (hat gedurft); **that ~ well be**   das mag wohl sein
**maybe**   vielleicht
**maximal**   maximal

**me**   mich *(acc.)*; mir *(dat.)*; **- too!**   ich auch!
**meadow**   die Wiese, -n
**meal**   das Essen, -; **Have a good ~ *(at lunch).***   Mahlzeit.
**mean**   böse; **to ~**   meinen; bedeuten; **What does that ~?**   Was bedeutet das?
**meaning**   die Bedeutung, -en
**meanwhile**   inzwischen
**meat**   das Fleisch
**mechanic (auto)**   der Automechaniker, -/ die Automechanikerin, -nen
**medicine**   die Medizin; das Medikament, -e
**meet**   treffen (hat getroffen); kennen lernen (hat kennen gelernt)
**member**   das Mitglied, -er
**memorial**   das Mahnmal, -e *(selten:* -mäler); das Denkmal, ¨er; die Gedenkstätte, -n
**merchant**   der Kaufmann, ¨er/die Kauffrau, -en; *(pl.)* die Kaufleute
**merry**   lustig
**message**   die Nachricht, -en
**meter**   der Meter, -
**Mexican**   mexikanisch; **~ (person)**   der Mexikaner, -/die Mexikanerin, -nen
**microwave oven**   der Mikrowellenherd, -e
**middle**   die Mitte, -n
**midnight**   die Mitternacht
**milk**   die Milch
**million**   die Million, -en
**mineral water**   das Mineralwasser
**minor subject**   das Nebenfach, ¨er
**minute**   die Minute, -n; **(five) ~s after (one)**   (fünf) Minuten nach (eins); **(five) ~s to (two)**   (fünf) Minuten vor (zwei); **Just a ~ please!**   Einen Moment, bitte!
**miracle**   das Wunder, -
**mirror**   der Spiegel, -
**Miss**   das Fräulein, - *(for young girls only)*
**missing: to be ~**   fehlen (hat gefehlt)
**mix**   mischen (hat gemischt)
**modern**   modern
**mom**   die Mutti, -s
**moment**   der Moment, -e; **at the ~**   momentan; im Moment; zur Zeit
**monarchy**   die Monarchie, -n
**Monday**   der Montag

**money**   das Geld
**month**   der Monat, -e
**monument**   das Denkmal, ¨er
**mood**   die Stimmung, -en; **magical ~**   die Zauberstimmung
**more**   mehr; **no ~**   kein ... mehr; **~ and ~**   immer mehr; **~ or less**   mehr oder weniger
**morning**   der Morgen; **Good ~.**   Guten Morgen.; Morgen. **this ~**   heute Morgen
**mornings**   morgens
**mosque**   die Moschee, -n
**most**   meist-, am meisten; am liebsten; **at the ~**   höchstens; **~ of the time**   meistens
**mother**   die Mutter, ¨
**motivated**   motiviert
**motive**   das Motiv, -e
**motorcycle**   das Motorrad, ¨er
**mountain**   der Berg, -e; **~ climbing**   das Bergsteigen; **~ peak**   der Gipfel, -
**mouth**   der Mund, ¨er
**move**   ziehen (ist gezogen) nach; um·ziehen (ist umgezogen); **to ~ away**   weg·ziehen (ist weggezogen)
**movie**   der Film, -e; **~ star**   der Filmstar, -s; **~ theater**   das Kino, -s; **to make a ~**   einen Film drehen (hat gedreht)
**movies: to go to the ~**   ins Kino gehen
**Mr.**   (der) Herr
**Mrs.**   (die) Frau
**Ms.**   (die) Frau
**much**   viel; **how ~**   wie viel; **too ~**   zu viel
**multicultural**   multikulturell
**multiculturalism**   der Multikulturalismus
**museum**   das Museum, *pl.* Museen
**music**   die Musik; **~ conservatory**   die Musikhochschule, -n; **~ store**   das Musikgeschäft, -e
**musical**   musikalisch *(adj.);* das Musical, -s; **~ instrument**   das Musikinstrument, -e
**musician**   der Musiker, -/die Musikerin, -nen; der Musikant, [-en], -en
**must**   müssen (hat gemusst); **I ~ not**   ich darf nicht
**my**   mein
**mystery story**   der Krimi, -s

## N

**nail polish**   der Nagellack
**name**   der Name, [-n], -n; **by the ~ of** namens; **first ~**   der Vorname, [-n], -n; **last ~**   der Nachname, [-n], -n; **What is your ~?**   Wie heißen Sie?; **to ~**   nennen (hat genannt)
**namely**   nämlich
**narrow**   eng
**nationality**   die Nationalität, -en
**naturally**   klar; natürlich; selbstverständlich
**nature**   die Natur, -en
**Nazi**   der Nazi, -s; der Nationalsozialist, [-en], -en; **neo-~**   der Neo-Nazi, -s
**near**   bei + *dat.*
**nearer**   näher
**nearby**   in der Nähe, nah(e)
**necessary**   notwendig
**neck**   der Hals, ⁻e
**need**   brauchen (hat gebraucht); **I don't ~ to**   ich muss nicht
**neighborhood**   das Viertel, -
**nephew**   der Neffe, [-n], -n
**nervous**   nervös
**never**   nie, niemals
**nevertheless**   trotzdem
**new**   neu; **What's ~?**   Was gibt's Neues?; **~ building**   der Neubau, -ten; **~ Year's Day**   das Neujahr; **~ Year's Eve**   das Silvester
**news**   die Nachricht, -en
**newspaper**   die Zeitung, -en
**next**   nächst; **~ Saturday**   nächsten Samstag; **~ to**   neben + *dat.*
**nice**   nett; schön
**niece**   die Nichte, -n
**night**   die Nacht, ⁻e; **Good ~**   Gute Nacht.; **last ~**   gestern Abend; **~mare**   der Albtraum, ⁻e
**nighttime**   nächtlich *(adj.)*
**no**   nein; kein; nicht; **~ longer** nicht mehr; **~ more . . .**   kein . . . mehr
**Nobel Prize winner**   der Nobelpreisträger, -/die Nobelpreisträgerin, -nen
**nod**   nicken (hat genickt)
**none**   kein; **~ at all**   überhaupt kein
**nonsense**   der Unsinn
**noon**   der Mittag

**no one**   niemand
**north**   der Norden
**North Sea**   die Nordsee
**nose**   die Nase, -n
**not**   nicht; **isn't that so?**   nicht?; nicht wahr?; **~ at all**   gar nicht; **~ any**   kein; **~ only . . . but also . . .** nicht nur . . . sondern auch . . .; **~ necessarily**   nicht unbedingt
**note**   die Notiz, -en
**notebook**   das Heft, -e
**notes: lecture ~**   das Skript, -en
**nothing**   nichts; **~ special**   nichts Besonderes
**notice**   bemerken (hat bemerkt), merken (hat gemerkt), auf·fallen (ist aufgefallen) + *dat.*
**novel**   der Roman, -e; **crime ~**   der Kriminalroman, -e (der Krimi, -s)
**November**   der November
**now**   jetzt; nun; **~ and then**   ab und zu; hin und wieder
**nowhere**   nirgendwo
**number**   die Zahl, -en
**nurse**   der Krankenpfleger, -/die Krankenschwester, -n
**nursery school**   der Kindergarten, ⁻

## O

**object**   der Gegenstand, ⁻e
**obtain**   bekommen (hat bekommen); kriegen (hat gekriegt); erhalten (hat erhalten); besorgen (hat besorgt)
**occupation**   der Beruf, -e; **~ zone** die Besatzungszone, -n
**occupied: to be ~**   beschäftigt sein
**occupy**   besetzen (hat besetzt)
**occur**   statt·finden (hat stattgefunden); **to ~ to someone**   auf·fallen (hat aufgefallen) + *dat.*
**ocean**   der Ozean, -e; die See, -n
**o'clock: at (six) ~**   um (sechs) Uhr; **It's (five) ~.**   Es ist (fünf) Uhr.
**October**   der Oktober
**of**   von + *dat.;* **~ course**   klar
**offer**   an·bieten (hat angeboten); bieten (hat geboten)
**office**   das Büro, -s; (military) die Schreibstube, -n; **~ hours**   die Sprechstunde, -n; **doctor's ~**   die Praxis, *pl.* Praxen
**often**   oft (ö)

**oh**   ach, ah; aha; **~ I see**   ach so; **~ my**   o je; **~ well**   na ja
**okay**   O.K.; alles klar; okay; ganz gut; **It's (not) ~.**   Es geht (nicht).
**old**   alt (ä) **~ town**   die Altstadt, ⁻e
**Olympic: ~ Games**   die Olympiade, -n; **~ Stadium**   das Olympiastadion
**on**   an; auf + *acc./dat.;* **~ account of** wegen + *gen.;* **~ foot**   zu Fuß; **~ one hand**   einerseits; **~ (this) Sunday** am Sonntag; **~ Sundays**   sonntags
**once**   einmal, mal; **~ more**   noch einmal; **~ upon a time, there was . . .** Es war einmal . . .
**one**   *(pronoun)* man; **~ another** einander
**oneself**   selbst, selber
**only**   nur; erst; einzig
**open**   offen, geöffnet; **to ~** auf·machen (hat aufgemacht); eröffnen (hat eröffnet); auf·schließen (hat aufgeschlossen); öffnen (hat geöffnet)
**opening**   die Öffnung, -en; **~ time** die Öffnungszeit, -en
**opera**   die Oper, -n
**opinion**   die Meinung, -en; **to have an ~**   meinen (hat gemeint); **What's your ~?**   Was hältst du davon?; **in my ~**   meiner Meinung nach
**opportunity**   die Gelegenheit, -en
**or**   oder
**orally**   mündlich
**orange**   die Apfelsine, -n; die Orange, -n; **~ juice**   der Orangensaft; **~ (color)**   orange
**orchestra**   das Orchester; **~ conductor**   der Dirigent, [-en], -en/die Dirigentin, -nen
**order**   die Ordnung; die Reihenfolge, -n; **in ~**   in Ordnung; **in ~ to** um . . . zu; **to ~**   bestellen (hat bestellt); **to put in ~**   ordnen (hat geordnet)
**orderly**   der Krankenpfleger, -; ordentlich
**organization**   die Organisation, -en
**organize**   organisieren (hat organisiert)
**origin**   die Herkunft
**original**   ursprünglich; **~ text**   der Originaltext, -e
**originate**   entstehen (ist entstanden)

**other** ander- (-er, -es, -e); **the ~ way around** umgekehrt

**otherwise** sonst

**our** unser

**out of** aus + *dat.*

**outdoors** im Freien

**outgoing** gesellig, kontaktfreudig

**outside** draußen

**over** *(time)* vorbei; ~ *(position)* über + *acc./dat.;* **-filled** überfüllt; **~worked** überarbeitet

**overcast** bedeckt

**overhead: ~ projector** der Overheadprojektor, -s; **~ transparency** die Folie, -n

**oversee** übersehen (hat übersehen)

**own** *(adj.)* eigen; **to ~** besitzen (hat besessen)

### P

**pack** packen (hat gepackt); ein·packen (hat eingepackt)

**package** das Paket, -e

**page** die Seite, -n; das Blatt, ¨er

**pain** der Schmerz, -en

**painkiller** die Schmerztablette, -n

**palace** das Schloss, *pl.* Schlösser

**pale** blass

**pants** die Hose, -n

**pantyhose** die Strumpfhose, -n

**paper** das Papier; ~ **(theme, essay)** die Arbeit, -en; das Referat, -e

**paperback** das Taschenbuch, ¨er

**parade** der Umzug, ¨e

**paradise** das Paradies, -e

**pardon!** Entschuldigung!; **I beg your ~?** Wie bitte?

**parents** die Eltern *(pl.)*

**park** der Park, -s; **to ~** parken (hat geparkt)

**parka** der Anorak, -s

**parking: ~ fee** die Parkgebühr, -en; ~ **garage** das Parkhaus, ¨er; ~ **space, lot** der Parkplatz, ¨e; ~ **stub** der Parkschein, -e

**parliament** das Parlament; **German Federal ~** der Bundestag; **German ~ building** der Reichstag

**part** der Teil, -e; **in ~** zum Teil

**participate (in)** mit·machen (hat mitgemacht) bei + *dat.;* teil·nehmen (hat teilgenommen) an + *dat.*

**particular** besonder-

**particularly** besonders

**part-time worker** die Aushilfe

**party** die Party, -s; das Fest, -e; die Fete, -n; **political ~** die Partei, -en; **to give a ~** ein Fest geben; **to go to a ~** auf eine Party (Fete) gehen (ist gegangen)

**pass: mountain ~** der Pass, ¨e

**passenger** der Passagier, -e; ~ **vehicle** der Personenkraftwagen, -; der PKW, -s

**passionate** leidenschaftlich

**passive** passiv

**passport** der Pass, ¨e

**past** *(in clock time)* nach; die Vergangenheit

**pastry** das Gebäck; ~ **shop** die Konditorei, -en

**path** der Weg, -e

**patience** die Geduld

**pay** zahlen (hat gezahlt); **to ~ for** bezahlen (hat bezahlt); **to ~ attention** achten (hat geachtet), auf·passen (hat aufgepasst)

**pea** die Erbse, -n

**peak** der Gipfel, -

**pearl** die Perle, -n

**pedestrian** der Fußgänger, -/die Fußgängerin, -nen; ~ **zone** die Fußgängerzone, -n; der Fußgängerbereich, -e

**pen** der Kugelschreiber, -; der Kuli, -s; der Stift, -e

**pencil** der Bleistift, -e

**pension** die Rente, -n

**pensioner** der Rentner, -/die Rentnerin, -nen

**people** die Leute *(pl.);* die Menschen *(pl.);* man

**pepper** der Pfeffer

**per** pro

**percent** das Prozent, -e

**performance** die Verstellung, -en; die Aufführung, -en/

**perhaps** vielleicht

**period** der Punkt, -e

**permit** erlauben (hat erlaubt); lassen (hat gelassen)

**permitted** erlaubt; **to be ~** dürfen (hat gedurft)

**person** der Mensch, [-en], -en; die Person, -en

**personality** die Persönlichkeit, -en

**personnel: ~ department** die Personalabteilung, -en; **head of ~** der Personalchef, -s/die Personalchefin, -nen

**pharmaceutics** die Pharmazie

**pharmacist** der Apotheker, -/die Apothekerin, -nen

**pharmacy** die Apotheke, -n

**Philharmonic Orchestra (of Berlin)** die Philharmonie

**philosophy** die Philosophie

**photograph** das Bild, das Foto; **to ~** fotografieren (hat fotografiert)

**photographer** der Photograph, [-en], -en/die Photographin, -nen

**physics** die Physik

**piano** das Klavier, -e; ~ **lesson** die Klavierstunde, -n

**pick: to ~ out** aus·suchen (hat ausgesucht); aus·wählen (hat ausgewählt); **to ~ up** ab·holen (hat abgeholt); **to ~ up (mess)** auf·räumen (hat aufgeräumt)

**picture** das Bild, -er

**piece** das Stück, -e

**pink** rosa

**pity: what a ~** schade

**place** der Platz, ¨e; die Stelle, -n; der Ort, -e; **to my ~** zu mir; **at my ~** bei mir

**plan** der Plan, ¨e; die Planung, -en; **to ~** vor·haben (hat vorgehabt); planen (hat geplant); **What have you got planned?** Was hast du vor?

**planetarium** das Planetarium, *pl.* Planeterien

**plant** die Pflanze, -n; **to ~** pflanzen (hat gepflanzt)

**plastic** das Plastik

**plate** der Teller, -

**play** das Theaterstück, -e; das Drama, *pl.* Dramen; **to ~** spielen (hat gespielt)

**playground** der Spielplatz, ¨e

**plaza** der Platz, ¨e

**please** bitte; **to ~** gefallen (gefällt, hat gefallen) + *dat.*

**pleased: to be ~ (about)** sich freuen (hat sich gefreut) über + *acc.*

**pleasure** die Freude, -n; die Lust; das Vergnügen

**plot (of a story)** die Handlung, -en

**plump** mollig

**pocket** die Tasche, -n

**poem** das Gedicht, -e
**poet** der Dichter, -/die Dichterin, -nen; der Poet, [-en], -en/die Poetin, -nen
**point** der Punkt, -e; der Zweck, -e; **to ~ to** zeigen (hat gezeigt) auf + *acc.*; **There's no ~.** Das hat keinen Zweck.
**pointless: It's ~.** Das hat keinen Zweck.
**poison** das Gift, -e
**poisonous** giftig
**police** die Polizei
**political** politisch; **~ party** die Partei, -en **~ science** die Politikwissenschaft, -en
**politician** der Politiker, -/die Politikerin, -nen
**politics** die Politik, -en
**poor** arm (ä)
**popular** populär; beliebt; **~ music** die Popmusik
**pork** das Schweinefleisch
**portion** der Teil, -e; die Portion, -en
**portray** schildern (hat geschildert)
**position** die Stelle, -n; **in your ~** an deiner Stelle
**position (job)** die Stellung, -en; der Job, -s
**positive** positiv
**possible** möglich; **It's (not) ~.** Es geht (nicht).
**possibility** die Möglichkeit, -en
**postage stamp** die Briefmarke, -n
**postal code** die Postleitzahl, -en
**postcard** die Postkarte, -n
**poster** das Poster, -
**post office** die Post; **~ box** das Postfach, ¨-er; **to go to the ~** auf die Post gehen.
**pot** der Topf, ¨-e
**potato** die Kartoffel, -n
**poultry** das Geflügel
**pound** das Pfund, -e; **to ~** pochen (hat gepocht)
**power** die Macht, ¨-e
**practical** praktisch
**practice** üben (hat geübt); **to ~ a profession** einen Beruf aus·üben (hat ausgeübt); praktizieren (hat praktiziert)
**pray** beten (hat gebetet)
**prefer: I ~ to work.** Ich arbeite lieber.
**preparation** die Vorbereitung, -en
**prepare (for)** (sich) vor·bereiten (hat sich vorbereitet) auf + *acc.*
**preschool** der Kindergarten, ¨
**present (gift)** das Geschenk, -e; **~ (time)** die Gegenwart; **to ~ oneself** sich vor·stellen (hat sich vorgestellt)
**presentation** das Referat, -e; **to make a ~** ein Referat halten (hat gehalten)
**president** der Präsident, [-en], -en/die Präsidentin; -nen; **German Federal ~** der Bundespräsident, [-en], -en/die Bundespräsidentin, -nen
**pressure** der Druck
**prestige** das Prestige
**pretty** schön; (*for women*) hübsch; **~ pale** ganz schön blass
**price** der Preis, -e
**prince** der Prinz, [-en], -en; der Königssohn, ¨-e
**princess** die Prinzessin, -nen; die Königstochter, ¨
**printer** der Drucker, -
**private** privat; **~ bath** das Privatbad, ¨-er; **~ lesson** die Privatstunde, -n
**probably** wahrscheinlich; wohl
**problem** das Problem, -e; **without a ~** problemlos
**proclaim** proklamieren (hat proklamiert); aus·rufen (hat ausgerufen)
**produce** her·stellen (hat hergestellt), produzieren (hat produziert)
**product** das Produkt, -e
**profession** der Beruf, -e
**professional** der Profi, -s
**professor** der Professor, -en/die Professorin, -nen; **assistant ~** der Dozent, [-en] -en /die Dozentin, -nen
**program** das Programm, -e; **TV or radio ~** die Sendung, -en
**programmer** der Programmierer, -/die Programmiererin, -nen
**project** das Projekt, -e; das Unternehmen, -
**projection screen** die Leinwand, ¨-e
**promise** die Versprechung, -en; **to ~** versprechen (hat versprochen)
**protect** schützen (hat geschützt)
**proud** stolz
**Prussia** (das) Preußen
**psychiatry** die Psychiatrie
**psychology** die Psychologie
**pub** die Kneipe, -n; die Gaststätte, -n; die Bar, -s; das Lokal, -e; **student ~** die Studentenkneipe, -n
**public** öffentlich
**publish** veröffentlichen (hat veröffentlicht)
**pudding** der Pudding, -s
**pull** ziehen (hat gezogen)
**pullover** der Pulli, -s; der Pullover, -
**punctual** pünktlich
**pupil** der Schüler, -/die Schülerin, -nen
**pure** rein
**purple** lila
**purpose** der Zweck, -e
**purse** die Handtasche, -n
**Puss-in-Boots** der gestiefelte Kater
**put** *(horizontal)* legen (hat gelegt); *(vertical)* stellen (hat gestellt); *(seated)* setzen (hat gesetzt); *(hanging)* hängen (hat gehängt); *(inserted)* stecken (hat gesteckt); *(general)* tun (hat getan); **to ~ up overnight** unter·bringen (hat untergebracht); **to ~ together** zusammen·stellen (hat zusammengestellt); **to ~ on (clothing)** an·ziehen (hat angezogen); **to ~ on makeup** sich schminken (hat sich geschminkt)

## Q

**qualified** qualifiziert
**quality** die Qualität, -en; **personal ~** die Eigenschaft, -en
**quarrel** der Krach; der Streit; **to ~** sich streiten (hat sich gestritten) mit + *dat.*; Krach haben (hat gehabt)
**quarter** das Viertel, -; **~ after (five o'clock)** Viertel nach (fünf); **~ to (five o'clock)** Viertel vor (fünf)
**queen** die Königin, -nen
**question** die Frage, -n; **~ word** das Fragewort, ¨-er; **to ~** fragen (hat gefragt); **to ask a ~** eine Frage stellen (hat gestellt)
**questionable** fraglich
**quick** schnell
**quiet** die Ruhe; die Stille; ruhig; still
**quite** ziemlich

## R

**race** rennen (ist gerannt)
**racism** der Rassismus
**radio** das Radio, -s
**railroad** die Bahn, -en
**rain** der Regen; **to ~** regnen (hat geregnet); **~ shower** der Schauer, -
**raincoat** der Regenmantel, ¨
**raise: to ~** heben (hat gehoben); **to ~ children** erziehen (hat erzogen)
**Ramadan** der Ramadan
**range (kitchen)** der Herd, -e
**rank** der Rang, ¨e; die Stellung, -en
**rare** selten, rar
**rather** ziemlich; **(in opposition)** sondern; **~ than** lieber als
**rave; to ~ about** schwärmen (hat geschwärmt) von + *dat.*
**raw material** der Rohstoff, -e
**razor: electric ~** der Rasierapparat, -e
**reach** erreichen (hat erreicht)
**react** reagieren (hat reagiert)
**reaction** die Reaktion, -en
**read** lesen (hat gelesen)
**ready** bereit; fertig; **to get ~** sich vor·bereiten (hat sich vorbereitet)
**real** echt; richtig; wahr; **~ estate agent** der Makler, -/die Maklerin, -nen
**reality** die Wirklichkeit, -en
**really** wirklich; richtig; ganz; echt *(slang);* **~ neat** echt toll; ganz toll; **~ bad** ganz schlimm
**rear** der Hintern
**reason** der Grund, ¨e; **for that ~** deshalb; deswegen; aus diesem Grund
**reasonable** vernünftig; **~ (price)** günstig
**reasonably priced** preiswert
**receipt** die Quittung, -en
**receive** bekommen (hat bekommen)
**recently** vor kurzem; neulich
**reckon with** rechnen (hat gerechnet) mit + *dat.*
**recognize** erkennen (hat erkannt)
**recommend** empfehlen (hat empfohlen)
**recommendation** die Empfehlung, -en
**reconcile** sich versöhnen (hat sich versöhnt)

**record** die Platte, -n; **~ store** das Musikgeschäft, -e
**record player** der Plattenspieler, -
**recover (from)** sich erholen (hat sich erholt) (von + *dat*).
**recuperate (from)** sich erholen (hat sich erholt) von + *dat.*
**recycling** das Recycling
**red** rot (ö)
**refrigerator** der Kühlschrank, ¨e
**region** der Bereich, -e
**register** sich ein·schreiben (hat sich eingeschrieben)
**regulate** regeln (hat geregelt)
**rehearsal** die Probe, -n
**related** verwandt
**relative** der/die Verwandte *(noun decl. like adj.)*
**relatives** die Verwandtschaft
**relax** sich aus·ruhen (hat sich ausgeruht)
**relaxation** die Entspannung, -en
**relaxed** locker
**reliable** zuverlässig
**religious** fromm (ö); religiös
**remain** bleiben (ist geblieben)
**remaining** übrig
**remedy: home ~** das Hausmittel, -
**remember** sich erinnern (hat sich erinnert) an + *acc.*
**renovate** renovieren (hat renoviert)
**rent** die Miete, -n; **to ~** mieten (hat gemietet); **to ~ out** vermieten (hat vermietet)
**repair** reparieren (hat repariert); **~ person** der Mechaniker, -/die Mechanikerin, -nen
**repeat** wiederholen (hat wiederholt)
**report** der Bericht, -e; das Referat, -e; **to ~** berichten (hat berichtet); sich melden (hat sich gemeldet)
**reporter** der Reporter, -/die Reporterin, -nen
**representative** der/die Abgeordnete, -n *(noun decl. like adj.)*
**republic** die Republik, -en
**request** bitten (hat gebeten) um + *acc.;* erfordern (hat erfordert)
**resistance** der Widerstand
**resort** der Ferienort, -e
**resource** die Ressource, -n
**respect** der Respekt
**respectable** anständig

**respectfully** *(at end of a letter)* Hochachtungsvoll
**responsibility** die Verantwortung, -en
**responsible** verantwortlich; zuständig
**rest** der Rest, -e; **to ~** sich aus·ruhen (hat sich ausgeruht)
**restaurant** das Restaurant, -s; die Gaststätte, -n; **town hall ~** der Ratskeller, -
**result** das Resultat, -e; das Ergebnis, -se
**resume (CV)** der Lebenslauf, ¨e
**return** die Rückkehr; **to ~** zurück·fahren (ist zurückgefahren); zurück·gehen (ist zurückgegangen); zurück·kommen (ist zurückgekommen); wieder·kommen (ist wiedergekommen); zurück·kehren (ist zurückgekehrt); **to ~ something** (etwas) zurück·geben (hat zurückgegeben); zurück·nehmen (hat zurückgenommen)
**reunification** die Wiedervereinigung; die Union
**reveal** auf·decken (hat aufgedeckt)
**rice** der Reis
**rich** reich
**ride** die Fahrt, -en; **to ~ a bike** Rad fahren (ist Rad gefahren); **to ~ horseback** reiten (ist geritten)
**right** das Recht, -e; **Is it all ~ with you?** Ist es dir recht?; **to be ~** Recht haben; **that's ~** genau; richtig; **on/to the ~** rechts; **~ around the corner** gleich um die Ecke; **~?** nicht wahr?
**ring** der Ring, -e; **to ~** klingeln (hat geklingelt)
**rinse** spülen (hat gespült)
**risk** riskieren (hat riskiert)
**risky** riskant
**river** der Fluss, *pl.* Flüsse
**rock: ~ music** die Rockmusik; **~ musician** der Rockmusiker, -/die Rockmusikerin, -nen
**role** die Rolle, -n
**roll** das Brötchen, -; die Semmel, -n
**rollerblades** die Rollerblades *(pl.)*
**roll-top shutter** der Rollladen, ¨
**Roman** römisch
**romance novel** der Liebesroman, -e
**romantic** romantisch

**room** das Zimmer, -; der Raum, ¨e;
(**space**) der Platz, ¨e; **bathroom**
das Badezimmer, -; **bedroom** das
Schlafzimmer, -; **classroom** das
Klassenzimmer, -; **living ~** das
Wohnzimmer, -; **~mate** der Mitbewohner, -/die Mitbewohnerin, -nen
**~ number** die Zimmernummer, -n
**round** rund; die Runde, -n
**routine** die Routine, -n; der Alltag
**rubble** der Schutt
**rug** der Teppich, -e
**rule** die Regel, -n
**Rumpelstiltskin** Rumpelstilzchen
**run** laufen (ist gelaufen); rennen (ist
gerannt)
**running** das Joggen; das Jogging; das
Laufen
**Russia** (das) Russland
**Russian** russisch; **~ (language)**
(das) Russisch; **~ (person)** der
Russe, [-n], -n/die Russin, -nen

## S

**sack** die Tüte, -n
**sad** traurig
**safe** sicher
**safety** die Sicherheit, -en; **~ helmet**
der Sicherheitshelm, -e
**sail** segeln (ist gesegelt)
**salad** der Salat, -e
**salary** das Gehalt, ¨er; **~ expectation**
die Gehaltsvorstellung, -en
**salesperson** der Verkäufer, -/die
Verkäuferin, -nen
**salt** das Salz
**same** (der/das/die)selbe, gleich; **It's
all the ~ to me.** Das ist mir egal.; **at
the ~ time** gleichzeitig
**sandal** die Sandale, -n
**sandwich** das Brot, -e; das Butter-
brot, -e; das belegte Brot
**satisfied** zufrieden
**Saturday** der Samstag; der
Sonnabend
**Saturdays** samstags; sonnabends
**sausage** die Wurst, ¨e
**save** sparen (hat gespart)
**savings: ~ account** das Sparkanto,
-konten; **~ bank** die Sparkasse, -n
**say** sagen (hat gesagt); erzählen (hat
erzählt)
**scarf** der Schal, -s

**scene** die Szene, -n
**scenery** die Landschaft, -en
**schedule** der Stundenplan, ¨e
**school** die Schule, -n; **elementary ~**
die Grundschule, -n; **high ~**
(**non-college**) die Realschule, -n;
**college prep. high ~** das
Gymnasium, *pl.* Gymnasien;
**technical-vocational ~** die
Hauptschule, -n; **~ days** die
Schulzeit, -en
**science** die Wissenschaft, -en; die
Naturwissenschaft, -en
**scientific** wissenschaftlich
**scientist** der Wissenschaftler, -/die
Wissenschaftlerin, -nen
**score (in a game)** treffen (hat
getroffen)
**screen** die Leinwand, ¨e
**sea** die See, -n
**search** die Suche, -n; **to ~ for**
suchen (hat gesucht) nach + *dat.*
**season** die Jahreszeit, -en; (**sports**) **~**
die Saison, -s
**seat** der Platz, ¨e; **Is this ~ taken?**
Ist hier frei?; **to ~ oneself** sich setzen (hat sich gesetzt)
**secretary** der Sekretär, -e/ die
Sekretärin, -nen
**see** sehen (hat gesehen)
**seem** scheinen (hat geschienen)
**seldom** selten
**select** wählen (hat gewählt)
**selection** die Wahl; die Auswahl
**self (oneself, myself, itself, etc.)**
selbst, selber; sich; **~ -reliant**
selbstständig; **~ -assured** selbstsicher
**sell** verkaufen (hat verkauft)
**semester** das Semester, -; **~ break**
die Semesterferien *(pl.)*; **~ bus pass**
die Semesterkarte, -n; das Semesterticket, -s
**seminar** das Seminar, -e; **~ room**
der Seminarraum, ¨e; **~ report** die
Seminararbeit, -en
**send** schicken (hat geschickt);
senden (hat gesendet)
**sense** spüren (hat gespürt)
**sentence** der Satz, ¨e
**separate** trennen (hat getrennt);
spalten (hat gespaltet)
**September** der September
**sequence** die Reihenfolge, -n

**serious** ernst; **Are you ~?** Ist das
dein Ernst?
**serve** dienen (hat gedient)
**set** setzen (hat gesetzt); **to ~ the
table** den Tisch decken (hat
gedeckt); **to ~ off (on a trip)**
los·fahren (ist losgefahren)
**several** einige; mehrere, manche
**sexuality** die Sexualität
**shake** rütteln (hat gerüttelt); schütteln (hat geschüttelt); **to ~ hands**
die Hand schütteln; die Hand geben
(hat gegeben)
**shampoo** das Shampoo, -s; das
Haarwaschmittel, -; **to ~** (sich) die
Haare waschen (hat sich gewaschen)
**share** sich teilen (hat sich geteilt)
**shared** gemeinsam; **~ bathroom**
das Gemeinschaftsbad, ¨er; **~
kitchen** die Gemeinschaftsküche,
-n
**shave** (sich) rasieren (hat sich rasiert)
**shaver (electric)** der Rasierapparat,
-e
**she** sie
**shelf** das Regal, -e
**shine** scheinen (hat geschienen)
**ship** das Boot, -e; das Schiff, -e
**shirt** das Hemd, -en
**shock** der Schock, -s
**shoe** der Schuh, -e; **athletic ~** der
Turnschuh, -e
**shoot** schießen (hat geschossen)
**shop** das Geschäft, -e; der Laden, ¨;
**to ~** ein·kaufen (hat eingekauft)
**shopping: to go ~** ein·kaufen gehen
(ist einkaufen gegangen); **~ bag** die
Einkaufstasche, -n: die Einkaufstüte,
-n; die Tragetasche, -n; **~ basket**
der Einkaufskorb, ¨e; **~ center** das
Einkaufszentrum, *pl.* -zentren; **~ trip**
der Einkaufsbummel
**short** kurz (ü); **~ (people)** klein; **~
story** die Kurzgeschichte, -n
**shorts** die Shorts *(pl.)*
**should** sollen (hat gesollt)
**shoulder** die Schulter, -n
**show** zeigen (hat gezeigt)
**shower** die Dusche, -n; **~ room** der
Duschraum, ¨e; **to ~** (sich) duschen
(hat sich geduscht); unter die
Dusche gehen (ist gegangen); **rain ~**
der Schauer, -
**shy** schüchtern

**siblings**   die Geschwister (*pl.*)

**sick**   krank

**side**   die Seite, -n

**sight-seeing attraction**   die Sehenswürdigkeit, -en

**sign**   das Schild, -er; das Zeichen, -

**silence**   die Stille

**silver**   das Silber

**similar**   ähnlich; gleich

**simple**   einfach; schlicht

**simply**   einfach; bloß

**simultaneous**   gleichzeitig

**since**   seit (*prep.*); seitdem, da (*conj.*); ~ **when**   seit wann

**sing**   singen (hat gesungen)

**singer**   der Sänger, -/die Sängerin, -nen

**single**   ledig; einzeln; ~ **-family home** das Einfamilienhaus, ¨er; ~ **room** das Einzelzimmer, -

**sink**   das Waschbecken, -; **to ~** sinken (ist gesunken)

**sister**   die Schwester, -n

**sit**   sitzen (hat gesessen); **to ~ down** sich setzen (hat sich gesetzt)

**situated: to be ~**   liegen (hat gelegen)

**situation**   die Lage, -n; die Situation, -en

**size**   die Größe, -n

**skate: roller ~**   der Rollschuh, -e; **ice ~**   der Schlittschuh, -e; **in-line ~** der Rollerblade, -s: **to ice ~** Schlittschuh laufen (ist gelaufen); **to roller ~**   Rollschuh laufen (ist gelaufen)

**ski**   der Ski, -er; **to ~**   Ski laufen (ist Ski gelaufen); Ski fahren (ist Ski gefahren); ~ **boot**   der Skistiefel, -; ~ **chalet**   die Skihütte, -n; ~ **parka** der Skianorak, -s; ~ **run, track**   die Piste, -n; **cross-country ~ track**   die Langlaufloipe, -n

**skin**   die Haut; ~ **color**   die Hautfarbe, -n

**skirt**   der Rock, ¨e

**slam shut**   zu·knallen (hat zugeknallt)

**sled**   der Schlitten, -

**sleep**   schlafen (hat geschlafen); **to go to ~**   schlafen gehen (ist schlafen gegangen)

**sleigh**   der Schlitten, -; ~ **ride**   die Schlittenfahrt, -en

**slender**   schlank

**slice**   die Scheibe, -n

**slow**   langsam

**small**   klein

**smart**   intelligent; klug (ü)

**smell**   riechen (hat gerochen); stinken (hat gestunken)

**smile**   lächeln (hat gelächelt)

**smoke**   der Rauch; **to ~**   rauchen (hat geraucht)

**smooth**   glatt

**snow**   der Schnee; **powder ~**   der Pulverschnee; **to ~**   schneien (hat geschneit); ~ **-covered**   verschneit; **Snow White**   das Schneewittchen

**so**   so; also; **Isn't that ~?**   Nicht?; ~ **that**   damit; ~ **long.**   Tschüss.; **I believe ~.**   Ich glaube schon/ja.

**so-so**   so lala

**soap**   die Seife, -n; ~ **opera**   die Seifenoper, -n

**soccer**   der Fußball; ~ **field**   der Fußballplatz, ¨e

**sociable**   gesellig; kontaktfreudig

**society**   die Gesellschaft, -en

**sociology**   die Soziologie

**sock**   die Socke, -n

**socket: electric ~**   die Steckdose, -n

**sofa**   das Sofa, -s

**soft drink**   die Limonade, -n

**software**   die Software

**soldier**   der Soldat, [-en], -en/die Soldatin, -nen

**solution**   die Lösung, -en

**solve**   lösen (hat gelöst)

**some**   etwas; einige; manch (-er, -es, -e); **at ~ point**   irgendwann

**someone**   jemand; irgendjemand

**something**   etwas, was; irgendetwas; ~ **like that**   so was

**sometime**   irgendwann

**sometimes**   manchmal

**somewhat**   etwas; ziemlich

**son**   der Sohn, ¨e

**song**   das Lied, -er

**soon**   bald; **as ~ as**   sobald; wenn

**sorcerer**   der Zauberer, -

**sore: ~ muscle**   der Muskelkater, -

**sort**   die Art, -en; die Sorte, -n; **to ~** sortieren (hat sortiert)

**sorry: to be ~**   Leid tun + *dat.* (hat Leid getan); **I'm ~**   es tut mir Leid; ~ **I'm late.**   Entschuldige die Verspätung.

**sound**   klingen (hat geklungen); **That ~s good.**   Das klingt gut.; Das hört sich gut an.

**soup**   die Suppe, -n

**south**   der Süden; südlich; **South American**   südamerikanisch

**southwestern**   südwestlich

**souvenir**   das Andenken, -

**space**   der Platz, ¨e

**spaghetti**   die Spaghetti (*pl.*)

**Spain**   (das) Spanien

**Spanish**   spanisch; ~ **(language)** (das) Spanisch

**Spaniard**   der Spanier, -/die Spanierin, -nen

**speak**   reden (hat geredet); sprechen (hat gesprochen)

**spectator**   der Zuschauer, -/die Zuschauerin, -nen

**speechless**   sprachlos

**spell**   buchstabieren (hat buchstabiert); **How do you ~ that?**   Wie schreibt man das?

**spend (money)**   aus·geben (hat ausgegeben); **to ~ (time)** verbringen (hat verbracht)

**spite: in ~ of**   trotz + *gen.*

**splendid**   großartig

**spontaneity**   die Spontaneität

**spontaneous**   spontan

**spoon**   der Löffel, -

**sport**   der Sport; **to engage in sports**   Sport treiben (hat getrieben); ~ **coat**   der/das Sakko, -s; die Jacke, -n

**spring**   der Frühling, -e

**stadium**   das Stadion, *pl.* Stadien

**stage (theater)**   die Bühne, -n

**stair**   die Treppe, -n

**stairwell**   das Treppenhaus, ¨er

**stamp: postage ~**   die Briefmarke, -n

**stand**   der Kiosk, -s; der Stand, ¨e; **to ~**   stehen (hat gestanden); **to ~ up** auf·stehen (ist aufgestanden); **to ~/put upright**   stellen (hat gestellt)

**standing**   der Rang, ¨e

**standard German**   (das) Hochdeutsch

**stanza**   die Strophe, -n

**stare**   an·starren (hat angestarrt)

**start**   an·fangen (hat angefangen); beginnen (hat begonnen); **to ~ a conversation**   an·sprechen (hat angesprochen)

**state (in Germany)**   das Land, ¨er; das Bundesland, ¨er; ~ **(in the U.S.A.)**   der Staat, -en; ~ **exam**   das Staatsexamen, -

**state-owned**   staatlich

**stay**   der Aufenthalt, -e; **to ~** bleiben (ist geblieben)

**step**   die Treppe, -; **to ~**   treten (ist getreten)

**stepbrother**   der Stiefbruder, ¨

**stepdaughter**   die Stieftochter, ¨

**stepfather**   der Stiefvater, ¨

**stepmother**   die Stiefmutter, ¨

**stepsister**   die Stiefschwester, -n

**steps**   die Treppe, -n

**stereo system**   die Stereoanlage, -n

**stick**   stecken (hat gesteckt)

**stiff**   steif

**still**   still; die Stille; noch; immer noch; noch immer

**stomach**   der Bauch, ¨e

**stomachache**   die Bauchschmerzen *(pl.)*

**stop**   an·halten (hat angehalten); auf·hören (hat aufgehört); halten (hat gehalten); stehen·bleiben (ist stehengeblieben); **(bus) stop**   die Haltestelle, -n

**storage room**   der Abstellraum, ¨e

**store**   das Geschäft, -e; der Laden, ¨

**storm**   der Sturm, ¨e

**story**   die Geschichte, -n; die Erzählung, -en

**stove**   der Herd, -e

**straight**   gerade; **~ ahead**   geradeaus; **~ hair**   glatte Haare

**straighten up**   auf·räumen (hat aufgeräumt)

**strange**   seltsam

**street**   die Straße, -n

**streetcar**   die Straßenbahn, -en

**stress**   der Stress; **to ~ (feel stressed)** stressen (hat gestresst); **stressed** gestresst; **stressful** stressig

**strict**   streng

**stroll**   der Spaziergang, ¨e; der Bummel, -; **to ~**   spazieren gehen (ist spazieren gegangen); bummeln (ist gebummelt)

**structure**   die Struktur, -en

**strong**   stark (ä)

**student**   der Student, [en], -en/die Studentin, -nen; **~ (university-level)** der/die Studierende, -n *(noun decl. like adj.);* **fellow ~**   der Kommilitone, [-n], -n/die Kommilitonin, -nen; **~ ID**   der Studentenausweis, -e;

**~ room**   das Studentenzimmer, -; die Studentenbude, -n

**student life**   das Studentenleben

**studies**   das Studium, *pl.* Studien

**study**   studieren (hat studiert); lernen (hat gelernt); **~ group**   die Arbeitsgruppe, -n; **minor area of ~** das Nebenfach, ¨er

**stuff**   das Zeug

**stupid**   dumm (ü), doof

**subject (academic)**   das Fach, ¨er; das Studienfach, ¨er; **major ~**   das Hauptfach, ¨er; **minor ~**   das Nebenfach, ¨er

**subway**   die U-Bahn, -en

**successful**   erfolgreich

**such**   solch (-er, -es, -e); **~ a**   so ein

**suddenly**   plötzlich

**suggest**   vor·schlagen (hat vorgeschlagen)

**suggestion**   der Vorschlag, ¨e; der Tipp, -s

**suit (man's)**   der Anzug, ¨e; **(woman's) ~**   das Kostüm, -e; **to ~** passen (hat gepasst) + *dat.;* stehen (hat gestanden) + *dat.*

**suitcase**   der Koffer, -

**summer**   der Sommer, -; **~ cottage** das Sommerhäuschen, -

**sun**   die Sonne, -n

**Sunday**   der Sonntag, -e

**Sundays**   sonntags

**sunglasses**   die Sonnenbrille, -n

**sunny**   sonnig

**supermarket**   der Supermarkt, ¨e

**supper**   das Abendessen; das Abendbrot; **for ~**   zum Abendessen; **to have ~**   zu Abend essen

**supposed: to be ~ to**   sollen (hat gesollt)

**sure**   sicher; bestimmt; **(agreement) ~!**   Natürlich!; Klar!

**surf**   surfen (hat gesurft)

**surprise**   überraschen (hat überrascht)

**surprising(ly)**   überraschend

**suspect: to ~**   ahnen (hat geahnt)

**suspense: to be in ~**   gespannt sein

**sweater**   der Pulli, -s; der Pullover, -

**swim**   schwimmen (ist geschwommen); baden (hat gebadet)

**swimming pool: indoor ~**   das Hallenbad, ¨er; **outdoor ~**   das Frei(schwimm)bad, ¨er

**swimming trunks**   die Badehose, -n

**swim suit**   der Badeanzug, ¨e

**Swiss**   *(adj.)* schweizer; **~ (person)** der Schweizer, -/die Schweizerin, -nen

**switch (to change)**   wechseln (hat gewechselt)

**Switzerland**   die Schweiz

**symbol**   das Wahrzeichen, -; das Symbol, -e

**synagogue**   die Synagoge, -n

---

**T**

**table**   der Tisch, -e

**take**   nehmen (hat genommen); **to ~ along**   mit·nehmen (hat mitgenommen); **to ~ care of**   erledigen (hat erledigt); bewerkstelligen (hat bewerkstelligt); **to ~ off**   aus·ziehen (hat ausgezogen); **to ~ place, occur** statt·finden (hat stattgefunden)

**talented**   begabt; talentiert

**talk**   sprechen (hat gesprochen); reden (hat geredet); diskutieren (hat diskutiert); *(dialect)* schwätzen (hat geschwätzt); **to ~ about**   reden/sprechen/diskutieren über + *acc.;* **to ~ to**   sprechen (etc.) mit + *dat.;* **to ~ over**   besprechen (hat besprochen)

**tall**   groß (ö); hoch (höher)

**tardiness**   die Verspätung, -en

**target**   das Ziel, -e

**task**   die Aufgabe, -n

**taste**   der Geschmack; **to ~** schmecken (hat geschmeckt)

**tasty**   lecker

**tavern**   die Wirtschaft, -en

**taxi**   das Taxi, -s

**tea**   der Tee, -s

**teach**   unterrichten (hat unterrichtet); lehren (hat gelehrt)

**teacher**   der Lehrer, -/die Lehrerin, -nen; **~'s degree**   das Staatsexamen, -

**team**   die Mannschaft, -en; das Team, -s

**telephone**   das Telefon, -e; **to ~** telefonieren (hat telefoniert); an·rufen (hat angerufen); **~ booth** die Telefonzelle, -n; **by ~**   telefonisch; **~ number**   die Telefonnummer, -n

**televise**   übertragen (hat übertragen)

**television**   das Fernsehen; **~ set** der Fernseher, -; **color ~**   der Farbfernseher; **~ program**   die Fernsehsendung, -en; **to watch ~** fern·sehen (hat ferngesehen)

**tell**   sagen (hat gesagt); **to ~ (a story)** erzählen (hat erzählt); **to ~ about** erzählen von + *dat.*

**temperature**   die Temperatur, -en; **the ~ is (ten) degrees**   die Temperatur liegt um (zehn) Grad

**tennis**   das Tennis; **~ ball**   der Tennisball, ¨e; **~ racket**   der Tennisschläger, -; **~ shoe**   der Tennisschuh, -e

**tent**   das Zelt, -e

**terrace**   die Terrasse, -n

**terrible**   schlimm; furchtbar; schrecklich

**test**   die Prüfung, -en; **to ~**   prüfen (hat geprüft); überprüfen (hat überprüft); **to take a ~**   eine Prüfung schreiben (hat geschrieben)

**than**   als

**thank**   danken (hat gedankt) + *dat.* (+ für + *acc.*)

**thanks**   danke; **a lot!**   danke schön; vielen Dank

**that**   dass; jen- (-er, -es, -e); **~'s why** deshalb; deswegen; **~ is to say**   das heißt (d.h.)

**the**   der; das; die; die (*pl.*)

**theater**   das Theater, -; das Schauspielhaus, ¨er; **to go to the ~**   ins Theater gehen; **~ play**   das Theaterstück, -e

**their**   ihr

**them**   sie (*acc.*); ihnen (*dat.*)

**theme**   das Thema, *pl.* Themen

**then**   dann; da; damals; (*particle*) denn

**theory**   die Theorie, -n

**there**   da; dort; hin; dahin; **over ~** dort drüben; **~ is/are**   es gibt (hat gegeben)

**therefore**   also; deshalb; daher; darum; deswegen

**these**   diese

**they**   sie

**thick**   dick

**thin**   dünn, schlank

**thing**   das Ding, -e; die Sache, -n

**think**   denken (hat gedacht); meinen (hat gemeint); glauben (hat

geglaubt); **to ~ about**   denken an + *acc.;* **to ~ of**   halten (hat gehalten) von + *dat.*/für + *acc.;* **to ~ over** sich überlegen (hat sich überlegt); **to ~ something over**   nach·denken (hat nachgedacht); **to ~ that**   finden (hat gefunden); **What do you ~?** Was meinst du?

**third**   das Drittel, -; dritt-

**thirsty**   durstig; **to be ~**   Durst haben

**this**   dies (-er, -es, -e); **~ morning** heute Morgen; **~ afternoon**   heute Nachmittag; **~ evening**   heute Abend

**thorough**   gründlich

**throat**   der Hals, ¨e; **to have a sore ~** Halsschmerzen haben (hat gehabt)

**through**   durch

**throw**   werfen (hat geworfen); **to ~ away**   weg·werfen (hat weggeworfen)

**thunder**   donnern (es donnert, es hat gedonnert)

**Thursday**   der Donnerstag

**thus**   also

**ticket**   die Karte, -n; **airline ~**   der Flugschein, -e; das Flugticket, -s

**tie (necktie)**   die Krawatte, -n

**time**   die Zeit, -en; das Mal, -e; **(clocktime)**   die Uhr; **at that ~** damals; **at the same ~**   zur gleichen Zeit; **for a long ~**   lange; **for the first ~**   zum ersten Mal; **What ~ is it?** Wie viel Uhr ist es?/Wie spät ist es?; **At what ~?**   Um wie viel Uhr?; **~ line** die Zeittafel, -n; **to have ~**   frei haben (hat gehabt)

**timely**   hochaktuell

**times**   mal; **[three] ~**   [drei]mal

**tip**   das Trinkgeld, -er

**tired**   müde; **dead-~**   todmüde

**to**   an; auf, in; nach; zu

**today**   heute; **What day is it ~?** Welcher Tag ist heute?

**toe**   der Zeh, -en

**together**   zusammen; gemeinsam

**toilet**   die Toilette, -n; das WC, -s; das Klo, -s (*colloq.*); **to go to the ~**   auf die Toilette/aufs Klo gehen (ist gegangen)

**toiletry**   der Toilettenartikel, -

**tolerable**   erträglich

**tolerant**   tolerant

**tolerate**   ertragen (hat ertragen)

**tomato**   die Tomate, -n

**tomorrow**   morgen; **~ morning** morgen früh; **~ afternoon** morgen Nachmittag; **~ evening** morgen Abend; **day after ~** übermorgen

**tonight**   heute Abend

**tongue**   die Zunge, -n

**too**   zu; **me ~**   ich auch; **~ bad** schade; **~ little**   zu wenig; **~ many** zu viele; **~ much**   zu viel

**tooth**   der Zahn, ¨e

**toothache**   die Zahnschmerzen (*pl.*)

**toothbrush**   die Zahnbürste, -n

**toothpaste**   die Zahnpasta, -pasten

**topic**   das Thema, *pl.* Themen

**tour**   die Tour, -en; **~ guide**   der Reiseleiter, -/die Reiseleiterin, -nen; der Fremdenführer, -/die Fremdenführerin, -nen

**tourism**   der Tourismus; der Fremdenverkehr

**tourist**   der Tourist, [-en], -en/die Touristin, -nen; **~ office**   das Fremdenverkehrsbüro, -s; der Verkehrsverein, -e

**towel (bath)**   das Badetuch, ¨er

**tower**   der Turm, ¨e

**town hall**   das Rathaus, ¨er; **~ restaurant**   der Ratskeller, -

**track (for skiing)**   die Piste, -n; **to track**   nach·spüren (hat nachgespürt)

**traffic**   der Verkehr; **~ light**   die Ampel, -n; **~ regulation**   die Verkehrsregel, -n; **~ sign**   das Verkehrsschild, -er; das Verkehrszeichen, -

**train**   der Zug, ¨e; die Bahn -en; **~ station**   der Bahnhof, ¨e; **main ~ station**   der Hauptbahnhof, ¨e; **~ track** die Schiene, -n; das Gleis, -e

**trait**   die Eigenschaft, -en

**transfer**   überweisen (hat überwiesen)

**transformation**   der Wandel

**translate**   übersetzen (hat übersetzt)

**translator**   der Übersetzer, -/die Übersetzerin, -nen

**transportation**   der Verkehr; **means of ~**   das Verkehrsmittel, -

**travel**   fahren (ist gefahren); reisen (ist gereist); **~ by train**   (mit der)

Bahn fahren (ist gefahren); ~ **agency** das Reisebüro, -s; das Reiseun-ternehmen, -; ~ **group leader** der Reiseleiter, -/die Reiseleiterin, -nen

**treasure** der Schatz, ⸚e

**tree** der Baum, ⸚e

**treaty** das Abkommen, -

**trifle** die Kleinigkeit, -en

**trip** die Reise, -n; die Fahrt, -en; die Tour, -en; **bike ~** die Radtour, -en; **to take a ~** verreisen (ist verreist)

**truck** der Lastwagen, -; der LKW, -s

**trunk** der Kofferraum, ⸚e

**true** wahr; **that's (not) ~** das stimmt (nicht)

**trust** das Vertrauen; **to ~** vertrauen (hat vertraut)

**truth** die Wahrheit

**try** versuchen (hat versucht); probieren (hat probiert); **to ~ on** an·probieren (hat anprobiert)

**T-shirt** das T-Shirt, -s

**Tuesday** der Dienstag

**tunnel** der Tunnel, -s

**Turk** der Türke, [-n], -n/die Türkin, -nen

**Turkish** türkisch

**Turkey** die Türkei

**turkey** die Pute, -n

**turn** ab·biegen (ist abgebogen); wenden (hat gewendet); **to ~ around** (sich) um·drehen (hat sich umgedreht); **to ~ in (a paper)** ab·geben (hat abgegeben); **to ~ on** an·drehen (hat angedreht); **to ~ off** aus·machen (hat ausgemacht)

**turn, turning** die Wende

**TV** das Fernsehen; **~ set** der Fernseher, -; **~ program** die Fernsehsendung, -en

**twice** zweimal

**type** die Art, -en; **to ~** tippen (hat getippt)

### U

**ugly** hässlich

**umbrella** der Regenschirm, -e; der Schirm, -e

**umpteen times** zigmal, x-mal

**unathletic** unsportlich

**unattractive** unattraktiv

**unbelievable** unglaublich

**uncle** der Onkel, -

**uncreative** einfallslos

**under** unter; **to keep ~ lock and key** unter Verschluss halten (hat gehalten)

**underpaid** unterbezahlt

**understand** verstehen (hat verstanden)

**understanding** das Verständnis; **international ~** die Völkerver-ständigung

**understood: to make oneself ~** sich verständlich machen (hat sich verständlich gemacht)

**undertaking** das Unternehmen, -

**underway** unterwegs

**underwear** die Unterwäsche

**undoubtedly** bestimmt

**undress** (sich) aus·ziehen (hat ausgezogen)

**unemployed** arbeitslos

**unfortunately** leider

**unfriendly** unfreundlich

**unhappy** unglücklich

**unification** die Vereinigung

**unified** vereinigt; vereint

**unique** einmalig

**unity** die Einheit

**university** die Universität, -en; die Uni, -s; die Hochschule, -n; **to attend a ~** an/auf die Universität gehen; studieren (hat studiert); **at the ~** an/auf der Universität

**unlikable** unsympathisch

**unlock** auf·schließen (hat aufgeschlossen)

**unmusical** unmusikalisch

**unpaid** unbezahlt

**unsure** unsicher

**until** bis; **~ now** bisher; **~ later** bis später; tschüss; bis dann; bis bald

**up: ~ to** bis zu; **~ front** da vorne; **What's ~?** Was gibt's?

**uprising** der Aufstand, ⸚e

**urgent** dringend; dringlich

**U.S.A.** die USA (pl.); die Vereinigten Staaten von Amerika; **from the ~** aus den USA

**us** uns (acc. & dat.)

**use** benutzen (hat benutzt); gebrauchen (hat gebraucht); verwenden (hat verwendet);

**to ~ up** verbrauchen (hat verbraucht)

**usual** üblich

**usually** meistens; gewöhnlich

**utensil** das Gerät, -e

### V

**vacation** der Urlaub; die Ferien (pl.); **~ trip** die Ferienreise, -n; **on/ during ~** in Urlaub/in den Ferien; **to go on ~** in Urlaub/in die Ferien fahren (ist gefahren); Urlaub nehmen (hat genommen); **~ home** die Ferienwohnung, -en; **ready for a ~** ferienreif

**vacuum** der Staubsauger, -; **to ~** staub·saugen (hat gestaub-saugt)

**valley** das Tal, ⸚er

**value** der Stellenwert, -e

**vegetable** das Gemüse, -

**vending machine** der Automat, [-en], -en

**very** sehr; ganz

**veterinarian** der Tierarzt, ⸚e/die Tierärztin, -nen

**vice versa** umgekehrt

**vicinity** die Nähe; **in the ~** in der Nähe

**victor** die Siegermacht, ⸚e

**video** das Video, -s; **~ camera** die Videokamera, -s; **~ game** das Videospiel, -e; **~ recorder** der Videorecorder, -; **~ store** der Videoverleih, -e

**view** die Aussicht, -en

**village** das Dorf, ⸚er

**violence** die Gewalt

**visible** sichtbar

**visit** der Besuch, -e; **to ~** besuchen (hat besucht); **to ~ (a museum, etc.)** besichtigen (hat besichtigt)

**volleyball** der Volleyball

**vomit** sich übergeben (hat sich übergeben); kotzen (hat gekotzt) (colloq.)

**vote** die Wahl, -en; **to ~** wählen (hat gewählt)

**voter** der Wähler, -/die Wählerin, -nen

## W

**wage rate**   der Tarif, -e

**wait**   die Wartezeit, -en; **to ~**   warten (hat gewartet); **to ~ for**   warten (hat gewartet) auf + *acc.*

**waiting period**   die Wartezeit, -en

**waiter/waitress**   der Kellner, -/die Kellnerin, -nen; **Oh, ~!**   Herr Ober! Fräulein! Frau Ober!

**wake up**   auf·wachen (ist aufgewacht)

**walk**   der Spaziergang, ̈e; **to ~** laufen (ist gelaufen); **to take a ~** einen Spaziergang machen; **to go for a ~**   spazieren gehen (ist spazieren gegangen)

**wall**   die Wand, ̈e; **~ (exterior)**   die Mauer, -n

**wallet**   das Portmonee, -s

**want (to)**   wollen (hat gewollt); Lust haben (hat gehabt)

**war**   der Krieg, -e; **(First, Second) World ~**   der (Erste, Zweite) Weltkrieg, -e; **Cold ~**   der Kalte Krieg

**wardrobe**   der Kleiderschrank, ̈e

**warm**   warm (ä)

**warn**   warnen (hat gewarnt)

**wash**   die Wäsche; **to ~**   (sich) waschen (hat gewaschen); **to ~ dishes**   ab·waschen (hat abgewaschen); Geschirr spülen (hat gespült)

**washing machine**   die Waschmaschine, -n

**wastepaper basket**   der Papierkorb, ̈e

**watch**   die Armbanduhr, -en; **to ~** an·sehen (hat angesehen); schauen (hat geschaut); **to ~ TV**   fern·sehen (hat ferngesehen); **to ~ out** auf·passen (hat aufgepasst)

**water**   das Wasser; **~ sports**   der Wassersport; **~ tower**   der Wasserturm, ̈e; **mineral ~**   das Mineralwasser; **to ~ ski**   Wasserski fahren (ist gefahren)

**wavy**   wellig

**way**   der Weg, -e; die Art; **on the ~** auf dem Weg; **this ~**   so; auf diese Weise

**weak**   schwach (ä)

**wear**   tragen (hat getragen)

**weather**   das Wetter; **~ map**   die Wetterkarte, -n; **~ report**   der Wetterbericht, -e

**Website**   die Website, -s

**wedding**   die Hochzeit, -en

**Wednesday**   der Mittwoch

**week**   die Woche, -n; **a ~ from today** heute in acht Tagen

**weekday**   der Wochentag, -e

**weekend**   das Wochenende; **on the ~** am Wochenende

**weightlifting**   das Gewichtheben

**welcome**   das Willkommen; **you're ~** bitte (sehr)

**well**   gut; wohl; **~?**   na?; **I'm not ~.** Ich fühle mich nicht wohl.; **to get ~** sich erholen (hat sicherholt); **Get ~!** Gute Besserung!; **~ (interjection)** Na!; Nun!; **~ now, oh ~**   na; naja

**well-known**   bekannt

**west**   der Westen

**we**   wir

**wet**   nass (a/ä)

**what**   was; **~ kind (of), ~ a**   was für (ein); **What?**   Wie bitte?

**when**   wann; wenn; als

**whenever**   immer wenn; sooft

**where**   wo; **~ (to)**   wohin; **~ do you come from?**   Woher kommst du?

**whether**   ob

**which**   welch (-er, -es, -e)

**while**   die Weile, -n; **in a ~**   in einer Weile; während

**white**   weiß

**who?**   wer?; **~ is that?**   Wer ist das?

**whole**   ganz

**whom**   wen *(acc.);*   wem *(dat.)*

**whose**   dessen; **~?**   wessen?

**why**   warum, wieso, weshalb; **that's ~** daher; deswegen; deshalb

**wife**   die Frau, -en

**win**   siegen (hat gesiegt); gewinnen (hat gewonnen)

**wind**   der Wind, -e

**window**   das Fenster, -

**windy**   windig

**wine**   der Wein, -e

**winter**   der Winter, -; **~ sports**   der Wintersport

**wish**   der Wunsch, ̈e; **to ~**   wünschen (hat gewünscht); **I ~ I had . . .** Ich wünschte/wollte, ich hätte . . .

**witch**   die Hexe, -n

**with**   mit; **~ it**   damit; **to live ~ a family**   bei einer Familie wohnen

**withdraw (money)**   ab·heben (hat abgehoben)

**without**   ohne

**woman**   die Frau, -en

**wonder**   das Wunder, -; **I ~ if . . .**   Ich frage mich, ob . . .

**wonderful**   wunderbar

**woods**   der Wald, ̈er

**word**   das Wort, ̈er

**work**   die Arbeit, -en; **to ~**   arbeiten (hat gearbeitet); **to ~ part time** jobben (hat gejobbt); **It doesn't ~.** Es geht nicht., Es funktioniert nicht.; **to ~ out all right**   klappen (hat geklappt); **~ experience**   die Arbeitserfahrung, -en; **~ environment**   das Arbeitsklima; **~ place** der Arbeitsplatz, ̈e; **~ quota**   die Arbeitsnorm, -en

**workbook**   das Arbeitsbuch, ̈er

**worker**   der Arbeiter, -/die Arbeiterin, -nen; der Arbeitnehmer, -/die Arbeitnehmerin, -nen

**workroom**   das Arbeitszimmer, -

**world**   die Welt, -en; **~-famous** weltberühmt; **~ war**   der Weltkrieg, -e

**worry**   die Sorge, -n; **to ~ about** sich Sorgen machen (hat gemacht) um + *acc.;* **Don't ~.**   Mach dir keine Sorgen.

**worth**   der Wert; wert; **to be ~ it** sich lohnen (hat sich gelohnt)

**worthwhile**   wert

**would**   würde; **~ like**   möchte; **I ~ be**   ich wäre; **I ~ have**   ich hätte; **That ~ be . . .**   Das wäre . . .

**wound**   verwunden (hat verwundet)

**wow**   Mensch!

**write**   schreiben (hat geschrieben); **to ~ to**   schreiben (hat geschrieben) an + *acc.;* **to ~ down**   auf·schreiben (hat aufgeschrieben)

**writer**   der Schriftsteller, -/die Schriftstellerin, -nen; der Autor, -en/die Autorin, -nen

**written** *(adj.)*   schriftlich

**wrong**   falsch; **What's ~?**   Was ist los?; **What is ~ with you?**   Was hast du?

**xenophobia**   die Ausländerfeindlichkeit

**year**   das Jahr, -e; **for ~s**   seit Jahren
**yearly**   jährlich
**yellow**   gelb
**yes**   ja; *(for emphasis)*   doch
**yesterday**   gestern

**yet**   noch; schon; **not ~**   noch nicht
**Yiddish**   das Jiddisch
**yogurt**   der/das Joghurt
**you** *(informal sing.)*   du *(nom.);* dich
  *(acc.);* dir *(dat.); (formal sing. & pl.)*
  Sie *(nom. & acc.);* Ihnen *(dat.);* ~
  **guys** *(informal pl.)*   ihr *(nom.);* euch
  *(acc. & dat.);* **You're absolutely right.**
  Du hast vollkommen Recht.
**young**   jung; **~ girl**   das Fräulein
**your** *(informal sing.)* dein; *(informal
  pl.)* euer; *(format sing. & pl.)*   Ihr

**youth**   die Jugend; der/die
  Jugendliche *(noun decl. like adj.);* ~
  **hostel**   die Jugendherberge, -n;
  **budget ~ hotel**   das Jugendhotel,
  -s; ~ **literature**   die Jugendliteratur

**Z**

**zero**   die Null, -en; null
**Zip code**   die Postleitzahl, -en

# Index

This index includes grammar topics, topics from the **Wissenswerte Vokabeln, Sprache im Alltag, Brennpunkt Kultur, Deutsch im Beruf,** and common communicative functions. References to student annotations are indicated as [SA].

**R-66**

# Permissions and Credits

The authors and editors of the second edition of *Vorsprung* would like to thank the following for their generous permission to use copyrighted material.

## Texts

**Deutsch im Beruf 1:** p. 113: Pier 39, San Francisco; p. 114 (*left*): Blazing Saddles Bike Rentals, San Francisco; p. 114 (*top right*): Cliff House, San Francisco; p. 114 (*bottom right*) Amtrak and Gray Line, San Francisco.

**Kapitel 4:** p. 136: Auszüge aus der Broschüre "Sicherheitsinfo Nr. 8: Fahrrad fahren," herausgegeben im Auftrage des Bundesministeriums für Verkehr von der Bundesanstalt für Straßenwesen, Bergisch Gladbach.

**Kapitel 5:** p. 178: The administrators of *crazy-board.net* and *freundschafts.net*.

**Kapitel 6:** pp. 215–216: Bastian Berkner, Michaela Chirila, Julia Dreja und Jenni Zwick, "Integration und Multikulturelles Leben an der FH: Eine Bestandsaufnahme" 10. Januar 2003. *www.campusmagazin.de*, Studiengang Online-Journalismus, Fachhochschule Darmstadt.

**Kapitel 7:** pp. 265–267: Carin Pawlak und Stefan Pielow, "Die Entdeckung des Benjamin Lauth," **FOCUS** 09/03 vom 24. 02. 2003.

**Kapitel 8:** pp. 308–309: Nikola Sellmair, "Die beste Uni für mich," **STERN**-Magazin, 16/2002, Germany.

**Kapitel 9:** pp. 350–351: Online texts for "Wien: Treffen Sie den guten Ton. Opernhäuser. Konzertsäle. Auf den Spuren weltberühmter Musiker." © Wien-Tourismus / Vienna Tourist Board.

**Deutsch im Beruf 2:** p. 379: Global Competence Forum, Tübingen.

**Kapitel 10:** pp. 406–407: Kur- und Verkehrsverein Braunwald for "Braunwald: Ein Wintermärchen … hoch über dem Alltag."

**Kapitel 11:** pp. 457–458: Zeitbild-Verlag GmbH, Bonn und München, for the model timeline "Unterrichtsprojekt Metropole Berlin," December 1990.

**Kapitel 12:** pp. 487–488: Sprachinstitut Treffpunkt *www.deutschkurse.com*, Alexandra von Rohr, "Warum Deutsch lernen?", April 2005.

## Photos

**Kapitel 1:** p. 1: Stuart Cohen; p. 13: Ullsteinbild/The Granger Collection, NY; p. 18: J. Douglas Guy; p. 19: Stuart Cohen; p. 20: Ullsteinbild/The Granger Collection, NY; p. 22 (*top*): David R. Frazier Photolibrary; p. 22 (*bottom*): Ullsteinbild/The Granger Collection, NY; p. 32 (*left*): dpa/ipol; p. 32 (*right*): Ron Sachs/Corbis.

**Kapitel 2:** p. 38: Martin Brockhoff; p. 45: UPI/Bettmann/Corbis.

**Kapitel 3:** p. 74: Stuart Cohen; p. 80: Ulrike Welsch; p. 90: David R. Frazier Photolibrary; p. 107 (*left*): Kathy Squires; p. 107 (*right*): David R. Frazier Photolibrary.

**Kapitel 4:** p. 115: Ullsteinbild/The Granger Collection, NY; p. 121: J. Douglas Guy; pp. 138 & 143: Ullsteinbild/The Granger Collection, NY; p. 152: J. Douglas Guy.

**Kapitel 5:** p. 157: Ullsteinbild/The Granger Collection, NY; p. 163: Ulrike Welsch; p. 173 (*top*): David R. Frazier Photolibrary; p. 173 (*bottom*): Kathy Squires; p. 174: Ulrike Welsch; p. 180: David R. Frazier Photolibrary.

**Kapitel 6:** p. 196: H. Mark Weidman; p. 210: J. Douglas Guy; pp. 215 & 216: *campusmagazin.de*; pp. 217 & 233: Ulrike Welsch.

**Literarisches Deutsch 1:** p. 236: Bettmann/Corbis.

**Kapitel 7:** p. 238: David R. Frazier Photolibrary; pp. 243, 261, 265: Ullsteinbild/The Granger Collection, NY; p. 268: J. Douglas Guy.

**Kapitel 8:** p. 284: David R. Frazier Photolibrary; pp. 290, 309, 311: Ullsteinbild/The Granger Collection, NY.

**Kapitel 9:** pp. 331 & 337: J. Douglas Guy; p. 347 (*left*): Bettmann/Corbis; p. 347 (*top right*): Planet-Vienna.com; p. 347 (*bottom right*): Roger Antrobus/Corbis; p. 350: Ullsteinbild/The Granger Collection, NY; p. 351 (*left*): Jim Zuckerman/Corbis; p. 351 (*right*): Herwig Prammer/Reuters/Corbis; p. 353: Ulrike

Welsch; p. 363: Robert Harding Picture Library Ltd./Alamy.

**Kapitel 10:** p. 381: dpa/ipol; p. 394: Peter Ginter/Getty Images; p. 409: Kevin Galvin; p. 417: The Stock Market/ZEFA/Damm.

**Kapitel 11:** p. 431: Ullsteinbild/The Granger Collection, NY; p. 434: The Image Works/Rudi Meisel/Visum; p. 438 (*top*): Ullsteinbild/The Granger Collection, NY; p. 438 (*bottom*): AP/Wide World Photos; p. 444: Ullsteinbild/The Granger Collection, NY; p. 454 (*left*): dpa/ipol; p. 454 (*right*): AP/Wide World Photos; p. 455: Ullsteinbild/The Granger Collection, NY; p. 457: AP/Wide World Photos; p. 458: Bisson/Sygma; p. 470: Kevin Galvin.

**Kapitel 12:** pp. 474 & 482: Ullsteinbild/The Granger Collection, NY; p. 480: Marc Rathmann; p. 489: Sony Pictures Classics / The Kobal Collection / Spauke, Bernd; p. 492: Tom Lovik.

**Literarisches Deutsch 2:** pp. 496 & 497: Ullsteinbild/The Granger Collection, NY.

## Illustrations

All illustrations by Tim Jones except pp. 136, 178, 379, 406–407, 487–488 by Steve McEntee and pp. 56 & 294 by Anna Veltfort.

## Realia

**Kapitel 1:** p. 6: © 1996 KFS/Distr. Bull's; p. 8: Quick, 14 Mai 1992, Karl-Heinz Brecheis; p. 26: Goethe-Institut; p. 30 (*middle*): Goethe-Institut; p. 30 (*bottom*): courtesy Himmel Haus, Elkhart, IN; p. 35: courtesy Stern.

**Kapitel 2:** p. 46 (*right*): Brillenmacher Preiß GmbH, Bremen, Germany; p. 46 (*middle*): moove-wohnen GmbH; p. 47: *Beim Analytiker* © Manfred von Papen, Fackelträger, Hannover; p. 48: Gastl Buchhandlung; p. 64: Hebbel am Ufer.

**Kapitel 3:** p. 92: real,- SB - Warenhaus GmbH; p. 93: Tourist Service Mannheim; p. 97 (*left*): Heidelberg City Revue '96; p. 98: Verlag *Heidelberg dieser Woche*, and Zum Seppl, Hauptstr. 213, 69117 Heidelberg, Rest. Kurpf. Museum, Tischer,

Unholtz, Schnitzelbank, Edm König & Bierkrug, Hauptstr. 147, Heidelberg.

**Deutsch im Beruf 1:** p. 113: Pier 39; p. 114 (*left*): Blazing Saddles Bike Rentals; p. 114 (*top right*): Cliff House; p. 114 (*bottom right*): Amtrak/Gray Line.

**Kapitel 4:** p. 117: Dr. Steinfels Sprachreisen GmbH; p. 121 (*top*): Goethe-Institut; p. 121 (*bottom*): Deutscher Akademischer Austausch Dienst; p. 127: Deutsche Bundespost; p. 129: SFB Berlin; p. 131: Fritz/ORB/SFB; p. 135: FahrRadLaden am Haagtor, Tübingen; pp. 136 & 139: Bundesministerium für Verkehr, Bau- und Wohnungswesen; p. 140: Uli Stein/Mice and More Marketing; p. 141: Bundesministerium für Verkehr, Bau- und Wohnungswesen; pp. 144 & 145: Deutsche Bundesbahn; p. 146: Verkehrsamt Frankfurt am Main.

**Kapitel 5:** p. 159 (*left*): Tourismus-Zentrale Hamburg; p. 159 (*right*): Universität Hamburg; p. 168: Uli Stein/Mice and More Marketing; p. 175: *Frankfurter Allgemeine Zeitung*.

**Kapitel 6:** p. 201: Eberhard-Karls-Universität Tübingen; p. 203: *Dschungelbuch,* Studentenwerk Uni Tübingen; p. 211: *Tübingen hat viele Seiten,* Handel- und Gewerbeverein Tübingen; p. 212 (*left*): Eberhard-Karls-Universität Tübingen; p. 212 (*right*): Studentenwerk Tübingen; p. 222: © E. Rauschenbach, Berlin.

**Kapitel 7:** p. 242: Verkehrsverbund Neckar-Alb-Donau GmbH; p. 249 (*top*): Breisach-Info; p. 249 (*bottom*): Tourist-Kongress und Saalbau GmbH Neustadt/Weinstraße; p. 251: Ihr Platz,

Osnabrück; p. 254 (*left*): Mercedes-Benz Museum; p. 254 (*center*): Wilhelma der zoologisch-botanische Garten Stuttgart; p. 254 (*right*): Stuttgart Marketing GmbH; p. 264: Fremdenverkehrsamt München; p. 274 (*right*): Köln Tourismus; p. 277: Filmnachte am Elbufer; pp. 279 & 281: Osiandersche Buchhandlung, Tübingen.

**Kapitel 8:** p. 291: courtesy Lätta; p. 302 (*top*): Uli Stein/Mice and More Marketing; p. 302 (*bottom*): Universität Passau; p. 304: Spiegel Special, 1/2005: Student 2005; p. 307: Friedrich-Schiller-Universität Jena; p. 319: Transparente Landeskunde, 5th edition, by Friedrich Bubner, Bonn-Bad Godesberg: Inter-Nationes, 1990; p. 320: Anzeige mit Titel Young Miss 3/93, BRIGITTE, Gruner & Jahr, Hamburg; p. 322 (*left*): Eberhard-Karls-Universität Tübingen; p. 322 (*right*): courtesy Schwartau Mövenpick.

**Kapitel 9:** p. 339: Siemens AG, München/Siemens Management Consulting; p. 341: Focus, 21/2003, 19. Mai 2003; p. 343 (*left*): Praxis Dr. Berger/ufafabrik; p. 343 (*right*): Philips GmbH, Hamburg; p. 344 (*left*): Skoda Auto Deutschland; p. 344 (*right*): Guter Rat, Berlin; p. 348: taz, *die tagezeitung* (Berlin); p. 357: Michael Gösler, Hamburg; p. 359: Die Neue Schule, Berlin; p. 360: Focus, 1/2003, 30. Dez. 2002, Illustration: K. Espermüller; p. 362: Internationale Stiftung Mozarteum, Salzburg; p. 362: Verlag Nürnberger Presse Druckhaus Nürnberg GmbH & Co.; p. 362: Thüringer Zoopark Erfurt; p. 362: Tierpark Hellabrunn; p. 362: Grazer Oper; p. 365: © Grundig; p. 368: courtesy Pro7; p. 370: *Deutschland – Zeitschrift für Politik,*

*Kultur, Wirtschaft und Wissenschaft,* Nr. 3, 12/93; p. 373: Wiener Staatsoper.

**Deutsch im Beruf 2:** p. 379: Global Competence Forum, Tübingen.

**Kapitel 10:** p. 383: Ekko Busch/Süddeutsche Zeitung; pp. 385–387: courtesy Margret Rettich, Vordorf, for illustrations originally published in WUNDER-Buch Nr. 69, *Aschenputtel* (Rechte beim Illustrator); p. 396: Deutsches Theater/Bühne der Stadt München; p. 397: Bild von Anny Hoffmann, aus "Der gestiefelte Kater" nach den Gebrüdern Grimm, © 1989, Pestalozzi-Verlag, Deutschland; pp. 399, 402, 403–407: Kur- und Verkehrsverein Braunwald; p. 401: Stern/Boris Thode/Picture Press; p. 412: courtesy Margret Rettich, Vordorf, for illustrations originally published in WUNDER-Buch Nr. 69, *Aschenputtel* (Rechte beim Illustrator); pp. 421 & 422: Kur- und Verkehrsverein Braunwald.

**Kapitel 11:** p. 453 (*right*): Berlin Tourismus Marketing GmbH; p. 447: © E. Rauschenbach, Berlin; p. 452: courtesy Maria Burg, originally in *Das neue Blatt,* Nr. 21, 18. Mai 1994; pp. 464–465: GO Druck Media Verlag/*www.go-kirchheim.de.*

**Kapitel 12:** p. 484 (*far left, middle right*): Goethe-Institut; p. 484 (*far right*): Landesmuseum für Technik und Arbeit in Mannheim.